FORT TECUMSEH AND FORT PIERRE CHOUTEAU

Fort Tecumseh and
Journal and Letter Books 1830–1850

Fort Pierre Chouteau

TRANSCRIBED AND ANNOTATED BY
MICHAEL M. CASLER and **W. RAYMOND WOOD**
with a Foreword by James A. Hanson

SOUTH
DAKOTA
HISTORICAL
SOCIETY
PRESS
Pierre

© 2017
South Dakota Historical Society Press.

All rights reserved.

This book or portions thereof in any form whatsoever may not be reproduced without the express written approval of the South Dakota Historical Society Press, 900 Governors Drive, Pierre, S.Dak. 57501.

This publication is funded, in part, by the Deadwood Publications Fund provided by the City of Deadwood and the Deadwood Historic Preservation Commission.

The paper in this book meets the guidelines for permanence and durability of the committee on Production Guidelines for Book Longevity of the Council on Library Resources.

Cover image: Frederick Behman's 1854 watercolor of Fort Pierre Chouteau. *South Dakota State Historical Society, State Archives Collection, Pierre*

Text and cover design by Rich Hendel
Typeset in Miller, Sentinel, and Egiziano by Kim Bryant

Please visit our website at sdhspress.com.

Printed in the United States of America

21 20 19 18 17   1 2 3 4 5

Library of Congress Cataloging-in-Publication Data is available.

CONTENTS

	Foreword *by James A. Hanson*	vii
	Preface	xi
	A Note on the Transcriptions	xiii
	Introduction	1
1	FORT TECUMSEH JOURNAL *by Jacob Halsey*	7
	Volume 1: January 31–June 13, 1830	7
	Volume 2: June 14, 1830–April 8, 1831	19
	Volume 3: January 27, 1832–June 1, 1833	35
2	FORT TECUMSEH LETTER BOOK	55
	November 1, 1830–May 10, 1832	
3	FORT PIERRE LETTER BOOK A	93
	June 17–December 14, 1832	
4	FORT PIERRE LETTER BOOK B	103
	December 20, 1832–September 25, 1835	
5	FORT PIERRE LETTER BOOK C	155
	June 25, 1845–June 16, 1846	
6	FORT PIERRE LETTER BOOK D	181
	December 1, 1847–May 9, 1848	
7	FORT PIERRE LETTER BOOK E	203
	February 12, 1849–December 4, 1850	
	Notes	235
	Bibliography	251
	Index	257

FOREWORD

Legend has it that when Pierre Chouteau, Jr., visited Fort Tecumseh in 1831, he cracked his head on a low door lintel and was so angry he ordered that a new fort be built. Chouteau had come up the Missouri River as a passenger aboard the American Fur Company's steamboat *Yellow Stone* on its maiden voyage. It was the only time that he ascended into the trading region he would eventually control as president of the fur company that bore his name. The new fort, replacing time-worn Fort Tecumseh, was also to be named in his honor—Fort Pierre Chouteau—and in turn it became the namesake of the town of Fort Pierre, on the west bank of the Missouri just downstream from the old fort's location. Decades later, the capital city of South Dakota—Pierre, on the east bank of the Missouri—took its name from Fort Pierre.

Central South Dakota was an important Missouri River crossing point for the powerful and numerous Lakotas, or western Sioux, who, at the end of the eighteenth century, were migrating westward in search of horses and buffalo. This movement corresponded with American efforts to open the trading potential of the Missouri following the 1803 acquisition of Louisiana Territory and its initial exploration from 1804 to 1806 by Lewis and Clark. Close on their heels came Manuel Lisa's Missouri Fur Company. Its traders built a post on Cedar Island, thirty-five miles downstream from present-day Pierre. Other trading firms occupied that site as late as 1824.

Whatever the truth of Chouteau's head-banging incident, work on Fort Tecumseh's replacement was soon underway. William Laidlaw, the *bourgeois*, or chief trader, at the American Fur Company post, wrote to Pierre Chouteau, Jr., on October 14, 1831: "We have got on but slowly with the New Fort, having the wood for building to bring from such a distance, and so very few hands to do it. Mr. Lamont expected that there was enough of wood, cut for all the buildings, but when it came to be collected, we had not enough for one store. I should like much to get a man who understands making brick, to make enough to build the chimneys, as there is so much risk, with mud ones: and when so much property is exposed, I think it highly necessary, as we have no lime here."

It is at about this point that the Fort Pierre letter books reproduced in this volume really get their start. Admittedly, the correspondence, or the log of letters sent from the post, is one-sided, but it is replete with observations on people and the details of fur trading that are available nowhere else. Editors Michael M. Casler and W. Raymond Wood have done a masterful job in preparing the surviving files of a major fur-trading fort's quarter-century of correspondence for modern readers.

In these documents, we encounter a host of fur traders not met elsewhere. As examples, Lewis Crawford, Modest Presley, Paul Kenning, Baptiste Fouchette, and Henry Maurice are all employees at the fort who are mentioned in the correspondence. Previously unknown beaver trappers such as Legris and Taudière also appear. The letters also mention luminaries of the western fur trade. As the years passed and the letter books recorded the passage of time, William Clark, the "Red Headed Chief" who functioned as Indian agent, became known to his charges as "the Gray head." Jim Bridger arrived at Fort John (Laramie) in 1845, delivering 675 deerskins, 840 pounds of beaver and castoreum, 52 horses and mules, and 1,400 California abalone shells. We also find a reference to Hugh Glass, the hunter and mountain man who was mauled by a grizzly bear and then left for dead by his companions.

Grizzly bears were a hazard of the job. In December 1834, Laidlaw wrote to Honoré Picotte: "Little carrier got most shockingly torn by a Bear; but is now doing well, though much disfigured, he was not expected to live at one time. Lebrun and he caught 92 Beaver skins before the accident happened, which was of course an injury to their hunt." We learn from the Fort Tecumseh journal that two other independent trappers, Lacomb and Leclair, became intoxicated in June 1830, and that one of them was so obnoxious that trader Francis Chardon flogged him. In December 1830, the journal describes how the Arikara Indians robbed a trading party led by Kenneth Mackenzie, *bourgeois* at Fort Union and self-styled King of the upper Missouri. The Arikaras took their equipment, though one of the party's mules came back to the fort, shot in the head with an arrow. Other famous mountain men such as Johnson Gardner and James Beckwourth also ramble through the pages.

Indians, too, receive lengthy mention. In a letter from Fort Tecumseh in November 1831, Laidlaw noted that "the Paunies" (Pawnees) had "shamefully defeated" the Cheyenne leader High Backed Wolf; thirty years later, his son of the same name was killed at the Battle of Platte Bridge, Wyoming, in an encounter with American troops near present-day Casper, Wyoming. An Indian named Dog's Shadow stole a horse from Fort Pierre; Laidlaw commissioned an Indian to recover the horse in February 1833, or, if that were not possible, to kill it. "I would rather he should kill him, than the fellow should have the use of him," he wrote. Yanktonnais had stolen Laidlaw's best buffalo horse in February 1832, but the animal escaped from them as they were crossing a river and returned to the fort; the same letter reports that Laidlaw had not been obligated to buy any fresh meat from the Indians because he and his charger had killed twenty-five buffalo cows that winter. An Indian murdered an employee named Gauslin in October 1830; a second Indian mortally wounded Gauslin's attacker. In gratitude for how that warrior had risked himself for one of the company's men, the traders presented the warrior "with every thing to ornament himself with, among the different articles was a sword." We also meet other interesting Indians; in December 1831, correspondence alludes to a "Mashed Testicles," for one, about whom I think we know too little.

The federal government's seeming absentmindedness to the needs of its Indian constituents is apparent. It dispatched Dr. Meredith Martin to the Sioux agency near Fort Lookout to vaccinate the Indians for smallpox. Unfortunately, Martin failed utterly in carrying out his duties; five years later, in 1837, the disease swept away thousands of upper Missouri Indians, including almost the entire Mandan tribe. We learn from the letter books that the diseases that carried away whole villages of Indians also killed thousands of whites. In November 1833, Laidlaw wrote trader Charles DeGray: "The Cholera has been very destructive in St Louis this summer and has carried off about 500 persons, poor Brasseau amongst the rest." Thus we learn of the demise of old Joseph

("Kiowa") Brazeau for whom Fort Kiowa, near present-day Chamberlain, South Dakota, was named.

There are a few references for those interested in the roles played by African Americans in the West. From Fort Pierre in December 1847, a letter mentions a "Mulatto or Negro man named Charles Barton," saying "this man is a slave" who must be returned to Saint Louis: "you could please keep an eye on him but not let him know it." Other blacks cross the pages. The Fort Tecumseh journal notes in February 1831, "James Parkins a Moletta arrived, he reports buffaloes to be plenty in every direction." Assistant trader Jacob Halsey wrote Chouteau in July 1832: "We are much in want of a cook here, Mr. Laidlaw wishes you to send him a good one, this fall if possible: a black man would be preferrd."

One of the saddest stories in the letter books is the accidental death of Thomas Sarpy, brother of both Peter (founder of Bellevue) and John (namesake of Fort John) at the Oglala Post on Cheyenne River in January 1832. A candle touched off a fifty-pound keg of powder, destroying three buildings. Sarpy, "so shockingly burnt and disfigured as not to resemble a human being," died shortly thereafter. The letters record his last words. Curiously, two men with him were not seriously hurt. Most pertinent, the Oglalas posted guards around the site to prevent looting and helped gather up the scattered property.

The letter books also reveal the mundane sides to a remarkable business. At many points, we are treated to studies in business leadership. Laidlaw was furious with one of his traders who had performed badly, writing from Fort Pierre in December 1834: "there would appear to be a great want of management on our [Oglala] post which must be evident to all *you are the sole Cause*." Or imagine Alexander Culbertson's dismay when he learned in summer 1845 that the man in charge of bringing in the winter's furs from Fort John had been stopped by low water, whereupon he and his crew simply abandoned the boats and cargo along the Platte.

Fort Pierre Chouteau grew in stature in the 1830s; upon its completion, it became headquarters for the American Fur Company's Sioux Outfit, and in 1837, it became headquarters of the Upper Missouri Outfit after Fort Union's Kenneth Mackenzie fell from grace. Even though Sublette and Campbell built opposition posts on both the Bad and White rivers in 1833 and 1834, Fort Pierre was the largest trading post ever built in the United States. It boasted workshops for a tailor, tinsmith, blacksmith, and saddlemaker. It had an icehouse, root cellar, saw mill, warehouses, lodgings, a mess hall for a hundred employees, a dairy herd, horse herd, stables, a major farm on Roy's Island (later Farm Island) downstream, and a large boatyard and lumbering operation up the river at Chantier Creek. Fort Pierre was not only a principal fur-trade warehousing and distribution center; it was a major transportation hub served by the keelboats and steamboats of the Missouri, the mackinaws and bullboats of the smaller rivers, the cart and wagon caravans supplying Fort Laramie and its dependencies, and even teams of dog sleds carrying goods to the frozen northern posts and essential dispatches all the way to Saint Louis.

In December 1845, opposition traders were smuggling liquor to the upper Missouri from the Saint Peter's River in Minnesota, and there were no federal agents to stop them. In September 1849, staff at Fort Pierre tried to straighten out a mix-up in which Fort Union received six hundred pounds of blue beads and no white ones. The chief trader at Fort Pierre, after supplying the beads to Fort Union, pleads for more beads from Saint Louis to replenish his own stores, noting, "This is a serious mistake as to its effect on the trade." Such revealing comments are the grist to our understanding of the fur trade; its success or failure might ride on whether a clerk somewhere along the line sent the right color of beads.

By 1850, the "new" Fort Pierre was falling apart. Pierre Chouteau, Jr., and Company had sold Fort John (Laramie) to the army—prematurely, many believed, for the Indian business picked up there as the California gold rush traffic declined. Chouteau learned from Alexander Culbertson in a letter of July 13, 1850, that he had examined Fort Pierre: "I find all the buildings more or less decayed and must be either rebuilt or repaired. For that reason I have most of the hands up the river procuring Timber and rafting it." Some repairs were made, but in 1855, the company sold Fort Pierre to the army. The officers on site complained bitterly that the fort was in bad shape and not suitable to the needs of the military. However, too much is probably made of their point; the army bought a trading post, not a military fort, and, for relatively little money, they had immediate access to protected lodging and warehousing just before a difficult winter.

In the spring, both the army and the fur company built new facilities (Fort Sully and Fort Galpin), but the memory of Fort Pierre as America's biggest trading post would remain. It had survived more than a quarter century as *the* anchor of the Missouri River fur trade. This book is the day-to-day recounting of that fascinating tale.

James A. Hanson

PREFACE

The Missouri Historical Society, now the Missouri History Museum in Saint Louis, has long been the repository for most of the records of the fur trade on the Missouri River. For more than a hundred years, historians have sifted through this collection for information about the operations of the Western Department of the American Fur Company and its later incarnation, Pierre Chouteau, Jr., and Company, which lasted until 1865. A wealth of letters and other information gleaned from these documents has been published in numerous books and articles over the years. In 1932, Annie H. Abel's edition of Francis A. Chardon's journal reproduced the Fort Tecumseh journal and the Fort Pierre letter books in part, but the full content of these rarest of fur-trade documents has never been published until now.

Letter books were common items at all fur-trade forts on the upper Missouri—so common, in fact, that they were rarely mentioned in company documents except for casual references in a few letters as documents to be carried to and from the satellite posts and the depot-level forts. A letter book is one side of a conversation, consisting of messages sent to direct the movement of men and trade goods from the managers of the company to its servants in the field. The reader browsing in these fur-trade documents today never sees the response to these letters but can make educated inferences that the directions in them were carried out by reading later letters to the same individuals or forts. These letters, besides relaying company business, also include personal information about individuals who, in many cases, had worked together for many years and were close friends.

Only a few of the letter books kept at the forts on the upper Missouri have survived—those of Fort Union and of Forts Tecumseh and Pierre Chouteau, the major depot-level posts—and then probably only a few of them. Although there are significant gaps in their coverage, these documents vividly illustrate the commerce of the northern Great Plains during the years 1830 to 1850. While there is much redundancy in these records, each letter or journal entry differs slightly from the others. Small details add value, and a number of passages in these otherwise mundane documents reveal information important to researchers. These texts, for example, offer new details about methods of transportation between Forts Pierre and John (Laramie) and proof that the redoubtable Hugh Glass had been at Fort Tecumseh on May 19, 1830—one of only a few references that place the legendary mountain man at a given location at a given time.

Many of the names of the fur-trade *engagés* employed on the upper Missouri do not appear in Saint Louis documents that record the men that were hired. Fort Pierre letter book B provides an explanation for this lack. William Laidlaw wrote to Pierre Chouteau on August 29, 1833, that the Canadian *engagés*, or "pork eaters," from Montreal did not travel through Saint Louis at all. That letter and others tell that the new employees came to the Missouri River by way of the Great Lakes to the Fox River in present-day Wisconsin, then portaged to the Wisconsin River and down it to Prairie du Chien on the Mississippi River. They traveled upriver to the mouth of the Saint Peter's River—the Minnesota River—at Fort Snelling in present-day Minneapolis and ascended that stream to Lake qui Parle in what is now southwestern Minnesota. Finally they pressed on to Lake Traverse before traveling two hundred miles overland to reach Fort Pierre. For this reason, their names will never be found in the lists of those workers recruited in Saint Louis. These men did not, however, prove to be satisfactory workers, and many of them deserted. In supplying such details, these documents from Fort Pierre prove their value.

The Missouri River in the heart of modern South Dakota was a major hub of the fur-trade industry throughout most of the middle of the nineteenth century; no other part of the West would see such a succession of trading posts by various firms as those at the confluence of the Missouri and Bad rivers. The first trading post at the mouth of the Bad (then called the Teton) was Fort LaFramboise I, which the mixed-blood French-Ottawa Joseph LaFramboise of Canada established in 1817 or 1818. Its site, somewhere within the modern town of Fort Pierre, has been lost to history and, perhaps, to the Missouri River. Today, its namesake LaFramboise Island occupies the center of the Missouri River channel between the towns of Fort Pierre and Pierre. In 1822, Fort LaFramboise met stiff competition from the Columbia Fur Company's Fort Tecumseh. Honoré Picotte, the *bourgeois* of the new post, was so generous in his trading with the Indians that he forced his less-well-financed competitor from the scene the following year. Almost nothing is known of Fort LaFramboise I.

Fort Tecumseh flourished for a few years, but erosion from the nearby Missouri River forced traders to plan and build a new fort in the winter of 1831–1832. Fort Pierre Chouteau opened for business in June 1832. Excavations by archaeologists from the South Dakota State Historical Society and work by researchers from elsewhere continues to add to what is known about this key location of the fur-trade era from 1830 to 1850. For the scholar or the ordinary reader who wants to learn about daily life at Fort Tecumseh and Fort Pierre, however, the journal and letter books from the forts provide information that is available nowhere else. Those documents are published in their entirety here for the first time.

A NOTE ON THE TRANSCRIPTIONS

The Fort Tecumseh journal and letter book and the Fort Pierre Chouteau letter books A to E have been known for more than a century. Charles E. DeLand abstracted them in the 1918 *South Dakota State Historical Society Collections*. His transcriptions did little violence to the meaning of the text, but there are massive deletions of material that he considered redundant. Furthermore, DeLand prepared his transcriptions using the "expanded" method in which spellings and case are corrected, periods are added where there are none, dashes are replaced by periods, and figures are often spelled out. Perhaps his major error in transcription was his identification of James Beckwith passing Fort Tecumseh on November 1, 1832, when, in fact, the text clearly gives the name of a trader named Dicoteaux or Decoteau. Later authors have published a number of significant letters from these documents, but the bulk of the originals remained unpublished and had to be consulted in microfilm or photocopies. While there is much redundancy in the Fort Pierre documents, each one differs from the others. We have tried to annotate the text so that the average reader can navigate the sometimes-difficult terminology and the wealth of new names and make sense of the documents. Fur-trade historians may wish for more annotations, but the material we present is the raw stuff of history, material that historians will consult for their own purposes.

The Fort Pierre Chouteau letter books posed a number of problems in transcription. We tried to follow the tenets of modern documentary editing, but the vagaries of the various documents by different clerk copyists posed many problems, the authors being entirely inconsistent in the use of periods, commas, and dashes. The writers almost universally used dashes as commas and as periods; here the editors render them as commas and periods. Where the editors have added single words or letters to clarify the text, they have enclosed those additions in brackets. The requisitions of goods for the Forts Pierre, John, Union, and Clark outfits for 1846 were especially troublesome, and despite our best efforts, much of the text could not be deciphered; here we left blanks in those lists. Several of the letters were written in French, authored by Kenneth McKenzie, William Laidlaw,

Alexander Culbertson, and Antoine R. Bouis. We are indebted to James A. Hanson for translating those letters as well as the occasional French phrase found elsewhere in the predominantly English text.

Trader Jacob Halsey wrote the Fort Tecumseh journal in a crisp hand that is easily read in photocopy. It is written in three separate record books, and we retain those divisions in this work as volumes 1, 2 and 3. There is an eight-month gap between the second and third volumes, but that does not necessarily mean part of the journal is missing. Letters from other fur posts indicate that Halsey was stationed at Fort Floyd, in what is now North Dakota, for a time, and he may have temporarily set aside his Fort Tecumseh journal for that reason. The text posed few problems in transcription, for Halsey generally used proper grammar with few misspellings, though the letters in many words lack real definition and the editors transcribed them in the spelling one would use today. Halsey was sparing in his use of periods, generally using them only in abbreviations. He universally denoted sentence endings and commas within sentences with dashes, which are here rendered as periods and commas. The dates for daily entries are modified by the addition of a colon before commencing the text. Readers will note that a few letters are chronologically out of order, which is how they occur in the letter books themselves; the original order has been retained.

The most serious problem in transcription in the remaining documents was spelling. The original authors of the letters generally used good grammar and spelling, but in their effort to save paper or because they were writing in haste, the copyists often ran letters together. The editors had to decipher many words because the letters sometimes became little more than a wavy line, though the length of the word and its context generally made its meaning clear. For this reason, another editor might perhaps render the text somewhat differently than presented here. Some words defied interpretation and are indicated with [word?]. The text of letter book D was especially difficult. Underlining in the text was rare, but underlined words are printed in italics. In many cases, a few words were struck out; these are likewise struck out in our text, though we leave the stricken text visible as being of potential interest to readers. On rare occasions, the letter writers repeat one or two words; in such cases, we have silently deleted the duplicate words.

Unlike with the Fort Tecumseh journal, the long gaps of months or years in between some of the letter books suggest that some of the letter books were lost or destroyed. The editors have written short "bridges" to summarize what was going on in the Missouri River fur trade in those periods.

The names of the principals in the fur trade are well known, and the writers invariably precede them with "Mr." When the names of the *engagés* are mentioned, however, either the author or the copyist spelled them inconsistently. Other editors might have filled in more of the blanks than we have done here. All we can say is that we have made an honest effort to offer fur-trade historians a useful document for further study.

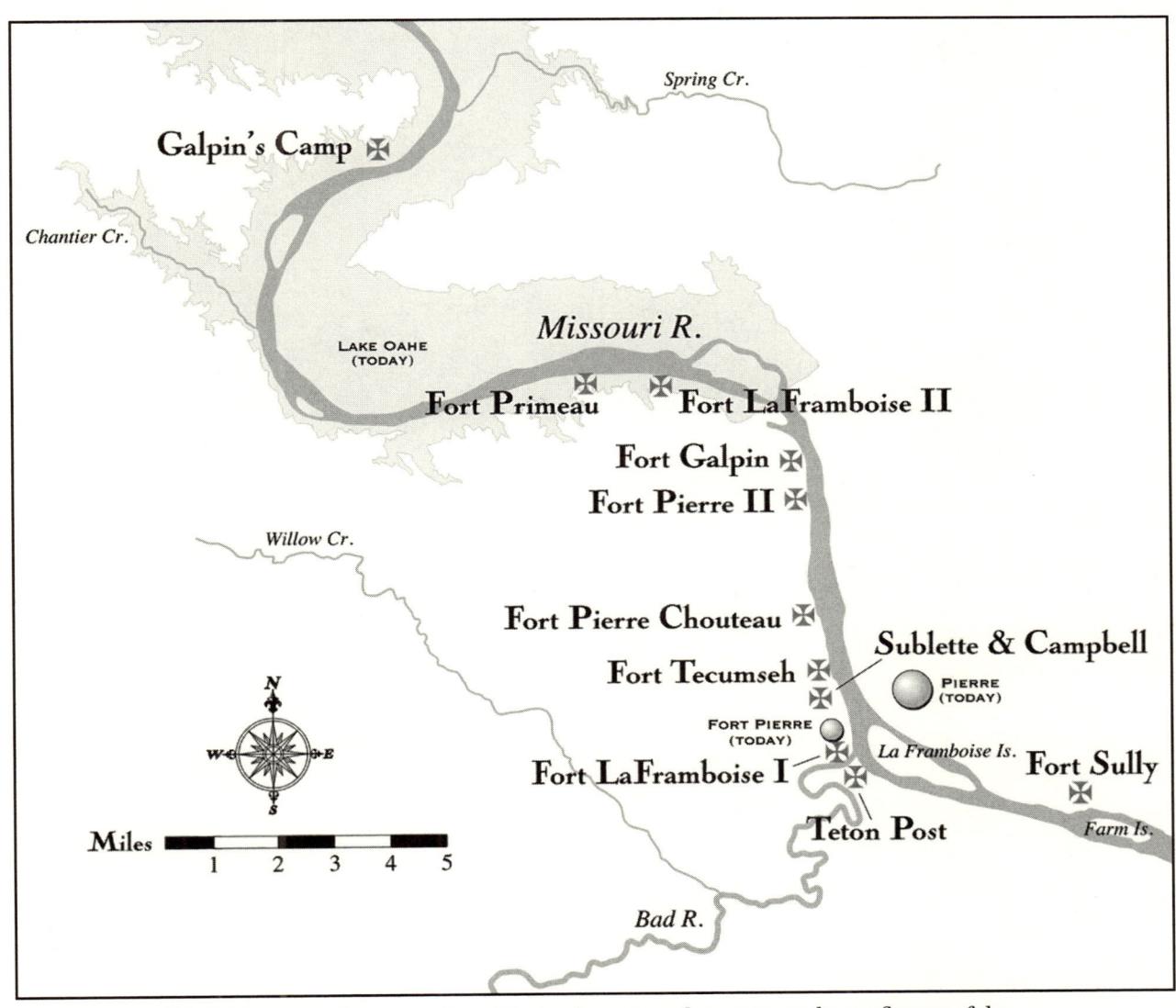

No other part of the West saw such a succession of fur-trade posts as the area near the confluence of the Bad and Missouri rivers in what is now South Dakota. *Map by Brian R. Austin*

INTRODUCTION

The vicinity of Pierre, South Dakota, capital of the "Mount Rushmore State," was a focus of the fur-trading industry on the upper Missouri for nearly two centuries, beginning with the establishment by Joseph LaFramboise of a fur-trading post on the west bank of the Missouri in 1817.[1] At this same location in 1804, the Lewis and Clark Expedition met with a party of Teton Sioux in one of the most tense episodes of the entire journey. On September 24, the expedition landed near the mouth of the Bad River,[2] and the following day its members assembled at noon and paraded under arms. Their council with chief Black Buffalo and his Brulé band did not go well, for at one time there was a mutual show of arms. They resolved their differences, however, and on September 29, 1804, the expedition cautiously moved on upriver.[3]

Trade in what is now central South Dakota, however, had begun long before LaFramboise opened his trading post. The Arikara Indians had lived in the vicinity for centuries, proto-Arikara groups having entered South Dakota from the Central Plains as early as A.D. 1300. Although the Sioux had recently driven the Arikara people from the area, their villages were once the hub of a widespread, intertribal trade network that brought the nomadic, tipi-dwelling nomads—principally the Cheyennes, Arapahos, Comanches, Kiowa-Apaches, Kiowas, and their immediate neighbors, the Teton Sioux—to their villages annually to exchange goods. The Sioux now controlled the intertribal trade in the region around the Bad River, and it was their fear that Lewis and Clark would interfere with their monopoly that led to their confrontation with the expedition in 1804. The Tetons were right to be concerned, for Lewis and Clark were part of the American effort to open the Missouri River trade to non-Indians.[4]

Lewis and Clark's return to Saint Louis in 1806 and their report of the vast number of beaver on the far upper Missouri led to what can aptly be described as a "fur rush." Saint Louis had been a major center for the fur trade on the lower Missouri River and its tributaries almost from its founding in 1764. One trader had even reached the Mandan Indians as early as 1792, and other traders were on their way upstream even as Lewis and Clark were returning home. The expedition's reports of the abundance of beaver farther upstream sent, at first, small groups of traders to exploit these aquatic mammals. Companies soon were formed for the same purpose.[5]

The first individual to establish posts on the upper Missouri expressly for trade was Manuel Lisa, an energetic Spanish merchant in Saint Louis. He ascended the Missouri in April 1807 with two keelboats and fifty to sixty men and built Fort Raymond for trade with the Crow Indians at the juncture of the Bighorn and Yellowstone rivers. The site is in present-day Yellowstone County, about twenty-five miles east of Billings, Montana. Lisa returned to Saint Louis after a successful winter's trade and founded the Missouri Fur Company (also known as the Saint Louis Fur Company). In the fall of 1812, he established what is today called Fort Manuel in Corson County, South Dakota, on the west bank of the Missouri a few miles south of the present North Dakota boundary. Most of the post's business was with the Arikaras, who lived in their villages near the mouth of the Grand River, some thirty river miles downstream. Traders occupied Fort Manuel only for a single winter. They abandoned it sometime after March 5, 1813, ostensibly because they feared that the British during the War of 1812 might inspire Indians to hostility. Lisa's Missouri Fur Company also built a post on Cedar Island, thirty-five miles downriver from the mouth of the Bad River, a site that was occupied as late as 1824.[6]

The first recorded Indian-white trade took place in the Pierre locality when Joseph LaFramboise built a stockaded fort, Fort LaFramboise I, for the Sioux trade beside the Missouri somewhere north of the mouth of the Bad River in about 1817. The date is derived from Sioux winter counts, yearly records collected by Garrick Mallery. LaFramboise, a Canadian of French and Ottawa Indian background, is believed to have continued his trade there until 1822. It was likely on the bank opposite the head of today's LaFramboise Island; perhaps its ruins are beneath today's town of Fort Pierre.[7] No record of it exists after 1822, for in that year, a powerful new trading company built a new post nearby.

In 1821, the two giant fur-trading companies in today's Canada, the Hudson's Bay Company and the North West Company, merged under the former company's name, leading to significant downsizing by both companies. Many of its former employees had to find other work. Some of these men emigrated from Canada and settled in Saint Louis. Manuel Lisa's success in the trade on the upper Missouri inspired the formation of new companies; prominent among them was Tilton, Dudley and Co., better known as the Columbia Fur Company. Some of the unemployed Canadian traders now living in Saint Louis organized the new company. Joseph Renville, aided by Kenneth McKenzie, formed the company in late 1821 or early 1822. Other prominent members of the company included William P. Tilton (its titular head, though McKenzie was its driving figure), Daniel Lamont, William Laidlaw, and Honoré Picotte. The new company immediately established several trading posts in Minnesota, and then expanded west, building Fort Washington on Lake Traverse and Fort Tecumseh on the Missouri River in 1822.[8] This competition from the Columbia Fur Company was surely the reason for the demise of Fort LaFramboise. Indeed, the two posts were so near the same spot on the Missouri that it is possible the Columbia Fur Company simply took over and rebuilt Fort LaFramboise, renaming it Fort Tecumseh.

At the same time, a rival firm, Berthold, Chouteau and Pratte (also known as the French Company) entered the scene. In 1822, it built Fort Lookout across the Missouri from present-day Chamberlain, South Dakota. When that fort became the property of the American Fur Company it took on the name of Fort Kiowa—from the nickname of its chief trader, Joseph Brazeau. The post initially was designed to compete with the Columbia Fur Company, although it was one hundred ten river miles downriver from Fort Tecumseh. To compete directly with Fort Tecumseh, the French Company also built Fort Teton on the south bank of the Teton River in 1828.

Fort Tecumseh quickly became the principal depot for the Columbia Fur Company on the Missouri; men were sent from it to wintering posts along the Missouri and its tributaries, returning their furs and robes to the fort in the spring. Steamboats stocked its inventories by first carrying goods up the Mississippi River to Fort Snelling, Minnesota. Goods were then boated up the Minnesota (then called the Saint Peter's) River to

Lake Traverse and finally overland by wagon to the Missouri. The Columbia Fur Company maintained its monopoly at Fort Tecumseh for five years. In 1827, Pierre Didier Papin was sent to Fort Tecumseh to help Kenneth McKenzie inventory its property for new owners.

America's first millionaire, John Jacob Astor, had his eye on the Missouri River fur trade. His American Fur Company—formed in 1808—could no longer tolerate the competition from the Columbia Fur Company. In July 1827, the two companies negotiated a merger on terms that were favorable to both organizations. Even though Kenneth McKenzie had been an active and aggressive leader of the Columbia Fur Company and was largely responsible for its success on the upper Missouri, the company was in financial difficulty. It was delinquent in repaying its suppliers, making it ripe for a takeover. The new coalition brought in fur-trade veterans Bernard Pratte and Company of Saint Louis, whose traders included members of the powerful Chouteau family. The old Columbia Fur Company became known as the Upper Missouri Outfit. McKenzie remained in charge on the upper reaches of the river, and other former employees stayed on as the workforce of the new unit. The Upper Missouri Outfit, as part of the Western Department of the American Fur Company, operated along the Missouri River from the mouth of the Platte River in Nebraska to the Missouri's source in western Montana.

Meanwhile, the "opposition" that the documents from Forts Tecumseh and Pierre Chouteau sometimes mention was growing. In 1828, the French Company built Fort Teton on the south side of the mouth of the Bad River. This post, too, had a short life, for its backers did not have the resources to compete with the Upper Missouri Outfit, but its limited success nonetheless led McKenzie to buy them out in 1830. The Upper Missouri Outfit's employees promptly dismantled Fort Teton and transferred its lumber and trade inventory to Fort Tecumseh. Later, bitter rivalry would develop between the competing companies, but good will and friendship existed between officers of the two firms in this era, for they often dined with one another. Traders even stayed overnight in the other company's post occasionally.

Fort Tecumseh was not to last, either, for the erosive power of the Missouri River began to undermine the river bank, and in February 1831, company employees moved its two-story trade house to prevent its falling into the river. They also had to move the stockade to keep the building in the fort's compound. But the cottonwood logs of the rest of the stockade and the building sills were nearing the end of their usable life, and some timbers were rotting in the ground. By 1832, the entire post was abandoned, and traders took up operations in a new fort constructed a few miles upriver. The new fort was built on higher ground, and traders began moving goods to it on March 26, 1832. The brand new Fort Pierre Chouteau (Fort Pierre, for short) was named for the president of the Western Department of the American Fur Company, Pierre Chouteau, Jr., and it became the most important of the company's posts on the middle reaches of the upper Missouri. Its only rival in importance was Fort Union, built in 1828 near the mouth of the Yellowstone River. Today, the site of Fort Pierre Chouteau is a National Historic Landmark.[9]

Fort Pierre Chouteau was the only trading post in the Pierre locality that travelers on the Missouri described in detail. Prince Maximilian and his artist-companion, Karl Bodmer, left not only a plan of the fort in 1833 and 1834 but also an image of its location and portraits of several of its Indian customers. John James Audubon and his companion, Edward Harris, also left valuable descriptions of the fort in 1843. Prince Maximilian prepared a sketch map of the new post to accompany his description of it and its surroundings. Fort Pierre, he wrote, was one of the largest of the American Fur Company's posts on the Missouri. Built in the form of a quadrangle, the fort and its buildings were surrounded by high pickets in a large prairie area. Blockhouses were set on two corners for the defense of the nearly one hundred people living there and of its inventory worth nearly eighty thousand dollars. The two large gates, facing the river and opposite it, were closed every night. The surrounding prairie provided pasture for the horses and for the cows that supplied the fort with milk and butter. Teton and Yankton Indian tipis stood at varying distances from the fort, and nearby were large numbers of burial scaffolds. Dogs were everywhere; they did not bark but bared their teeth if visitors came near them.[10]

Ownership of the post changed over the years. In 1834, John Jacob Astor sold the Western Department, including the Upper Missouri Outfit, to Pratte, Chouteau and Company. After Pratte's death in 1839, the firm was reorganized as Pierre Chouteau, Jr., and Company, which continued in business until 1865. The fort served as the headquarters for the surrounding region under the supervision of a succession of directors, or *bourgeois*—William Laidlaw, Honoré Picotte, and Alexander Culbertson. The letter books for Forts Tecumseh and Pierre Choteau not only reveal the day-to-day details of the business transacted between the traders and the Indians, but they also afford a peek into the lives and problems of the men who staffed these remote outposts.

By 1854, Fort Pierre Chouteau had grown old in its turn. Frederick Behman's bird's-eye view of the post in 1854 is especially helpful for visualizing layout just before it underwent major renovation. The United States Army purchased the post in 1855 to garrison and supply forces under the command of Brigadier General William S. Harney, who was then engaged in a campaign against Sioux Indians. Charles E. Galpin was the agent for the Chouteau firm at the time, and sometime before August 7, 1855, he established a camp of some sort about four miles above Chantier Creek "with the party that vacated Fort Pierre on the arrival of the troops." The camp's location is well known, for it was marked on a contemporary map of the locality. Why it was established is not clear, for in November 1855, Galpin himself had written, "Fort Pierre is a barren and exhausted place."[11] The camp appears to have been in use for only a short time.

Despite the establishment of this camp and Galpin's dismal appraisal of the local trading scene, the sale of the old fort prompted traders to erect a new one. In 1857, Galpin began building a post that came to be called Fort Galpin, but it, too, was short lived, and in 1859, workers started building a third fort about two miles north of the site of old Fort Pierre Chouteau, one that is today referred to as Fort Pierre II. The builders scavenged the old fort for lumber to supplement the new timbers used in construction. Its occupation "was of relatively short duration," and "the post itself was of relatively minor importance even during its own period—one of rapid decline in the trade as a whole."[12] Beginning in the summer of 1862, events in the Missouri Valley were focused on the subjugation of the Sioux, and over the next few years, Fort Pierre II faded into obscurity.

In 1863, a military post—Fort Sully—was established adjacent to Farm Island and, since Fort Pierre II apparently was abandoned, traders gravitated to this post, for the military would not defend traders in another locality. The traders rafted goods from Fort Pierre to the new fort, but firsthand accounts say the workers left much material behind that they could not easily transport. With this move, as Hubert Smith commented, "the traders doubtless assumed more the role of sutlers for the military, less that of Indian traders," effectively ending the Indian-white trade in the Bad River locality.[13]

South Dakota historian Charles E. DeLand wrote of another fort, the ruins of which the construction of the Oahe Dam obliterated. Francois ("Frank") LaFramboise, a nephew of Joseph, built and managed it. That fort is referred to here as Fort LaFramboise II to distinguish it from the one that Joseph built in 1817. DeLand wrote that LaFramboise operated the post for a time for the firm of La Barge, Harkness and Company, but he gives no dates for its operation.[14] A second elusive post is "Fort Primeau," which, according to DeLand, Charles Primeau built in the early 1860s. The conflicting testimony about this alleged post is such that archaeologist G. Hubert Smith was skeptical that it existed, at least in the locale claimed for it, because the site described is on land quite unsuitable for a post. In any case, in June 1862, Primeau was in charge of Fort Pierre II, making it unlikely that he would have a second post at the same time.[15]

Fort Pierre's location was again an asset starting in 1875, when freighting firms started locating warehouses in the town of Fort Pierre in order to supply mule and ox trains heading for the Black Hills mining camps via the Fort Pierre-to-Deadwood Trail. The firms shipped goods by steamboat to Fort Pierre, then loaded the merchandise into wagons for the rest of the journey. Later, merchants shipped goods by rail to the railhead on the opposite shore of the Missouri, then ferried the goods across. Pierre, South Dakota's capital city, sprang up in 1880 around that railhead and took its name from an early settler's listing of his shipping address as "Pierre, east of Fort Pierre." Because the railroad was unable to bridge the river and because Fort Pierre remained part of the Great Sioux Reservation for years longer, Pierre soon became the larger city.[16]

Pierre has been the capital since South Dakota became a state on November 2, 1889, and the Pierre/Fort Pierre community remains a hub of commerce even today—as the region has been for hundreds of years. Archaeologist Smith was certainly correct in his assertion: "[F]ew geographic locations in the West exhibit a greater concentration of sites of . . . historic fur- and Indian-trade establishments, or one covering a longer time span, than that of the junction of the Bad and the Missouri Rivers."[17] The present volume will help add to what is known about that proud legacy.

1

FORT TECUMSEH JOURNAL

Jacob Halsey

Volume 1: January 31, 1830–June 13, 1830
Fort Tecumseh, Jany. 31st, 1830

Sunday: Throughout the day Strong gales from the N.W. and moderate weather. Put up Mdse. for the trade of the Chyennes.[1] At dusk the wind fell and it commenced snowing

[February 1830]
Monday, Feb. 1: Begins with a light fall of snow. At 10 A.M. an appearance of clearing off. J. Jouett with one hand, and three Chyenne Indians left here with 6 Horses & mules laden with Mdse. for the trade of the Chyennes. Mr. Laidlaw and myself[2] visited Messrs. Papin and Noble.

Tuesday, 2nd: Fine pleasant weather. Mr. Papin dined with us. J. Letaud & F. Montaigne arrived from the Navy Yard[3] in quest of Provisions, Nails, &c. Through the night strong Northerly winds.

Wednesday 3: Throughout the day Cloudy and Moderate weather.

Thursday 4th: Strong N. West wind, and very cold weather.

Friday 5th: Clear and very cold weather.

Saturday 6: More gales from the southeast and moderate weather.

Sunday 7: Clear and Cold. Mr. Laidlaw and my self rode down to Mr. Papin's house,[4] a family of Yanctons[5] arrived and camped on the other side the Missouri. Sent off an Indian to White river with dispatches.

Monday 8: Clear and fine. Alexis Tibaut and four men arrived from White river with 30 horses and 589 Buffalo Robes.

Tuesday 9th: Pleasant and clear. At night Strong gales from the north with snow—two men arrived from the Little Chyenne[6] with one horse loaded with ammunition.

Wednesday, 10th: Moderate winds and pleasant. Alexis Tibaut with four men & 13 Horses left here for White river for the purpose of bringing in peltries. Crossed the remainder of our horses at a point of woods nearly opposite the fort.

Thursday 11: A continuation of fine pleasant weather. Mr. Papin dined with us.

Friday 12th: Clear & pleasant. At dark Mr. J. Holiday with one man and a mule loaded with Mdse. arrived from the Little Chyenne river.

Saturday 13: Roy & Paquette with two dog trains arrived from Apple river. they brought ammunition, Scarlet, &c.—the weather still continues remarkably pleasant. Mr. Laidlaw and myself rode down to Mr. Papins house.

Sunday 14: Still continues fine Pleasant weather overhauled our meat and found about 25 p[ound]s: mouldy. Prepared dispatches for St Louis. Joseph Bary and an Indian left here for the forks of Chyenne river with a mule loaded with Mdse.[7]

Monday 15: Dispatched Roy to Council Bluffs[8] with letters for St. Louis, also a man to the Poncas with Porcelaine. Mr. J. Holiday left here for the Little Chyenne. Mr. Laidlaw and myself paid a visit to Mr. Papin. At night we had a light fall of rain.

Tuesday 16: Moderate weather and Cloudy. Francis Quenel and Louison an Indian arrived from Forks Chyenne with 9 Horses.

Wednesday 17: Westerly winds and Cloudy. Drounded one of our best horses in attempting to cross the Missouri with a load of hay.

Thursday 18: Moderate and cloudy weather throughout the day. Letand and Montaigne came down from the Navy Yard. 3 Men arrived from Hollowwood[9] with 18 Horses & Mules loaded with Robes

Friday 19th: A little snow fell last night. Throughout the day strong Northerly winds and cool.

Saturday 20: Clear and cool with strong N.W. winds. Mr. Noble and Mr. L. Cerre[10] dined with us.

Sunday 21: In the morning three men left here for the Forks chyenne river—the day was clear with strong N.W. winds.

Monday 22: Strong N.W. winds & cool. Four men arrived from Apple river[11] with dispatches from Mr. Lamont

Tuesday 23: Northerly winds and cold—at day light crossed the Missouri for the purpose of bringing over some hay—succeeded in crossing two cart loads—the ice is still dangerous.

Wednesday 24: Cold and cloudy. 6 men left here for Hollowwood with 18 Horses for the purpose of bringing in Packs belonging to white River outfit—crossed two loads of hay to day. A Yancton Indian arrived with two Robes.

Thursday 25: Clear and fine. Mr Pascal Cerre dined with us, crossed all our horses on this side the Missouri. At 4 P.M. Bary and Toin with two men and 21 Horses and mules arrived from the forks Chyenne River.

Friday 26th: Clear and very pleasant weather

Saturday 27: Clear and pleasant with Strong Southerly winds.

Sunday 28th: Still continues clear and pleasant, a man arrived from Forks Chyenne river with 2 horses—and four men with 12 horses from White River with Robes.

[March 1830]

Monday 1: Strong Northerly winds and moderate weather—sent off 13 Horses to Hollowwood for a load of Robes belonging to the White river outfit, at the same time Baptiste Dourian left here for forks of Chyenne river.

Tuesday 2: Hard gales from the Southeast and moderate weather.

Wednesday 3d: First part hard gales from the South Middle and latter part fine pleasant weather, several Indians past the fort from above and encamped at Papins house

Thursday 4th: Moderate northerly winds and fine pleasant weather.

Friday 5: Northerly winds and Cloudy. Mr. Holliday & 9 men and 35 Horses arrived from White River outfit with furs, Peltries, Meat, Mdse. &c.

Saturday, 6th: Northerly winds and snow throughout the day. Cut our keel boat free from the ice. The Missouri has rose a foot the last 48 hours.

Sunday 7: Cloudy and Cold. At 11 A.M. a man arrived from St. Louis—he said he left the Prince of Wattenburgh[12] with 7 men and 10 horses at Cedar Island destitute of Provisions. Mr. Laidlaw, Mr. R. Holliday, myself and an Indian took horses and provisions and started to meet the party—we went five miles below Cabri creek[13] but saw no signs of travelers. Mr. Laidlaw returned to the fort, and Holliday, myself and the Indian camp'd at Cabri creek—the night was cold and our bed was light.

Monday 8: In the morning I returned to the fort, Mr. Holliday and the Indian proceeded on in search of the Prince—at 4 P.M. Holliday returned without finding the Prince, he delivered over the provisions to the Indian and told him to continue the search down the river Missouri — weather clear and cold

Tuesday 9th: At 7 A.M. the Indian arrived without success. At 9 A.M. a man arrived who announced the safe arrival of his majesty at Mr Papin's house, arranged a house for his reception. At 3 P.M. the Prince and part of his men arrived at the fort with Mr. G. P. Cerré, who introduced us to his majesty — on his arrival we hoisted our flag — the day was clear and moderate with a north wind.

Wednesday 10th: It commenced snowing in the morning and continued at intervals throughout the day — at 10 the remainder of the prince's party arrived. The Prince is a fine looking man, he is about 6 feet high and somewhat corpulent — he styles himself Paul Prince of Warttenberg, nephew to the present King of England. In the evening Louis Gagnier and an Indian arrived from Dicksons establishment (la Riviere a Jacque)[14] in quest of Mdse.

Thursday 11th: Strong Easterly winds and cloudy weather

Friday 12th: It began to snow before daylight, and continued at intervals throughout the day — the weather was cold, with hard gales from the Eastward.

Saturday 13th: The weather was clear and cold. The Prince packed up his things with the intention of starting for the Mandans[15] tomorrow. Six of our horses died last night.

Sunday 14th: Clear and pleasant. The Prince left here in the morning — one of his men deserted last night — we were obliged to furnish him with another to go with him a far as the Little Chyenne river. At dark Michel Debruille & Francois Faye arrived with two horses from the head of D'Leau que course river[16] — where they left Frederick Laboue[17] trading with the Souix and Poncas. They brought in 8 horses loaded with Robes as far as Co[mpany]s house on White river — from thence they came here with two horses light. They have been five days without eating a mouthfull.

Monday 15: Strong westerly winds and warm weather. The snow and ice melting fast. Mr. Noble dined with us to day. Mr. Laidlaw, Holliday and myself were weighed to day. I weigh'd only 130 [pounds].

Tuesday 16th: Strong Northwest winds and warm. Jos. Jeutt and family arrived from Forks Chyenne river — he says the snow is very deep in that neighbourhood. I have now been nearly four years absent from home. I left there the 16th June 1826 — proceeded on to St. Louis in company with Mr. Crooks — on my arrival there I engaged myself to the Am. Fur Cy. in capacity of clerk in the business of the Indian trade. In August I left St. Louis on the stage for Franklin (a small town in Missouri state) when I overtook the companys boats, and embark'd aboard and proceeded up the Missouri river. I continued in good health until we reached Kansas river, where I was taken ill with the fever & ague and continued very sick untill the middle of December — during my sickness I was very much exposed to the weather, being in an open boat and having no place to shelter me from the inclemency of the season. I arrived at the Ariccarras village in November — remained there till the middle of December when my health was so far recovered, that I started for the Mandan villages, where I arrived safe after travelling 5 days. I remained there till spring of 1827 when Mr. P.D. Papin and myself left with 5 skin canoes and one Batteau laden with the fruits of our trade (300 Packs robes, 5 of Beaver and 5 of Musk Rats). The C[olumbia]. F. C[ompan]y had two Batteaux and two skin canoes laden with Furs & Peltries. We arrived safe at St. Louis the beginning of June — my reason for descending this year was sickness. I applied to Doctr. Lane[18] of St Louis for medical aid and in one month was restored to excellent health and have continued to enjoy that great Blessing (with little intermission) ever since. In August following I again left St Louis for the Upp. Missouri — we arrived at Ft. Lookout[19] in November. The boat I was on board of was stopp'd here by the ice. I was ordered to prepare myself to start a foot for Vermillion river (a distance of about 300 miles) accordingly on the 25th Novr. myself, two men and an Indian family, with two horses to carry our baggage started on the voyage which we were 19 days in performing — we had very bad weather, the snow was so deep that we were frequently obliged to make roads for our horses — we often passed a day with out eating. In fact I never knew what it was to suffer before. I remained at Vermillion river till March 1828, when I went to the Poncas[20]—made the spring trade with those Indians, and returned to the Vermillion the latter end of May. I remained there living in an Indian Hut, till July, when one of the Cos. boats arrived from St Louis. I embarked on board and proceeded on to this place, where I remained till fall I then embarked on a Keel boat with Mr. Laidlaw and proceeded up the river Missouri as far as the mouth of the H[e]art River[21]—where Mr Laidlaw wintered with the Yanctonnas, and I proceeded on to the Mandans by land and wintered there. In spring of 1829 I left the Mandans and descended as far as this place where I have been ever since.

Wednesday 17th: The Mandan Indian live in Wigwams they are from 30 to 60 feet in diameter made in the form of a bowl turned upside down—the frame is made of wood. over the top small branches are thickly laid, and over this about six in[ches]: of dirt—in the center there is a hole dug in the ground, which serves as a fire place, immediately above this is another made for the smoke to pass through. On the side of the Wigwam (or as it is called by the french, dirt Lodge) their berths are placed, and all the furniture is kept—the other side is appropriated for their horses. They are obliged to stable their horses because they have allways more or less enemies to contend with. They have at present the Assiniboines in the north, the Chyennes south, and the Sioux and Ariccarras east, and the Black feet Indian west of them—all of these nations they are now at war with. The Mandans are of a lighter complexion than the Indians south and east of them. The men are in general tall and well proportioned, neat in their appearance and kind and affable at home, but when met in the plains on a war excursion they are not to be trusted. Some of these Indians have blue eyes, and I have seen children of about 12 or 13 years of age with gray hair.[22] The women are generally stout, well made and rather neat than otherwise in appearance—they are however much addicted to fornication, in fact they are so much depraved, that there are few among them who are free from the venerial disease.[23] The men do not scruple to lend their wives to the whites without solicitation. The great superstitions of these Indians constrains them in many instances to rigorous suffering. A Young man before going to war will have two holes cut in his back near the shoulders, through these holes a cord is passed, at the two ends of which a Buffalo Bulls head is attached—thus arranged he will proceed at a little before midnight, without any thing to defend him from the sharpness of a cold winters night, and walk round his village, training the Bulls head after him till the weight of it tears his flesh away, alternately crying and imploring the Great Spirit or Master of Life, to grant him success in war, and not to let him return to his village without bringing trophies of his having been victorious. They have many other modes of torture equally severe all of which the[y] sustain with extraordinary calmness. It was formerly a custom among this people to cut off a joint of one of their fingers at the death of a relation, beginning with the little finger of the right hand, but, I believe it has of late years been nearly, or quite abolished. However, be this as it may, you seldom or never see one of the men who does not bear evident signs of his having been burnt, cut or Mangled in some part of his body, for without such proofs he would not be considered under the appellation of Man. The women at the death of a relation cut of[f] their hair, and scarify their head and legs in a shocking manner.

They do not bury their dead, but, after dressing the corpse in its best clothes, wrapped in skins, and place it on a scaffold outside the village. They state that their tradition says they were once a powerful nation occupying 13 large villages but were reduced to their present number (which is two villages, one of 30 and the other of about 60 wigwams) by the small pox which raged among them about 30 years ago—since that time they say their number has neither increased or diminished.[24] Superstition induces them to say that their ancestors formerly lived under ground, that at a certain time a grape vine was discovered to have grown up to the surface of the earth—a young man more daring than the rest, attempted to climb the vine and succeeded in reaching the top without accident—he then to his infinite gratification and delight discovered that the face of the earth was covered with Buffalos, he immediately made known the joyful tidings to his nation upon which most of them succeeded in reaching the surface of the earth in safety—the last who attempted to ascend the vine was a Fat old woman with a child on her back, but her weight was too great, for the vine broke, and she was precipitated with her charge to her former abode. After death they suppose their souls are wafted back to this, the ancient abode of their Forefathers, and there live anew. A Gentleman of my acquaintance who recently passed a summer with the Mandans, informed me that while walking one day in the village he observed an old man setting outside the wigwam, wrapp'd in a white Buffalo Skin, and who appeared to be speaking with a good deal of vehemence, he also observed the Indians presenting him different things, upon which he asked them the meaning of it, they replied that a great while ago their country was destroy'd by a flood, and many of their people perished, since which time those who escaped, sacrificed yearly, a part of their property, believing that by so doing, the Great Spirit would look on them in pity, and not punish them again by inundation, as long as the[y] continued the ceremony.

The Mandans are extremely fond of bathing, at all seasons of the year—boath men and women are good swimmers. In the spring of the year, when the ice in the river breaks up, there is allways more or less Buffalo drownded, by attempting cross the river when the ice is weak—at this period the young men keep a good lookout, and if they discover the dead carcass of a Buffalo drifting down the river, they immediately strip, take a cord and pole, jump on to the drifting ice, and leap from cake to cake, untill they come within reach of the object of their pursuit, which they secure with the cord, and then return to the shore, in the same manner—they frequently fall in the water, but as they are expert swimmers, the[y] contrive to catch the ends of the pole, on two cakes of ice, which supports them till they have an opportunity of getting out, they generally land about 1/2 mile below the place from whence they started. The flesh of a Buffaloe that has been drownded about a week is considered a delicious morsel by these Indians. In war, the Mandans are brave and expert—some Years ago 44 Assiniboines[25] proceeded against them, they hid themselves in holes about 2 miles from the South village and killed one or two women before they were discovered. When the Mandans attacked them they kill'd 37 in their holes, and 6 they slew in the river with their knives, so that only one escaped to carry the tidings to his nation. The Mandans lost 4 men in this battle.

The first time I visited the Mandans, I saw their chief in his most stylish Habiliments—he wore round his neck as a token of his bravery, a complete sett of human fingers, which he had taken from the body of one of his enemies, after killing him in battle. I also saw a drum at the Mandans, which the Indians told me, was made out of the skin of an Arriccarras Indian.

The Minniterees (or as they are called by the french Grosventres)[26] live but a short distance above the Mandans (which is situated in Latitude 47 degrees and some minutes north). They have three villages and are rather more numerous than their neighbours the Mandans. I suppose both nations can raise 600 fighting men—they are allways at peace with each other, and have the same enemies. In their appearance, manners and customs they differ but little from the Mandans but there is a great difference in their Language, that of the Mandans is very difficult to learn. Most of the Mandans speak the Minniterree language, but I never saw one Minniterree that could speak the Mandan tongue, although they have lived near each other a long time and see each other dayly. The Minniterrees are great thieves and are much more troublesome to the traders than the Mandans—both nations raise corn, Beans & Pumpkins in great abundance.

Wednesday March 17th 1830: First part of the day northerly winds and Snow. At 11 A.M. Clear weather, but Strong gales from the north, which continued throughout the day. I forgot to mention that Louis Gagnier and an Indian started yesterday for Dicksons establishment, Riviere a Jacque.[27]

Thursday 18th: Fine pleasant—they have gone there for the purpose of bringing Furs & Peltries. I saw several flocks of Geese and ducks this day.

Friday, 19th: Continuous fine Pleasant weather. In the morning Jacque Letand arrived from the Navy Yard—he says John Gamlin (one of our men at work there) is very ill—his complaints a severe pain on the left side. In the afternoon Messrs. Laidlaw, Holliday and myself played at cross ball with the squaws—they bet Moccasins against beads—we came of[f] victorious—two men and 4 horses arrived on the other side and camp'd there—the Missouri ice is too weak for them to cross at present.

The Arriccarra Indians lived in dirt Wigwams on the banks of the Missouri River,[28] about 60 Leagues below the Mandan villages—they have two villages and can muster about 550 warriors, they differ very little in their manners and customs from the Mandans and Minniterrees, but in their character they differ much. They are deceitful and treacherous in the extreme, cowardly in War, and faithless in peace. They are at present surrounded by enemies, for which reason they are afraid to go far from their villages—therefore they frequently starve, when buffaloe are near at hand. Their language is soft and harmonious to the ear & is easily acquired. They have heretofore kill'd many white men—at present a white man would be safe in their village but if caught alone in the plains they would be sure to rob or kill him—seldom a year passes without their killing one or more of our men, in the winter of 1828 they kill'd one at the Mandans. About 8 months ago a boat hand in the employ of this company was stabbed to death with a knife about a half mile above their village—the assassin was a Souix Indian, but he was (according to his own words) instigated to commit the act by an Arriccarras, to assuage the Wretchedness of an old chief who had formerly lost a favorite son in battle. While I was at the Mandans in the winter of 1828 & 9 the two nations were at war with each other. Some time in the middle of the winter an Arriccarree arrived at the village—he had several strong relations among the Mandans, consequently he did not apprehend much danger of being slain. He was not molested, on the contrary, he was treated with a great deal of kindness. He told the Mandans he was sent by his nation to entreat for peace, they assured him they were ready to comply with his proposal or entreaty—he then pledged himself on the part of his nation that the Mandans and the Grosventres (or Minniterrees) should be no more molested by the Arriccarras. He was afterward loaded with presents and sent back to his village, before he had proceeded far on his journey he fell in with a Mandan boy, who he treacherously murdered and scalped, and then made the rest of his way home.

Saturday March 20th 1830: Strong Northwest wind and pleasant. Jacque Letand left here for the Navy Yard. Sent up a Blister Plaster and other medicines for Gamlin. The ice in the Missouri commenced breaking to day.

Sunday 21st: Begins with easterly winds and cloudy weather. In the middle part of the day a little snow fell. Latter part Northeast wind and an appearance of more snow. The ice in the Missouri stopped running last night.

Monday 22d: Clear and Pleasant. At noon the rest of the Missouri ice in the vicinity of this place broke up, and continued drifting at dark.

Tuesday 23d: Fine pleasant weather. The Missouri rising a little—the ice still continues drifting.

Wednesday 24th: A continuation of fine pleasant weather—very little ice drifting. At 4 P.M. one of our men arrived from the Navy Yard, one from Little Chyenne river, and two of P. D. Papin & Cos. men, the two latter are the same who arrived on the other side with 4 horses on the 19th ultimo. They were from the Sanchannas,[29] they say that Mr Lamont came near being kill'd by one of the Indians at his place, he was fired at, in his own house, but the intended blow was fortunately warded off, by his negro Boy, and the ball passed above his (Mr. Lamonts) head—they also state, that they left an Indian on the other side the Missouri with dispatches from above. Our man (Francois Montaigne) from the Navy Yard announces the melancholy tidings of the death of John B. Gamlin, [two words struck out] who departed this Life without a struggle about 12 oclock last night.

Thursday 25th March 1830: Fair pleasant weather—the Missouri fell about 6 inches to day, in the morning Montaigne & Lataille returned to the Navy Yard. At dark two of the men who left here on the 18th ultimo returned from White River with 9 horses loaded with Robes.

Friday 26th: throughout the day strong gales from the Northwest and pleasant weather. At Meridian an Indian called the Mauvais Bouef, and two squaws arrived from White River. This Indian is a man of considerable consequence among the Brules, he had the misfortune to have the end of his nose bit off in a drunken frolick last fall at Messrs. P. D. Papin & Cos. house on the Teton River. He who committed the act was a Yancton, he was shot dead by the relations of the Mauvais Boeuf about an hour after he bit him. The circumstance excited a good deal of enmity on the part of Yanctons at the time, but I believe they are now quite pacifick. The Missouri rose about 2 feet last night and the ice is drifting thick to day. Messrs. No ice drifting

Saturday, 27th: Calm and fine. The Missouri rose about 2 feet last night, and the ice is drifting thick today. Messrs. Noble and Cerre dined with us.

Sunday 28th: First part of the day light, winds and cloudy weather. At 2 P.M. hard winds from the Northeast. The Missouri fell about two feet this day—no ice drifting.

Monday March 29th, 1830: Throughout the day strong Gales from the Northwest and Cloudy weather. At night saw some persons arrive and camp on the other side the Missouri

Tuesday 30th: Still continues Strong Gales from the N.W., attended with cold weather—a little snow fell last night, the Missouri has rose about two feet since last evening and was still rising at 6 PM. Large bodies of ice commenced drifting at 12 A.M.

Wednesday 31st: The Gale continued all last night, and a little snow fell, the Missouri rose about 2 feet, and the ice is coming down in very large bodies to day. At 12 A.M. the gale had abated to a moderate breese, which continued decreasing gradually till evening when it was nearly calm. The Missouri still continued rising fast, and the ice drifting at sunsett.

[April 1830]

Thursday April 1st 1830: Moderate Southeast winds and cool. Ice still drifting thick and the Missouri falling—caught a good deal of drift wood to day. Hands employed pressing Packs. At 4 P.M. 8 or 10 Indians arrived on the other side the river. Pressed 46 Packs Robes to day.

Friday 2d: Light Easterly winds and warm weather in the morning crossed 9 Indians from the other side the Missouri, they brought with them a quantity of Robes and dry meat which we traded. At 3 P.M. Pierre Dauphin arrived from Little Chyenne river—he was sent by our trader there for a boat to bring down his Furs, Peltries &c. At 5 P.M. crossed 3 of the Indians who came in to trade this morning. Louis Lagrave arrived from Vermillion, he says he parted with Francis Roy 5 days ago (each supposing they were taking the best road) since which time he has tasted no food. We pressed 28 Packs of Robes to day.[30]

Saturday 3d: Cloudy weather and moderate. South easterly winds. Hands variously employed. Pressed 16 Packs Robes this day. At dusk saw a fire on the other side the Missouri, the river rose about 6 in. to day.

Sunday, 4th: Moderate westerly winds and pleasant weather. Ice drifting again and the Missouri rising fast. At 4 P.M. crossed 4 Indians to the other side the river. Louis Roy arrived from Council Bluffs. Caught a considerable quantity of drift wood[31] to day, also a drownded Buffaloe, which we presented to our starving friends.

Monday 5th: First part of the day northerly winds, with rain and snow at intervals. Middle and latter part clear and cool. No ice drifting, the Missouri now a little. Pressed 19 Packs of Robes.

Tuesday 6th: Cloudy, with Northerly winds and cold weather. In the morning dispatched Alexis Tibaut and 3 men for the Little Chyenne river for the purpose of bringing down what Packs the company may have there. Two Indians left here with them. The [word?] is falling to day. Pressed 27 Packs Robes.

Tuesday 6th: At 8 P.M. Joseph Juett arrived from la Riviere Leau que course.[32] He left Mr. LeBoue with Furs, Peltries, &c about 2 days march from here on his way in from Trading.

Wednesday 7th: Cloudy at daylight. At 6 A.M. Northwest winds and snow & rain which continued with little intermission throughout the day—men employed making Packs. The Missouri falling very fast.

Thursday 8th: Strong Northwest winds and rain the first part of the day. Middle and latter part clear. At 6 P.M. Frederick Leboue and 3 men arrived from Leau que course river with 12 Horses laden with Furs, Peltries, &c.

Friday 9: Light Northerly winds and cool weather. At 6 P.M. Mr. F. A. Chardon arrived from Forks of Chyenne river with 7 skin canoes laden with 4360 Buffaloe Robes and a quantity of Furs, Mercandise &c. Mr. P. D. Papin of the Firm of P.D. Papin & Co arrived at the same time with two canoes—he camped here for the night. Mr. Chardon unfortunately lost a canoe with 400 Robes in descending Chyenne river. Pressed 22 Packs of robes to day. Three or four Indians arrived from the other side the Missouri with fresh meat, they state that Buffaloe are in great abundance in the neighbourhood of Medicine hill.[33]

Saturday 10th: Mr Papin departed at daylight for his establishment. At 10 A.M. Strong S.E. winds, which continued throughout the remainder of the day. The Indian who arrived yesterday left here in the evening.

Sunday 11th: Moderate Northeast winds and cool weather. Messrs. Papin, Cerré and Noble dined with us—in the after part of the day sent 6 horses across the Missouri—a party of gentlemen contemplate going to hunt Buffaloe tomorrow. The river is now very low and continues falling.

Monday 12th: It commenced snowing last night and continued with a strong N.E. untill 5 P.M. to day, when it turned to rain.

Tuesday, 13: The first part of the day cloudy weather. Middle and latter part clear and cool with a strong North wind. Sent three men on the other side the Missouri in the morning to see to our horses. Made and Pressed 69 Packs Robes to day.

Wednesday 14th: Clear and pleasant. At 6 A.M. our men arrived from the other side. At 10 A.M. Messrs. Laidlaw, Papin, Cerré, Chardon & Laboue with 6 men and 10 or 12 Horses left here for Medicine Hill on a hunting excursion. At 1 PM an Indian arrived from Medicine hill. Made and Pressed 86 Packs Robes to day. Sett 3 men at work making a fence for a garden. At sundown some men arrived on the other side the Missouri.

Thursday 15th: Sent the skiff across the river in the morning and brought over the men who had arrived last night. Joseph Juett and Francois Montaigne, the latter came in quest of men to help turn the Batteaux at the navy Yard. The day was pleasant with a moderate easterly wind. Made and pressed 94 Packs of Robes to day. I understand that one of Messrs P. D. Papin & Cos. men (Derocher) died last night at their establishment on Teton river.

Friday April 16th 1830: Strong Southerly winds and cloudy weather. At 12 A.M. Messrs. Laidlaw Chardon and Laboue arrived from hunting. At 2 P.M. the rest of the party arrived on the other side the Missouri, the wind has been blowing so strong that they have not yet been able [to] cross. They state that they found Buffaloe in great plenty about 20 miles from here—they succeeded in killing six. Made and pressed 73 Packs Robes to day. In the early part of the day F. Montaigne and 8 men left here for the Navy Yard.

Saturday April 17th: Moderate Southerly winds and warm weather—in the morning got our meat over from the other side the Missouri. At 5 P.M. 11 Ree Indians[34] and 1 squaw arrived from their village they descended the river in canoes and say they are bound for the Pawnee villages. Made and pressed 80 Packs Robes to day.

Sunday April 18th: Throughout the day Strong Southerly winds and Cloudy weather. In the morning the Indians who arrived yesterday left us—they proceeded down the Missouri in skin canoes.

Monday April 19th: A combination of Strong Southerly winds, at intervals attended with light showers of rain. Made and pressed 83 Packs Robes to day. At dusk Pineau le Yancton (who left here on the 15th instant to hunt) returned with the flesh of two Buffaloe. He says cattle are in great plenty, not more than 10 miles from here, on the other side the Missouri.

Tuesday April 20th: Southwest winds and rain. At 10 AM Joseph Juett and 1 man left here for Medicine Hill with a small equipment of goods to trade meat and Robes. At 1 P.M. Messrs, Laidlaw, Chardon, Holliday, Laboue and myself rode down to Mr Papins house—we returned in the evening accompanied by Messrs. Papin, Cerre & Noble.

Messrs. Primeau and J. Holliday arrived from the Little Chyenne river with a Batteaux laden with Peltries, Mdse &c. Joseph Longeau arrived from the Navy Yard in quest of Pitch, Cordage,[35] &c for Batteaux. Middle and latter part of the day hard showers of rain at intervals.

Wednesday April 21st: Throughout the day Strong Northerly winds and rain. It stopped raining about sunsett and there was some appearance of its clearing off. Messrs. Papin, Cerre & Noble returned home. The Missouri has rose considerable during the last 48 hours.

Thursday, April 22 — In the morning cloudy weather — unloaded the Batteau that arrived on the 20th ultimo. Three men left here in search of Mr. Thomas L. Sarpy[36] who we presume is descending the Chyenne river in skin canoes, and in want of assistance, as it is now a long time since we suposed he must have left his wintering ground. 2 men also left here for the Navy Yard with two Jack asses loaded with Pitch, Cordage &c for the Batteaux. Middle and Latter part of the day Strong Easterly winds and rain at intervals.

Friday April 23rd: Strong Northeast winds and rain and snow at intervals throughout the day. At 3 P.M. sent the Batteaux across the Missouri after hay — it returned in the evening with a load.

Saturday April 24th: Strong Northerly winds and cloudy weather. At dusk the clouds faded away, but the wind still continued blowing hard. Saw the new moon to day. Commenced taking Inventory of Stock.

Sunday April 25th: Strong Northerly winds and cool weather. Latter part of the day clear and calm. Joseph Juett arrived from Yanctons camp at Medicine Hill, with Robes & Meat — he also brought with him a living young Buffaloe calf.

Monday April 26: First and Middle part of the day Clear and pleasant with a strong Southerly wind. Messrs. Laidlaw, Chardon, Laboue and three men cross'd the Missouri for the purpose of hunting Buffaloe. Messrs. Papin & Noble dined with us. Latter part of the day light airs from the South and fine weather. Made and pressed 75 Packs Robes to day.

Tuesday April 27: Calm and Cloudy. At 9 A.M. Messrs. Picotte & Chenie passed here with four Skin canoes loaded with Robes. At 11 A.M. Strong northerly winds our boat Builders arrived from the Navy yard with four Batteaux. The gentlemen who went out hunting yesterday returned with a quantity of fresh Buffaloe meat and 5 living Calves. They say Cattle are still in great plenty about twenty miles from here. Made and pressed 35 packs Robes to day.

Wednesday April 28th: Disagreeable rainy weather. Messrs. Papin, Picotte, Chenie, Noble and 7 other gentlemen, all our opponents in trade dined with us. They all returned home in the evening except Mr Noble who passed the night with us. The day ends with thick cloudy weather and an appearance of more rain.

Thursday April 29th: First part of the day Cloudy, mid- and latter part disagreeable rainy weather. In the morning Messrs. Picotte, Chenie, Winter, Baird with 5 interpreters and indians rode up and passed the night with us.

Friday April 30th: Pleasant weather and moderate winds Messrs. Laidlaw, Chardon, Primeau, J. M. Holliday and 7 Men attended my Mr Picotte's party left here with horses for a hunting excursion on the other side the Missouri. Middle and latter part of the day light [word?] winds and pleasant.

[May 1830]

Saturday May 7th: Cloudy weather and light winds about noon Mr Noble returned home. One of the Buffaloe calves died to day and we have another which I think will not live long.

Sunday May 2d. 1830: Commenced with cloudy weather and Easterly winds, with rain at intervals. Latter part of the day Strong N.E. winds and rain. Messrs. Picotte Laidlaw & Chardon arrived from hunting — they left the rest of the party behind — some of them arrived late on the other side the Missouri and have camped there for the night. They kill'd 23 Cows and 9 calves and are bringing in 6 living calves. Cattle continue in great abundance not more than 25 miles from this.

Monday, May 3d: It rained hard the first part of last night and afterward turned to snow, which continued till about 10 A.M. to day. The wind was blowing very strong from the eastward, and the weather was cooler than any we had last winter — we were much concerned for the safety of the hunters who left here on the 30th of last month—they have however all returned in safety—some of them passed the night under the snow—the severe weather killed two of their horses. About 12 A.M. Mr. Picotte and his party retuned home with the fruits of their hunt. Our men brought in four living calves, they had more, but were obliged to abandoned them in the Prairie.

Tuesday May 4th: Fine pleasant weather—men are employed overhauling the Robes and making a new Baggage outside the fort. Sent two men across the river in the morning to look after property left behind by the hunters in the Storm. In the evening they returned without finding any thing.

Wednesday 5th May 1830: A continuation of fine pleasant weather. Dispatched 3 men across the river in the morning, on the same errand as those we sent yesterday—they found the property and returned in the evening. At 9 A.M. Mr. Emillian Primeau[37] left here alone in a canoe for St. Louis. Hands employed to day overhauling Robes, making Packs pressing them &c.

Thursday 6th May: Light winds and cloudy—finished making and pressing Packs. At 4 P.M. the man who we sent in quest of Mr. Sarpy on the 22d of last month, returned without any inteligence of him, they followed the river Chyenne, as far as up as Mr. Chardons wintering ground, when they found themselves destitute of Provisions, and nearly bare-footed, and consequently returned. We now think that both himself & those who were with him have been killed by some war party. At 5 P.M. Strong Southerly winds, Messrs. Lamont, Pilcher, Sandford, Dickson & Campbell arrived. The[y] left two Keel Boats and one Batteaux loaded with Robes &c opposite the Island about 3 miles above this.

Friday May 7th: Calm and Hot. At 7 A.M. the Keel boats arrived, unloaded one of them. At 12 A.M. we were visited by Messrs. Picotte, Papin & Winter—after dining with us they returned home. Crossed our horses from the other side the Missouri.

Saturday May 8th: Strong Southerly winds and cloudy. At noon Louis Piton arrived from the Chyenne river where he left Mr. T. L. Sarpy with his peltries—he has unfortunately lost a skin canoe loaded with Robes. It is now about two months since he left his wintering ground during which time the weather has been so unfavourable, that he has not made more than 60 miles. His canoes are rotten & he has sent in Piton for a supply of horses to bring in his returns. In the evening Messrs Pilcher & Sandford & servant left here for St. Louis in a Skiff.

Sunday May 9th: Finished loading three Keel boats with Furs & Peltries for St. Louis. Hard Gales from the east throughout the day, we were unable to load the Batteaux. At noon Piton, Dickson, Degrey and Lachapele with one man left here with 52 Horses, Mules and Jack asses to bring in the remainder of Sarpys packs.

Monday May 10: Last evening Mr. William Dickson & family arrived. We crossed them this morning. Dickson Brought with him 27 Packs Robes and a few other Furs—loaded 5 Batteaux to day.

Tuesday, May 11th: Light winds and pleasant—in the morning 3 Keel Boats & 5 Batteaux left here for St. Louis—they have on board upwards of 2000 Packs furs & Peltries—passengers, Messrs. Laidlaw, Lamont, R.T. Holliday, Bouck, Hay, & Laboue, Middle part of the day strong winds from the south. One of the Buffaloe calves died to day.

Wednesday May 12th 1830: Strong northerly winds and pleasant. In the morning rode down to Mr. Papins house—in the evening ~~rode down~~ [word?] return'd in company of Messrs. Papin Picotte, Winter, L. Cerré & Mr. Avaripe who passed the night with us.

Thursday May 13th: First part light winds and pleasant. Middle part Strong Northerly winds. Our visitors returned home in the morning. Pineau kill'd a cabrie to day. Ends with calm and pleasant weather.

Friday May 14th: Light winds and cloudy weather. Baptiste Dorion and Pineau le Yancton killed each an antelope to day.

Saturday May 15: Disagreeable rainy weather, with strong Northerly winds. At 4 P.M. 10 Yanctonnas arrived on the other side the Missouri, sent over boat and crossed them—they are encamped about two days march from here, say they have plenty of Buffaloe, in their neighbourhood, and came in quest of a trader.

Sunday May 16th: Throughout the day cloudy & Gales—we were visited by Messrs. Papin, Picotte, Winter & Alvaripe. 6 more Indians arrived from the other side the Missouri about two days march from here, they also, came in quest of traders. Put up two Equipments of Mdse: one for each camp.

Monday, 17th: In the morning J. M. Holiday & Baptiste Durion left here with goods to trade with the Yanctannas and Saons.[38] Pineau le Yancton crossed over the river with them, and returned this evening with fresh Buffaloe meat. The weather was clear and pleasant, with light variable winds. I forgot to say that the Indians all left here with Durion & Holliday—the most distinguished man among them was a young chief called "He that speaks the truth."

Tuesday 18th May: Light winds and Cloudy weather. Chardon & myself rode down to Papins house where we dined—in the evening we returned to the fort—towards sunsett a little rain fell. Hands employed to day planting Potatoes.

Wednesday 19th: Moderate winds and cloudy weather. At 4 P.M. Hugh Glass[39] and Francais Vione with 9 men arrived from Fort Union,[40] they came in a Skiff & wooden canoe & were sent in quest of horses &c.

Thursday 20th: Cloudy and cool weather. Holliday and Dourian returned with about 10 Packs Robes. 5 Indians came in with them, saw a large band of Buffaloe on the opposite side the Missouri to day. Kill'd 4 of them.

Friday, 21st: Cloudy and light winds, at 10 A.M. Mr. T. L. Sarpy and party arrived with fifty odd horses loaded with 108 Pack Buff. Robes a little Beaver, Mdse, Tallow &c. In the evening 11 Indians arrived from the other side the Missouri.

Saturday May 22d. 1830: Cloudy and moderate wind. Engaged packing horses to sent to Fort Union.

Sunday May 23d: In the morning Messrs. Glass, Vione, Winter, Holliday, Degray & Lachapelle left here with 12 men and 58 Horses & Mules for Fort Union, Yellowstone river the day was cloudy with Strong Southeast winds. All the Indians left here to day.

Monday May 24th: First part cloudy, at 10 am a little rain fell, at 12 Clear & Pleasant. I forgot to mention that our old Bull died yesterday morning, he was cut about 15 days ago, from which time he has been dwindling away till the time of his death. We are afraid some of our horses have been stolen, thirteen have been missing for some time past, 6 belonging to the company, 3 to Mr. Dickson, & 3 to his Uncle and 1 to Baptiste Dourion. One of our men discovered an encampment on the little river opposite the Navy Yard, where Indians had been but a short time previous. Last evening Joseph Villande one of the Yellow Stone party returned to exchange a Kettle which had been fired through by Laurent Lerretti [?]. It appears from Villanders statement that the party encamped early and were all taking a frolick when the Kettle was broke.

Tuesday May 25: Pleasant weather. L. Cerre & two of his clerks dined with us. 5 more horses missing to day have no doubt they are stolen. Yesterday we commenced bringing the horses in the fort at night.

Wednesday May 26th 1830: First part Thick Cloudy weather. Middle and Latter part pleasant. Henrie Angé and Pieau le Yancton and J. Jutt went on the other side the Missouri to hunt buffalo, they were quite close, we saw two bands this morning, about 3 PM, the hunters returned, having killed six. 13 Yanctonnas arrived at the same time, from the camp on the opposite side the Missouri with Robes. Hands employed repairing the roof of the high Store.

Thursday May 27th: First part ~~first~~ of the day a little rain fell. Middle and Latter part clear & pleasant, hands employed variously.

Friday 28th: Clear and Hot. Hands employed making a pack for the [word?]. In the morning crossed all the Yanctannas on the other side the Missouri. At 6 P.M. we had a fine refreshing shower. The Missouri is rising fast.

Sunday 30th: First part Cloudy. W. P. May and Wm. Miller (two furriers) arrived in a canoe from the Mandans. At 12 A.M. Thomas Dumond and Oliver Leclair with a squaw came in from hunting Beaver, they have had all their horses stolen except one which they brought in with them. Middle and latter part of the day rainy weather.

Monday May 31st 1830: Throughout the day Strong Northerly wind and cool weather. Hands employed repairing houses. At 4 P.M. about 50

Indians (Yanctonnas and Saons) arrived from the other side the Missouri with Robes, they say that the Buffaloe have all disappeared from their neighbourhood. Throughout the night engaged trading with the Indians, traded twenty three packs Robes. Joseph Vasseur sick and off duty, this man has done nothing since the 20th instant.

[June 1830]

Tuesday June 1st 1830: Northerly winds and pleasant weather. In the morning traded a few more packs Robes, at 12 A.M all the Indians left us on their return home. They all behaved well while with us, with the exception of a scoundrel called the handsome Feather (Saon) who tried to frighten us with his threats, but I believe he left us with his martial feelings pretty well abated for we handled him [word struck out] somewhat roughly.

Wednesday June 2d. Pleasant weather. At 9 A.M. 8 or 10 Indians arrived from the camp on the other side the Missouri, they brought us three of the horses stolen on the 25th last month, and twenty two Robes which we traded. At 1 P.M. saw two men on the hill behind the fort, as we supposed them to be horse thieves, we each took a horse and went out in pursuit of them, but were unable to discover their hiding place. At 4 P.M. we crossed a part [of] the Indians who arrived this morning and the Skiff and canoe returned with 6 more Red skins with Robes. The Missouri has rose a foot since Yesterday morning. The Indians say they saw a Band of Buffaloe to day on the other side the Missouri about 15 miles from here.

Wednesday June 2d 1830: At 9 P.M. Mr. May left here in a canoe for the settlements below council Bluffs.

Thursday June 3d: Fine pleasant weather, in the evening 4 more Indians arrived from the other side the Missouri with Robes, they say there is plenty of Buffaloe quite close to this place.

Friday June 4th: Pleasant weather. In the morning the Indians left here. Angé, Miller and Pineau crossed over on the other side the Missouri to hunt. Baptiste Dourion went out on this side and kill'd a Bull, he says he saw a band of about 12. Throughout the night strong gales from the Eastward & ~~stormy weather~~ hard squalls of rain attended with Thunder & Lightning.

Saturday 5th: Our Batteaux broke loose from her moorings last night and nothing is to be seen of her this morning. Sent Lagrave down the river in search of her, at noon he returned, having found her opposite the second Island below this. At 4 P.M. sent off 5 men in the skiff to bring her up. 2 lodges of Indians arrived on the other side the Missouri and camped there. The Missouri continues rising it is now about 4 feet above low water mark. Throughout the day pleasant weather.

Sunday 6th: A little rain fell last night. Throughout this day the weather was windy. At 12 A.M. our men returned with the Batteaux, at the same time Angé and the others came in having kill'd 3 Buffaloe Cows and two calves. The Missouri continues rising.

Monday June 7th 1830: Clear & Hot. At 9 A.M. 10 or 12 Indians arrived here from the other side the Missouri, they brought in three more of the stolen horses. (Dickson's property) They have not as yet returned any of the compy's horses. Besides the horses the Indians brought some Robes and fresh Buffaloe meat. At 4 P.M. recrossed the Indians. Messrs. Cerré, Bouchet & Recontre called on us, the Missouri still continues rising.

Tuesday June 8th: Clear & Pleasant. At 10 A.M. Pierre Garrow & Amable Lacomb arrived from the Rees, the latter brought with him a small pack of Beaver, after selling Lacomb & Leclair two or three bottles of Liquor they became noisy and wished for more but Mr. Chardon refused to let them have it, upon which a quarrel arose, and Chardon gave Lacomb a flogging and they have both left us with their Beaver for Messrs. P. D. Papin & Co. establishment. At 4 P.M. 10 or 12 Indians arrived from the other side the Missouri with Robes. At 6 P.M. 5 or 6 more arrived from the same camp with Robes. At dusk strong Easterly winds & hot, sultry weather with an appearance of rain. Missouri still rising.

Wednesday 9th: Clear and fine, in the morning finished trading, and recrossed the Indians. At 4 P.M. saw a band of Buffaloe on the hills back of the fort, killed one in the act of crossing the Missouri. The river still rising.

Thursday June 10th 1830: Throughout the day cloudy weather. Saw several bands of buffalo crossing the river from the other side.

Friday 11th: Continues cloudy with easterly winds. Saw several large bands of Buffaloe crossing from the other side the Missouri, we all equipted ourselves and proceeded out against them and kill'd 24 Buffalo caught their calves & a young antelope. At 5 PM strong squalls from the east and hard showers of rain attended with thunder and Lightning. The Missouri still continues rising. The bank on which this fort stands has been daily caving in since the Missouri began to rise, if it continues to fall in much more we will be obliged to move a part of the fort.

Saturday June 12th: Hot, Sultry weather. Saw several large bands of Buffalos on the other side the Missouri. A band of about 150 crossed within one hundred yards of us but were prevented from landing by some of our men who frightened them, they returned again to the other side the river, we, however succeeded in ketch catching 5 calves, and in killing 5 cows. The Missouri still rising, it has rose about 2 ½ feet since yesterday morning. The latter part of the day light showers of rain with thunder & Lightning.

Sunday 13th: Hot, Sultry weather. Saw several bands buffaloe crossing the Missouri, the river still continues rising.

Volume 2: June 14, 1830–April 8, 1831

Monday June 14, 1830: Throughout the day cool and cloudy weather. At 4 P.M. 5 Indians arrived from the other side the Missouri with Robes. Saw several bands of Buffaloe to day. Kill'd two.

Tuesday June 15: Fine pleasant weather In the morning Pierre Garrow[41] left here for the Rees, and Baptiste Dourion left here to search for horses below Teton river, we have some hopes of finding a part of the horses we thought were stolen last month. At 5 P.M. Mr. Chardon, Angé and myself rode down to Mr. Cerré's house, on our return we found that 5 or 6 more Indians had arrived from the other side the river with Robes. The Missouri still continues rising.

Wednesday 16th: Still continues pleasant. Saw a band of Buffaloe crossing the river, killed six cows and three calves. Through the night Strong Gales from the East, with rain and Thunder & Lightning.

Thursday 17th: Throughout the day Strong Easterly winds and cloudy weather. The bank opposite the fort gate, has fell in so much that we will be obliged to pull down the blacksmiths shop and move back the picots [pickets] of the fort. Our batteaux was found sunk this morning, and our Skiff has gone adrift or sunk, this was owing to the falling in of the bank last night. The Missouri six feet above low water mark. Baptiste Dourion arrived this evening but brought us no news of our horses.

Friday 18th: Cool and cloudy, rain at intervals, employes pulling down the blacksmith's shop and moving back the east side of the fort. Missouri 5 feet above low water mark.

Saturday, June 19, 1830: Fine pleasant weather, finished arranging the fort. Missouri 6 feet above low water mark. Madam Dickson very sick.

Sunday 20th: Fine pleasant weather. Messrs L. Cerré and Bouchet dined with us. At Meridian 7 Poncas Indians arrived with one of the horses stolen last month, they say they have nine more of our horses in their possession which makes up the number missing, according to their story they were stolen by the Paunees of whom they say they took them after a slight skirmish in which one of their people was kill'd, but we are inclined to believe that they were stolen by the Poncas.

The Poncas say they are encamped on L'eau que course and have a considerable quantity of Beaver Skins, accordingly we put [up] a small equipment and dispatched Baptiste Dourion with them and a cart and one man to their camp for the purpose of trading with them, and to bring back our horses if Possible. Henri Angé accompanied them as a part of the horses and the property with W. Dickson his employee. Dicksons uncle, a Sonte Indian also was one of the party, two or three of the horses his property. Missouri is 5½ feet above low water mark.

Monday 21st: A continuation of pleasant weather. At 4 P.M. about 40 Ree & Paunee Indians arrived here on their way to the Ree village, they camp'd in the point above this. At 8 P.M. Angé, the Sontee Indian and two Poncas Indians returned to the fort. The Poncas started after the Rees and paunees this morning for the purpose of stealing horses, they have ten. The Pauneees deny having stole our horses. Missouri 5½ feet above low water mark.

Tuesday June 22d: Pleasant weather and Strong Southerly winds. Hands employed variously. Missouri 5 feet above low water mark. Madam Baptiste Dourian was delivered of a fine boy at 6 A.M. this morning.

Wednesday June 23d. Southerly winds and hot sultry weather. Hands employed variously. Missouri 5 feet above low water mark. At dusk cloudy weather with thunder and lightning. We find the flies trouble our horses [so] much to day that they are very restless.

Thursday June 24: First part of the day Cloudy. Messrs. Sarpy, Juett, Pineau, Miller & Dumond left here with all our horses for Medicine river,[42] where we intend keeping them for a month or two. Middle and latter part of the day Light Northerly winds and hot weather, the Mosquitos begin to be troublesome. Some of our people say they saw 4 men on the hill back of the fort this evening. Missouri 4½ feet above low water mark. Hands employed putting up a Blacksmiths Shop.

Friday June 25th: Through out the day warm, with light Showers of rain at intervals. Began making Packs, pressed fifteen. Missouri 3½ feet above low water mark.

Saturday June 26th: Clear & Hot. Hands employed working at the Blacksmith's shop & making and pressing packs, pressed 53 Packs. Missouri 3½ feet above low water mark.

Sunday June 27th: First and Middle part of the day Pleasant weather. At 7 A.M. saw a band of Buffaloe on the hill back of the fort, Chardon & Angé went out in pursuit of them and kill'd five. At 11 A.M. James Parker and Pierre Detaillier (two trappers) called on us, it appears that these two men in company of with [name blank] Carrier another trapper arrived at Cerré's house last evening with about two packs of Beaver. Latter part of the day hard showers of rain attended with thunder and Lightning. Missouri 4½ feet above low water mark. At sunrise this morning several Indians arrivd on the other side the Missouri with two or three horses, but as the wind blew strong from the east we were unable to cross them, & they went off about 11 A.M.

Monday June 28th: Fine pleasant weather, men employed working at Blacksmiths shop and pressing Packs. Pressed 15. At 1 P.M. Paul Dourian and his squaw arrived from the Mandans in a Skin canoe. Missouri 4½ feet above low water Mark.

Tuesday June 29: Hot Sultry weather, at intervals hard showers of rain, finished the Blacksmith Shop. Missouri 4½ feet above low water mark.

Wednesday 30th: Same weather as Yesterday At 12 A.M. Baptiste Daurion arrived with all our horses, 11 Packs Robes and 2 lbs. Beaver from the Poncas. The Hoe (a Poncas Chief) and 8 of his young men came in with Baptiste. The Hoe acknowledged that it was [h]is own people who stole the horses. Baptiste says that the Poncas have still about 20 Packs of Robes and that they are now on their way to White river with their lodges. Finished pressing one packs to day, find we have 166 of Robes and one of Beaver Skins. Missouri is 4½ feet above low water mark.

[July 1830]

Thursday July 1st: Hot sultry weather, with showers of rain at intervals. Hands employed variously. At 12 A.M. J. Juett and Thomas Dumond arrived from Medicine river where our horses are. Missouri 4½ feet above low water mark.

Friday July 2d: First part of the day Cloudy weather and very hot. At 7 A.M. Baptiste Daurion and the Ponca left here. Daurion has an equipment of Goods to trade what the Poncas may have. At 10 A.M. 5 men arrived in a canoe from the Mandans. They say, they with two other men were turned out of the fort at the Mandans by Mr. McKnight, and after remaining six days with the Indians, they succeeded in getting a canoe, and departed with the intention of descending to St. Louis. We endeavoured to persuade them by fair means to remain here untill Mr. McKenzie arrives from above, but in this we failed, consequently Mr. Chardon and Myself armed ourselves, took two of our men, had the canoe unloaded and hauled in to the fort, the Mandan men made no resistance. Missouri 4½ feet above low water mark.

Sunday July 4th: The Anniversary of the declaration of Independence of the United States was ushered in upon us with fine pleasant weather. At 10 A.M. manned our canoe and Mr. Chardon and myself proceedd down to Mr. Cerré's house where we were received with a salute of their guns, we passed an hour there and returned home, where we were again saluted. At 1 P.M. Thomas Dumond arrived from Medicine river where the horses are. They intend leaving Medicine river with the horses and to camp somewheres in the Grand Detour for fear the Poncas will find out their present situation. The day ends pleasantly. Missouri 3 feet above low water mark.

Monday 5th: Pleasant weather and moderate northerly winds, in the morning Sent Letand and 4 men up to the navy Yard to make a Boat to cross horses in. The rest of our men employed variously. The Blacksmith repairing beaver traps, &c. &. Missouri same as yesterday.

Tuesday 6th: Very Hot. At 4 P.M. T. L. Sarpy and Henri Augé came in from the Big Bend[43] with four horses loaded with fresh meat, plenty of cattle where our people are encamped. Sent Alexis Dusman up to the navy Yard this morning to bring down our canoes. Missouri same as Yesterday, in the evening Dusman return'd with the canoe.

Wednesday 7th: A continuation of hot Sultry weather, in the morning T. L. Sarpy and J. Vasseur left here for the Big Bend. Men employed cutting wood to make charcoal. Missouri same as yesterday.

Thursday 8th: Same weather as Yesterday. Men at the same employment. Missouri 3½ feet above low water mark, in the evening Mr. Miller arrived from the Big Bend.

Friday 9th: Hot weather, at 3 P.M. Antoine Chesnie and Alexander Matthews arrived from Fort Union in a canoe they gave us a letter from McKnight at the Mandans & then proceeded on to Mr Cerré's establishment. Latter part of the day hard showers of rain. Missouri 3 feet above low water mark.

Saturday July 10th: Light southerly winds and pleasant weather. Baptiste & Party arrived from the Poncas camp with Peltries &c. A Poncas chief called La Bouchanne and another Indian came with him. We hear by Darion that the Brulés are not more than 30 miles from here with their Lodges. Sent off a man to the Big bend to tell our people to come in with all our horses. Missouri as Yesterday.

Sunday 11th: Hot Sultry weather, in the morning the Poncas left here. Missouri as yesterday.

Monday 12th: Same weather as yesterday. At 9 A.M. our people arrived with all our horses. Missouri 3 feet above low water mark. At 12 A.M. our men arrived from the Navy Yard with a Batteaux.

Tuesday July 13th 1830: Fine pleasant weather, with Moderate Southerly winds, in the morning T. L. Sarpy & L. Lagrave left here for the Brulé's camp with a small equipment to trade what he may find, in the evening 2 Indians arrived from the Brulés. Missouri 3 1/2 feet above low water mark.

Wednesday 14th: Light S.W. winds and Hot.

Thursday 15th: Fine pleasant weather and moderate southerly winds at 9 A.M. Kenneth McKenzie, Esqr. Arrived from Fort Union with a keel boat laden with furs & Peltries, he was accompanied by Messrs. Leclair, Fallon, Garves, Lachapelle & Degray.

Friday 16: Left here with Mr. McKenzie in Keel boat Otter bound for St. Louis.

[no entries for Saturday, July 17, through Saturday, July 24]

Sunday, 25th: On the 21st ultimo we arrived at Vermillion river where we found two of the cos. traders (Colin Campbell[44] and Joseph Lacompt).

On the 22d. met a Keel boat belonging to the Coy. loaded with mdse. and bound for Fort Union. At Meridian on the 24th we arrived at Council Bluffs, or rather at Cabaneés establishment[45] 7 miles below the Bluffs, here we expected to receive some intelligence of a [word?] boat from St. Louis, which was to have left that place eight days after the first, but nothing has been heard of her. Keel boat Otter proceeded on her voyage this morning and if I hear nothing of the other boat tomorrow I shall prepare myself to return above by land.

Monday 26th: Hot weather toward evening Shower of rain and thunder and Lightning.

Tuesday 27th: Same weather as Yesterday, had the [word?] all the last night.

Wednesday July 28th: Strong South winds and Hot, at night a thunder shower. This morning I sent off Mongrain a half Indian to fort Tecumseh with a letter to Mr. Chardon. I should have went above with him but sickness prevents me. I am sure in my present state of health I never would be able to reach Fort T. a horse-back, therefore I cannot reproach myself for not going above at present.

Thursday 29, Friday, 30, Saturday, 31st: A continuation of Strong S. winds & hot weather, but a Thunder Shower every day. This is the most disagreeable hole I ever was at in my life. The Mosquitos are not only very thick, but the fleas are still in greater abundance. My health continues bad I have the fever at night, and a violent headache throughout the day.

[August 1830]

Sunday August 1: Hot weather with a shower at night.

Monday [August] 2. Same weather as yesterday.

Tuesday [August] 3d. Clear & Pleasant, and what is wonderful no rain. But plenty of fleas & Mosquitoes.

Wednesday August 4th: Pleasant weather. A man arrived from Belview,[46] Pilchers old establishment, he says a party of Iowas arrived there a few days ago who report that a Keel boat was lost in ascending the Missouri about 50 Miles above cantonment Leavensworth, if this news be true it is no doubt the Cos. boat loaded with Mdse. from St. Louis which we have been for some time expecting here.

Thursday 5th: Same weather as Yesterday with a Strong South wind. I forgot to mention Yesterday that a canoe passed here from above with four men in it, as they made no stop here, I think they are deserters.

Friday Augt. 6th, 1830: Fine pleasant weather, a man arrived from St. Louis with dispatches from Mr. Cabanies, he says he left Mr. Picotte with five mules loaded with Mdse. at the Riviere Platte, he also brought the news of the loss of one of Cos. boats a short distance above Cantonment Leavensworth.

Saturday 7th: A continuation of fine pleasant weather, at 10 A.M. Mr. Picotte of the firm P. D. Papin & Co. arrived with five mules and one horse laden with Mdse. for the trade of the Upper Missouri, he will leave here tomorrow for Teton river as my health is now better I shall accompany him.

Sunday 8th: Fine pleasant weather. At 10 A.M. left this establishment in company of Mr. Picotte, two of his clerks, one hand, and a Souix Indian called the Mauvaise Boeuf who is returning from a visit to his father the "Gray head" (Genl. Clark).[47]

Thursday 12th: We had pleasant weather since we left Cabannes establishment. At 1 P.M. sent W. Rodgers and the Souix Indian ahead of us to the Mahas[48] village, we however do not expect to find Indians there, but are in hopes of finding a Saddle or two which we are much in want of, at dusk we were disagreeably disapointed by meeting with two Indians (Mahas) they informed us that the most of the Mahas were at the village. Rodgers has sent them to us to recommend us to camp and not attempt to go to [the] village to night, consequently we encamped 2 miles from the village.

Friday 13th: At Sunrise arrived at the village, [word struck out] ~~that~~ where we found the Mauvaise Boeuf was in danger of having his scalp taken by the Mahas, his nation having but a short time previous killed two Mahas, through the influence of the braves of the tribe his life was spared, about twenty of the principal men accompanied us 4 or 5 miles from the village, to accomplish this object, at 8 P.M. we encamped after hiding ourselves a few mile out of the road.

Sunday 22d: At 8 P.M. arrived at Mr. Cerre's house on teton river where I passed the night.

Monday 23d: At daylight crossed Teton river and arrived at Fort Tecumseh at sunrise, where I found Messrs. Gordon, Chardon, Holliday, Campbell and several other clerks of the Coy. Throughout the whole of the trip from the Bluffs to this establishment we had pleasant weather and no rain. I however enjoyed it but little as I was several times attacked by the intermittent fever.

Tuesday 24th: Fine pleasant weather, we have 10 or 12 Lodges of Indians here. I have just heard that three white men have been recently kill'd by the Rees, viz. Pierre Bouchet, Jos. Passiche and another man whose name I do not know, they were kill'd between the Rees village and the Mandans by a war party of Rees, they had Mdse. and horses to the amount of $1000.

Wednesday 25th August: Strong Southerly winds and pleasant. Lachapelle and Pineau arrived, it appears that Lachapelle was sent up to join the Keel boat "Twin Males" which left here on the 19th Ultimo bound for fort Union, and to make every endeavour to affect her passage by the Rees village, in case those Indians should prove to be unwilling to let her pass, he says he made a strict search after the boat for one day and a half without finding her, or even discouvering any trace of her. Mr. Picotte Came up and dined with us to day. Indians are poring in from every quarter.

Thursday 26th: Strong westerly winds and Clear. Dispatched Lachapelle again for the Ree village on the same errant he was sent before. Mr. Picotte accompanied him, he goes to see if anything can be saved of the property which the Rees must have plundered the white man they recently murdered.

Friday 27th: Cloudy weather, and Strong easterly winds.

Saturday 28. Same weather as yesterday, at dusk a little rain fell. The Indians have play'd great havoc in our Garden, stoled Corn, Potatoes, Pumpkins &c. &c., spoke to the Soldiers[49] about it but it seems to be of little use.

Sunday August 29th: Pleasant weather. Several lodges of Yanctons arrived to day. Hands employed in bringing in our hay and Stacking it.

Monday 30th: A continuation of pleasant weather, hands employed as yesterday.

Tuesday August 31st: Strong Northerly winds and pleasant weather. 5 Black feet Indians arrived here yesterday with several Lodges of Brulés.[50] The Indians have Stole about half our potatoes.

[September 1830]

Wednesday Sept: 1st: The Indians stole nearly all our potatoes last night, at 10 A.M. Lachapelle arrived from the Rees. The boat passed that place the 8th day after the[y] left here. Piccotte returned with Lachapelle, several more Lodges of Indians arrived to day, in the evening several more Indians arrived.

Thursday, Sept: 2d: In the morning a thick fog. Middle and latter part fine, pleasant weather, at 11 A.M. Messrs Laidlaw, J. L. Bean[51] (U. S. Sub Indian Agent) Mitchel, Primeau, Laboue, T. & W. Dickson, and Hamilton with 4 men arrived from St. Louis. Mr. Hamilton is an English gentleman traveling for curiosity.[52]

Friday Sept: 3d: First part of the day a little rain fell, Middle and latter part fine pleasant weather. Men employed in digging potatoes, the Indians continue stealing potatoes as usual, they are much more troublesome this year than I ever knew them to be. At 12 A.M. sent Lachapelle & Boulé with an Indian and 3 Horses, to the Sawons camp for Dry Meat.

Saturday Sept 4th: First part of the day a little rain fell. Middle and latter part fine pleasant weather. J. L. Bean U. S. Indian Agent held a grand council with the Yanctons and Brulés, he presented each nation with a barrel tobacco, he contemplates leaving here in 7 or 8 days for St. Louis with 8 or 10 Yanctons, and says he expects to return to this place with the Yanctons some time in November next, when he will make his present to the different bands.

Sunday Sept: 5th: Fine pleasant weather. Hands employed digging potatoes. The Indians still continue stealing them before our faces.

Monday Sept 6th: Cloudy weather. Hands variously employed. I forgot to mention that Messrs. T. Dickson, J. M. Holiday & F. Laboue left here yesterday for the Brulé's camp to trade what they may find.

Tuesday Sept 7th: Disagreeable rainy weather, many of the Indians left us Yesterday.

Wednesday 8th: Clear & pleasant n the morning. Maj. J. L. Bean left here for St. Louis in a Batteaux with 21 Indians (all Yanctons except one the "Broken leg" (Brulé). Mr. W. Gordon also accompanied him. At 9 A.M. Michlin Primeau started in a Batteau with Mdse: and four men for the Rees, to trade corn. At the same time sent off Baptiste Dourion and Louison Brulé to hunt some horses which were lost by Mr. Laidlaw's party.

Thursday 9th Sept: 1830: Clear with a strong wind from the north which increased till 4 P.M. when it blew a hard gale. Mr. T. Dickson and party arrived from the Brulé's camp with 4 Horses loaded with meat.

Friday 10th: Throughout the day Strong north winds, and Cold weather.

Saturday 11th: Same weather as Yesterday although not quite as cold. Baptiste Daurion and party returned without news of the horses.

Sunday 12th: Clear and a Strong Northerly wind, went out to gather plums, found but few fit to eat, a Lodge arrived on the other side the Missouri.

Monday 13th: Cloudy and cool with a strong Northerly wind.

Tuesday 14th: A continuation of Cloudy weather. Cardinal Grant arrived from hunting with a few Beaver Skins.

Wednesday 15th: Northerly winds and cloudy weather with an appearance of a storm J. B. Derain (a Beaver Hunter) arrived.

Thursday 16th: Still continues cloudy with northerly winds, put [up] an Equipment of goods for the Saons and Chyennes.

Friday 17th: Same weather as Yesterday. Chardon, Dourion and Gontieras left here for the Sawon camp with 6 horses loaded with Mdse. J. B. Deroin left us in the morning early.

Saturday 18th Sept: 1830: Fine pleasant weather, hands variously employed.

Sunday 19th: First part of the day cloudy weather, Middle and latter part of the day fine pleasant weather. Mr. Laidlaw visited with Mr. Cerré. We are at present very anxious about Lachapelle and party who left here on the 8th Ultimo for the Sawons camp; one of Mr. Cerré's men arrived from there, the day before yesterday, and he says Lachapelle left the camp on his return three days before him, he had a good guide with him, therefore we do not think he could have got lost. The present presumption is that he has been kill'd by some war party.

Monday Sept: 20th: Throughout the day strong Northerly winds and cloudy weather.

Tuesday Sept: 21st: Cloudy weather throughout the day, at night a little rain fell.

Wednesday 22d: First part of the day cloudy weather. Middle and latter part light Airs from the Southward and fine pleasant weather. Millien Primeau and party arrived from the Rees with about 100 bushels Corn and a quantity of fresh meat. Primeau met Lachapelle and party at the Mouth of Chyenne river, descending in a skin canoe with three hundred p[iece]s. Dry Meat.

Thursday Sept: 23d. Southerly winds and Fine pleasant weather.

Friday Sept: 24th: Light airs from the South and fine weather in the Morning. Lachapelle & Dufond arrived from the Souix camp on cheyenne river in a skin canoe laden with Dry Meat. At 10 A.M. sent out Pineau le Yancton and one or two men to hunt.

Saturday Sept 25th: Fine pleasant weather, and nothing new, hands employed variously.

Sunday 26: Same weather as yesterday.

Monday Sept: 27: Throughout the day fine pleasant weather. At dusk Mr. P. N. Leclaire and Bapt. Defond arrived from St. Louis with 7 horses. On their arrival at the poncas they fell in with two Yanctons who expressed their wish [to] accompany them to this place. Mr. Laclare without hesitation immediately consented, they accordingly sett out together. Mr. Leclaire taking with him a boatman of the name of Pierre Golsin to assist him on the journey. On the 25 Ultimo about 4 P.M. as they were riding along Poncas river they were suddenly attacked by the two Yancton Indians. Pierre Goslin the first attacked was dangerously wounded by an arrow, they also fired at Leclare, but owing to the fleetness of his horse he escaped injury after they had fired 5 or 6 shots at Leclare and his party, he (Leclaire) succeeded in stopping his horse, dismounted and was preparing to fire on the Indians when he perceived them retreating with all possible speed. As the place where they were attacked was thickly wooded and the Indians had concealed themselves in the bushes. Mr. Leclare and two mounted companions thought it best to proceed on their journey with all possible dispatch, after travelling about two hours Goslin became worse, declared his utter inability to proceed further, as none of the party had an axe, and as Lecliare was situated, without any help whatever & Golsin unable to ride, he was [word?] forced to the heartrending necessity of leaving the poor fellow in the prairie, after having placed him on the banks of Poncas river,[53] and given him a sufficient quantity of biscuit to keep him alive 5 or 6 days. Thus it is, the Yanctons, Who have always been very friendly with the whites, and have never before attempted the life of a White man have at length commenced.

Tuesday Sept: 28th: First part of the day Southerly winds and cool weather. Middle and latter part fine & pleasant. A man came up from Mr. Cerré's house with news that the two yanctons who attacked Leclaire's party had arrived there, what hardihood, what an insult. A party of us armed ourselves and proceeded out in pursuit of them, but they discovered us and fled to the plains, we consequently gave up the chase and returned home at 7 P.M. Our only object was to frighten the Scoundrels.

Wednesday Sept: 29th: Southerly winds and pleasant weather. Hands variously employed.

Thursday Sept. 30th: Same weather as yesterday, employees overhauling the potatoes find a good many of them are rotten.

[October 1830]

Friday Oct: 1st: Light southerly winds and Hot weather.

Saturday Oct: 2nd: Fine pleasant weather. F. Roy arrived from our Keel boats which he says he left in the Grand detour, on Thursday last.

Sunday Oct: 3rd 1830: First part of the day light Easterly winds and fine. Middle and latter part calm and pleasant. Messrs. Picotte and Cerré dined with us, at dark saw a fire on the river some distance below, the mouth of Teton river, we suppose it to be on board our boats, from St. Louis.

Monday Oct 4th: Keel boats Beaver and Musk Rat arrived from St. Louis, the Musk Rat at 10, and the Beaver at 12 A.M. unloaded both boats, J. Holliday and the Indian sent in Search of Pierre Gauslin returned without success.

Tuesday 5th: Put up an Equipment of Goods for the Brulés on White River.

Wednesday 6th: Emillien Primeau started with 7 horses & a mule laden with goods for the Brulés on White River. Put up two Equipments of Goods 1 for the Sawons and Chyennes and 1 for the Ogallallas.

Thursday 7th: Put up two Equipments of goods 1 for Rees and 1 for the Oncpapas.[54]

Friday 8th: Put up an Equipment of goods for the trade with the Yanctonnas. At 10 A.M. loaded Keel boat "Muskrat" with three Equipments goods one for the Rees, one for the Oncpapas and one for the Yantonnas, at 2½ P.M. the musk Rat left here with Mr. D. D. Mitchel for the Yantonnas, R. T. Hilleday [Holliday] for the Rees and F. Laboue for the Oncpapas, and twenty five men for the three different posts.

Saturday Oct. 9th: First part of the day thick Foggy weather, Middle and latter part Cloudy. Sent off goods for the Ogallallas, Sawons, Chyennes Outfits. A sunsett Messrs. McKenzie, Lamont, Fallon, May and five or six men arrived from St. Louis.

Sunday 10th October 1830: Clear and Hot weather. F. A. Chardon left here with three horses laden with Mdse. for the Sawon and Chyenne Outfits.

Monday Oct: 11th: A continuation of hot weather. Sent off a Cart For Sawon & Chyenne Outfit with Mr. Laidlaws property. I forgot to mention that Messrs. P. D. Papin & Cos. boat arrived here on the 9th Ultimo, on the 10th Mr. Hays left here in a Skiff with six men, he is ordered to proceed down the Missouri till he falls in with Keel boat "L. Valle" he is then to use all his influence to expedite her arrival here.

Tuesday Oct: 12th: Strong Gales from the North west and Cold weather. Hands variously employed.

Wednesday Oct 13th: Same weather as Yesterday in the evening Messrs. Beemer, Papin, Picotte, Chenie and the two Cerre's called on us.

Thursday Oct: 14th: Throughout the day Strong Northerly winds and pleasant. Bought out P. D. Papin & Co, engaged Papin, Cerre & Picotte, the other two are to return to St. Louis.

Friday Oct: 15th: Mr. Laidlaw Started early this morning for forks Chyenne river, At 12 A.M. Messrs. Papin & Co. delivered us their Keel boat laden with Mdse. &c, and at the same time we sent down one of our own boats to bring up what they may have remaining.

Saturday Oct: 16: At 10 A.M. Messrs. Papin & Co. delivered us the bal[ance] of their property, commenced unloading boats and weighing the cargoes.

Sunday Oct: 17th: Engaged taking the count of Papin & Co property. First and middle part of the day Northeast winds and cloudy weather, at night a little rain fell.

Monday Oct: 18th: Cool and windy, finished taking account of Papin & Co property.

Tuesday Oct: 19th: Throughout the day Moderate and fair, employ'd bailing and packing up goods. Several Free hunters arrived with Beaver viz Lacomb, Gagnier, Dumond, Leclair.

Wednesday Oct: 20th: Same weather as yesterday, sent a boat down [to] Papin's & Co old establishment to bring up our two buildings, the boat returned at 12 A.M. and we immediately sett the men to work raising two houses.

Thursday Oct: 21st: Fine pleasant weather, several Indians arrived from the other side the Missouri, hands employed variously, in the evening Pierre Garrow left here for the Rees with dispatches for Messrs. Holliday & Mitchell.

Friday Oct: 22d: Clear and warm commenced loading Keel boat Fox, for the Mandans. Hands employed as Yesterday.

Saturday Oct 23d: Finished loading Keel boat "Fox" at 4 P.M. she left here bound for F. Clark,[55] 21 men and Messrs. Picotte, P. Cerré, and I. Brasseau Clerks on board.

Sunday 24th: Light Southerly wind and fine, several lodges of Yanctons arrived and camp near the fort, they have with them one of the Indians who attacked Leclerc and party some time ago, they wished to surrender him to Mr. McKenzie, but he told them to keep him till their father came up and deliver him to [word struck out] him.

Monday Oct: 25th: Fine pleasant weather for this season, hands variously employed.

Tuesday Oct: 26th: Same weather as Yesterday. Dithonette and a Yancton (Campbells comrade) arrived from the Brulés with two of our horses which were lately stolen by that band.

Wednesday 27th: Cool with the appearance of a storm. Engaged preparing papers for St. Louis, at night Campbells comrade wounded the murderer of Gauslin, some little excitement was shown by the Indians at the moment, consequently we all prepared ourselves for an attack, but all was quiet at Midnight. The Indian I believe is mortally wounded.

Thursday 28th: The Yanctons raised their lodges and left us, the murderer of Gauslin not dead yet, but it is not thought he will live long. Mr. McKenzie dressed the Indian who risked his life so much for us, he was presented with every thing to ornament himself with, among the different articles was a sword, he left here late in the evening for White River. A Batteaux left for St. Louis.

Friday 29th: Clear and Warm. Mr. Laidlaw arrived from the Sawons. Several Yanctonnas arrived yesterday from the Chyenne river, in the evening some men came in from Primeau's establishment on white River.

Saturday Oct: 30: Throughout the day Cool and pleasant weather. I forgot to mention that the murderer of Pierre Gauslin died yesterday morning.

Sunday Oct: 31st: Cool and pleasant Throughout the day. Wind Southerly.

[November 1830]

Monday November 1st: The morning cold, a hard frost last night, hands employed variously. Sent of[f] three men and 7 horses loaded with Mdse. for White River Outfit.

Tuesday November 2d: Strong Westerly winds throughout the day,

Wednesday 3d: Same weather as yesterday.

Thursday 4th: Moderate winds and Cloudy, 4 men arrived from the Sawons with four carts laden with Dry Meat, Robes, &c.

Friday 5th: Strong N.E. winds and cold.

Saturday 6th & Sunday 7th: Clear & cool
On Saturday Mr. Laidlaw left here for his

establishment on the Chyenne, on the 7th Leclair, Gagnier & Dumond [word?] left here for the same place.

Monday 8th: Southerly winds and cool weather. Employed variously.

Tuesday 9th: Light southerly winds and cool, at 2 P.M. Keel boat "Louis Vallé" arrived from St. Louis, unloaded her and put the goods in the Store.

Wednesday 10th: Cool & Cloudy with an appearance of Snow. Blacksmith employed shoeing horses.

Thursday 11th: Same weather as Yesterday, hands variously employed. Blacksmith shoeing horses.

Friday Nov. 12th 1830: Cool weather and Strong Southerly winds. Finished Shoeing the horses.

Saturday Nov. 13th: Messrs. Leclerc, Lafierre, May and 7 men and 22 horses & mules left here for the Upper Country.

Sunday 14th: First part of the day Cloudy. Mr. McKenzie accompanied by Thos. Dickson left us For Ft. Union. An Indian left here for the Riviere Bois blanc[56] for dispatches to William Dickson. Middle and latter part of the day raining or Snowing. 5 or 6 Yanctons arrived here yesterday and left us today.

Monday 15th: Moderate and cloudy, an Indian arrived From Sawon camp on Chyenne river, hands employed variously. Carpenter making a desk and cooper making Kegs.

Tuesday 16th: Hard Frost last night, throughout the day cool with moderate westerly winds hands employed cutting fire wood, plastering the houses, &c.

Wednesday 17th: It Snowed hard throughout the day, sent Alexis Tibiaut with one of the boats after a load of Fire wood at night clear and cold.

Thursday 18th: Clear & Cold ice drifting in Missouri. Sent off Keel boat "Louis Vallé" with 13 men For the Chyenne river to cut timber for a Fort.

Friday 19th: Ice drifting thick to day in river, Cold and cloudy.

Saturday 20th: Fine pleasant weather, ~~but the~~ last night was cold, ice drifting much thicker to day than yesterday, sent off 5 men to the Navy Yard with all our horses (43 including private property), in the morning an Indian and squaw who arrived here on the Fifteenth from the Sawons left us (as they say) for the Brulés camp on white river, two Yanctons who went out hunting 5 or 6 days ago returned to day. I understand the[y] kill'd six deer, they gave us the Flesh of one.

Sunday Nov: 21st: Throughout the day thick cloudy weather and an appearance of more Snow. Not so much ice drifting to day as Saturday.

Monday 22d: Cool & Cloudy weather. L. Lachapelle and Louis Obachon arrived from the Rees in the evening with dispatches from Mr. R. S. Holliday in Charge of the Cos. establishment at that place.

Tuesday 23rd: Same weather as yesterday, but not so much ice drifting, in the evening Antoine [Name?] Pierre Detaillier, and Alexander Matthews, beaver trappers arrived with something less than a pack Beaver. Hands employed variously, some cutting fire wood, others making Balls. &c.

Wednesday 24th: Sent off Louis Obachon to the Rees with letters to Frederick Laboue and R. S. Holliday. Weather cloudy, with southerly winds, no ice drifting. Hands employed as yesterday.

Thursday 25th: A continuation of Cloudy weather. Hands employed, Cutting firewood, making Balls. and melting Grease,[57] & Julien Chouquette sick, off duty. At dark one of our men, and two Indians arrived from [word?] establishment on White river with 5 horses and much loaded with dry Meat, they left three men behind with [two words?] loaded with the same article.

Friday November 26th: In the morning the cart from White River with 48 ps Dry Meat which (including that received yesterday, makes in all 171 pieces, the weather throughout the day cloudy and moderate, but the ice drifting thick. In the evening put up some Lances and Powder for white river Outfit, through the night strong N.W. winds and Cloudy, hands variously employed. Julien Chouquette Sick and off duty.

Saturday 27th: The men belonging to White river Outfit left here this morning with 4 horses and a mule. Weather mild and Clear. In the evening Jacob Mayotte arrived from the Navy Yard after [word?]. Hands employed Cutting and hauling Fire wood &c &c. Julien Chouquette Sick and off duty.

Sunday 28th: Sent off Mayotte & Vachard to the Navy Yard with 54 ps. Dry Meat. At noon three lodges Yanctonnas arrived on the other side the Missouri. Sent over three men with Skiff and crossed them.

Monday 29th: Fine pleasant weather, hands employed Cutting fire wood, making Balls &c.

Tuesday 30th: Same weather as Yesterday. One Lodge of Yanctons left here for White River, hands employed cutting wood, making balls &c Julien Chouquette sick and off duty.

[December 1830]

Wednesday Dec. 1st. 1830: The Yanctons who arrived from the other side on the 25th inst. left us. Giroux arrived from Mr. Papin's establishment at Straw Cabin creek.[58] Weather fine. Hands employed cutting wood and making Balls. Mr. Hay and Bapt. Boyer arrived from White river with four Indians and a Squaw no ice drifting.

Thursday 2d: Throughout the day Strong N.W. winds and rain and snow. No ice drifting in the Missouri.

Friday 3d: Cool, with N.W. winds and passing clouds, hands employed variously.

Saturday 4th: Fine pleasant weather, 3 of the Indians went out a hunting but returned unsuccessful. Hands employed Cutting wood making balls, lying corn &c., a little ice drifting in the Missouri.

Sunday 5th: Same weather as yesterday, ice drifting thick in the Missouri.

Monday 6th: Southerly winds and Cold. Hands variously employed.

Tuesday 7th: Southerly winds and Cloudy weather. Hands employed as usual. Messrs. Lamont and Hamilton went out walking and returned with a wolf, which Mr Lamont [words ?].

Wednesday 8th: Throughout the day Moderate N.E. winds, and Snow, at 10 pm wind at N.W. and Clear.

Thursday 9th: Cloudy weather Northerly winds and snow. Pierre Detallier and Albert Paquette arrived from the Yancton trading house on White River.

Friday 10th: Throughout the day cold and Cloudy, two men arrived from the Navy yard for provisions. Zephine and two Indians went out hunting, Campbells comrade kill'd a Deer, the others were unsuccessful. Hands employed making a coal kiln &c. &c.

Saturday 11th: Strong N.E. and Snow throughout the day. The last night was the coldest we have had his winter. Thermometer at 13 degrees above Zero. The Missouri closed At 9 P.M. Still continued Snowing.

Sunday 12th: Northwest winds and very cold, sent the two men back to the navy yard with provisions &c. At 10 P.M. Cloudy, Thermometer at 4 degrees above Zero.

Monday 13th: Cold and Cloudy at intervals light falls of snow, at daylight the thermometer was at Zero, at Meridian 8 degrees above and at sunsett 4 above Zero. Hands employed as usual throughout the day.

Tuesday 14th: Same weather as Yesterday. At daylight Thermometer at Zero, at Meridian 6 above and at Sunsett 4 degrees above Zero. At daylight Mr Hay was dispatched to Mr. Laidlaw's establishment with 4 men in quest of provisions at 6 P.M. an Indian arrived, he says he is from the Honcpapas who are camped on the head of Moreau's River and have plenty of Buffalos.

Wednesday December 15th 1830: Still continues Cold, at daylight thermometer at 10 degrees above Zero, at daylight at dark 4 above. Jacques Mayotte arrived from the Navy Yard for Iron bolts for traces &c. Hands Variously employed.

Thursday December 16th: Throughout the day strong gales from the North very Cold weather, 2 more men arrived from the Navy Yard for Provisions &c.

Friday 17th: Moderate North winds and pleasant at daylight Thermometer at 10 above Zero, at Meridian 16, and at Sunsett 12 above Zero. Sent off two men to the Navy Yard with provisions &c, the Indian who arrived from the Honcpappas on the 14th left in company with them. Hands employed as usual.

Saturday 18th: Throughout the day Cloudy weather. The Thermometer variated but Little from 10 degrees below freezing. Two of the Indians went out to hunt today, one of them returned in the evening without Success. At 9 P.M. Louison Raboin arrived from Laboue's establishment on Moreau's river with a letter from him, and one from Mr. R.S. Holliday at the Rees. Mr. Holliday states in his letter that Mr. McKenzie's party was pillaged by a war party of Rees the second day after their departure from their Villages. It appears from what Mr. Holliday has been able to learn, that the party was stopped in open day and their Saddles, Blkts. Tomahawks &c were forcibly taken from them. One of the party's Mules returned to the Ree village with an arrow sticking in his head. God send that this may be the worst of the story.

Sunday Dec: 19th: Southerly winds and Cold. The Thermometer 12 degrees below Freezing. In the morning the Indian who went out hunting Yesterday, returned with a fat deer. James Parker, Beaver Trapper arrived at the same time, he was sent in by Michel Cassier for the purpose of conducting out Lachapelle to his encampment something less than two days march from here, it is said they have 90 Beaver Skins.

Monday Dec: 20th: Strong N.E. winds and snow throughout the day. At daylight Thermometer at Zero. Meridian 3 below, and at 10 P.M. 7 degrees below Zero. Joseph Lemay arrived from the Navy Yard, he says he kill'd a Bull in that neighbourhood a few days ago.

Tuesday Dec: 21st: Strong North wind and very Cold. At daylight thermometer 10 degrees below Zero, at Noon it had risen to Two, and at 10 P.M. fell down to 10 degrees below. In the morning Chenier, Zephine and Campbells comrade went out to hunt. Hands employed variously.

Wednesday 22nd: Fine pleasant weather, at Sunrise the Thermometer 12 degrees below Zero, at 12 A.M. and 9 P.M. at Zero. At 12 A.M. Saw a Band of antelope on the opposite side the Missouri, sent off three Indians in pursuit of them they returned about an hour afterward with them, it is supposed there was at least 200 in the band. Started Louison Robain with two other men, for Laboues establishment on Moreau's river with letters to him and R.S. Holliday at the Rees. Also sent off two men to look for lost horses in the neighbourhood of White River where they were last seen.

Thursday Dec: 23rd: Pleasant weather [word?] Hamilton, J. Holliday and myself went out hunting but were unsuccessful. Chenise and Campbells comrade returned from hunting. They Say they have kill'd three deer and want a horse to go out and bring in the meat. Zephine remained to take care of it.

Friday Dec: 24th: Light N.W. winds and [word?] throughout the day. Chenise commenced work today. Sent off an Indian with a hand to bring in the deer kill'd buy Zephine and Campbells comrade, and [word?] Zephine and the Indian arrived with the deer and two Porcupines. In the evening an Indian arrived, he says he is from the neighbourhood of Dickson's establishment on the Riviere Bois Blanc, and there is three Lodges coming here from the same place, all of them Starving. At 10 P.M. Moderate and Clear.

Saturday 25th: Throughout the day clear and pleasant weather, two Indians arrived from the other side the Missouri where three Lodges Yanctons from La riviere Bois Blanc are camped.

Sunday 26th: Pleasant weather, the three Lodges from the other side the river came over and camped along side the fort. Chenise did not work Yesterday or to day. Moderate weather this day

Monday 27th Dec: Several of the Indians went out to hunt on the other side the river, at 2 P.M. they returned having seen a band of Buffalos and kill'd t[w]o females.

Tuesday Dec: 28th 1830: Fine mild weather, 2 men arrived from the Rees with letters from Mr. McKenzie and others at the Mandans. The Rees pillaged Mr. McK and party of every thing they had except their horses, and they took one of them. He has heard news of Mr Vanderburghs party, they have had a Battle with the Blackfeet Indians, they were victorious, it is supposed they kill'd between 30 & 40 Indians, and they lost but one man.[59] Several Indians went out to hunt to day and at 10 P.M. they had not returned.

Wednesday 29th: Mild weather, the Indians came in from hunting they saw a small band Buffaloe and kill'd two Cows. Lachapelle and the men who brought the express, left here to day for the Rees. Noel Richard left here for the Navy Yard with sundry Tools &c.

Thursday 30th: Still continues mild weather. Light fall of snow throughout the day. Letand and another man arrived from the Navy Yard. Engaged preparing dispatches for St. Louis.

Friday 31st: Moderate with snow at intervals. Zephine Recontre and Cyprian Denoyer left here with a Dog train with dispatches for St. Louis. Chenier worked ¾ of a day.

[January 1831]

Saturday Jan. 1, 1831: Throughout the day Strong S.E. wind and Cloudy weather. At 6 P.M. Giroux Indron arrived from the Yancton post with 25 ps. Dry Meat and 2 Horses, at the same time the Big Soldier (Yancton) arrived from St. Louis. He is one of the Indians who left here with [Major] Bean last Sept: two or three of the deputation have arrived at the Yancons camp, the Bal[ance] conducted by W. Gordon may be expected here to-morrow or next day. At 7 P.M. Two men arrived from the Yanctonnas Apple river. According to a/cs from that neighbourhood the snow is so deep to render communication between them and the Mandan post infrequent.

Sunday January 2d 1831: Throughout the day Strong N.W. winds and Clear, Chenier off duty. An Indian kill'd a Buffaloe about 15 miles from here.

Monday Jany. 3d: Giroux and an Indian left us for Yancton Post with Four and Lances. The Little Soutier another of the St. Louis deputation arrived he says Gordon will be here in day or two with the rest of the Indians.

Tuesday Jan 4th: North winds and Cold. Letand left here for the Navy Yard. Sent back two men who arrived from the Yanctonnas on the 1st. Chenier worked ¾ of a day.

Wednesday 5th: Cold and Cloudy. Messrs. Lamont and Hamilton went down the river on the ice in the Sleigh with the expectation of meeting Gordon and the rest of the Indians from St. Louis. Chenier off today.

Thursday 6th: Clear and Cold. Three of the Indians went out to hunt Buffaloe. Hands employed variously. Chenier and Chouquette off duty.

Friday 7th: Cold and Cloudy. Philbert and two men arrived from the Navy Yard with three broken axes and we have none to replace them neither have we any coal to repair them. One of the Indian hunters returned to day, he brought with him the Tongues of four Buffalos which he kill'd in the neighbourhood of the Village de tens, he says Buffaloe are plenty in that neighbourhood. The other two Indians remained to take care of the Meat. Chenier Shod a horse to day.

Chouquette Sick and off duty. Messrs. Lamont and Hamilton arrived at 10 P.M. they saw no signs of Gordon. One of our [two words?] this evening.

Saturday Jany. 8th: Throughout the day clear and pleasant. Thermometer in the morning 10 degrees above Zero, at noon 15 and at night at Two. Lemay, Vachard, and Hilbert returned from hunting the horses lost by McKenzie and party in Route from St. Louis to this place, they saw no signs of them but fell in with Gordon in the neighbourhood of Bijou hills,[60] he delivered them a package of letters and papers from St. Louis, by which we have tidings of a late revolution in France in which many thousands were kill'd and wounded. Charles X driven off and the Duke of Orleans proclaimed King.[61]

Sunday Jany. 9th: Cloudy weather Thermometer in the morning at Zero, at noon 10 above at 9 P.M. at Two.

Monday 10th: Clear and Cold Thermometer at Sunrise 14 below Zero, at noon 10 and at night 10 above Zero. Phillibert and Richard left for the Navy Yard.

Tuesday 11th: Cloudy and mild with a strong westerly wind. Thermometer in the morning 20 degrees above Zero, at noon 30, and at night 20 above. Mr. Hay arrived from Mr. Laidlaws establishment with 230 pieces of dry Meat and 13 horses and Mules. He left one horse on the road. Buffaloe in abundance not more than a days march from here.

Wednesday 12th: Continues moderate. Thermometer 20 degrees above Zero. Two men arrived from the Breaks with 4 horses loaded with Robes, at night Cloudy with an appearance of rain. Sent off two men in the morning to the Yanctonnas, Apple River for Beaver Trade.

Thursday Jan 13th 1831: Still continues moderate and cloudy weather, Sent of[f] four indians to hunt Buffalos, if they find plenty they are to camp and endeavour to kill us a good supply. Thermometer throughout the day 20 degrees above Zero. Hands employed taking care of the horses, making a coal kiln, &c. &c.

Friday Jany. 14th: First part of the day clear and cold. Thermometer 10 above Zero. Sent back the two men who arrived from the Brulés on the 12th inst. the[y] have four horses loaded with Mdse: Middle and latter part of the day cloudy at noon thermometer 20 above Zero, at night 30. Hands employed as yesterday.

Saturday Jany. 15th: Cool and pleasant the first part of the day, Middle and latter part Strong gales from the north and cloudy. At Sunrise Thermometer at 10 above Zero, noon 30 above at night 10 above, one of the Indian hunters came in he says they have killed 4 Buffalo and want horses to bring in the meat. Hands employed as usual.

Sunday 16th: Cold and Cloudy at daylight the Thermometer stood 10 above Zero, at noon 20 and at night 10 above. At intervals throughout the day a little snow fell.

Monday 17th: Clear and pleasant, but cold, at daylight thermometer at Zero, at meridian 20 above and at dark ten above Zero.

Tuesday 18th: Moderate weather. Mr. Gordon and lady arrived from St. Louis. Sent off Dauphine with two men and 8 horses laden with Mdse. for Sawon and Chyenne Outfit.

Wednesday 19th: Throughout the day clear and mild weather, some of our Indian hunters came in with fresh Buffaloe meat, they say they (Buffaloe) are in abundance about 15 miles from here.

Thursday 20th January 1831: Fine pleasant weather for the season. Gagnier and Paul Dourion came in from hunting with four horses laden with fresh Buffaloe meat. Hands employed variously, Chenier off duty.

Friday 21st: Same weather as yesterday, Chenier at work mending Axes. Middle and latter part of the day cloudy with Strong North wind and snow at intervals.

Saturday 22d: Cold and cloudy throughout the day with the appearance of Snow, 2 men arrived from the Navy Yard with broken axes, they also brought two Beaver Traps and a letter from Mr Holliday at the Rees. Three of the Indians went off to the Yancton Camp on White River.

Sunday 23d: Same weather as yesterday, at intervals a little snow fall.

Monday 24th: North wind and cold with snow at intervals. Giroux arrived from the Yancton Post. Hands variously employed.

Tuesday 25th: Begins with N.E. winds cold weather and Snow. Giroux left here for the Yancton camp.

Sent t[w]o men back to the Navy Yard with axes Ammunition &c.

Wednesday 26th: Cold with North winds and cloudy weather and snow at intervals. Hands employed as usual.

Thursday 27th: Moderate and Clear, the first and middle part of the day. Joe. Jouett with two men and 5 horses, and mules arrived from Mr. Laidlaws establishment with 250 Buffaloe Tongues. Latter part of the day very cold thermometer below Zero.

Friday Jany. 28th 1831. Clear and Cold. Dispatched Juett and Hay with pack horses loaded with Mdse. for Sawon and Chyenne outfit. Mayotte arrived from the Navy Yard with 4 Broken Axes.

Saturday Jany. 29th: Clear and Cold, hands employed making a coal kiln &c.

Sunday 30th: Same weather as yesterday Lacharite arrived from Papins establishment on White river in search of provisions, he has been six days without eating.

Monday 31st: Lacharite left here, the weather throughout the day Mild and clear, the Snow and ice melting fast.

[February 1831]

Tuesday February 1st: Throughout the day strong N.E. winds and snow. Larcharite with a lodge of Yanctons has encamped at the mouth of Teton river, he will remain there till good weather comes on and will then proceed out in search of Buffaloe, he has three horses, and if he makes a successful hunt will return with them loaded with meat to Papin's establishment on White river.

Wednesday 2d: Cold weather with passing clouds, sent two men down to an Island in the neighbourhood of Old Cedar Fort[62] for a horses belonging to the company. left there in charge of a Yancton Indian by Mr Gordon, hands employed making coal, cutting wood &c. Cooper making Kegs. One Indian went out hunting.

Thursday 3d: Clear and cold. Sent off Mayotte for the Navy Yard. Hands employed as usual.

Friday February 4th 1831: Clear and then coldest day we have had this season, employed burning [word?] coal kiln &c. Cooper making kegs. One of the Indians killed a Buffaloe about 10 miles from here.

Saturday February 5th: Clear and cold. Vachard and Hebert arrived from the Rees and Yanctonnas with Beaver Traps.

Sunday 6th: Our Indian hunter killed a Buffaloe cow on the other side the river. Weather Same as Yesterday but not quite so cold.

Monday 7th: Still continues Cold, and throughout the most of this day it was snowing and blowing Strong gales from the North.

Tuesday 8th: As yesterday Cold and strong Gales from the North, but no snow. Sent of[f] two men with a Dog train and 16 Beaver Traps for Sawon and Chyenne Outfit.

Wednesday 9th: Weather more moderate, hands employed burning a coal kiln &c. Saw a large band Buffaloes on the other side the Missouri.

Thursday 10th: Clear and cold. Plenty Buffaloes on both sides the Missouri not more than three miles from here. Messrs. Hamilton, Holliday and our Indian went out, they kill'd two between them. At noon Mr. and Mrs. Gordon left here for Mr. Laidlaws establishment on the Grand Chyenne river.

Friday 11th: Moderate and Clear, with Strong N.W. winds. Messrs. Hamilton and Holliday went out hunting but were unsuccessful, although they saw plenty of Buffaloes about 5 miles from here. A Yancton Indian arrived, he say his lodge is encamped at Village de terre.[63]

Saturday 12th: Cold and cloudy with Strong S.W. winds. Holliday and our Indian hunter went out. Saw Buffalos but kill'd none.

Sunday 13th: Cloudy with snow at intervals, the two men who were sent down to the neighbourhood of old Cedar fort for a horse belonging to the Coy. returned accompanied by a Yancton Indian, the horse died some to time previous to their arrival at the place w[h]ere Gordon left him, they report Cattle to be numerous between this and fort Lookout.

Monday 14th: Fine pleasant weather. Hamilton and Holliday went out hunting again but were unsuccessful. Our Indian hunter killed 2 Cows and Mr "Whiskey" kill'd one.

Tuesday 15th: Same weather as Yesterday. James Parkins a Moletta [Mulatto] arrived, he reports buffaloes to be plenty in every direction, he left Carries and Matthews on Teton river where they [are] making a supply of dry Meat.

Wednesday 16th: Strong Gales from the North and Snow, 4 men with 3 Dog trains loaded with fresh meat arrived from Mr Laidlaws establishment. Alexis Thibeau the patroon[64] and Nowl Richard the Carpenter arrived from the Navy Yard with broken axes.

Thursday 17th: Clear and Cold. Dispatched Mr. Laidlaws men for his fort with 2 Dog trains loaded with Mdse: also Tibeau and Richard with repaired Axes for the Navy Yard. Messrs. Lamont and Hamilton went hunting at 11 A.M. they returned a short time after dark, and succeeded in killing a Young Bull.

Friday Feby. 18th 1830: Mild and Clear, several hunters out. Mr Hamilton and our Indian kill'd each a Buffaloe. A Lodge arrived from the Ogallallas. The chief man of the family is a Brulé called the Magic Soul.

Saturday Feb. 19th: Mild and Cloudy. One of our Hogs died yesterday with the Hydraphobia [rabies], it was bit by a mad wolf a few days ago and our Bull appears to be mad also, it is possible he was bitten by the same animal. Saw a band Buffaloes on the other side the Missouri.

Sunday 20th: Found our Bull so much worse this morning that we were sure he would not recover, and therefore shot him. The weather throughout the Day cold and Cloudy.

Monday 21st: Moderate and Cloudy. Sent off Louis Vachard with 100 lb Salt for Ree Outfit. At 8 P.M. Provost[65] arrived from Fort Union with dispatches from Mr McKenzie Campbell arrived at the same time from the Yanctonnas.

Tuesday 22d: Still continues moderate and cloudy. Sent a man up to the Navy Yard for the purpose of bringing down all the horses which are in good order and can be spared. Provost requires 40 or 50 to take on towards the Rocky mountains where Mr Vanderburg is wintering with a party of Trappers, in the night Bary arrived from the Navy Yard in search of Files.

Wednesday 23d: Sent off two men to Mr. Laidlaws establishment with dispatches for that Gentleman. Hands employed pulling down our two story Store for the purpose of putting it up again on the hill back of the fort. From the latest accounts from above we have every reason to apprehend being inundated here after the Breaking up of the ice in Spring in consequence of which we intend moving all the property of a perishable nature to a spot about 200 Yds: Back of the fort which stands about 5 feet higher than our present situation. The weather throughout the day fair and mild.

Thursday Feb 24th: Same weather as yesterday, 8 men arrived from the Navy Yard with 8 or 10 Horses. Our Indian and one hand with a Train and Dogs went out Buffaloe hunting. Bary returned to the navy yard, at 12 P.M. our hunters returned with their train loaded with fresh Buffaloe Meat. Our Indian kill'd two.

Feb. 25th: At 4 P.M. Mr. Provost with 10 men and 9 Horses laden with Mdse. left us for Powder river where he expects to meet Mr Vanderburgh with a party of Trappers. The weather throughout the day Cloudy and Mild. Hands employed freeing the boat from the ice by sawing it round her, others removing the timber of the high store to the hill back of the fort where they will begin to put it up tomorrow.

Saturday Feby. 26th 1831: Same weather as yesterday, employed erecting the high store in the prairie back of the fort, in the evening a man arrived from the Rees with a letter from Mr Holliday.

Sunday February 27th: Southeast winds and rain throughout the day. Saw a large band Buffaloes on the other side the Missouri, in the night the wind shifted to the N.W. and a little Snow fell.

Monday February 28th: Throughout the day strong gales from the North and cloudy weather, hands employed making a canal to carry of[f] the water back of the fort, sent off 4 men to the Rees with Dispatches to Messrs. McKenzie, McKnight, Mitchell and others, to be forwarded from post to post.

[March 1831]

Tuesday March 1st: Moderate and cloudy. Gordon's Father in law (Yancton) arrived with a few Robes, he says the Yanctons are in encamped at the fork White river and have plenty of Buffaloes, we also hear by him that the ice has broke up in Teton river and that the water has already begun to rise. Hands employed variously. Prudhomme arrived from the Navy Yard with a saw to be repaired. Saw plenty Buffaloes on the opposite side the Missouri, our Indian hunter kill'd one.

Wednesday March 2d: Strong North wind and Mild weather. Emillien Primeau and three men arrived from White river With 13 horses laden with Mdse: belonging to Brulé's Outfit. Hands employed variously.

Thursday 3d: Moderate north winds and Clear. Mr. Laidlaw arrived from Fork Chyenne river with his family. Mr Hay and Baptiste Dourion with 5 men accompanied him, they brought with them 48 Horses, Mules and Jack Asses the property of the Co:, three or four Yanctons also arrived in the early part of the day, they say they are bound for the other side the Missouri in search of their people. Cattle Still continue in great abundance in every quarter.

Friday March 4th: Moderate and cloudy. Primeau and his men left here on his return to his post on White river, it is expected he will descend to the Poncas with his returns and there wait the arrival of the boats from this quarter, at 10 A.M. two men arrived from the Poncas with a letter from Mr. G. Sebelle, no News of Zephine, he left the Poncas for Council Bluffs on the 11th January and up to the 15th Febr. he had not returned, nor had any tidings been had of him. Two of Mr Laidlaws men who remained behind with them or four horses arrived this evening.

Saturday March 5th: Mild and pleasant. Traded 25 pieces Dry Meat and a few Robes of 5 lodges Yanctons who arrived yesterday.

Sunday March 6th: Same weather as yesterday, the 5 Lodges yanctons left us for Medicine river.

Monday March 7th: Mr Laidlaw with Campbell, B. Daurion and 5 men and 6 horses and Mules left here for his establishment on Chyenne river Pineau le Yancton from his establishment arrived about an hour after his departure.

Tuesday 8th: It commenced snowing last night and continued throughout the most part of to day. At noon Zephine Recontre and Denoyer arrived from C. Bluffs with letters from St. Louis. Zephine states that he was robbed of his bedding, ammunition and provisions by the Mahaws on his return from the Bluffs. Letand arrived from the Navy Yard. I forgot to mention that Alexis Tibout arrived from the Navy with all the horses excepting two or three that our men are working there. Louis Vachard also arrived yesterday from the Rees.

Wednesday 9th: Moderate and Clear. The Big Leg (Brulé) and Lodge arrived here, hands employed moving our Mdse: to the high store back of the Fort.

Thursday 10th: Mild and pleasant the first part of the day, middle and latter part Cloudy. Letand left us for the Navy Yard, hands employed as yesterday. one of our Goats was delivered of 2 Young ones.

Friday 11th: Strong Westerly winds and mild weather. Several Yanctons arrived.

Saturday 12th: Cloudy with Snow at intervals.

Sunday 13th: A Little Snow fell last night. Throughout the day cloudy with snow at intervals. Hands employed making packs. Saw a flock of Ducks yesterday going south, another of our Goats was delivered of a young one.

Monday 14th: A continuation of unsettled weather. Hands employed as yesterday.

Tuesday 15th: Strong N.W. wind and cold. Zephine Recontre left here for the Yancton camp on the Little Missouri with a Small adventure to trade Lodges and Meat, hands employed removing Indian Departments goods to the Store back of the fort. Mr Hay arrived from the Yancton's camp with 75 ps. Meat.

Wednesday 16th: First part of the day cold with a Strong North wind. Middle and latter part Moderate Hands employed making and [word?] packs &c.

Thursday 17th: Cold and windy, finished packing Packs, have on hand 1857 Packs Robes.

Friday 18th: Throughout the day cold and cloudy with snow at intervals. Hands employed variously.

Friday [sic] 19th: Still continues cold with a Strong N.W. wind. Baptiste Defond arrived from the Mandans. Joseph Lemay from the Navy Yard, and Zephine Recontre from the Yanctons camp. Zephine made no trade whatever. But he and the Indian who accompanied [him] kill'd 7 Buffaloes and brought us six horses laden with their flesh. At night the wind fell and the weather moderated.

Sunday 20th: Fine pleasant weather, the Indians went out to hunt. Lemay return'd to the Navy Yard.

Monday 21st: Same weather as Yesterday, the Indians returned from hunting after having kill'd 7 Buffaloes. Saw a flock of Geese Goding to the north, the Dogs kill'd one of the Kids today.

Tuesday 22d: A continuation of fine pleasant weather. Hands variously employed.

Wednesday 23rd: First and Middle part of the day Strong N.E. winds and rain, in the night a little snow fell. Saw one or two flocks of Geese and Ducks to day. Our remaining Buffaloe calf disappeared this day, we suppose the Indian dogs have destroyed them.

Thursday 24th: Light northerly winds and Moderate weather. An Indian arrived from Ash wood point[66] with two Robes which he traded and left as immediately.

Friday 25th: Fine pleasant weather. Sent off Zephine Recontre with 3 hands, 3 Indians and 12 Horses to hunt Buffaloe. Mr. Laidlaw arrived from forks Chyenne river, he left Gordon and three men behind with horses and Mules.

Saturday 26th: Clear and fine, in the morning Mr. Gordon arrived and in the evening the remainder of the party with two or three horses and Mules. 2 Indians also arrived one from the south and one from the north.

Sunday 27th: Moderate north winds and cloudy the first part of the day, at 3 P.M. the ice in the Missouri broke up and continued drifting thick at 11 P.M.

Monday 28th: Southerly winds and pleasant. Ice still drifting a little. Zephine Recontre and the hunters arrived with 11 Horses lo[a]ded with fresh Buffaloe Meat, at night a little rain fell.

Tuesday 29th: Light westerly winds and rain throughout the most part of the day. At 9 P.M. Clear and pleasant.

Wednesday 30th: Strong north winds and Clear. Sent two men down to Cimmerians Island[67] to bring up a canoe in that neighbourhood, a considerable quantity of ice drifted by last night and the water rose a little.

Thursday 31st: Throughout the day Strong north winds and cloudy, a little ice drifting. Madam Recontre delivered of a fine Heiress last evening at 10 oclock.

[April 1831]

Friday April 1st: Fine pleasant weather, three men left here with 19 Horses for mountain expedition under charge of E. Provost, we expect they will overtake Provost on Cherry river.[68]

Saturday 2d 1831: Throughout the day rain and snow at intervals. Gordon left us to join the men who left here yesterday with horses, he is to conduct them to Cherry river, where it is expected they will fall in with Provost, in the evening two men with 2 mules arrived from the Yancton post on White river.

Sunday April 3d: Strong north winds and cold. Hands employed variously.

Monday 4th: Clear and cool. Baptiste Dufond left here for Ottos Establishment[69] with dispatches for St. Louis and the intermediate places.

Tuesday 5th: First part of the day a little snow fell. Middle and latter part moderate and cloudy. At A.M. Messrs. Laidlaw, Hamiltton, Hay, Halsey and Recontre with 4 men and 9 horses and mules left here for a Buffaloe hunt.

Wednesday 6th: Throughout the day cloudy. Joseph Vaseur arrived from forks Chyenne river with 5 horses, he states that Mr. Chardon left there on the 1st instant with 11 skin canoes containing 440 packs Robes, in the evening Philibert and 4 men arrived from the Navy yard with Keel boat "Louis Vallé."

Thursday 7th: Cool and cloudy with a strong north wind, at meridian the hunters returned with 9 horses and Mules loaded with Buffaloe meat.

Friday 8th: Moderate and cloudy with snow at intervals.

[journal lacks eight months of entries; begins again on January 27]

Volume 3: January 27, 1832–June 1, 1833

[January 1832]

Friday January 27th 1832: Cold South winds and clear weather, at 4 P.M. James Parker, Pineau le Yancton and Louison Brulé arrived from the Ogallallahs Post with the Melancholy news of the death of Mr. Thomas L. Sarpy, the Cos. trader at that Station. From what we can learn it appears that on the 19th inst: about 5 P.M. he entered his Store accompanied by two of his men with a lighted Candle for the purpose of putting it in order. The Candle was placed on the counter under which was a Kettle containing a quantity of Powder. It appears that either the candle or a spark from it was thrown into the Powder while they were in the Act of passing some Robes over the counter, which of course blew up the building and the three persons engaged in it. Mr Sarpy was found lying on his back a considerable distance from where the building stood, the first words he spoke were "Quel Mathew que ji fast" [What evil did this? or What malevolence made this happen?] the second "Vené mois de beau sur le corps" [Pour water on my body], the third and last was a demand for a drink of water, as it was given him, his spirit fled into eternity. Cut off in the prime of life, he has arrived at his eternal home, and is fixed in an unchangeable state. Man giveth up the g[h]ost, and where is he, what has become of him who but a short time ago we saw and conversed with. He has gone to the bar of God, to give an account of the time, the means and advantages he has enjoyed, and to receive his doom. Mr. Sarpy was one of the Cos. most useful Clerks, his loss will be felt, and much regretted by his employers. The Other two men were much injured but they are now considered out of danger.

Saturday 28th: Snow throughout the greatest part of the day. Put up some goods for the trade of the Ogallallahs.

Sunday January 29th 1832: Moderate and cloudy weather. At 10 A.M. a man arrived From Fort Lookout with news of the arrival of Leclerc at the Sioux Agency. At the same time Mr Laidlaw and Parker left here for the Ogallallahs with goods, and Braseau Duchonquette and Bapte: Daurion for the Honcpappas & Yanctonnas camp with goods to trade what they may find. At 1 P.M. 1 Lodge of Yanctons arrived and camped along side of us. Plenty of Buffaloe to be seen on the hills opposite here. At sun sett clear and pleasant.

Monday 30th: Throughout the day Cloudy with an appearance of a storm. At 8 P.M. Last evening 2 men arrived from the Brulé post for goods. At 11 A.M. 2 men arrived with letters from Fort Union and the intermediate posts.

Tuesday 31st: Still continues cloudy, hands employed at the New fort, putting down piccotts of this fort, and hauling them to the new one for building logs. At 12 A.M. Sent of[f] Louis Renville to Council Bluffs with dispatches for St. Louis. The 2 men from Brulé post Returned yesterday with 4 horses loaded with goods.

[February 1832]

Wednesday February 1st 1832: Commences with Strong Gales from the North East and snow, throughout the day a continuation of the same weather.

Thursday 2d: Cold and Cloudy, with moderate north winds and snow at intervals.

Friday 3d Febuary: Clear and Cold. Cyprian Belcom started For the Yancton post, with a train laden with provisions. Sent Quenel to hunt Buffalos.

Saturday 4th: Mr Picotte and the Indians went out to hunt Buffaloes, the day Clear and moderate. Mr. Picotte returned in the evening with the flesh of 5 Cows. 4 Yancton Indians with 3 horses and several dogs loaded with 40 ps: dry Meat arrived and traded. Buffaloe in sight from the fort this evening.

Sunday 5th: Two of our men arrived from Cedar Island with 2 Trains loaded with 140 plank. The first part of the day a considerable quantity of Snow fell. Middle and latter part pleasant. Several more Indians arrived with Dry Meat to trade. Traded 100 pieces. Buffalos to be seen from the fort.

Monday 6th: Clear and Cold. Hundreds of Buffaloes to be seen from the fort to day. Hands employed raising a building of 36 ft. by 20 ft. Cooper making Kegs.

Tuesday 7th: Cold and Cloudy with Snow at intervals. Hands Variously employed. Noel Richard sick and off duty. Buffaloes still in sight from the fort.

Wednesday 8th: Still continues cold and Cloudy with Snow at intervals. Noel Richard still unable to do duty. Sent two trains down to Cedar Island for Plank. Hands employed cutting fire wood &c. &c.

Thursday 9th: Clear and Cold. Baptiste Dufond and Baptiste Gallieau arrived from the Sawon Post with 2 Mules in quest of goods.

Friday 10th: Dispatched defond and Gallieau for the Sawon Post with 5 Horses and Mules loaded with Merchandise. The day Clear and Cold. At 4 P.M. Louisan Brulé and Gabriel Fefer arrived from Brulé post in quest of Merchandise.

Saturday 11th Febuary: First and Middle part of the day Mild and pleasant. Latter part Cold N.W. winds. In the morning sent Fefer and Phillip Yancton with 5 horses loaded with goods for the Brulé Post. Men employed as usual. Finished raising a building of 36 ft: by 20 ft intended for Indians and Interpreters.

Sunday 12th: Cloudy with Snow throughout the greatest part of the day. Our Men arrived from Cedar Island with two trains Loaded with 120 plank.

Monday 13th Febuary 1832: Clear and pleasant. Sent two men below to Cut wood For the Expected Steam Boat.[70] Hands employed variously. Buffalos to be seen from the fort.

Tuesday 14th: Clear and Cold. One of our men arrived from Roys Island,[71] he says that four of Leclerc's men are coming up the river with two sleighs loaded with goods, they are bound to the Sawon post on Cherry River. In the evening Mr Laidlaw and an Indian arrived from the Sawon Post.

Wednesday 15th: Cold and Snow throughout the day. Leclerc's men with 2 sleighs loaded passed here. Employed making up dispatches for Fort Union and the intermediate posts. Hands employed at the Fort.

Thursday 16th: Cold and Cloudy throughout the greatest part of the day. Employed as yesterday. 2 Indians arrived with meat to trade. Saw more than 10 thousand Buffalos.

Friday 17th: Strong North winds with Cold weather. Sent off two men to Apple river post with dispatches for Fort Clark[72] and Fort Union. 1 Lodge Yanctons arrrived.

Saturday 18th Febuary: Strong North winds and cold. Thousands of Buffalos to be seen from the Fort gate. Hands employed variously.

Sunday 19th: Mild and Cloudy. Still plenty of Buffalos in sight.

Monday 20th: Strong Gales from the north and cold weather. Commenced duplicate Ledger.[73] Sent off 3 trains to Cedar Island for plank.

Tuesday 21st: Moderate and Cloudy. Brasseau Duchonquette and 3 men arrived from the Ogallallahs post with 35 Horses and Mules and 130 pieces dry Meat.

Wednesday 22nd: Strong Gales from the N.W. and Cold. I forgot to mention that J. Deshonnette and an Indian arrived from White River last evening with 2 horses in quest of more goods.

Thursday 23d Febuary 1832: Clear and Cold with moderate airs from the north. Mr. Picotte with 8 men left here for Crook's point[74] to Cut pickets for the new fort. Deshonnette and two Indians left here for the Brulé's post with 2 horses loaded with Merchandise. Toward morning a Yancton (called the 4 hands) and his family came in with Robes and Meat to trade.

Friday 24th: Clear and Cold with Strong S.E. winds. Two teams arrived from Cedar Island with plank.

Saturday 25th: Moderate and Clear.

Sunday 26th: Same weather as Yesterday. Some Indians came to trade meat. Sent two trains to Cedar Island for plank.

Monday 27th: Clear and Moderate with Southeast winds.

Tuesday 28th: Clear and Mild. Mr. Laidlaws son Robert very low not expected to live long.

Wednesday 29th: Moderate and cloudy. At 10 A.M. Robert son of Wm. Laidlaw departed this life in the 5th year of his age. It can I think be truly said of him and all others who are taken away at this age "Oh Grave where is thy Victory:" Oh death where is thy Sting. At 4 P.M. his remains were interred.[75]

[March 1832]

Thursday March 1st: Moderate and pleasant.

Friday 2d: Same weather as yesterday. Plenty of Buffaloes in sight, in fact, they have been in sight without intermission for the last two or three days. Mr Laidlaw and a few indians went out to Surround[76] and returned about noon having killed 4 Cows. 15 Gens de paches came in with Robes to trade.

Saturday 3d. Fair pleasant weather. Mr. Laidlaw and the Indians went out to surround, they returned at 1 P.M. having kill'd meat enough to load their horses.

Sunday 4th: Moderate and cloudy with rain at intervals. Gabriel V. Fifie and 5 indians arrived from White River post with 7 horses and mules and 200 Buffaloe Tongues.

Monday March 5th 1832: Clear and Fine pleasant weather. Some Indians arrived from Above; they say that all the "Gens de paches" are encamped about 10 Miles above here, they are all coming here in a few days. Hands employed Variously. Joseph Vasseur who was hired for 1 Month, on the first of March, sick and off duty.

Tuesday March 6th: Fine pleasant weather. Sent off 2 men to White River post with a horse loaded with goods for the trade of the Indians there. 5 Lodges Yanctons arrived and camped here. At 3 P.M. 10 Indians of the Blackfoot [Sioux] nation arrived to beg, &c. The snow is melting away very fast, the small rivers in this neighbourhood are all free of ice and very high. On the Missouri there is more than a foot of water over the ice. Hands variously employed. Joseph Vasseur sick again and off duty.

Wednesday March 7th. Weather continues the same as Yesterday. Several Indians of the "Gens de pache" band arrived on a begging visit. The Blackfeet Indians who arrived yesterday, left us to day. One of them stole a kettle, we fortunately missed it before the fellow had proceeded far. Mr Laidlaw and some Indians went out after them and succeeded in recovering the kettle. The "Gens de pache" who arrived to day, say that Baptiste Daurion has been lately kill'd by a Sawon Indian, but we have reason to suppose the story to be fictitious.

Thursday 8th: The weather still continues as yesterday. 5 more Lodges Yanctons arrived to day. Also several more of "Gens de paches" came in to trade.

Friday, 9th. A continuation of Fine pleasant weather. 5 more Lodges Yanctons arrived and camp'd. There is now about 3 feet water on the top of the

Missouri Ice. 2 Men arrived from Cedar Island, they were obliged to leave their plank [for the new fort] and trains on the way, the ice being so bad that they could not travel on it.

Saturday 10th March 1832: The weather is still warm and pleasant and if it continues a day or two longer the ice in the Missouri will probably break up. At Meridian 4 men with 3 horses arrived on the other side the Missouri, we suppose them to be our sawyers from Cedar Island. In the evening Mr. Picotte and two Indians arrived from the other side the river, they made a skin canoe and crossed.

Sunday 11th: Same weather as Yesterday. The water falling a little.

Monday 12th: Cold North winds with Snow and rain at intervals.

Tuesday 13th: Still Continue strong Gales from the north and Colder, but the weather is now clear and the Indians are ~~now~~ crossing on the ice in great numbers with Robes to trade, "Gens des paches."

Wednesday 14th: Clear and Moderate weather. The "Gens de puches" are still crossing with Robes to trade. Traded about 10 packs. Mr Picotte left us for the Navy yard.

Thursday 15th: Clear and pleasant. Still continue trading with Gens de puches.

Friday 16th: Strong North winds cold and Cloudy with snow at intervals. Baptiste Dufond arrived last evening from the Sawon post with Horses and Mules.

Saturday 17th: Cold and Clear, still continue trading pretty brisk with the "Gens de puches."

Sunday 18th: Moderate and clear. 2 Indians arrived from White River post with a letter from Mr. Papin the Commandant.

Monday 19th: Mild and clear throughout the day nothing new. Finished duplicate Ledger.

Tuesday 20th: Still mild and pleasant weather. Employed making packs and pressing them.

Wednesday 21st: Strong North winds and mild weather.

Thursday 22d: Same weather as Yesterday.

Friday March 23rd 1832: Still continues fine weather. Most of the Lodges left us to day, they have gone up the little Missouri [the Teton]. The Missouri is broke up at this place.

Saturday 24th: Weather same as yesterday. No ice drifting and water low, which induces us to think that the ice is not gone, more than two or three miles above this place.

Sunday 25th: Cool and Cloudy. The ice drifting thick throughout the day, and the water 4 feet above low water mark.

Monday 26th: Clear and fine. Commenced moving the goods to the New fort [Fort Pierre Chouteau]. Ice still drifting thick and Water 6 ft. above low water mark.

Tuesday 27th: Clear and fine, employed as yesterday. Ice still drifting thick. Missouri 5 ft. above low water mark.

Wednesday 28th. Same weather as yesterday. Ice still drifting a little, Missouri 4 ft. above low water mark. Mr Picotte and a Voyageur arrived from the Navy Yard in a canoe.

Thursday 29th: Fine pleasant weather. No ice drifting in Missouri. 3 ft. above low water mark.

Friday 30th: Fine weather. Ice commenced drifting thick at 9 A.M. and the water rose about 4 feet from Sunrise to Sunsett. In the morning Baptiste Dufond departed down stream to meet the Steam Boat Yellow Stone.

Saturday 31st: Cloudy with rain at intervals, no ice drifting, the Missouri still rising at 6 P.M. it was 7½ feet above low water mark.

[April 1832]

Sunday 1st April: Strong Gales from the North and Clear Weather. The Missouri still rising. At 5 P.M. it was nearly 8 ft. above low water mark.

Monday 2d: Moderate and pleasant. The Missouri about 8 feet above low water mark.

Tuesday 3d April 1832: Moderate and pleasant. Missouri still rising. It is now 8½ ft. above low water mark. Last Evening J. Jouett arrived from the Ogallallahs post with horses & Mules (in all 16).

Wednesday 4th. A continuation of fine pleasant weather.

Thursday 5th. Same weather as yesterday. Messrs. Laidlaw and Halsey moved up with their baggage to the new fort.[77]

Friday, 6th. Still fine and pleasant. Hands employed variously. 2 men arrived from the Yanckton post with 3 horses. They report the arrival of Mr

P. D. Papin at the mouth of white river with 2 Skin Canoes laden with Buffaloe Robes.

Saturday 7th: Mr. Wm. Dickson arrived from Riviere au Jacques with 12 Packs Furs.

Sunday 8th: 2 Men arrived from the Navy Yard with the News that the Indians have stolen all the Cos. horses at that place.

Monday 9th: Clear and moderate with North wind. Missouri Falling fast, on the 6th inst. the water was so high that the old fort was nearly surrounded with water. Employed Variously, hauling property from the Old Fort, &c, &c. At 11 A.M. 5 Skin Canoes loaded with Buffaloe Robes under Charge of Colin Campbell arrived from the Ogallallahs post on Chyenne river. The[y] bring News of the Murder of Francois Quenell by Frederick Laboue the Cos. trader at Cherry river. Laboue arrived in the Canoes.

Tuesday 10th: Strong Gales from the north and pleasant weather. Finished unloading the Canoes. The Missouri has fell 5 feet since the 8th inst: it is now about 3 feet above low water mark.

Wednesday 11th: Moderate north winds and pleasant. Sent the skiff with two men to Roy's Island for Cedar plank. 4 or 5 Sawon arrived with 8 or 10 Robes to trade.

Thursday 12th: Strong south winds and pleasant, several Sawons arrived last evening. The Missouri rising.

Friday 13th: Strong Northerly winds and pleasant. Mr. Dickson left for Riviere au Jacques.

Saturday 14th April 1832: Fine pleasant weather, hands employed variously.

Sunday 15th: Variable winds and Cloudy with rain at intervals.

Monday 16th: Clear and pleasant with light S. Easterly winds. Employed making and pressing Packs &c.

Tuesday 17th: Same weather as yesterday, but wind Westerly, hands employed as yesterday.

Wednesday 18th: Strong N.W. winds and Cloudy, at 3 P.M. Degray, Juett, Lainvian and Belcom arrived from the Brule Post with 24 horses loaded with Mdse. Robes &c. &c. Hands employed as yesterday.

Thursday 19th: Cool and Clear. A man arrived from the Navy Yard in quest of provisions, hands employed making and pressing Packs, &c. &c.

Friday 20th: We had a shower of rain in the morning. At 10 A.M. it cleared off. Hands employed variously, at 3 P.M. 4 men arrived from Navy Yard. Buffaloe in sight from the houses. Mr. Laidlaw and some Indians went out and they return'd at 4 P.M. having kill'd 4 cows.

Saturday 21st: Calm and cloudy. Sent of[f] Campbell and 22 men to Cherry river to bring down the peltries at that place.

Sunday 22nd: Clear and moderate winds from the N.W.

Monday 23rd: Fine pleasant weather.

Tuesday 24th: Same weather as yesterday.

Wednesday 25th: A continuation of fine pleasant weather.

Thursday 26th: Still fine pleasant weather, nothing new.

Friday 27th: Weather same as yesterday, at five o'clock P.M. Messrs. McKenzie, Kipp, and Bird[78] with 9 Blackfeet Indians arrived in a Batteau from Fort Union. McKenzie brought down 111 packs Beaver Skins.

Saturday 28th: Still Continues fine pleasant weather, employed Variously.

Sunday 29th: Strong Gales from the South and pleasant.

Monday 30th April 1832: Same weather as yesterday, hands employed making packs &c. &c.

[May 1832]

Tuesday 1st May 1832: Cold and Cloudy throughout the greater part of the day, hands employed pressing packs &c. &c. Mr. Bird and the Blackfeet Indians left here in the morning on a visit to the Sioux Camp. Mr. Laidlaw went out to hunt Buffaloes and in the Evening he return'd having kill'd a Bull. The Missouri is rising slowly. At 5 P.M. a man arrived from the Navy Yard for nails.

Wednesday 2d May. Cloudy with rain at intervals. Mr. Cerré arrived Yesterday from the Yanctonnas with 90 odd Packs Robes, hands employed making and pressing them.

Thursday 3d: Clear and pleasant, nothing new, hands employed pressing packs, &c. &c. The Indians are now coming in every day to trade.

Friday 4th: Moderate and clear. Mr Bird and the Indians returned from the Sawon Camp.

Saturday 5th: Strong winds from the South and Cloudy weather.

Sunday 6th: Strong Easterly winds and raw throughout the day.

Monday 7th: Moderate winds and disagreeable rainy weather. Colin Campbell with eleven skin canoes laden with Buffaloe Robes, arrived from Cherry river. Mr. Campbell while at Cherry river disinterred the body of the deceased F. Quenel and as 7 wounds were found in the body Frederick Laboue was put in Irons immediately at the arrival of the canoes.

Tuesday 8th: First part of the day strong North winds attended with snow. Middle and latter part strong Gales from the same quarter and Cloudy weather. A man arrived from the Re[e]s Yesterday in Quest of Mdse. for the trade of those Indians.

Wednesday 9th: Clear with strong Southerly winds. Made and pressed 220 packs Buffaloe Robes.

Thursday 10th May 1832: Strong South wind and cloudy, hands employed as yesterday.

Friday 11th May: Fine pleasant weather. Sent off two men to the Rees with Goods for the trade of those Indians. Pierre Octubise and two men left in a skiff in search of the Steam boat. Hands employed making and pressing packs.

Saturday 12th: Strong Southeast winds and rain throughout the day.

Sunday 13th: Same weather as yesterday attended with Snow.

Monday 14th: Clear and pleasant crossed 64 Horses to the other side the Missouri. At 4 P.M. had a thunder shower. Indians coming in from every quarter to trade.

Tuesday 15th: Clear and pleasant. 3 or 4 hundred Lodges Sawons arrived and camped here. Hands employed variously.

Wednesday 16th: Same weather as Yesterday. Indian trading pretty brisk.

Thursday 17th. Clear and fine. Employed crossing more horses for Fort Union, &c: &c:

Friday 18h: Same weather as Yesterday, nothing new.

Saturday 19th. Still continues Clear and pleasant weather. But no news of consequence, at 4 P.M. two men arrived. Halsey's child was born.[79]

Sunday 20th: Cloudy with rain at intervals.

Monday 21st. Clear and pleasant, sent off 20 men to the Navy Yard to cut timber and bring it down in rafts.

Tuesday 22d: Fine pleasant weather. Mr. Fontenelle with 20 men and a number of horses Arrived here from St Louis, they bring news of the S. B. Yellowstone she is now between this place and the Poncas.

Wednesday 23d: Cloudy with rain at intervals. 18 men arrived from s. b. Yellowstone. She has stopped for want of water about 60 miles below White River. William Dickson and family arrived from Riviere au Jacques.

Thursday 24th: The first part of the day a little rain fell. Middle and Latter part pleasant.

Friday 25th: Clear and fine. B. Defond arrived from the S. B. at the Big Bend. Messrs. McKenzie, Fontenelle and others left here in a Keel Boat to meet her.

Saturday 26th: Cloudy with rain at Intervals.

Sunday 27th: Same weather as Yesterday and nothing new.

Monday 28th: Cloudy weather and rain at intervals.

Tuesday 29th: Same weather as Yesterday. Missouri rising a little.

Wednesday 30th: A continuation of cloudy weather with rain at intervals.

Thursday 31st May: Same weather as Yesterday. Missouri still rising 4 Men with horses arrived from White river post with Robes, &c. &c.

Thursday 31st [sic]: S. B. Yellowstone arrived at 5 P.M.[80]

[June 1832]

Friday June 1st: A continuation of disagreeable rainy weather, sent off men to cut wood for the Steam boat.

Saturday 2d June: Throughout the day disagreeable rainy weather, part of the men arrived with a boat load of wood.

Sunday 3d: Strong Gales from the north and Clear.

Monday 4th: Same weather as Yesterday. The Sawons lifted their Lodges and went off. The Missouri has rose about 3 ft. in the last 4 days.

Tuesday 5th: fine and pleasant. S. B. Yellowstone left here for F. Union, water falling.

Wednesday 6th. fine and pleasant weather. Mr. Fontenelle left here with 40 and odd men for Ft. Union with 110 or [1]15 Horses. Water rising.

Thursday 7th: Still continues fine and pleasant, water rising. Four or 5 Lodges Indians left us, and there now remains but three or four.

Friday 8th June 1832: Hot sultry weather. Employed making packs &c. &c. Water still rising. Three men are employed planting potatoes.

Saturday 9th: Same weather as Yesterday. Richard and Gagnon arrived from the Navy Yard for Oakum. Water still rising.

Sunday 10th: A continuation of hot sultry weather. Keel boat Flora arrived from Council Bluffs with a cargo of Mdse. &c.

Monday 11th: Fine weather with south winds. Keelboat Flora left here for Ft. Union with a cargo of Mdse: &c. Keel boat "Male twin" left here for the Navy Yard to bring down timber.

Tuesday 12th: A continuation of hot sultry weather, the Missouri falling. Degray and Pineau le Yancton went out hunting and in they returned having kill'd 3 Buffalos.

Wednesday 13th: Same weather as Yesterday, last night we had a thunder shower, Missouri still rising.

Thursday 14th: Still continues hot sultry weather. Water still rising, hands employed variously.

Friday 15th. Hot and sultry the first part of the day, keel boat Male twin arrived from the Navy Yard. Latter part of the day we had a fine refreshing shower. I forgot to say that 4 Batteaux also arrived from the Navy Yard to day they as well as the Male twin were loaded with pickets for the fort.

Saturday 16th: Loaded Keel "Twin Male" and 4 Batteaux with cargos Buff. Robes for St Louis, at night had a heavy shower of rain and hail.

Sunday 17th. Keel boat "Twin Male" and 4 Batteaux conducted by Mr. Honoré Picotte left here for St Louis loaded with 1410 packs Buffaloe Robes.

Monday 18th: Strong North winds with cold cloudy weather, hands employed hauling up timber from the river bank &c. &c.

Tuesday 19th: Fine pleasant weather water still rising. Hands employed as yesterday.

Wednesday 20th. Fine pleasant weather with Moderate Southerly winds. The Missouri still rising, it is now nearly over the bank. Joseph Jewett who left on the 10th arrived to day from the Ogallallahs with dry Meat, lodges &c. 480 lbs. dry Meat was left there in the spring, but the wolves broke in that house and eat it all except about 20 pieces.

Thursday 21st: The weather still continues pleasant. Water falling. Hands employed making and pressing packs &c. &c.

Friday 22d: Joseph Juett left here with pack Horses for White river to bring in the balance of the Robes, Meat &c. left at that place. The weather same as yesterday.

Saturday 23d: Same weather as yesterday. Water falling.

Sunday, 24th: S. B. Yellowstone arrived from Fort Union sent down 600 packs Robes on board of her.

Monday 25th: S. B. Yellowstone left us for ~~fort Union~~ St. Louis with a Cargo of 1300 packs Robes and Beaver. Mr Laidlaw went on board he is to go down as far as Sioux Agency and return by land. Ortubise has got a Keg of Whisky and is continually drunk himself and he tries to make as many of the men drunk as will drink with him.

Tuesday 26th: Stormy Southery winds and Clear Weather. Two Lodges Indians went off and there now remains but one. Ortubise and [Name?] went out hunting. Jos Juett returned.

Wednesday 27th: Same weather as yesterday and nothing new. In the evening Mr Laidlaw returned.

Thursday 28th: Fine pleasant weather till 4 P.M. when we had a thunder storm.

Friday 29th: Heavy squall of rain attended with thunder and Lightning throughout the last night. This day was clear and the weather hot and Sultry. 6 men arrived from Navy Yard with three rafts [of] fort Timber.

Saturday 30th: We had another shower last evening. This day was cloudy & sultry. Men employed hauling up timber.

[July 1832]

Sunday 1st July 1832: Messrs. Laidlaw and Dickson left us for Lac traverse[81] in quest of some Canadian pork eaters[82] expected here this summer. Castongi sick and off duty.

Monday 2d: Sent our men for the Batteaux at Roy's Island.

Tuesday 3d: The wind is strong from the north our men returned without the Batteau, commenced hauling the pickets from the river bank. Carpenter not at work, Missouri Falling.

Wednesday 4th: Cool and cloudy at night, a little rain fell. Men employed hauling pickets, putting lodges on the Stores &c. &c.

Thursday 5th: Northerly winds and fine weather. Sent the men down to try a second time to bring up the boat from Roys Island, at 12 A.M. they returned with the boat, set three of them at hauling the pickets, and the other three at putting Lodges on the store.

Friday 6th: Hot Sultry Weather. Musquitoes very thick, finished hauling the pickets. Missouri rising a little.

Saturday 7th: Fine Weather, Men employed carrying 200 packs from the Baggage into the Store.

Sunday 8th: Same weather as Yesterday, with the exception of a light shower in the morning, at 9 P.M. Messrs. Brown, Durand and 2 American's (all beaver trappers) arrived here with about a pack of Beaver.

Monday 9th: fine weather at 6 A.M. Henry Hart arrived from Fort Union with 3 Batteaux loaded with Robes &c. Loaded one boat with 120 packs Beaver & other skins, and put on board of another 30 packs of Robes, she is to take in 120 or 130 packs at Yancton Post.

Tuesday 10th: Strong Gales from the North. 4 Batteaux ready to start for St Louis, but they were detained here all day by the wind.

Wednesday 11th: 4 Batteaux laden with 355 packs Buffaloe Robes and 10,230 lbs. Beaver Skins left here for Saint Louis, they will take in 120 or 130 packs Robes at Yancton Post. Water rising fast, it is now 5 feet above low water mark.

Thursday 12th: Sent 6 men above to bring down the Bal: of timber cut at the Navy Yard last winter. Missouri falling.

Friday 13th: Fine pleasant weather. Employed clearing up the store.

Saturday 14: A continuation of Fine pleasant weather. Missouri falling.

Sunday 15th: Same weather as Yesterday, but a strong south wind.

Monday 16th: Pleasant weather with Southerly winds. Sent down to Roy's Island in the canoe (Ortibuse and Demay) to see what is going on there, and also to bring up the Balance of our chickens. Our men arrived from the Navy Yard, with them rafts [of] 200 pickets.

Tuesday 17th: Hot sultry weather, men employed hauling up the rafts.

Wednesday 18th: Sent 5 men to the Navy Yard for the Balance of the timber there. Also Ortibuse and Juett to hunt Buffaloe or any thing else they may fall in with.

Thursday 19th July 1832: Jewett and Ortubize returned from hunting having Killed 2 Bulls. On their arrival on this side the river we discovered two more Bulls on the opposite side when we immediately recrossed them, at night they returned having Kill'd one more Bull.

Friday 20th: Cloudy and hot sultry weather. Vasseur and 2 men belonging to LeClerc's Co.[83] arrived at the mouth of Teton river for the purpose of building, and establishing a trading house there. Leclaire a free man arrived here from Ft. Lookout.

Saturday 21st: The men arrived from the Navy Yard with the Balance of the pickets, we have in all now 900 hundred; and it will require about 400 more. Weather clear and pleasant, Missouri about 4 ft: above low water mark.

Sunday 22d: fine pleasant weather, sent off 6 men to the Navy Yard to Cut more pickets.

Monday 23d: Strong gales from the north and clear weather, the men for the Navy Yard left here to day instead of yesterday.

Tuesday 24th: Clear and pleasant, and nothing new.

Wednesday 25th: Sent off 3 Men to cut hay, towards night weather cloudy, with appearance of rain.

Thursday 26th: Had a shower of rain last night. The weather to day fine and pleasant. Saw a Band of about 200 Buffalos on the bank of the river. 6 of our people went out on horse-back to hunt them and succeeded in killing 6 Bulls. We have two men cutting hay on the other side the river, and one on this side.

Friday 27th: A fine pleasant day, the Missouri now begins to fall fast.

Saturday 28th: Same weather as Yesterday nothing new.

Sunday 29th: Pleasant weather and Light northerly winds, at 10 A.M. Mr Laidlaw arrived on the other side from the East with 36 Pork Eaters; he lost two on the road. Employed the greatest part of the day crossing the men and their Baggage. At 12 A.M. Cardinal Grant arrived from the Yankton Post.

Monday 30th: Clear and windy, sent out t[w]o men to hunt Buffalos. Missouri falling.

Tuesday 31st: Strong southerly winds And pleasant weather. Mr. Brown left us with 26 pork Eaters to cut fort timber about 12 Miles above this. A party of two of them went out and Killed 3 Buffaloes.

[August 1832]

Wednesday Augt: 1st: Strong Gales from the south and Hot weather. Juett left for the Yancton camp.

Thursday August 2d: Calm and pleasant. Plenty of Buffaloe. Mr. Laidlaw went out to hunt them and Killed 3.

Friday 3d: Same weather as yesterday. A man arrived from the Navy Yard with news that two of our horses at that place have been stolen. Sent him back with 2 horses, to replace those missing.

Saturday 4th: 4 Brulé Indians arrived in search of a trader, they are encamped 5 days march from this.

Sunday 5th: Fine weather Banal Suoux arrived from the Navy Yard in quest of sundry articles wanted there. In the Evening he returned and 8 Brulé Indians arrived from another camp in search of a trader.

Monday 6th: Baptiste Daurion, Charles Primeau and Hipolite Neissell left here this morning accompanied by the 4 Indians, who arrived on the fourth with Mdse: to trade Meat, &c: &c: Sent up Ortubise to the Navy Yard (or Shanty) to hunt for our men at work there.

Tuesday 7th August 1832: Weather cool and pleasant. Louis Demaray laid up with the Venerial disease. C. V. Cerré left us for the Brule camp, accompanied by the 8 Indians who arrived the day before [word?] with goods to trade what he may find in their camp.

Wednesday 8th August: Fine pleasant weather. Mr. Laidlaw went out and killed a Buffaloe. One of the Indians also killed one.

Thursday 9th August: Fine pleasant weather. Mr. Brown arrived from the Shanty.

Friday 10th: In the morning Mr. Brown returned to the Shanty. The weather clear and pleasant.

Saturday 11th: 11 Souix Indians arrived from the other side the Missouri (they belong to the Band called the Blackfeet).

Sunday 12th: At daylight a heavy shower of rain fell. Middle part of the day pleasant.

Monday 13th: Joseph Juett arrived from the Yancton Camp last [word?] with 4 Carts loaded with dry Meats 420 ps: 2 Brulé squaws arrived at the same time, they say that they were attacked by a war party while the camp was moving with their Lodges. To day the weather is hot and an appearance of more rain, hands employed variously.

Tuesday 14th: Messrs. Catlin and Bogart arrived from Ft. Union on their way to St Louis.[84]

Wednesday 15th: A fine, pleasant day. Bapt. Daurion and G. P. Cerré arrived from the Brulé camps with dry meat, Robes &c.

Thursday 16th: Light Southerly winds. Mr Catlin left us for St Louis, accompanied by Mr. Bogart in a skiff.

Friday 17th: A fine pleasant day with a refreshing shower in the Evening. In the early part of the day News Was brought in of a band of Buffaloe not being far from the fort, consequently a party went out to hunt them. Bapt: Daurion was ~~Saturday~~ one of the party; they all returned without ~~having~~ killing any Buffaloe; but Daurion fell in with a strange Indian riding off with one of the companys horses, after a little skuffle, he killed the Indian and we got back [t]he horse. We suppose he was a Ree. Durian did not fire at the Indian, till he had fired two arrows at him.

Saturday 18th: Hot sultry weather. Hands Employed variously, finished Hay Making and have 5 mud chimnys underweigh. Brown arrived from the Lumber yard, also two rafts of timber.

Sunday 19th: Clear and pleasant, a party went out and Kill'd two Buffaloe Bulls.

Monday 20th: Mr Brown and the raft-men returned to the Lumber Yard, the day clear and fine. Hands variously employed.

Tuesday 21st. Weather as yesterday, at 11 A.M. Mr. Brown arrived from the Lumber yard, two of the men there (Louis Turcot and James Durant) having stolen a canoe and deserted last evening. Mr. Brown with one man left here in a canoe at 12 A.M. in pursuit of them. Several Lodges

Yanctons and Esontis [?] arrived on the other side the Missouri and camped there.

Wednesday 22nd: 4 or 5 Lodges crossed over. Weather Cloudy with rain at intervals.

Thursday 23rd: fine weather. Mr. Brown arrived with the two deserters Turcot and Durant, he caught them in the middle of the big bend.

Friday 24th: A continuation of fine pleasant weather. 12 or 15 Lodges Indians crossed the river and camped along side of us, commenced planting the pickets of the fort.

Saturday 25th: Several more Lodges crossed from the other side and 12 Lodges Brulé and Ogallallah arrived and camped here.

Saturday 25th August: Mr Brown with 5 men left here in the Batteaux for the Lumber yard, the day clear and fine, with a moderate south wind.

Sunday 26th: Weather as Yesterday, a few more lodges of Indians crossed from the other side and camp'd here also 8 or 10 Lodges of Brulé's, Ogallallahs and bad Arrow points arrived from teton river.

Monday 27th: Cool and windy, 2 of our men arrived from the Navy Yard with a raft of timbers, a few Lodges went off and some more arrived from the other side the Missouri. Sent out Juett and some Indians to hunt Buffalos.

Tuesday 28th: Same weather as Saturday, some more Lodges arrived from the other side, and some 5 or 6 went of[f] from here to day.

Wednesday 29th: Disagreeable rainy weather, the Batteau arrived from the Navy Yard last night with pank Coals [?].

Thursday 30th August: Still continues cold weather, 3 men arrived from the Navy Yard with a raft of timbers.

Friday 31st: Cool and pleasant, 2 Indians arrived from the Sawon camp on Bear river in search of a trader.

[September 1832]

Saturday 1st Sept: 1832: A fine pleasant day, one of the Carpenters sick and off duty. Mr Brown arrived from the Lumber Yard with a raft of timber.

Sunday 2d: Same weather as Yesterday, and nothing new.

Monday 3d: Mr Brown left for the Lumber Yard, Cerri and Luett with 2 men from the Sawon and Ogallallahs camp on bear river[85] to trade what they may find, at 4 P.M. 8 Ogallallah Indians arrived from the[y] came over the river.

Tuesday 4th: Lachapelle arrived from the Ree Villages, weather [word?] fine and pleasant. Daurion and the Indian arrived with fresh Buffaloe.

Wednesday 5th: Weather still fine, the Ogallallahs who arrived on the 3rd left here this morning. 2 Honcpapas arrived with 2 of our horses recently stolen from here.

Thursday 6th: Weather as Yesterday, and nothing new.

Friday 7th: A continuation of fine pleasant weather, some Indians arrived on the other side the Missouri.

Saturday 8th: Same weather as Yesterday. Mr. Laidlaw went down to Roy's Island in a Batteau to bring up a Load of Corn. Mr Brown arrived from the Lumber Yard with a raft of timbers.

Sunday 9th: Southerly winds and pleasant weather. The prairies are on fire in every direction. G. P. Cerré arrived from the Sawon Camp.

Monday 10th: A continuation of fine pleasant weather.

Tuesday 11th: Same weather as Yesterday. Mr. Brown left us for the Navy Yard otherwise called the lumber yard. In the Evening Charles Degray and Colin Campbell arrived, Degray from St Louis and Campbell from the Yancton camp.

Wednesday 12th: Charboneaux, Bellehumeur and Durand with two Arriccaras squaws arrived from the Mandan village, the day Clear and pleasant, hands Employed Variously.

Thursday 13th: A fine pleasant day.

Friday 14th: Charbonneau, Bellehumeur and Durand with the Arriccarras squaws left us for the Mandans. At the same time G. P. Cerré With 6 men left us in a skin Canoe for the purpose of meeting the Keel boat and giving her assistance, which from accts: they appear to be in want of several of the Crew having deserted.

Saturday 15th: Weather still fine. The prairies are on fire in every direction. 3 men with a raft arrived from the Lumber Yard.

Sunday 16th: A fine pleasant day.

Monday 17th: Weather as Yesterday. Wind strong from the south throughout the night rain.
Tuesday 18th: Cool and Cloudy with an appearance of more rain. A Lodge of Yanctons arrived.
Wednesday 19th: Still continues cool and windy weather and nothing new. Degray went out hunting.
Thursday 20th: Cool, windy and Cloudy weather. 2 men arrived from the Navy Yard with a raft of timber.
Friday 21st: Strong North winds and Cloudy, hauled out the raft, and the raftmen left for the Navy Yard.
Saturday 22d: Cool and Cloudy.
Sunday 23d: Weather as Yesterday. J. Fillion and J. Landry arrived in a Canoe from Fort Union, they brought us no news of importance.
Monday 24th: Laidlaw, Halsey, Campbell Demaray and an Indian left us for Sioux Agency near fort Lookout and on Sunday the 30th they returned accompanied by Doct: M. Martin[86] who visits this place for the purpose of Vaccinating the Indians. Messrs. McKenzie and Fontenelle with several others arrived from Fort Union in a Batteau having on board about 6000 pounds Beaver Skins. In the evening Wm. Dickson arrived from River Bois Blanc in quest of Mdse: for the trade there.
[no entries for September 25 through 30]

[October 1832]

Monday Oct: 1st: A very pleasant day.
Tuesday 2d: Same weather as Yesterday.
Wednesday 3d: A continuation of fine weather.
Thursday 4th: Cloudy and windy. Doct. Martin left us on his return to the Sioux Agency. Provost with horses arrived from fort Union. In the night a little rain fell. Campbell with the Ogallallah Equipment.
Friday 5th: Cloudy weather with rain at intervals.
Saturday 6th: Still continues Cloudy. Sent out Charles Degray with a party to hunt. Also Bapt: Daurion to trade meat at the Ogallallahs.
Sunday 7th: A continuation of Cloudy weather.
Monday 8th: Mr Lamont arrived the Keel boat, which he left at Ft. Lookout.
Tuesday 9th: Rainy with Strong North winds.
Wednesday 10: Windy, hands variously employed.
Thursday 11th: Clear and windy.
Friday 12th: Cool and Cloudy, with rain at intervals.
Saturday 13th: Same weather as Yesterday. Messrs. Papin, Bijoux and Duchonquette arrived from St Louis.
Sunday 14th: Clear and pleasant, several Lodges Yanctons arrived.
Monday 15th: Messrs. McKenzie, Fontenelle and Party left us for St Louis. Keel boat Argo arrived from St Louis. A few Lodges Yanctons arrived.
Tuesday 16th: Keel boat was unloaded.
Wednesday 17th: Indians arriving from all quarters all starving.
Thursday 18th: Mr Lamont with 8 men left here in a Batteau for Ft. Clark, weather fine. Indian visitors pouring in from all quarters.
Friday 19th: Cardinal Grant and another man arrived from fort Lookout with Horses & Mdse belonging to J. P. Cabanné. Emillien Primeau arrived from Riviere au jacques, he left Louis Demaray on the road to Riviere au jacques so much indisposed that he could not travel. Several Lodges of Yanctons arrived and camped.
Saturday 20th: Employed putting up goods for J. L. Bean U.S.I. Agent as also for the trade of the Sawon Indians. Weather clear and pleasant.
Sunday 21st: Strong gales from the South and Clear weather. Mr. Papin Left here with 5 men for the Sawon Post on Cherry river with an Equipment of goods for the trade of those Indians.
Monday 22d October 1832: Light wind and pleasant. Mr. G. P. Cerré left here in Keel "Argo" with a Supply of Merchandise for J. L. Bean U.S.I.I. Indian Agent.
Tuesday 23d: Light wind and pleasant. Two men arrived from the Lumber Yard with a raft.
Wednesday 24th: Still Continues light winds and pleasant weather.
Thursday 25th: Weather as Yesterday. A few Lodges Yanctons arrived and camped along side of us. 21 Chyenne men and women arrived on a visit. Louis Demaray arrived very sick.
Friday 26th: A continuation of fine Pleasant weather. 2 men arrived from the Lumber Yard with a raft timber. The Chyennes arrived today, not Yesterday.
Saturday 27th: Same weather as Yesterday the most of the Chyennes left us in the evening.

Sunday 28th: A continuation of fine pleasant weather. The Balance of the Chyennes left us. Demaray continues very low.

Monday 29th: Cloudy weather several Lodges of Sioux went off and we have now but few remaining. 2 Lodges arrived on the opposite side the Missouri and camp'd there. Ortubise and two men arrived yesterday from the Ogallallah Post with horses &c: but no meat, he says the Indians in that quarter are Starving.

Tuesday 30th: Cloudy with an Appearance of rain. Sent out a party of Indians to hunt.

Wednesday 31st: Still continues Cloudy weather. Braseau Duchonquette and three men arrived from the Lumber Yard with a raft Timber.

[November 1832]

Thursday 1st November: 2 men arrived last evening from Fort Lookout or Sioux Agency with News of Mr Picotte's arrival there with Keel boat Atlas. Mr. Picotte requests assistance to aid in bringing up the Atlas to this place, the most of his crew of his crew having engaged to bring the Boat no higher than Sioux Agency and to return from thence to Council Bluffs. At 10 A.M. dispatched 10 men for Mr. Picotte, at 11 A.M. A. Harvey and Dicoteaux arrived from Fort Lookout on their way to the Mandans (they are both freemen). At 1 P.M. put them across the river and on the return of the Boat our Indian Hunter arrived with fresh Buffaloe meat, they say they saw several bands of Buffalos not far from here.

Friday 2d: Cloudy with rain at intervals, and strong Northeast wind. Hung the front gates of the [new] fort.[87]

Saturday 3d Nov: It commenced Snowing at 10 A.M. and continued for an hour or two Middle and Latter part of the day Cold and Cloudy.

Sunday 4th: Mr. Laidlaw and a party Whites and Indians went out hunting. Harvey and Dicoteaux returned from the other side having concluded not to go to the Mandans. They left here again at 4 P.M. for the Chyenne river where they say they will Winter.

Monday 5th: Cool and Cloudy throughout the whole of the day. 2 Lodges arrived. Hands variously employed. A. Vallin sick and off duty.

Tuesday 6th: Cloudy with snow at intervals, at 8 P.M. Mr. Laidlaw & party returned from hunting, they did not see a Buffaloe and consequently returned light. Ice commenced drifting in the Missouri to day.

Wednesday 7th: A fine pleasant day. Some Indians arrived from Sioux Agency, the[y] say the Agent Bean has gone to St Louis. Two rafts arrived from the Lumber Yard. Keel boat Argo was in sight at sun sett.

Thursday 8th: Same weather as yesterday, hauled up the rafts and unloaded Keel boat "Argo" of Plank from Roys Island.

Friday 9th Nov: 1832: Same weather as Yesterday the man left with our hunter on the other side the Missouri returned with some fresh Buffaloe Meat. Sent the boat across the river for a load of Hay.

Saturday 10th: The Boat returned with a load of Hay. Put up an Equipment of Goods for the trade of the Blackfeet and Huncpapas (Band of Sioux) Indians. Charles Degray and 3 men with a Cart and several horses ~~left here~~ arrived from Sawon Post.

Sunday 11th: Clear and Fine. Emillian Primeau with 5 men left here for the Blackfeet and Honcpapas camp on Chyenne river with an Equipment of goods to trade with them.

Monday 12th: Same weather as Yesterday. Men commenced working at the Stable. Others employed, hauling hay from the bank of the river, daubing the houses,[88] making fort Gates &c. &c.

Tuesday 13th: A fine pleasant day. Mr Picotte arrived with Keel boat Atlas, he brought back the goods that were loaned Mr. Beau last month.

Wednesday 14th: Cool and clear.

Thursday 15th: Clear and Fine. J. D. Begeu arrived from the Blackfeet and Honcpapas camp on Chyenne river he says the Indians there have plenty of Buffalos. An Indian arrived from the other side with meat, he stated that there was Buffaloe a short distance from here on the other side the Missouri.

Friday 16th: Mr Laidlaw and a party went out to hunt Buffaloe on the opposite side the river. Several Lodges Yanctons arrived. Weather cool and cloudy. Mr Laidlaw J. B. Daurian returned without success.

Saturday 17th: The last night was very cold. Ice drifting thick in the Missouri. One of our Keel boats is on the opposite side the river and the other is at Cedar Island where we fear they will both have to winter. At sunset ice drifting thicker than in the morning and weather colder.

Sunday 18th: Still continues very cold with the Missouri is in many places stopp'd up with drift ice.

Monday 19th: Weather much the same as yesterday. Mr Picotte and the rest of the men came across from the other side the Missouri when one of the Keel Boats ("Atlas") is frose up in the ice. Mr Brown and the men who went down with Keel boat "Argo" to bring up Cedar all returned by land except one man who was left to take care of the Boat she is also "frose up" a short distance above Cedar Island. Employed putting up Goods for the trade of the Brulé's.

Tuesday 20th: Mr. Pascal Cerré with 4 men left here for the Brulé Post with 11 horses, Mules and Jack asses loaded with Mdse: for the trade of those Indians. Mr. C Primeau arrived from Roys Island.

Wednesday 21st: Mild and Calm weather. Mr Picotte with 20 men on horse-back left here for Cedar Island to make an attempt to bring up the "Argo." Sent out P. Ortubise to trade meat.

22d: Cloudy Weather.

~~Thursday~~ Friday 23d: Cloudy with an appearance of a Storm. Wind strong from the N.W., finished raising the Stables. Sawyers arrived from Roys Island.

~~Friday~~ Saturday 24th: Same weather as yesterday. Mr. Picotte with 5 men left here for fort Clark at the same time Mr. C. Primeau with 10 men left here for the Honcpapas Post, provisions being so scarce here that we were obliged to send them out to live on what providence may chance to throw in their way.

Sunday 25th: Mr Laidlaw and a party went out to hunt Buffaloe.

Monday 26th: A fine Pleasant day.

Tuesday 27th: Same weather as Yesterday, sent off two men to cut timber for Saddles & Kegs.

Wednesday 28th: Weather as Yesterday.

Thursday 29th: A man arrived from Mr Laidlaw's camp with 2 horses loaded with fresh meat.

Friday 30th: Lachapelle arrived from the Mandans, he was stopped by the ice with a boat Load of Corn &c: near Beaver Creek[89] between the Ree and Mandan Village, he "cached" the cargo of the boat and came on with two men by land.

[December 1832]

Saturday December 1: Strong east wind and cold with Snow throughout the day.

Sunday 2d: Weather clear and pleasant.

Monday 3d: Same weather as Yesterday and nothing new.

Tuesday 4th: A continuation of pleasant weather, a man arrived from Mr. Laidlaws camp with 2 mules loaded with dry Meat. Buffaloe are said to scarce where he is, but plenty in the neighbourhood of Little Chyenne river.

Wednesday 5th: Clear and cold. Lachapelle with two men and two mules left here for Mr. Laidlaws camp, Michel Hebert, Louis Demaray, Louis Monigen, James Boyle, and Samuel Delpai sick and off duty.

Thursday 6th: Cloudy with an appearance of a Storm. 3 Lodges Yanctons arrived.

Friday 7th: Same weather as Yesterday, a man arrived from Mr. Laidlaws Camp with dry Meat.

Saturday 8th: Clear and fine 2 Lodges Yanctons arrived and 3 went off.

Sunday 9th: Same weather as Yesterday and nothing new.

Monday 10th: Weather as Yesterday, J. Juett & 2 men arrived from the Ogallallahs Camp with horses and mules laden with 100 pieces dry Meat. Lachapelle also arrived from Mr Laidlaws camp with news that himself and party have killed 17 Buffalos.

Tuesday 11th: Cold and Cloudy with snow at intervals.

Wednesday 12th: Sent off Pineau le Yancton and two men to Mr. Laidlaws camp with 5 mules and a horse to bring in meat at 4 P.M. Mr Laidlaw and party arrived from hunting, with the exception of a few who he left to "keep up the camp."

Thursday 13th: Clear and, the Missouri closed Last evening and the ice is now strong enough to cross horses on. Put up goods for Ogallallahs Post.

Friday 14th: A fine Pleasant day. J Juett with 2 men left here for the Ogallallahs post, with Mdse. for the trade of the Indians there.

Saturday 15th: Pierre Ortubise arrived from the hunters camp the other side the Missouri with 5 horses loaded with fresh meat.

Sunday 16th: Lachapelle Left here for E. Primeaus establishment on the Chyenne river a man left here at the same time for Mr Papins establishment at cherry river with Mdse: &c.

Monday 17th: Moderate and Cloudy, nothing new.

Tuesday 18th: Same weather as Yesterday.

Wednesday 19th: Cold and Cloudy, the first part of the day a little snow fell. Middle and Latter part clear. A Lodge Yanctons arrived.

Thursday 20th: Clear and cold, nothing new.

Friday 21st: Clear and Cold with strong Easterly winds.

Saturday 22d: Clear and fine pleasant Weather for the season.

Sunday 23d: A continuation of Mild weather. 4 men arrived from E. Primeaus establishment, and 3 men from the hunting establishment with 3 mules loaded with Meat.

Monday 24th: Strong Easterly winds and mild weather. Braseau duchonquette arrived from the hunting camp on the other side the Missouri.

Tuesday 25th: Cloudy weather, 2 Buffalos were killed on the hills back of the fort, through the night strong gales from the N.E. and snow.

Wednesday 26th: N.E. winds and snow throughout the greatest part of the day.

Thursday 27th: Clear and cool with a north wind, a Lodge Yanctons arrived from the other side the Missouri.

Friday 28th Dec: 1832: A fine pleasant day for the season of the year H. Auge with 2 horses laden with Mdse: left here for Riviere au Jacques. Lachapelle with 8 or 10 horses and mules left here for a Yancton Camp on Serpent river[90] to trade meat.

Saturday 29th: Mild and Cloudy, a few Lodges Yanctons arrived from Medicine Hill; no Buffaloe in that quarter. Mr Crawford arrived from F. Clark with dispatches from Fort Union and Fort Clark for Saint Louis.

Sunday 30th: A Fine pleasant day. The ice thawing fast. A Lodge of Indians arrived from the other side the Missouri.

Monday 31st: The Express[91] left us for St Louis; the bearers Vincent, Guitard and Antoine Raboin. Mr. Brown also left us for the Island (Roy Island) with 8 or 10 men to Clear a spot for a Garden, weather fine and Clear.

[January 1833]

Tuesday 1st Jan: 1833: Was a Cloudy day with an appearance of a storm.

Wednesday 2d: Bapt. Daurion & Pierre Ortubise arrived from the Sioux Camp at the little Chyenne river with 80 ps: dry Meat.

Thursday 3d: The first part of the day rainy. Middle and Latter part a considerable quantity of snow fell, in the morning Mr. Crawford left us for fort Clark and B. Duchoquette for Beaver creek after the corn left there by Lachapelle who stopped by the ice last fall, at 4 P.M. Lachapelle & Pineau arrived from the Yancton camp on Serpent river with about 50 ps: dry Meat.

Friday 4th: Cloudy with an appearance of a storm.

Saturday 5th: A considerable quantity of snow fell the first and Middle part of the day. Latter part pleasant. Mr. Brown returned from Roy's Island.

Sunday 6th: Baptiste Daurion left here for the Yancton camp on the Little Chyenne river. The weather Cloudy with an appearance of snow.

Monday 7th January 1833: Clear and Cold, 2 Indians arrived last evening from the Brulé camp, finished raising a Kitchen.

Tuesday 8th: Cold and cloudy with a strong N.E. wind.

Wednesday 9th: Cloudy with snow at intervals. 2 men arrived [from] E. Primeau's establishment they bring letters from F. Clark and fort Union from which we learn that Mr W.H. Vanderburg and A. Pillon were killed by the Blackfeet Indians on the 14th Oct: last.[92]

Thursday 10th: Clear and Cold Mr. P. Cerré and a voyageur arrived from the Brulé post on White river. No Buffaloe in that neighbourhood. Baptiste Daurion arrived from the little Chyenne camp Yanctons with about 130 ps: Meat, Dry and fresh.

Friday 11th: Sent off Louis Lagrave and Antoine Delude to Council Bluff with letters for St Louis to communicate the death of Mr Wm. H. Vanderburg. At the same time sent off papers for Fort Clark Fort Union and the intermediate posts. The day was clear and cold.

Saturday 12th: A fine pleasant day, but nothing new.

Sunday 13th: Fine weather Mr Cerré and his man left us on their return to the Brulé Post. At 4 P.M. J. Lacompt arrived from the Yancton post near the Sioux Agency in search of a few articles of Mdse.

Monday 14th: Weather the same as Yesterday, a lodge of Indians arrived from below (they are as usual starving).

Tuesday 15th: 7 men arrived from E. Primeaus establishment on the Chyenne river with a few bales of meat, from all accounts all the Indians west of us are starving and there is no prospect of making any [of] them a trade in that direction.

Wednesday 16th January 1833: Clear and fine about 20 Lodges Yanctons & Brulé Indians arrived here to day they are all starving.

Thursday 17th: Clear and remarkably mild weather for the season. As many of the Indians as were able to travel went off to day, sent off 3 men to Primeau's establishment on Chyenne river with a horse train loaded with Mdse: for the trade of the Indians in that quarter. Mr. Laidlaw is preparing for another [word?]

Friday 18th: Same weather as Yesterday. Sent off B. Daurion, Pineau and some other Indians to hunt for us on the other side of the Missouri, we have but three or four lodges now remaining here.

Saturday 19th: About 20 Lodges of Brulé and Yancton Indians arrived here from White river, they are all starving. Weather Clear and pleasant.

Sunday 20th: A few more lodges of Starving Indians arrived. Weather as Yesterday.

Monday 21st: All the Lodges moved off to day in quest of Buffaloe, the weather still continues fine and pleasant. In the evening an Indian arrived from Primeau's establishment with a letter.

Tuesday 22d: Weather as Yesterday 5 or 6 Lodges Brulés and Yanctons arrived from below (as usual they are starving) Baptiste Defond with three men and 6 horses loaded with Robes &c. arrived from Cerré's post on White river.

Wednesday 23d: Defond and the men and horses from Cerres post returned left on their return to day. Weather mild and cloudy.

Thursday 24th: A little snow fell, but the weather still continues mild.

Friday 25th: Mild and cloudy 8 or 10 Lodges of Miserable half starved Indians (Yanctons & Brulés) arrived here.

Saturday 26th January 1833: All the Indians went off except two Lodges, 2 men arrived from the Hunters camp with a few horse loads of fresh meat, as also 2 men from Primeau's establishment on Chyenne river with horses loaded with 60 ps: dry Meat.

Sunday 27th: Braseau Duchonquette & 6 men with 6 horses loaded with Corn arrived from Lachapelles cache near Beaver creek, fortunately not more than 10 or 12 Bushels are missing. Weather mild and cloudy.

Monday 28th: Weather the same as Yesterday, no news stirring.

Tuesday 29th: A continuation of mild weather and no news stirring.

Wednesday 30th: Weather as Yesterday. Joseph Juett arrived from the Ogallallahs Post with 45 horses and mules. Alexander Haury (trapper) arrived from Ft Union but he brought no news or letters. P. Cerré and his men arrived from the Brulé post with the Mdse: intended for the trade of those Indians, the Brulés are a long distance out in the plains and nearly in a state of starvation.

Thursday 31st: Mr. G. P. Cerré with 2 men left here for Primeau establishment with Mdse: to trade in that quarter. Weather moderate and Cloudy with snow at intervals.

[February 1833]

Friday February 1st 1833: Weather the same as Yesterday. Joseph Juett with Lachapelle and 6 men left here for the Ogllallah Post they took with them a supply of Mdse: &c. for the trade of the Indians there.[93]

Saturday Febuary 2d: The weather still continues mild and cloudy.

Sunday 3d: A continuation of mild pleasant weather.

Monday 4th: Still continues mild Weather, 2 Yanctons arrived from above, they say that Buffaloe are getting scarce.

Tuesday 5th febuary 1833: The weather still continues very mild for the season. Two men arrived last morning from Primeau's establishment with horses loaded with 40 pieces dry Meat.

Wednesday 6th febuary 1832 [*sic*]: Three or four Indians arrived from the Little Chyenne river with meat &c.

Thursday 7th: The weather still continues as yesterday although if any thing it is milder.

Friday 8th: Weather as Yesterday and nothing new.
Saturday 9th: Cold and cloudy with snow at intervals.
Sunday 10th: Cloudy with snow the first part of the day. Middle and Latter part pleasant.
Monday 11th: A fine Pleasant day. Sent off a man with a letter to Sawon Post, also one with a letter to Lacompt at Yancton Post. Also sent of[f] Baptiste Defond with an Equipment to trade Meat at Medicine Hill camp.
Tuesday 12th: Clear and cool, no arrivals or departures.
Wednesday 13th: Weather fine and pleasant.
Thursday 14th: Weather as Yesterday.
Friday 15th: J. D. Bigué and 3 men arrived from Primeau Establishment with 3 Trains loaded with Meat, Skins &c.
Saturday 16th: Filled our Ice house with Ice. Champeau and the dog (Capeue de fleches) arrived from Chyenne Establishment.
Sunday 17th: Cold and Cloudy with snow at intervals.
Monday 18th: Cold and cloudy with a strong Northerly wind.
Tuesday 19th: Cold with snow throughout the middle and latter part of the day.
Wednesday 20th: A Clear and pleasant day, 2 Indians arrived from the Yancton camp at Medicine Hill.
Thursday 21st: Weather the same as Yesterday. One of the Indians who arrived yesterday left us this morning.
Friday 22d: Strong North wind and Cloudy weather.
Saturday 23d: Several Lodges of Yanctons arrived from above on their way to Medicine Hill on the other side the Missouri.
Sunday 24th: Weather cool and cloudy with an appearance of a storm.
Monday 25th: Clear and cool. Mr. and Mrs. Brown left us for Roys Island. Also all the Lodges went off.
Tuesday 26th: Cold and cloudy with snow the first part of the day. Sent off P. [Name?] for the upper Camp in search of provisions.
Wednesday 27th: Weather clear and cold, a considerable quantity of snow fell last night, five or 6 staving Yanctons arrived from above.
Thursday 28th: The Coldest day that we have had this winter, a Lodge of Indians arrived from above, those who arrived yesterday left us to day.
~~Friday 29th~~: The weather is still very cold.

[March 1833]

Friday March 1st: a few Indians arrived from above on their way to Medicine Hill.
Saturday March 2d: Weather moderate and pleasant 8 or 10 Lodges of Yanctons arrived from above, and camped on the opposite side the river.
Sunday March 3d: Was a pleasant day for the season.
Monday March 4th: Weather as Yesterday. Charles Primeau and 1 man arrived from Yancton Post in quest of provisions.
Tuesday March 5: weather still continues pleasant.
Wednesday March 6th: Mr. Laidlaw and a party of Whites and Indians went out in search of Buffaloe, in the evening one of his men returned with the flesh of Bull which they fell in with and killed. At the same time 2 men with 8 horses and mules arrived from Chyenne river establishment loaded with 800 lbs. dry meat.
Thursday 7th: Weather cloudy with rain at intervals.
Friday 8th: Weather Mild and pleasant.
Saturday 9th: Still fine pleasant weather. The Missouri very bad. Mr. Laidlaw and party returned from hunting, he was not successful, in the evening Mr. Brown arrived from Bloomfield farm (Roys Island)[94] as also some 6 or 7 Indians arrived from Serpent river with about 15 Pieces dry Meat to trade.
Sunday 10th: Weather as Yesterday. Mr. Brown left us in the afternoon on his return to Bloomfield farm at which place however the unfortunate gentleman never reached alive, the ice was so weak that he broke through and was drowned not more than 20 paces from the shore of the island, he had men with him but they were too far from him to render him any assistance.
Monday 11th: The first part of the day a little snow fell, middle and latter part Cold and cloudy, the Indians from Serpent river left us. Baptiste Defond and Two men left us for Cedar Island to look after our Keel boat laying at that place.
Tuesday 12th: First and middle part cool and cloudy. Mr. Braseau Duchonquette left here for Bloomfield farm to fill the vacancy occasioned by

the death of Mr. William L. Brown. 5 or 6 indians arrived from above with Robes to trade. Latter part of the day Clear and pleasant.

Wednesday 13th: Stormy Southerly winds and moderate weather.

Thursday 14th: Weather as Yesterday. Baptiste Defond arrived from keel boat "Argo" at Cedar Island.

Friday 15th: Strong Gales from the East and moderate weather. All Intercourse to the opposite side of the Missouri is obstructed by the extreme weakness of the ice.

Saturday 16th: Mild and pleasant. The ice opposite this place made a move.

Sunday 17th: Louis Lagrave arrived from Council Bluffs with dispatches from there, the Missouri is clear of ice the balance moved off about meridian. The day clear and pleasant.

Monday 18th: First part of the day Strong Easterly winds and Cloudy weather middle and latter part rainy and windy. Sent five men across the river to bring over Keel boat Atlas but the wind is too strong for them to get the boat over to day.

Tuesday 19th: Strong Gales from the Northeast and snow the first and Middle part of the day, latter part Calm and Cloudy. The men arrived in the evening from the other side the river with Keel boat Atlas.

Wednesday 20th: Light northerly winds and pleasant weather. The Little Soldier's (Yancton) son in law left here with one of his daughters quite sick.

Thursday 21st: Clear and calm throughout the day. Baptiste Defond left here for the lower country in a canoe he goes in quest of the expected Steam Boat, and is to return in her.

Friday 22d: Same weather as yesterday and nothing new.

Saturday 23d: Strong Gales from the west and Cloudy weather.

Sunday 24th: Clear and pleasant.

Monday 25th: Same weather as Yesterday. [Name?] (a Brulé) arrived from above with Lodges.

Tuesday 26th: Strong Northwest wind and snow throughout the day.

Wednesday 27th: Clear and Calm. Mr Campbell from the Ogallallah Post and Mr. Papin from the Sawon post arrived with 7 skin canoes laden with 280 packs Robes, Mdse: &c. &c. [Name?] Roland, Prudent Boudieu, Francois Duchaim, Louis Turcot and James Durant stole a skiff last night and deserted.

Thursday 28th: Clear and fine. Ice commenced drifting thick, and water rising fast.

Friday 29th March 1833: Still continues fine pleasant weather. Water falling. Ice still drifting a little.

Saturday 30th: A Continuation of Fine Pleasant weather. Missouri Still falling. 2 Lodges Indians arrived on the other side the Missouri and camp'd there.

Sunday 31st: Weather still pleasant.

[April 1833]

Monday 1st April 1833: Weather mild and Cloudy. Missouri rising.

Tuesday 2d: A Continuation of mild pleasant weather. E. Primeau arrived from Tonala Caxal[95] with two skin Canoes laden with Mdse: and 70 Packs Robes. Missouri 3 ft: above Low water mark.

Wednesday 3d: The Weather is still very pleasant. The Missouri 3½ ft. above low water mark and still rising.

Thursday 4th: Auguste Boenbomt and Peter Hill not relishing a corn diet left here this morning for Fort Clark (Mandans) in quest of better fare. Weather as Yesterday. Ice drifting and the Missouri rising.

Friday 5th: Strong Northerly winds and fair weather, completed our Robe Baggage, it contains 830 Packs. Missouri still rising.

Saturday 6th: A Cloudy day with an appearance of rain. Missouri falling fast.

Sunday 7th: A Continuation of Cloudy weather, with an appearance of rain. Missouri still falling.

Monday 8th: Cloudy weather. 4 Buff. Bulls made their appearance on the opposite side of the Missouri. Mr Laidlaw and a party went over and he succeeded in killing two.

Tuesday 9th: A considerable quantity of snow fell last night, the weather throughout the day disagreeable, rainy.

Wednesday 10th: The weather the same as Yesterday.

Thursday 11th: Strong Gales from the North East and snow throughout the day.

Friday 12th: Weather Calm and pleasant, but nothing new.

Saturday 13th: A fine pleasant day, caught 240 fish with the seine at Little Missouri.

Sunday 14th: Weather Clear and cold. I forgot to mention that two Indians (Brulés) arrived yesterday from the Brulé camp on White river. They stated that they have plenty of Buffalos in the neighbourhood and plenty of meat and robes in their Lodges and that the[y] would like to have a trader. At 12 P.M. Messrs. Lamont Picotte, May & Moncravie arrived from Fort Clark, they left keel boat Louis Vallé about 40 miles above here.

Monday 15th: Messrs. Papin, Primeau and 6 men with the Brulé Indians left us with an assortment of goods to trade with that band. At 4 P.M. Keel boat Louis Vallé arrived from the Mandans with a cargo of Robes, Meat, Corn &c.

Tuesday 16th: Cold and cloudy. A little snow fell last night, unloaded Keel boat Louis Vallé. T 10 P.M. Louis Morgan died.

Wednesday 17th: A fine pleasant day. At 4 P.M. interred the remains of Louis Morgan.

Thursday 18th: Weather as Yesterday, a party went to Teton river with the seine and succeeded in taking about 60 fish.

Friday 19th: Strong Easterly winds and cloudy weather.

Saturday 20th: A Little rain fell last night, but to day the weather was pleasant. A party Sent down to Teton river with seine and succeeded in taking 240 fish.

Sunday 21st: A fine Pleasant day. Bigué & Duchonquette arrived from Bloomfield farm with a loaded boat of Plank &c.

Monday 22st: The ~~weather~~ day cloudy with hot sultry weather, and an appearance of a storm.

Tuesday 23rd: Strong Gales from the North and cloudy with the appearance of a storm. L. Frenier left here with a Keel boat for Cedar Island to Cut wood for the purpose of making shingles.

Wednesday 24th: A Continuation of windy weather, nothing new.

Thursday 25th: Hot sultry weather for the season, during the night Thunder and Lightning, and a little rain fell.

Friday 26th: A Party went down to Teton river with the Seine and succeeded in taking 250 fish.

The weather as Yesterday. 2 Lodges Yanctons arrived on the other side the Missouri and camped there.

Saturday 27th: Weather Cloudy and windy. Crossed the two Lodges of Indians from the other side, they are starving.

Sunday 28th: The weather still continues cloudy and there is every appearance of a storm.

Monday 29th: The same weather as yesterday, at night a little rain fell.

Tuesday 30th: Still continues cloudy weather with the appearance of a storm. The Missouri rising a little. A party went down to Teton river with the seine but only succeeded in taking about 40 fish. The Keel boat arrived from Cedar Island with timber for the purpose of making Shingles.

[May 1833]

Wednesday May 1st: A disagreeable rainy day. Auguste Bourbont and Peter Hill arrived from the Mandans. No news of importance from that quarter.

Thursday 2d: Cloudy with rain at intervals.

Friday 3d: Hot Sultry weather (Clear and calm).

Saturday May 4th: Same weather as Yesterday. Mr. D. D. Mitchell arrived from Ft. Union with a Batteaux loaded with dressed skins &c. &c.

Sunday 5th: Fine pleasant weather and nothing new.

Monday 6th: Same weather as yesterday four men arrived from below they say they are Beaver Trappers. A Lodge of Indians arrived on the opposite side the Missouri.

Tuesday 7th: The strangers who arrived last night have confessed themselves to be traders they say their employers Messrs. Sublett, Campbell & Leclerc have two Keel boats now on their way up the river laden with Merchandise. Pierre Garrow and one of them left here for the Mandans this morning, the others took the road down the river. The day was Clear and fine.

Wednesday 8th: Weather as Yesterday. Missouri rising.

Thursday 9th: Cool and cloudy, appearance of a storm.

Friday 10th: A fine pleasant day Mr. W. Dickson arrived from Riviere a Jacques with 9 carts laden with 58 packs Robes &c. &c.

Saturday 11th: A fine pleasant day. But no arrivals. A party went down to Teton river with the seine and took upwards of 100 fish.

Sunday 12th: A Continuation of fine pleasant weather.

Monday 13th: Cloudy with Strong Northerly winds and an appearance of rain. Missouri falling.

Tuesday 14th: A little rain fell last night. To day the weather is cloudy and there is an appearance of more rain. 15 Sawon Indians arrived.

Wednesday 15th: Throughout the day fine weather, at night a considerable quantity of rain fell.

Thursday 16th: Cool, Cloudy and windy. 2 American Beaver Trappers arrived in a canoe from the Upper Country on their way to St Louis.

Friday, 17th: A fine pleasant day. At noon Mr. Wm. P. May and the two American strangers left us for St Louis in a canoe.

Saturday 18th May 1833: Cool and pleasant weather, at night we had a light shower of snow, we caught upwards of 100 fish with the seine to day, and yesterday upwards of 200.

Sunday 19th: The weather throughout the day was very pleasant, at meridian Charles Primeau arrivd from the Yancton Post, no news from St Louis yet.

Monday 20th: Cool northerly wind and clear weather, the Missouri rose 3 inches.

Tuesday 21st: Clear and Pleasant. Missouri rising a little, at 2 A.M. Mr. L. Fontenelle and man arrived from Council Bluffs. Two steam Boats he states that two S. Boats are now on their way up here somewhere between this and the Poncas Village.

Wednesday 22d: Weather as yesterday, ay Meridian a man arrived from Yancton Post with news from the steam Boat on the 11th inst. they were stopped for want of water. Some where near the Three [?] Island. Missouri rising.

Thursday 23d: Weather cloudy with an appearance of rain. Commenced baling goods for Mountain Outfit. 2 Sawon Indians arrived from their camp on Chyenne river, they report to be still scarce.

Friday 24th: Clear and pleasant the Missouri still rising. Employed as Yesterday.

Saturday 25th: Cloudy with rain throughout the greatest part of the day. Missouri still rising a little.

Sunday 26th: A disagreeable windy Cold and cloudy day.

Monday 27h: A fine Pleasant day. Several freemen arrived from the upper country to day. Mr. Adams[96] one of the party remained here and the others proceeded on down the river. Mr Lamont and Mr Mitchell left here in a skiff to meet the S. Boat

Tuesday 28th May: A Cold disagreeable day. Missouri falling.

Wednesday 29th: Steam Boat Yellowstone arrived from St Louis.

Thursday 30th: Steam Boat Assiniboine arrived from St Louis.

Friday 31st: Employed discharging Cargo of Steam Boats.[97]

[June 1833]

Saturday June 1st: Employed as Yesterday. Missouri rising.

2

FORT TECUMSEH LETTER BOOK

November 1, 1830–May 10, 1832

[translated from French]
Fort Tecumseh Nov: 1st 1830
Mr. E. Primeau

You will receive by Ortubise the baggage that you outlined as well as a Standard of the Fur Trade. But if you believe that the red blankets and vests might be too high, I advise you not to show them. Legé and Ortubise there with you are already in debt[;] I beg you to do nothing to increase this advance. Only if they have absolute need. You also have the accounts of others, and there are dear ones that could be more interesting [of greater value].

Tell the Brulés that they will have only one trading house this year. They are the ones responsible for this because of their actions and that, if they don't comport themselves better it is likely that they won't have any next year; it depends on them entirely.

Take extra care of your horses, because it is impossible to get more of them here, you should wash them and take special care all the time.

Your men left a horse on the road they followed to here, and the others were in bad shape.

I beg you to exercise your Authority
and [I] remain your [servant] etc.
(Signd.). K McKenzie

❖ ❖ ❖

Fort Tecumseh Novr. 21st 1830
Mr. Emillien Primeau
White River
Dear Sir

My present purpose for sending to your establishment is the want of provisions. We have been for some time out of our common provisions (Dry Meat.) and our little stock of Corn & Pork diminishes rapidly. I hope you will be able to send me by the return of Mr Hay a considerable Supply, for I have a great many mouths to provide for.

I wish you to send in the Cart by the present opportunity. I do not think it probable you will have a better one. I would also advise you to send in all your horses, without you have good feeding for them at hand, and can have them well taken care of.

I do not know whether Mr. Laidlaw told you what manner he thought most advisable to bring out the returns of your outfit, the present supposition is that you will trade an unusual number of Packs, and if it should prove to be true, you will be obliged to make canoes and descend white river. I make this remark so that you may make all necessary preparation in time, but You are no doubt aware that the present season, is not the time to purchase Skins for that purpose.

I have nothing more to add except that Mr. Hay will deliver you a lot of Fancy Beads, for the price of which I refer you to the enclosed bill. All the goods you left him were charged in Invoice rendered, but have been recently placed to the credit of your outfit.

Yours Respectfully
Danl: Lamont
To
Mr. Emellien Primeau (Signd) per Jack Halsey
White River

❖ ❖ ❖

Fort Tecumseh Nov: 21st 1830
Mr. Pierre D. Papin
White River
Dear Sir

Inclosed you have your Invoice of Mdse: and a Statement of the advances made to our men: Sent you so that they may be kept within limits of their wages. Giroux you will perceive is already in debt. I would advise you to let him have nothing, except such articles as he may possibly stand greatly in need of.

There is but little doubt that Lataille has received advances in St. Louis, but, as no account has been forwarded us, it is impossible for me to say how he stands with the Company.

I have nothing of import to communicate. Mr. McKenzie left here a few days after your departure, for Fort Union, since that time we have been destitute of Dry Meat, and, having already been obliged to broach upon our little stock of Corn and Pork

Yours Respectfully
Danl: Lamont
(Signd) per Jacob Halsey

❖ ❖ ❖

Fort Tecumseh Novr. 23d. 1830
Mr. Frederick Laboue
Moreau River
Dear Sir

I acknowledge the receipt of your favour pr. Lachapelle dated 17th inst.

You have no doubt seen Mr. McKenzie before this time, he left here on the 14th inst: and must have arrived at your establishment the third or fourth day afterwards.

Your horse was claimed by Mr. Chardon as a gift from you, and he has him now in his possession

I hope you will see your Indians soon, and get a Supply of Dry Meat. We are, and have been, for some time, destitute of that provision and, if we do not soon get relief we shall be badly off.

In case you should fall in with any furriers, I do not wish you to make them any advances without a written order from someone belonging to the concern.

Yours Respectfully
Danl. Lamont
(Sign'd.) per Jacob Halsey

❖ ❖ ❖

Fort Tecumseh Novr. 23d. 1830
Mr. Richard T. Holliday[1]
Ree Village
Dear Sir

Your favour of 14th Ultimo was received yesterday pr Lachapelle, Mr McKenzie left here the same day your letter is dated, and, as you have no doubt seen him ere this, and received all necessary instructions from him, with regard to the trade, it is unnecessary for me to say any thing on that subject.

I send you by the bearer Louis Obachon, two swords, and, would furnish you with all the articles you have written for, if I had the means of sending them.

Our horses were in such miserable bad order, and as proper attention could not be paid to them here, I sent [them] to the mouth of Chyenne river, where we have a party of men cutting timber for a Fort. You remark that you was not absolutely in want of the articles ennumurated in your letter, at the time you wrote. I would advise you to send to Frederick's establishment for such articles as you may be in immediate want of, he has an unnecessary quantity of goods, and, it is more than probable he will be able to supply you with many, and, perhaps all, of the articles you stand in need of.

In case you should be visited by any furriers, I do not wish you to make them any advances, without an order from some one belonging to the concern.

Yours Respectfully
Danl: Lamont
(Signd.) per Jacob Halsey

❖ ❖ ❖

Fort Tecumseh Novr. 26th 1830
Mr. Emillien Primeau
White River
Dear Sir

I acknowledge the receipt of your letter dated 22d. inst: per Ortubise, with 171 pieces dry Meat. I shall not depend upon you for another Supply, but, in case you Should at any time have more on hand, than you think necessary for your own consumption, you will no doubt send it in to us. According to your request, I send you 30 Lances, 50 lbs. Powder and some medicine for your crippled man. You will perceive on reference to the inclosed bill, that the Lances cost a high price: to make a profit, they should be sold for two Robes each. I wish you to make the trial, and, if you find the Indians will not buy them at that price, let them have them for one.

I sent all your horses back except one, which I do not think able to return.

Ortubise & Legé say you have the means of having them well taken care of, otherwise I should have sent them to the Mouth of Chyenne river where we have a party of men cutting timber for a Fort. I sent the whole of our horses there, some time ago.

In case any free hunters should pay you a visit, I do not wish you to make them any advances whatever, without an order from myself or Mr. Laidlaw

Yours Respectfully
Danl. Lamont
(Signd.) per Jacob Halsey

❖ ❖ ❖

Fort Tecumseh Dec. 1st 1830
Mr. Pierre D. Papin
White River
Dear Sir

Yours of the 27th November last, I received per Giroux this morning. I send you as requested 2 Bush: Corn & 10 lbs. Grease, nothing has been seen of the Wampum Hair Pipes, which you say, you think, were left here, but I send you some others to replace them.

Your Invoice and a Statement of your mens A/cs. were forwarded to Primeau's establishment, and, from thence they will be sent to you. Mr. Hay who arrived from there to day, informs me, that the Yanctons have plenty of Buffaloes and were daily looking for your arrival at their camp, to trade dry Meat.

I do not wish you to make any advances to Freemen, without an order from myself, or Mr. Laidlaw. Pierre Detaillier left here yesterday for your establishment. Halsey wrote you a few lines by him, and notified you of this request of mine, but in case you never should see this letter, it is mentioned again. We have had no arrivals from St. Louis yet, nor, do we look for any, before the tenth of this month. If we should receive any letters for you, they shall be forwarded by the first opportunity afterwards.

If you should be fortunate enough to get more meat from the Indians, than is necessary for your own consumption, I hope you will send us the Surplus, for we are poor in Provisions

Yours Respectfully,
Danl: Lamont
(Signd.) per Jacob Halsey

❖ ❖ ❖

Fort Tecumseh 13 Dec: 1830
My Dear Laidlaw

I did not calculate when you left here to have sent to you previous to your chrismas visit, but necessity which as old Col. Dickson[2] used to say has no legs compells me to call upon you for a Supply of provisions. We are now almost destitute of every description of the provisions of the Country, having only received since you left us a small Supply of Meat from Primeau, with a notice that nothing more can be looked for from that quarter.

Our Navy Yard party which consists of 20 Men are like to starve us out here, and unless Buffalos make their appearance, I fear it will be impossible to Support them.

A few days from your departure the small boat arrived, and two days after McKenzie left us for Fort Union taking with him all the horses in condition to make the trip. I have heard nothing of him since, but presumed he must be at his destination some days since. The remaining horses (your own included) have gone to the Navy Yard where it is said the feeding is good: they are all under charge of Tibout the patroon, and as many of them will be required for hauling timber for the contemplated new fort below the mouth of the Chyenne. I have given directions to have yours exempted.

In the Shape of news I have not a sentence to offer you as we are quite in the dark regarding what is passing as yet at any of the posts.

Our Indian deputation has not yet returned from St. Louis, but are hourly look'd for, when you pay the promised visit, we may possibly have something worthy of communication.

Detaillie and Mattheu arrived here from their hunt about ten days ago, they have made out by hard squeezing to pay their debits to papin, but have not a dollar left, nor are they likely to obtain any aid in this quarter. Carrier has not yet made his appearance, tho' much beyond his usual time, in case he may pass by your establishment, I inclose you a small a/c against this man, amounting to twenty-eight dollars, which I hope you will be able to secure.

By the Small boat I have received the articles deficient in your St Louis purchases, and send you by this opportunity, those most likely to be required during the Winter, to wit, 2 small [word?] suits of Clothes, and some Scarlet Bombasette [worsted cloth of twill or plain weave]. I also send you a pair of Pistols ordered for Joseph Juett, an a/c of which you will find as charged your post.

The Season untill a day or two past has been more like Spring than Winter, the river ceased running the 11th without the usual uproar with floating ice, but gradually like Stagnant water. We can now have a wider range for our rambles, for indeed we have little else to occupy our time.

Mr. Hamilton who tenders you his respects, joins me in the hope of your promised visit to us not being abandoned, be not frightened at the coy of [word?], for we shall find for you, notwithstanding our poverty, a "bit and a sup" while you sojourn with us

In the hope of seeing you soon
Believe me my Dear Laidlaw
Yours Sincerely
(Signd.) Danl. Lamont

❖ ❖ ❖

Fort Tecumseh 19 Dec: 1830
Mr. Richard Holliday
Dear Sir

Your favour of the 12th Ultimo came Safe to hand last night by a man from Fredericks establishment, the uncertainty which yet envelops the affair of the robbing of the robbing of Mr. McKenzie's party by the Rees makes it very disturbing and consequently I am under the greatest anxiety to learn all the particulars possible, still I think had any of the party fallen by the hands of the savages we should have had intelligence from some quarter in this as bad news generally makes rapid strides. As McKenzie at the time this unfortunate accident occur'd must have been close to the Yanctonnas trading post and would go there for succor. I have written to Mr Mitchell for an account of the particulars, have the goodness to forward him the inclosed and send his reply as far as Fredericks with as little delay as practicable. I observe what you say with regard to Garrow and from my own knowledge of his character, can amply warrant your suspicions. Your situation I am aware must be very disagreeable and perhaps a critical one, but yourself who are on the spot must be the best judge how to act. For your own safety and that of the property under your charge endeavour to put the best face on matters possible and by no means lose any time as soon as the navigation will permit [you] to leave the vile place. Skins cords and poles for your canoes have in readiness which the articles can be procured without inconvenience. I inclose you a tariff of prices, by which you will be regulated: had I not supposed you had been furnished with one on leaving here, it would have been sent you sooner.

I have nothing in the shape of news to communicate to you, the Indian deputation to St. Louis has not yet returned tho' much beyond the time contemplated. God preserve you and Believe me

Most Sincerely
Your friend and Obdt.
(Signd.) Danl. Lamont

❖ ❖ ❖

Fort Tecumseh Dec: 28th 1830
Mr. Richard T. Holliday
Dear Sir

Your favour of the 20th Dec: Came to hand this morning and I hasten to fill your [two words?] so far as your two men will be able to carry. The letters from Mr McK. Brought by your men gave us all great relief as from the reports our minds were far from being at ease.

On the subject of boats going up in spring I have heard nothing but presume Mr McK. misst the Steam boat, but had no [word?] to your remaining till its arrival. As I stated to you in my last make all necessary preparations and start as soon as the ice will permit.

Lachapelle goes up with the men for a Supply of traps to enable him to make a spring hunt with Carrier, if you have any furnish him with 8 and charge them to this depart, he has settled his a/c here and should he have any dealing with you send me an a/c by him.

I have no intelligence to offer you that is of note. If sympathy for your unpleasant situation would add to your present ease or future safety you should riot in enjoyment but alas it can be of little benefit.

Your Letter for Mr Langham shall go with the express in a day or two and will be attended to in St Louis by Mr Chouteau, with the compliments of the season and hopes of your safe arrival here in Spring believe me my

Dear Holliday
Yours Sincerely
(Signd) Danl: Lamont

❖ ❖ ❖

Fort Tecumseh Dec: 28th 1830
Mr. David D. Mitchell
Dear Sir

The morning brought the express which I assure you gave us all great relief and will supercede a reply to my letter written a few days ago to you.

I rejoice at the prospect of a good return being made by our post it will be much wanted, for so far the prospect of most others is very unfavourable.

Halsey will put you up an assortment of such medicines as we have, and be sure to make those who use them pay the transit. I send Campbell a phial of Love Essence so much wanted by him last winter, but I suppose it will now be of Little service. I send you the Files you request say ½ doz: Pitsaw.[3] Nothing new yet from Saint Louis

Yours Truly
(Signd.) Danl. Lamont

❖ ❖ ❖

Fort Tecumseh Dec: 30th 1830
Mr. John Sibelle
Dear Sir

Herewith you will receive your Invoice and a Statement of your mens a/cs sent you so that they may be kept within limits of their wages. By the return of the express I wish you to send me a minute account of the property you have received from Messrs. P.D. Papin & Co.

The news of the surrounding country is somewhat of an interesting nature, but time prevents me from giving you a relation of it, you will have it all from the [word?] of dispatches Zephine Recontre. Whatever advances you make to persons belonging to this post or who are journying hitherward you will please to send me an a/c of. Do not make any advances to Denoyer except such articles as he may possibly stand in need of for the completion of his voyage, he has already taken the most of his wages and would soon be in debt if we were to furnish him with every thing he asks for

Yours &c.
Danl. Lamont
Per Jacob Halsey

❖ ❖ ❖

Fort Tecumseh Dec: 30th 1830
Pierre Chouteau Jr. Esqr.
Dear Sir:

I have just received dispatches from McKenzie dated at the Mandan Villages accompanying orders for the Supply of the ensuing year to avoid the risk of any accident in the transit of the documents hence to St. Louis. I have had copies made of each and send a sett of each by the two men sent to Council Bluffs. Mr Cabanne will than take whatever precaution he may deem necessary for their safety.

Mr. McKenzie has given you a detail of the unfortunate occurrence with Mr Vanderburg at the forks of the Missouri, and also of the outrage committed on himself and party by the Rees; the former much as it is to be regretted has many palcating [?] circumstances but the latter is without parallel, to be pillages and maltreated by a nation in whose Village we now have a trader, and that too before our people were fairly out of the smoke of their Lodges and by the very persons who made a shew of hospitality to them but a day or two previous. Assuredly in this instance no provocation could be alledged, not even the flimsy one assigned for the destruction of Bouchi and party for they had not been unfortunate in War but left their Village for the purpose of committing depredations.

Mr Holliday who is in charge at the Ree village is daily insulted and threaten'd, nay a [word?] that neither himself or his people will be allowed to depart in spring as the determination is to do as much mischief as possible ere quitting the Missouri, which they contemplate next spring and joining the Paunees on the Platte. That some severe step should be taken by the strong hand of Government calculated to strike terror in the minds of the Indians is no longer problematical. While the Ree are suffered to commit outrage upon outrage with impunity other Indians view the appathy of the whites in the most unfortunate light, already saying and with much apparent truth that Cowardice and not philanthropy is the cause. This spirit has already shown itself among those whom we have hitherto considered the staunchest friends of the Whites. It is in vain for Government Agents, Cival or Military to attempt any longer pacific measures the blood of too many white men cries aloud to the empolicy [?] of the Government heretofore and nothing but a War and that to extermination will avail to give security to the lives and property in this country. Much as it may be the policy generally to conciliate the Friendship of Indians, as regards the Rees this doctrine does not apply, for they are not only a great inconvenience in the intercourse between posts above and below them, but their trade has ever been a losing one, at least since known by any of the men engaged in the commerce of the Upper Missouri. I trust (and it is the hope of all in the Country) that Government will do something and that speedily to afford us safety. I cannot help stating my perfect conviction that it would be for the companies interest, and that they will do themselves countless injustice if they do not use all their ennergies to promote it.

The Robe trade in this quarter I fear will fall much short of the return last year, untill lately the weather has been unusually mild, the Missouri having kept open untill the 11th of the Month, the inland posts will make their usual proportion I think fully, but up to this time there has not been a Buffaloe kill'd on the Missouri river, the few free hunters from this quarter have made but indifferent hunts, they were presuming an opposition and knew they would be secure in board and lodging during the Winter go where they might, they have been sadly undeceived and now invoke imprecations on their own heads and those of their [word?] when too late.

Mr McK. ignorant at the time he made out the general order, of the situation of the posts below in Minutia has neglected a number of articles highly necessary, the inclosed list have the goodness to have packed, and addressed as in the order.

I also at Mr McK. request inclose you a copy of observations made by Mr. Laffinue on board the "Louis Vallé" on her voyage from St Louis, the loss of time and conduct of the hands from the Patroon down, is really Melancholy.

By Mr Bean you should have received the first of his draft on Kennedy & Co. for the amount of his a/c here, but to prevent accidents I now inclose you the second of the same draft, which when paid will go to the credit of Outfit 1830.

For some time past it has snowed almost constantly, the quantity now on the ground is unusually great, the result will be very favourable for the Steam boat trial which I trust is still your intention to make. I am altogether at a loss to conjecture a cause for the detention of "Beaver" and his Indians, by whom you have no doubt written, it is now almost a month beyond the time calculated for their return and their relations are getting quite uneasy.

Accept Dear Sir, the complements of the season and Believe me ever
Your Most Obdt.
(Signd.) D. Lamont

❖ ❖ ❖

Fort Tecumseh Dec: 30th 1830
Mr. Jean P. Cabannie
Dear Sir

The Bearer Zephine Recontre will and you the dispatches from Mr McKenzie containing the orders for the supplies of the ensuing year, to prevent or guard against accidents I have forwarded duplicates of each document which you will have the [word?] to dispose of as may seem most advisable to insure their arrival at their destination.

Mr McKenzie in his letter to you has no doubt informed you of all that has transpired above Mr. Vanderburg's unfortunate affair together with the outrages committed on himself by the Rees in his route to the Yellowstone, the latter was the most unprovoked attack I have ever known and together with the murder of Bouchi and party last summer calls loudly for revenge. If the Government persists purcuing the same course they have hitherto done in regard to the Indian here will be little security for either life or property, from the Rees we have everything to dread so long as they are allowed to exist, or at all events to inhabit the Missouri and have no advantage to [word?] from our intercourse with them, for all their trade even without opposition since I have known them has been a losing business.

So far the season has been unusually mild the Missouri closed here the 11th inst:, in consequence of the fine weather Buffaloe have remained far in the large, not one having yet been seen on the Missouri, in consequence of which I fear the return of Robes will fall much short of last year, to give you any idea at present of the probable quantity is altogether impossible, the inland posts from the latest in intelligence will make their usual proportion, but those on the river from which nearly half of the whole return usually comes have not yet made a pack, nor moreover, is there much prospect of their doing any thing. The free hunters from here have done little or nothing, they are all now arrived, and have brought only two packs Beaver.

Thus Sir, you see the appearances from this department are very gloomy but there is yet a considerable portion of the season to come in which Robes are good, we must trust in better results.

On examining your a/c settled last summer in Saint Louis, I find the eight dollars I requested you to pay "Gallerman" have been already paid him, as you will see by refferance to your book. He must have been paid by Mr. Fontenelle and the Rogue supposed you would not have detected him, or that I would not take the trouble of examining.

We are much in want of paper and Candlewick here, if you can spare me some of each, or either, you will greatly oblige me.

The men who carry the express are both in debt, have the goodness to advance them nothing more than is necessary for them to return
Yours Truly
(Signd.) D. Lamont

P.S. Should you have received any news papers of a later date than our leaving St. Louis, you will greatly oblige me by sending up such as you have procured. We are here almost bookless and will be thankful for any thing.[4]

❖ ❖ ❖

Fort Tecumseh Jany 2d 1831
Mr. Pierre D. Papin
White River
Dear Sir

Yours of the 28th Ultimo came safe to hand last night per Giroux with 25 pieces Meat, and the other articles mentioned. I cannot send you any of our horses, as they are all at the mouth of the Big Chyenne where we have a party of men cutting timber for a fort, neither do I think it advisable for you to attempt to send me another supply of meat, without you have horses able to stand the trip, although we are much in need of provisions.

Giroux wishes me to give him his freedom he says he has had an offer to go trapping with Cardinal. I do not object to his proposition, that is to say if Cardinal will hold himself responsible for the debt he owes us, and for five months time, which he has yet to serve at the rate of $160 per annum. Your letters for St. Louis arrived two days too late for the express, they shall be forwarded by the next opportunity. Gordon has not arrived yet, if he should bring any letters for you, I will send them to you by the first occasion.

Gendion is already in debt nearly 180 dollars he says he is much in want of a horse, if you think there is a prospect of his making enough in Spring to square his account you may furnish him with one at what you consider a fair price, provided you have one you can spare without putting yourself to any inconvenience. Do not give Giroux his freedom on any account if you stand in need of his services. With the compliments of the season I remain

Yours Truly
Danl. Lamont
(Signd.) per Jacob Halsey

❖ ❖ ❖

Fort Tecumseh Jany. 3d 1831
Mr. John McKnight
Fort Clark
Dear Sir

Yours of the 8th December addressed to Halsey came safe to hand on the 28th together with Mr McKenzie's dispatches which I forwarded from him in the 31st Ultimo.

The Invoice of Mdse: for Keel Boat "Fox" as forwarded you by Mr McKenzie is incorrect, most of the goods are part of the Stock of the late Messrs. P. D. Papin & Co. and in the hurry and confusion of the moment the Invoice was made out without charging an advance of 6 per Cent on the Blkts:, 10 per Cent on the Liquor and Tobacco and freight on the whole at the rate of five cents per pound. The copy which I now inclose you I believe to be correct.

In order for you to be able to take an accurate account of Stock in spring it will be necessary for you to keep the "Fox's" cargo separate from your other mdse:

Do not fail to send me an account of the advances your post has made to individuals up to the last Settlement day.

I have nothing in the way of news to communicate by the present opportunity. No arrivals from Saint Louis yet, but are in daily expectation of Gordons arrival from that neighbourhood.

We have had thus far a great deal of snow in this quarter, an unusual quantity is now on the ground, and from what I can learn it is still deeper South of us.

Yours &c.
Danl. Lamont
(Signd.) per Jacob Halsey

❖ ❖ ❖

Fort Tecumseh Jany. 3d 1831
Mr. David D. Mitchell
Dear Sir,

Your two men arrived here the day before yesterday. I am exceedingly sorry it is not in my power to send you a single Axe, as we have but one for the use of the fort. I send you a couple of pieces of Iron and some steel, and must recommend you to have it made up at the Mandans. I have no news to offer you, Gordon is reported to be near, with the Yanctons who went with "Beaver" to Saint Louis.

I send you by the barer all my wealth in books, I am sorry to say it is not more, for I know well what you suffer.

As with you, the Snow here, is very deep and keeps us housed: add to which we are almost as low in the provision way, and know not where to look for a Supply, but I presume the God who presides over all, will have a care to his good people of Fort Tecumseh

Believe me always
Yours Truly
(Signd.) Danl. Lamont

❖ ❖ ❖

Fort Tecumseh Jany. 11th 1831
Mr. David D. Mitchell
Dear Sir

Inclosed you have two letters recently received from St. Louis, they were brought here by one of our men who received them from Gordon some distance below this place when he was met on his return from St. Louis with the Yanctons. "Beaver" has remained at Cantonment Leavensworth, Gordon and a part of the Indians have not yet arrived, they of course have horses and on account of the unusual depth of snow are unable to travel fast.

I wish you to send me with as little delay as possible all the Beaver traps you have, I am in want of fourty which I fear is more than you will be able to send me.

By our letters and papers from St. Louis we have received news of an interesting nature we learn that considerable excitement has lately existed in the civilized world from a late civil war in France which broke out in July last. The revolt of course took place in Paris. Many thousands were kill'd and wounded, the existing Charles X was allow'd to leave the Capital without being molested by the revolters who look'd upon their late Monarch with an eye of contempt, and thought him too insignificant to punish or detain he fled to England for succor but was there received as a private individual and treated accordingly. The Duke of Orleans was raised to the throne as first constitutional King of the French under the title of Philip I. The Veteran Lafayette it is said [to have] held a conspicuous part in the revolution, his bravery and disintrestedness on the occasion will allways insure him in france (at least under the present administration) the good wishes of his countrymen and a high station in the Government of the Kingdom as well as the admiration of Europe and America.

I beg of you not to advance Vachard any thing more than is necessary for his return here, he is already deeply in debt

Yours Truly
Danl. Lamont
(Signd.) per Jacob Halsey

❖ ❖ ❖

Fort Tecumseh Jan 11th 1831
Mr. Richard S. Holliday
Dear Sir

By a letter I have received this evening from Mr. Laidlaw, I find he is in want of about fourty beaver traps, to equip some trappers in his neighbourhood. I wish you to collect with as little delay as possible all the traps you have loan'd out to Indians or Whites, and send the whole of them to me on the return of my men from Mr. Mitchells establishment to whom I have written to the same effect.

The news recently received from St. Louis is of an interesting nature. Inclosed is a letter from your brother he tells me he has given you a detailed account of every thing worthy of communication consequently it is unnecessary for me to repeat it.

I beg you to make no advances to Vachard, he is already in debt

In Haste

Yours Truly
Danl: Lamont
(Signd.) per Jacob Halsey

❖ ❖ ❖

Fort Tecumseh Jany. 12th 1831
Mr. Emillien Primeau
White River
Dear Sir

Yours of the 7th inst: per Seger I received yesterday with eighty Buffaloe Robes.

I send you all the articles requested, but as the Snow is unusually deep, I do not think it prudent to load your horses so heavily as otherwise would do, you will receive only 100 lbs. Tobacco instead of the quantity you have asked for.

I am gratified to hear there is a prospect of your trading a large supply of Meat, we will require a goodly quantity of provisions here in spring and from appearances at the other posts we have not much to hope for.

From the annual depth of snow, I should think it a difficult matter to send in your returns with horses without killing a part or perhaps the whole of them; from present appearances we certainly have a right to expect very high water in Spring, and it appears to me it would be a saving of expense and labour to descend White river in canoes. However you are on the spot and are best able to judge which would be the wisest plan to pursue. If you should conclude to make canoes and try the river, I wish you, after the trade is over to send in your horses, with what Mdse: you may have remaining, and descend with your packs to the Poncas, and there wait the arrival of the boats

Yours Truly
Danl: Lamont
(Signd.) per Jacob Halsey

❖ ❖ ❖

Fort Tecumseh Feby. 20th 1831
Mr. Richard F. Holliday
Dear Sir

Yours of the 28th January last came to hand the beginning of the present month, and should have been answered sooner had I not been delayed from day to day for the arrival of Zephine, that I might make one job of all in sending the express above, up to this day I have no tidings of him and begin seriously to think some accident has happened him. On refference to your 1st letter I perceive what you say regarding Lachapelle, when I received your letter it was too late to give you any opinion about the propriety of trusting him further, and I was in hopes he had got as deep in your debt as he would for this trip, he deceived you abominably about the $70 he said he had in Carrier's hands, and on the whole I think he has treated him badly.

I am much pleased at the prospect of a large amount of Robes from your post, and my object at present, is principally to concut [concoct] some plan by which your and Fredericks returns, may be got down as I know the great difficulty you must have in procuring Skins even for your own packs. Frederick writes me that he will be compelled to send to you for Skins to make canoes, in consequence of his Indians being too great a distance from the river, tho' I know it will be very difficult if not impossible for you to accomplish. I therefore think it advisable that you should Club your own forces and send to the Navy Yard for the boat that is there, by which means you will save time, and much expense and be able to man such number of Skin canoes as you will require with the hands you already have, for it is altogether out of my power to send you any additional force, the boat will carry about 300 packs or perhaps a trifle more if well packed, so that you will be able to estimate very nearly the extent of your skin conveyances necessary. I shall notify Frederick and you and him must concut your plans accordingly, the men should be at the boat before the breaking up of the ice, and provisions to bring up the boat are indispensable as there is none either there or here. The Patroon is directed to hold himself ready, and to obey your directions. I rejoice at the prospect of receiving from you a large canoe load of provisions, we are living here completely from hand to Mouth, and have no stock of either dry meat or corn, for Spring or for descending the river, for [word?] sake strain every nerve to procure as much as possible, no matter of what, provided it be eatable that you may not be disappointed in the Fall. I send you a couple of Bush: in my Sleigh, my pony is the only animal here able to make the trip, and it is even doubtful if he can stand it, the return of the sleigh will be a good opportunity to send me a load of corn. Should you have more Salt than you require you can notify mr Mitchell and if he is in want he will send for it, by the bye, it strikes me very forcibly that you can by previous arrangement with Mitchell (who has a very large boat) get all your packs, Goods &c down, without the help of Skin canoes at all. I shall mention the subject to him and request him to let you know what spare room he will have.

Have the goodness to forward the inclosed to Mitchell without delay, as it is of consequence he should have it with as little delay as possible

Yours Truly

(Signd.) Danl. Lamont

❖ ❖ ❖

Fort Tecumseh Feb: 20th 1831
David D. Mitchell
Dear Sir

Your favour of the 22d Ultimo I recd. Here on the 5th inst:, together with 7 Beaver Traps. I am much pleased to learn from you that on your first essay on the Upper Missouri you have a pleasing prospect of getting enough to eat at least, if your situation in other respects should be less enviable. I know well my good fellow what kind of company you have go[t] into, they are sad dogs but on the whole I believe, are more inclined to bark than bite. Since the arrival of Gordon we have heard nothing from below although Zephine is now out 22 days to Council Bluffs, from the former I received a file of papers from Mr: Pilcher, containing a tolerable account of the french Revolution which I send you for your perusal and when you have finished be good enough to inclose and address it to Mr McKenzie at the Yellow Stone. I am a little surprised at Mr. Chouteau stating having sent you a packet of papers, be assured no such came here, or I should have been held sacred.

By this time I presume the principal part of your trade is over and I hope it is worthy of the abundance of the season. The only post in this quarter that appears to be doing any thing is Mr. Laidlaw's, and to judge of his arrangements he will do a handsome business. I have just received from him a requisition for 30 men to be at his post by the 12th March at latest. Now as I can only raise 10 here, I have to request that you will send me immediately every man you can spare over your boats crew, and if possible furnish them with Shoes sufficient to take them to the fork of the Chyenne. For here we have not a pair. It is all important that no delay should take place in getting the men to Mr. Laidlaw, as he must start in the breaking of the ice in order to benefit by the high water.

Holliday and Frederick are apparently much [word?] about getting out their packs in Spring. I have placed at their disposal a Small boat now at the Navy yard which will carry about 300 Packs, but she will be too small to take all their plunder. I have stated to Holliday my belief that you will be able to give him a lift in passing, please have the goodness to let him know early what you can take for him, that he my make his arrangements accordingly, your boat well stowed should carry equivalent to 500 Packs, in that part of the river.

I trust (and let me impress it on your mind) that you will bring here a grand lot of Dry Meat or something eatable our only hope is from your post not only for our living here, but for a supply of provisions to take the boat to St Louis.

The severity of the winter has been such that we have reason to calculate on an early spring, as you are little acquainted in the Missouri, let me warn you of the necessity of a most vigilent attention to your boat, as the danger at the breaking of the ice is very great. I have just sent Mr Holliday a supply of Salt, should you be in want I presume he can spare you some. In hopes of seeing you early after a successful campaign believe me my dear Sir
Sincerely Yours
(Sign.) Daniel Lamont

❖ ❖ ❖

Fort Tecumseh 9th March 1831
Mr. Pierre D. Papin
Sir

Your letter of the 5th instant per Giroux, came safe to hand yesterday and solves they mystery of Lacharte's conduct, his arrival here, and still more the delay he made a few miles above on the Little Missouri was to me very extraordinary, but by his account, having been sent by you to find his living in the prairie, I could not order him to return, suffering as a matter of course that the want of provisions was the cause. When Provost arrived here on his way to the mountains of the 20th Ultimo, Lacharite made an offer of his services to accompany him as a hunter, this I objected to, conceiving his services probably necessary to you, but on the reassurance of his being in no way required, either himself or the two horses he had, I consented to his going, and sent the horses along with him. I certainly must say his offer of going to the mountains surprised me not a little, nor can I account for it in any other way, than the fear of returning to you after having been guilty of so much rascality.

I am happy to find by your letter there is yet a prospect of your making a few packs, and think you may with great safety wait untill you finish the trade, the immence quantity of snow in the mountains and Black Hills, will keep up for a long time all streams heading in this direction.

Emillien was here a few days ago with a part of his goods, the remainder he keeps in the expectation of yet seeing a band of Brulés; but in [the] event of their not coming to him, he will be compelled to take his goods to the Poncas, there not being a horse here capable of making the trip; out of nearly 100 horses here at present, there is scarcely one able to go to your post light, much less to bring a load back. In such can all I can advise you, is to decend your goods and Furs to the Poncas, and in event of the Steam Boat passing previous to the arrival of the boats for St Louis, you will ship the goods on board of her, and send an account of them to this place. On your arrival at the Poncas it will be necessary to send up as many men as will be necessary to take down such Boat or Boats, as will be required to carry your own, Primeau and the Poncas returns. This you will ascertain, taking care, however to retain a sufficiency to make the packs, that no detention may take place on the arrival of the boats.

I send you by Giroux the articles required in your letter, the handsaw is but indifferent but the best we have.

The express brings no news of consequence from St Louis, I expect another however shortly, and should it bring any thing for you, it shall be forwarded by Dufond, who will pass here shortly after the opening of the navigation
I am Sir
Your Most Obedient
(Signd.) Danl. Lamont

❖ ❖ ❖

Fort Tecumseh 4th April 1831
Pierre Chouteau Jr. Esqr.
Dear Sir

A few days after writing you last (30th Dec:) I received your letter by Bean previous to your starting for the Ohio on the Steam Boat business, since then I am sorry to say we are totally in the dark as to your movements below, and consequently at a loss to calculate the arrangements for the coming year, at the time I last wrote you the weather had continued unusually mild, and consequently Buffaloe remained at a great distance: indicating a great deficiency in the Robe return, this however took a fortunate change almost immediately after, and up to the present moment the season has been altogether without a parallel. Cattle have been in the greatest abundance at nearly all the trading posts, and the returns I think will be fully equal if not surpass all made in the river last year. Our mountain party after their disaster last fall passed the winter at the forks of the Yellow Stone (Powder river) from whence they will commence their spring hunt, but in consequence of the great depth of snow it will be sometime yet ere they can commence operations. I have just sent them a supply of horses to replace those lost in the Blackfeet attack.

Presuming it still [is] the intention of the Co. to make the trial of the Steam Boat, I send Defond who will act as pilot from the Bluffs up, the water will be in a fine stage and is likely to continue so during the Season on account of the great quantity of Snow in the Mountainous regions.

Inconsequence of the lateness of the season, it will in all probability be far in the month of June before the returns get to St. Louis. Mr. McKenzie being anxious that the mountain returns shall go at the same time. In hopes hearing from you yet ere I start, believe me Dear Sir

Your Most Obt. ser

(Sign's) Danl. Lamont

I inclose you an A/c against F. Pencinneau a fur hunter, who I understand arrived at St Louis last fall with Sublette & Co., should he yet be there, have the goodness to have it presented to him

❖ ❖ ❖

Fort Tecumseh 4th April 1831
Jean P. Cabanné Esqr.
Dear Sir

I received your favour of the 5th Febuary by Zephine on the 8th March, he was most inhumanely treated by the Omahas in passing and in consequence came very near starving.

I am sorry to have no late intelligence from St Louis, but presuming on the Steam Boat expedition going forward, I have sent Defond who will pilot her from Council Bluffs up. Should she not have arrived by the time he gets down, but in certainly of her coming, I think it would be well to let him proceed until he meets her.

As we will be scarce of men when our boats start, I have sent Francois to assist Baptiste down and inclose you an account of necessaries furnished him since he has been in the service of the Outfit.

The latter part of the winter has been uncommonly severe and the quantity of snow immence. Buffaloe shortly after I wrote you, came in great abundance, and instead of falling short of last year I think the Robe returns will surpass those of any season on the Upper Missouri.

I have had no intelligence of note since I wrote you from the Mountain post, in fact none could be expected, they pass the winter on Powder River, and will commence operations as soon as the snow will permit. I have just sent them a Supply of horses to replace those lost by the Blackfeet attack. In hopes of hearing from you before my departure believe me Dear Sir

Yours Sincerely

(Sign'd) Danl: Lamont

Last summer we omitted obtaining a supply of Garden seeds in St Louis, should you have a surplus, you will greatly oblige me, by sending such as you can spare.

❖ ❖ ❖

Fort Tecumseh April 4th 1831
Mr. John Sibelle
Dear Sir

I acknowledge the receipt of your favour dated 15th Febuary last, and send you as requested 40 lbs. Grease, 10 lbs. Sugar, and 5 lbs. Coffee. I notice what you say with regard to the credits made [at]

the Poncas last year, and am sorry it is not in my power to furnish you with a memorandum of them, however, I presume Primeau is acquainted with the most, if not the whole of the debts due by the Poncas, and you can learn from him who the individuals are.

As I was much in want of men on the arrival of Lajuniss and Seblond, I have detained them here, have the goodness to send up their a/c by the first opportunity.

Endeavour to collect all the Beaver traps remaining in the hands of your Indians, and by no means let them retain any, without paying you for them

Yours Truly
Danl. Lamont
(Sign'd.) per Jacob Halsey

❖ ❖ ❖

Fort Tecumseh April 4th 1831
Mr. Pierre D. Papin
Dear Sir

I have yours of the 27th Ultimo with 2 Mules, 1 Horse, 6 Saddles and 12 dam'd Robs. according to your request, I send you letters herewith.

If you have an a/c against Sachanté or Paquette you will oblige me by forwarding both, or either by first opportunity in haste

Yours Truly
Danl. Lamont
per Jacob Halsey

❖ ❖ ❖

Fort Tecumseh 21st April 1831
Mr. Pierre D. Papin
White river
Dear Sir

Yours of the 16th instant I received this morning per Giroux and I hasten to send him back with 3 Galls: Alcohol as requested.

At the expiration of your trade I wish you to send in, and let me know how many horses it will require to bring in what Mdse: you may have remaining, and I will endeavour to supply you with the means of transporting them here by land, as it is more than probable that you will be too late to meet the Steam Boat.

We have every reason to Suppose that White river will be sufficiently high for Skin canoes to descend on it, throughout the remainder of this month, however you are on the Spot, and are best able to judge which will be the most prudent course to follow.

Believe me Yours Truly
Danl. Lamont
per Jacob Halsey

❖ ❖ ❖

Fort Tecumseh April 28th 1831
Pierre Chouteau Junr. Esqr.
Dear Sir

On the 4th instant I had the pleasure of addressing you, since which nearly all the returns have come to hand, and I am happy to confirm my anticipations in regard to returns.

The Bearer (Benoit) a free hunter who has just arrived from the Mandans where he delivered a small quantity of Beaver, has a draft on you for $441.25 which you will please charge to Outfit 1830, he brings us no intelligence of importance, only that the upper Indians will make fully their usual proportion of Robes.

All possible precaution an and will be taken to expedite the Steam Boat, and be assured your presence in here will be very gratifying

In truth, believe me ever
Your Most Obedient Servt.
(Sign'd) Danl. Lamont

❖ ❖ ❖

Fort Tecumseh May 2d. 1831
Mr. Pierre D. Papin
Dear Sir

Yours of the 30th Ultimo by Vital came to hand last evening, and I send you as requested the articles mentioned in the inclosed bill. Blue Blkts: are articles I have not got.

Your plan of getting out the packs with horses cannot be accomplished at present, in consequence of the great poverty of those we have here, they are however, recruiting and may probably be able to make the trip in 20 or 25 days. Should you then consider the river dangerous, by giving notice I shall be able to send a Sufficient number to take the whole at one trip.

Your brother in law arrived here two days ago, and starts to day for the Rees, to trade the balance of their Robes

Yours Respectfully
(Sign'd) Danl. Lamont

❖ ❖ ❖

Fort Tecumseh June 7th 1831
Jean P. Cabanné Esqr.
Otto Establishment
Dear Sir

Your two favours of the 6th and 21st Febuary I received on my arrival here from Fort Union on the 4th inst. I am happy to say our returns this year will exceed in the quantity of Robes, that of any other year previous, the returns of Fort Union turned out much better than I had any right to expect, and I am pleased to add the prospect of the next year, is still more favourable.

The Mountain expedition has not come in yet, nor is it possible for me to form any idea what will be the probable returns of their Spring hunt, however, I think if they meet with no unforseen accident our Beaver returns this year will be fully equivalent to that of the last, notwithstanding the unfortunate accident, which happened t[o th]em in the fall. The Sioux, Rees and Chyennes have made full as many Robes, this year as they did the last.

The Steam boat has not yet reached here, she was Stopped by the low water, at the Poncas about 13th Ultimo. Mr. Lamont left here on the 29th with two Keel boats for the purpose of expediting her arrival here, and, as the water has risen considerably since his departure, I hope to see her here in a few days, but I am very fearful she will be unable to proceed higher up the river, for the water is still unusually low for this season of the year.

The only news I have heard of Mr Fountanelle, was given me by a young man of the name of Harvy.[5] Mr Harvy says he left Mr Fountanelle in the month of August or September last on Sweet water; that, upon his leaving him he promised he would meet him at the Crows village on the Yellow Stone, and there pass the winter, this is all I have heard of him. Mr Harvy delivered to Leclerc a quantity of Beaver and Mdse: to take down, with instructions who to deliver it to. I endavoured to persuade Mr Harvy to go down himself but he declined.

Mr Harvy has been trading at the Crows all winter at the place Mr Fountanelle promised to meet him, the Bearer he declined Leclerc the fruits of his trade with them

Yours Respectfully
(Sign'd.) K. McKenzie

❖ ❖ ❖

Fort Tecumseh 7th June 1831
Agent American Fur Compy:
Western Department
Saint Louis
Dear Sir

I arrived here on the 4th inst: from Fort Union with the returns of that depot and those of Fort Clark, which I took in passing, the returns of Fort Union have turned out much better than I had any right to expect, and I am happy to add, the prospect of the next year is still more flattering. The Mandan Post does but a poor business, the Robes traded there this year, fell much short of the usual quantity.

The Mountain expedition has not come in yet, neither have I had any late information of them, so that it is impossible for me to say what their prospects are. I shall not look for them before the last of July, I think I may say with safety that if they are not molested by the Indians, our Beaver returns this year will be at least equivalent to that of the last, notwithstanding the unfortunate affair of last fall.

The Sioux, Rees and Chyennes have made as many Robes this year as they did the last.

I inclose you a Statement of the mens A/cs, and a bill of Lading of Two Keel boats and three Batteaux sent you under charge of Mr. Picotte.

I would send you the whole of our returns immediately, had not Mr Lamont been obliged to descend the river to the Poncas, with two of our largest Keel boats, for the purpose of assisting the Steam boat, detained there on account of the remarkable low state of the water. It has been rising for the last few days, and I hope not many more will elapse before we will have the pleasure of seeing you here.

On my arrival at Fort Union last fall I fortunately found a Blackfoot interpreter, and by this means have been enabled to make these Indians acquainted with my views regarding them. I sent him with four or five men to their villages, where they were kindly received and well treated, on their return to the fort, they were accompanied by some of the principal chiefs, they expressed great satisfaction and pleasure at the idea of having a fort at their villages, which I promised and assured them they should have this fall, and in order to strengthen my promise I have sent a Clerk with four or five men to them, to take what they may have. It is impossible to say what may be the result of this enterprise, but I am very sanguine in my expectations. I hope and have no doubt I shall be well paid for our risk and trouble[6]

 Yours Respectfully
 (Sign'd) K. McKenzie

P.S. The Balance due P. N. Leclerc and John McKnight, I do not wish to be paid them, before Mr. Chouteau arrives in St Louis.

❖ ❖ ❖

Fort Tecumseh June 14th 1831
Pierre Chouteau Junr. Esqr.
Steam Boat Yellow Stone
Dear Sir

Yours of the 10th inst: addressed to Mr McKenzie, I have just received, and I hasten to send back your men with 9 horses, and I now hope to have the pleasure of seeing you here in a few days.

Messrs. McKenzie and Sanford left here in a skiff on the 13th, and they are no doubt with you before the present period.

We have but one keel boat here, and as Mr McKenzie wished to send her above without loss of time, I think it would be imprudent to send her down, particularly as I expect to hear from him to day or tomorrow.

Please give my compliments to Majr. Bean, and tell him his children are impatiently waiting his arrival, stealing horses from us, and committing the like depredations every day.

If there is no coffee on board the Keel boats, it will be well for you to bring up a supply for we have none here.

 Yours Most Respectfully
 William Laidlaw
 (Signd) per Jacob Halsey

❖ ❖ ❖

Fort Tecumseh June 21st 1831
To the Agent Amer. Fur Cy.
Western Department
Saint Louis
Dear Sir

Herewith you have the packing accounts of 5 Keel boat and five Batteaux shipped to your address, under charge of R. F. Holliday, also an A/c of Mdse: &c received of Papin and Co. at the Poncas, and a list of the persons employed by this Outfit last year, upon reference to which you will perceive that remarks have been made opposite the names of those who are good men, as well as of those who are unworthy of being engaged again.

I have lately given these drafts on you, one in favour of Ignace Grondieu for $13. Pierre Lebrun for $25. and the other in favour of Madame Richard for $75 which you will be pleased to pay and charge as therein mentioned. I have given several other drafts on you of which, I neglected to advise you in my last.

I refer you to Mr Chouteau's letter for all the news.

 Your Respectfully
 (Sign'd.) Kenneth McKenzie

❖ ❖ ❖

Fort Tecumseh June 21st 1831
Jean P. Cabanné Esqr.
Otto Establishment
Dear Sir

Having reason to suppose that Pineau Gagnin, Thomas Dumond, Oliver Leclair and James Parker (four free hunters, who are indebted to this Outfit) will come in to your establishment after their hunt. I inclose you their A/cs and beg you to collect them if you should see them and they have wherewith to pay. They are great rascals and by way of returning thanks for our having supplied their wants for several years past, I have been told they have expressed their intention of making an effort to cheat us.

I have not time to write you to any length, and must refer you to Mr. Holliday for all the news.

 Yours Respectfully
 (Sign'd.) K. McKenzie
 Pierre Gagnin's a/c, Amts. To $90.35
 Thomas Dumond 10.25
 Oliver Leclaire 117.88
 James Parker's Note 27.---

❖ ❖ ❖

Fort Tecumseh 4th July 1831
To the Gentlemen in
Charge of Fort Clark
Dear Sir

I wish you to send down Keel boat "Louis Vallé" with as little delay as possible. It will require 6 men to bring her down as low as the Rees, from thence here four will be sufficient and two of your men can return by land. Baptiste Leclaire is said to be a trusty man I wish you to send him down and give him care of the boat

Yours Respectfully
Wm. Laidlaw
(Signd.) per Jacob Halsey

❖ ❖ ❖

Fort Tecumseh 24 July 1831
To J. L. Bean Esqr.
Dear Sir

Mr Dickson who arrived here a few days ago, informs me that Pineau and Duchomette are employed by you: I presume you are not aware that they are both deserters, from the American Fur Company otherwise you would not employ or harbour them, as such a precedent, cannot fail to be very injurious to the Cos. Interest, therefore I beg you will turn them adrift without loss of time; they both owe the Compy: to a very considerable amount. I have but very little doubt, but Duchomette has been seduced from here by Zephine, but in this, perhaps I may be mistaken. I send Sarpy and three men for the boat. I am in hopes by this time that you have got under cover. I am in much want of the boat, or I would not have sent so soon. I return your log chain with many thanks, the other you mentioned I might keep, for the present, if in want of it. Nothing new has transpired, since you left here, only, that we have got seven of our best horses stole, by whom I cannot imagine.

I wish the men to bring the boat loaded with plank for Fort Lookout.

Four Sawons arrived here the other day from Bear river, they were very anxious to know if you had not left a talk for them. I told them that you had said that you expected to meet them here this fall.

I should be glad if you could make it convenient to pay us a visit and spend a few weeks with us. If you can possibly spare me one of your Grind Stones, I should feel much indebted to you. I will either pay for it, or be particular in having you one returned next Spring by the first boat

Accept my best wishes
and believe me yours most Truly
Sign'd W. Laidlaw
To J. L. Bean Esqr.
Fort Lookout

❖ ❖ ❖

Fort Tecumseh 4th August 1831
Mr J. L. Bean Esqr.
Sioux Agency
Dear Sir

Your favour per Giroux I have just received and I hasten to send him back with the articles requested.

Leston has not yet arrived, I presume you wrote by him about the houses in Fort Lookout, and consequently I am unable to say any thing with regard to that affair before his arrival. I shall dispatch him again without delay and will thus give you an answer. I am sorry to hear you are in ill health, hope you may be spedily restored. Believe me ever

Your Friend & Servant
Wm. Laidlaw
(Sign'd) per Jacob Halsey

You will receive the following articles per Giroux. All your Bacon (10 hams) and the Salt. 2 fine Candle moulds. 1 Pad Lock and say 45 Fish Hooks. 2 Leather Bags. 1 Calf Skin Bag 2 Cords. 1 Blister Plaster. 5 doses Salt Emetec. 5 doses Calomel and Tallow.

❖ ❖ ❖

Fort Tecumseh August 6th 1831
Pierre Chouteau Junr. Esqr.
Agent Amer. Fur Copy.
Saint Louis
Dear Sir

Last evening I received a few lines from Mr. McKenzie, by five freemen on their way to Saint Louis, they have five drafts on you for the sum of $1557.87 in all, which you will be pleased to pay.

I presume Mr. McKenzie has given you all the particulars from the Yellowstone.

Nothing worth relating has taken place here since you left us. I have not seen or heard of an Indian since that time, however, they have made out to steal eight of our best horses, by what tribe I cannot imagine unless by the Paunies, a few of whom passed the winter with friends the Rees.

I have been looking for Defond for some time passed, but as he has not made his appearance, I presume you have taken him to St Louis with you. I am extremely anxious to hear the news from that quarter, for many reasons, if we are to be opposed I have no doubt you will let us know without loss of time.

I sent down to Fort Lookout for the Batteaux we lent Mr. Bean and to my great disappointment found she was sunk, and could not be raised, this is quite inexcusable in Mr. Bean, as it must have occurred from pure negligence. So much for lending. We have been busily engaged rafting timber for the new Fort ever since you left us. The Missouri rose considerably after you left us, the Sandbar opposite this place was entirely covered for the space of about a week.

Mr. McKenzie in his letter to me, remarks, that Mr Vanderburg neglected to send in an Inventory of the stocks, remaining on hand from the equipment given the mountain expedition, but he advises us to credit his post for the sum of $20,000. as he has no doubt that it will amount to that sum at least. Be kind enough to forward the letter addressed to my brother, and you will much Oblige

Your Obt. And Humble Servant
(Sign'd.) Wm. Laidlaw

❖ ❖ ❖

Fort Tecumseh 14th August 1831
To J. L. Bean Esqr.
Sioux Agency
Dear Sir

I send F. Laboue with a party of men to try if possible to bring up the boat, but I am told she is very much shattered, and unless she has been repaired, it is very doubtful whether they will be able to get her up or not.

Respecting the houses in Fort Lookout, I am much afraid that this will be too late for you. I cannot possibly spare any of the plank nor the house in the S.E. corner as I wish to bring them up to this place, should any of the other suit you, Frederick is authorized to treat [?] with you

Believe me ever
Your Friend & Servant
Wm. Laidlaw
(Sign'd.) per Jacob Halsey

❖ ❖ ❖

Fort Tecumseh 21 Sept: 1831
John L. Bean Esqr.
Sioux Agency
Dear Sir

Yours of the 19th Ultimo I duly received, and according to your request I send our Licence for 1831. The Ogallallah have requested a post at or about the mouth of Eau-qui-Courre,[7] they particularly object to coming to Hollowwood to trade, therefore, I would wish to have a trading establishment at that place. The Chyenne have also requested a post somewhere between the forks of the Chyenne, and the Bear Hill,[8] which I would also wish to establish. If I do not succeed, we will lose their trade, as they cannot agree with the Sawons. I have not yet seen the Brulés, but I am of the opinion, they would like to have their post higher up than the Forks of White river. If so you will much oblige me by complying with this, and the before mentioned alterations.

Your Most Obt: & Humble Servt.
William Laidlaw
(Sign'd) per Jacob Halsey

P.S. Should you be in want of Flour or Pork, I have directed Fredk: to let you have, what you may want, or any thing else, that they can conveniently come at, that you may be in want of. I am entirely ignorant as to the Cargo of the boat, not having received any letters from St Louis by Defond.

Halsey desires to be remembered to you, we would have paid you a visit but have been dayly looking for our people from St Louis, for some time past, and consequently did not like to leave the Fort, which we regret exceedingly.

Yours &
Wm. Laidlaw
Per J. H.

❖ ❖ ❖

Fort Tecumseh 14. Oct: 1831
Pierre Chouteau Junr. Esqr.
Agent Amer. Fur Cy:
Saint Louis
Dear Sir

I embrace the opportunity of Mr Sanfords going down of addressing you a few lines. Nothing of any importance, has taken place here since I [was] last with you, it being a season of the year we scarcely see an Indian, however, they now begin to approach, as also the cattle begin to make their appearance.

Mr. McKenzie writes me that it is rather uncertain whether he will send down a winter express or not, and advises me, to make out my order for goods, for the ensuing year, from the Rees down. I am rather at a loss, how to make it out having heard that a boat is on her way to this place, and being entirely ignorant as to her cargo, however, that difficulty you will easily get over in St Louis by deducting from the order, whatever may be in the boat, intended for this place.

Baptiste Defond arrived here three weeks ago, the boat had then passed the Bluffs 13 days, he informed me that they were still getting six Fillets [?] per day, and making very free with Flour &c:, after having eat[en] up all the biscuit, immediately on his arrival, I sent off Frederick Laboue with a Skiff, and provisions to meet them, and just a stop to such unnecessary waste.

I have been anxiously looking for Mr. Picotte and the other gentleman from St Louis, for Six weeks past, and still no tidings of them, which is rather extraordinary, the post at the Yanctonnas ought to have been established before this time, in order to collect provisions as they could now be got easily and cheap. I was much disappointed in not getting any letters from Defond, I was greatly mortified to hear the fate of the Keel that Guinelle steered; but he could give me no satisfactory account, how many packs were saved, or how many lost, it is really provoking, after all the trouble and expence in collecting them, and what is worse, the pick of our Robes. I was much gratified to hear that you got down so well with the "Yellow Stone," and am glad that Buffaloe calves got down safe, and in fine order.

We have got on but slowly with the New Fort, having the wood for building to bring from such a distance, and so very few hands to do it. Mr. Lamont expected that there was enough of wood, cut for all the buildings, but when it came to be collected, we had not enough for one store. I should like much to get a man who understands making brick, to make enough to build the chimneys, as there is so much risk, with mud ones: and when so much property is exposed, I think it highly necessary, as we have no lime here.

Louis Gagnin and Francois Leoulli deserted from this, on the 31st August, they stold a Canoe, Axe, Kettle and a quantity of Corn from the Island, the former owes $279.25 exclusive of his equipment, which was paid here; the latter $87.81. If you can lay hold of them, I hope they will be punished accordingly. If not it will be an encouragement to others to follow their example. I should like to have a Copy of Mr. Lafieneu's engagement; I also wish to know if the men engaged in St Louis for 18 months, are obliged to furnish themselves with arms; and how many of them were furnished with Guns in St Louis.

Mr. Sanford has settled his Account here, every thing except the freight, which he says is to be settled by Genl: Clark and yourself, by mutial agreement.

I have said nothing regarding the Upper country as McKenzie wrote me that he has wrote you fully on that Subject, when you come to pay us a visit next spring, I assure you that you will not break your head on the beams of our houses, as you did when you was here last.[9] I shall have a comfortable room prepared for you.

Enclosed you have a statement of Mr Sanfords freight, left blank by your order last Summer.

I have drawn upon you in favour of Mr. Sanford for $206.65 which you will please to pay. Since writing the foregoing Messrs. Papin Picotte and Cerré have [word?] in upon us, also Lafleur, he lost your letter, however I have engaged him and he starts to day for the Poncas. I shall have an eye after Mr Leclerc you may depend. Yours of the 30th August I received with the other papers sent; I have not had time to look over them. Mr Sanford is just about pushing off, he has had a good deal of trouble with his Indians here, in consequence of the report of the Smallpox below. I believe a good many of them will return from this. I remain

Dear Sir
Your Most Respectful
& humble Svt
(Sign'd.) William Laidlaw

❖ ❖ ❖

Fort Tecumseh Oct: 17th 1831
Kenneth McKenzie Esqr.
Fort Union
Dear Sir

Inclosed with this you have several A/cs appertaining to F. Union. I believe all necessary explanations accompany each.

I regret exceeding that it is not in my power to complete the Invoice Mdse: &c. for "Beaver," we have as yet received no bill of the articles furnished you, from the Stores of S. B. Yellowstone; you have the prices of all the other articles, in the account forwarded you herewith.

By the first opportunity you will please send me a Statement of Omissions, Overcharges &c., for I am persuaded there are many.

I have forwarded Pancinneaus and Portalans and these Men's A/cs; to Fort Clark, with directions to take a Copy of them, and forward the Original to you, as it appears to be uncertain, whether they will come out at your establishment or the Mandans. I have done the same, with Bordeau's, Miller's and Durant's A/cs.

Be good enough to inform me if you promised Frederick Laboue when you engaged him, to erase the sum charged him, as expences coming up from St. Louis last fall, also if you promised to make him a present of a Squaws dress, he states this to be the case; and we have supplied him with these articles, and they will remain to his debit till we receive your advice on the Subject
Most Respectfully
Your Obdt. & hum: Svt.
Jacob Halsey
(Sign'd) per Wm. Laidlaw

❖ ❖ ❖

Fort Tecumseh 24th Oct: 1831
John L. Bean Esqr.
Dear Sir
I had a letter from Mr: Dickson the other day from Riviere O Jaques, wherein he mentions, that Mr. Rolette has sent people and built along side of him, for the purpose of trade with the Indians. Mr Dickson as well as myself, is under the impression that he cannot have a licence from that quarter, without interfering with your agency, therefore I think it a duty incumbent upon me, to give you this timely notice, so that you may have time to take what steps or Measures you may deem most proper.
I am Dear Sir
With Great Respect
Your Most Obt. & huml. Svt.
(Sign'd.) Wm. Laidlaw

❖ ❖ ❖

Fort Tecumseh 24th Oct: 1831
J. P. Cabanné Esqr.
Dear Sir
By A. Mackquie a free hunter on his way to Sant Louis, I avail myself of droping you a few lines. I doubt much whether the fellow will deliver it or not, at all events I shall run the risk.

Many of the Accounts of 1830–31 from your establishment against the department have been forwarded here without prices, so that we cannot possible balance the Account of your place, unless you forward a full statement with the prices annexed; may I beg of you to forward them in that way, by the first opportunity.

Since writing you last, a band of the Sioux and Rees have had a skirmish, and a good many kill'd and wounded on boath sides, which will no doubt injure the huts considerably. The Buffaloe are coming in, in great abundance. I am very anxious to hear something of Leclerc. I am in hopes he will not get up this far.
I am Dear Sir,
Your Most Respectful & huml. Svt.
(Sign'd.) Wm, Laidlaw

❖ ❖ ❖

Fort Tecumseh Oct: 31st 1831
Kenneth McKenzie Esqr.
Fort Union
Dear Sir
Herewith you have Invoice of Merchandise per Keel "Beaver" 4th July last, and "Louis Vallé" 17th October, together with a statement of Mens A/cs: and A/c. Current from June 4th. By the present

opportunity I shall forward a book to Fort Clark containing the A/cs. of Men who went up by land with you, as well as all those per "Beaver" and "Louis Vallé" in detail; with instructions to Mr. Mitchell to take a copy of A/cs. of such men as remained at his establishment, and to forward the book to you with as little delay as possible.

Invoice Mdse: for "Beaver" is no doubt full of errors, can you tell me if the White Barley corns were received per Yellowstone, or if they are old Stock, or if they are assorted, there is a great difference in the price of those beads. I also think there is a mistake in the number of Chopping Axes charged you, but you will no doubt send us a Statement of all errors by the first opportunity, after the receipt of the Invoice.

Your statement of advances to hands at F. U. as transferred this post I am last differs widely from that made out by Mr. Hamilton. Our book have been regulated according to his statement, which we presume to be correct. I will give you a sketch. Baptiste Dufonds A/c. was transferred last June $44.31 as per Mr. Hamiltons statement $98. Henry Hait, June last $41.25 as per Mr. Hamilton, $44.25. Joseph Howard June last $99.88 per Mr. Hamilton $116.88. I could mention many other differences but it is unnecessary.

I cannot balance Michel Gravelles[10] A/c, according to our books he is three hundred dollars in debt, if there is any error in his A/c, I think it must be in the amount of is advances at F. U. July 1830 $671.32. I send you his Acct. in detail from the commencement on our books.

Isidore Sandoval[11] Leroy balance due him July 1830 according to Mr. H. [Hamilton] statement $21.25 the balance due him at that time as per Genl. Ledger $71.25 making a difference of $50. I send you his also in detail.

I Have Charged your Outfit 1831, with all the Notes which appear from Accts. rendered unpaid, I have also charged you with Fallons Dechamps and Sheppelands A/cs., but think it will save unnecessary trouble to charge no more A/cs. of freemen until we receive advices of their having been paid. A/cs. of men that went up in keel "Fox" at the Mandans have been rendered and charged to the Genl. Accts.

On Settlement with Mr. Sanford, he stated that the Mdse: loaned him at this post, last Summer was settled for at F. U., if this is true, Ft. T. should have credit for the same, and be advised of such settlement, so that proper entries can be made.

The Accounts of Minard and Leclair as forwarded you some time ago, have been recently paid at this depot

Believe me Dear Sir
With Great Respect
Your Obdt. And humle Servant
(Sign'd) Jacob Halsey
for Wm. Laidlaw

❖ ❖ ❖

Fort Tecumseh Oct: 31 1831
Mr. D. D. Mitchell
Fort Clark
Dear Sir

Herewith you have your Acct. Current from June 4th 1831. Statement Men's Accts. supposed to be in your neighbourhood, and A/c. sundry Mdse: &c delivered F. C. by J. F. A. Sanford Sept: last.

Invoice Mdse: for Keel "Louis Vallé" was forwarded you per Mr. Picotte, if you should discover any errors in it (of which by the by I fear there are some) be good enough to advise us of them, as soon as practicable.

Mr. McKenzie has requested us to furnish a statement of all advances to men, at this place in detail. I have made them all out, and the Accts of those remaining at your post, you will find in the book, you will receive herewith, after taking a copy of them, you will please to forward the book to F. U. by the first opportunity I will thank you to let me know, the amount of advances you have made to Pierre Leveque; so that it may be placed to the credit of your Outfit. The last Acct. received from Mr. Sanford, you say his Acct at F. C. amounts to 80.25 but in the amount a charge for lost time is included. In hopes of hearing from you soon. I believe myself

Most Sincerely
Your friend & Servant
(Signd.) Jacob Halsey
(Official.)

❖ ❖ ❖

Fort Tecumseh 23d. Oct: 1831
Pierre Chouteau junr Esqr.
Dear Sir

So as not let skip an opportunity of writing you, I avail myself of one that now offers by a free hunter Alexr. Matthews. I have very little confidence in him, so shall be very laconick, he takes down about a pack of Beaver with him, there is no such thing as getting a Skin of it here. Since last writing you a band of Sioux (Le Gens de Peche) have had a skirmish with the Rees, and a good many kill'd and wounded on both sides, so it is to be presumed there will be a general war between the two contending tribes, which will no doubt affect our trade considerably.

I had a letter from Mr. Dickson a few days ago from Riviere a Jaque, he complains bitterly, Rolette having sent there and built along side of him, this intrusion is certainly breaking in upon the arrangements we have with the Amer. Fur Cy:. I shall annex a copy of Rolettes letter (as forwarded me) which I think very unhandsome in him, true I could not look for anything better from the source whence it came, it will also affect our trade even here, it will no doubt encourage many of the Indians to carry their Peltries and Robes there.

Pierre Welch's Acct. differs $20 from the Acct. against him in the Book of advances made to men, given us by you last Summer.

The Amount of Advances made to Baptiste Defond (if any) has not been received, nor do we know any thing about his present engagement with the Cy:. There was a balance in his favour of upwards of $100 when he went down, and he says he only received $60 odd dollars in Skins, how far this Statement is correct I cannot say, I should like to know the particulars. Many of the Accts. of Men per S. B. Yellowstone received per Picotte and Zephine, differ in amount from those in the book, this will cause a deal of trouble, and dissatisfaction amongst the men, most of whom went to the Yellowstone, and of course their Accts. were settled before their leaving this place. The "Male twin" arrived here safe on the 14th inst:. Piccotte and Cerré went off on the 16th. I sent with them, the "Louis Vallé" to go as far as the Mandans, as Mr McKenzie writes me he was defficient in many articles, from there he will be able to get up on trains, what he may be most in want of.

I Remain Dear Sir
Your Most Obdt. & huml. Svt.
(Signd) Wm. Laidlaw

❖ ❖ ❖

Lac Travers. 15th Augt: 1831
Pierre Chouteau junr. Esqr.
St Louis
Copy of Rolettes letter
Dear Sir

I am compelled to send an Outfit to your place as the most part of the Indians that were Ceded to me by the Col. Fur Cy: make their hunts in that country. My Dear Sir if you have no arrangement for the future, I have empowered Mr. Moon to make an arrangement with you and him to give you the two posts for next year in Co. with the A.M. Fr. Co. it will put an end to competition and we will make money.

Mr. Wm. Dickson   Respectfully
James River   Your Obt: Servt.
                              (Signed) Jos. Rolette

❖ ❖ ❖

Fort Tecumseh Nov: 27th 1831
Mr. David D. Mitchell
My Dear Sir

Your favour of the 9th inst: I received last evening, with those from F. Union all Safe; the Beaver was taken by the ice some where about the Ree Villages, and [Hart] was obliged to leave his canoe and take it on foot, one of his legs is very much Swelled; so much so, that he will; not be able to return, therefore by the first opportunity, it will be well to send his Acct. down.

I trust you have received all the letters and papers that was forwarded from this place, although you do not acknowledge having received them, but I am in hopes, it may be a little oversight on your part. I hope you are particular in forwarding Portalance and Pincennans Accts:, as Mr. McKenzie wants them particularly. The inclosed paper I return you, as I presume you must have sent it by mistake.

My Dear Friend you surprise me with the long apology you make of having opened by mistake a letter addressed to me, had you been a stranger to me, it might have been necessary; but as it is, the bare mention of [the] thing would have been sufficient, and quite satisfactory. I assume you it is a thing that may easily happen to any one, and very often does happen. The packet addressed to F. Union, I beg you will forward as soon as possible. Mr. McKenzie writes me if possible to send him a man who understands cooking, and I have not one that knows any thing about it. I wish you would send him Bapt: Yeo. Yeo. As you have Maxan, who cooks well and your family cannot be so large as his.

I sent a Grey Horse to the Little Crow a Mandan Chief that returned from this, he promised to deliver him to you, and another with him, by way of interest; if he has not delivered him, please jog his memory.

There is a great many mens papers addressed to Mr McKenzie, if you feel inclined to read them, you can peruse them, and forward them afterwards. This is a dull season of the year; anything going on, I have heard nothing of Leclair since Picotte and Papin came up.

I have not seen a Buffaloe since you left us, they are said to be plenty in the large, but the Indians are so much taken up about their war; that I do not suppose they will hunt much, the Sioux say that they will oblige the Rees to leave their Villages, and this part of the country. I thought we ought all to encourage them to do so, the country would then be quiet and they are now very destitute of arms and ammunition and easily fall a prey to their enemies. Cant you make some of your boys turn out. Since writing the above I have resolved to send Braseau's Black boy, who I am told is a good cook, so that it will not be necessary to send Baptiste.

Ours Most Truly
(Sign'd.) Wm. Laidlaw

❖ ❖ ❖

Fort Tecumseh 27th Nov: 1831
Mr. Henry Picotte
Dear Sir

I received your favour of the 10th inst: yesterday. I approve of your having taken Lachapelle up with you, as I think he would have run a considerable risk had he remained below. There is nothing but war and rumours of war here, scarcely a day passes, but some war parties are out, the Sioux are determined to drive them from their villages, and that they will very easily do, as they are now destitute of Arms and ammunition. I think it would be highly imprudent to send Lachapelle there in the winter. Should they return to their Villages (as you say) it will be an easy matter to trade with them in passing, but, I sincerely hope that the Sioux will oblige them to abandon this part of the Country; and, I think it would be the duty of all of us, to encourage them to do so as much as possible, we would thus be in peace and quietness.

Hart is lame and not able to return, I shall send another man in his place, to go as far as your establishment; from thence, I wish him to return, and you to send another man in his place. Since you say that you cannot be employed advantageously where you are; I would wish you to come down to this place, with 5 or so good men. I should think two or three quite sufficient for that place until spring; when we can send more. I wish you to come down without a moments delay if possible, and if you can bring us any provisions, so much the better. Your Indians (Yanctonnas) have stole from us since last spring a great many horses, I wish to make them pay for them on the trade; and tell them, that in every band where there is an stolen horses, I mean to adopt this plan, if we do not do something there will be no such thing, as keeping a horse. I hope you will not lose sight of this; and, be particular not to trade any bad Robes. I would write Pascal but am much hurried, therefore, I beg you will hand him this, which will answer every purpose.

Lachapelle took us in most abomably with his Robes, that he traded at the Rees last Summer. "Ah E. son de Bulle Robe lont a fete" they are of all others, the most villanous Esuchimous I ever saw, they are here, and will speak you themselves. The Gens de Puche that you thought had gone to Riviere le Jaque, are somewhere about the Painted wood

I remain
Dear Sir
Yours Most Respectfully
(Sign'd.) Wm. Laidlaw

P.S. When writing the foregoing, I have resolved to send John Douchouquette above; so, that one more from your place will be sufficient. I think upon second consideration that three more, will be a great abundance for that post, with the interpreter and Lachapelle will make six in all. If old Letand is still with you, he ought not to be encouraged or assisted, in any way: as he deserted without any cause whatever.

❖ ❖ ❖

Fort Tecumseh Nov: 27. 1831
My Dear McKenzie

Your favour of the 29th October, I received yesterday, with letters from the intermediate posts. I wrote you on the 16th Ultimo pretty fully concerning our affairs in this quarter. I trust by this time you are in possession of mine and all the news I could then rake and skrape was therein related.

Mr Picotte no doubt wrote you from the Mandans as well as Mr. Mitchell, giving you a statement of the Warlike appearance of things, in this part of the country, there is nothing but wars, and rumours of wars with the Sioux, and the Rees, there has been about 100 of the latter kill'd and wounded, and there is no doubt but they will be thin[n]ed considerably before spring, the general opinion is that they will clear out for the Paunies as soon as the weather will permit. I shall do all in my power to effect that; as we would then be in peace and quietness, now that they have no trader; they have neither arms or ammunition, the Sioux got about 60 of their Guns, and a great many bows and arrows in a late skirmish they had, in that affair the Gens de Puche kill'd 18 and wounded 36 some mortally, this statement I have no doubt is correct, the gentleman that was partisan, when they pillaged you got [k]nocked over, also one of Hollidays soldiers, the Sioux have his sword. Picotte thought it imprudent to have Lachapelle with his Equipment, as the Sioux told him, they would certainly take his goods from him; if they found him, and if they had not, I think it more than likely the Rees would, so, that upon the whole, I am well pleased, that he has taken him above. Should they return to their Village, what Robes they may have, can be traded in passing, which will answer every purpose. Buffalos are said to be plenty, in the Large, but I think it is not Likely that the Sioux, will make much of a hunt, as they are so much occupied with their war excursions.

My Dear friend, I am much at a loss how to act. I am afraid you will ride me rough shod: Picotte, Pascal and Lachapelle, are all at our post, and of course cannot have employment, for more than one of them, rather than they should do nothing at all I mean to order Picotte down to take charge of the People at the Navy Yard, which will ensure us getting the wood Sufficient to finish the fort: However, I think there is very little prospect. I think I hear you exclaim; a pretty business, to set a man at $1000 per year, to take charge of a few wood cutters, it will be a dear fort, all true; but, then again, of two evils, choose the least. I cannot employ him here; I have not heard that you are in want of him; but should you want him, you can have him by giving me notice, at all events, I do it for the best.

We get on very slowly, that skamp Montaigne, deserted about a month ago, with master Alexr. Matthews, who took down with him about a pack Beaver; at the same time, Old Letand disappeared; I was of [the] opinion that he had gone along with him, but understand that he has gone up the river and is at Apple river; on his way up to the Yellowstone. I think the poor fellow [word?] if not, he must be a worthless fellow, at least. Big Gagnin and Seviellé deserted on the 8th Augt. and stole Chardons canoe, and various other articles; I have not a man that can handle a tool, except Richard, and he is hardly compass Mentus, at times, and a great Maladraite[12] at least, unless you can send me a man or two to make the boats; I do not know what I shall do, every thing will be at a stand; it is really too bad to be drauling on in this sluggish manner, I put myself half to death, and all to no purpose, for Gods sake try and assist me with some workmen. I have heard nothing of Leclair since I last wrote you; and as the ice is now drifting a little, I am in hopes he will not get up this far; but even if he should, I am well prepared for him. I shall have some one at his heels, all the time, he told Papin that nothing would do him so much good, as to go puffing a Span[ish]: Segar, along side of you, and, put on a dignified look. I expect the gentleman will take care, and not go too close. Lacharite went down with Sanford to meet him, nothing less than $40 would satisfy him; so I thought it best to let him go. Jack our famous hunter, is his head Clerk, he used to ride about in St Louis with him in a Dearbourn; he has also the two Dauphins and Fouchtte. Old Lacompt is at Ft. Lookout, whom I instructed to give me [word?], as soon as he would make his appearance, but as yet, have had no tidings of him. Bean got tired of living there, and cleared out for the Bluffs, a few days ago, with Cardinal.

I must now come to a disagreeable part, we have got 36 Horses stolen, there is no such thing as Keeping one, only in the Stable; as near as I can learn the Sioux have about 30, and the Rees 6 or 8. Your Colt, and the Young Capeue des fleches is among the rest. I really do not know how to punish the Rascals; I am only waiting to see if Leclaire comes; if he does not, I mean to make such bands, as have our horses, pay for them in the trade. I think of no other means, that will protect them so effectually, and such of the bands, as have no stolen horses; will inwardly rejoice, those that stole the most, are Yanctonna and Gens de Puches, the Sawons, Brulés and Ogallallahs have not stolen one. All the Chyennes have come in, except about 30 Lodges, that remained out with the High Backed Wolf; he got shamefully defeated last summer, by the Paunies, and is doing pennance. Portalance and Pencinneaus Accts. have been sent up to you; as to their Agreement with the Cy: I know nothing about it, only what you told me yourself last Summer, their Agreement must be still in St Louis, as no such paper has been sent here. You know more about it, than we do. Baptiste Daurion has been at deaths door, from an absess in his side; but has now nearly got over it, it is really astonishing the Matter it discharged. Leclaire. (hunter) Carrier, and Ménard kill'd nearly 2 packs Beaver which we have got, and rigged them out for another hunt.

I had a letter from Mr. Dickson some time ago, wherein he complains bitterly, Rolette having sent Narcess Frenier there, with a strong equipment to oppose him. Bailey[13] was dayly expected, to send there also; he passes the winter at Lac Traverse; he has had a rumpous with Rolette, and is now in partnership with Culbertson, the sutler they have a house at Lac-qui-pach, and intend sending to riviere broache to oppose young Renville, who is there so that there is a bad prospect, in that quarter. Mr Halsey has wrote you concerning some Acct. which I think correct.

I do not know how we are to get out our packs next Summer, as all the Men that were engaged in St Louis are free the 1st of June.

Baptiste Marchands wife is not dead, as reported. I would send you up John Braseau, but he knows nothing about cooking; and besides he is the only man that can assist Richard a little. I shall write Mitchell to send up Yeo. Yeo; he has Maxan there, and does not require two. Hart is lame and cannot return. I shall send another in his place.

Since writing the foregoing, I have found out that John Douchouquette can cook, and will send him.

I understand that old Cabanné and Pratte are quite against Steamboating;[14] they say it is all a "deponce from arien" ["to give evidence for nothing or about nothing"]

Believe me My Dear friend
To be Yours Most Sincerely
(Signd.) Wm. Laidlaw

P.S. The two Hollidays have gone to the Spanish country; I understand they are equiped by Powells, McKnight has gone with them.

❖ ❖ ❖

Fort Tecumseh Dec: 3d 1831
Mr. Frederick Laboue

I received your favour of the 3d. by Charles Degray the day before yesterday, with the horses and the meat you sent me. I wrote you some days past by Wah-man-ny-too I forgot to tell you I lent 2 small Rigs to the one horn, 1 to the Cut Ear; 1 to the No Heart. 1 to the Little Bear and 1 to the Mashed Testacles; try and get them back and give this post credit for them.

I think it possible for you to send here without sending a Guide every time, if your men cannot come by the large, let them follow the Chyenne and the Missouri; in that way they cannot get lost.

You ought to procure your skins for your canoes, for it is very difficult to procure them in spring, I assure you. You ought also to procure poles, have them cut by your men, enough for your canoes, have them well arrainged and dryed. I adopted this plan last year, we found them much better than the Pinette poles which we bought of the Indians, at the same time, it saves a good deal of expence.

I hope you will not forget to collect as much meat as possible.

I have heard that B. Defond drinks terribly, if this is true, I hope you will let him have no more liquor, you ought not to have forgotten already, that the orders are very strict this year, all Clerks in charge of a post, are forbid advancing to any person, more than the amount of their wages, without an order. I do not know the exact amount of his Acct. as we have not got the amount of his Acct in St Louis, not only this; a man that drinks hard; as they say he does, cannot do his duty, as he should do it. I have paid the Indian who came with Charles Degray. I send you the Acct of Joseph Vasseue in detail.

    Your very humble Servant
    (Sign'd) Braseau Duchouquette
    for Wm. Laidlaw
    A true translation of the Original
    (Sign'd) Braseau Duchouquette

❖ ❖ ❖

    P.S. I opened your letter to tell you the news of Leclaire, he has arrived at the Poncas, he has sent to the large to the Brulé's to trade horses, to bring up his goods, try and collect all the Beaver. If the Corbeau dans le Coup must absolutely have horses, try and buy some to give him. The Mauvaise Baouf has a good deal also, he can come after that if he will. If the Indians do not know this news; I think you had better not tell them.

❖ ❖ ❖

    Fort Tecumseh 4th Dec: 1831
    To Mr. P. D. Papin
    Dear Sir

    I have long been waiting with the greatest impatience to hear from you, but presume that you have not been able as yet to procure provisions, which has occasioned such a delay. We are on very short allowances so that a supply in that way, would be very acceptable. I have this morning been informed that Leclerc has sent to the Brulé's and Ogallallahs, eight horses loaded, it is said, that he intends purchasing horses and returning to bring up his goods. I beg that you will be on the alert, and throw every obstacle in his way that you can devise, by fair means; You need not want for goods, put him up to high water mark and let us check him in the bud. We have many advantages over him, and afford to sell cheaper than he possibly can. I have sent Campbell to get all the information he possibly can; he will be ready to render you any assistance in his power. Should they have gone to the Chyennes or Ogallallahs, I wish Campbell to proceed there without a moments delay. I shall look for your men to get new supplies soon, it is well to be fully supplied in time.

    I have every confidence in your activity and exertion, and will rest satisfied that you will do your utmost, for the benefit of your employers, there is more of those who are to oppose you, much renowned for either capacity, or activity as traders. Campbell will give you my views in general, with regard to Leclerc.

    I had a letter a few days ago from the Yellow Stone, and the intermediate posts; every thing appears to be getting on smoothly; Messrs. Picotte, Cerré, and Lachapelle are all at our post at Apple River. Picotte thought it imprudent to have Lachapelle, as they did not see a Ree, and the Sioux threatened to pillage him, if they found him in that neighbourhood. The Rees are all camped somewhere upon Grand river. In hopes of hearing from you soon I remain Dear Sir

    Your Most Obt. Servant
    (Sign'd.) Wm. Laidlaw
    P.S. Inclosed you have your Invoice and your mens Accts.
    Wm. L.

❖ ❖ ❖

Fort Tecumseh Dec: 5th 1831
Mr. Pierre D. Papin
White River
Dear Sir

    I have yours of the 28th Ult. And hasten to fill up your requisition, so far as the horses will be able to carry. I am only able to send you 100 pounds of Flour by the present opportunity; by the next, I will send you some more.

    According to your request, I send you Charles Degray. When you send us a supply of provisions; I wish him to come in, so that the horses may be properly taken care of, that is to say; if you can dispence with his services, for the time he will be absent. Campbell left here for your establishment: by him I wish you fully, and sent your Invoice and Mens Accts.

    Herewith you have a bill of Mdse: &c. sent you by the present opportunity. I regret that I have no small

Kegs to send you. Your Letters for St Louis, Shall be forwarded by the first opportunity. Believe me to be
 Yours Very Truly
 (Sign'd) Wm. Laidlaw

❖ ❖ ❖

 Mr. P. D. Papin
 White River
 Continued
 P.S. I have settled with Deshonnette, he was in debt 18.55; I have (for his faithful services this year) made him a present of $50 besides his debt. A part of this sum he has taken here; and the Balance which will be due him next spring is $36.50.
 (Sign'd) J. Halsey
 for Wm. Laidlaw

❖ ❖ ❖

 Fort Tecumseh 21. Dec: 1831
 Mr. Thomas S. Sarpy
 Dear Sir
 I received yours of the fifth inst: a few days ago by J. Juett, and have completed our memorandum as far as practicable; I send you fo[u]r guns more than you ask for, at the particular request of the Ogallallahs, they have this seamingly well pleased. I have been obliged to let the Chyennes have a trader as they objected trading at the Ogallallahs post. Joe is in charge of the [word?] for the Chyennes; the goods will be charged to your post, and the returns credited accordingly, therefore I trust you will render him every assistance in your power, and supply one another as circumstances may require from time to time. I think you ought to pay him a visit as soon as possible, and see how he is fixed, and give him what advice you may deem necessary. I send three men, two, to remain with Joe till he gets properly arranged, the other, will proceed to your place with Minard.
 I already wrote you that you might make some advances to Leclair, say sixty, or seventy dollars. You will also furnish Pineau with a horse suitable to make his hunt in spring, he will also require a little Ammunition and Tobacco. Minard also requests to be furnished with Ammunition and Tobacco, or any, ~~other any~~ other trifling thing they may be in want of.
 Leclerc's men have been wandering about the country for 6 weeks past, with 6 or 7 horses loaded.

Minard will give you all the particulars; I do not apprehend that any of them will get to your place. I have promised the Chyennes 80 Balls for a Robe, so as to encourage them to hunt. I presume you will be obliged to give the same. Mr. Halsey sends your Invoice and a list of Memorandums
 in haste
 Your Obdt. Servant
 (Sign'd) Wm. Laidlaw

❖ ❖ ❖

 Fort Tecumseh Dec: 28th 1831
 Mr. Louis Lafleur
 Dear Sir
 Yours of the 27th Nov: and 15th inst: came safe to hand, and I should have sent you the provisions requested before, but for the want of conveyances, the horse you sent up by Chattilion having died of thirst on the trip up; he says you refused to give him an axe, in consequence of which, he was unable to cut the ice, for the purpose of giving his horse drink. According to Chattilions account, it would appear that you have been squandering away the Company's property at a great rate; and making but feeble endeavours to promote the interest of your employers in any way. Do not suppose that I am induced to believe this man's statement; no; I think better of you; but, you must be aware, that such intelligence is very disagreeable.
 I send you a horse loaded with Flour, Meat &c. as per A/c. herewith. I shall have an opportunity of sending you some more flour before long.
 I understand Leclerc has traded a large quantity of Corn, if this is true, I am much surprised, that you have not been able also, to lay in a store of that article, as you arrived at your post some time before your opponent.
 I do not think that Leclerc will be able to procure horses in this quarter; if he should attempt to trade any at your place, you should make him pay well for them; his you know can be easily done (if you find he will get supplied) by trading, or offering for one, a high price yourself.
 Mongrain is in charge of the articles sent you, if he delivers them safe you can pay him two or three dollars for his trouble.
 It is absolutely necessary, that you should have 10 or 12 cords of Ash wood cut at your place, or in

that neighbourhood, for the Steam Boat. Relying on your endeavours for the interest of your employers, I remain

    Yours Very Truly
    Wm. Laidlaw
    Per Jacob Halsey
    Mr. Louis Lafleur
    Poncaws Village

❖ ❖ ❖

    Fort Tecumseh Dec: 26th Dec: 1831
    Pierre Chouteau Junr. Esqr.
    Dear Sir

I received your favour of the 28th October two days ago, you will perceive by mine of the 14th of same month, by Mr. Sanford that I was apprised of the Opposition upon Riviere au Jaques; by recent accounts I understand that Bailey never once thought of sending there until Rolette had established a house there, nor Have I yet any certain intelligence that Bailey has sent there. Rolette, I have no doubt wrote you in the way he did to clear himself of reproach; I do not apprehend their coming here this winter, in fact it is next to an impossibility.

I have no doubt, that long in this you are in possession of our order for next year, in case that the Steam Boat should be too much loaded. I think we could do without the part of ammunition and Tobacco, ordered for this section of the country, as we have a great stock on hand, say 6000 pounds Tobacco, and liquor a pretty reasonable stock. I am sorry to say that we have been able to do very little work at our New Fort lately, our best Carpenter (Montaigne) having deserted with that fellow Matthews, by whom I wrote you, and so long as the system of making such heavy advances to our men, is continued we can never pretend to get any work done by them; as they are by far the greater proportion of them without principal, and seeing themselves indebted, get discouraged and wont work, and if found fault with clear out; and I have been told that P. Gagnin and Levull's are in the employ of the Compy: at Black Snake Hills[15] if so such a precedent cannot fail to encourage others, to follow this example. The number of men I have, is merely nominal, half the number would do more work, if they knew that they had the greater part of their wages due them. Richard is merely an apology for a workman; and if we wish to get on with the fort, we would require two good Carpenters.

Leclerc I hope will have reason to repent his wild scheme; he was taken by the ice at the Poncas village, three or four of his men have got up this far, with six horses loaded; they find great difficulty in getting horses, and can never get up with their own means; but I am informed that Maj. Bean has proffered them all his horses, and Mules, to assist in bringing up their goods. I have every reason to believe this information correct, as Zephine his interpreter told Mr. Papin so, if this is the case, it is not Leclerc we have to fear as an opponent, but the Agent and he combined together.

I had a letter from Mr. McKenzie some time ago under date of 29th October, wherein he mentions that the prospects in that quarter, are rather gloomy, having but few Buffaloe, and a great many of his Indians have gone to the north; the H. Bay Cy: having established all their old posts, on Riviere que Appell,[16] and are determined to annoy us as much as possible; he says, that he has no news from Ft. Peagon, Kipp had got up safe, as far as the mouth of Mussel shall River on the 16th Sept:, he no doubt by this time has had news from him.

Our prospects in this part of the country are flattering, as we have plenty of Cattle in every direction; they have seldom, or perhaps never been in greater abundance; and we have got the Indians to make much better Robes, than they ever did, since I have known them. The Rees have no trader; the Sioux positively objected to our sending them a trader. In hopes of seeing you sometime in the latter end of April, I remain

    our Most Obdt. & humle Servant
    (Sign'd) Wm. Laidlaw
    Pierre Chouteau Junr. Esqr.
    Saint Louis

❖ ❖ ❖

    Fort Tecumseh 25th Dec: 1831
    J. P. Cabanne Esqr.
    Dear Sir

Your favour of the 3rd inst. I duly received last evening, and thank you for the information contained therein, however I was long ago apprised of the opposition upon Riviere au Jacques; I apprehend no danger of their coming here, by the last accounts I had from Wm. Dickson he wrote me that our worthy friend Rolette,[17] had established a post there, and that Bailey also spoke of establishing a post, at the same place in consequence of Rolettes having sent there, otherwise he says that Bailey would never once have thought of it, as it must now be a losing business to all those concerned.

Leclerc I think will have reason to repent his wild experiment, particularly had he not Mr. Beans people, to aid and assist him in every way as they do; I understand that his Interpreter Zephine, who has been living with the Indians for a month past tries every means in his power to injure us, the Indians say that he told them not to trade with us; that we were Englishmen,[18] and if they did, that they would not be looked upon by their father Major Bean, as a proof of this he goes on to say, that Mr. Bean had ordered him or given him instructions, to send all his horses to assist Leclerc, in getting up his goods, now if this be really the case, it is not Leclerc we have to fear, as opponent, but the Gent or his Subs; but even admitting that they should combine their forces against us; I hope to be able to stand our own ground. I should be sorry to think that their kind of proceedings were encouraged, or permitted, by Major Bean; I am convinced they would not, if he ever presents himself; it is unfortunate he should have left his post at this time, as we will no doubt be the sufferers. You say if you thought I was on better terms with the Agent, you would request of me to ask him, if it is to him you are to apply for the horses &c that were forcibly taken from your men last Summer. I have no knowledge of being on bad terms with Mr. Bean; if so, it must be on his part; I know of no good reason why we should be on bad terms; and would be willing to go great lengths to strengthen the friendship and good understanding between us, please tell him so if [its all right] with you.

Mr. Bean sent two of the horses that were taken from your people here, also a Mule, one of the horses was stolen next day, the other two I have still got.

I wrote you twice, since last fall by Mr Sanford and the second by A. Matthews. I am afraid neither of which you received, not having acknowledged the receipt of either.

I had a letter from Mr. McKenzie some time ago dated 29th Oct:, wherein he mentions that the prospects in that quarter, are rather gloomy, having but few Buffalos; and a great many of his Indians having gone to the north, the H. Bay Cy: having established all their old posts, on qu Appell river, and are determined to annoy us, as much as possible; he says that he has had no news from Fort Peagan; Kipp had got on safe as far as Mussell shell river on the 16th Sept:,[19] and did not expect to hear from him again, till the ice took.

Our prospects here I think very flattering, as we have plenty of Buffalos in every direction, they have seldom or perhaps never been in greater abundance.

I understand that two of our men that deserted from here last Summer, are engaged by the Cy: at Black Snake hills, Louis Gagnin owes the Cy: $190. Louis Seveilli $90, which sums I beg you will interest yourself to get, or any part of it.

With the greatest respect
Your Obdt. & humbe Servant
(Sign'd) Wm. Laidlaw
P.S. I am much at a loss how to get wood cut for the Steam Boat below the Vermillion, may I beg of you to have wood cut up that far, any expense, or trouble, you may be at, we willingly pay. I shall endeavour to get enough cut down to that place. I am sorry to hear that the prospects of your post are so poor, but hope it may turn out better than you expect. Wishing you all the compliments of the season I remain,
Yours Very Truly
Wm. L.

❖ ❖ ❖

Fort Tecumseh Jany. 7th 1832
Mr. Pierre D. Papin
White River
Dear Sir
Your several favours of the 17th 20th and 21st ultimo all came safe to hand. I send off Charles Degray to remain with you till spring; you will receive by him 18 Galls. Alcohol and 47 lbs. Flour. With regard to our opponents, it is unnecessary for me to say any thing, you are aware that the main point is to obtain the peltries, and to crush the competition in its infancy. With the means you have, and experience in times of opposition will enable you to do many things to promote our interest, to

the disadvantage of our opponents. If you should be in want of more goods, you have only to send in for them; and they shall be forwarded with all possible dispatch.

It is unnecessary for you to trade any more horses, without you are in want of them or the use of your establishment. We have plenty for our own use (such as they are). By a letter recently received from St Louis, we learn that the S. B. Yellowstone is to leave there the 15th March next for Yellowstone river, we expect Mr. Chouteau will come up in her. On the return of the Express to Otto Establishment, on the 28th Ulto., I forwarded you a letter. Mr. Picotte is here, he has written to you, and I presume given you all the Upper Country news. Wishing you all the compliments of the season, I subscribe myself
Your Friend and Servant
Wm. Laidlaw
Per Jacob Halsey

❖ ❖ ❖

Fort Tecumseh 18th Jany. 1832
Mr. Frederick Laboue
Dear Sir

I received yours dated the 18th inst: to day; Baptiste Defond left this a few days ago, with three trains loaded with such articles as I thought you would be most in want of; I hope by this time that he has arrived at your place, but in case you should not have enough liquor, I shall send off Mr. Campbell tomorrow with three Mules loaded; he will remain and assist you some time, he is best able and willing. Since he left off drinking, I trust you will not be so self sufficient, as to despise his assistance, as I am convinced that it will be very much to the interest of the Company. I am much mortified by the accounts I have daily, from your post; the Indians seem all much dissatisfied with your treatment towards them, and would not approach your house, if they could possibly avoid it; such tidings as this, so often repeated, I assure you is very displeasing to me, particularly as we may Expect to be opposed every day; I am well aware that they exaggerate some; at the same time, have little doubt, that they have too much reason to complain; I would advise you to try and restrain your temper or feelings a little; and have no doubt you will, if you have the interest of your employers at heart. We don't come here to quarrel with the Indians Mall appropos, but to try and gain their good will, by mild gentle and kind treatment; besides what does it serve to be always showing ones teeth, when we dare not bite, even if inclined.

Now I beg that you will take nothing amiss in this, as I mean nothing more than a kindly advice. Since writing the foregoing I have resolved to send Campbell with one train [since] the ice now appears good; You ought to get the indians to come in and trade as soon as possible, before Leclair gets up. Should Letand want any supplies you will furnish him as far as possible, as you are so much nearer us, and can be supplied at all times; I beseech you to look out ahead and not get out of any thing that you may require for the trade. Should you not have sent the trains (that Defond took from here) to Letand's place, I wish you to send one of them here without delay along with the one Campbell now takes. Send two careful men with them; I also wish you to send me two or three Chopping axes as you cannot now be much in want of them and they are much wanted here.

Mr Holliday will inclose you a list of Articles sent by Campbell. Nothing more for the present
I remain Your Servant
Wm. Laidlaw
(Sign'd) per: Honoré Picotte

❖ ❖ ❖

Fort Tecumseh Jany. 31. 1832
Pierre Chouteau Junr. Esqr.
Agent Amer. Fur Cy.
Saint Louis
Dear Sir

An Express has just arrived from Fort Union with a packet addressed to you which you will receive herewith.

Mr. Laidlaw wrote you on the 26th Ulto. Acknowledging the receipt of your favour of the 28th October, which letter if no unforseen accident has happened must now be making its way towards you the other side of Council Bluffs.

It is with deep regret that I have to inform you of the death of Mr. Thomas L. Sarpy who was trading on a branch of the Chyenne river with a band of Sioux called the Ogallallahs. It appears that on the 19th inst: after he had been busily engaged trading throughout the day he entered his store in the evening accompanied by two of his men with a lighted candle, for the purpose of putting it in order; the candle was placed on the counter under which was a kettle containing about 50 or 60 pounds of Powder, either the candle or a spark from it was accidentally thrown into the powder, while they were in the act of passing some Robes over the counter, which blew up the building, and the three persons engaged in it. Mr Sarpy was found lying on his back, a considerable distance from where the building stood, he lived about an hour after the Explosion took place, and his spirit fled into Eternity. The other two men were severely injured, but they are now considered out of danger. From what we have been able to learn the loss of property by the explosion was not so great as might have been expected.

In consequence of this destressing occurrence Mr. Laidlaw left here yesterday morning, for the purpose of arranging things in that quarter, he will visit the other Sioux Station before his return here, which may be expected about the 26th Febuary.

I am happy to say, the prospect in this part of the country is flattering; Buffaloe have never been more plenty in the Sioux country, than they are now; and have been, for the last month; consequently, we have every reason to expect the Robe return will be fully equal, if not Surpass, all made by the Sioux last year; say 2000 packs. I am sorry the same cannot be said of the Assiniboine and Mandan posts, at which stations Buffalos are said to be scarce. Leclerc was taken by the ice at the Poncaws Village, three or four of his men have got up as far as Sawon post, with 6 or 8 horses loaded with Goods; and we have just heard that he has arrived, at the Sioux Agency near Fort Lookout, with 3 trains loaded; where he says he is waiting with the dayly expectation, of the arrival of three more trains, with goods from his boat, when they arrive, he is to proceed to the Sawon post. I am told he is living in the Agents houses; and has been proffered the use of his Men, Horses and Smith's Shop to assist him in opposing the Company Maj. Bean left here some time ago, for Mr. Cabannés establishment, where we suppose he still is; it is to be regreted he is not at his station; for we cannot suppose he would sanction such proceedings.

In reference to Mr. Laidlaws letter to you of the 14th Oct: and 26th Decr; I see you have been advised of the desertion of Francois Leveillé, Louis Gagnier and Francois Montaigne, since the desertion of the latter, we have been able to do very little work at the new Fort. We have two building raised, of 120 ft: long by 20 deep; One of 72 by 24 ft: an office of 20 ft: by 18 ft: and at present are employed raising two of 36 ft: by 20 ft: each.

Be good enough to deliver the enclosed letter, and believe me to be, Dear Sir
Your Most Obedient & humble Servant
(Sign'd) Jacob Halsey
Pierre Chouteau Junr. Esqr.
Saint Louis

❖ ❖ ❖

Fort Tecumseh 31. January 1832
J. P. Cabanné Esqr.
Otto Establishment
Dear Sir

Mr. Laidlaw wrote you on the 25th Ulto. per Mongrain, acknowledging the receipt of your letter of the 3d., which you have no doubt received before the present period.

It becomes my painful duty to inform you of the death of Mr. T. L. Sarpy, who was trading on a branch of the Chyenne river with a band of Sioux called the Ogallallahs. It appears that on the evening of the 19th inst:, he entered his store accompanied by two of his men, with a lighted candle, for the purpose of putting it in order; the candle was placed on the counter, under which was a kettle containing 40 or 50 pounds of Powder, either the candle or a spark from it was by some means or other, thrown into the Powder, which of course blew up the building, and the three persons engaged in it. Mr Sarpy was found a considerable distance from where the building stood, the first words he spoke, were *Quel Mallieu que le fact* ["What evil did this?" or "What malevolence made this happen?"] the second, *Versé mois de leau sur le corps*, ["Pour water on my body,"] the third and last, was the demand for a drink of Water; as it was given him, his spirit fled into Eternity. The other two men were much injured, but they are now considered out of danger. The loss of property is not known to any accuracy, but it is not supposed to be so great as might have been expected.

The prospect from this part of the country, is flattering. Buffaloe are plenty, at all the Sioux Stations, and it is to be expected that the Robe return, will fully equal if not surpass all made by the Sioux last year. I am sorry the same cannot be said of the Assiniboine and Mandan posts, at which stations Buffaloe are said to be scarce.

You are apprised that Leclerc was taken by the ice at the Poncaws Village. Three or four of his men, have got up this far, with 6 or 8 horses loaded with Goods. Leclerc, we have just heard, has arrived at the Sioux Agency, near Fort Lookout; he has taken possession of the Agents houses; and it is said he has Mr Bean's permission to make use of his Men, Horses and Smith's Shop; to aid in opposing us. His Interpreter Zephine Recontré, does all in his power to injure the Company. Mr. Laidlaw left here yesterday, for the purpose of arranging the affairs of the deseased, T. L. Sarpy. I conclude by wishing you health and prosperity.

 Your Very Humble Servant
 (Sign'd) Honoré Picotte

❖ ❖ ❖

Fort Tecumseh Jany. 31st 1832
Mr. Louis Lefleur
Poncaws Village
Dear Sir

Mr. Laidlaw wrote you on the 28th Ulto. By Mongrain, by which he sent you a supply of Meat &c:, which if no accident has happened, you have received before now. I should like to send you some Flour by the present opportunity, but it is impracticable; however, I hope to be able to send you some in a short time.

The only news I have to give you, is of a Melancholy nature; it is the death of Mr. Thomas L. Sarpy, it was caused by an Explosion of Powder at his station the Ogallallahs.

Mr. Laidlaw is at present absent from here. Please write us by every opportunity, and let us know your prospects &c. &c. It is necessary that the Bearer of Dispatches, should proceed down to Mr. Cabannés Establishment, with all possible dispatch. The Season is now advanced, and he has no time to lose. Do not forget the wood for the Steam Boat.

 Believe Me Very Truly
 Your Friend & Servant
 (Sign'd) Jacob Halsey
Mr. Louis Lefleur
Poncaws Village

❖ ❖ ❖

Fort Tecumseh 16th Feb: 1832
Kenneth McKenzie Esqr.
Fort Union
Dear Sir

Herewith you have the Account of Provost in detail from the commencement on the Genl: Ledger; You will recollect that [Etienne] Provost arrived at this place from St Louis in October 1829. On his arrival, he stated he had been equiped for trapping by the Amer. Fur Co., and, that this Outfit had an interest in the business. As he brought no letters but little attention was paid to his assertions. We however advanced him such articles as he stood in need of to prosecute his hunt, and charged them to his private Acct.; amounting in all to $232.52. A copy of this Acct. was forwarded to Fort Union for adjustment the same fall. In July 1830 upon settlement of your post A/c I observed that you had only charged him with half the sum advanced him here on Viz: 11th 25 [?], in consequence of which his Acct. was settled here in the same way: but upon second consideration I certainly think this must have been done, by Mr Leclaire without your knowledge or approbation; as it appears evident to me, that many of the articles furnished him here at that time; should have went into his private Acct. for Items be good enough to look at Page 6. October 8.9.10th 1829 in accompanying Acct.[20] You will see it still remains as settled at Fort Union.

October 10th 1830, his Acct. in Saint Louis, the preceding year was received here; the balance Against him stated to be $582.6. You will observe this Acct. was not received here, little more than one year after it was contracted. When you left him in November 1830, a copy of this Acct. was presented you, with some other documents appertaining to Fort Union. I now send you the original as received from Saint Louis. What his agreement, or an

Engagement was we do not know. In much haste Believe me Dear Sir

   Your Obedt. And Humble Servant
   Jacob Halsey
   P.S.

Do you not recollect, that I delivered you 8 lbs. Glauber Salts a few days before you left last summer; Mr. Hamilton says it was never received; be this as it may; I am very sure they were not left behind.

❖ ❖ ❖

Fort Tecumseh Feb: 15th 1832
James A. Hamilton Esqr.
Fort Union
Dear Sir

I received your favour of the 21st December on the 30th Ulto., the day after which the Express was forwarded to Mr Cabannés establishment.

In answer to your several inquiries, I will begin with George Gray, he is one of the Four men furnished Portolance & Co. the names of the other three, are Etienne Bertrand, Frederick M. Phillips, and Baptiste Trotten. The A/c's of their Engagements as well as the accounts of Pincinneau and Portolance were forwarded to Fort Clark in October last with directions to Mr Mitchell to take a copy of them, and Forward them to Fort Union, with all possible dispatch: and if no unforeseen accident had occurred, you no doubt have them, before the present period.

You ask for abstract, or Copy of the engagement with Pincinneau and Co.; it would have been forwarded with their Accts. had it been in our possession. All that I know relative to their Engagements, is what I was told by Mr McK. last Summer. Viz: that they were to be furnished with men, horses and Ammunition &c:, for trapping, for Acct. and Risk of themselves and Upper Missouri Outfit, as you will see upon examination of their Accts.

In your favour of 1st Sept: last, you mention Peter Miller, as one of the men who remained at Fort Clark, or returned here for Louis Vallé; consequently, the term of his engagement ($90 for services ending fall of 1832) was forwarded to Fort Clark.

I send you herewith abstract of the agreement with Papin & Co., A/c Current with Fort Union. Jacques Letand's and Boneventure Lebrun's accounts upon reference to that of the latter, you will perceive, that the sum of $56 alluded to in your letter, was not included in the Amt: of his A/c, forwarded you last July. As he is a great Blackguard; I was advised to say nothing about this debt, with the expiration of his term, when if he had herewith to pay, he was to have been charged with it.

You will also receive herewith E. Provost's Acct. in detail, from the commencement on our books Believe me dear Sir, with Great Respect
   Your Friend and Servant
   (Sign's.) Jacob Halsey
   (Official)

❖ ❖ ❖

Fort Tecumseh Feb: 15th 1832
Mr. Pascal Cerré
Dear Sir

I received your favour of the 20th Ulto. On the 28th on my way to the Chyenne. I regret much having been obliged to detain your men so long, but It could not be helped. It is with much regret that I have to inform you of the death of T.L. Sarpy, who came by his death, by the explosion of Gun Powder after having traded considerably during the day; he was putting away the Robes in the evening; had a candle upon the counter; had a fifty pound keg of Powder immediately below it; it is presumed that in passing the Robes, a spark had fallen from the candle, into the powder, and of course in a moment the explosion took place; and blew the store and two other houses in every direction, and burnt and shattered him, in the most shocking manner; he only lived about five minutes afterwards. The loss of property you may immagine has been very considerable.

Should you have no instructions from Mr McK. how to act in the spring; I think you[r] best plan will be to get Mr: Mitchell, to send down for the boat, and come down yourself with your returns in Skin canoes; and leave Lachapelle at the Rees, with one or two men to make his trade; I can think of no other plan that will suit so well. The Rees winter upon Grand river where they were last winter, and think long for spring, to get back their trade. I saw Lacomb the other day, he tells me that Pierre Garrow, is now the head man of the Village, having made two have cors.[?] Your Yanctonnas did not kill one of them, in the last skirmish they had with them.

I wish you had been a little communicative, and have told me what your prospects are, try and get a sufficiency of wood cut, for the Steam Boat, should you be detained by wind in coming down; you ought to get wood cut in every convenient place. When you leave Lachapelle at the Rees, he ought to get wood cut there, tell him to interest himself, to get back 7 Horses the Rees stole from him last fall. A Colt belonging to Mr McK is among the number. I think we will make about 12 Hundred packs in this part of the country, and generally Robes of the first receipt. Please tell Lachapelle not to trade such Epechimons[21] as he did last Summer, And Believe Me

    Yours Truly
    (Signd) Wm. Laidlaw
    Mr. Pascal Cerré
    Apple River

❖ ❖ ❖

    Fort Tecumseh Feb: 15th 1832
    Mr. David D. Mitchell
    My Dear Sir

Your favour of the 18th Ulto. I received on the 29th while on my melancholy errant to the Ogallallah post to see after the affairs of the disceased Thomas L. Sarpy, who I am sorry to say was blown up by Gun Powder on the 19th of the last month; he had been busily employed trading throughout the day, and was putting away the Robes in the evening; put a candle on the counter, and had two men handing him Robes when it happened, it is presumed that a spark from the candle, had fallen into a fifty pound keg of Powder, which was immediately below the counter, when in an instant the explosion took place, and blew the Store and other two houses into a thousand directions, he was so shockingly burnt and disfigured as not to resemble a human being; he only lived about 5 minutes and uttered a few words; and then closed his eyes for ever; no doubt in great agony, it is a singular circumstance that the other two men that were along side of him recd. little or no injury. The loss of property has no doubt been very considerable, but not so great as might have been expected. The conduct of the Indians upon the occasion cannot be to much applauded, the Soldiers mounted guard, and collected the goods in every direction and would not allow man, woman, or child to approach the fatal spot, not even a dog was allowed to approach with impunity. Our Opponent Leclerc has got up this far with a few pack horses loaded; I think he will have reason to repent his folly. Father Bean it is said, employs all his means, to render him every assistance possible; but I do not fear them, great as our fathers power may be.

Mr. McKenzie writes me for the "Louis Vallé" to go up to your place, I can devise no other plan than your sending down men, to take her up; with the goods. Pascal may have left, and he must try and procure skin canoes, and come down. I have no means of sending you any of the small articles you ask for; perhaps Pascal could furnish you with a small supply; I shall write him to that effect.

The way 100 per cent came to be charged on the White Buffaloe skins; was, they were only charged half price which comes to the same thing. You have charged $29 of lost time of P. Levegen [?] to this post, which ought not to be; it is hard that this post should pay for the lost time of your men. I shall send you some pitsaw files; I never was so much at a loss for men; how to get boats made and the returns out of the Chyenne and White river, I know not. I would require at least 60 men; I expect we will make 12 hundred packs below the Rees, no person ever saw cattle in greater abundance

    Now my dear friend Except
    My Best wishes for your welfare
    And Believe Me Most Truly Yours
    (Signd) Wm. Laidlaw

P.S. I am sorry you did not send the letters you had prepared for your friends; I should have forwarded them without fail; nay I am angry with you, Mr. McKenzie writes me that [he] had wrote you to do so. Our fort building is at a stand for want of men. Be particular in forwarding the Express without a moments delay.
    (Sign'd) Wm. L.

❖ ❖ ❖

Fort Tecumseh 15th Feb: 1832
Dear McKenzie

Your long and interesting favour of the 12th Dec: I only received on the 28th January a little below Crook's point, on my way to visit the different posts, on the Chyenne. I opened the packet upon the ice, and what with anxiety and cold together, I began to Shake long before I got through with your dispatches. From there I wrote to Mr. Picotte and Halsey to forward the packet to St Louis the next day, which was accordingly done; it must be by this time [be]low the Bluffs.

It becomes my painful duty to announce the death of Mr T. L. Sarpy, who was stationed at the mouth of Eau-que-court, after being busily employed, trading throughout the day, in the evening of the 19th January he was putting away some Robes, with two of his men; he put the candle upon the counter, had a 50 pound keg of Powder immediately below the counter, which he had opened in the morning, it is presumed, that a spark from the candle must have fallen into the band and of Course the Explosion immediately took place, it blew three houses all in a line to shivers, and he was so completely burnt, and mangled, as not to bear the resemblance of a human being; he only lived a few minutes, uttered a few words, and then expired without a strug[g]le; it is singular that the men who were along side of him should have escaped without injury; save one, that got one side of himself a little scorched; the loss of property you may imagine has been very considerable, tho' by no means so much as I would have expected. The conduct of the Indians upon the occasion, cannot be too much applauded; the soldiers immediately mounted guard, and did not allow man, woman or child to approach he fatal spot, all that night, and next day, and collected every thing that they possibly could, and delivered them to J. Juett who is trading about 15 miles below, with the Chyennes. I left Campbell there to trade with the Ogallallahs, and Jos Juett with the Chyennes, the former are very tenacious of their rights, and insisted upon having the goods that were intended for them; their conduct has been so meritorious, that I could not help humouring them. Campbell trades in a lodge, along side of Joe: and every thing seemed to go on well, when I left them, a few days ago.

I wrote you fully on the 27th November last. I trust long in this, you are in possession of it in a few days after it left this; I got news of Leclerc's having sent pack horses to White River, and the Chyenne from the Poncaws, where he was sett fast by the ice; I immediately sent out people after him "a tout bon a tout cotté" ["we covered all the angles"] however he made out to get both places after a great deal of trouble, and I have no doubt vexation; he did not come up himself, but sent the Dauphins and Lacharetté; and moved himself snugly, along side of D. Lamont Poncaw squaw, and sent out three Pork eaters, to seek his fortune; a pretty fellow, to be trusted at the head of a concern, without making a single effort to save himself, or ass[o]ciates; his men have just this moment passed him, with two trains for Cherry river, one of them, had made very free with my name, in fact, had abused me in a most outrageous manner to my own men, and, threatened to shoot me, sooner than he would a dog; and so on; when I saw them passing, I went to give him an opportunity of putting his threats in execution; but he begged off; now says I my good fellow; strife, and we will take a tiff by ourselves; blackguard as you are; I will give you a chance; all would not do, he still declined; well then defend yourself, and I boom'd away at him, and gave him some marks, that he will carry with him to his grave; I could have wished his master in his place; I would have had a little more satisfaction. "Le Corbeau dan Coup" gave them 50 Beaver Skins immediately upon their arrival; there was no such thing as getting a skin of it; it is not yet paid for: they have also about 20 packs of Robes on credit; so upon the arrival of his trains, he will be put up to high water mark. I made them a harrangue in camp, that I would give two yards of Scarlet for a Beaver, large or small: knowing that there was none in camp. I am determined to make him pay for it; for Robes and every thing else in proportion; we will trade him out in two days; we have got 400 packs there, at the old prices, and can afford to make a speck. I think we will bring out of the Chyenne about 900 packs, White River 250 or 300, the Yanctons and Rees I can form no idea of what they will make. I expect to be able to muster about 7 or 8 packs of Beaver from the different posts.

Father Bean has given us our opponents every assistance in his power, in furnishing them with men, horses and the use of his Blacksmiths shop; it is said he allows his men to voyage for them, Interpret &c., now this has a very bad effect, I assure you; and has given us a great deal of trouble. Gendron who is engaged to Bean, passed here to day with Leclaires men; I asked him, how he came to be there, and he told me, he was hired to Mr: Bean, and obliged to obey orders. I have no doubt, they will try to pass their goods, as belonging to Government; otherwise I am persuaded, they will never reach Cherry river as the Gens de Puches are all camped near the mouth of Chyenne river. I shall follow them tomorrow, or send Picotte to see how they get on; Leclaire I am told is lodged in Bean's houses, at Fort Lookout. Bean went down to the Bluffs, last fall, and left Mr: Zephine as his Sub. It is unfortunate, that every Indian in the country are going out there, next spring, to see their Father, and as Cattle are very plenty, every where, they cannot fail to make an immence quantity of Robes, of which Leclair will no doubt get a great many, being under the roof, and protection, of our Father; so that it is not Leclair that we have to fear, as an opponent; but the Agent and all his means, combined with that of Leclaire's: will such coniving proceedings, be allowed to pass, without being taken any notice of, if it does, I shall say like Rose. ("this I think very funny").

Should the Indians have the quantity of Robes that I expect they will make when they come out, we must concentrate all our forces, to that place, and make them pay for their [word?]

Pascal is at a loss how to get down his returns, from his post: I shall write him providing he has no instructions from you, to get Mr: Mitchell to send some men for the boat; and him to bring down his returns in skin canoes; and leave Lachapelle at the Rees; as he passes; I can think of no other plan, that will suit so swell. The Rees winter upon Grand river, and have a great many Robes, they have been in the midst of Cattle all winter, and think long for spring, to get back their trader. Lachapelle traded 100 packs last summer, to good account; but the Robes were very indifferent, the Sioux in general make excellent Robes, which cannot be excelled even by your Assiniboines, which is saying a great deal. I must wait the arrival of the Steam Boat, to send up the "Male twin," as I have no means of sending [word?]. I observe that you wish Picotte to go to the Mandans, in spring. I hope that he will be time enough, to go in the Steam Boat, as I cannot easily dispense with his services, before that time; however, should it be absolutely necessary, that he should be there sooner; continue to let me know, and I will send him at all hazard.

My Dear Friend you greatly upbraid me, for not having sent you news papers; but be assured, the fault is not with me; as I forwarded a packet without even reading them; and by the last express, forwarded the rest; true, they were addressed to Mr. Hamilton, for reasons that will readily occur to you; if any fault there is, I am inclined to believe, it must be with Mitchell. I now forward you a bundle of Greenock papers,[22] which I hope you may find interesting; particularly if you are fond of reform. I received a letter from Mr. Chouteau about Christmas; wrote last fall; nothing in it of consequence. I would send it to you; but as there is one here addressed to you; I presume he writes you more particularly; there is also one from Powell.

Excuse me my Dear Sir if I do not give you any opinion, with regard to the arrangement made with Fountinelle and Drips;[23] as I am not well enough versed, in the politics of that part of the country, to offer an opinion. I confess it appears to me, to be rather an intricate business; which I will not attempt to unravel; the common arrangement no doubt means, the Upper Missouri Outfit.

I am glad to hear that your prospects are so flattering in the Beaver way. Iron you can have, in place of the Axes you mention.

I am sorry to inform you, that our potatos crop misgave entirely; they had a fine appearance, and promised a luxuriant return; but unfortunately some vermin eat them up, just as they began to bloom; so that we did not save one. I wrote to St Louis for 10 Bushels, for seed and if they come, you shall have part of them, with a great deal of pleasure.

The Sioux kill'd only 20 Rees in all; and are now about making peace, with them; so much for Indian Warfare.

I cannot immagine how I am to get enough boats made, to get our packs out of the Chyenne, and White river. I got back my "Casseur des fleches" last fall, it was the Yanctonnas that Stole him; he got away from them in crossing the Chyenne, and they were not able to catch him again. I have kill'd 25

Cows with him this winter; so that I can keep the fort in fresh meat, without buying a bit. I kill 2, 3 and 4 Cows at a surround, that is "Wa-u-pi."

I shall write Pascal and Lachapelle, to interest themselves, to get your colt from the Rees.

You shall have Provosts Acct. in detail, for years back. It is with extreme sorrow, that I learnt the melancholy tidings, of the death of Your son Alexr. poor little fellow, I do not know, when I had my feelings so much hurt.[24]

I shall endeavour to get you 100 prs. Horse shoes made. I have got about 70 Horses here; but am afraid there will be no such thing, as keeping them; when the Indians begin to Collect in such numbers. I am half inclined to sell the half of them; rather than they should be stole.

I beg you will make my excuse to Mr Hamilton for not writing him, as I only arrived late last night, and propose being off again tomorrow: and am of course much hurried. I know, or at least think, he will be generous enough, to Forgive me. I am well aware, that it is ungrateful in the extreme, on my part, in not even acknowledging the receipt, of his of very polite and interesting favour. Give my best to him, and remember me to Chardon, and all the other good folks, that you may think of, and accept of my best love

For yourself, and believe me your
Affectionate Friend, while
(Sign'd) Wm. Laidlaw
Kenneth McKenzie
Fort Union

❖ ❖ ❖

Fort Tecumseh 22d. Feb: 1832
Mr. Pierre D. Papin
Dear Sir

I received your favour of the 14th inst: last evening by Deshonnette; your memorandum for Goods shall be completed as far as practicable, but some of the articles, I am sorry to say we have not got; such as Axes, Wampum Hair Pipes, Shells and Cock feathers. I returned here a few days ago from the Ogallallahs post, where I saw a letter from you, requesting a lock of hair of the disceased T. J. Sarpy. Your letter arrived too late, and even had it been in time before he was interred, it would have been impossible to have got it; as the hair was completely burnt off his head, and so shockingly disfigured as scarcely to bear any resemblance to a human being.

I observe what you say, with regard to your opponent, and particularly the ill timed interference of Father Bean; he is certainly deviating from his duty, and will I have no doubt, be called to account for his conduct. If your opponents still hold out that the goods they have under their charge, belong to Bean, I would have no hesitation in telling the Indians, that they are robbing them of their just rights, and selling the goods to them, that was explicitly sent by Government, for their annuities and presents.

In place of your giving away for nothing; I would advise rather to make a reduction in the price of our goods; in this way all would share in the Jubilee; as it is impossible to give presents to all, it generally creates a jealousy, and does more harm than good, in like cases, I have invariably adopted the plan I have suggested, and found it to answer well; but I by no means wish to dictate to you: You must only be guided by your own good sence and experience. They certainly cannot annoy you much, with five horse loads; Cannot you trade him out, and then you would be at ran. [?].

Gendron and three of Leclercs men are camped about three miles above this, with two trains; their horses having given out, they have sent on to Chyenne river for others: I scarcely think they will reach that place, as all the Gens de Puches are camped near the mouth of the Chyenne; but even if they should, I do not fear tem: I think we can continue to trade them out in two days, and then resume our old prices

I am Dear Sir
Yours Most Respectfully
(Sign'd) Wm. Laidlaw
Mr. P.D. Papin
White River
P.S. I would not wish you to trade any more horses.

❖ ❖ ❖

Fort Tecumseh 2d. March 1832
Mr. Colin Campbell
Ogallallahs Post
Dear Sir

I wrote you on the 27th Ulto. By the "Four Spiders." I now send you five men from this, which with those from Frederick's will make fourteen in all, which is all I possibly can send.

I cannot pretend to give you any instructions or advice how to act, but you must do what you think best, taking every precaution for the security of the property.

I send you Ten spikes, for your poles, and also your hat by Lagrave.

Believe Me Dear Sir
Yours Respectfully
(Sign'd.) William Laidlaw
To Mr: Colin Campbell
Ogallallahs Post

❖ ❖ ❖

Fort Tecumseh 4th March 1832
Mr. Pierre D. Papin
Dear Sir

Yours of the 28th Ulto. I received last night by Deshonnette with the horses and other articles therein mentioned. When I last wrote you I thought it unnecessary to say any thing more regarding our opponents, as we had talked over that subject so often. I did not think it necessary to write you, as I would a green boy of no experience, but left every thing in a great measure to your own discretion and prudence, well aware that you knew my sentiments, with regard to them, and the views of the Company: I felt fully satisfied that you would in every means in your power, to meet these views. It was never my intention that you should buy their goods, when I talked of your trading them out: I was governed intirely by your former letters, wherein you mentioned that there was still an immence quantity of Robes in Market, in which case it would have been well to do so, as they seemed to annoy you so much; but as it is, it is the last thing I should think of.

It is our business to prevent them from getting a Robe if possible, and to force the trade as far as your means will allow.

You said nothing to me with regard to men to take down your canoes; however, it is of no consequence as I could give you no assistance; all I have got here, are old Mayance and Ledoux, the rest all having gone to the Chyenne: You will be strong enough to take down two Canoes, and the remainder you will be obliged to leave at your house, in charge of Charles Degray or Lauviere; I shall endeavour to get the whole to this place, as soon as the Snow goes off; with pack horses; I would advise you to take down a sufficiency of Meat for your hands while they remain with the packs, at the mouth of White river. Also a little for Joseph Lacompte, as he is almost in a state of Starvation.

When once you have arranged your baggage in safety, I wish you to go and remain with Lacompte and give him a hand, as I think there will be a great many Indians there; and a good many Robes; and you know old Josey, is not a very bright genius. In the expectation that you will get there as soon, or sooner than the Indians I shall not [be] satisfied, that Master Leclerc will have no advantage over us, even at Fort Lookout; although under the wing and care of Father Bean.

There is nothing new here from any quarter. Lacompt's man is here in quest of provisions, he says; they, as well as our Sub Agent Monsieur Zephine are starving. Picotte with 6 men have gone to the Navy Yard some time ago

I am, Dear Sir
Yours Most Respectfully
(Sign'd.) William Laidlaw
M. P. D. Papin
White River

❖ ❖ ❖

Fort Tecumseh 5th May 1832
James A. Hamilton Esqr.
Dear Sir

Mr. McKenzie's favour of the 13th Febuary came safe to hand on the 1st inst:, four or five days after his arrival here, the Accounts have been regulated according to the instructions laid down in that letter, and I hope that ere long we will be able to make our books agree.

From Explanation made by Mr: Kipp it appears that Greenwood is in debt to the A.F. Coy. 753.76 instead of 445.76 the amount includes his Note for

	354.76
his Note for	61."
and sundry advances Afterward	338."
making in All	753.76

for further particulars relating to this account I refer you to Mr. McKenzie.

If our Books are correct the A.F.Co. are indebted to William Rodgers this sum of 12.75 instead of his being indebted to them the same Amount. Amable Bertrand's Acct. as we have it amounts to 43.25 instead of 43.75.

Believe Me Most Respectfully
Your friend and Sert:
(Signd.) Wm Laidlaw

❖ ❖ ❖

Fort Tecumseh May 10th 1832
To the Gentleman in Charge
of Otto Establishment
Sir

Tomorrow I shall dispatch one of my Interpreters (Pierre Ortubise)[25] with two men down stream, with the hopes of getting some news of the long expected Steam boat, he has instructions to proceed down as far as your establishment, if he should not meet her, before his arrival there; I wish him to return, with all possible dispatch, be good enough to furnish him with the means, of making as expeditious a voyage back, as possible, it is of the utmost importance, that I should know whether the S. B. is coming up or not.

Louis Preville is with you, please send him with Ortubise, as he knows the road, and is a good voyageur. If he should not be with you, I must beg of you to keep one of my men, and furnish Ortubise with another, capable of guiding him to this place.

Mr. Ortubise is a good young man; but he has one failing, he is fond of liquor, please keep him from temptation.

Be good enough to write me, and give me all the news. We have not had a word from St Louis since October last

Believe me
Most Respectfully
Your Obdt. & Humble Servant
(Sign'd.) Kenneth McKenzie

3

FORT PIERRE LETTER BOOK A

June 17–December 14, 1832

Fort Pierre June 17th 1832
To The Agent American Fur Co.
Saint Louis
Sir

Herewith you have a statement for the number of Robes &C: to be shipp'd to the address of the American Fur Company, on board Keel boat "Male Twin" and 5 Batteaux conducted by Mr. Honoré Picotte; as also a Statement of the Accts. of Men descending with him. Some few of the men, have wintered below this, and may have recd. advances not included in Statement herewith inclosed. Mr. Picotte has been instructed to see into the business, and will notify you accordingly.

The "Yellowstone" left here for Fort Union on the 5th inst: Mr. Chardon was in good health and fine Spirits. As I am in great haste, you will be good enough to excuse the brevity of my letter. Allow me to refer you to Mr. Picotte for all the news

And Believe Me
Yours Most Respectfully
Sign'd Wm. Laidlaw

❖ ❖ ❖

Fort Pierre July 7th 1832
Pierre Chouteau Jr. Esqr:
Saint Louis
Dear Sir

Herewith inclosed you have the Inventories of Stock remaining on hand at Fort Union and Clark, as also sundry other documents appertaining to Upper Missouri Outfit. Viz: Additional requisition for fall of 1832. J. L. Beans letter and acceptances, Packing acct. of Furs &c: shipp'd to the address of the American Fur Company, under charge of Charles Lebuge.

Mr. Laidlaw has given two drafts on you; one payable to the order of Honoré Picotte for $64, and the other two Pascal L. Cerré for 1148.24. He left us on the first inst:, accompanied by Dickson for the East,[1] in quest of the expected Pork-eaters.

The rumour which was circulated about the time you left him, that Ortubise had obtained a ½ barrel of Whiskey of the Engineer, proved to be true; he and Angé were intoxicated with very little intermission, from the time the S. B. left, till the 30th of Ulto. when we succeeded in finding the keg, which they had taken the precaution to hide;

their conduct during this time was dastardly in the extreme but comment is unnecessary.

I understand from Lebieg and others, that the Engineer belonging to the "Yellowstone," traded several Beaver Skins while at the Mandans, as also some Buffalo Robes. Mr. Laidlaw requests me to say, that if we are to have competition the approaching season, he advises you to Put up the Outfit for the Poncaw tribe, in St. Louis, and to forward it by the Keel boat, with such person to take charge of it, as you may deem prudent. Mr. Picotte or Papin, can give you an idea, of what goods will be necessary for that Post.

The following are the names of others, he requests you not to engage for the Outfit. Viz: Francois Roy, André Bonnetiere, Benjamin Hart, Pierre Laccovere, A. F. Boillot, Francois M. Broit and Francois Demant. Four or six good Saursus [Sawyers] are wanted at the Depot. I can recommend to your notice as such: Joseph Bary, Edward Boulé, Etienne Papin and Joseph Berthiencu, men who descended with Mr. Picotte.

I do not know how you intend to [deal with] Little Laloues Acct. After crediting him with his salary for services ending Summer of 1832, the Balance to his credit appears to be 365.36 (Ice Lodges) it had been intimated that he has (by abandoning his post when there was about $400 worth of Property exposed to the mercy of the Sioux Indians; who might easily carried off all, if they had been so disposed) forfeited all claims to salary, however you are no doubt acquainted with Mr. McKenzie's statements on the subject. After the departure of the boats, there will remain but 5 men, to pass the Summer here, among which are the Blacksmith and Carpenter, one of the other three men has the Venerial Disease, and will without doubt, be useless all summer; it will require at least two men to make hay; and the other two, will find sufficient employment in hauling wood and water, and taking care of the cattle.

Joseph Lemoin (a Steam Boat man who came down in the boats,) says he is sick, and wishes to return to Saint Louis; at all events, he appears to be good for nothing, and we think it best to let him go; I have recd. an Acct. from Fort Clark against a man called Cenion Carr, I understand he returned to St. Louis per "Yellowstone" also a charge Against Mr. Sanford from the same post.

Items not known here, Charles Landry, Michel Leccette, John Demant, David Paur and Amable Tisdale, canadian Pork-eaters engaged in Montréal Spring 1829, go down with Leberge; by Agreement their time does not expire till August 1832, no date specified. I requested them to remain here, as their time is not out till next Month, but they objected to, saying that by agreement made by them, with Mr: Pratte at Prairie-de-chien Jan 1829. they were to be free on arrival of Cos. boat in St. Louis , the Summer of 1832.[2] In accordance with Mr. Mckenzies instructions, I have charged them with 53 days time unserved, as you will Perceive on reference to their Accts.

The Americans who arrived here a few days ago, from the Rocky Mountains, go down with Leberge on condition that they shall work for their passage, they take with them a small lot of Beaver Skins, which we were unable to get from them; their price was $5, and our instructions is, to give no more than $4.

We are much in want of a cook here, Mr. Laidlaw wishes you to send him a good one, this fall if possible: a black man would be preferrd. Bapt. Leclaire[3] the cook who was at the Mandans when you passed there, is said to be good for nothing, he is too great a friend to the Indians, and squanders away provisions, he offered to remain here, on conditions that we would allow him to take a squaw.

You will also receive herewith inclosed, the Inventory of Stock remaining on hand at Fort Union 17,777.90 dollars. I have not had time to examine it; we do not wish to delay the boats, as the water is now falling; therefore I hope you will excuse me. We shall send down a boat from here nearly light, for the purpose of taking the packs at Fort Lookout; the last Accts. from there, they had on hand 22 Packs Robes.

We have remaining here 373 packs Robes, without the means of shipping them. Allow me to refer you to the letter addressed to you from Fort Union, for all the Upper Country [word?]. Mr McKenzie appears to have been much engaged in putting up Outfits &c: at the time the boats departed from his establishment.

We had instructions from a Mr. Laidlaw, to send down 1500 pounds Tallow to Mr. Cabanné´s establishment, and 1000 pounds to St Louis.

Lebrige says the boats are already sufficiently loaded therefore we do not think it prudent to send any.

July 10th. The wind commenced blowing a Gale at daylight, and there is now (9 A.M.) every appearance that it will continue throughout the day; but the Missouri rose a foot last night which is some consolation.

I shall give each Steersman an Acct. of the loading of his boat, with directions that they exhibit them, on their arrival in Saint Louis.

It is now 12 A.M., the wind is moderating, and I shall close the packet, so that in case they think it safe to Start; I shall be ready. I believe I have communicated every thing of import. Believe me Dear Sir
    Your Obdt. and Humble Servant
    Jacob Halsey
    For Upp: Missouri Outfit
    Pierre Chouteau Jr. Esqr.
    Agt. Amer: Fur Co.
    Saint Louis

❖ ❖ ❖

Fort Pierre July 9th 1832
Pierre Chouteau Jr. Esqr:
Agent Amer: Fur Co.
Saint Louis
Dear Sir

This will be handed you by Francois Vaillant, who has a draft on you for 2204.07. He claims payment for a Note of Smith, Sublette & Co. in his favour taken down to St Louis by Mr. McKenzie, in July 1830, and paid by them, to the Co. In Acct. current 1829, date Oct 25, 1830 the Outfit is endebted. By cash recd. of Smith, Jackson and Sublette[4] for their two notes 835.75, perhaps it is one of theirs; he says the Amt. of the Note is $60. If his statement is correct, that is to say, the note has been paid, this Outfit is in debt to him the Amt: of it, independent of the draft above mentioned.

    I have the honour to be
    Your Most Obedient
    (Sign'd.) Jacob Halsey
    For Upp: Missouri Outfit.

❖ ❖ ❖

Fort Pierre July 12th 1832
Kenneth McKenzie Esqr:
Fort Union
Dear Sir

Dumond will leave here tomorrow accompanied by Durand; he will take charge of the letter, and I have written Mr. Kipp to Forward it to you, from his establishment by the first opportunity.

The S. B. "Yellowstone" arrived here on her return the 24th Ulto., and departed the 25th with a fine stage of Water, having onboard 1200 packs Robes, and the Beaver Skins taken in at your establishment, and Fort Clark.

Messrs. Laidlaw and Dickson left us on the 1st inst: for the East, in quest of the expected Pork-eaters. The arrangement with Dickson was completed on Mr. Chouteaus return. It was made agreeably to the proposition you made him before you left. He took with him a few goods, and will return in the fall for his winter supply.

Henry Hart and others from your establishment, arrived here safe on the 9th inst:. Charles Lebuge was left here by Mr. Chouteau, for the purpose of steering the boat containing the Beaver; on the 10th he picked out the best boat, and all the Beaver Skins, Rats &c: we had here, was put on board of her, generally to Mr. Laidlaws instructions. (10,209 lbs. Beaver Skins.) We sent down the boat "Marias" nearly light from here, she will have to take in 130 packs Robes at the Yancton Post.

The Brigade left here on the 11th inst: conducted by Charles Lebuge; the water high, and rising. Batteaux #1 Capt. Hart, #2 Capt. Vaillant, #3 Capt. Lebuge, "Marias" Capt. Chevalier. I am sorry to say there still remains here, and without the means of shipping them, 373 Packs Robes.

We have Six men to pass the Summer here including Castongé and Demeray, who is laid up with the Venerial Disease. Mr. Laidlaw took four with him, he talk'd some of going to St: Louis, if he did not meet the "Pork eaters" at prairie-du-chien.

The Pork eaters who came down with Hart were all anxious to go to St Louis; indeed we could not have sent the boats down without all of them except two. However, on the arrival of Hart, I requested them to remain and serve out their time; this they all objected to, and there was no one among them, who was willing to pay for the Balance of his time, alledging that by Agreement made by them, with Mr. Pratte at "Prairie-du-chien" June 1829 they were to be made free on the arrival of Co. boat at St Louis the Sumr. of 1832. According to the instruction laid down in your letter to Mr. Laidlaw, (which I took the liberty to open,) I have charged them all (except Hart and the Samotts) with time unserved, and have written to Mr. Chouteau on the subject.

Joseph Lemoin, who said he had been sick since the S. B. left St. Louis, begged to go down; as he is utterly useless, and as provisions are now very scarce here, we thought it best to let him go. We were obliged to reengage old Mayaneu; Bapt: Leclair (otherwise called "Soyo") would not remain. Three American Trappers arrived here a few days ago from the Mountains; they say, they left Vanderburgs camp in April; their names are Wm. L. Brown, C. Shanks and Wm. Thompson. Brown remains here till the arrival of Mr. Laidlaw, he seeks employment; the other two, went down with Lebuge on condition, that they work their passage, they took with them 30 or 40 lbs. Beaver Skins, which we were unable to get, their price was $5, and our instructions are, to give no more than $4.

Mr. Hamilton in his letter to Mr. Laidlaw (which I also took the liberty to open.) says Francois Vaillant claims payment for a note of Smith Sublette & Co. taken down to St Louis in July 1830, and paid. On Examination of Acct. current, I see this Outfit is endebted, Oct: 25th 1830 with cash received of Smith, Jackson and Sublette or their two Notes 835.75. Perhaps it is one of these. I have given him a letter to Mr. Chouteau on the subject. Fort Union the (S. B. Yellowstone") was advised of the payment of these two Notes, and has recd. credit for the same. Please send me abstract of Lachapelle's engagement, by the first opportunity; he denies having recd. A 3 Point Green Blanket, on board the Steam Boat.

Lecompt and Cardinal are still at Fort Lookout, Mr. Laidlaw wrote to Mr. Papin, by Picotte, requesting him to remain with Lecompt till the arrival of the S. B., and he went down that far in her, fully expecting to find him there; but he had gone down with Picotte. We sent Lecompt a small assortment of goods for Lebuge. Leclerc left two men at the Sioux Agency, with a few Goods to pass the Summer. Dishouette is living with them; Joseph Vasseur is [word?] on late.

Pineau, Parker, Leclaire and Ménard came in from hunting about a month ago; they did not make more than one Pack of Beaver altogether, having lost the most of their horses, at the beginning of the hunt. We got their Beaver, which when divided among them, would not pay their debts to the Company. They wished Mr. Laidlaw to furnish them with horses, but he refused to do so; as they are already deeply enough in debt. Ménard and Leclair have gone on a visit to Vasseur, in order I suppose, to see how the Land lies in that quarter. Old Carrier and Parker (otherwise called Jim the Mulatto) have two or three horses remaining, and have gone out in the "large" to pass the Summer. When you engaged me last Sumr. you requested me to let you know before hand, when ere I should make up my mind to go down, in order that you might make your arrangements accordingly. It is my wish to go down next Summer. Believe me Dr. Sir, I do not say this in order to get a raise of Salary; but, for no other reason than because I have business to settle at home, as also, a desire to see my relatives and friends once more. If you should feel so disposed I should be willing to return to your employment the year following; or, if you could so arrange matters as to let me go down this fall, I would be ready to return again in the spring.

Please remember me to Mr. Hamilton; I recd. his Polite and friendly letter pr Hart; and would answer it now, but time will not permit. Compliments to Chardon and Lafrierer, and all who take the trouble to enquire about me.

Believe me dear Sir
Your Obedient Servant
(Sign'd.) Jacob Halsey
For Upp: Missouri Outfit.
Kenneth McKenzie Esqr.
Fort Union

❖ ❖ ❖

Fort Pierre July 12. 1832
Mr. James Kipp
Fort Clark
Dear Sir

This will be handed you by Thomas Dumond, who will leave here tomorrow for your neighbourhood.

I inclose you a letter to Mr. McKenzie which I

must beg you to forward by the first opportunity. I have not yet had time to settle your post acct. Messrs. Laidlaw and Dickson left here on the 7th inst: for the East in quest of the expected Pork eaters Picotte for St Louis on the 17th S. B. Yellowstone on the 25th Ulto. and Hart on the 11th inst: Durand abuses you like a pick pocket, if you had heard him, I think you would not allow him to enter your fort again.

Dumond says he will perhaps be in want of some little articles at your place. You will I presume, act in accordance with your instructions from Mr. McKenzie, however, I can inform you that he has money in St. Louis, to the Amt: of about $600. We have advanced him ten dollars here, which if an opportunity should offer you will be good enough to collect: and place to the credit of Fort Union. Durands Acct. at Fort Clark $6.63 has been paid.

I would write you a long letter but time, and not inclination, prevents me; Remember me to Crawford. Excuse hurry, and Believe Me, Your friend
   (Sign'd.) Jacob Halsey
   For Upp: Missouri Outfit.

❖ ❖ ❖

   Fort Pierre July 25th 1832
   Mr. James Kipp
   Fort Clark
   Dear Sir

I do not know when dispatches will be made up for your neighbourhood, but as I am at present employed settling your post acct. I think it a fitting time, to advise you of several errors and deficiencies, in your document dated July 3rd last. Under date of Sept: 30th you charge Fort Tecumseh with Amt. of James Kipp Acct. from 12th Jany. 1831 to 16th July inclusive, 143.38. Also (same date) with Amt: of James Kipps Acct. from 12th Jany. 1831 to 21st July, charged by order from Fort Union 143.35.

June 4th 1831 Your Acct. at Fort Clark up to the departure of Mr. McKnight 133.24 was transfered to Fort Tecumseh; entered to your Genl: Acct., and credit accordingly given Fort Clark for the Amt: Now it appears to me that after the transfer was made, and up to the date of 16th June or 21st July, which ever it may chance to be; you took for the sum of 10.14, and then again, your Acct. commencing December following $29, which makes the Amt. against you at Fort Clark this year 39.14 instead of 315.76. You also charge this post with Pierre Levigues Acct. 80.25, you should only have charged us with the Amt: of advances made to him; and not with his best time.

Your Acct. against Fort Union up to the 21st ulto.: you state to be 1303.16½ Fort Union in Acct. current up to 30th Ulto:, allows you only a balance of 711.15, is this correct or not.

I understand Nicholas Durand has paid his old debt amounting to 364.72, if such is the case, F. Union should be advised of such Settlement; so that proper entries might be made. I have however, charged your post with his a/c, but will make no entire [entries] to his credit, till I receive your advises on the subject. Inventory of Merchandise recd. from Yanctonnas post as you state it, is incorrect; as also that of the goods delivered you by Lachapelle, which you state to be 524.20 the correct Amt is 1078.28.

You sent me per Hart an Acct. against C. Cerré for 12.62 this man went down to Saint Louis in the Steam Boat, and it is now more than probable, too late to recover it. You say Louis Bissonnett has a outfit of 480 dolls: as also Bellhumeur one of 380 dolls: Bissonnetts wages is $400, and Bellhumeurs is $300. Be good enough to let me know, what the Balance is for. Bissonnette told me he gave the Co. some Beaver Skins; if so, it should have been deducted from the Amt: of Advances made to him.

You sent down your Inventory without prices; I have made it out, and you will receive it herewith inclosed, but I fear it is imperfect; I see no Blacksmiths tools, neither do I see many articles in use of any kind mentioned in it. Be good enough to furnish me with abstract of the Engagements of persons at Fort Clark for season 1832.33, as also with the items of J. F. A. Sanfords Acct. A detailed Acct. of the articles furnished S. B. Yellowstone, and a Copy of you[r] Post Acct. against Yanctonnas Outfit, season 1831.32 is much wanted here. I believe I have communicated every thing of a business nature, and will close with
   My Best wishes for your health
     and prosperity
   (Sign'd.) Jacob Halsey
   For Upp: Missouri Outfit.

❖ ❖ ❖

Fort Pierre Augt: 14th 1832
Pierre Chouteau Junr. Esqr.
Agt. Amer. Fur Compy:
Western Department
Saint Louis
Dear Sir

Mr. Catlin has just arrived from Fort Union and was the bearer of letters, which contain nothing, but news of an unpleasant nature. Mr. McKenzie did not write, but from what I can gather from Mr. Hamiltons letter, and from Mr. Catlin, it appears to me that our affairs in that neighbourhood, present a very unfavourable, and alarming aspect On the 7th July the Keel boat for the Blk: feet, under Mr. Mitchell with a splendid Equipment, and 50 Picked Men, started for River Marias, 8 or 10 days after her departure from Fort Union she was completely wreaked; the Cargo nearly all lost, one man (DeBennoit) and a Blk:foot Indian drowned. Fortunately the "Flora" arrived about the same time they were apprised of the Melancholy tidings; all hands were immediately summoned to make up fresh Equipment for the Blk:feet, and the Flora left Fort Union for "Marias," on the 19th Ulto. The Untoward delay it is to be feared, will be very detrimental to the trade of the infant post; however, we must hope for the best; news will go ahead of the disaster, and Mr. Bird who departed with a party on horse-back, having Tobacco and ammunition, it is to be hoped, will do his utmost to content the Indians.[5]

I left here on the 1st Ulto. in quest of the Pork Eaters. I met them (41 in number) one days march this side of Fort Snelling, and arrived here safe on the 29th with all the party, except two, who were lost in the prairie, by leaving the party while under march, they have all thus far behaved themselves well, and I hope they will give us less trouble, then those of 1829.

If it is not too late, I wish you to send us by the fall boat, as large a supply of Corn as possible, we have now many mouths [to] provide for, and provisions are scarce. I have written a note to the gentleman in charge of the boat, to the same effect.

You will receive herewith inclosed, Mr. Catlins Acct. which you will have the goodness to collect, and place to the Credit of U.M.O. 1831. It was contemplated when Mr. Catlin left Fort Union, that an express would be sent us 10 or 12 days after his departure, when I presume Mr. McKenzie will write you fully, and make amends for putting you off at this time, without a line.

I sincerely hope a pleasanter theme, will be matter for my next communications, believe Me Ever
   Very Truly Yours
   (Signd) Wm. Laidlaw
   Pierre Chouteau Junr: Esqr.
   Agt. Amer. Fur Co.
   Western Department
   Saint Louis

❖ ❖ ❖

Fort Pierre Augt: 14. 1832
To the Gentleman in Charge
of Upp: Missouri Outfit
Keel Boat "En Route"
Missouri River
Sir

If this letter does not reach you too late, and your boat is not too heavy loaded, I wish you to purchase a Supply of Corn; as much as your boat will be able to carry without risk. Provisions are low, and we have reason to expect they will continue to be, very scarce at this depot
   (Sign'd) Wm. Laidlaw
   Aig: Agt: for U.M.O.
   at Fort Union

P.S. If you have passed the Settlements, it is very probable, that you can get a supply of Corn at Mr. Cabannés Establishment; if not you can try at the Poncaw Village. Mr. Bogart will deliver you a Keg, belonging to the Co.

❖ ❖ ❖

Fort Pierre September 13. 1832
Mr. James Kipp
Fort Clark
Dr. Sir

I recd. Mr. Crawfords letter of the 8th on the 14th inst:, and have according to his request made out a statement of our selling prices at this post, which with sundry other documents appertaining to Fort Clark you will receive herewith inclosed. I always understood that the rates of selling at the Mandans; were higher than at this place, however, you must know more about the matter than I do; having no doubt been made acquainted with Mr. McKenzies sentiment on the subject. I shall enclose you a blank list for Yanctonnas Outfit: you will be good enough to have it fill'd up; the prices of that post, should not differ from those of your own.

We have not yet recd. the accts. of Mdse: per S. B. "Yellowstone"; so soon as they come to hand, I will attend to your request regarding your Invoice. It is impossible to send you any Vermillion before the fall Boat goes up; as we have ourselves recd. none from St. Louis this season; none was to be procured there, and all sent from N. York was lost by Shipwreck. You will however receive pr: Belhumeur $5 Needles.

If it is possible Mr. Laidlaw wishes you to send us a supply of Corn this fall, we got none from the Rees this year, and we have many mouths to provide for.

We recd. news from St Louis a few days ago. Mr. Lamont is on his way up with the Keel destined for your place. We suppose he is now as high up as the Poncaw Village. Maj. Bean has arrived at his place with a doctor, who is busily engaged Inoculating the Indians. The Small Pox is still raging among the Lower Indians (Otto &c). Leclair is on his way up with an Equipment about as Extensive as his last, which you know was small. F. Labeaus trial for the murder of F. Quenel, was to have commenced the 1st Monday in this Month in the U.S. Court.

Tell Crawford I would write him, but I really have not time. I hope he will Excuse me, remember me to him, Excuse hurry, and Believe me

Yours Truly
(Sign'd) Jacob Halsey
(Official)

P.S. Since writing the foregoing we have procured 2 lbs. Vermillion and it will be sent to you Pr. Belhumeur. Mr. Laidlaw is unwell today, otherwise he would write you as also Mr. McKenzie, he arrived here with 3 "Pork Eaters" on the 29th July, they have, with a few exceptions all conducted themselves thus far very well, 2 of them deserted, but were overtaken in the "Big Bird," and brought back. Our work has not progressed fast, as many of them have been sick, and we have now 6 or 8 unable to do duty. Belhumeur is detained while I am writing these hurried lines, and I shall keep on till he calls on me. The S. B. got down safe, and returned as far as Council Bluff with the keel in tow. Picotte and Brigade had 150 Buff. Robes Parcially damaged, on the trip down, but lost none. Lebuge and Bogarde were met by the "Yellowstone" on her return up the river, some where about the "Hill without design"[6] (all well) it is to be presumed, they reached St Louis without accident.

We have reason to think that Mr. McKenzie will descend this fall; if he should arrive at your place after the receipt of this, be good enough to hand it to him for Perusal.

Yours &c.
(Sign'd:) J. Halsey

❖ ❖ ❖

Fort Pierre Oct: 10. 1832
Mr. William Dickson
Dear Sir

Narcisse Frenier arrived here the day before yesterday, the weather was so bad yesterday that I could do nothing, or I would have sent an express after you to inform you that I keep him here. I order you to take all the Mdse:, Horses, Carts &c. which he left at your post belonging to the American Fur Co. to take an Inventory of them, and have every thing Witnessed, and deliver the property to E. Primeau who has instructions to bring them here. The men who are there, can either come here or return to Lac Treverse.

I wish you to keep within our limits, which you are well acquainted with. The following articles belonging to Narcisse he wishes to be given to his woman, Viz. 100 lbs: Flour, 30 lbs: Sugar, 5 bags Sweet Corn, 3 lbs: Powder, 6 lbs: Shot, 50 lbs. Balls 12 Plugs Tobacco and his double barrel Gun to be given to his father-in-law. Take Pineaus wife and family into your house, and provide for them, and pay some little attention to his father-in-law

Your Truly
(Signd.) Kenneth McKenzie
Agt. Amer fur Co.
For Upp: Missouri Outfit
To Mr. William Dickson
Riviere-au-Jacques

❖ ❖ ❖

Fort Pierre 18th October 1832
James A. Hamilton
Fort Union
Dear Sir

Herewith inclosed you will receive a detailed a/c of advances to men at this place in June last; A/c current up to 9. July, a/c of errors in your Inventory of Stock, accts: of Baptiste Lebrun and Geo: Simonds and D. D. Mitchell, as per General Ledger Oct: 1. last; as also an Invoice of Mdse: furnished Upper Missouri Outfit last spring, Per S. B. Yellowstone. We fully expected that we would have been furnished with seperate Invoices, as the several Equipments were prepared and packed in Saint Louis; but we have been disappointed. I have no acct: whatever of the goods &c furnished Fort Union per S. B. and Keel "Flora"; and must beg you to furnish me with a statement thereof, as soon as convenient; as also, to return me the Invoice when you have done with it. I have at present my hands full of business, and am unable to Furnish you with a/c current up to the present prices; but hope to be able to do so ere long. Meanwhile, I must beg your indulgence.

I will send you some Tracts, and late news papers by Mr. Lamont, who goes up in a boat as far as Fort Clark from here, you will hear every thing new and interesting.
    Dear Sir
    Yours Most Respectfully
    (Sign'd) Jacob Halsey
    (Official)

❖ ❖ ❖

Fort Pierre 18th Nov: 1832
James A. Hamilton Esqr.
Fort Union
Dear Sir

Herewith inclosed you will receive several documents for Fort Union Outfit 18.31.32 to 30th June, and Outfit 3.2.33 to 26th Ulto. I have compared your Duplicate with the General Ledger, and find that most of the accts. correspond with each other; a statement of those that do not, you will find inclosed (No 5) upon reference to which you will find out where the difference lies, and be able to make the necessary entries, and consequently our books will agree. Francois Bellair and Baptiste Cheralins accts: I neglected to send you by last opportunity; I hope you will suffer no inconvenience from the neglect. They left here on the morning of the fourth Uto: I gave them each at parting a [word?] of papers, on which was written the amt: of their advances at this place; the night following they returned, and Chevalier got whisky for $3 and Bellair Whisky $3 and Blue Cloth $4, making in all $7 for the latter and $3 for the former, not included in the accts: given them. I was not aware of their having returned, untill they were off gain, or I should have given them new accounts.

On the book of advances to men in St Louis, sent you per S. B. "Yellowstone"; if I mistake not, there was one of the name of Gotlib Guesel mentioned, engaged for 18 months wages $240. Can you tell me the amt: of his advances in St Louis. Please Excuse hurry,
    and Believe me Dr. Sir
    Yours Most Respectfully
    (Sign'd) Jacob Halsey
    (Official)

❖ ❖ ❖

Fort Pierre 10. Dec: 1832
Mr. Pierre D. Papin
Cherry River
Dear Sir

I only sent yours of the 10th a few days ago, having been absent on a hunting expedition at the time your men arrived here, consequently, your men have been detained here longer than I could have wished. It is useless for me to mention to you, that we have been in a starving condition for some time past; necessity drove me to the plains in quest of Grub, with a small party, we have been able to kill about 30 animals, which will keep us a going for a few days; our work is nearly at a stand in consequence; I sent 12 or 15 men to E. Primeaus establishment to make a living the best way they could.

Mr. Picotte started for the Yanctonnas about 3 weeks ago. Lachapelle was set fast with his load of Corn, somewhere near Apple river, where he put the corn in cache; am much afraid that our friends the Yanctonnas, will find it out; then adieu to our corn. I expect the express daily from above; I am under the necessity of keeping Vincent here, to send down with the express, as all the men I have are "Pork eaters." Deshonnette has been sick for some time past. I have filled your memorandum as far as practicable for the present, but should you be in want of any further supplies, you can let me know; and I will still endeavour to supply your wants; if you are not opposed, you ought to be as saving as possible of your dry goods, and Guns, and let them trade ammunition and Tobacco, and other dimentives [?], comparatively of less value; but you no doubt are the best judge, how far this can be done with propriety.

I got the shoes and nails made, all ready to shoe your horses, but they are so poor that I think it would be imprudent to shoe them, as it would be impossible for them to make a voyage, and to have them shod, would be certain death. Should you get meat, your best plan I think would be to send some pack horses by the Chyenne; it is fine travelling in the bottoms, and they can easily come to the mouth, in two days. I am surprised that you did not send in pack saddles for your horses; I do not know how to rig them out; as we have neither saddles or cords; in future should you want any thing from this, you will be good enough to send them rigged, as well as provisions for the voyage for your men. Have the goodness to write me in future in English, as I have a great deal of trouble in making out your letters; and then very imperfectly. You write English equally as well, as you do French. I shall inclose you a memorandum of goods sent you. I have not yet heard from Pascal. In the Mean time believe Me,
Your Most Respectfully
(Sign'd.) William Laidlaw

❖ ❖ ❖

Fort Pierre 14th Decr. 1832
Mr. Emillien Primeau
Dear Sir

I have been for some time past expecting a supply of Meat from you, what made me expect it more confidently, is that I understand the camps in your vicinity have plenty of Meat, say some at the Little Chyenne; and a little further up, they have meat in great abundance; therefore I hope you will make every exertion in your power to send us a supply as soon as possible.

I wish Alfred Traverse to be sent to Mr. Papins in place of Vincent, who I have kept here. I will inclose you a list of the men I wish sent here; it will be necessary that your Brother accompany them, as I shall find use for him in a few days. Let me know by the first opportunity, what goods you think will be required for your post; as I think I shall have an opportunity of sending them up before long, when the balance of your flow shall be sent you. We have been living here from hand to mouth, ever since your brother left us; and still have very little before hand. I expect the Express from above in a few days.
I remain
Yours Most Respectfully,
(Sign'd.) William Laidlaw

[There is a break of five days until letter book B commences.]

4

FORT PIERRE LETTER BOOK B

December 20, 1832–
September 25, 1835

Fort Pierre 20th December 1832
Pierre Chouteau Jr. Esqr.
Agt: Amer: Fur Co.
Dear Sir

The favour of the 1st September was duly recd. as well as all the papers mentioned therein. I have for some time past waiting for the express from above; I have no doubt that Mr Hamilton and Mr. Lamont, have given you all the news of that country in detail; therefore I shall confine myself principally, to the occurrences of this district. When Mr. McKenzie left this last fall, he wrote me from Fort Lookout to supply Maj: Bean with goods sufficient to pay the Indians their annuities; which I did. Mr. Picotte arrived at Beans only three days after the boat I sent down; consequently, he made use of but few of our goods, which was fortunate for us; as his goods were much inferior to ours.

Majr. Bean left his place very abruptly; without seeing any of the Indians except the Yanctons; the consequence is, that all the plain Indians are very much dissatisfied, and no doubt we will be the sufferers; they complain that they are overlooked, and cannot be worse off; and have kill'd and stolen about fourty horses and Mules, (I believe in consequence.) However; there is nothing else for it, but to put up with it patiently.

I am sorry to inform you that our prospects for making Robes, in this part of the country is far from being flattering; true the season is not yet far advanced, and the weather so very mild that the Buffalos keep out on the plains; we have had a sad struggle to make a living this far, and if the Cattle do not soon make their appearance, we shall be placed in a most deplorable situation; my men are mostly all scattered about the different camps, and barely make out to subsist. I have not been able to get more than 100 pieces of meat, since Mr. McKenzie left us.

I only returned from a hunting excurtion a few days ago; necessity drove me to the plains; I packed wood upon horses and Mules four days out in the plains; our little party was fortunate enough to kill thirty Buffalos, which will keep us going for a few days, we were fortunate in having tolerable fine weather; as a severe snow storm would have killed every one of our horses; for we were destitute of any thing like shelter.

There appears to be some kind of mystery about

Mr. Papin's acct:, he is credited in this way; to full amount of his wages; Mr. Halsey says that he explain[ed] it in this way, that $50 of that was what Dickson owed him, which is correct; and that the other fifty, was a debt that Louis Ménard owed him; how he came to Cr[edit]. himself with that amount, I know not, as Ménard owes the Company upward of $150, and I told mr. Papin myself last year, when he asked me to Cr. Him with that amt:, how Ménard was situated, and that I could not give him Cr.; neither did I. Mr. Papin Brought here last fall 2 Horses, saddles, bridles &c:; he says you promised to take them, at the price he paid for them; if so, be kind enough to let me know, as it places me in a rather awkward situation.

Mr. Picotte brought up with him Jean Duchouquette a black man, which he says was verbally engaged by Mr Sarpy for the Co., of which I have no accounts; I thought that it was distinctly understood, that this black man was too expensive, and was not to be employed for this Outfit in future; I told him that if he was engaged by Mr. Sarpy, that it was all very well.

Be kind enough to let me know if Charles Vachards a/c in Saint Louis March 1832. $145.62 includes his advances there in August 1831. $44.50. I wish also that you would forward Baptiste Defonds A/c in fall, and abstract of his engagement for the present year. We would also like much, to have the Retai[l] Store Acct:.

John Sibelle came here last fall with two Pack horses, and the little remains they had from last year & with one hundred dollars worth of goods, which Mr. Picotte tells me father Bean let them have, will enable them to make some little trade. Hart is still at Fort Lookout, and Sibelle at Cherry river, where I understand he has a good many Deer Skins.

I have made out the order for the ensuing year, which you and Mr. McKenzie can curtail, or add to, as you think proper, when you find out how we are to be opposed.

I would fain Hope that you will not give up the idea, of paying us another visit in the spring. The paint store mentioned in the requisition is not wanted: we have found one, which will answer my purpose.

Yours Most Respectfully
(Sign'd.) William Laidlaw

❖ ❖ ❖

Fort Pierre 24th Dec: 1832
Mr. Emillion Primeau
Dear Sir

I this afternoon recd. yours of the 20th inst: I was very much provoked upon the arrival of your men here to find that they had lamed the mule from inattention; so much so, that it is impossible for her to return; indeed I dont think she will be fit for service this winter, which is a severe loss. It would appear that the time of the Clerks you have with you is very precious, why did not you send Bigéu or your brother along with them, to see that the companys property should be taken care of; I am far from thinking the property safe, under charge of such fellows, as I am well convinced even at the appearance of Indians, that they would run off and leave the goods; therefore if you wish the goods immediately that you mention, you will be kind enough to send some responsible person, to take charge of them, also to furnish them with provisions for their voyage.

If you cannot send in my meat, the men you have may remain with you for the present, as I have not the means of supporting them. With regards to your Keg having leaked out, is certainly being very unfortunate; I am much afraid that it has leaked by the bung on its way out; as I understand that it was perfectly light when it left this; if not by the bung, it must have got some hard usage, there can be no mistake about that. If you do not want the goods immediately, it is likely that I may have an opportunity of sending them up to your place, as soon as the express arrives from above; that is to say if the corn is safe.

I shall send a few of the articles requested, and every man who brings a mule or a horse here, with his back hurt from negligence, shall have the pleasure of packing a little himself. This plan ought to be generally adopted, then you would that sore backs would be a rare occurrence. I shall inclose you a list of articles sent by the men. Try and Trade as many good cords and parfleches[1] as possible.

I remain
Yours Most Respectfully,
(Sign'd.) William Laidlaw
To E. Primeau

❖ ❖ ❖

Fort Pierre 30th Decr. 1832
Jean P. Cabanné Esqr.
Otto Establishment
Dear Sir

I have been long waiting or the dispatches from above, to send off the Express for Saint Louis, the arrival of which affords me an opportunity, that I have not had before, of sending down your man (A. Raboin). Mr. Picotte would have sent him with the others, but there was no room in the Skiff for him, which was an unfortunate circumstance, as I have had no earthly use for him here.

We had a good deal of trouble, in procuring provisions necessary for the consumption of this fort. Buffalos have been scarce, and in consequence of the protracted mild state of the weather, they are still a great distance from us; and upon the whole, the prospect of the Robe return from this district, is far from being flattering, however, the season is not yet far advanced, and we must trust in better results; from the Accts: we have received from above, the prospects there, are equally poor. Be good enough to send back Guetard by the first opportunity; I shall inclose you his Acct:, as also that of Antoine Raboin. Be good enough to forward the accompanying packet without delay. Accept of the compliments of the season, and believe me Dear Sir,
 faithfully yours
 (Sign'd.) William Laidlaw
 To J. P. Cabanné Esqr.

❖ ❖ ❖

Fort Pierre 27th Decr: 1832
Mr. William Dickson
Dear Sir

Three days ago I duly recd. yours of the 15th inst:, and have given due attention to its contents. I have fulfilled your memorandum in full, and have sent you several other little articles; an account of which I shall inclose you. My object in sending these articles, is in consequence of what Henri he told me; that is, that you can procure about any quantity of meat from the Indians; it is an article that we have been, and are still, very short of: therefore I have to request that you will trade all that you possibly can; as it will be emmence the quantity that will be required here next spring.

With regard to the Blankets which you say were left in the store, I have no knowledge of them; neither have any of the Clerks that were in the store at the time, I very much fear, that they were stolen after your good men crossed on the other side.

In a former letter of yours, I observe that you wish me to say something regarding the rights of your trade; I think it unnecessary to say any thing on that head, as Mr. McKenzie made you fully acquainted with his sentiments on that subject. All that I would advise on the subject, is not to be the first aggressor; if they continue to entrude on your rights, you must then act on the defence; which is the first law of nature.

I have kept Lagrave here, in order to assist in getting out the canoes in the spring, as all the men I have are "pork eaters," one of whom I send you in his place.

I beg you will make your "pork eaters" no advances, except what is absolutely necessary, and keep them at work, should it be even to cut cord wood.

I hope you will keep a bright Lookout, not to get short of goods in the spring, but send here as early as possible for a supply, should you be in want.

Picotte tells me, he gave you[r] spy Glass and watch to Billon in St Louis, neither of which he could repair, and sent both to New York; so that you will not be able to get them before spring.

I have no news from above or below for some time past, but daily look for an express from both quarters. Cattle have been, and are now very scarce in this part of the country; I have been obliged to send the most of my men out to the different posts to live.

I would willingly send something for the "Black Lightening," but I am afraid to hunt. Hence with it, after what you told me last summer, so you must try and satisfy him; the best way you can, and if he comes here in the spring, I will endeavour to satisfy him. I am glad to hear that you have got back part of the horses which were stolen from here last fall, and I have no doubt that you will do every thing in your power, to get the rest of them. Wishing you all the compliments of the season, and my best wishes for yourself and family

I remain,
Your Most Obt. & humble servant,
(Sign'd) W. Laidlaw
To Mr. Wm. Dickson

❖ ❖ ❖

Fort Pierre January 1st 1833
Danl: Lamont Esqr.
Fort Clark
Dear Sir

Herewith inclosed you will receive your post account up to this date; upon reference to which you will see that all charges have been made and entered, in accordance with your directions; as also you will receive a note, given by W. P. May in favour of Scott and Gayon or order; I presume he will pay it without difficulty, it has already been charged to Upper Missouri Outfit.

I last had the pleasure of addressing you on the 23d. November per Mr. Picotte, at that time all documents for your place and Fort Union were forwarded, and I presume they came to hand, in due course. I shall go to work immediately, and prepare Ft. Union Account regulated as yours, a copy of which I hope to be able to send, by the St Louis Express. With the compliments of the season, Believe me Dr. Sir

Your Obt: & humble Servant,
William Laidlaw
(Sign'd) Per Jacob Halsey
To Danl. Lamont Esqr.
Fort Clark

❖ ❖ ❖

Fort Pierre 1st January 1833
Mr. Henri Picotte
Dr. Sir

Your favour of the 16th Ulto:, came safe to hand on the 29th, with regard to Mr. Lamonts to you I can say nothing on the subject, not knowing his views or object; however, all I can do for you, shall be done with pleasure. I shall send you two men to replace those he requested from you, I also send you a good long saw complete, which I hope will enable you to get two boats made; and if you succeed in making them, I hope they will be such as will answer to carry out our returns in the spring, (if we made any.) I would also have sent you some nails and old cordage, but as you say nothing about that, I have concluded that you expect to be supplied with these articles from F. Clark. Brasseau will leave this tomorrow with 6 trains, to go in quest of our corn; no "Pork eaters" could have acted more injuriously in that business, than Lachapelle done.

Inclosed you have a list of flour and Groceries sent you, I wish I had it in my power to supply you more liberally; but having such a host of people about me, I am short of these articles; however, every little helps in these squally times; we have been living here from hand to mouth, ever since you left us. I have not got a piece of Meat from one of our outposts, except 90 which J. Juett brought in. I have not heard from Pascal since he left this, I expect he must be (Booding). I heard by some indians that he has three or four of his horses killed, and two stole; he is always in "Misire," go when he will; I regret much that I cannot find his Credit book of last year. I expect that he was ashamed to shew it, as the Doctor says, that he never gave it in to the office; the only thing you can do, is to be as foxy as possible; by "sifting" them, they will declare upon each other.

We have as yet had no news from below; our express left this yesterday. I am glad to learn that you have the prospect of making some trade, I assure you our prospects in this part of the country, are of a very gloomy nature. Wishing you all the compliments of the season, not forgetting Frience [?].

I remain Dr. Sir,
Yours Truly
(Signd) William Laidlaw
To Honoré Picotte

❖ ❖ ❖

Fort Pierre January 1st 1833
James A. Hamilton Esqr.
Fort Union
Dear Sir

Your favor of the 24th November came safe to hand on the 29th Ulto:, and the express started for Saint Louis on the 31st. I sincerely trust that it may get down in time.

With regard to Mr. Roque, when I saw him last summer, we talked over a good many subjects, and amongst other things, the different tribes of Indians that inhabit the Upper Missouri; I think he told me that he spoke Blackfoot well, and two or three other languages, and could trade with several of their bands without the aid of a Interpreter if necessary; he then I believe inquired what Wages we gave; I told him from three to ten hundred dollars, and that I had no doubt but Mr. McKenzie would be glad to employ him; he then agreed to come to Fort Union in the spring, which I encouraged him to do; saying, that I was confident that he might make an advantageous arrangement for himself, and be useful to the company; but how he could come to say that I had engaged him for $100 for Fort Union, I know not.

I think the best thing he can do now since Mr. McKenzie is absent, is to return to Ree river, when Mr. McKenzie arrives, he can then write him the terms he would engage him on, and if they suit him, it is no great distance for him to come back.

Mr. Roque is a decent respectable man of his standing, and is considered generally to have a good deal of influence amongst the Indians he is acquainted with; I understand by Crawford, that he is much in want of some little supplies, if so, I think it would be well to advance him for $30 or $40.

J. D. Begué says that he heard something about our order, but for what, or how much, he does not know, but believes it was only for a trifle.

I shall send you some old news papers, notwithstanding they are old, they will still serve to beguile a little of your spare time (if you have any.) We have had no news from below since Mr. Picotte came up, as soon as the express arrives, I shall lose no time in forwarding it, when I hope to be able to send you some papers of a later date. I have no doubt that long ere this reaches you, that Mr. Lamont will have opened his budget to you; I regret much that his stay was so short in this place; however, I hope we shall all met in spring once more. We have had a hard struggle to make a living here, the weather has been, and still is so fine, that the Cattle keep far out in the plains. All our Outposts in this part of the country are in a starving situation. I am much affraid that our returns will make but a sorry appearance in spring. Accept my dear sir of the compliments of the season, and Believe Me to
   remain Yours Most Truly
   (Sign'd.) William Laidlaw
   To J. A. Hamilton Esqr.

❖ ❖ ❖

Fort Pierre 4th January 1833
Mr. G. P. Cerré
Dear Sir

I have been long expecting to hear from you, but have been hitherto disappointed. I have had various reports of you from the Indians, but there is so little confidence to be put in their reports in general, that I have paid little attention to them. Amongst others, I heard that you had got two of your Jackasses killed, and 1 Mule, and that you had plenty of meat, and might have, and if you chose to send for it to the Brulé camp; the latter report I can scarcely believe, knowing that you were well aware of our destitute situation at this place for want of provisions; at all events, I think you ought to have let me know how you were getting on, and if there be any chance of getting a supply of provisions from you soon. I hope you will make it convenient for you to write me, immediately on the receipt of this. I have heard from all the other posts except yours; I think if I remember right, Mr. McKenzie complained of you on the same ground last year.

The Express left this on the 31st Ulto: for St Louis, and if they meet with no accident, I think they will get down in good time. I look for one dayly from below. Buffaloe are scarce in this part of the country, the only place where I hear of their being plenty is a the Little Chyenne, but even there, they cannot make meat fast enough for us, I have upwards of 70 mouths to feed here daily. In hopes of hearing from you soon, with a good stock of meat. I remain
   Yours Truly
   (Sign'd.) William Laidlaw
   To Mr. G. P. Cerré

❖ ❖ ❖

Fort Pierre January 5th 1833
James A. Hamilton Esqr.
Fort Union
Dear Sir

Herewith inclosed you will receive your post a/c up to the present priced, upon [word?] to which you will perceive that we have done away with the advance of 100 Per cent usually charged on Outfits, and charged you with the advances made to the men furnished last summer, the accounts of whom I have closed by a charge to your post, when they will of course remain open for continuations. As also I have charged you with the time of sundry persons, whose engagements either expired last fall or December. By the first opportunity have the goodness to let me know whether all is understood, and if the balance in your books corresponds with that which you will receive herewith.

I do not recollect whether I have heretofore furnished you with Jean Marchands Account here last spring; however, I think I have not, consequently I have made it out, and you will now receive it; as also those of Michel Carrier and Janus Parker (beaver trappers,) who I understand are in your neighbourhood; I have thought it best not to charge their notes, till you advise us of the payment thereof.

I have not recd. your invoice of Mdse: per S. B. Yellowstone yet, but I presume it is forthcoming.

We have been for some time looking for the Express from below, but it has not yet made its appearance; so soon as it comes to hand, dispatches will be made up for Fort Union, when I hope to be able to send you some News from the civilized world, in the Meantime, Believe me Dear Sir

Yours Most Truly
(Sign'd.) William Laidlaw
James A. Hamilton Esqr.
Fort Union

❖ ❖ ❖

Fort Union 10th January 1833
Daniel Lamont Esqr.
Fort Clark
Dear Sir

I have yours of the 15th Ulto, and hasten to give you the accounts and explanations required, all of which you will find herewith.

When the papers sent you for Mr. Crawford were to hand, you will perceive that the sum of 112 in Phillip Gaillaucys account is an overcharge, instead of additional advances made him; the amt: of his advances here is $35.01 instead of $39.13; as also, you will see that my acct: for horses &c: furnished H. Picotte amounts to $190.60 exclusive of groceries, provisions &c. fwd. him for the trip up, the account of which, amounts to $3.67, making in all $198.27.

I have made enquiry of Mr. Brown regarding the Pitsaw files delivered you; he says that you took 14 doz:, the number kept here was 6 doz:, making in all 20 doz:, which is the quantity sent from Saint Louis; they were charged to Fort Clark, as it was supposed you might probably retain a few, for the use of that post.

Mr. Halsey says Mr. McKenzie never spoke to him of the new mode of keeping the books, neither did he even receive orders to do away the advances of 100 per cent, untill the reception of your letter from Mr. Crawford; otherwise, it would have been done in the first instance.

The amount of Alexis Dusseau a/c you will receive in detail, if it is erroneous the mistake must I think be, in his account at Fort Clark as transferred here, when he last left for above, his a/c was forwarded; but if I recollect right, he disputed he correctness of it.

I forwarded an account against Charboncais per Crawford, who surprised me by saying that there was no charge against him at the Mandans, which I cannot account for, as the same was forwarded per "Yellowstone" last June; fearing he will dispute it, I send it also in detail.

In your a/c current you have omitted crediting this post with 1 frying Pan $1, delivered you last October; when this is done, our books will agree.

I am at present much occupied in preparing documents for Saint Louis, and must beg you to excuse me for not forwarding a/c current by the present opportunity. I will not fail to do so by the next.

Believe me Ever
Yours Truly,
(Sign'd.) William Laidlaw
To D. Lamont Esqr.
Fort Clark

❖ ❖ ❖

[translated from French]
Fort [Pierre] 15th January 1833
Mr. Emillien Primeau
Sir

Your letter via Bigué arrived today as well as the goods you mentioned. I am surprised you write that I had picked a soldier to guard your establishment, something I am entitled to do in any event; but since I wrote you not to mention this matter I don't know on what basis you are so bold as to give me such reproach. As for the Indians of whom you speak, I believe that it is left to my decision to make such gifts to him as I find useful without fearing rebuke on your part. I do not believe that I am required to deal with you over a trifle. However, Sir, since you believe the appointments and favors that I make are done to your prejudice I will make pains to give you notice on this matter that no doubt you will [not take?] a perverse pleasure when I [word?].

I believe it necessary to turn the discussion to another subject[;] all the reports are that it is absolutely impossible to obtain provisions at your establishment. It seems to me that it will be better to take your goods and to go to the houses on the Little Cheyenne, or to Point of Rocks at Cibelle's post which should be in good enough shape except for the chimneys, and then you will be useful to us for provisions, furs, and if the animals continue to be abundant.

I hope that you will condescend to my wishes and if you cannot take all your goods and your robes, you can send to me via Mr. Brasseau what he can carry and also the meat that you don't need to haul with you when you go. the animal business will do me a great deal of good at this time because provisions are very scarce.

I send you an inventory of what I have sent for the present and I propose sending you Pierre Ortubise as soon as possible to help with the trade or with dealing with the Indians. And recommend to you that you keep an eye on the drinking of which you should be aware. As soon as you are in your houses I will send you all the goods you need to trade at your house. You will send me a list when you know what you are lacking something and I will send it to you by return mail.

I am Sir your servant
Signed William Laidlaw
Mr. Emillien Primeau

❖ ❖ ❖

Fort Pierre January 31st 1832
Mr. Emillien Primeau
Dear Sir

The meat which you left at your establishment I duly received; the Robes I am sorry to say I found a great defficiency in their being 14 Calves, and One Epichimore [Apishimore] worth 6¼ cts. I have to request that in future you will not trade Epichemors for Robes; if obliged to trade them, not to give more than one fourth, or one fifth of the price, of a merchantable Robe for them, neither can we afford to give the full value of a Robe, for a Calf Skin.

As Mr. G. P. Cerré has been obliged to abandon his post in consequence of the Indians having left that part of the country, I send him up with his outfit, to cooperate with you in using every exertion possible, to procure provisions; his Equipment will no doubt be wanted at your place, should he not go father up, which rests with himself; he will be governed by circumstances when he gets to your place. We are entirely out of meat, but I expect to get relief from you soon, as I understand that you are surrounded with that article.

I hope you are in a place of safety in case of high water. If not, you ought to take measures to get the property placed out of danger, try and send me by the first opportunity a few Parfleches, 40 or 50 would not be too many. I remain
Yours Most Respectfully,
(Sign'd.) William Laidlaw
Mr. Emillien Primeau

❖ ❖ ❖

Fort Pierre 6th Febuary 1833
Mr. Henry Picotte
Dear Sir

Mr. "Sunga-Wites" dropt in upon us yesterday afternoon, but as he has no pasport or letter of introduction from you, I have paid but little attention to his "histories," notwithstanding I have paid him some attention, having known him formerly to be a good Indian.

Since I last wrote you, Pascal has been obliged to abandon his post on White river, in consequence of all the Indians having been obliged to leave that part of the country; they have been in a state of starvation all winter, and have suffered most dreadfully, many of them have gone towards the Platte, and others somewhere about the Ree Villages; I have not heard a word of Mr. Papin for two months past; Campbell has been starving all winter, he has lived a good deal of the time on four dogs; the Chyennes and Rees have all crossed the Black hills some time ago; we are here living from hand to mouth, God only knows what we shall do in spring, if we can make out a living till that time; we cannot eat meat of any consequence of the Indians, neither for love nor money; they appear to be determined to starve us out; let me again impress upon you the necessity of procuring a large stock of provisions at your place, if there be any possibility of getting it. "Coute que Coute." ["Cost what it will"] If any opportunity should offer, I wish you would write Mr. Lamont to try and procure some corn for us in the spring; perhaps the best way of making him acquainted with our situation, would be to forward him this. It is generally reported that a great many of the Indians with you, intend carrying their Robes to some place appointed by Moore, where Narcisse Funier is to meet them with goods; I have no doubt you will keep a bright lookout.

I would write Mr. Lamont were I sure of its reaching him, which I think is very uncertain. We have had no news from below yet, I have given up all hopes of a winter Express. I send you by this opportunity Pascals Credit book; I hope it will still be in time for you to recover, at least a few of the debts. The Bearer of this has promised to take the horse the "Dogs shadow" stole from here, or kill him if he cannot get him; I would rather he should kill him, than the fellow should have the use of him.

I remain
Yours Truly,
(Sign'd.) William Laidlaw
To Mr. H. Picotte

❖ ❖ ❖

Fort Pierre 6th Febuary 1833
Messrs. Primeau & Cerré
Gentlemen

Your two men Girard and Vinette, arrived here on the 4th inst: with 1 mule, and three horses, with only about 30 pieces of Meat, after having been lost for some time, they also lost the letter you gave them, and cannot tell why, or wherefore, they were sent here; however, I think it advisable to send them back with all the horses except one, which they allowed to get astray while here. You must make a bold effort to get some meat, if you should be obliged to send me Bigéu, Alfred, Ortubise and Vinette, all to be at this place by the 15th of this month, I shall send you others in their place if necessary.

We will require at least 100 good Parfleches, and as many good cords as possible; also a few green hides to cover riding saddles, in the Meantime, Believe me to be
Yours Most Respectfully
(Sign'd.) William Laidlaw
To Messrs. Primeau and Cerré

❖ ❖ ❖

Fort Pierre January 31st 1833
Danl: Lamont Esqr.
Fort Clark
Dear Sir

When I last had the pleasure of addressing you, I had not examined your Inventory of Nov: last; Multiplicity of business prevented me from doing so before that time; however, since then, I have had leisure to go over it, and have discovered the following errors, the balance of which will be a charge to this post, and it has been accordingly entered to credit of Fort Clark Outfit. In the first place 3½ lbs. of Candlewick @ 29c pr. lb. was extended 91c. instead of 100c, difference 10 cts., 2d. 1/6 doz: 8 in: ½ round files @ 252 pr. doz: was extended 43c. instead of 42c. difference 1c, and 3d. 14 doz: Oval fire steels @ 72c was extended 1708 instead of 1008, difference $7 making in all the sum of 6.91 to credit of your Outfit.

I have balanced C. Greenwoods a/c; as also, I have charged your post with the sum of $233.50, which sum you say in your letter of 29th Ulto., has been received for the same.

On the 3d. July last, Mr. Crawford sent us an account against James Kipp, amounting to $143.38 for advances made him at Fort Clark, from 12th January 1831, to 16th Febuary following, on my examining his general a/c, I found that he had previously been charged with $133.24 of the former amount, which left a balance of $10.14 there chargeable to him; as also, at the same time, we were furnished with his a/c at F. C. December 1831, in amount $29. making in all $39.14 which sum was accordingly charged to Kipp, and Fort C. duly credited for the same. Then again in October, we received sundry accounts for A. Harvey and among them James Kipp at the Mandans, which was there stated to be from 16th June 1831, to 24th June 1832 amounting to $86.38 which of course included the $9 in December 1831, leaving a balance chargeable to Kipp of $57.38 after the reception of the documents per Harvey. I had strong hopes of being able to rectify this troublesome a/c, but since I have had leisure to examine those of 10th November last, at which period his acct: was again transferred $39.28, I have been led to Show, that I am as far from right as ever, his a/c here at the present moment, stands thus, Viz:

10.14 to 16th June 1831
29.14 to December 1831
57.38 to 24th June 1832
39.25 to 10th Nov 1832

135.80 which sum is balanced by charge to Fort Clark; consequently I have charged your post with $56.53 which with $79.27 heretofore charged with his account here, as also I have charged F. C. with the sum of $20 paid Mr. G. Catlin, for a portrait delivered [to] James Kipp,[2] and have given him credit for the same, in all $155.80.

By first conveyance, please have the goodness to give me the means of correcting this a/c, if it is still erroneous. You have given us Cr. For the amount of Mr. Belhumeurs a/c of $238.70, which does not agree with his a/c here. You shall have it in detail, so that you will be able to discover the error. Upon reference to the account current herewith, you will perceive the [word?] that has taken place since my last communication; among sundry late charges, you will find one for advance to Thomas Dumond at this place last summer, amounting to $9.85. When he left here for the Mandans, I wrote Mr. Kipp that he was indebted to the Co. $10, a few days after his departure, I discovered that our store keeper had made an error in his a/c of 15 cts, which make the difference.

I have charged you with Lewis Crawfords a/c $299.41 and have given him Credit for the same amt: although we have not that much to his debit on the books here. Kipp in his a/c current of 10th November last, claims credit for advances to him $256.41, his a/c at Ft. Union as transferred here 30th June last, is $36.75, making only $293.06, how is this? Mr. Kipp has also sent us an account of advances to Ely Harding (Nov: 11th last) as you have not given fort Pierre credit for the amount of his a/c $105.13, I presume he is at Fort Union, and have consequently, made my entries accordingly.

Be good enough to furnish me with abstract of James Kipps engagement with the Co. for the present year. We have as yet received no news from below, and begin to give up all hopes of a winter express; consequently, I know not when dispatches will be made up for your neighbourhood, and will close my letter, with the intention of forwarding it, by the first opportunity

Believe me Dear Sir
Most Respectfully,
Your Obdt: and humble servant,
William Laidlaw
(Sign'd) Per Jacob Halsey
To Danl: Lamont Esqr.

❖ ❖ ❖

Fort Pierre 10th Febuary 1833
Messrs. Lacompt and Primeau
Gentlemen

I send Demeray the bearer of this, for the purpose of guiding Chatillion and Steboiné to this place, I wish you to send them here without a moments delay; you no doubt by this time have got all the wood necessary cut for the Steam Boat, at the different places that I mentioned to you; if not, you must get it done with the other two men.

You will require to keep a sharp lookout for the Poncaws, it is likely they will have a good deal of Beaver, take care that your opponents do not get the start of you; dont let your men know that you have any idea of going after them, as they would be sure to let the thing leak out.

There is a Yancton called the Pipe, who stole a mule from this; I understand that he is somewhere in the neighbourhood of Fort Lookout, if so; I hope you will be able to recover it, and send it up by the men, if you can get it in time to send by them.

We are still very short in the way of Provisions, I hope you have been more fortunate in that respect. Again let me impress upon your mind, the necessity of keeping a bright Lookout for the trade; every other kind of work must give place to that.

Yours Truly,
(Sign'd). William Laidlaw

❖ ❖ ❖

Fort Pierre 11th Feby. 1833.
Mr. Pierre D. Papin
Dear Sir

Your favour of the 2d. inst: I duly recd. Per Champeau; I have detained him here for some time, being in daily expectation of men from below, it is now a month and a half since our men started with the express, and yet we have had no tidings of them; so with regard to news from that quarter, we are as much in the dark as Yourself.

I am sorry to hear that you have been so situated, so as to put it entirely out of your power, to lay up a stock of provisions; it has been pretty much the same all over this part of the country, we have been living from hand to mouth all winter; we cannot procure any meat of consequence from the Indians; they keep continually threatening to kill our horses, so we were obliged to abandon the chase altogether, from the Mandans down to the Little Chyenne, the Missouri has been [word?] with Buffaloe all winter.

Pascal has been obliged to abandon his post on White river, in consequence of the Indians having left that section of the country, being compelled to do so, from starvation. Pascal is now above, somewhere about Dog Island[3] below the Ree Village, trying to lay in a stock of Meat for the spring. J. Juett was here about ten days ago from the Ogallallah. I hear from Campbell that they have been on the eve of starving all winter; but notwithstanding, he expects to make about 400 packs of Robes, and requests me to send him 20 efficient men to bring down his canoes; he says that the Chyenne at his place, has been open for some time past; he means to make light loads as far as your place, when he proposes taking in a full cargo; I think his plan good, and as we cannot supply him with a sufficient number of men; I wish you to send back Champeau to this place, without a moments delay, and another man with him if you possibly can; the men will leave this, on or about the 16th.

The doctor will send you the Castor oil and salts. Picotte has had plenty of Cattle all winter, and expects to be able to make a good deal of meat. Wishing you all manner of happiness, and a good trade, I remain
Yours Truly
(Sign'd) William Laidlaw
Mr. Pierre D. Papin

❖ ❖ ❖

Fort Pierre 12th Febuary 1833
James A. Hamilton Esqr.
Fort Union
Dear Sir

On the 5th Ulto. I last had the pleasure of addressing you a few lines, when I duly notified you of our new mode of keeping the books, and furnished you with an account of mens Wages and advances, chargeable to your post; in lieu of the advance of 100 per cent, which has been exploded; all of which, I hope have been duly received before the present period.

Since the date of my last, a very considerable alteration has taken place in the a/c; for particulars of which, I refer you to the inclosed account current. Among other changes, you will find an additional a/c of Wages of Clerks, Interpreters & Voyageurs belonging to your Outfit. As also, you will perceive that I have charged you with the Equipment fusd. [furnished] Clerks, Interpreters and voyageurs at F. U. $532.22 which sum, was previously to credit of Fort Union.

The Equipments furnished men engaged in St Louis last March, will be charged you, so soon as the Amer. Fur Co. retail store Acct: comes to hand; which by the bye, ought to be forthcoming. We have not had a word from Saint Louis, since the last of August. The men sent down with your first Express, left here the 31st of December; and the bearer of the sad intelligence of the melancholy end of Mr. Vanderburg, left us in the 11th ulto; still, we have this far, had no tidings of either party.

I have not charged you with Mr. Lafreniers[4] Salary, as I am unacquainted with the amount of it for the present year. I have written to the office of the Amer. Fur Co. in St Louis, more than once, for an abstract of his Engagement, but have as yet not received it.

Buffaloe have been very scarce in this section of the country all winter; we have had much difficulty in procuring provisions for our men, and we find it impossible to lay up a stock for the spring, so that our present condition is by no means flattering, for we expect lots of folk here in April.

Please remember me to Chardon and Lafraniere, and Believe me ever,
Very Truly Yours,

William Laidlaw
Per Jacob Halsey
James A. Hamilton Esqr.
(Official)

❖ ❖ ❖

[Fort Pierre: no date]
Mr. Emillien Primeau
Dear Sir

I have been long looking for some arrivals from your place with a supply of Meat, but as they do not make their appearance and we are getting scarce of meat, I send P. Ortubise with 2 horses in the expectation that you have laid up a stock; if so, you will be good enough to send down as many horses loaded as you possibly can, I am very anxious to get a little good fresh meat to put into our Ice house to give the S. B. folks a treat when they come; If you have none, I told Pierre to try and get some.

I am much surprised at the question you put to me, to know whether Pascal or yourself is in charge of the post you know very well you was put in charge of the post and untill such time as that charge is taken from you [you] must consider yourself responsable.

By the return of Pierre if you are in want of any thing for the trade let me know and I will send up again such things as you may be in need of.

I intend to write Pascal to get one or two canoes made, you will require to furnish him with a man or two for that purpose. I have been out to surround but was not successful. No news yet from below. I heard from your brother who is at Fort Lookout a few days ago, he was well

Believe me Yours
(Sign'd) William Laidlaw

❖ ❖ ❖

Fort Pierre 23d. April 1833
Mr. James Kipp
Fort Clark
Dear Sir

Herewith inclosed you will receive Ft. Clark a/c current up to the 18th inst: and A: Bellhumeur a/c in detail.

On the 3d. July last Mr. Crawford sent us an a/c against you, amounting to $143.35 for advances made you at F. C. from 12th Jany. 1831 to 16th June following; on my examining your general a/c, I found that you had previously been charged with $133.26 of the former amount, which left a balance of $10.16 there chargeable to you; as also at the same time, we were furnished you're a/c at F. C. Dec: 1831 in amount $29, making in all $39.16 which sum was accordingly charged to you, and F. C. only credited for the same.

Then again in Oct: we recd. Sundry a/cs per A. Harvey, and among them yours at the Mandanes, which was then stated to be from 16th June 1831 to 24th June 1832, amounting to $86.38 which of course included the $29 in Dec: 1831, leaving a balance chargeable to you of $57.35; and Nov: 10th we recd. You're a/c at F. C. $39.25 at the present moment it stands thus, exclusive of a/c at F. C. while under charge of Mr. Lamont, Viz

$10.14 to 16th June 1831
29.14 to Decbr. 1831
57.38 to 244th June 1832
39.28 to 10th Nov: 1832
135.80

$79.27 of this sum was charged to F. C. while under charge of Mr. Lamont, the balance which I now charge you is $76.53, which sum includes $20 paid Mr. Catlin for a Portrait, as M. Bellhumeur a/c dos not agree with our Books here, You shall have it in detail so that you may be able to discover the error; upon reference to it, you will perceive it does not include his a/c at the Mandanes as transferred here by Mr. Lamont.

Among other charges you will find one for advances to T. Dumond at this place last summer, amounting to $9.55; when he left here for the Mandan's last summer, I wrote you that he was indebted to the Co. $10, a few days after he left this, I discovered that our store keeper had made an error in his a/c of 15 cts. which makes the difference.

Believe me ever
Your Most Humble Servant
William Laidlaw
(Sign'd.) per Jacob Halsey
Mr. James Kipp
Fort Clark
(Official)

❖ ❖ ❖

Fort Pierre 20th April 1833
James A. Hamilton Esqr.
Fort Union
Dear Sir

Your favour of 19th Jany. Came safe to hand on the 16th inst: at which time Mr. Lamont arrived from Ft. C. with the returns of that post; Upon returning to a/c current herewith you will perceive I have paid due attention to your advices.

Among other documents you will receive Chevaliers, Belloires, & Decotemes a/cs. but I think it probable we will see them, before you do.

We have not yet recd. The particulars from St. Louis of A. Lutemans Engagement and advances; so soon as they come to hand, I will attend to your request regarding them.

You will perceive that I have given you credit for Harvey's a/c. I thought it prudent to do so, as it is more than probable that he will not return to Ft. Union, he is now here, and talks of going down to St. Louis.

I have made enquiries regarding the goods charged to Ft. Union by Ree Outfit. Lachapelle says there can be no mistake about the matter; that they were delivd. Ft. Union by S. B. Yellowstone June last.
Believe me Ever
Yours most Humble Servant
(Sigd.) Jacob Halsey
(Official)

❖ ❖ ❖

Fort Union June 26th 1833
Mr. Laidlaw
Dear Sir

I have received from J Halemont two mares and one colt which he was received of [word?] river per Steamboat with his woman, but I have thought it better to request [word?] to deliver to her on her arrival at Fort Pierre Two good mares one with a colt at her side which you will charge to this Post. Untill Halemont Woman can find her people, please give her board and lodging in pursuance of my promise to her husband.
Ever Yours faithfully
K/ McKenzie

❖ ❖ ❖

Fort Pierre 2d. Augt 1833
Mr. James Kipp
Dear Sir

Your per Steam Boat *Assiniboine*[5] I duly received, this will be handed to you by Mr Crawford whom I sent up with Louis Frenier with letters for Mr. McKenzie. I have to request you to forward them without a moments delay, you must try and furnish Frenier with a canoe to return to this place. By the time this reaches you I have little doubt but our opponents will have arrived[6] at Your place & it is unnecessary for me to say any thing on that head. I hope it will be with you as it has been with us, the nature of their coming was much more injurious than the reality itself, they no doubt will have a little [word?] at the first outset, but it will not last. You know a new broom sweeps clean, them that have remained here are, as far as I can judge entirely ignorant of the Indian Character and are not calculated in my opinion to do much injury.

Mr. McKenzie no doubt has told you how to proceed with things, therefore I shall rest asured that you will do every thing for the best, untill the Mandans change very much their mode of preceeding I think it highly probable that they ~~might~~ may find themselves without a fort next spring, which if they know it is their only safety if we have no fort there the Sioux would make a general attack upon them, the Sioux feels quite indignant at the attacks the Grosventres made upon this place, and I am persuaded before long will pay them honed [?] with interest.

If Sublette leaves a post at the Yanctonay You will require to look after it for the present as I have not the means of establishing it just now, and Crawford will give all the news of this place, in the mean time,
believe me
Dear Sir Yrs. Most truly
Wm. Laidlaw
To Mr. James Kip

❖ ❖ ❖

Fort Pierre 29th August 1833
Pierre Chouteau Esqr.
Dear Sir

On this day Mr. Provost arrived from the Mountains bringing with him [blank] packs of Beaver. Mr Fontenelle in his letter to me stated that he laboured under some disadvantage by being so late and that he lost 5 or 6 packs of Beaver in consequence of Mr Subletts caravan arriving there before him 8 or 9 days. I would send the beaver down immediately but there is no person here that can steer a boat well, nor no persons that I can safely put in charge of the cargo, neither have I any craft sufficiently strong to car[r]y it with safety, But I expect a Mackinaw from the Yellow Stone soon.

I see a letter addressed to You from Mr Fontinelle which suppose contained all the intelligence relative to his expedition.

Mr Sublettes Boat arrived here on the 17th of July, one of which stoped a little below old Fort Tecumseh and commenced building,[7] the other proceeded up the Missouri and arrived at the Mandans, on the 7th or 8th of August. I thought that at first they would have a considerable men of [word?], but time has proved it otherwise. A few days ago 60 or 70 Lodges of the Ogallallahs, encamped part here and part at his house.

They had but few Robes and I believe I got the most of them. Upon the whole the Indians appear to be much dissatisfied with their reception and with the whole concern. At the Mandans they were received in the following manner. They held a council for the distributions of presents at which *"The four Bears"* presided. Sublette gave them a little powder and a few balls tied up in a handkerchief. They asked him if this was the great present they expected from the Americans, and upon being told it was all they were to get, they Knoked it to one side and told him to go away as soon as possible. He then gave them a Keg of Powder, but they remained as much exasperated as before, for upon examination the Keg was found to be tap[p]ed and about the half taken out. However they took his present and Dougherty is left in charge of that post. This much I had from Mr Crawford who was there at the time. I went to "Lake qui Parle"[8] on the 11th of July but cold hear nothing of the news from Montreall. (They arriv'd here however, on the 18th of August in charge of Dr M Kenny). He says they were [word?] much on account of the Cholera and, that 7 of them died of that disease, amongst whom was Mr Rosson, the Clerk there in charge. [Two words?] directed and the remainder consisting of 29 arrived here in good health. The Men unfortunate in not receiving by then their accounts of advances and their engagements of the men. They were lost or stolen at the Portage of the "Ouis coulis" and Fox River [in Wisconsin]. You will please write for them and forward the same as soon as possible as it is indispensably necessary that they should be here.

I have Started our traders to their wintering grounds and experienced much inconvenience from the abscence of Messrs Papin Picotte &c who should have been here before now. However I have done the best I could with those here. We are much in need of Provisions just now. There are no Buffalos nearer than 5 or 6 days march and owing to the scarcity of meat nearly all our provisions of flour & pork has been consumed.

The goods at the "Bluffs" are much needed. We can scarcely make out an entire equipment without them, and look anxiously for the arrival of the Boat. I recd your letter from Prairie du Chien, and will attend to the contents immediately. The water has been in a fine stage for Steamboating from the time the Assiniboine left here untill the 15th of August when it commenced falling gradually. I have received no late news from the Yellow Stone but expect a boat soon

Mr Respectfull
Your Most obt Set
Wm Laidlaw
Fr P. Chouteau Esqr.

❖ ❖ ❖

Fort Pierre 28th September 1833
Pierre Chouteau Jr Esquire
Dear Sir

By the bearer Mr Patton you will receive the beaver sent you by Mr Fontenelle from the Mountains. You will also receive all the papers and letters designed for St Louis. Paper #1 is a statement of accounts of the men who are going down in the boat. It was drawn by Mr Hamilton. I have examined the accounts on our Books, and find they are correct. #2 is a recapitulation of balances of the same accounts, drawn by me and which correspond with those sent to you from Fort Union. #3 is a memorandum of Outfit required for the Rocky Mountain Expedition of 1834. I do not know how many Horses he will require: he says in his letter to me (of which a copy is hereby sent you) that he had sent me a memorandum of Horses Mules &c &c, required for his expedition, but I immagine that he must have forgotten to send it, for no such memorandum arrived here by Mr Proveau. Paper #4 is W. E. Primeau's account with the AFCoy. #5 is a Bill of Lading of the Furs, &c. sent down by the Mackinaw Boat of which Mr Patton has charge. The account of Eli Harding is attached to paper #2, that of Alfred Travers is not needed he stopping at Fort Clark. Those who have got advances here, you will find the sum set opposite their names on paper #2 which accounts please deduct from the balances due them. All of which papers &c &c I hope will in due time be received by you.

Messrs. Papin & Picotte with their [blank] consisting of 22 Horses arrived here on the 21st of this month. The Keel Boat had passed the Bluffs 10 days before they got there, and Mr Papin did not get on board of her as directed by you. Today Mr Picotte leaves this with some men to meet her and assist in bringing her up as soon as possible. I cannot yet give you any account of the prospects of this year's trade. Buffaloe begin to make their appearance 2 days march from here. Mr McKenzie will I have no doubt give you all the country news from above as he is busy writing. I send you a copy of Mr Fontenelle's Letter to me, from his Rendezvous: and refer you to that for the news of that quarter. We are all well here.

    Most Respectfully
    Your Obedient Servant
    Wm. Laidlaw
    Per E. T. Denig

❖ ❖ ❖

Fort Pierre 18th October 1833
Mr J. A Hamilton
Dear Sir

I hereby send you the accounts of the men, which you requested me send, by Mr Crawford, part of them are the same accounts that have been sent up twice before, but there was something about them which could not be understood, that something I have explained to Mr McKenzie to his satisfaction. It consisted in giving Beaugard and others Cr. For more than the amount of their annual wages; now, upon examination of Beaugard's a/c as I now send it you will see he has a credit for $57.62 "by charge to Fort Clark." There, the same $57.62 is charged back again to Fort Pierre and are included in the "a/c of Fort Pierre" against Beaugard. He has therefore been first charged with the articles here to the amot. of 57.62; afterwards he was charged at Fort Clark for the same amot. which is an entry twice made, for the same articles consequently he should receive Cr. For $57.62. I think that this is sufficiently plain, and the others are in the same state. You may depend upon these accounts being correct and fix your Books to correspond with the same.

Paper #2 is an Invoice of Goods taken to Fort Union from Fort Pierre in Steam Boat Assiniboine being part of Outfit 1833, for Fort Union. The accounts now standing charged to Fort Union are, as marked on Paper #3, which are the same as before with the addition of Alfred Travers $22. These you will observe are only those who are in debt here which is all I can charge Fort Union with, and the Credits stand in the others favor untill balanced by the acts. from Fort Union against them. The statement of mens wages I cannot now furnish you with, the book or papers on which they were entered cannot now be found, but as soon as Mr Halsey arrives and I can find their act: of wages for ending 1834, I will forward it to you. The weight of Iron and Tobacco I cannot furnish at present as it has been confused with other articles of the same kind before me in the store. The sash was credited to the act: of F. Dechaine as you will perceive by reference to his account. Also this man has been charged with loss of wages by desertion. The errors in Buffaloe Robes, Tallow, & Calico, are rectified. In your letter to me of May last you advise to give J. Lajunnesse five dollars and charge the same to Fort Union. In your last per Mr Crawford you say it must not be charged to that Post which is the proper place. If there is any other accts. yet wanting or if these be not sufficiently plain I will furnish you at any time others and answer any questions concerning them you think proper to propose. You will also receive per Mr McKenzie an "Invoice of Goods sent from here by Keel Boat "Argo," which I was not able to complete in consequence of the Invoices of Goods for 1832, having not arrived from St Louis, as soon as they do arrive, you may expect the prices to the articles above referred to.

Most Respectfully
Your Mo: Obedt. Servant
(signed) Wm Laidlaw
per E. T. Denig
(Official)

P.S. Please examine whether Mr Chardon was charged with 10 yds fancy calico, an a/c of which was sent to F. U. some time since.

Wm. L.

❖ ❖ ❖

Fort Pierre 17th Octr. 1833
Mr James Kipp
Dear Sir

By Mr McKenzie you will receive the papers and Letters designed for your Post. Paper #1 is an Invoice of the articles shipped for F. C. from F. P. per Keel Boat Argo. As most of the articles sent were goods of this year, and the Invoice not having arrived I could not send you all the prices of the goods and have left them blank, untill the Invoice comes, then at the first opportunity you may expect ~~to have~~ a Bill of the same with the prices thereof.

There is in the Boat a small parcel for you, also a Bundle, Bandbox and Trunk for Belhumeur, but for these and all the rest of the goods for Fort Clark, have reference to the "Bill of Shipment." I have charge Bonaventure Lebrun with the amots. of his a/c from Fort Union, as directed by Mr Hamilton, you will therefore please *not* make an entry against him for the same a/c. Also the Accts. of Pierre Ortubise and L. Crawford from Fort Union are charged against them at this post. Please send me the amount of B. Lebrun's salary, for the year. I have a Note in my hands against Denius Angé Guerin for the sum of seventy four Dollars and 96 cents, please take a memorandum of the same in order that you may regulate his advances accordingly. Alfred Travers is in debt for this year, you will therefore be carefull about advancing him.

Most Respectfully
Your Mo. Obt. Servant
(signed) Wm. Laidlaw

❖ ❖ ❖

Fort Union 30th October 1833
Mr Colin Campbell
Dear Sir

Yours of the 23rd Inst., I duly received per Joe Juett yesterday. I am sorry to learn that the Buffaloe keep at such a distance from you but I am in hopes that they will come nearer as the season advances. I have completed your memorandum and even sent you more than you requested in order that you may have every advantage over your opponents. I am fully persuaded that you do not require to be better assorted than them to give you an advantage over them, but still am willing to give you every advantage if we do not come out with flying colours this year, it is of no avail to have people fully acquainted with the Indian character and speak the Language as fluently as themselves, & who has had experience enough to know them from within. You no doubt are well aware of the confidence I have in your experience in the way of maneuvering the Indians and your opponents at the same time I beseech of you not to leave a stone unturned Robes and peltries are the order of the day and from your acknowledged vigilence & activity I have no doubt but you will meet my most sanguine expectations spare no trouble nor expense to accomplish the views of the company. I was much disappointed that Joe did not bring in any Horses for us but he explained the impossibility of getting any for the present however I have no doubt but in the course of the winter you will be able to pick up a good many. We had a visit from Mr McKenzie lately and he took along with him every one that was fit for service. Messrs Papin and Picotte arrived from St Louis about 8 weeks ago, the Cholera has made sad havoc there last summer, God only knows when it will end. I send you Bellair's a/c in full I hope he will find It correct. I send him a little flour, sugar and coffee which I beg he will accept of from me he is one of the few freemen that I have found honest and upright which I believe to be strictly so. Should Mr Lamont come here this fall it is likely that I may pay you a visit during the winter. Joe will give you all the news of this place and perhaps a little more but you know him and can make a little allowance. I have promised him the mare he brought in here for 7 large Beaver one small & six Robes which when paid will be in full. I strongly suspect that Ménard is going to take Dumond's place: you can easily play tricks enough upon him to turn his mind any where but to the advantage of his employers. You well know that most of Sublettes people are the refuse of our people that we would not take upon any account and is it possible that they will make any thing against our choice

    Believe me
    Dear Sir
    to be your's most truly
    Wm Laidlaw

    N.B. you can have as much wine as you chose to send for

❖ ❖ ❖

    Fort Pierre 30th October *1833*
    Mr Wm. Dickson
    Dear Sir

I received yours of the 20th Inst last night, per Joe Juett. I am sorry to learn that your Indians are at such a distance from you, should they not come near you it cannot but be injurious to your trade but I think there is little doubt but the cattle will come your way as soon as you find it convenient. I wish you would send in for your grocery &c and any thing else you may be in want of, I can let you have as much wine as you choose (it has a ready market) only send the means of carrying out such articles as you may want as I can render you no assistance. Mr McKenzie has been here and remained with us about three weeks he left this ~~about~~ eight day ago and took all the Horses with him that were fit for any thing, he has wrote you fully regarding the trade so I shall say nothing more on that head. I do not think that you will be opposed at your place but it is well to be prepared for it and let Robes and Peltries be your watch word and be wide awake. Mr Papin & Picotte arrived from St Louis about a month ago the Cholera has made great havoc there poor Brazeau died 3 days after his arrival in St Louis and several of our men eight or nine died about Mr Cabannes establishment. Major Dougherty was taken with it when they passed his sub died of it and his son John died of the same complaint at the Blackfeet and 3 or 4 of our men. We have been looking for Mr Lamont for him some time past but still no tidings of him I am much afraid that some accident has befallen him. Picotte has gone to winter with the Yanctonay Papin with the Houcpapas near the ree village. You need not put yourself to any extra expense or trouble about getting meat for us as I think I shall be able to hold out till the spring or the opening of the navigation only try to lay in a good stock for spring. Picotte brought back your watch but took it along with him your spy Glass is not yet repaired. You can have what tea you want when you send in. Your friend the Eclare Noir caught 7 Beaver and traded them with Dauphine. With regard to the Horses 6 in number that was found by our people near the Mandans, I have wrote Kipp to deliver them to the owners whenever they call for them I offered to pay them all two Robes each here for the Horses but those that came here declined taking the price. In hopes of hearing good news from you soon

    I remain
    Yours Truly
    Wm. Laidlaw

❖ ❖ ❖

    Fort Pierre 3d. November 1833
    Mr Charles Degray
    Dear Sir

Your men and Louison arrived here Yesterday with the meat you sent us. Enclosed you have an account of the goods sent you for the post. I have sent you such articles as I thought you would stand in need of, but should you be in want of any thing else you can have it at any time for the sending, for it will be well to keep always a good supply on hand.

I lend you a Young Gentleman the bearer of this (Mr Kennedy)[9] who will keep your accounts, take care of the horses when you may have occasion to go out, or anything else you may have for him to do, he is a new hand and knows nothing about the trade, give him all the insight you possibly can.

I have made an arrangement with Louison, he is to remain with you till spring, that is to say till after the trade, and is to be commanded as an engaged hand, or rather as an interpreter, and of course subject to your command, and can be very usefull if he chooses he has given me a horse here that he has not been paid for, should he be in want of anything from you during the winter you may let him have to the amount of Forty or fifty dollars.

The Pork Eaters that you have must have nothing but what is absolutely necessary. I send you some new articles of trade which I have no doubt you will find ready sale for, I have told Mr Kennedy the prices which he will show you. You can have as much wine as You can send for.

The Cholera has been very destructive in St Louis this summer and has carried off about 500 persons, poor Brasseau amongst the rest.

Mr Lamont has not yet arrived Mr McKenzie has been here from the Yellow Stone and left us about 12 days.

We have already talked so much about the trade that it will not be necessary for me to enlarge on that subject. I Trust that you will use every exertion in your power, to get your full share of the Robes and Peltries that may be made in your part of the country, and that you have Mr Kennedy with you, you must write to me very fully and give me all the news you can think of, and keep the boys a moving let me know what your prospects are and believe me to be Yours

Most Respectfully
Wm. Laidlaw

❖ ❖ ❖

Fort Pierre 5th Septr 1833
Mr. Colin Campbell
Dear Sir

Wm. Dickson is just in the act of starting for the forks of the Chyenne with 9 carts. By him I send the articles you requested. There is not one of the poor miserable horses you sent is able to move. I am persuaded it was not [in] your Interest. In future I would not have such, on any account. Give Bellair $6.00 for his Beaver in Merchandise if you cannot get it for less, at all events our opponents must not have it. Provost arrived here some time ago with 120 Mules & horses they Brought in 60 odd packs of beaver. They have gone down to winter their horses at the Bluffs, to make an early start in the spring. Dickson will be able to let you have a couple of men if you stand in need of them, for the news from the "*Mandans*" I enclose you a copy of Crawford to me for Your amusement. I hope you will not fail to read it to your Indians and make the most of it to show them how sensible the Mandans are that this opposition is an imposition, upon them and no doubt will be the means of making many of them miserable in future. Charles Degray & Disonnette had gone to winter with the [blank] high on White River. They are opposed by Biguer & Lachauitay. Dauphine has gone to Cherry River. Hart I suppose is with you before now. The "Wa-na-ucoe-tu-nae" that passed us here are quite displeased with their new traders and cry them down as much as they were accustomed to extoll them, and left this apparently better pleased with us than usual. True I received them well but all this news you will get from themselves, which will have a better effect. After that I have already said to you with regard to the trade, I think it unsatisfactory to say more to you being fully persuaded. You will do every thing for the best and not have a store [word?] for Gods sake and send me some meat as soon as possible. If you could send the meat to [word?], he could send it on by the return for the Cash.

Truly Yours
Wm Laidlaw

❖ ❖ ❖

Fort Pierre 12th Novr 1833
Mr Wm. Dickson
Dear Sir

Yours of the 7th inst I duly received by Peneau and have fulfilled your memorandum as far as practicable, enclosed you have a list of the articles sent you. The Brittania [word?] and sea shells ought to be sold for two robes each if possible but if not take one rather than not sell them. The Large Hot Plates cannot be sold for less than two, the small ones for one. The fine Gun I send you is bespoke by the "One Hand" and sent at his particular request, the price I put upon it is 15 robes, the other two are 12 each. The two Barrells of wine are very strong and I have no doubt but you will make the most of it if you can possibly purchase 10 or 12 good horses I would wish you to do it.

Peneau talked some thing to me about clothing some Indians to which I am realy at a loss to reply, but upon the whole I think it bad Policy, as it never fails to create a jealousy but however I shall leave that entirely to your own discretion & Good sense. When an Indian has wherewith and wishes to purchase a dress, of course there can be no jealousy in that case.

You mention in yours that Mr McKenzie is rather touched [word?] upon a tender point, but I think if you were to take the trouble to study his letter attentively you will find that there is nothing at all personal; but a mild statement of fact that might occur to yourself or any one else that will serve them impartially.

Messrs Lamont and Halsey arrived from St Louis last night, they brought some things for you & no doubt will write you a few lines, there is nothing new of any consequence.

I send by Peneau a smal Keg of butter and a bag of Potatoes for Mr Dickson with my best respects & a meat for yourself which I have no doubt you will find a treat particularly when you come to understand that the greater part was made by myself, accept my best wishes for Tercelf and family, and believe me to be Your

Most Truly
Wm. Laidlaw

P.S. Find all the good cords and Parfleches you possibly can, and lodges to cover your robes coming across the Cheyenne, you ought to lay up skins enough for four canoes, without loss of time & get your Poles cut and prepared, so that they will have sufficient time to dry. If your men have any spare time during the winter I think it would be well to cut and prepare timber for a small fort.

W L.

❖ ❖ ❖

Fort Pierre 16th Nov 1833
Mr James Kipp
Dear Sir

By the express which is to start tomorrow morning I avail myself of the opportunity of addressing you a few lines though nothing worthy of relating to communicate by Mr McKenzie I send you the papers requisite for your place and if any thing be found necessary they will be forwarded by the same conveyance.

I hope you will forward the express without a moments delay as it is of the greatest consequence that it should get up before Mr McKenzie sends off the winter dispatches. By the first opportunity let me know how many horses you think you can dispose of to advantage in the Spring and when you think would be the best time to send them.

Our prospect for Cattle in this section of the country I think is good, true it is yet early in the season and they may clear out. I send you a few newspapers and an almanac which I hope you will find interesting.

I understand we are to have the pleasure of ~~Your Company~~ seeing you in the spring. I hope you will not disappoint us ~~in~~ Mr Lamont desires to be remembered to you

Believe Me to be Your friend
Wm. Laidlaw

❖ ❖ ❖

Fort Pierre 16 Novr. 1833
Mr P. D. Papin
Dear Sir

I only received yours of the First by the "Medicine Ear" and have been anxiously looking for the boat and men every day since; their long abcence has put me to a great deal of inconvenience, and a considerable loss. You have put it entirely out of my power to send you liquor or any thing else, as I have not men enough to furnish the Fort with firewood, but by your securing for such articles as you may be in want for the trade, you can have at any time.

I send you by the express a paper of Ink powder, & some letters from St Louis. I beg of you to forward the express without a moments delay, send a good carefull man and an Indian, with it as far as Mr Picottes, and write to him to forward it in like manner to the [word?]. Mr McKenzie also expects to hear from you. Write to me by any opportunity and

believe me to be
Truly Yours
Wm. Laidlaw

❖ ❖ ❖

Fort Pierre 16 Novr 1833
Mr H. Picotte
Dear Sir

I duly received your note by the two Indians, you sent with the fort Union express. I am much afraid in consequence of your tedious passage that you would not see Mr McKenzie, if so of course the tin Smith remained on board, and as he is indispensably necessary I think it would be well to send him up, with those that take up the express, which I beg you will forward with all *possible speed see that not an hour is lost,* as I am afraid it will not reach the Yellow Stone, before the winter and ought to leave that. Mr Lamont & Halsey arrived here on the 12th inst. I forward some letters for you which they brought from St Louis, where I forwarded You have all the news from that Quarter, be sure you write to Mr McKenzie and let me hear from you by every opportunity that may offer in the course of this winter Cattle are said to be plenty in the neighborhood of our [word?] posts, nothing worth relating has taken place here since you left us,

 I remain Yours
 Most Truly
 Wm. Laidlaw
 P.S. Remember me to Mr Crawford if with you.

❖ ❖ ❖

 Fort Union 16th Nov 1833
 Mr P. D. Papin,
 Sir

Since writing the above the Boat and men arrived with yours of the 11th inst. I am much disappointed that you did not send down the meat you can spare. I think it unnecessary to say any thing more regarding the trade as we have talked that subject over so often you know the views of the Company and must do for the best. I have every confidence in your zeal and experience, and am in hopes you will make your Young opponents look foolish in the spring. Let me only know your needs and I will endeavour to supply them. Your letters will no doubt announce to you the death of your mother [two words?] who died before Mr Lamont left St Louis. Mr Lamont Desires to be remembered to you.

 Except my best wishes &c
 Wm L.
 P.S. to the letter on the other leaf or line of the same date

❖ ❖ ❖

 Fort Pierre 20th Nov 1833
 Mr. P. D. Papin
 Dear Sir

When the express left this for above it seems that some papers of great consequence to Mr McKenzie have been left here through mistake, which I now forward to you and beg of you that you will forward them with all possible speed, so that they may overtake the express, as they are of the greatest consequence.

I have settled accounts with the "Big Kitch-away" as he calls himself, and as we now stand he owes you three Robes which you will please see that he pays; he used to be very punctual and *I have* no doubt that he will be so in this instance. His brother is "*Le Ouise qui Sorte*" owes a horse that Emillion lent him last year, try and get payment from him viz; 10. Robes or a horse, he says that he gave some Raw hides to Daurion but that is a bargain between them, & Baptiste will pay him for them when he sees him. The other that accompanied the big Corenade appeared to be a good American [horse].[10] Why did you keep the Cordell[11] that belonged to the boat & the handle that belongs to the whip saw. If you can spare me a good Buffalo Runner, I wish you would send him down by the Bearer of this. Should you want a pack horse to replace him I can furnish you. Send down "Delorea" as I want him to saw.

The liquor that you sent down tastes so much of Peppermint that it is not easily to say, which if it is Whiskey or Peppermint, try and get some from the same place, and put it into a clear bottle. I am much hurried, so excuse haste &

 Believe Me Yours Truly
 Wm Laidlaw

As I was out hunting and did not settle with the "Medicine Ear" I owe him 14 Robes and 6 Pieces of meat and one of Primeau, if he wishes to get payment from you, try and settle with him.

 Wm L.

❖ ❖ ❖

Fort Pierre 10th June 1833[12]
Pierre Chouteau jr Esqr
Dear Sir

I wrote you a few lines by steam boat Yellow Stone which I hope you will duly receive. The Assiniboine left this on the 5th inst and only got ~~past~~ about 8 miles above this place when they found they could not get further without the help of another Keel Boat to lightener her. Consequently they sent back to this place and got one, so she has gone with two large Keels in tow, Whilst I was aboard of her, she passed over a sand bar [with] 4 feet water on one side and 3½ ft: on the other. So that I have no doubt but she will get on well. We are still in hopes that we shall have a rise,[13] if you remember the first year you come up, we had nothing of a rise before the 6th of July so we must not despair however discouraging.

Louis Prouvoucier [?] will leave this to day with the keel boat "Acyces" with the remainder of our packs, the amt of which you have enclosed as well as a statement of the mens accounts that go down with him. He has but an Indifferent Crew, but the Boat is nearly light. He is instructed to leave the Boat at Mr Cabannés, to bring up the Goods that are left there. I shall write to Mr Pilcher to furnish them with the means of getting down. Mr McKenzie desired me to press upon you the necessity of Picotte's being at Prairie du-chien[14] in time to met the Pork Eaters. Mr Papin ought to be here by the first of September. I do not see why we ought to have any kind of delicacy in making them do their duty, they are well paid for it and I have no doubt if not [word?] they will attribute it to fear and not to indulgence.

Mr Fontenelle left this on the 8th inst with about 170 mules and Horses well rigged. I have never been able to find out what became of the goods that were taken down from the Poncaws last year, please let me know if you know any thing about them. I shall be glad to hear from you the first opportunity if you have not forgotten me altogether in the mean time believe me to be Your Most Obedt. & Humble Servant

Wm Laidlaw
per E.T. Denig

❖ ❖ ❖

Fort Pierre 5th Decr 1833
Mr Henry Picotte

Your letter of 24th Ulto. By Mr Papin was only received here on the 2d. Inst two days having elapsed after his arrival on the opposite side before we could get him across in consequence of the drifting ice.

You could not possibly sent for horses at a more unpropitious time than the present our stock being very small and much harassed transporting the Outfit to the different inland posts monthly as I am exceedingly anxious to give you eve[r]y facility to compete successfully, I have selected from the brigand 13 of the best today which will start by Papin, assisted by Vachard, with instructions to proceed [word?] from one Good feeding place to another, the closing of the river [word?] as Each as necessary to arrive at your post You are well aware of the difficuty of procuring horses from he Indians and without liquor, and the high prices, consequently given for each, as can be had paid as they must be by merchandise at opposition prices. You will therefore be governed as far as practicable by this knowledge, in disposing of their horses, 10 Large beaver they ought to average. Mr Kipp is likewise an applicant for horses for which his Indians have Beaver to pay, should you have more than can be sold to advantage in beaver, I would recommend sending them to Fort Clark when sufficiently [word?] to [word?] the Voyage. I enclose you a descriptive list of horses, ennumeraing their good qualities On the strength of Papin's statement he has in your possession 33 Beaver Skins, I have sold him two horses, one an American Dark Sorrell, white spot upon his neck near side for $80, the other a bright Sorrell Indian horse with [word?], and [two words?] for $40. I am thus particular in describing them that to prevent [word?] you on the trip, or these horses I have agreed to take Beaver at the rate of 350 per lb, and to allow $5.00 per lb in merchandise, as you have probably no steelyards [scales] to weigh the Beaver you can keep it seperate from your stock and have it weighed in the spring. In your arrangement as to advances, always keep on the safe side. In the event of being hard pressed for horses in the spring you may calculate on an additional supply the articles per Invoice enclosed have been furnished agreeably to your request all in your memorandum which we have not probably it may be found at fort Clark. You will find noted below your Invoice the balance of account due by Papin of $8.00 which include in your settlement with him, and also a saddle $10, the latter is considered as cash and paid at the same rate as the horses, the former being for merchandise; Beaver at $5 per lb will suffice. I have no Instructions to give you with regard to trade, you know our views amply on that subject. Foreign news we have had none since I last wrote you.

Believe Me always
Yours truly
Wm Laidlaw

P.S. Papin has received in addition to the amount before mentioned $4.00 in Merchandize, making in all $10 which is charged to your post
W. L

❖ ❖ ❖

Fort Pierre 5th Decr 1833

Wrote Dominique Lachapelle with Invoice of goods per Henry Angé, directing him to send Angé to the Gens-Arc camp for winter, but no wine to be sent; my Indians requiring the article to give their Robes and take an order on Lachapelle for the necessary quantity.

(Sg) M. L.

❖ ❖ ❖

Fort Pierre 5th Decr 1833
Mr Collin Campbell
Dear Sir

Yours of the 30th Novr I received two days ago by Bellair, he will start in the morning with the different articles you requested with the exception of Battle Axes which I have not got, enclosed you have a list of the goods sent you &c.

I cannot help thinking that it would be very wrong in you to remove to the forks of the Cheyenne for many reasons, one very good one is, that it would give Hart an opportunity of opposing both you and Dickson at the same time, but you say that he had no horses but in a very few days he would get a sufficient number to [word?] his [word?] to that place. If you think it necessary to remove any where else, for instance toward the "Dear Hill" where the Indians are, I would have no objections, in that case you might cause your opponent some trouble. But as Mr. Dickson is all alone it would be a thousand pities to distrust him. Bellair tells me that you[r] need of Opium was that William was drawing your Indians to the forks to trade This I can scarcely believe but even if it was so it would be so much the Better, as one should be [word?] of getting all the Robes Dickson being all alone. The flour, coffee & sugar you requested for your men is packed up in the Flora and has been charged to your equipment therefore you will charge it to their private accounts. What [word?] Salt for has been charged to [word?].

I cannot possibly spare you more than one [word?] for the present which I hope will answer your purpose in the mean time.

I had a letter from Mr Papin some days ago, the Indians beat Sublette badly and threaten him a good deal, he has only traded one Robe and that Papin sent to him for Alcohol, I have got the liquor here. I wish you would try and trade some [word?] as we have not an ounce here, we will require also a great many parfleches and cords. I send you a list of clothes that came from St Louis last fall and was ommitted to be sent you by Joe last ~~fall~~ time.

Believe Me ~~Your~~
Dear Sir
Most truly Yours
Wm. Laidlaw

P.S. It will be necessary for you to put your wine in a cellar or else it will freeze and become Sour.

If you see the "Sparrier de Fere" or "Iron Sparrow" you can tell him that I have heard of his [word?] welfare, that the Pawnee delivered him up to the Omahas and that he is well. I sent Baptiste to get him from them by fair means if possible, and if not I sent a fast horse by Baptiste for him to clear out with, but unfortunately Daurion could not find them out, but I will send back again as soon as I can find out where they are, tell the Old Man to keep up his courage, that I have no doubt but he [i.e., we] will soon see him. Our Medicine is strong for those that we take a fancy to, you know better than I can tell you how to make the most of this.

Wm L.

Bellair has just told me that Oacoteaux has offered you a pack of Beaver, three good horses, saddled & two [word?] & five traps for six hundred dollars, if his Beaver is good I would advise you to give him that sum for his Beaver and other articles before mentioned *provided you cannot get it for less*, at the same time try and make a bargain with him for the beaver that he has at the store of Mr Sublette at this place I believe about $45 lbs.

Yours W L.

❖ ❖ ❖

Fort Pierre 28th Decr 1833
Mr P. D. Papin
Dear Sir

I this afternoon received your letter of the 26th inst: per Vachard, and hasten to send you the [word?] you so earnestly request. I send a horse by Primeau which you can keep if in want. The man that accompanied Primeau I wish to be sent back with the express when it comes from above but if you think you can employ him to advantage you may keep him also. You are no doubt aware that you will require to get cut a sufficient quantity of wood, for the Steam Boat, say one or two days march above and below your [word?]. I am sorry to hear that Crawford is so badly Furnished in goods for the Trade. Why does he not send to you for a supply of such articles as he may be in want of. You too can easily [be] furnished at any time. If an opportunity offered I wish you would write to him to this effect, he w[r]ites to me for a sett of pierced Broaches which I send by Primeau, please forward them By the first opportunity. With regard to Leclairs [word?] at White river, that it is a little "Coo de vent,"[15] he gives himself and perhaps he does need to do so, as [I] believe no one else would be satisfied in doing so, if his trip to White River was worth 20 packs to him, I am said it is not worth the fourth of that to Sublette, judge for yourself, here is an abstract from Charles Degray's letter.

"This moment I hear that Leclair is going to the Fort to bring out his Squaw, and intends to return soon, of this I will be glad, as I am sure his being here will be very expensive to them as he seemed not to stick at trifles, while at the same time does little as a Trader."

The Brulés have not yet come in to Charles Degray, they are four days march from this house, and are said to have plenty of Buffaloe, I have not heard from any of the posts since I last wrote you, if you can find me any news about Augé, they would be acceptable particularly if good. Your letter per Zabette I only received and have noted your remarks about the Three Merchants.

Wishing you all the compliments of the season, I remain

Yours Truly

(Signed) Wm Laidlaw

P.S. Decr 31st. Since writing the foregoing I find the snow too deep to send the horse, but I furnished Primeau with two dogs in place of the [word?].

W L.

❖ ❖ ❖

Fort Pierre 10th Jany 1834
Mr Bapt Defond
Sir

I avail myself of the express going to the Bluffs, of addressing you a few lines. I beg that you will render the express every facility of getting on as fast as possible as I am much afraid that it will be too late. I hope Roy arrived safe with his crew and horses, should you require one or two more I know of no other way of your getting them, but by sending them to Mr Pilcher where Mr Lamont left some on his way up; I wish you to try and find out the Poncaws as they have had no traders since last summer and must have a good deal of Beaver and Robes, I sent Daurion out upon *Eau qui Court*, to try and find them out but he did not find them out, nor any Trace of them therefore I hope you will use every exertion in your power to find them *and get their Trade*. A Boat will leave this early in the spring, in it will be time enough for you to go and meet the Steam Boat in it I will endeavour to send someone to take charge in your absence. I am in hopes that you will make a good trade, let me know what furs you have by the return of the express and give me all the other news you can collect.

We heard from Fort Union Yesterday, it seems two of our men were killed near Fort Cass[16] by the Blackfeet; During the late snow storm we have been so unfortunate as to get three of our men badly frozen, I doubt much whether any of them will recover they Suffer dreadfully.

We have no Buffaloe near this; but at all the outposts they are tolerably plenty and if they continue I think it is likely we will make a good Trade, I believe I wrote to you last time by Roy, not to advance any thing to the Pork Eaters which I sent you, except what is absolutely necessary, he deserted once therefore we can have no confidence in him.

I Remain
Your Friend
Very Respectfully
Wm Laidlaw

P.S. Porier and Ravalette must not be advanced any thing except what is absolutely necessary for him to perform his duty

Wm L.

❖ ❖ ❖

Fort Pierre 10th Jany 1834
Pierre Chouteau Esqr
Dear Sir

I only received your favor of the 20th Sept, on the 12th of Nov per Mr Lamont, and shall pay every attention to its contents, with regard to the

Inventory of this place, it shall be made out as you [word?] as far as practicable

The order which accompanied this for 1835 (if Filled) will I am persuaded be amply sufficient for the trade of that Year, even should it be one of the best [word?]. I am at a loss what to say about wine, for if our opponents are Supplied with alcohol as they have been this year we cannot expect to sell our wine so long as that article is to be had, so I shall leave it entirely to your better judgment & trust you will act accordingly. I am happy to say that the appearance for the Robe trade in this section of the country thus far looks flattering, but it is impossible for me even to give you an idea what will be made at this early season, as the trade is scarcely well begun, my own opinion is if the cattle continue as they now are that we may make from the Mandans down about fourteen hundred packs of Robes, but this is a mere guess and I do not know that I am Yankee enough to come within some hundred packs.

Our opponents do not seem to be doing much and are not by any means popular with the Indians, but time can only determine how they will come out one thing certain is that they will not make money by their Indian trade, but their returns from the mountains may save them if they get down safe.

I understood from the Sioux that Charles Bent had built a Fort[17] upon the Arkanzes for the purpose of trade with the different bands of Indians, that he may be able to draw about him, and if judiciously carried on cannot fail to be very injurious to the trade in this part of the country.

The Cheyennes have remained in that part of the country depending I have no doubt on that very establishment and if kept up I have very little doubt not a great many of the Sioux will follow their example.

When Mr McKenzie last wrote you we were both under the impression that the necessary number of horses for the Mountain expedition could be furnished from this place, but in consequence of the Cheyennes not coming in I find it will be useless for me to furnish any; as it is with the greatest difficulty that I can get enough to carry on our own business here

I am ignorant as to whether Mr Fontenelle has furnished you with his order for the goods he may require for the ensuing year, if not I can throw very little light upon the subject, having received nothing of that kind from him. All I can do is to send you a copy of his last years Invoice so that you may have some kind of data to go by.

Is there no possibility of recovering or punishing in any way those men that deserted from here last spring, I understood they are all doing well in St Louis, and their getting clear in that manner must be a great inducement for other to follow their example. I shall send you a statement of their accounts, you can then act as you think proper.

I do sincerely trust that this may be the last brigade of Pork eaters, that we will ever get from Montreall as the expense is enormous, and the men good for very little for the two first years, and will desert every opportunity they get, the last that came across were only here a few days, when three of them cleared out, however we were fortunate enough in overtaking them, and bringing them back, but can place no dependence in them.

The express has just arrived from Fort Union and have no doubt but Mr McKenzie has given you a full detail of every thing in that quarter, when he sent of the express, it appeared by a note that he sent to overtake it, that he omitted to make a requisition of the necessary number of men, that is required for that post, I am afraid that the letter may have been lost, and as I am entirely ignorant myself of the number he may wish I send you a copy of his to me on that subject. I am of opinion that we have enough of men to carry on the trade in this section of the country.

The enclosed packing act of goods for the rocky Mountain Outfit shipped on board the S. B. Assiniboine 18th March 1833. I am uncertain whether it is included in the general Invoice or not please let me know.

We have had no buffaloe in this immediate neighborhood this summer but collected a good stock of dry meat this fall and with the assistance of our garden stuffs we are pretty independent, our garden turned out much better than I could have expected, say 110 bus[hels] corn, 200 bus: Turnips & 400 bus. Samips &c.

I am sorry to inform you that three of our men got froze in the most shocking manner, ten days go, on their way from Cherry River to this place, there is very little hope of their recovery, we are all of opinion that the consequences must prove fatal, two Pork eaters in particular, Debbris a young man from St Louis may possibly live but will lose his toes if not his feet; Colin Campbells daughter was because of her death by her clothes catching fire, a fine child about two years of age.

We are all very anxious that you should pay us a visit next spring, if such a thing could be it is needless for me to assure you have my gratifying & would be to all of us.

    Believe Me
    Dear Sir
    Your Most Obdt Servant
    Wm Laidlaw

P.S. I neglected to mention that there is an error in the addition of the [two words?] of £200 [pounds sterling]. I have no doubt it by this time has been [word?]. I forward you the accounts of two Pork Eaters, one of whom was left at lake Frances in 1829 and the other at Lac qui parle last summer, they have had the services of the former and have no doubt they get the services of the other and of course ought to pay for their expences.

The mule which Mr Lamont brought here belonging to the Mountain Expedition will be sent back next spring

    Wm. L

❖ ❖ ❖

    Fort Pierre 14. January 1834
    Mr. Pierre D. Papin
    Dear Sir

Your favor I duly recd. by the express which left this two days ago for below, should the matter prove favourable I shall look for them a month from this.

This will be handed you by Mr. Denig whom I send up with a train load of goods for Mr Picotte. I am much surprised that Picotte would trust to this place for the means of conveying supplies to him he knows or ought to know, that when all the different posts get their equipments from him in the fall that they ought not to trust to means of that kind but furnish them themselves, they have certainly this better in their power than I can have, who has not seen a strange Indian since the river closed. I have heard from the men who brought the express that Charles Primeau got his feet froze on his way up which I regret exceedingly, but I am led to believe they are but slightly froze which is so far lucky, please let me know all about it, by the first opportunity.

It appears that Mr. McKenzie and Campbell could come to no arrangement so we must push on in the old way, and let Robes and peltries be the watch word. Coute que Coute.[18]

During the last seven snow weather we unfortunately got three of our men so much froze on their way from Cherry River to this place, that they cannot possibly live; Raboin may probably live, but he will undoubtedly lose his toes if not his feet, their sufferings are beyond any thing you can imagine.

Send the Broaches by Mr. Denig and Believe me
    Yours Most Truly
    (Sign'd.) Wm Laidlaw

P.S. Two of our men were killed by the Blackfeet at Fort Cass, Fitzpatrick got all his horses taken from him by the Crows 100 in number some beaver and all his goods. Chardon has built a Fort near milk river which he calls Fort Jackson[19] I presume he will go the *whole hog*.

    W. L.

❖ ❖ ❖

    Fort Pierre 14th January 1834
    Mr. L. Crawford
    Dr. Sir

Your favor of the 22nd and 29th Ulto. Came to hand in due time, it is flattering to me in the extreme to learn that you offered your neighbours with so much success, long may it continue, you ought to use every means in your power to get them along side of you otherwise they will have the advantage in spite of all you can do; I should think that your soldiers would have influence enough to accomplish that; you can tell them that such treatment as that, would not be allowed in a Sawon Camp. I have fulfilled your memorandum as far as practicable, arm bands and sea shells we have got now, every thing else I believe you have got; I trust you will not have occasion to use the medicine.

I am sorry to hear that you have such a limited supply of goods, it was my intention you know that your equipment should have been left when the boat passed, and got the equipment put up seperate for that purpose; I have wrote Mr Picotte to endeavour to supply you more liberally in future, Mr Denig will be able to bring you a load when he returns. I wish you could load his trains on his way down with grease as we have not an ounce to make a Candle with; Should you be in want of any part of his load for your trade you can make free with it, and send Mr. Picotte an account of such articles as you take; the prices you trade at is beyond all bounds, but so as you are sure that your opponents give the same price, so much the better, ("the hotter was the sooner peace") have you got no Epichlimores [Apishamores] that you could trade with them for some of the most sailable goods you must have many articles to trade that they have not, in that case you can make your own price, only find out what the articles are.

I hope Mr. Picotte will furnish you with the groceries that were intended for you, if not it would be well to jog his memory. Do not forget to get Steam boat wood set in convenient places for getting it aboard, and be sure you have enough; there were great complaints last year.

The last account I had from our outposts here was that cattle were beginning to come in, since the cold weather I have no doubt but they will be plenty, at most of the trading establishments. We have unfortunately got three of our men froze in the most shocking manner. Mr D. will inform you of all the particulars, as well as all the news of this place. I intend to pay Mary[20] a visit in a few days I shall not fail to make mention of you to her, shall I tell her that you are married. Write me fully by every opportunity, and believe me to be you friend and well wishes

(Sign'd) Wm Laidlaw

❖ ❖ ❖

Fort Pierre 14th January 1834
Mr. Henry Picotte
Dear Sir

Your favor of the 29th I duly recd per the Express on the 9th inst: which left this on the 12th for below, and if they have favourable weather, I shall look for them in a month from this.

I cannot help being a good deal surprised at you sending him for goods &c. without sending the means to carry them; I thought that you had known the situation of this place better, all the best of our horses I have already sent you and there is no possibility of our getting dogs, being no Indians about, however, I have made out to purchase them at an exorbatant price at the same time I very much doubt if they will be able to perform the trip they are so wretchedly poor; from this you will perceive that it is impossible for me to fulfill your memorandum. I therefore sent you a part of such articles as I think you will be in most immediate want of; would it not be much more convenient for you to get your wants supplied at the Mandans, as it is certainly much nearer, and they must have such articles as you appear to be in want of; the order from that place last year included the Outfit for the Yanctonnas; at all events should you want any thing else from here you must send the means to carry it to your place, as it is utterly impossible for me to do it.

I am sorry that you sold the two young horses I sent you so cheap, as they were both runners, and I could easily have got 15 Robes for each.

How do you intend bringing out your returns, the expence of skin canoes are so great, that I think you ought to continue to make some wooden craft to bring them down; any thing of that kind will do to bring them this far. I can supply you with saw, nails, pitch, or any thing else you may be in want of to make such a craft.

Mr. Crawford writes me that he is put to the great inconvenience of the want of goods, it is a great pity that he should lose any of the trade on that account, is there any possibility of sending him a good supply.

I have not the least doubt that Mr Kipp could furnish you all the necessities for Boat building, and very likely spare you a boat builder also; I have authorized mr Crawford to take some things from the trains, should he be in want. I wish the dogs sent back immediately, they can bring down a load from your place to Crawfords if necessary, I hope you will not forget the Steam boat wood, I wish you could bring us down a few good sticks of oak for carts, Mr Denig will give you all the [word?]; we have unfortunately got 3 of our men so much frozen that I do not expect they can live.

I can say very little about our prospects of trade in this quarter, not having heard from any of the posts for a great length of time

I remain Yours Most Truly
(Sign'd) Wm Laidlaw
P.S. Your letter I forwarded by the express, inclosed you have a memorandum of goods sent you.

❖ ❖ ❖

Fort Pierre January 14, 1834
Mr. James Kipp
Dear Sir

I duly recd your favor of the 26th per the express which arrived here on the 9th inst: I[t] gives me much pleasure to hear that you oppose your opponents so successfully, true the trade in all is but trifling, but that you cannot help. I am in hopes that after this cold weather that you will have Buffaloe all around you. I regret that the horses were in such bad order that Picotte sent you, they were all in good order when they left this; during the severe snow storm that we had on the 29th & 30. we lost several that got smothered in the snow, and have lost them as four since, but in spite of all that, I will endeavour to supply you with twenty in the spring. Also three or four American horses, which we can afford to sell for the price you mention, when I send the horses I shall send a discriptive list, and their characters. Mr. Picotte appears to be much in want of goods, I hope you will be able to supply his wants, also materials for boat building should he be in want, could you not spare him Boihan for a month.

I can say very little about our prospects for trade here, but the last accounts I had from any of the Outposts they had plenty of Cattle, and I am sure you never saw such cold weather upon the Missouri, "does it not bring you in mind of Big Salt river."[21]

I am sorry you have given up the idea of coming down next spring, I should like much to see you, surely you cannot be afraid to come this far; Come I am not going to let you off in that way. I am told the Cholera is nothing at all when once accustomed to it.

Mr. Lamont is writing you, and I presume will give you all the political news from below, he is sending you a sample of Blue Beads, let me know if they will take the market, Your Memorandum has been sent on with the express.

I am sorry to inform you that we have got three of our men dreadfully froze, so much so that I can scarcely think that any one of them will survive; they must at all events lose their feet, two of them "Pork eaters" from Montreal this year. The razor strop I recd safe. I am much surprised at your taking Old Charbonneau into favour after showing so much ingratitude, upon all occasions (the old knave what does he say for himself.)

Wishing you a good and pleasant new year, and many of them, Believe me to be yours most truly
(Signd.) Wm. Laidlaw

❖ ❖ ❖

Fort Pierre 14th January 1834
Mr. Charles Degray
Dear Sir

In the afternoon received your favour of the 7th inst: and hasten to send you all the relief possible, I beseach you not to have any scruples about sending for wine, or any thing else you may be in want of; now that you are doubly offered you must not stick at trifles, but get the Robes and Peltries Coute que Coute; profit I cannot expect, you will make any, if you do it is all good and well, but if not there is no harm, so [long] as you get the Robes. I wrote you some time ago by an Indian which letter I hope you are in possession of before this time. Let the dogs and train be sent back as soon as possible, when I shall fulfil your request or any thing else you may want. I intend to pay a visit to the forks of the Chyenne, and will pay you a visit if Practicable, I mean to cross over from Campbells to your place. I shall Inclose you a memorandum of the articles sent you in the meantime believe Me Yours Truly.
(Sign'd) Wm. Laidlaw
P.S. Do not forget to send us in a little meat and grease, by the train and particularly grease as we have not a ounce.

❖ ❖ ❖

Fort Union January 16th 1834
Kenneth McKenzie Esqr.
Fort Union
Dear Sir

Herewith you will receive all the accounts I know of which appear to be wanting at your establishment, all errors that have as yet been discovered have been corrected and I hope you will find them sufficiently plain, however a few observations regarding them may possibly save you the trouble of more inquiries.

Paper #1. Is an account of sundry Merchandize delivered this post by you in June last as also sundry Fancy articles recd per Crawford 20th August last.

#2. Is an Invoice of Sundry Horses and Equipage

furnished you for your trip to Fort Union in October last.

#3. Is another charge to your post for Merchandize sent up pr Keel boat "Argo" last fall and which were intended for the trade of Ft. Union.

#4. Is an account of Merchandise shipped at Fort Pierre ex S. B. Assiniboine in June last.

#5 Is a Credit for sundries received from your establishment in August and September last.

#6. Is a statement of wages of Clerks, Interpreters, Hunters and voyageurs which appear to be chargeable to your post for the present season upon refference to which you will find I have charged Fort Union with the Equipments of 35 men hired in St Louis last spring, as also with a fair proportion of the equipments of several other men on your establishment.

There are a few persons attached to Fort Union whose salary for the year ending 1834 I am not yet acquainted with, namely D. D. Mitchell, Dr. G. W. McKenney, James Beckwith and J. B. Lafontain and possibly others who may have escaped my memory be good enough to furnish me with abstracts of their Engagements, of all such as you find I may have omitted in paper # one

#7. So Fort Pierre in a/c current with Fort Union from 1 July to 20th November. I believe it sufficiently clear and that it needs no explanation.

#8. Is another Credit to Fort Union for sundry sums in paper #4.

#9. You will perceive in a statement of a/c which do not correspond with your Duplicate Ledger 1833. The summer or fall of 1832 you sent me a statement of advances to men in St Louis Spring of that year which you say was taken from the St Louis book in this statement you say Justin Grossclaude a/c then is $96.20 as for duplicate Ledger, it is said to be $90.20 and according to General Ledger he stands charged with $96.20 advance in St Louis and Moccasins on board "Flora" $1, making in all $97.20. The same applies to Antoine Laduoute in list before mentioned his advances stated at $105.12 and Per duplicate Ledger it is $103.13, this needs explanation before I can take upon myself the responsibility of altering the General book.

I make the Balance due by Johnson Gardieu [Gardener] to the Company $880.10 instead of $930.10, he is credited with a note of smith, Jackson and Sublettes Paid to the American Fur Company in St Louis $1371.48 in the document recd here explaintory of this mans account the amount of the note is more than once mentioned as $1371.48 but in one instance it is said to be $1321.48 and if the latter amount is correct, we are wrong, consequently it is mindful you should give us some further information on the subject.

#10. Is James Beckwiths a/c in detail, I understand he disputes his debt and consequently have collected all the old books together and overhauled them carefully. In an old Ledger Kept by Kipp and McKnight at Fort Clark I find there has been errors made in his a/c amounting in all to $137.38 in his favor, which no doubt will please him exceedingly. Upon refference to the paper you will perceive he was in debt to the Company on the 26th January 1830. $67.49, this was at the Ree Village, according to settlement made with him by Lachapelle he owed but one dollar, but in reality he owes $67.49. I shall now proceed to state how this happened, as clearly as I can with the documents I have before me.

Mr Lamont previous to his leaving the Ree Village for his wintering station at the Yanctonnas in Dec. 1829, made a serious bargain with Beckwith for his beaver, to be paid at the rate of $4 per lb. such supplies of Merchandize as the said Beckwith might require while there, and an Equipment for prosecuting his hunt was to be furnished him, at a discount of 20 per centum, on the rate charged the engages of the Company, that is to say, so far as his beaver would cover such supplies. Lachapelle was fully acquainted with this arrangement, and ordered to settle with him accordingly notwithstanding Lachapelle thought proper to pay $5 per lb. for only part of the Beaver (a part having been sold to Picotte) and made the 20 per cent discount; this proceeding was altogether unauthorized, in as much as it was for the particularly explained both to Lachapelle and Beckwith that the discount of 20 per cent was only [word?], in consideration of the whole of the Beaver being sold to the Company, and at the rate before mentioned namely $4 per lb. consequently the a/c is stated as per Paper #10, agreeably to the original bargain, which is considered just to both parties.

#11. Is an abstract of the engagements of the

men hired in Montreall spring of 1832. I hope this account will give you no further trouble, and regret that the manner in which they were previously made out, has a tendency to confuse those [word?] per S. B. Assiniboin.

#12. Is a statement of the accounts of Jacques Biyer, J. B. Moncravie and Alexander Harvey in detail, the a/cs of Baptiste Marchand and Henry Leblane will also be found on the same paper. I hope they will prove satisfactory, if not and you should discern wherein they are incorrect be good enough to advise us hereof and they shall be rectified accordingly.

#13. Will show what alteration has taken place in account, since the rectification of your favor dated 13th December last.

In your list entitled "Names of Clerks and men on Fort Union establishment 1833.1834" you state Baptiste Jackmans Wages to be $150 for services ending summer 1834, it should be (without you have granted him extra wages) $125, his time commenced in July 1832 when he was engaged for $250 for the 2 years, in the same a/c you make mention of J. Papin and state his wages to be $220 for services Ending summer 1834. Be good enough to give me his christian name or let me know whether Joseph Papin the trapper or the man you alude to.

In duplicate Ledger you mention Mr. Dubrielles a/c $19.41 this a/c has been closed by charge to Lucien Fontinelle. I shall be glad to know whether the sum of $145.62 advanced to Charles Vachard in St Louis March 1832 includes his a/c there in August 1831 $44.50. I presume it does as the amount of both the sums namely $190.12 has been previously forwarded to fort Union and no notation appears to have been taken of it. As per duplicate Ledger he stands charged with only $145.62. You have the Saint Louis Book of that year in your possession and will be able to enlighten me on this sub[j]ect. The man is still in the country, and if the old a/c of $44.50 has not been paid it can easily be collected, it is best to be sure on all occasions when there is no necessity for guessing.

If you would show me the Saint Louis Book of Advances to men spring 1833 it would be rendering me a great service. The following is an abstract from Mr Chouteaus letter to me regarding Inventories. I give it to you as it is possible he may have said nothing to you on the subject.

"On a former occasion [I] spoke to you as well as the gentlemen concerned with you, respecting the manner of making up your inventories, and at the same time objected to it, but I find them made in the same way this year again; I hope that in future they will be made according to the currency in which your Invoices go to you Viz: when the actual costs sterling, let it be sterling, and dollars and cents, let it also be so, taking care to distinguish between New York goods and those furnished here, which latter are termed fixed goods. It is in this way that all our traders and clerks of the Outfits make their Inventories, and allways have made them; and I think the only correct way. I hope therefore in future they will come from your quarter in this way."

It is in consequence of this information that when changed our system of keeping the a/cs upon refference to yours you will perceive their made out in the currency which the American fir Company makes out our Invoices, it will facilitate matters when you come to make up your Inventories in the spring. We have made a calculation of the general average of starting advances on goods in the country and find it amounts to 82.92 per cent. Should you require any further information or explanation I will endeavour to answer all of your inquiries, at present I can think of nothing more in the way of business

Ever Yours Faithfully
(Signd.) William Laidlaw

❖ ❖ ❖

Fort Pierre 22d January 1834
Mr. William Dickson
Dear Sir

I duly recd your favor of the 4th inst. and am sorry to learn that you have had so little trade, but from the late severe weather we have had, I think there can be little doubt but your Indians have plenty of Buffalos, therefore must not yet despair of making a good trade. I think it would be desirable if you could visit their camp and have a talk with them, and encourage them to go to your place to trade as soon as the season will permit; explain to them the consequences of abandoning and their post, and should they seem anxious about the Agent Bean, tell them to keep themselves perfectly easy, if they assemble themselves at the forks of the Chyenne, I will give them notice as soon as I hear of the fathers aproach, this I would think much preferable to their coming here in the spring, when they would undoubtedly suffer from starvation and in all probability be obliged to clear out without seeing the Agent; after visiting your indians, if you find that you will be in want of any thing for the trade, you ought to lose no time in sending for such articles as you may want, but be sure you send the means of carrying it to your place, as I cannot possibly render you any assistance in that way. I have sent there Barrels of Wine for Lachapelle, probably he will be able to spare you a barrel or perhaps more.

Henry Hart and suit have abandoned the post at the Ogallallahs, and if I can judge from appearances have been much reproached by Leclerc, as Dumond is now living here.

Your Memorandum for St Louis arrived a few days to late, the express having left this some days before yours arrived. We heard lately from Fort Union, but as I see a letter addressed to you from Mr. McKenzie I presume you will get all the news from it, at the same time he wrote me Buffalo were then scarce, and at a great distance. At Fort Cass two of our men got killed by the Blackfeet, the Crows have robbed Fitzpatrick and party of one hundred horses some Beaver and all the Merchandize. I was all prepared and ready to start on a visit to you, when Henri arrived and told me that there was not an Indian on the Chyenne, In consequence of which I abandoned the scheme which I much regret; let me hear from you soon and give me all the news in your quarter, I am very anxious to hear from Campbell. I remain Dr. Sir

Yours Truly
(Sign'd) William Laidlaw

P.S. Try and trade as many cords and [word?] as possible, as we will require an immence number to fit out the mountain expedition.

W. L.

❖ ❖ ❖

Fort Pierre 22d. Jany. 1834
Mr. Colin Campbell
Dear Sir

I embrace this opportunity of Angé going to Williams of dropping you a few lines. I have been long expecting to hear from you for some time past. I understand that you are now without opposition, Hart having gone on to Degray with his Outfit, I am glad you have got rid of them in that way. Your old friend Baptiste is quite proud to hear that you have gained the victory over them, but still he thinks it inferior to the *Ree Co*. Notwithstanding that you are alone I would not advise you to trade too hard with the Ogallallahs, as it might be apt to disgust them; and after the disposition they have shewed, I think it would be unfair to do so; but your own good sense and experience in the trade, will I have no doubt point out to you the advantages and disadvantages of such a measure.

I am much afraid that Charles Degray will be hard pushed; if you could make it convenient to pay him a visit I wish you would, and give him some of our wise council, and endeavour to furnish him with such supplies as he may want, (or that you can spare) without injuring your trade, the roads from his place to this, are so bad, and our house so poor, that I cannot possibly furnish him with sufficient supplies for the trade. In the mean time I shall not [be] satisfied that you will render him any assistance in your power.

You have no doubt heard by this time that we got three of our men dreadfully froze on their way from Chyenne to this place about the beginning of the year. One of them Bernard, one of the "Pork Eaters" of this year I do not think can live many days, another has got both his legs Cut off, and the 3d will lose his toes at least, they suffer terribly.

I heard from the Yellowstone about the 9th inst: buffalo were there scarce, and at a great distance, but I am in hopes that this severe weather may bring them near. Two of our men were killed near fort Cass by the Blackfeet. The Crows have robbed Fitzpatrick and party of one hundred horses, some Beaver, and all their goods, but I have not heard the particulars; I cannot imagine how they could rob such a large party, without a good many being killed. The Express started for below on the 12th inst, write me a long letter on the receipt of this and let me know your prospects, and what you have already traded. You can forward your letter to William and direct him to forward it. Do not forget to procure as many cords and parfleches as possible and Believe me to be Your friend

and Well wishes
Sign'd Wm Laidlaw

❖ ❖ ❖

Fort Pierre Febuary 6th 1834
Messrs Fontenelle & Drips
Gentlemen

Herewith inclosed you will receive all the accounts appertaining to your Outfit, which we have it in our power to furnish at the present period. No a/cs of the sales of Beaver Skins &c: have as yet come to hand, but I presume some a/c of the kind is forthcoming; and so soon as we receive it, you shall be furnished with a copy.

Paper # 1. Is an Invoice of the goods, horses &c delivered Mr Lucien Fontenelle at this place in June last. I hope you will find it correct in every particular.

#2. Is an account of the advances and wages of men who were furnished last June. Upon reference to this paper, you will perceive I had charged you with the wages of the men Viz: S. Delpant Vinitte and P. Bastian, but when you come to examine the account current, you will find I have given your Outfit Cr. for the wages of Bastian, and charged you with the Balance of his a/c. The same applies to Peter Hill, in the first instance his wages was charged; but when it was ascertained he was indebted to the Co., credit was given for the amount of his wages, and the debt was charged. Delpar and Vinitte were engaged to the company for two years, the first year expired last summer, at which time the both had money due them, for the which I have given your Outfit credit so that they have no further claim on us for the balance due them, when they left here in June last.

#3. Is the a/c. of Expedition 1832.33 the balance of which is transferred to new account.

#4. You will perceive is an account of the Salaries of the persons belonging to your Outfit season of 1832.33. It was charged in the a/c we received here from Fort Union. As some of the men with whose wages in your Outfit is charged in this a/c went down to Saint Louis last fall, and had in their possession drafts on the Agent there, and as all their drafts have been likewise charged to your Outfit, I am fearfull that paper # 4 will turn out to be erroneous in more instances than one; If you should discover wherein it is incorrect be good enough to advise us on the subject, and it shall be rectified.

#5. Is a Statement of a few accounts I send you, and which I am in hopes you will be able to collect. The first is a charge against Mr. Fitzpatrick amounting to $17.45, the second is Baptiste Chevaliers, he is indebted to us $336.34 and the third is August Durocher $61.17. On the same document you will find a charge against Joseph Vissina $42.06, his advances in St Louis the summer of 1831, he may possibly have paid this account in St Louis, but we have not been advised of such a payment being made, and consequently he still remains charged with the above sum exclusive of the amt: of his advances in St Louis last spring.

#6. Is our a/c current with your Outfit up to the present period $71. 183.35 on examination of this document you will see a charge of $3958.34 for something in St Louis March 23d. last, which charge we know nothing about.

#7. Is our a/c with Fontenelle and Drips you have as plain as it came to us from Saint Louis, on this paper will be found also the a/c of Fontenelle, Drips & Co., which is likewise as clear as we have it in our power to give you.

By the first opportunity be good enough to furnish me with a statement of the advances you have made to men who went down stream last fall, so that we may be able to close this account.

Should you discover any errors in the documents you will receive herewith, be good enough to point them out to me and they shall be corrected, or should any further explanation be required, I shall very cheerfully answer all your inquiries, for the present allow me to subscribe myself

Very Truly Yours
(Signd) Wm Laidlaw
Acting Agent for Upper Missouri
Outfit at Fort Pierre

❖ ❖ ❖

Fort Pierre 24th Febuary 1834
Mr P.D. Papin
Dear Sir

Being absent at the time your favour of the 10th Inst arrived. I of course was deprived of the pleasure of answering it, but understand from Mr Lamont who answered it, has also fulfilled your memorandum. I am sorry that I have little or nothing to offer you in the way of news, I was just a month gone on my trip, and made the round by Degray's, Campbell's, Dickson's & Lachapelle's &c, our returns I am afraid upon the whole will be small but at the same time we cannot complain, as we get nearly all that there is; our opponents do little or nothing any where (In fact I believe they will do less than nothing) as they must make considerable less. You no doubt must have heard that Hart was compelled to leave the post at the Ogallallahs; they starved him out. I have left Daurion to assist Degray, as our opponents seem to be concentrating all their forces at that place, and I have no great confidence in Dechonnette. I am afraid he has acted a double part, I am fully persuaded that Leclair has been tampering with him, which is rather a mean trick after the arrangements I made with Mr Sublette; as I before mentioned to you, Leclair did not get a single Robe while at White River. Charles Vachard the bearer of this, send on to Mr Picotte's for the purpose of bringing down a Skin Canoe with provisions as we are nearly out, and I am afraid before and will be able to get a supply that we will suffer greatly. If you could possibly spare a man to go down up with him to bring down the Canoe it would be well, but if not, he must just do the best he can: be good enough to see that he losses no time, at your place, and write to Mr Crawford to the same effect. Try and collect as much provisions as possible, and believe me yours most Truly

(signed) Wm Laidlaw

❖ ❖ ❖

Fort Pierre 24th Febuary 1834
Mr. L. Crawford
Dear Sir

I have just returned from a trip of a month and made the rounds by Degray's, Campbell's, Dickson's, & Lachapelle's, I much fear that our returns, will fall short of what we expected, our opponents are doing little or nothing any where, I congratulate you on the victory you have gained over your neighbours, it ought and will no doubt be a feather on your cap, and long may you continue to gain laurels in that way. The Bearer of this, Vachard, I wish sent on to Mr. Picotte without a moments delay, for the purpose of bringing down a Canoes Canoe load of meat as I understand he is ordered to go to Fort Clark with his returns and goods; I am much afraid that we will not be able to hold out in the provision way till the opening of the navigation. If it be practicable for you I would wish that you would send a man, with Vachard to bring down the canoe, as far as your place, in which case you could come down together, which would be preferable to [a] man coming all alone such a distance had I had the means I would willingly have sent another man with Vachard, but really I do not know what hand to turn to get a man men to bring the canoes down the Chayenne.

Trusting that you will do every thing in your power to forward my views
I remain
Most Truly Yours
(signed) Wm Laidlaw

❖ ❖ ❖

Fort Pierre 24th Febuary 1834
Kenneth McKenzie Esqr
Fort Union
Dear Sir

Since the date of my last Official Letter (6th Ulto.) several additional errors have been discovered in an account with your post Outfit, for explanation of which I beg leave to refer you to the enclosed document.

5 Brass Medals and 80 wooden Bowls, are noted in your Invoice dated 10th April last. It would appear that the price of these two articles were not known in St Louis as late as September, at which period the Invoices were copied from the American Fur Company's Books and delivered to Mr Lamont.

I have nothing much to offer in the way of news, prospects of the returns of this District not so good as anticipated. Provisions are getting scarce with us, we have not more than a month's supply in the Fort, and no expectation of getting relief from the posts "in large."

Believe me ever
Yours Most Truly
(signed) Wm. Laidlaw

❖ ❖ ❖

Fort Pierre 24th Febury 1834
Mr H. Picotte
Dear Sir

I regret much that it is not practicable for me to send you the Goods requested in your last, owing to the great depth of snow in the plains; and I think it would be wantonly sporting with the lives of both man and beast to attempt it by the ice in its present state.

Having learned by your last that you have instructions from Mr McKenzie to carry your returns and goods to Fort Clark, I send Vachard to your place for the purpose of bringing down a Skin Canoe loaded with meat; I much fear that we shall be entirely out before ~~we can receive~~ a ~~supply~~ a supply reaches us; I trust that you will furnish him with a canoe, and as much meat as you think he can bring down with safety. I have wrote Mr Crawford if possible to send a man with him, to assist him in bringing the canoe down as far as his place; from thence they can come in company

Your's Respectfully
(signed) Wm Laidlaw

❖ ❖ ❖

Fort Pierre 24th Febuary 1834
Mr James Kipp
Dear Sir

On my return here from the posts I was much disappointed in not hearing from you, having heard from all the other establishments down. I have little in the way of men to offer you; our opponents are doing little or nothing any where, the ~~first~~ only Robes they have got they got with their alcohol, which the Indians prefer to our wine; had we been well furnished in that article, I do not believe they would have made more than 20 or 30 packs in all, but as it is they cannot possibly make their men's wages. (not including their mountain trade)

I expect Mr McKenzie down early in spring, should he not come himself, he will no doubt send down a boat by which opportunity I wish you to send me 40 or 50 Bus: Corn, as I have not been able to get a piece of meat since last fall, and I much fear will be out of every thing like provisions before the opening of the navigation. By the same opportunity I wish you would let me know the exact number of horses you wish to send, and what time you wish them to be at your place. The Mandans I have no doubt if they have Robes, will give you Credit, I can supply you with from 20 to 40 if necessary. When at Campbell's I understood that the Soux lately stole from the Gros Ventres 28. The Crows a few days ago stole 21 from the same band, that stole those from the Big Bellies.

I wish you could purchase for me two first rate Mandan Robes. Accept of my best wishes for your prosperity and welfare, and Believe me to remain
Most Truly Yours
(Signed Wm Laidlaw

❖ ❖ ❖

Fort Pierre March 4th 1834
Mr Colin Campbell
Dear Sir

I regret much that I could not send the men sooner but I trust they will still be in time, they are instructed to take what men Dickson can spare in passing. I have fulfilled your memorandum an account of which will be sent you. As soon as convenient for you, you will send Joe and all the Horses to Degray's, tell him not to force the Horses, but to take plenty of time with them as we are in no hurry for them here. I hope you will be able to bring us a good stock of meat, as we are nearly out. I think the Missouri will be clear of ice in a few days, some wild fowl passed here yesterday. In hopes of seeing you soon I remain
Truly Yours
(signed) Wm Laidlaw

❖ ❖ ❖

Fort Pierre 4th March 1834
Mr Wm Dickson
Dear Sir

I find that three men is all that can be spared from this place, you will therefore require to send ~~all the~~ Campbell all the assistance you possibly can; after his arrival at your place you can consult together what will be the best way for you to get out your returns, and act accordingly. By the men I send the articles you requested a memorandum of which I shall enclose. I have picked out a gun horn for the little (Cassuer de fleche)[22] which I hope will please him. I have inquired about the Vent que arrivés Bones which were brought here by a Yancton

(Smaka on Cully) and have been well tied up and put upon a scafold, with the little soldier's child; I wanted to wrap them up in Scarlet and get a coffin made to put them in, but the Indians advised me not to do it as his brothers might perhaps wish to look at the bones; but should they wish it, I can get it done at any time.[23] I send a little Flour sugar and (Washteminy) for the little Cassuer de flesh with his name marked on the bundle. In spite of the late fine weather there is still a great quantity of snow near this place. I presume about your place it is all gone long ago. The express has arrived from St Louis, and gone above before I arrived here, there is no news from below that would be interesting to you. Send all the Horses to Campbell's that you can spare, but by no means put yourself to any inconvenience, should you be assured that the Indians will go to trade at your place in any number as it would be well for you to send for a supply of wine, so as to be prepared for them when they come out. I send an Ermine skin by John for Mary [Laidlaw's wife] to finish the saddle

I remain
Truly Your's
(signed) Wm Laidlaw

P.S. If you think you can to secure the heavy articles you may have remaining in spring it would be well to cache them, such as axes Tobacco and Ball

Wm Laidlaw

❖ ❖ ❖

Fort Pierre 28th April 1834
Pierre Chouteau Junr Esqr
Dear Sir

I avail myself of the opportunity of Baron Braunsberg's [Prince Maximilian's] going down of dropping you a few lines. I yesterday received a letter from Mr McKenzie wherein he mentions that he has given you a full account of our affairs above therefore I shall confine myself to things immediately connected to this place since Mr Lamont's departure. I am sorry to inform you that the returns from here will fall much short of what we [word?] time expected, I do not think that they will exceed 11 or 12 hundred packs of Robes, true the Indians have still a good many amongst them but they have been obliged to scatter about in every direction before they got them dressed on account of the great scarcity of provisions we have been living from hand to mouth for some [time] past and living principally on poor dogs

Inclosed you have a list of accounts of several persons who have I understand gone to St Louis without settling with us perhaps you will be able to get payment no limits ought to be shewn to any of them for they dont deserve it with the exception of William Marten of whom I know very little, he has been acting as SubAgent for Major Bean for some time past. Alexis Durant is one of our men whom I have permitted to go down on account of bad health his time is not out till August 1835 he has always behaved well and wishes to return in the fall if his health will permit the men above who did to are Louis Minard, Zephier Recontre, Michel Ducoteau

I remain
Dear Sir
With greatest respect
Yours Very Truly
(Signed) William Laidlaw

❖ ❖ ❖

Fort Pierre 30 April 1834
Mr James Kipp

Your two favours the one under date of the 13th March and the other 18th April I only received two days ago I have to regret that the former did not come to hand sooner as you could have had the Horses you request a month earlier I now lose no time in sending them, three American horses and 10 Indian, there are four of the Indian horses first rate Buffaloe runners indeed most overtake cattle with ease where reposed.

I regret exceedingly that you did not send us down some corn as we are in a state of starvation and our opponents have traded a good many robes for one quart of corn each and I have no doubt if I had the corn that I would trade 50 Bushels at that price, I wish you to send down Lachapelle and the man that go along with him with one hundred or a hundred and fifty Bushels of corn without a moments delay. Mr Kennedy you can keep with you for the present. Mr McKenzie when he comes down will tell you how to dispose of him. The Horses you mention that the Gros Ventres brought to their village belonged to Bellair and Landrie they found them out hunting and pillaged them but did not harm them otherwise. I can supply you with 20 or 30 more Horses if you dispose them to advantage please let me know how you sell those I have now sent. How does the sample of Beads I sent you please the Mandans?

Our return here will fall much short of what we at one time expected our Indians are starving in every direction.

For God's sake try and send us the corn as soon as possible, perhaps you can spare us a few [word?]. May has gone out a hunting about 10 days ago, because the shortness of this as I am much hurried. What became of the Horses that Bellhumeur & H ortubise found belonging to the Sawons?

Yours truly
(signed) Wm Laidlaw

❖ ❖ ❖

Fort Pierre 25th Augte 1834
Joshua Pilcher Esqr.
Dear Sir

This will be handed you by Mr Lachapelle who is sent from this as express to Saint Louis, to give information of the desertion of a number of our men from this post. As it is necessary that he should reach there as soon as possible, you will please supply him with provisions if he stands in need of them; or any thing else he may require to pursue his journey with as little delay as possible

Respectfully Yours
Jacob Halsey
For Pratte, Chouteau & Co.

❖ ❖ ❖

Fort Pierre 25th August 1834.
Messrs. Pratte, Chouteau & Co
Saint Louis
Gentlemen

This will be handed you by Lachapelle who is sent from here to bear information of the desertion of 13 Pork eaters from this post; so that you may take what measures you think proper to supply others in their place. They started out last night with a small Mackinac boat and skiff, and have no doubt supplied themselves plentifully with provisions at Bloomfield farm, a few miles below this place.

I have as yet nothing regarding trade mostly of communication of Buffaloe continue very scarce, and all the Indians we have had news from are starving. We have had no news from Fort Union since Mr McKenzie left there, Please Excuse hurry, and Believe me Ever

Yours Most Respectfully
Jacob Halsey

❖ ❖ ❖

Fort Pierre 25th Augt: 1834
William Laidlaw Esqr
Saint Louis
Dear Sir

The purpose of this conveyance is to give you information of the desertion of 13 Pork eaters from this post some time during the past night in the small Mackinac Boat and skiff; I presume they will take in a supply of Provisions at the farm in passing. The scoundrels have no good reason for leaving us, they have been well treated in every respect we having always been able to give them plenty of good dry Buffaloe meat and corn; the inclosed list will shew you who they are, how they stand with the Co., and what they stoled. I also include you a list of the men remaining here, so that you may be better able to judge what number will be sufficient for you to bring, or send into the country this fall. We have not had a word from above since Mr. McK. left, neither have I any good news to give you regarding trade, or the prospects thereof. Buffaloe are quite as distant as usual.

I am happy to inform you that your family are well, and that the general health of the Fort is quite as good as I ever knew it: although we have already consumed a good many melons, Cucumbers &c. J. Juett brought in 150 Pieces of dry meat, the balance of which we are now living on, and in a few days we will be again reduced to a corn diet. However the farmers at Bloomfield tell us that it will be time for the gathering in, the commencement of the [word?] week; how the crop will turn out I cannot say, but I fear from what I have heard that the Potatoes will not meet with your expectations as I am told that many of the vine have nothing on them, which is also the case in the field along side the fort.

We are desirous to send off Lachapelle with as little delay as possible, therefore you cannot expect a lengthy letter from me, and I beg leave to refer to Lachapelle for all the news.

Believe me Yours Most Truly
Jacob Halsey
William Laidlaw
Saint Louis

❖ ❖ ❖

Fort Pierre 1st October 1834
Mr. Francis A. Chardon
Fort Clark
Dear Sir

Inclosed you will receive particulars of stock remaining on hand at Fort Clark last summer showing the price of each article; you will find it convenient when you go to make out Equipment for the Groventres, and other Indians you will likewise receive herewith Invoice of Mdze. del. F. C. by Sublette & Campbell 18th June 1834. W. P. Mays note for $265.50, Michel Bellhumeurs a/c in detail, a/c amount between this post and Feb. and your own a/c up to June last.

By the first opportunity, I wish you would gave the goodness to let me have a list of the persons in the employ of the Co. at your Post, showing the amt.: of their wages and the term of their engagements, this is an absolutly necessary I should I have, in order to make out your post a/c completely; the a/c current will show the names of such of your people, with whom engagements I am acquainted.

I have charged your post with Mays note and a/c, as it is probable it will be paid at your post. Some Invoice of Mdse: per Steam boat, shall be sent to you as soon as it is recd. from St Louis; in the mean time I hope you will be able to get along without it.

I have nothing more to say to you in the way of business, and will now close by [word?] myself.
Very Truly Yours
Jacob Halsey
(Official)

❖ ❖ ❖

Fort Pierre 1st Octr 1834.
James A. Hamilton Esqr
Fort Union
Dear Sir

Inclosed you will receive all the papers appertaining to Outfit 1834, which I have the means of furnishing at the present period, so soon as the documents we are expecting from below come to hand, I will endeavour to supply you with whatever may seem [to] be wanting; In the mean time I hope you will not suffer much inconvenience from the want thereof.

With Great Respect
Believe me Yours Very Truly
Jacob Halsey
For Pratte Chouteau & Co.

❖ ❖ ❖

Fort Pierre October 1st 1834.
James A. Hamilton Esqr
Fort Union
Dear Sir

In settlement of the F. Union Outfit 1833. I have according to my instructions, directed in several instances from the statement formulated by you, consequently it is unnecessary I should give you explanations thereof, in order that you may be satisfied that what a situation we have made, are strictly fair and equitable. The first instance in which we differ is in your own a/c which is $12.27 instead of $10.21 which latter is the sum you give this post Cr. for in your a/c current under date of 18th October 1833. April 7th you charge F. P. with Pan, Cap, Plate; Epichimore and piece Lodge per Chardon, no such articles were recd. here. May 10th you charge advances to F. Croteau $61.50 he being indebted to the Co. it has been taken off the Co. side of the a/c. From charge of $25. 288.53 a deduction has been made of $5209.38 for advances made to freemen, as also "engages" above the amt. of their wages as will appear in Statement you will receive herewith. A deduction of one third has been made from the charge called proportion of expences of Montreal men.

Your charge against this post a/c a Baron de Braunsberg nine [day] passage from Saint Louis to Marias River, is thought a severe one, consequently, a deduction has been made of cf 150 there from; as also even advances to men accompanying him to Saint Louis, has been struck out. Mr. McKenzie could not remain long enough with us to take a perfect copy of your Inventory of stock on hand last June, therefore you will please have the goodness to let me have one, as soon as practicable.

A List of the men engaged at Fort Union last

summer, is also much wanted here; as also abstract of Michel Sudlows Engagement.

In hopes that the enclosed account current will prove satisfactory, I subscribe myself
Yours Very Truly
Jacob Halsey
For Pratte, Chouteau & Co.

❖ ❖ ❖

Fort Pierre 6th Octr. 1834.
Messrs. Pratte, Chouteau & Co.
St. Louis
Gentlemen

Herewith you will receive a Batteau laden with Robes &c. shipped by Colin Campbell this day, for particulars of which I refer you to the accompanying Bill of Lading and Packing a/c.

I also send you herewith inclosed a small account against Mr Whitten, for sundry articles paid to P. Ortubise per order of Mr. W. it was not presented at the [word?] place, untill after the departure of Messrs. McKenzie and Laidlaw, and consequently was not forwarded to you with the other charges against him.

A charge recently discovered against Fontenelle, Drips & Co. M. C. a (Girard a/c $210.45) is now sent you for collection, F. U. only gave us notice of this debt lately, consequently we could not send it to you before.

Andreu Lacompte is indebted to the Co. 68.87. as per note which you will receive herewith.

A statement of the mens a/cs. now descending is now sent you, in order that settlement may be made with them. I. Derois one of the Fort Union men has been engaged for this post: he has $100 coming to him for services ending this fall, which sum he wishes to have paid to his wife in St Louis on demand at the office, and we have promised him it should be done; indeed, it was only in consideration thereof that he engaged to the Co.; he is a good man, and I hope you will have the goodness to attend to his request.

In the packet from Fort Union there is no letter addressed to you, but there is one for Mr. McKenzie which you will receive herewith. Mr Hamilton in his letter to me gave me no news of consequence; nothing having yet having been done in the way of trade. I have made out Bills of Lading for the Fort Union boat and had them signd. Here, it being my impression that the skins sent out of the country were all insured.

I last wrote you a few lines on the 25th August informing you of the desertion of 13 men from this post. Lachapelle was sent down with the letter, he had instructions to proceed on to St Louis with as little delay as possible, but he finding the day after he passed Otto Establishment, that the most of the deserters had been engaged by Mr. Cabanné, and were ascending the river aboard of a Steam Boat with Mr. C. he thought it useless to go any further himself, as there [word?] be an opportunity of forwarding the letter in his possession by the return of the Steam Boat, and there was a reasonable prospect that she would get down to St Louis fully as soon, as he could reach there in a small canoe; consequently, he set out on his return, and finally reached here on the 22d. Ultimo.

The last news we had from the Indians "En Large" they were all starving, a Buffaloe was rarely to be met with in the plains. Frederick Laboue was at the Sawons, trying as we suppose, to persuade them to accompany him to the Riviere Platte; indeed the Sawons, Ogllallahs, Cheyennes, Brulés and Yancktons all say, they are going to visit that section of the country early in the spring.

There is a band of Sioux say 100 Lodges encamped on the Missouri, in the neighbourhood of the Ree Village, who we understand have Plenty of Buffalos; I am told they say they are coming in immense herds from the north, and I am in hopes that this years trade will exceed that of the last.

Bloomfield farm was of very great service to us this year; indeed without its aid we would have suffered severely for the want of Provisions, however, notwithstanding it has been valuable, it does not meet with our expectations; it has brought us in 300 Bushels of corn, and I presume we will have about the same quantity of Potatoes.

What has been done at Vermillion farm I know not we having no news from them since early in the summer.

I understand that Emillien Primeau and A. Leclair are on their way up the Missouri in opposition to each other, we suppose they are now somewhere in the neighbourhood of the P[onca?] Village.

I can think of nothing more worthy of communication at the present moment.

Allow me gentlemen to subscribe myself with my best wishes for our health and happiness.

Your Obt. and Humble Servant

Jacob Halsey

P. Since writing the foregoing Indians have arrived from the Large for Traders, Viz: Sawons, Ogallallahs, & Brulés *they all say* they have now plenty of Buffalos, indeed, they tell me they are so plenty, that they think the dead ones have all come to life again. I hope that next springs returns, will in some measure verify their assertion

I. L C. [?]

❖ ❖ ❖

Fort Pierre October 6th 1834

Messrs. Pratte, Chouteau & Co.

Saint Louis

Gentlemen

This will be handed you by Mr. J. P. Winter who has a balance due him for some Beaver skins &c: delivered at this post.

I have given him a due bill for the amount coming to him, which he will present to you for payment on his arrival in St Louis.

Respectfully Yours &c

Jacob Halsey

❖ ❖ ❖

Fort Pierre Oct 21 1834

Messrs Pratte Chouteau & Co

St Louis

Gentlemen

This will be handed you by Mr Francois Bellair to whom the Co. are indebted Seven Hundred dollars for Beaver Skins delivered at this Post at various times; his last hunt was eighty five pounds of this falls Beaver, for which we have allowed him three dollars and a half per pound, thinking it better to do so than to let him take it elsewhere, which he certainly would have done. He has a due bill for the amount coming to him.

Two Mackinac boats left here on the 6th inst, with robes &c. Shipped to your address which I hope will reach you without accident in due course of time. I understand Primeau and Leclair are on their way up the Missouri in Opposition to each Other, the last news we had of them they were Somewhere in the neighbourhood of the P[onca?] Village. We have had no arrival from St Louis yet, and begin to fear some thing has happened to the Gentlemen we have been looking for from thence; Otherwise it appears to me Some of them would have been here before the Present period. Their [word?] with you is quite necessary in order to send out the equipment "En Large" which by the bye, ought to have been started a month ago; happily for us however, we have had no opponents to contend with since last spring, and I hope nothing will be lost to the Co by their being Sent out a month later this year. Gardner is still at the mouth of Running Water River, waiting for the Poncaws, he has passed the summer there, and done nothing whatever in the way of trade, there Being no Indians at that point.

I have no news to give you regarding trade having wrote you fully ~~regarding trade~~ on that Subject by the Boats on the 6th inst, since which nothing has happened worthy of Communication

With my best wishes for

Your health & Prosperity

Believe me Gentlemen

Yr obedient & Huml Servt

(Signd) Jacob Halsey

Messrs. Pratte Chouteau & Co

Saint Louis

Misso.

❖ ❖ ❖

Fort Pierre 23d. Novr 1834

Mr. E. T. Denig

Dear Sir

Yours of the 21st I duly recd. and have noted the contents. It was not my intention that you should go or send to the camp immediately but only to watch the motions of Ménard and Laboue in case of their going along with them, knowing that the name of the people at a distance is much worse to contend with than their presence in reality; this you will no doubt find out. You must not attempt running out to the different camps from your place this winter, for we have not the means, it would require at least fifty good horses to do that, that you know we have not got, my object is to get them thoroughly established at Cherry River where they will in all probability send back their horses, then in that case

I would advise sending a trader into each camp, to be stationary for the winter.

Mr. Picotte is fully acquainted with my views on the subject, and will act accordingly. You ought to try and persuade them to remain quiet when they are shewing to them the difficulty of getting out the returns in spring, if they go further, but even this I scarcely think it necessary knowing Ménard not to be a man of great enterprise, the ideas or sugetions you ought to keep to yourself, for I confess I have no great confidence in Vasseur, I am much afraid you have been too hasty in forming a favourable opinion of him, and would advise you to keep a very sharp Lookout after him. The Indians that came in lately to Leclaire, were much disappointed and displeased at the reception they met with, and have gone off growling like a Bear with a sore head.

I have neither got man or horse to send you but as soon as [word?] returns from Mr. Dickson I shall send him to you; I now look for him every day, I do not believe that Leclair has got any liquor, if such is the case I shall not send out a drop any where this winter.

I have understood that Leclair has given or has not to date a Blanket under 3 Robes, and 3 pt. Blkts: four; this you will soon be able to ascertain at all events whatever he sells at, we must sell a little cheaper, so as to secure the trade. The Bearer of this is hurrying me so much that I must conclude by
 Assuring you I remain
 Yours Truly
 Sign'd Wm Laidlaw

❖ ❖ ❖

Fort Pierre 3d. Decr. 1834
Mr. H. Picotte
Dear Sir

I have been anxiously expecting to hear from you for some time past, but I heard of you through the medium of Mr. Denig, which was so far satisfactory, but it would still have been more so to have had a few lines from yourself; I was glad to hear that you made such an expeditious trade, and I have no doubt a good one, it was also pleasing to me to learn you had been at Cherry river. I like the plan of sending Angé to the Sans Arc,[24] but keep always in mind, that it is necessary you should be yourself [two words?] are opposed, any person will do when there is no opposition; then Ménard is not a very Bright genius, but still Mr. Denig has not had experience enough, and it cannot be expected he would do so well as one of your experience and Knowledge of the trade; and if I can believe report it appears there will be a very considerable trade made at Cherry River; I sent Mr. Denig three horse loads of Goods the other day, and intend sending him four or five more tomorrow by Big Leclair, whom I understand you have engaged, I hope he is bound by his engagement to help out with the returns.

I am very anxious to hear from Wm. Dickson, should he be in want of another trader or two, I can supply him. Mr Papin sent in for more goods a few days ago; the Brulés and Yanctons are near Eau-qui-court and have plenty of Cattle; consequently will make a good many Robes; I have heard nothing of Campbell since he left this, Joe sent in from the Ogallallahs for a further supply of Goods; but has neither Indians or Cattle near him; little Carrier got most shockingly torn by a Bear; but is now doing well, though much disfigured, he was not expected to live at one time. Lebrun and he caught 92 Beaver skins before the accident happened, which was of course an injury to their hunt. Write me on the receipt of this, and let me know your prospects and your different movements, I am much afraid that the Indians will come in to trade at Cherry River before you get back
 In the mean time believe Me Yours
 Sign'd. William Laidlaw

❖ ❖ ❖

Fort Pierre 3d. Decr. 1834.
Mr. Colin Campbell
Dear Sir

I have been waiting with the greatest impatience for ten days back, to hear from you and cannot immagine what has become of your people, that some of them do not make their appearance with the horses, after the strict injunction I gave you about sending them back without delay, I have heard from all the other posts. Bombonet arrived here a few days ago from the Ogallallah in quest of goods, he tell me that they had no tidings of you, as Joe appeared to be in immediate want of the goods I sent him a supply which I regret being obliged to do, being well persuaded that you have more than you will both require of most [word?].

By all that I can learn it appears that the Minni-co-jux will nearly all trade at the Cherry River, as well as a great part of the Little Bears and No heart band; if this report is correct, you can have but few Indians to trade at your place, but I cannot allow myself to think that such will be the case, otherwise you would certainly have given me notice before this time. Mr. Denig is labouring under a great disadvantage for want of men and goods; and you have put it entirely out of my power of supplying him by not sending back the Horses as was contemplated, should this report turn out [to] be true, you will require to send him some supplies of such articles as you can spare, but I am in hopes that things will turn out better than the present appearance of affairs would lead us to believe. Write me immediately on the receipt of this, if you could come in with propriety yourself so much the better, if not write me a long explanatory letter do not fail to send in Newmans horse (*light*) as he has been waiting for him for 10 days past he killed 45 Beaver and Mr. May who is also with him 160. Mr Picotte traded 100 packs of Robes at Grand river in one night and day, and better than half a pack of Beaver. You no doubt have been to see Joe before this time. I bought Lebruns and Carriers beaver for $4 per pound and sent you a statement of their a/c from this place, so that you will have no difficulty in settling with them. I told Bombonet to tell Joe if he had more ammunition and Tobacco than he required, to send all he could spare to you. You need not be afraid of having any opposition, as they have neither men or goods to send. I shall send you a memorandum of the goods I sent to Joe by Bombonet. In hopes of hearing from you soon I remain Truly Yours

Sign'd Wm Laidlaw

❖ ❖ ❖

P.S. Be sure you let me know what are your prospects for trade. Our stock of Dry Meat is getting very low, is there no possibility of sending us a little, but however much we may be in want I would by no means wish to interfere with your trade. What has become of all the hickory [word?] I bought last summer, I find only four in the store.

W. L.

❖ ❖ ❖

Fort Pierre 3d. Decr 1834
Mr. E. T. Denig
Dear Sir

Yours of the 1st inst. I duly recd. last evening by Leclair, and hasten to send you a supply of goods as much as I possibly can, which I think will be sufficient or all the demands that may be upon you for the present, I sent you three horse loads a few days ago, which I have no doubt you have recd. before this time. I think Leclair's wages very high for the winter, and it would appear that he is to get an Equipment over and above the sum you mentioned in your last; this I grudge more than all the rest for it is a thing that ought to be done away with altogether, I would rather give double the amount in money; I never considered him a very dangerous opponent, and would not fear him much, but however the thing is done and of course was done for the best.

That of Squaw influence with a band of Indians I must confess is intirely a new thing to me; I have often known it have a very bad effect, but never in one instance did I know it to have a good effect; but nevertheless there is no such without excepting the thing may *be possible*, the longer we live, the more we learn.

I am glad to hear that you get on so well in the Trade, but let me suggest one thing, you may be in being too stingy as well as too extravagent, as you are situated and what appears to you to be a profit or gain, may ultimately prove to be a loss, throwing more of the trade into your opponents hands. You mention that he has only 6 or 8 Robes. (I am afraid he has more than that) and those he got by giving double price, now if you trade a Robe for 25 cents, as you say, why not give six times that rather than he should get the Robes, you must not allow him to undersell you, unless he sells much below [word?] cost, and that I know he will not do. Let Robes be your password, and let the guard be wide awake, and have the Robes, (Coute qui Coute) cost what they will, goods you can have as many as you chose, only get the trade. I certainly strongly recommend enconimy [economy] when it can be done with propriety; you have every advantage over Ménard, and one in particular, that is his goods are nothing like assorted, you ought to inform yourself well what he has got; and what he has not got, such things as he has not got, you can Keep on old prices, which will enable you to undercut him in those articles [he] has got, all this it is true requires a good deal of maneuvering, and a great deal of discretion, however simple it may appear to you. Send back John with the horses I no send as soon as possible. I send by Leclair a letter addressed to Mr. Picotte & another to Campbell, which I beg you will have forwarded without a moments delay.

I thank you for the Tobacco that Leclair handed me, although I am sorry to say it is no better than our own, still my obligation to you is the same as if it had been the best. With regard to the Indian whose lungs come out, he gave back his Hat and Packamagan[25] in a Fit, because he did not chose to pay for them, but I think the best way to settle that with him for the present is to tell him that I will arrange the matter with him when we meet, that you know nothing of the transaction and that Lachapelle has gone above.

Yours Most Truly
(Sign'd) Wm. Laidlaw

❖ ❖ ❖

Fort Pierre 11th Dec. 1834
Mr. Collin Campbell

Yesterday I was much surprised by the arrival of your men with four horses & six Carts all in the worst possible order. I had long given up hopes of either seeing or hearing from you this winter. And on perusing your letter you may judge of my Surprise upon seeing that you have taken on that extensive Equipment to the Ogallalla post. When there was no earthly occasion for it & besides I took such pains in explaining to you that that Equipment, was to be left at the fork of Chayanne, in order to draw the Indians to that place to prevent their Coming to Cherry River where we are strongly opposed; you have therefore thwarted my plan intirely, and the consequences can not fail to be very injurious to the Company's interest; it was Ceartainly a great want of forethought on your part, and I [am] much at a loss how to rectify it at this late hour.

in the first place you have more than double the quantity of goods that will be required for that place, in the second place you have set yourself down in a place where we have no opposition (Contrary to my express order) with a retinue that might [have] established three post in case of necessity. Consider for one moment, how this will look in the eyes of the world, while we have Mr. Denig and Joe Vallonce, only ([word?] Homs) without a single man to help them to oppose Frederick and Ménard; taking all this into consideration there would appear to be a great want of management on our post which must be evident to all *you are the sole Cause*; my understanding with you was that you were to visit the different camps yourself, upon your arrival at the fork, in place of Complying with my instructions, you allow Frederick who left this fourteen Augt after you did, to come behind you and trade up every thing that could be found, this is certainly very galling, and I must say I feel ashamed of it (*however you may feel*) by not sending back the Horses & Carts immediately as you was directed, you put it intirely out of my power to supply Mr. Denig with such goods as was necessary for the trade, it would have been lucky any of the Horses you had, had broke their necks the day you passed the Fork, however enough of this. The business is how to rectify all these evils; I cannot see the necessity of your sending a trader to the Bear hill, as they must be compelled to come & trade at your place, therefore I wish you to send [Name?], Pineau and one man to transport the goods from your place to Cherry River, that is to say every thing that you have an surplus of, and you to remain there to assist in the trade see and get there put in motion as soon as possible, I understand part of the Oggalles will trade at Mr Papin upon White river, he is built in the mavis Terre,[26] when I left [two words?] last year; Deshonnette knows the place if you can assist in supplying him with goods do so [as] it is much nearer there to get there from this place.

There is a small a/c that was not included in Bonaventure Lebruns last a/c which Mr Halsey will forward you; you can make the freemen that are with you small advances if necessary, say 20 or 30 dollars. I cannot send the small Boxes nor beads having no Horses able to perform the trip.

I understand that the Oggalles are making a great many [word?] about going to the Platte (at least Joe says so), if so, do not try to prevent them but tell them that it is cattle that we are in want of, not indians, that if they abandon their lands, that they will soon be taken possession of by the Indians, that would be glad of the departings such as the Yanctons & Esautus I think this is the best way to treat threats of that kind and not to be making [word?] & entreating them to remain which I am persuaded would have no good effect; so it is best to appear quite indifferent, whether they leave the country or not, as good fish in the sea as are good out of it, send in one ball [word?] to Cherry River so that I may git it.

I remain yours
(signd.) Wm. Laidlaw

❖ ❖ ❖

[Fort Pierre: no date]
Mr. Edwin T. Denig
Dear Sir

I duly received your letter of the 6th Inst per John; I have spoke to Dafond & Ortubise about the flour sugar & coffee &c; they say the men were obliged to make use of two mugs of your flour, but did not touch the sugar & coffee. I am sorry that I have not a man to send you, the articles you requested in your last, but you say if hard pushed you will send for them, and if an opportunity offered I should not fail sending them, you and I appear to be playing at cross purposes, I have all along been striving to get the "merce co cus": to go and trade at Campbells when we have no opposition, and you doing in your power to induce them to come to Cherry River, which was very inconsiderate on your part; I am surprised that the impropriety of this did not occur to you, had it been Leclair of Valduce it would not have surprised me, I am exceedingly [word?] that Diéitte should pay you a visit, and have wrote him to that effect, however, should he not come and you expect the Indians to come in to trade in any considerable bands, let me [have] Yenny, and I will pay you a visit, to lend you a hand; if we allow one opponent such as you have to make any thing of a trade, I think it is time to shut up shop if you have not yet sent the letter addressed to Campbell, which I requested you to forward, it is not necessary to send it express, but wait an opportunity during the winter, I have heard from him yesterday, and to my great surprise and disappointment he had gone on to "Eau qui Court" I have directed him to send

a great part of his Equipt. To you, but you must not depend upon that.

If the Horse you mention, be a good Buffaloe runner sound and in good order, he is not too dear, his services will be of some value, and then we can always sell him for more than he will cost you, and a more ready sale than goods.

The little Yancton has just arrived from Mr. Dicksons in quest of goods he tells me that "Gachauty" is Stationed on grand River near where Mr Picotte is established, Dickson has traded 50 packs of Robs & 2 Packs of Beaver, Primeau it seems traded 5 Kegs of liquor, but is supposed to have no more, however, this is uncertain.

I spoke to the 'black eyes" to day about his having threatened to cut the Robes of those that moved off to trade at your House, he denied the charge point blank, and says that it is jealousy that makes them talk in that way, I told him that I thought it would be rather a dangerous undertaking, & that I did not think it could be done with impunity. Should Mr. Picotte be at your place, or whenever he may come, if he could make it convenient to pay me a visit I should be glad to see him, but not if he thinks it will interfere with his trade, please notify him of this. I would write him, [two words?] he would be at Cherry River, the doctor will send you some papers; continue to write me long letters and believe me truly Yours
(Sign'd) William Laidlaw

❖ ❖ ❖

Fort Pierre Dec 13th 1834
Messrs Pratte Chouteau & Co
St Louis
Gentlemen

After examining the several documents, some of them of long standing, which in all probability have been paid or settled, but as we have never been ordered of such payment or settlement, they still remain open, where perhaps if the truth was Known they should be now closed. I have made out a list of the names, and shall inclose it herewith, if all or any of these have made settlement, you will please have the goodness to advise me thereof, so that our Ledger may be regulated there from.

A copy of the Fort Lookout and Vermillion Inventory is much wanted here; it was altogether out of my power to send down a proper person to take an account of the stock there in Company with Mr. Whitten, consequently we have never had a Copy of these documents. Mr Denigs a/c in St Louis summer of 1833 has not yet come to hand, although I have written for it more than once, it is absolutely necessary that we should be furnished with a copy of it, or with at least the ammounts of it. Bernard Ray otherwise called "old Mayonce" says he has an account with you in St Louis, if it is chargable to this outfit, it would be well to furnish us with a Copy of it, as he is already in debt to a considerable amount. In a/c current with American fur Company, Outfit 1833, under date of 14 April 1834 we are charged with the sum of $592.33 cash paid Michel Chapman as pr account sent by him; it appears upon reference to one Ledger that, when he left here he had but $275 due him, this was some time in Oct. 1833, it is possible, however, that he delivered some Skins at the Vermillion Post, although I should rather think he would have taken them with him to St Louis. Cardinal Gruest delivd. Some furs to mr. McKenzie at the Vermillion when he passed there, if he left a statement of this delivery at your office, send it to us, if it can not [be] found, please be good enough to speak to Mr. McKenzie regarding it on his return to you, so that he will not forget to bring or send it to me in the spring.

The account against Rocky Mountain Outfit for summer find at Otto Establishment is sent you for collection. In this Bill herewith included drawn by Mr. Fontenelle in favor of M. P. Lefrenier for $162 you will please place to the Cr. of Outfit 1834, the a/c of Kanzas Outfit against U.M.O 1834 you will likewise receive herewith, I believe them to be current.

In these Forwarded to Fort Pierre by Mr C. Chouteau, there was several mistakes in the calculations. I have nothing more in the way of business, to Communicate at the present moment.

Believe me Gentlemen with my best wishes
For Your health & happiness
Your Obedient & humble Servant
(Sign'd) William Laidlaw
acing agent at Fort Pierre

❖ ❖ ❖

Fort Pierre Dec 16th 1834
Mr F. A. Chardon
Dear Sir

Your favour of the 6th Nov came duly to hand, I paid the order you gave Mr Newman after Mr and Mrs May pays the debt which Newman had contracted at this place; the note which you mention against Mr May was sent up to you by Mr Lamont. Mr May has been waiting here patiently for some time past, in expectation that Newman would return and join him, but as he has not made his appearance Mr M. has given him up, and will accompany our trains as far as Wm Dickson, from thence to your place by whom I will forward this letter as also his accounts.

It is Very probable that Wm Dickson may get short of goods and send to you for a supply, in which case I beg you will render him every assistance you possibly can. I hope you have got Legris and Taudieres Beaver, I have heard from all our out posts but they have done little or nothing as yet, Picotte traded 100 packs of Robes & 5 packs of Beaver, the others have traded nothing worth mentioning, I expect to hear from you soon, I hope your [word?] will be longer than your last; I hope you received the Butter & onions safe, I understand Emillien is making dog trains to go & pay you a Visit, I think here is little probability of his passing the "gen de Panie"

I remain
Truly Yours
(Sign'd) William Laidlaw

❖ ❖ ❖

Fort Pierre 17th Dec 1834
Mr. William Dickson
Dear Sir

Yours of the 5th inst: I duly recd. a few days ago per the Little Yanchnna, as also your horses, but you omitted to say how many you sent by him, however, he brought all of yours except your big sorrel; him he tells me you have sold.

I have fulfilled your memorandum, and even sent you down [a] few articles more than you requested, as you will see by the memorandum sent you. I send you B. Defond who will arrange to take charge of an outfit such as you may think proper to give him, you will of course send him where his service will be of most use to his employers; If Primeau starts

FORT PIERRE
am Missouri.
FORT PIERRE
on the Missouri.
FORT PIERRE
sur le Missouri.

Karl Bodmer's overlook view of Fort Pierre, 1834, Tableau 10, showed the fort shortly after it had been built to replace Fort Tecumseh, which was falling into the Missouri River. *Lewis & Clark Fort Mandan Foundation, Washburn, N.Dak.*

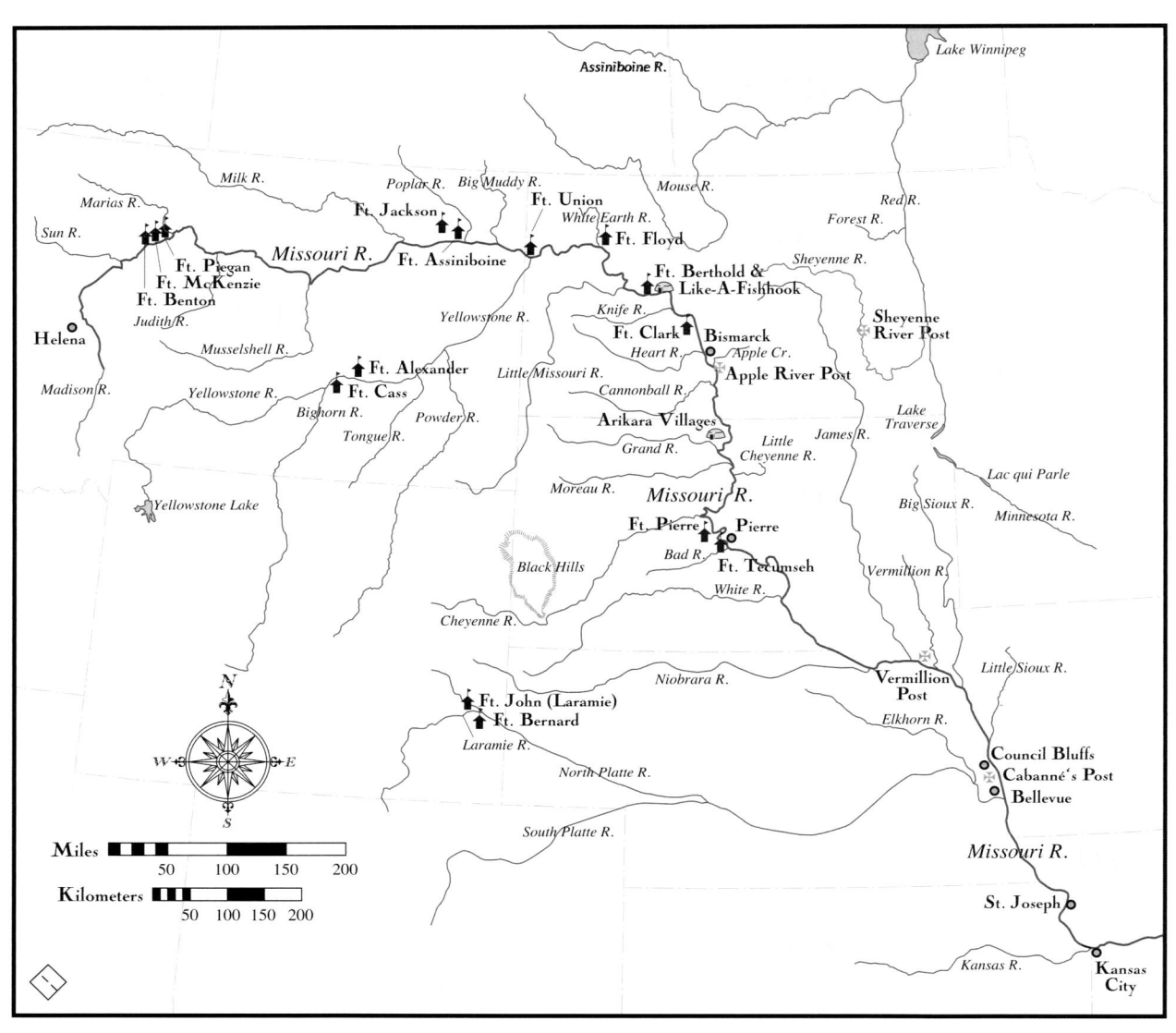

The places frequently mentioned in the journal and letter books from Fort Tecumseh and Fort Pierre range from Saint Louis to the Rocky Mountains. *Map by Brian R. Austin*

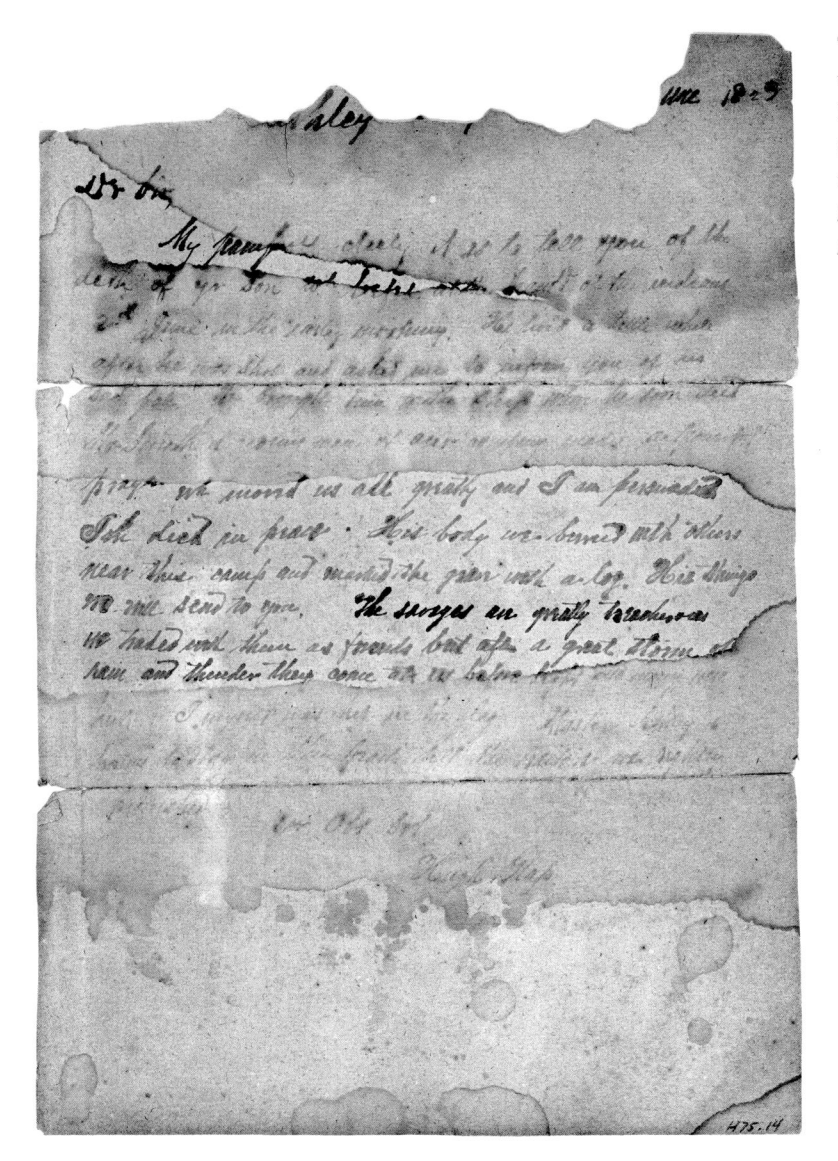

The only extant letter (dated 1823) written by legendary mountain man Hugh Glass informs the father of John S. Gardner that his son has been killed by the Arikaras at the mouth of Grand River. *South Dakota State Historical Society, State Archives Collection, Pierre*

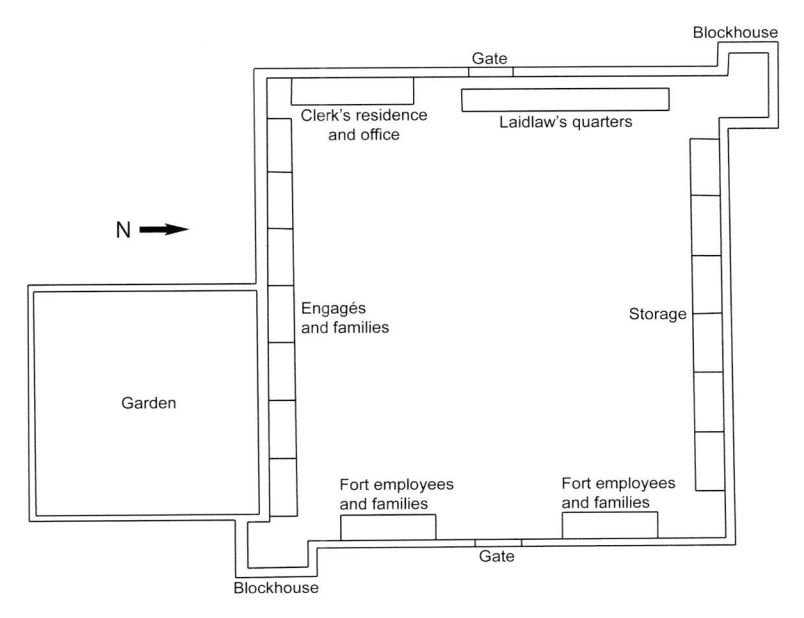

Maximilian's May 31, 1833, plan of Fort Pierre was made about a year after the fort's construction. *Redrawn and labeled by Amy Bleier*

The clientele at fur-trade posts such as Fort Tecumseh and Fort Pierre was composed of American Indians from many tribes, including this Yankton Sioux warrior depicted by Karl Bodmer in 1833, Tableau 8. *Lewis & Clark Fort Mandan Foundation, Washburn, N.Dak.*

This engraving of Fort Pierre, based on an 1844 pencil sketch by Alexander H. Murray, appeared in *Forest and Stream* in 1856.

Pierre Chouteau, Jr. *South Dakota State Historical Society, State Archives Collection, Pierre*

Joseph Rolette. *Minnesota Historical Society, Saint Paul*

The steamboat *Martha*, 1847. Collection of the Public Library of Cincinnati and Hamilton County, Ohio

Pierre Garreau. *South Dakota State Historical Society, State Archives Collection, Pierre*

Grave of William Laidlaw, 1800–1852, Mosby, Clay County, Mo. *David L. Cowell*

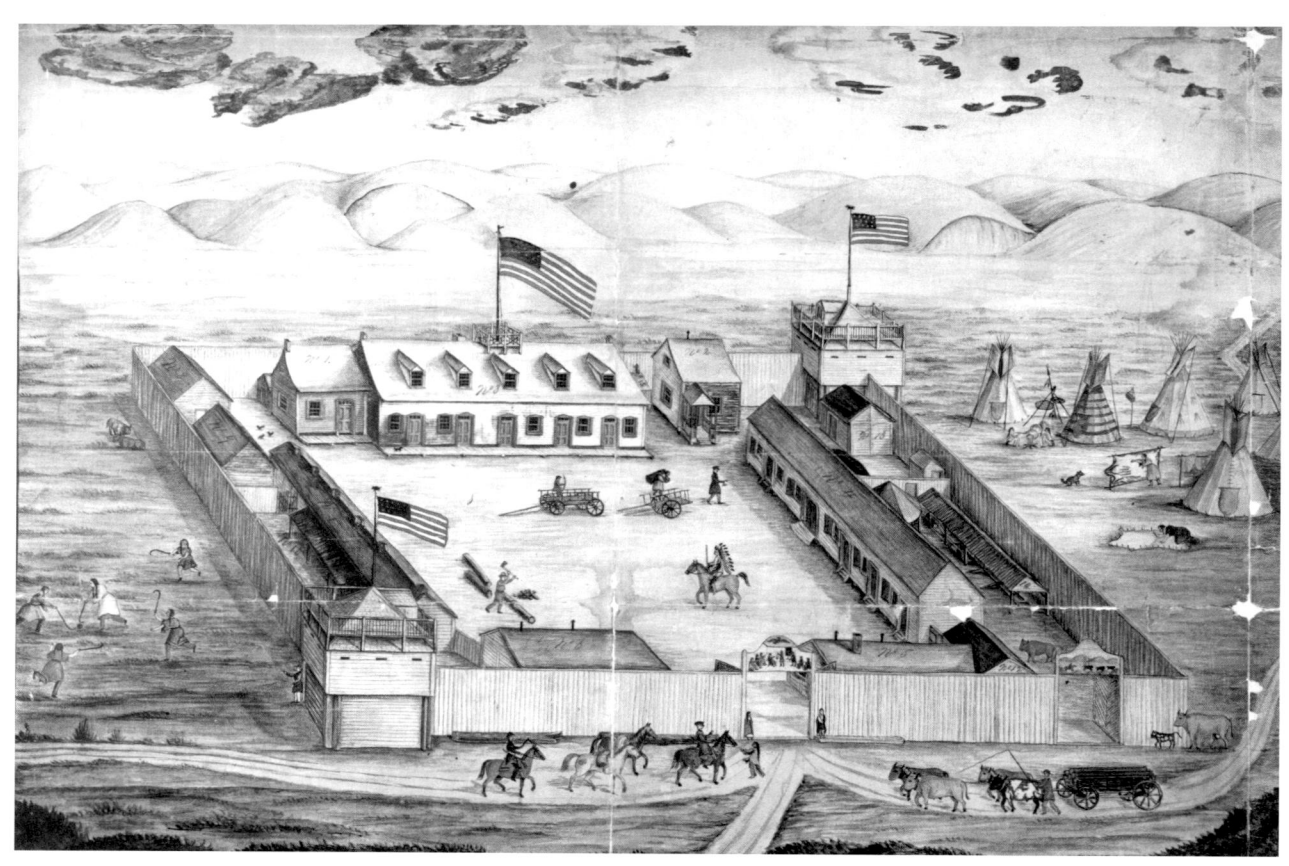

Frederick Behman's 1854 watercolor of Fort Pierre Chouteau shows the fort as it appeared four years after these letter books ended. *South Dakota State Historical Society, State Archives Collection, Pierre*

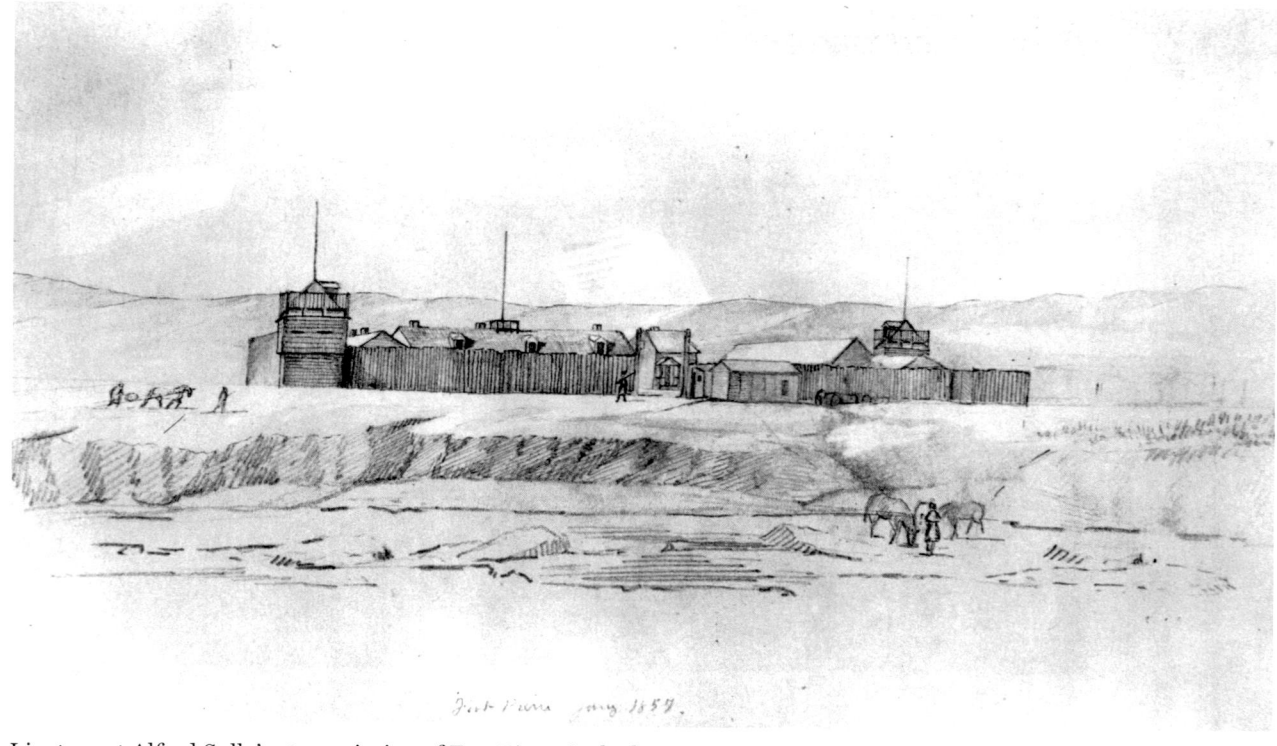

Lieutenant Alfred Sully's 1857 painting of Fort Pierre is the last recorded image of the fort. *South Dakota State Historical Society, State Archives, Pierre*

to go to the Mandans I am afraid he will come in for a good share of the trade of the "Gens de Pain" who have not yet traded I understand, if this be the case I have no doubt you will keep a sharp lookout after him, I have every confidence that you will use all exertion in your power to secure the trade, and even should you be obliged to sacrifice goods, it is of no consequence in comparison to getting the Robes; you [k]now the views of the company is to get the Robes "Coute que coute," so I beg you will spare no trouble or expence to accomplish that end; take special care not to get short of goods but send for more in time should you want any more. I think you had better send to the Mandans for a supply, it being considerably nearer your place; I have wrote Mr Chardon to render you every assistance in his power. I am extremely sorry that I have been obliged to send back your mare with the trains, but should she be injured in the least I will willingly pay for her, or give you another in her place, as it may suit you at the time; (it is an old proverb that necessity has no law.) I send Charles Primeau and a man for the purpose of bringing back the trains loaded with meat, as our stock is getting low; I understand that Lachapelle has a good deal, if he has enough to load the trains I think it would be well to take their load at his place, as he is trading in a lodge, and if the Indians get short of meat, they might be apt to impose on him.

I wish you had been a little more explicit about the beaver that the Little Yanctonna gave you mainly say 20 Beaver and 3 others, but do not say what kind or size, so I have been obliged to take his word, and have paid him for 19 Large Beaver 1 Small, and 2 others.

I have sent you three Sorrels, I would sell them for 5 Robes rather than bring them back, even four, though it would hardly pay for them.

"Wan-na-ta" came here a few days ago and goes up to your place along with Defond, I have no doubt but he will assist you as usual; I need not remind you to make no credits to Indians, nor advance any of the men more than their wages, in fact those you have ought to have nothing except what is absolutely necessary.

If you could possibly get me a few pairs of garnished moccassins made, I should be much obliged to you, without tops for ladies use, about the size of Jeans [?] foot would answer.

I send you a recipe for salting tongues, which if you follow you will be sure to cure them well; try and collect as many as you possibly can. If you send Defond above to the "Gen de Pain" I think it would be well for you to go up yourself to establish him.
Yours Most Truly
(Sign'd) Wm. Laidlaw

❖ ❖ ❖

Fort Pierre 22d. Dec 1834.
Mr. Pierre D. Papin
Dear Sir

I have this moment recd. yours of the 18th Inst:; I have recd. the Bearer w. you requested and given him several little things, with a great deal of good advice whether he will follow it or not is another thing. The old "E. C. ke see ga" that accompanied him, did not come here which is no great loss. I am glad to hear that you have such a successful trade, and I presume from your letter that you are by this time near the camp; but we again impress upon your mind the necessity of your keeping a good deal of goods on hand. So that your opponents will have no advantage over you, at the same time I am persuaded that you will look out for [word?]; I beseach you to make no credit to Indians. *I look upon any profit* you can *make as trifling* in comparison to getting the trade, *and defeating our opponents*, therefore I beg you not to spare the goods, but secure the trade, trouble, I am well aware you will undergo to accomplish that end; but if your indians make any thing of a hunt, I am of opinion that you have not half goods enough: do send in time, so that you may lack nothing. Campbell is at "Eau qui Court" Picotte is now here from Cherry River in quest of goods; Cattle are said to be plenty but far out; bad weather I have no doubt will bring them nearer.

Emillien was set fast with his boat a little below Beaver river. I hope I shall have the pleasure of hearing from you soon.

Be sure you trade all the meat you can, also grease. Is it true that the Cheyennes and Brules have been killing each other. Try and make Lesshin pay for the horses he got from the Brules last year.
In the mean time I remain Yours Truly
(Signd) Wm. Laidlaw

❖ ❖ ❖

Fort Pierre 23d. Decr. 1834.
Mr. E. T. Denig
Dear Sir

Your last I duly received pr Mr Picotte I have had a good deal of conversation with him regarding the trade, and he will adopt such measures as we have agreed upon, therefore it is unnecessary for me to enter into a detailed account; as he will explain I have fulfilled your memorandum and sent several articles more than you requested, thinking they will come in [word?] before the winter is past. I have seen the horse the "Little Capein de fleche" sent you If you call him a first rate horse I must say you are easily pleased; he is certainly the most miserable looking animal I have seen for some time, and not worth accepting as a gift.

I am much satisfied and at the same time much displeased to hear that you have already advanced Vasseur for nearly the amount of his wages; I should like to know what services you can expect from a fellow of that kind, when paid in full, be careful for the future not to advance him any thing except what is absolutely necessary for the performance of his duty.

I thought I had been very particular in telling you to give no credit to Indians and not advance any more to the full amount of his wages.

Should you go to grand river be particular in seeing that your horses are well attended to.

Yours Truly
(Signd.) Wm. Laidlaw

❖ ❖ ❖

Fort Pierre Jany. 12. 1835
Mr. William Dickson
Dear Sir

Your favor of the 21st December I duly received, as well as the packet of letters from above and yours of the 31st. I received yesterday, and embrace the opportunity of Mr. Newmans going to the Mandans of sending you the 2 doz: Red stone pipes[27] you requested in your last, I regret much that you have not been a little more communication as your last, you do not acknowledge the receipt of mine to you per Charles Primeau (perhaps you thought it not worth answering) but at all events I think you might acknowledge the receipt of the goods at least, taking it for granted that you received them, neither have you sent an a/c of the meat you sent by Charles. I must confess this is rather a loose way of doing business, and hope that you will be a little more particular in future.

You give me no idea what your prospects are for trade, not even a word on the subject; a person in charge of a post ought never to trust the occurrences of his post to be related verbally which he is able to write them himself.

I am much surprised and disappointed at the same time to hear from Charles that Emillien Primeau has opposed you so successfully, he has now got a much greater portion of the trade than I ever expected he would; considering the advantage you had over him in every respect, and after the instructions you had to push the trade so that what Furs or Robes he might get would be a losing concern for him. You well know that you are under no restraint with regard to prices but to get the trade even if the returns you make should not pay the first cost of the goods, it is of no consequence so [long] as you secure the trade; you are well aware that this is the object of the company and their position instructions.

I understand from Charles that the indians have nearly all left your place, and gone above on account of the scarcity of Buffaloes; if this be the case and [there is] little or no trade at your establishment I think you ought by all means to go yourself to where the force of the trade will be, and let every thing be done possible to secure it; I am in hopes that the necessity of such a step will occur to you before this reaches you. It is possible that I may be misinformed with regard to the Trade that Primeau has made, which I sincerely hope may be the case.

Every exertion ought to be made to recover the Horses which have been stole from you. If you can possibly spare Jim or anther man, I would like you to send him down as soon as possible; you know how very short of men we are, but short as we are do not send him if it will injure the trade in the least. Your man looks nearly as well as when he left this, I sent him to the Island where all our other horses are doing well.

I remain
truly Yours
(Sign'd) William Laidlaw

❖ ❖ ❖

Fort Pierre 11th January 1835.
Mr. F. A. Chardon
Dear Sir

This will be handed you by Mr Newman who leaves this tomorrow for your place in hopes of finding Mr. May; he has not been here for some days past, and in a pack of troubles about his Bubbly *Jack*, which he leaves in charge of P. A. Leclerc. Charles Primeau arrived here to day from Wm. Dicksons with two trains and a little dried meat, he tells me that his brother Emillion was about to set out for the Mandans as he came down; if so he must be with you by this time, I shall avoid saying any thing to you regarding the trade, as you will know the views of the Company and am persuaded you will do every thing in your power to forward them; profit you know is of little consequence when put in the scales of opposing them effectually, his assortment of Goods (if he even has one) must be much broke [word?]; as I understand he has opposed William Dickson very successfully, considering the disadvantages he laboured under.

I have nothing to offer you in the way of news, not having heard from any of our outposts since Mr. May left here, I put this down as the most dull winter I ever passed in the Indian country. I cannot even hear of a Buffaloe; what would I give for a month of such pleasant time as we passed at the Forks of the Cheyenne together.

Mr Halsey will send you a statement of Newmans a/c. I wish you would write me a long letter by the first and every opportunity. I intend writing a few lines to Mr. Lamont; if an opportunity offers from your place to Fort Union, send it up. If not keep it till spring. Please tell Mr May that his horses are both sound and well. Wishing you all the compliments of the season

I remain Yours Most Truly,
(Sign'd) Wm Laidlaw

P.S. If you think you can sell a few horses in the spring to advantage let me know. I can easily furnish you; mention the time they ought to be at the Mandans; I expect a good stock of corn from you by the first boats that come down, remember the scrambling we had last spring

WmL

❖ ❖ ❖

Fort Pierre 19th January 1835
Mr. H. Picotte
Dear Sir

I last evening recd. your favour of the 16th inst: per your man Friday I cannot immagine how he made out to find his way I now hasten with pleasure to supply your wants and am glad that I am so situated as to have it in my power. I send Ortubise and an Oto acquaintance of ours (B. Lebrun) who Newman [word?] from Gardner to go a hunting with him upon his arrival here. I took the liberty of claiming him which no doubt disappointed his new master should you be in want of men you can keep him for the present as I can do without him, untill I send out the men to Campbell which will be about the 20th of Febuary, that is to say I would wish them to leave this about that time, should you be absolutely in want of Pinie to make a trip away when you may also keep him for some time, but if you can do without him I would wish him to return, as I want him much for hunting, but the trade is the first thing to be looked after, in case you should be in want of horses I had told him to have you send as [many as] you may wish, as I think we will be able to hold out to spring in the provisions way I think it will be better not to send the trains as you are short of men and horses, but I beseach of you to save all the meat you possibly can, as we will again have a scrabbling in the spring if we do not get a good supply in that way from you, no hopes of getting any from either Papin or Campbell; I hope Juette and Angé will be able to collect a good many tongues in the different camps; is there no possibility of getting a little smoakd Beef.

Chenie and one of Leclercs men have been on a trading expedition some distance above Dicksons and have returned with not more than 5 or 6 Robes, and their mule completely knocked up; I send you only 10 Guns as Denig recd. the case I sent from this to Grand river, however shortly you still be of opinion that they will be wanted let me know by Pinie and I shall send them. I wrote to Dickson to try and furnish you with 2 men to assist in bringing out your returns.

I wrote you by the Comrade of Bozeu who delivd. me your letter after keeping the letter I wrote you for two days he declined returning but I shall now send it. Write me fully by Piene and let me know your plans how you mean to get out your returns and how you will be off for men not that I can assist you but still it would be a satisfaction to know from you how you are situated.

[Word?] the indians from [word?] you as [word?] I send you two Kegs trusting you will keep always in view what I told you the last time I had the pleasure of seeing you. I have sent you Castors brother in law to remain with you thinking he may be usefull as a guide or to run errands.

I send you some sugar, Coffee and Tea; the Tea you asked for on our a/c I have not sent should you still want it let me know by the return of Piene.

I send you a piece of Blue S. L. Cloth thin [word?] good quality which cannot fail to sell well try and send us some grease as we have not an ounce to make a candle with, dont allow Ortubise to smell the Kegs he is a fine boy while we can keep him sober.

Believe Me Truly Yours
(Signd,) William Laidlaw

❖ ❖ ❖

Fort Pierre 22d. Febuary 1835
Mr Colin Campbell
Dear Sir

I received your letter addressed to Mr. Laidlaw per Deshonette on 18th inst:, Since then the weather as been so bad that he could not leave here on his return. He will leave here tomorrow with Charles Primeau and five men to assist in bringing out your returns. I do not send you the accounts of any of the men, I presume they will not wish to get in debt; however, I think it desirable to let you know that James Andrews has already taken the Half of his wages, and his time you know, does not expire till next November. The two horses which Deshonette brought in are most miserably poor and both of them have sore backs, so they will not be able to return; and I fear this bad weather will kill them, with regard to the wine you ask for, I am sorry to say that I cannot comply with your request. Mr Laidlaws orders to me were *positive* not to send out a *drop*; he left here on the 16th with Picotte for the Sawon camp on Grand river, or in that neighbourhood; they took with them 14 Horses loaded with goods for the trade there.

As we have no one point Blankets I have sent you a few more pairs of the Two and a half point that you ask for. In one of the bales you will find 5 lb. of Sugar, and a pair of Goggles for yourself; as also a Phial of Spi[ri]ts. Of Campher for Bonebonet, for further particulars I refer you to the inclosed memorandum.

I am Glad to hear that Buffaloe are plenty among your Indians, and that they have all returned from the west, that you may still make a good trade, and in the spring bring us a good Supply of meat, is my sincere wish, and confident hope.

I am sorry it is not in my power to send you an extra man to assist in bringing in your Horses. After Primeau and his party started there will remain here Vallin, Boyer, Ladorese. May and James the Cook; so that you will perceive that our forces will be weak. Primeau will give you all the news of the day.

[Name?] he has been up as far as Dicksons Establishment. Lebruin left here about Five days ago. Mr Laidlaw wrote you by him. I presume he arrived in the course of time.

Believe Me Your Friend
(Signd.) Jacob Halsey
To Mr Colin Campbell

❖ ❖ ❖

Fort Pierre July 3d. 1835
Wm. Laidlaw Esqr
Saint Louis
Dear Sir

On the 28th Ulto. The Steam Boat Diana arrived here from St Louis after a passage of 36 days. Since then she has been detained here waiting for Defond who is at Cherry River with Picotte but he is expected here any moment and as soon as he arrives the Diana will leave us on her return to St Louis. The cholera has made some havoc on board the D[iana], but at the present we have no person on the sick list if it should break out among us we will be pretty well prepared for it.

Since your Departure I have reengaged Defond & Peneau; old Daurion has been here he is at present with Pilcher at Fort Lookout, our men are just now variously employed. Some of them cutting firewood and others building Mackinaw Boats to take up the Fort Union Goods. I have ordered Picotte in from

Cherry River for the purpose of taking up these Boats. If they should meet a keel boat on the way down from Fort Union I think it will be best to exchange cargos and let the keel boat return to F. U. with the merchandize.

The mdse for this post has been delivered in good order and the packages received agree with the packing act: Book Of the fort Union goods however there is a package missing said to have contained tin smiths tools &c

Yours Respectfully
Jacob Halsey
For Pierre D. Papin

❖ ❖ ❖

Fort Pierre July 3. 1835.
Messrs Pratte Chouteau & Co
Saint Louis
Gentlemen

Louis Cointer's Huns [?] one of the men engaged on St Louis this season has been sick nearly all the passage up and bid fair to be of little use to the Company, consequently I will give him permission to return with Capt Halstead, his note I will enclose you.

G. Huneau one of the men who descended with Mr Laidlaw has 20.86 coming to him instead of 9.86 which I think was the amt: of the balance sent down when he left here Therefore there will be 20$ more coming to him than it is possible he received.

We have Shipped on board the Diana 31 Packs of Buffaloe Robes which is all the skins we have here at the present moment. I shall enclose you one of the Bill of Lading as also a memorandum of advances made to persons attached to the Diana.

I have re engaged Bapt Defond for one Year ending Summer 1836 for 400$ and a double equipment. He refused to go on board the Diana without the Company agreed to allow him extra pay, whilst acting in the capacity of a pilot, which he says is the agreement Mr Chouteau formerly agreed with him. I told him that if the company had formerly allowed him extra pay while on board the Steam Boat he would get it again this year. Under these circumstances I have prevailed on him to go on board the Diana in the morning.

Respectfully

Your Obedient & Humble Svt
Jacob Halsey
For P. D. Papin
Messrs Pratte Chouteau & Co
Saint Louis

❖ ❖ ❖

[No place or date]
Messrs Pratte Chouteau & Co
Saint Louis

This will be handed to you by J. Carlisle from whom you will learn the lamentable fate of the Assiniboine and her Cargo[28]

In case of accident I have taken copies of all the papers brought down by Him. The a/c of the men going down with him you will receive herewith

Mr Lamont left here on the first inst: in a Batteaux ladened with all the [word?] furs, he must be now below the Bucases, by him I wrote you; Nothing but the late disastrous end of the Assiniboine has transpired since his departure

Respectfully Yours
(Signd) William Laidlaw

❖ ❖ ❖

Fort Pierre 16th June 1835
Messrs Pratte Chouteau & Co
Gentlemen

I have within a few days past drawn upon you personal drafts in favor of the following persons viz:

One draft in favor of C. Vachard for Forty Dollars
One do " "   "[Name?] Dauphine Fifteen "
One " " " " Wm Dickson " One hundred "
One " " " " D. Lachapelle " Seventy three dolls 50c
One " " " " P. Dauphine for " Fifty doll

All of which you will please pay when presented and charge us directly

Respectfully Yours
(Signed) Wm. Laidlaw

❖ ❖ ❖

Fort Pierre 20th June 1835.
James A. Hamilton Esqr
Dear Sir

The extra charge of a Barrell of Tallow shipped in September last has been placed to the Credit of Fort Union.

We have given Fort Union Credit for the article received here in July last $98.80 there was a Bushel of corn and a barrel of Tallow charged in your bill of 7 July 1834 but I assure you that no Such article came to hand.

From your bill of 20th July a deduction has been made of [word?] for error in price of any meat charged at 3 cts instead of 2 ½c per lb making the amount of that bill only 16853. As also we al[l]ow you nothing for stores ennumerated therein they having been all used by Mr McKenzie during his trip down.

I will endeavour to find out what has become of the packages of Mdse: taken to St Louis by Mr McKenzie last summer and if they are not returned your post shall have Credit for them. Your Invoice Mdse &c from Fort Clark outfit since 1834 is correct with the exception that you have allowed that post nothing for [word?]

The same applied to your Bill of Guns and Hoop [iron] show 181.52 Please have the goodness to credit us with insurance at the usual rate of three per cent.

The error made in P. Lafluers wages has been corrected. ~~Your post has been corrected~~ Your post has been credited with wages of A Massaur $200, and F. U. is now only charged with the amount of his advances in St Louis.

L. Crawford was according to orders given me Credited last year for Services ending 1834 $400. Consequently I charge F. Union with his salary for services ending 1835 $500.

Regardding your remark relative to Modest Presley I have but little to say if you think it advisable to [word?] 250$ you can do so, but you say yourself it may be made for 250$ or 210$ I have thought that the most prudent plan to pursue was to pass the latter amount only to his credit untill the fact of the matter can be ascertained from St Louis If it should prove to be 250$ the man will not fail to let us know soon enough to rectify the mistake.

The Bearer of this J. Dauphine may possibly remain some time at Fort Clark, I shall however enclose your F. Union account current to the present time.

The clothing shipped by you per Steam Boat Assiniboine having been all consumed by the late disaster which happened to that Boat, and not having been noted in the bill of lading, has of course been struck of the credit side of F. U. account. Goods retuned to St Louis per Mr Lamont will be credited when it is ascertained what prices the company will allow for them

If the Fort Clark & Fort Union Invoice per S B Assiniboine last year are with you, be good enough to forward them to me. They have not yet been entered in the Invoice Book

Believe Me Very Truly Yours
Jacob Halsey
For Pratte Chouteau & Co.

❖ ❖ ❖

Fort Pierre 18th July 1835
Mr Francis A Chardon
Fort Clark
Dear Sir

You will receive per Batteaux Experiment & Enterprize your supply of Groceries for this year for particulars of which I refer you to you're a/c current herewith Enclosed. I also enclose you the bill of Lading of Majr Fulkerson's goods;[29] when the goods are delivered to him you will please request the Majr to give you a receipt for them on the back of the bill of Lading and send it to us by the first opportunity after, so soon as it reaches St Louis the Company will be able to get payment for the freight. When Mr May was here he took for 22.50 it will remain charged to him in our Books untill you advise us of the payment thereof which I hope you will not fail to do so that the general Ledger may be regulated accordingly

Mr Papin will send you a horse per H Auge, he says he is a first rate Buffaloe runner and he is certainly in fine condition. I send you a bundle of Cloth for Belhumeur it is a present from Mr Lamont there is 2 Yds. of it.

I said in the commencement of this letter that you would receive all the Groceries intended for your post by Experiment & Enterprise we now find that it will be impossible to send you all your flour at the present moment There will be another boat going up in the fall and the three barrels left here belonging to Fort Clark can then be sent up, in the mean time Mr Picotte will deliver you two Barrells of that article. There remains here one Mackinac boat load of goods for Fort Union perhaps they will be sent up as far as Fort Clark the coming fall.

I have nothing more to communicate at the present moment/ I wrote you a few lines per Mr May who left here with Major Fulkerson a few days ago, and will if no accident happens there be shortly with you.

 Believe Me Yours Sincerely
 Jacob Halsey
 To Mr Francis A Chardon
 Fort Clark
 (official)

❖ ❖ ❖

 Fort Pierre 18th July 1835
 James A Hamilton Esqr
 Fort Union
 Dear Sir

The Steam Boat Diana arrived here on the 28th Ulto. With the Fort Union Fort Clark and Fort Pierre Merchandize for season 1835 & 36 She was 36 days in performing the trip to this post, and if Mr McKenzie had been here when she arrived I have no doubt but she would have proceeded up the river to Fort Union. The water has been high all summer and the Diana only draws 3½ feet of water when loaded. She did not bring up a single letter from any of the members of the Company The commander of her told us, that he had determined to go no higher up consequently our only [choice] was to go to work and make Batteaux, for the purpose of taking up the goods intended for ~~the trade~~ Fort Clark & Fort Union, the Capt having left the keel boat he had in tow at Ottos Establishment. Batteaux have been made but they prove to be too small to take up all the goods for fort Union consequently Mr Papin will send you such Articles as he thinks you will be most of need of. The St Louis Packing act: calls for a box containing [word?] tools &c but no such package came to hand here.

I will Enclose you the Fort Union a/c current up to this day, also Bapst Marchands act in detail & a charge against Mr Culbertson for postage

Mr Papin wishes you to send back the two Batteaux per Messrs Picotte & Auge and to furnish them with Bapt. Fouchette, Henry Mischall & Philip Gillaury, any supply of meat, [word?], or grease will be thankfully received, in fact if you cannot send us a supply of those articles I am afraid we will be again reduced to corn diet

Mr Picotte will deliver you a book left here by Mr Lamont for you. I will send you a book of the mens acts: they are all made out in detail I will inclose you a small memorandum which if you can fill up will be a benefit to Fort Pierre & we will be obliged to you Please let them be brought down by Mr Picotte if possible. Among the papers sent you you will find a memorandum of the articles left here intended for Fort Union. I hope & trust that you will suffer no inconvenience for the most of them

 Yours Most Respectfully
 Jacob Halsey
 James A. Hamilton Esqr
 Fort Union

❖ ❖ ❖

 Fort Union 31st July 1835
 Messrs Pratte Chouteau & Co
 Gentlemen

Four Mackinaw boats arrived here yesterday from Fort Union laden with Robes &c for particulars of which I beg leave to refer you to memorandum which I shall enclose. The Mackinaw boats manned by 24 men under H. Picotte passed here on the 18th inst: with a part of the goods recd per Steam Boat Diana for F Union, they were not able to take all shipped by you for that post, for your satisfaction I will enclose you a memorandum of such articles as were sent up. Mr Brazeau tells us he met Mr Picotte a short distance below the Ree Village. All well. In book of advances to men in St Louis, Mr Sarpy has not mentioned the wages of Paul Kenning and Baptiste Fouchette please have the goodness to remind him of this, so that he may be advised on the subject by the first opportunity. Modest Presley one of the men now going down has been Credited by Mr Hamilton with wages 250$ in the St Louis book of advances there is a blot on the figure, so that it may be read for 250$ or 210$ if the latter should prove to be the true sum allowed him for services you will please charge him with 40$ before he is paid off

I have examined some few of the F. P. Packages received per Diana I find several mistakes in Box #7. I will enclose you a memorandum of them

Mr Hamilton writes us that the trade at the Crows has turned out much better than was expected. 320 Packs of Robes & 1200 Lb of Beaver &c Mr Tullock was to remain at Fort Union under the expectation that Mr McKenzie will continue to trade or supply him with merchandize on his own account

Mr H. makes a remark in his letter regarding H. Maurice I will give it to you word for word.

"Henry Maurice who steered the Keel Boat to Fort McKenzie came down with Pellot, no man on board having skill to steer a Mackinaw boat down this far, and there being no one here of whose steering capabilities I have any knowledge, I have deemed it most prudent to send H. Maurice with the boat as far as F. Pierre he goes with some reluctance having been promised by Mr. Culbertson that he should return to Fort McKenzie immediately on his arrival here, his services will be relied on to steer the Keel Boat down next spring You will of course arrange for his return here this fall if possible as we have no person here capable of steering a boat Mr Papin has made up his mind to let him proceed on to St Louis from whence he will no doubt have an opportunity of returning in the fall. Bapt & Joseph Fouchette are the Steersmen of the Mackinaw boats which left here for Fort Union on the 18th inst. Papin requests Mr Hamilton to send down B. Fouchette on the return of Mr Picotte in the fall.

In settlement with C Latusiere Mr K has allowed him $250 for services ending fall 1835. I presume he feels confident that it is the correct sum although I am sure that the amount of the mans wages were not mentioned in the St Louis Book of Advances. Would it not be prudent to make Inquiry of Mr Sarpy before he is paid.

Upon Examination of the documents I send you herewith you will perceive that many of the men sent down from Fort Union are not free till the fall, and I have struck the balance that would be there and then, if they served their full time, having been informed by Mr Brazeau that nothing was paid to these persons previous to their leaving F. U. on the subject of paying for their time.

If I am wrong and you think it proper to charge them with time unserved it can be easily done in St Louis before they receive their pay

I am Gentlemen With the Greatest respect
Your Obedt & Humble Servant
Jacob Halsey

P.S. We have recd no Black Ink Powder from St Louis this year and have scarcely any on hand. I think it would be well to send up some papers in the fall, if an opportunity should offer

H[alsey].
Messrs Pratte Chouteau & Co
Saint Louis
Official

❖ ❖ ❖

Fort Pierre 25th Sept 1835
James A. Hamilton Esqr
Fort Union
Dear Sir

Herewith you will receive all documents appertaining to Fort Union which can be furnished at the present moment. I hope they will prove Satisfactory

Mr Brazeau left here on the 3d. of the present month with his four Boats, me not having any person here capable of steering a boat, Henry Maurice accompanied him to St Louis, from where I presume he will return to Fort Union in the fall.

It appears that when Mr Picotte [was with] us he had with him a man named Fernuire Lapana, he was not intended for Fort Union and as he left here without my knowledge of [word?] his account was not sent us. You shall however now have it in detail. With the following exception the General Ledger agreed with your duplicate

Viz: Henry Maurice, the balance due by him to the Co 25th June 1834 pr General Ledger was 40.25 per duplicate $31.25 making a difference on nine dollars, presuming your statement to be the correct [one] and I have made the Genl book agree with it. Charles Chalue. The balance he was in debt to the Co: 25 June 1834 per Genl Ledger is 104.12 in which amount his a/const at Fort Clark 2.75 is included. You may rely on this statement as correct & you can safely [word?] him with the difference 3.75 You have it 107.87.

Then Alexander Kennedy is charged with cash, paid postage of a double letter to New York 50c our books will agree viz Balance [word?] 93.68. The Error made by me in Charging postage to yourself and Mr Kennedy have been rectified. It would appear from your duplicate Ledger that you have credited James [Name?] with his wages for services ending June 1835, $340, in your list of salaries of Clerks & men you state it as $257, and sumr 1835.

I have regulated his a/c as stated in your duplicate & have charged Fort Union credit 1834 with the difference. If I am wrong please have the goodness to set me right. I have discovered some trifling errors in the Fort Union & Ft. McKenzie Inventories of this year, for particulars of which I refer you to a/c current herewith.

On the arrival of Mr Lamont here from Fort Union it was found that a pack of muskrat Skins #30. F McK. was missing from the Boats Cargo. In coming down the river I am told several of the packs got wet & among them muskrat skins which were spread out to dry on a windy day while the boats were wind bound, the presumption is that #30 was born off by the wind. Will you please to have the goodness to forward by the first opportunity Bapts Deguires a/c at Fort Union & Fort Cass in detail, his a/c of June 1834. 71.79 he tells me he has paid, but I do not believe a word of it, he however says that if it is procured from you in detail, & if it does not show that he has paid this debt, he is still willing to settle it

Respectfully Yours &c
Sig Jacob Halsey
James A Hamilton Esqr
Fort Union
Official

P.S. Mr Campbell who had charge of the retain Store here about the time Mr. Picotte left here for your post made an entrie in his book to the credit of Joseph Ramsay $12 for services as free man on board S. B. "Diana," and I forwarded Ramsays a/c to you agreeably to this entrie, which I have since discovered is incorrect, he should have been credited with but $6, please have the goodness to [word?] his account. Viz: Charge him with $6 error.

5

FORT PIERRE LETTER BOOK C

June 25, 1845–June 16, 1846

There is a ten-year gap in the letter books, and the documents are presumed lost. During this time, the fur trade on the upper Missouri was in transition. Bernard Pratte and Company had purchased the Western Department in 1834 when John Jacob Astor retired from the fur trade. The American Fur Company was split into business units, with the name going to Ramsey Crooks and the Northern Department of the upper Mississippi and Great Lakes. Pierre Chouteau, Jr., the leading partner of B. Pratte and Company of Saint Louis, purchased all of the trade along the Missouri River and into the Rocky Mountains. Kenneth McKenzie, now the head of the Upper Missouri Outfit, a semi-independent business under the Western Department, had had a series of embarrassing missteps in 1833. The United States Congress had totally banned liquor in Indian country in 1832; yet, McKenzie thought that bringing a still to Fort Union in 1833 would allow him to exploit a loophole in the law. He was wrong. When news of the still and its violation of the law reached Washington, it put the trading license of the company in jeopardy.

In an effort to show the Indian Department that the company would comply with the law, Pierre Chouteau, Jr., ordered McKenzie out of Indian country for one year. The contract renewing the Upper Missouri Outfit as a separate business was then allowed to expire in 1834. The Upper Missouri Outfit became an accounting entry on the books in Saint Louis. Pierre Chouteau, Jr., then split off a new Sioux Outfit along the Platte River, with Honoré Picotte in charge. This move angered the last two holdover managers from the old Columbia Fur Company, William Laidlaw and Daniel Lamont. The two quit, with Laidlaw selling his shares to Jacob Halsey and Lamont to David D. Mitchell, and then went into business trading robes on the Arkansas River.

In 1838, the firm of B. Pratte and Company reorganized as Pierre Chouteau, Jr., and Company. The new company's partners also changed at this time. Bernard Pratte had died in 1831, and Jean P. Cabanné was embroiled in his own liquor scandal and had been pushed out. Pierre Chouteau, Jr., John B. Sarpy, Joseph Sire, and John F. A. Sanford made up the new partners. The new company instituted new management along the Missouri

River. Honoré Picotte took over the Sioux Outfit and ran it from Fort Pierre. Fort Union, which from 1828 to 1835 had been the headquarters of the Upper Missouri Outfit, now slipped to a secondary position as Fort Pierre became the primary management post under the reorganized company.

Steamboat transportation during this decade also began to change. The Missouri River was a much shallower river than the Mississippi, but construction of steamboats had favored the deeper hulled side-wheels, with low-pressure boilers. New technology developed to meet the unique requirements of the Missouri River. Spoon-billed bows allowed construction of a shallower draft hull, and stern paddle wheels soon replaced side wheels to reduce damage to the buckets from debris floating in the river. Engine technology developed pressure-release valves on the high-pressure boilers, reducing the risk of the boiler explosions that had been common with older engine designs.

Steamboats still traveled only as far as Fort Union, which remained the head of steamboat navigation on the Missouri River. Above Fort Union, keelboats were the main means of transportation to Fort McKenzie. All of the large posts on the Missouri and Yellowstone rivers continued to build mackinaw boats in their chantiers (boatyards) and to send the packs of furs downriver in the spring. In 1839, over one-hundred-thousand-dollars worth of robes and pelts made its way downriver in fleets of mackinaw boats destined for Saint Louis. The improved transportation was a two-edged sword when, in 1837, a steamboat named the St. Peter's carried smallpox to the upper Missouri. The small, cramped conditions of steamboats were perfect vectors for contagious disease. The 1837 smallpox epidemic devastated both Indian and white populations alike, with an estimated fifteen thousand people succumbing.

The company retained a policy of assisting scientific expeditions up the river, hosting the parties at various posts, and providing room on company boats. In 1840, Father Pierre de Smet, Jesuit priest, made his first of many trips up the Missouri to minister to the Indian tribes. John James Audubon and party traveled upriver aboard the company boat Omega to Fort Union in 1843. That year, the Omega also set a new record by only taking fifty days to reach Fort Union and two weeks to return to Saint Louis.

In 1837, Pierre Chouteau, Jr., and Company acquired Fort John (later Fort Laramie) on the Oregon Trail. The management at Fort Pierre provided direction to Fort John until its sale to the United States Army in 1849. Pierre Chouteau, Jr., and Company saw no real competition on the Missouri until 1842, when Fox, Livingston and Company (Union Fur Company) began to build a series of forts to vie for robes and pelts. At this time, traders began to use adobe as a building material, influenced no doubt from the Southwest. Forts George and Mortimer featured adobe building materials, and the later Fort Benton, high on the Missouri, would be constructed entirely of adobe.

The year 1843 had its share of troubles when Francis Chardon and Alexander Harvey fired a cannon into a crowd of Blackfeet Indians waiting to trade at Fort McKenzie. The killing of Chardon's slave that winter by some Blackfeet had provoked the surprise attack. The move made Fort McKenzie untenable as a trading post, and it was abandoned later in the summer of 1843. In the fall, Chardon built Fort Francis Chardon at the mouth of the Judith River in Montana, a poor location where the Indians would not cross the river, nor would they come in and trade because of the killings. In 1842, Kenneth McKenzie became a minority shareholder in Pierre Chouteau, Jr., and Company, and in 1844, the company dispatched him to straighten out management issues that had developed at the forts on the Missouri. Alexander Culbertson was sent to Blackfeet country to restore the trade. He abandoned and burned Fort Francis Chardon and moved operations upriver to build Fort Lewis.

William Clark died in 1838, leaving vacant the position of superintendent of Indian Affairs in Saint Louis. Joshua Piltcher was appointed to the position in 1839. He was a man with a history in the fur trade going back to Manuel Lisa. However, when administrations changed in Washington, Piltcher was out, and in September of 1841, company trader David D. Mitchell was appointed superintendent of Indian Affairs in Saint Louis.

Fox, Livingston and Company, which had been opposing Pierre Chouteau, Jr., and Company, found that the company's hold along the river was *too strong. They had been losing money since they started in 1842, so when an offer came to sell out in 1845, they took it. The letter books now pick up in June 1845 with a letter to Joseph Picotte from Alexander Culbertson.*

❖ ❖ ❖

[translated from French]
Fort Pierre 25 June 1845
Mr. Jos. Picotte

It has been agreed between myself and Mr. Picotte that I would wait here for your arrival; but the joint instructions left by Mr. Picotte have several details that I am adding here, making it needless for me to prolong my stay. In giving you similar instructions we are persuaded beforehand that you cannot follow the letter and fail to take action should you have an unexpected meeting on the Platte since the last news we received. Upon your arrival at Fort Pierre you will find a man retained for the purpose of accompanying you on your trip. He will be able to take charge of everything so that you may rejoin the wagons that left the 22nd. If you think that the slow pace of the wagons will slow you too much, you must stay at Fort John[1] and take charge of our business for the next season, except for depending on personal things. When you are about to leave the Fort to get your baggage, leave Bourdau in charge. All that I have read makes me believe that you will find all the wagons and carts [charettes] in good condition. In loading your wagons you need to adjust as much as possible for the number of packs that I designate here by wagon and cart that you have. Wagon with the wide wheels and five pairs of oxen, 45 packs. 3 [wagons] with narrow wheels, 4 pairs of oxen, 40 packs. Each 1 with 6 mules 35 packs. 3 with 4 mules 25 packs. Each one with 6 mules 35 packs. 3 with 4 mules 25 packs each. 2 with five mules 30 packs each. 3 to 4 mules 25 packs each, 6 carts two horses, 12 packs each. In place of boxes for the wagons, it will be necessary to use the shafts that you will find completed, as much as you can. They will hold more robes and are longer. In loading your wagons you will place lots of loose robes as tarpaulins in all their length, by 6 or 7 [feet]. These are to be put across the wagons and tied to the second row of packs. I protect in this manner the loads of the small wagons up to those with 35 packs of robes without the least difficulty and without disordering anything, if after all you follow the instructions that Mr. Picotte has left.[2]

As soon as possible after your arrival at Fort John you will return with the baggage and with all the wagons and carts, except for one wagon that you will leave at the Fort for hauling hay. You will load them higher as stated and you will leave the post under the direction of Mr. Kellog. You will stay then with the baggage with the number of men required to bring down the rest of the packs. In case a rise in the water occurs, in that event you will accompany them to St. Louis, at least until you encounter Mr. Frederick Laboue who is on the road from St. Louis with men and the necessary instructions to see when you meet on the Platte. If that occurs Laboue will bring down the baggage and you will return to take your place at Fort John. If Fred Laboue arrives before you are ready to leave, you are to turn over the baggage to him with the injunction to stay there until fall at the minimum, always mindful that there might be a rise in the water. In that case, he should take the barges and take the packs down to St. Louis. If the water does not rise enough before fall, Laboue should put the baggage in order to protect it from all danger; let him accomplish it carefully with some trustworthy men from here. If by chance you have some difficulty in order to secure the number of animals needed for the wagons, you can take cattle in order to make the complement. If you receive our joint letter of instructions, pass it on to Fred Laboue if you see him before you descend the Platte, and another copy for you to leave in case high water requires you to leave and the instructions might be missed enroute. The wages for the men who stay with you and the baggage will continue the same; that is to say that the extension of their contracts will be paid at the same wage which is written in their engagement, until the animals and you no longer have need for them to deal with the baggage. As their engagements will run out before this work, you will reengage them at the same wages if you can. In the contrary case, you will act according to your judgment and for the best, considering the needs that you will have. As I presume you will be at Fort John before the wagons pass by the White River with the trade goods you should find out if Mr. Bourdeau has chosen his winter employment on the White River; send us at the same time the list of equipment that he should have for his wintering in order that Mr. Kellog be able to supply him when he returns to Fort John with the trade goods.

Yours, Signed A. Culbertson

❖ ❖ ❖

Mr. J. Bourdan
Fort John

The unfortunate fate of my boats which were stopped by low water and abandoned on the banks by Major Hamilton[3] reached me by Laroque, you are well aware of my instructions to Hamilton and the men, that if they were stopped by low water, to remain with the boats & never think of abandoning them; also that if they wanted me to pay them, they must assist me to get down my returns, instead of this, I understand Hamilton waited but 6 days & that not satisfied with leaving the boats himself, he carries more than half my men with him, by which depriving me of the means of getting down our returns.

I left you in charge of the company's business, you being the most experienced hand in the country: I thought you would know better how to act in case of an accident, but I am sorry to tell you that I was a good deal surprised that instead of your writing me that 26 of the men had left, you would say you had kept the men until the river rose, or further orders from this place. I am sorry I left so soon, but it cannot be helped now. I send Mr. Jos. Picotte to take charge of Fort John with instructions how to act in relation to the Robes &c; you will therefore give him any aid to facilitate him in accomplishing the wishes of the compy. The Groceries I sent by the wagon are sent over for sale, to be sold to the men or any person wishing to purchase them for Cash, hoping that a due consideration of the predicament in which we have been left with our returns will be sufficient stimulant not only for you but the other gentlemen at the post, now in [word?] and waiting to get those robes to market.

The hat you asked for is sent, the sugar & Coffee you can take out of the quantity sent.

Yours &c Culbertson
(Original)

❖ ❖ ❖

[Translated from French]
26 June 1845
Mr. Frederic Laboue
Fort John

Upon receipt of these favors given to you by Mr. Jos Picotte, you will have to take charge of the goods that he will give you and you will have to stay until fall with the necessary number of men, i.e. 3 for one hundred packs of robes, unless a rise occurs before then allowing you to carry down the boats to St Louis. Mr Jos. Picotte leaves from here with instructions to carry down the boats if there is enough water in the Platte and since we think that you will go up the river in order to meet him, you will take his place if it happens and you will let him go back to Fort John, as you yourself will go down to St. Louis. If you arrive at the goods, you will take care of it, as said before and you will stay there until you lose any hope of a rise. You will then arrange the goods to keep it safe of all dangers and you will leave it in charge of a trusted man with 2 others to help him; you will also take care to have the boats placed in a safe location for the winter. Before you pack your goods carefully, and be sure to examine the robes and to have them pressed before packing them again.

(Signed) A. Culbertson

❖ ❖ ❖

[Translated from French]
26 June 1845
Mr. Fred. Laboué
Fort John

When you arrive at Fort John, if you find that Mr. Jos. Picotte has gone down with the barges, without you being able to meet him on the way, take care to stay there until further orders.

Signed A. Culbertson

❖ ❖ ❖

17th August 1845
F. A. Chardon Esqr
Fort Clark
Dear Sir

I take the opportunity of B. Labrun who leaves for the upper post to write you a few lines.

I am sorry to inform you that our Corn crop has suffered considerably from the drought, we will not gather more than 150 Bushels, a quantity altogether insufficient for this place: therefore, I think it advisable that you trade 3 or 400 Bushels for this place & forward them as opportunities offer, otherwise the company will suffer a severe loss.

I expect the waggons from Fort John in ten days, the boats are ready & I will dispatch the Robes immediately upon their arrival. La Brun will give you all the news from St. Louis, everything goes on well here, no desertion.

Respectfully your obedt. servt.
A[ntoine] R. Bouis
acct. of B. La Brun $7 which he says he will settle with you.

❖ ❖ ❖

19th August
Messrs P. Chouteau Jr & Co.
Saint Louis
Gentlemen

Messrs. Lurty, Harper & Fairwell arrived yesterday from Fort John, they left Mr. Kellog on white river with 13 waggons & carts laden with 387 Packs Robes, he is progressing but slowly; I will start five carts to-morrow to meet him, in order to lighten his loads. I expect him here about the 1st September and as soon as possible after his arrival, I will start two mackinaw boat (the Boats are ready) with 550 Packs for St Louis.

I draw on you this day favor Robert F. Harper for ninety seven 62/100 Dls. ($97.62) & E. V. Penville for Twenty five Doll[ar]s. ($25.) which you will please pay & charge to Upper Missouri Outfit 1845, it is for Balance due on mules which I purchased from him very cheap. No news from Fort John. I close for the present, as I do not consider the present a safe opportunity, all goes on well at this place. I will write fully By the mackinaws.

Respectfu. Your obedt Servt.
A. R. Bouis.

❖ ❖ ❖

August 30, 1845
Jos Picotte
Fort John
Dear Sir

You will receive herewith a/cs sundries forwarded you, acs men &c &c all correct. I am really sorry that it did not lay in my power to make Mr. Bourdeau's outfit at this place. Mr. Montalant will explain.

In the a/c of March 1 received from St Louis per Steamer Genl Brooke 2 cases Vermillion are charged to your post & but one was found. I think however that the other was sent by Manta some time since.

We have had to make three boats and repair several that came from above, our rosin is out & if you do not send us some tar, we will not be able to make boats next spring. I wanted to give Mr. Kellogg a whip saw but he said it was not good & left it behind.

Yours &c. Signed A. R. Bouis

❖ ❖ ❖

Fort Pierre 31st August
Honore Picotte Esq
St Louis
Dear Sir

Mr. Kellog arrived here on the 27th Inst: with 12 Waggons & 2 carts loaded with 387 Packs Robes. J. Picotte writes that he has made baggage of the blce [balance] of the robes remaining at the [word?] (520 Packs) and has left three trusty men to take care of them; he has lost all hopes of a rise in the Platte this season, the Boats have been filled with water and secured he says they will answer very well for next spring. Mr Cabanne has abandoned fort Platte,[4] Bissanet is stationed a few miles below that fort with a few articles of trade that remained on hand last spring: it is supposed that if Cabanne comes up next fall it will be with but a small outfit. The prospect of trade in that section of the country is very flattering, plenty of Buff:, and there will be more Indians there this season than ever, part of the Miniconaujous[5] & 200 Lodges of Chayennes will winter in the neighbourhood of the Fort, I think that he will trade from 12 to 15 Hundred Packs. The trade with the Oragen [Oregon] emigrants was confined chiefly to exchange of horses, mules & cattle for skins & robes, and about $250 in cash & dfts the latter J. P. disposed of for horses and mules. Vasquez writes from Platt's fork that in consequence of Bridgers[6] party not having been heard from, he will not come to Fort John this season. He had traded five packs of beaver 600 do Deer skins &c. He is very sanguine in his expectations and thinks Bridger will make a first rate man. Since Mr. Culbertson's departure from Fort John, Bourdeau has traded 100 packs. No news from F. Laboue. It is reported that Marcelin St. Vrain[7] is coming with an outfit, the north forks of the Platte. The Indians in the district are not yet settled for the winter. The Yanctons are part at their cornfield, some have gone to the Punchas for corn, and the remainder on Riviere au Jacques. I believe they will make a good many robes, there will be more Esantes on Riviere a Jaques and on the Missouri than usual. No news from the upper Yanconais. The lower Yanconais have been all summer at Red Stone quarry but are now coming to their winter hunting grounds. The Oncpapas are at Three Buttes with a small band of Blackfeet. Not many Buff; there, there, but a small band of Miniconojous are at Bute D'Ores, the balance of that band are gone to the Platte. Poor prospects at forks of Cheyenne this year. All the Sawons are on White river with a band of Brules, we have not heard from them lately. I have not heard from the Upper Posts since your departure. Frenier will leave in a few days for the Yanctonais, the other traders will be sent to their differnt destinations as you ordered. All the wood necessary for the blacksmith shop is ready and will be put up in a few days. The coal (500 bbls) is finished and in the coal house, the meat will be hauled in a few days. We have not lost a horse or cow since your departure. I am sorry to inform you that the potato is an entire failure, we will not save a single one. The corn crop will also yield but little, say 400 bushels, this is all owing to the extraordinary drought this season. I found it impossible to set fire to Fort George,[8] there are now and have been since your departure 15 families of the Two Kettle band living in the fort, the remainder are on White river en mecana and have left their plunder in care of those that remained behind, however, so soon as I hear that the opposition is coming I (if such should be the case) I will send down a trader with a few goods to take possession of the place. The bbl of apples intended for this place has not been received. We have traded 110 packs since your departure. Kellogg left this morning for Fort John with balance of Outfit. All goes on well, no desertions. For further particulars I refer you to my letter to Messrs P. Chouteau & Co herewith

    Yours &c

    (Signed) A. R. Bouis

❖ ❖ ❖

Fort Pierre Septr. 1. 1845
Messrs P. Chouteau and Co
St Louis Mo
Gents

You will receive herewith a/c of present shipment & accts men going down. J. Jewette, B. Cadotte & Taussin Bergenau are to return per first opportunity as their term of engagement will not expire till sumr 1846. The boats are well manned and every care has been taken in the loading of them. For particulars respecting trade &c I refer you to my letter to Mr. Picotte herewith.

Mr. Laidlaws a/c is 69.92 Dollars for sundries furnished Mr. R. K. Lutz, which you will please collect & credit this outfit, the account [word?] has been handed Mr. Lurty

    Yours &c (Signed) A. R. Bouis

❖ ❖ ❖

Fort Pierre 4th Septr 1845.
Mr Jos. Picotte
Fort John
Dear Sir

Mr. Charles Primeau with four men arrived from St Louis yesterday. Mr. Picotte writes me to inform you that it will be necessary to haul up all the packs from the Chimneys to Fort John, and if you can possibly spare any waggons to send them to this place loaded with robes by Mr. Laboue & his men. You will see by this that the plan first given you in your instructions stands for naught. I have nothing further to tell you on the subject, you are on the ground & no doubt will do for the best. I write to ~~you by Laboue~~ Laboue by the present, in case he should be on his way before the present reaches you.

    Signed A. R. Bouis

❖ ❖ ❖

[Translated from French]
Fort Pierre 4th Sept 1845
Mr Fred. Laboue
Sir.

Messrs. Goulais and Primeau arrived from St. Louis yesterday. Mr. Picotte wrote me to not lose a moment in informing you that it will be necessary for you to stay with the baggage on the Platte River until all the packs have been carted to Fort John.

Once there Mr. Joseph Picotte should furnish you with wagons [and] that you should use the men bringing the robes to load them. One hopes that you do not lose courage when at the same time you will not be able to take your post at the Brulees house before the month of Decr. One says that there will be time. I have not any instructions to give you, you are on location [literally, on the spot] and I do not doubt but that you will make the best of it. You will receive a letter from your family.

Signed A R Bouis

❖ ❖ ❖

Septr. 16th 1845.
Messrs. Bridger & Vasquez.
Gentlemen

Mr. Bridger's letter of 3rd Inst: has been duly received and Contents noted. A Copy of what was furnished Mr. Bridger at Fort Union Novr. 1843 was recd. at this place in December of the same year and charges made in Conformity with said account, one of the principle reasons for wishing to see either of you at this place was to come to an understanding in order to settle that account equitably, as to what respects sundry drafts amt [word?] gives [word?] Chouteau for Collection, no advice has been received from St Louis on this Subject, although Messrs. P. Chouteau Jr: & Co. have been written to, however Mr: Picotte will have no doubt bring an answer this winter, as he has taken a memorandum to inquire into the Matter, as there are other charges in your account Current, which require explanation, it is impossible for me to send you that account correct. I have therefore thought it best to deffer it until either, or both of you come here. You have been credited with every thing delivered Mr. Jos: Picotte at Fort John on the 22nd Inst, but I can not affix prices to the California sea shells until I see Mr. Honoré Picotte on the subject. $3791.21 has been charged to your account for Blces due divers persons as per statement of Mr. James Bridger, I will give drafts to those men on Messrs. P. Chouteau Jr: & Co. Jacarie has paid us 92.75 Dollars and Mr. Kipp collected 2 Horses from James Hawthorn last winter [for] $50 for which amounts you have been Credited. F. Douville did not pay us 41$ he said when asked if he was indebted to you, that he had settled in full, I will keep his note & make him pay when he comes next spring.

Lewis Willcocks is here, but not employed by the Company, he has nothing & you stand but a poor Chance to get paid. You will receive herewith the a/c of what is forwarded you by Mr: Pope

You may rely that there will be no difficulty in settling your account, but it will be necessary for either or both of you to come here next spring.

signed H. Picotte
per A. R. Bouis

❖ ❖ ❖

Sept: 17th 1845.
Mr: J. Picotte
Fort John
Dear Sir

All you sent by Mr. Pope has been recd. I would as soon as practicable forward you Fort John a/c [word?] since Mr. Mortalon's departure. You will please not neglect and send the a/c of what you will furnish Mr: Bridger for: 1st opportunity in order that the necessary changes be made on Fort Pierre books. Mr Pope is taking out all the goods Mr: Bridger asked for together with those intended for Fort John; all the Brass and Copper kettles which we had on hand have been sent you by Mr. Kellogg, we have no rifle locks nor sand paper.

signed A. R. Bois

P.S. Please send us some Tar per first opportunity.

❖ ❖ ❖

Fort Pierre 17 Septr: 1845
Messrs. P. Chouteau Jr & Co.
St Louis
Gentlemen

Mr. James Bridger arrived at Fort John on the 2d. Inst: and delivered to Mr. Jos Picotte 840 lb of Beaver & and Castorum, 675 dressed deer skins, 28 mules, 24 horses, 1400 California sea shells &c &c the whole amounting to about $5000 exclusive of the California shells, as I did not know what Mr. Picotte would allow for them. Mr. Bridger remained at Fort John, and Mr Pope was sent to get some few articles of trade for him, amounting to $700, he says that they have nearly all their Outfit of last year on hand. Mr. Bridger was in California, he found plenty of beaver there, but he could not trap, as the Indians stole the Traps as soon as the hunters had set them. Vasquez is gone with 10 men to hunt on Wind river

Mountain.[9] There is a balance of $3570.50 due Bridger's men, they are all going down, and I have given them a/cs for the amount due each, which you would please pay and charge this Outfit. The Balance due Bridger & Vasquez July 1844 was 4271$ it is now is 3500$ & not counting the 1400 shells. The following is a list of the men going down & the amts due to each.

Leonard Benoist two dfts 750.63, Vincent Tibeau 994.50, François Boissert 949.20, George Hudson 377.08, Charles Lapointe 316.63, Amable Carifille 119$, Charles Levellier 11$, Baptiste Derosier 12.50.

Mr. Charles Primeau arrived here on the 3d. Inst: two days after J. Jewett had left for St. Louis.

An Indian has just arrived from the Forks Chayenne, plenty of Buffaloe there. I will start a trader for that place in a few days. No news from the Upper country since my last.

signed A. R. Bouis.

❖ ❖ ❖

Fort Pierre 9 Octr 1845.
Alexr. Culbertson Esqr
Dr. Sir

Mr. Picotte at his departure in June last requested me to advise you that J. B. Moncravie in June 1844, while going up with the keel Boat to the Blackfeet had got drunk several times and given upwards of 20 gallons of Liquor to the men, after Mr. Picote had ordered him positively not to dispose of a single drop. You are therefore requested to charge Moncravie $400, for the Liquor he expended, to seize upon all that he may bring from his Customers expedition in payment of same and not to employ him any more. The informers are Messrs. Chardon, Harvey, Champagne & Etienne Prousain.

You have herewith letters from St Louis, which no doubt will give you all the news from that place.

Yours &c A. R. Bouis

❖ ❖ ❖

Fort Pierre 10 Octr 1845.
Mr E. T. Denig
Fort Union
Dear Sir

A press of business renders it impossible for me to forward Fort Union a/c current at present. You will receive herewith a/c sundries furnished Mr Kipp for trip, together with a/c men going up.

A medium light Leather Trunk belonging to Mr. Welden was it I supposed landed at some of the Upper posts from Steamer Genl. Brooke, should the [item?] be at Fort Union please forward it to this place next spring. Mr Welden will be obliged to you by so doing, it appears that there are papers of value in it.

Yours &c
A. R. Bouis

❖ ❖ ❖

Fort Pierre Nov: 9th 1845
P. D. Papin Esqr:
Fort John
Dear Sir

Your two communications of the 5th and 13th Oct: have been duly received and Contents noted. Proveau [Provost] arrived here on the 2nd. Inst: and I have detained him until now in expectation of the arrival of Mr. Picotte, but as the latter has not arrived, and the season is far advanced I have deemed it prudent to dispatch him with a part of what you ask, an a/c of which you will find herewith. It is to be regretted that Mr. Picotte has not yet arrived, as in that case he could answer your several inquires respecting Wards California shells. Your views of consentrating your Packs on the head of white river &c, &c, questions which it is impossible for me to answer, the importance of the subject is such, that I doubt not Mr. Picotte will immediately upon his arrival dispatch an Express with his instructions

The Inventory which you took on your arrival at Fort John does not interfear with the account Current of that Post (which a/c you will receive herewith) as it was done for the mutual satisfaction of yourself & J. Picotte. I have compared the a/cts since Mr J. Picotte took charge of Fort John until your arrival at that Place, and find that the Post has gained a trifle during his administration.

Your Post is not charged with the Furs, Horses &c delivered by Bridger & Vasquez, that is the Prices are not affixed to the articles, this will be settled when Mr: Picotte arrives; and an a/c sent you per: first opportunity thereafter, for the same reason the articles brought by Pope (except Horses) have not been priced as you will observe from the a/c herewith

signed A. R. Bouis.

❖ ❖ ❖

Fort Pierre 7 Decr 1845
Messrs P. Chouteau Jr & Co
St Louis Mo:
Gentlemen

I arrived here on the 20th Ulto. All well; not having met with any accident except that one of my men Simon Dufrin deserted from me at Kanzus. I see that it is promised to pay J. B. Cousiman 20¢ on his account in six months from the 15th Octr., you will please stop the payment of the same.

No news from the Blackfeet since Harvey's arrival, Mr Culbertson got up safe with his Boat, there is every appearance that he will make peace with the Blackfeet and make a good Trade. I hear from Mr Kipp, under date of 4th Ulto. The Crow Boat reached her destination in safety: there are more Buffaloe in the neighborhood of Fort Union this season than ever, but the Assiniboins will not hunt, no whiskey, no trade at that place; there is no doubt if Mr Kipp had some of that article he could turn out this season upwards of 800 Pack, as it is he will make little or nothing, as I said above the Indians will not hunt except for what will provide them a little Tobacco and ammn.

Mr Chardon is with the Gros Ventres at L'ours qui dance,[10] fair prospcts of a good Trade there, I am sorry however to inform you, that the Rees are very much dissatisfied that Mr Chardon has left them, they threaten vengence, but as Mr Deasutels is to winter with them with some goods, we may perhaps content them. Mr. Kipp writes that the Hudson Bay Co. are trading Liquor in plenty with the Assiniboins for small furs, fortunately they will not trade Robes. I need not here again tell you how important it is that we should have plenty of that article next season. In this district the Indians are all settled for the winter, and every thing bids fair for a good trade, there is this drawback however; Mr. Sybliers people are on Rivieré a Jaques opposing our Traders strongly, not only with a good assortment of goods but with Liquor which they succeed to smuggle from the St Peter. I earnestly request you to put a stop to this, the injury to the Outfit is Considerable. I will leave in a few days to visit the Yancton Post and the Post on Riveré a Jacques and in two or three weeks will go to Fort John, but before I start for the latter place I will see Kancillen and buy him out as I promised if possible. The Yanctons prefer to have their goods purchased in St Louis and freighted up in the Cos Boat next spring, I told Maj Drips that I am willing to bring them up at whatever terms Capt. Jim thought proper to make; I consider this an advantage to me, if we had paid the Yanctons this season, they would not have been so industrious in their Hunt, and what few Robes they would have made would have cost me very dear.

I find that we have more Carts & waggons in this country than necessary. I wish you therefore to dispose of what we now have at Kanzes River even at a loss of 25% upon Cost price.

I draw on you this day favor of abnr. Harvey for 4186.72 Dollars, it being balance due him for services which you will please pay and charge this outfit

Signed H. Picotte

❖ ❖ ❖

Fort Pierre 7 Decr 1845
Jno. B. Sarpy Esqr
St Louis
Dear Sir

When I left this place to go down last summer, I advised with Mr Culbertson and we thought it best to order Mr Harvey to finish his term at this place; Harvey was sent here accordingly, but I am sorry to say that he appears to be very much dissatisfied, he swears there was a plot made to assassinate him at the head of which is Mr. Chardon, this I know nothing of. James Lee, M. Clark & old Berger attacked him and all three tried their best to kill him but could not succeed, he is now going down to procure an order to have these men brought down in order to prosecute them. I have done every thing in my power to keep him here until next spring, but he is determined to go down; I also wished to re-hire him for two years, but he declined for the present, if it is possible to come to some terms with him do so provided he is reasonable. You may offer him the Charge of the Blackfeet Post as he informs me positively that Mr Culbertson is going down next Spring, and I know of no other as efficient as he is, besides I believe nothing else but the Charge of the Post will satisfy him. I wish you to keep Harvey quiet, if he has difficulties with some of the people in the Country and ought not to run down the Company for that reason; he has promised to speak to no one but yourself about his difficulties.

Signed H Picotte.

❖ ❖ ❖

Fort Pierre 14 Decr 1845
Mr P D. Papin
Dr. Sir

Your favor of 25th ulto. For Decotae was duly recd and contents noted. You do not inform me whether the Bills produced by Capt Finch at the Transfer are original or true Copies, there are four of the goods which appear to me extraordinarily high.

The contract says that "all the men who are now in the Employ of said Pratte & Cabanné in the Indian business are to be kept & employed by the said Honoré Picotte agent H; and their wages from this month of August last are to be paid by the said Honoré Picotte agent H." Now this does not imply that we are to assume the debts of the *employes* of P. & C., Capt Finch should have settled with his men and if they were in his debt, it was his business to collect such debts from them; we pay their wages from the 1st August, and whatever they may take in the country after they Come into our Employ, we wish and it is nothing but right that we should have the benefit thereof. You were right in not giving Capt Finch the rate he requested of you, I will be with you about the 10th next month at which time I will explain to Capt Finch my views on the subject. It is useless now to enter with the details of this business as I will see you soon, in the meantime I wish you to keep this strictly secret. I recd. along with your letter a note from Capt finch & hereby give him an answer, please be particular and let neither Capt Finch or Hodgkiss have any thing to do with your Books. You will receive herewith several letters.

Yours Respy. Signed H Picotte

❖ ❖ ❖

Fort Pierre 14 Decr 1845
Capt D. Finch
Dr. Sir

Your favor of the 24th ulto was duly recd. and Contents noted. As I will start in a few days for Fort John, I deem it necessary at this time to give you my reasons why I cannot empower Mr Papin to terminate the business in question as you desire. I will be with you on or about the 10th next month.

Yours Respy. Signed H Picotte

❖ ❖ ❖

Decr. 18th.
James Kipp Esqr
Fort Union
Dr Sir

Your two favors of the 4 & 15 Ulto were duly recd. and contents noted. Your requisition is just such as I wished to send, Keep a tight hand on your English goods such as Blkts Cloth Guns and all other costly articles, as it is our intention to order of these articles only what will be absolutely necessary to carry in the trade, I will increase the quantity of Groceries and am'ntion, but in other respects will order but what you ask for. You can rely that a sufficiency of goods will be brought up next season and you may tell your Indians that they will have more than they can trade, by the by cant you not [give] me some artifice to make the Assiniboines hunt? tell them for instance that you will have grog soon, perhaps by that means you may make them come near the Fort and induce them to hunt, you can afterwards get out of the scrape by telling them the grog was pillaged on the way by the Sioux or Rees, we must try and do something, it is really a great pity now that there are such good prospects with you that we cannot take advantage of it. I have sold all our returns of last year 32 000 Robes which reached St Louis at an average of 255, had we been fortunate enough to get all the platte Robes down, we would have had a small [word?] in our favor, as it is the Outfit (1844) loses 8000$ but we have more of last years trade in the Country than sufficient to cover this loss. As to our arrangements for the next two years I say nothing about as you seen the contract in St Louis. I have no hesitation in saying that robes will be worth three dollars all round in St Louis next season, and from appearances we may safely Calculate that our returns will not be far short of Good Robes counting the packs of last year which remained in the Country, at the Platte our people Calculate upon 12 to 15 Hundred Packs at this place about 2000 and the Balance will be made up from the upper posts. We have bought out Messrs. Pratte & Cabannés interest at Fort Bernard[11] in the Platte, we therefore have all the Country to our selves; excepting Wm Kancellin who is opposing us at this place with a small outfit, we find Messrs Pruth Cabanné 25% advance on the St Louis cost for goods delivd. in the Country, and they were very glad to accept this proposition as they are tired of the business you will recollect that we were strongly opposed last season and our returns comparatively speaking small, still from the advance on robes we would as I said before would have had a small dividend in our favor had all the Robes got down; if we take down good robes this year as I have every reason to believe we will and they average 3.00 our dividend I think be sufficient to cover all our loss.

I request you to send up to Culbertson the men who carry this express and more if you can spare them, in order to enable him to bring down all his returns to Fort Union, it is of importance that all the packs from the Blackfeet and Crows be consontrated at F U, when there if you have not men enough to send them all down in Mackinaws they can be shipped by the steam Boat, by following this plan no packs will remain in the posts above, if you want men to bring down the Crow returns let me know and I will find the number you will ask let me know also if you can spare some dried meat & how much. I have plenty of men here at present but I have established a Chantier in order to have [a] timber boat down in the spring to make new Houses and put up new pickets. I hope by next spring you will have F. Union in good repair. I understand by Harvey that the freemen above Fort Union were not allowed to come in the Fort to Trade, this is Certainly wrong, we come here for Furs, & we ought to buy them it makes no difference who from, you should on the Contrary invite them to come & trade, & if you absolutely require the [word?] of some of them why not employ them, as soon as Jacain & douville arrive with them. Jaquis dispatch them down. We have no nail rod Iron & we have not ordered nails for the Bottoms of Boats for several years as we make them with small pieces of Iron that are always about a Blacksmith Shop, please do the favor. The draft for 500$ which Hunot gave Mr McKenzie for collection has been garnished in the Hands of Mr. McK; you will therefore please no advances to Hunot on a/c of said Dft. Please when you have your Beaver packed for St Louis to mention the Quantity of skins in each pack as well as the number of pounds. Was there not an Error in the quantity of P. C mirrors recd. last spring pr S B Genl. Brooke? You will receive herewith a/c of what is now sent up a/cts men a/c of F. Bercier and an order from Loise on Vilandy for a Rifle, also F. U. of current Otft [Outfit] 1835.

Justin GossClaude the Bearer of the present was in the employ of Pratte & Cabanné and in the transfer of useless articles, I had to take him, he goes to the Blackfeet as I do not wish him to go to the Crows he is engaged to a trader but I have put him at the Second Table[12] please do the same thing & hurry him up as soon as possible

Yours &c
Signed H Picotte

❖ ❖ ❖

Decr. 18
F. A. Chardon Esqr
Fort Clark
Dear Sir

Your two favors of the 11th & 26th ulto have been duly recd. and contents noted. I am pleased that you have removed to your present place and effected the same without any serious difficulties with the Rees, I have no doubt but what we will eventually be the gainer by it.

Mr Kipp was mistaken when he told you beaver were worth but 150¢ pr pound I sold all ours on an average 275¢, robes Furs & all small ones bring a good price encourage your Indians to hunt them. I will early in the spring send up men to bring down them. Corn you traded for this place, I assure you we will want it, the Indians here are not willing to give us meat at fair prices and our Corn Crop was nearly a failure. You will please send your order for next years trade in time to be forwarded to St Louis at he breaking up of the ice next spring, I would advise you to hold on to your English goods as much as possible, such as Blankets Cloth Guns and all other Costly articles, as it is our intention to bring up as little of these articles next season as will be Consistent with the Trade.

Here is written the same about Justin GossClaude as in Mr. Kipps letter

Yours Respy.

Signed H Picotte

❖ ❖ ❖

Decr 18
Alexr. Culbertson Esqr
Fort Honoré
Dear Sir

Your esteemed favor of 19th Octr last was recd. two days ago & contents noted. I am really well pleased to hear that you have removed to your present location, it will no doubt be beneficial to the Company as it is more in the Center of the Indians for whom it was built success to you.

Mr. Kipp has sent down his requisition he asks but for very few Blankets Cloth Guns & other English goods. I have therefore to request you to hold on to that description of goods as much as possible as it is our intention to order only what will be absolutely necessary for the trade, as to grog Console yourself and you may tell your indians they will not want for any next season

Harvey is gone down to procure (so he says) an order from the Supt. Ind: Affairs, to have Clark, Berger & Lee taken down to St. Louis on plea that they formed a plot to assassinate him he wants the following men brot down as his witnesses, F. Archembeau, Bernabe, Pussi Crenier, Iagen Enuth, & Henry Robert, now as some of these men will not wish to go down I think you can take advantage of this Circumstance to hire them Cheap if you want them; my opinion is that Harvey is comg. up in the spring to oppose us at the Blkfeet trade as few Horses as possible we have plenty in every post for this years trade. I have written to Mr Kipp to send you up as many men as he can spare in order to enable you to bring down all your returns to Fort Union it is of importance that all the packs from the Blackfeet and Crows be concentrated at F. U.; when then if Mr Kipp has not men enough to take them down in Mackinaws they can be shipped by the Steam Boat, and in that way no packs will be left at any of the posts above.

Tell Berger his debt due him by the dobies is lost, I arrived too late in St Louis.

Respy. Yours &c

Signed H Picotte

❖ ❖ ❖

Fort Pierre Febry 2, 1846
Pierre D Papin Esqr
Fort John
Dear Sir

Sometime ago I wrote to Robt Pope advising him that his brother Mr W H Pope had deposited Three Hundred Dollars (300$) in the hands of Messrs. Pierre Chouteau Jr & Co of St Louis, for his use and subject to his order; upon examination, I find that Messrs Pierre Chouteau Jr & Co have transferred the account to Credit of Upper Missouri Outfit 1845, you will please therefore give Robt Pope Credit for Three Hundred Dollars on fort John Books, and when paid charge the same to Fort Pierre.

I find that four of your traders eat up the Tongues they trade, I request you to put a stop to this, you know they are a cash article in St Louis & should be taken care of. The Two Hundred Robes Kellogg brought here from the head of white River are certainly the meanest lot I ever saw, not one robe in the lot which can be Called prime, please use every exertion to induce your Indians to do better. You will receive herewith sundry a/cs. Fort John a/c current will be made by first opportunity

Signed H Picotte
pr A R Bouis

P.S. I have no traps to send you, you will receive 210 Trap springs, please have traps made.

❖ ❖ ❖

Fort Pierre 24 Febry 1846
Francis A Chardon Esqr
Fort James [later Berthold]
My dear sir,

I write today to Louison Freniere to start four men for your place immediately upon the recpt of my letter, these men you will keep until the breaking up of the ice and as soon thereof as practicable dispatch them in a *Bull Boat* for this place with 150 or 200 Bushels of corn, it is of importance that I should receive that article as soon as possible as we have now but very little left. I wish you also not delay and send me down your requisition for next year as soon as you receive the present, you can hire Beauchamp or Detaillie to bring it down to Frenieres post, and from there it will be brought to this place by one of F's men, it is my intention as soon as the River opens to start an Express in a canoe for St Louis.

You will receive a small package which your sister gave me for you in St Louis and which was overlooked by me when I sent up Goss Claude & party. The trade in this district will not be as much as I had at first had reason to expect, I fear it will not exceed 200 packs the extraordinary mild weather we have had for the last two months and a half, has caused the Buffaloe to move into the interior & what is worse, we could not keep the Indians stationary, they were travelling about from one place to the other all winter. The Balance of the corn which you traded for this place will be brought down by the S Bt next spring. If you want a Boat to bring down your packs, you will write to Mr Kipp and he will provide you with one. Please let me know how many packs you expect to trade

 Yours &c
 Signed H Picotte

❖ ❖ ❖

Requisition Merchandise for the Trade at Fort Pierre Outfit 1846.

[column 1] [originally in two parallel columns]

100 pr	3 pt	Comn. Whi Blankets
200 "	2 ½ pt	Large " "
250 "	1 "	" " "
50 pr	Indigo Bleu Stroud	
50 "	yd Lt Bleu Cloth	
1 "	Fancy Lt	
60 "	Comn. Fancy Calico	
20 "	good " "	
20 "	4/4 unbleached shirting	
10 "	4/4 Bleached "	
5 "	4/4 Apron chick	
15 "	7/8 Plain Domestic	
10 "	Fancy table covers	
3 pr	Co ___ ___ Bright cols	
4 "	Comn. Black silk Hdkfs [Handkerchiefs]	
5 doz	woolen comforters	
2 "	good Palm Leaf Hats	
5 "	Blk Leather Belts	
30	Very Large flushing Capots	
30 pr	" " Comn. fat Pants	
20 "	" " Summer "	
50 "	" " Blk seal skin caps	
20 pr	Comn. Duck Pants	
20 y	Red 10 Bleu 5 & Green 5 Ribbon #4	
3x Ea	Bleu wht & ___ Col Patent Thread	
½ "	good Black sewing silk	
½ "	" _____ " "	
25 "	Cot. Candle wick	
10 "	wrapping Tissue	
10 "	Holland "	
20 "	silver Gorgets No 1	
20 "	" " No 2	
70 doz	P. C. Mirrors	
2 "	6 in H[an]d saw files	
1 "	8 " Cross cut saw files	
1 "	14 " flat Bastard " Cross	
1 "	14 " H[al]f Round files "	
6 "	6 " flat Bastd " "	

[column 2]

1 doz	6 " flat Bastard files	
½ "	6 " H[al]f R[oun]d "	
100 gro:	Brass Finger Rings	
1 gro	½ in wood screws	
1 "	¼ " " "	
2 doz	good strong nail gimlets	
½ "	" " fluke gimlets	
1 ¢	fish hooks	
2 M	Gun Flints	
60	Beaver Traps	
5 doz	Beaver Trap chains	
2 ¢	Garmt needles in 10 to 12	
1 doz	Large shop scissors	
2 setts	Knives & forks	
100 doz	____ ____ Knives	
100 "	Comn. " "	
100	P___ Hawk Bells	
25 #	Rough Horse Bells small	
100 doz	Crambo Combs	
50 "	Boxwood " ___ on both sides	
10 M	12 oz Saddlers Tacks	
5 "	Brass nails	
24 doz	Bright oval fire steels	
12 gro	gun worms	
1000 #	Wht P[oun]d Beads as per samples	
500 "	deep Bleu " "	

6 doz	Comn. snaffle Bridles	
1 "	Glass Tumblers	
3	Large ____ Pitchers	
1 doz	Collins Choppg. Axes (Heavy)	
1500 "	Tobacco 1 in Plug	
2000 "	" 1/8 in Twist	
500 "	Bar Iron 2 by ½	
200 "	" " 1 ½ by 3/8 in	
100 "	Round Iron 1 In diameter	
700 "	Hoop Iron ½ in wide	
300 "	4 ½ in wrought spikes as per sample	
300 "	12 p[enn]y wrought nails "	

❖ ❖ ❖

Fort Pierre Requisition Oft [Outfit] 1846 Contd.
[column 1] [originally in two parallel columns]

300 lb	12 py Cut nails as per sample
400 "	Oakum
1 Bbl	Rosin
1000 #	Pig Lead
3000 #	Gun Powder in 25 lb Kegs
4 Bags	Shot No 3
4 " "	" 1
12 gro	Good Clay Pipes
5 galls	a . . . . . . for mid___
80 Bbls	flour
6 "	Pilot Bread
10 "	Navy "
2 "	Butter Crackers
3 "	Dried apples
2 "	" Peaches
1 "	White Beans fresh
6 "	Early Potatoes for seed
3 "	good molasses
25 "	asstd. Candy for Children
6 Bags	G. A. salt
4 Boxes	Castile Soap
1 "	Shaving "
7000 #	Br: Havana sugar
5500	Green " Coffee
10 Boxes	muscatel Raisins
100 "	Fresh Y. H. Tea
3 Bbls	Rice
100 #	Black Pepper
6 dz	Kentucky Mustard in tin cans
½ "	Steel Back scythes
50	Belgians Guns
½ doz	scythe stones
10 #	Epsom Salts
1 Bot	Paregoric
2 gro	Phial corks

[column 2]

2_4	Twin Day Books
12-1 "	Blank " Ruled
1 Ream	Ruled Letter Paper
1 "	" fools cap
1 "	Hard____ ____
50	good quills
1 doz	Lead Pencils
2 "	Red Tape
50 #	Verdigais
233 1/3	Chinese Vermillion
150 #	Am[erica]n. Vermillion
300 #	Chrome Yellow in Boxes of 5 ea.
1 good	Carpenter | To be first rate
1 "	Blacksmith | 2d@ Table 250$
1 "	Tailor | wages comp @ ___ &
200$ Tailor	
15	Voyageurs
200 Bu	Corn

The above order is made out to
Include the goods per trade from
Pratte & Cabannés which are now
In St Louis —
The following is to be left at Bellevue
By Capt. Sire —

12 Bls	good Pork	
10 "	Navy Beans	
1 "	sugar	

Fort Pierre March 10th 1846
Signed H. Picotte

❖ ❖ ❖

Requisition Merchandise for the Trade at Fort John Offt [Outfit] 1846.

[column 1] [originally in two parallel columns]

120 prs	3 pt Comn. White Blankets
150 "	1 ½ pt " " "
60 "	3 pt Bright scarlet
40 "	2 ½ pt " "
5 ps	Comn. Red flannel
2 doz	wht wool Hats
36 pr	Comn. Pants Large
36 "	Summer " "

2 doz	Calico night Caps	
6 "	Comn. Night caps	
6 "	Cot: Pocket HdKfs	
1 pr	Black silk HdKfs	
10 pr	Cotton Candle wicks	
600 "	White pd. Beads as per sample	
600 "	Bleu " " " "	
50	Best N.W. Guns 2 ft 6 in	
100	Powder Horns	
20 #	Rough Horse Bells	
20 gro	Brass Finger Rings	
50 doz	P.C. Mirrors 4+ 5 Inches	
40 "	Warranted scalp Knives	
40 "	Comn. " "	
20 "	____ C____	
2 "	14 in flat Bastard files	
10 ___	Brass nails	
1 Keg	4 in wrought spikes	
1 "	12 py Cut nails	
100 #	Round Iron 1 in diameter	
1___	Coarse Sand Paper	
2 doz	a____ B____ B____	
1 "	____ ____	
1	Flat foot adze	
700 #	Gun Powder	
5000	Pig Lead	
8 Boxes	1/8 Twist Tobacco	

[column 2]

10 #	Spanish Tobacco	
1 Coil	Manila Rope 1 in thick	
200 #	Oakum	
6 Boxes	Brn Havana sugar	
8 Bags	green " Coffee	
25 Barrels	fine Flour	
3 "	Navy Bread	
3 "	Pilot "	
2 "	Rice	
1 "	Dried apples	
4 Boxes	Raisins	
4 "	Com__ Soap	
3 Bags	G.A. Salt	
5 gals	Paint oil	
1 "	Spts Turpentine	
1 gro	1 oz Phials	
1 "	Phial corks	
5 #	Wrapping Tissue	
5 "	____ "	
1 Ream	Wrapping Paper	
½ "	Ruled Letter	
1/2 "	foolscap	
1-4	Twin Day Book Bound	
1-6	Twin Ledger "	
1-6	Invoice "	
½ doz	Blank Books 8 by 12 inch	
25	good quills	
1	small Phial Red Ink	
1 doz	Lead Pencils	
1 "	Red Tape	
1	grind stone	
2 Boxes	Chinese Vermillion	
25	Verdigris	
100 #	Chrome Yellow in 5# Boxes	
1	Tailor & 1 waggon maker	
12	Voyageurs	

Fort Pierre 10th March 1846
Signed H. Picotte agt U.M.O.

❖ ❖ ❖

Requisition Merchandise for the Trade at Fort Union Offt [Outfit] 1846.

[column 1] [originally in two parallel columns]

70 pr	3 pt. Hudson Bay Blkts	
20 "	2 ½ " "	
100 "	1 pt White	
15 pr	Sd Lt Bleu Cloth	
10 "	Indigo Beu Stroud	
5 "	Bleu ____	
6 "	Red Flannel	
5 "	White do	
5 "	____ Calico	
30 "	Fancy "	
15 "	4/4 Bleached ____	
10 "	4/4 apron check	
60	Check shirts	
100	Calico do	
5 pr	Large ____ Red HdKf [Handkerchief]	
2 "	Fine silk "	
3 doz	good woolen socks	
2 "	Mens Brogans	
36 pr	Summer Pantaloons	
2 doz	Palm Leaf Hats	
20 "	Cot: Candle wicks	
1 doz	Collins Chopping axes	
300 #	white pound Beads	
50 doz	____ Col. Cut Glass	

10 #	white garnishing	
10 "	Bleu "	
90	Best N. W. Guns	
40	Belgian "	
150	Powder Horns	
6 doz	6 in Pit saw files	
2 "	8 " Flat Bastards	
3 m	6 oz Saddlers Tacks	
7 Kegs	4 ½ in m ____ ____ ____	
6 "	12 py Cut nails	
1 "	8 py " "	
400	____ Rod Iron	
60 ft	Bar Iron 2 + ½ in for tin	
30 "	" " 2 ½ + ½ " "	

[column 2]

200 ft	Bar Iron 2 x ½ in	
3 B____	Clay Pipes	
10 m	Good Percussion Caps	
3000 #	Gun Powder	
5000 "	Pig Lead	
1500 "	Tobacco 1 n Plugs	
325 "	" ½ " "	
500 "	" 1/8 " "	
500 "	" ½ " "	
500 #	Oakum	
2 Barrels	Raisins	
5000 #	Br Havana sugar	
3500 "	Green " "	
3 Bls	molasses	
40 #	Y. H. Tea	
2 Bags	G. A. Salt	
60 #	Black Pepper	
8	B____ Raisins	
2 Barrels	Dried apples	
2 "	" Peaches	
60 "	Fine Flour	
2 "	Rice	
40 "	A.......	
3 Gals	Linseed oil	
2 "	Lamp Black	
10 #	Epsom Salts	
1 "	Cinnamon	
½ "	Cloves	
½ "	Nut meg	
1 "	Allspice	
3 doz	Kentucky Mustard	
2 "	C____ ____	
1 "	____ ____ ____	

3 doz	Turlingtons Balsam	
4 Bot	Castor Oil	
3 doz	____	
3 "	Good Steel Pens	

Forward
Fort Union Requisition Offt 1846 Contd.
[column 1] [originally in two parallel columns]

½ "	Red sealing wax	
1	Ruled Blank Books	
½ doz	2 ____ Blank Books	
½ "	scythe stones	
1/3 gro	Brass Thimbles	
1	Keel Boat Cordelle	
1	Blacksmith (same remark as Ft. P.)	

[column 2]

2 ¢	Fish Hooks as pr sample	
24 doz	Bright oval fire steels	
1 "	Large ____ ____	
½ "	Good strong Pad Locks	
100 "	Open Brass Kettles	
12 "	Cavendish Tobacco for Mr Kipp	
40	Voyageurs	

Fort Union March 10th 1846
Signed H. Picotte U.M.O.

❖ ❖ ❖

Requisition Merchandise for the Trade at Fort Clark Offt [Outfit] 1846.
[column 1] [originally in two parallel columns]

15 prs	3 pt. dark Bleu Blankets	
10 "	3 " ____ " "	
20 "	3 " Green " "	
20 "	3 " Bright Scarlet "	
100 "	3 " Eng[lis]h white "	
80 "	2/oo L____ " "	
30 "	2 ½ " Scarlet "	
10 "	2 ½ " deep Bleu "	
50 "	1 pt white " "
15 pr	____ ____ Bleu Cloth	
5 "	Indigo Bleu Stroud	
10 "	____ ____ Scarlet Cloth	
1 "	Fancy Lt Bleu Cloth	
1 "	Comn. Red Flannel	
1 "	4/4 Apron Check	
10 "	4/4 Bro: _____	

5 "	4/4 Bleached "	
1 "	Union strops	
15	Fancy Calico	
4	Fancy Table Cloth covers	
2 pr	Comn. Blk silk HdKfs	
3 "	Cot mattress	
3 "	Ea: Ind Bleu & Green Ribbon ___	
2 doz	woolen comforters	
15	Large ___ Coats	

[column 2]

24	Red Flannel Shirts
48	Calico "
12 pr	Summer
24 "	Comn. ___ "
24	Large Blk seal Skin Caps
10	Cot: Candle wick
2 doz	Red Cock feathers
3 M	Percussion Caps
10 doz	7 in But[cher] Knives
30 "	6 " " "
10 "	M_ Scalps "
40 "	Comn. " "
30 doz	P.C. Mirrors
30 "	Crambo Combs
2 "	Fine Tooth Combs
5 M	Brass nails
4 gro:	Ind: awls
6 doz	Bright oval fire steels
2 gro:	Gun worms
4 doz	[Iron] Corn Hoes
10 gro	Brass Finger rings
150 #	wht pd. Beads
3 doz	Comn. Curb Bridles
30	Belgian Guns
30	Powder Horns

[Fort Clark continued]
[column 1] [originally in two parallel columns]

2 doz	Black Leather Belts
1 Box	Clay pipes
10	silver Gorgets No 1
10	" " " 2
3-2	Twin Blank Book
½ Ream	Ruled Letter Paper
½ "	" foolscap
½ doz	Lead Pencils
1 "	Steel Pens
¼	Common Quills
3 doz	Turlingtons Balsam
1 Bot	Spts Camphor
1 "	Essn Peppermint
1500 #	Br Havana sugar
1000 "	Green " "

[column 2]

13 #	Y H Tea
1 Bag	G. A. Salt
20 #	Black Pepper
1 Bbl	Dried apples
1 "	" Peaches
10 "	Fine Flour
1 "	Rice
4 ___	Comn. ___
25 #	Verdigris
100 "	Chrome Yellow
1 Box	Chinese Vermlr.
50 #	Am[erica]n Vermillion
8	Voyageurs

Fort Pierre March 10. 1846
Signed H Picotte
Agt U. M. O.

❖ ❖ ❖

Fort Pierre March 10. 1846
S. A. Sarpy Esqr
Bellevue
Dear Sir

Mr Harding promised me on my way up last fall, to deliver you 5 Bbls Potatoes; should he do so please [do] not fail & ship them up by the Steam Boat this spring they are much wanted for seed.

Should our Express Devinie Guion be in want please let him have what provisions he may require and charge same to this Outfit.

Wishing you good health & prosperity
Yours &c
Signed H Picotte

❖ ❖ ❖

Fort Pierre 10th March 1846.
Mr Theophile Bruguire[13]
Fort Vermillion
Dear Sir

Immediately on receipt of the present you will make your order for merchandise for next years trade and forward it down by our Express Vincent Gouin, should Guion be in want of provisions, give him sufficiently to take him to Bellevue and hurry him off as it is desirable that the Steam Boat should come up as soon as possible.

I had promised to stop at your place on my way up, but at Bellevue I heard that to do so I would be obliged to pass through the Potawatomies, Otto & Omaha Camps and as I feared some of the Indians would steal my Horses I thought it prudent not to risk it.

In making out your order you will ask for more Sugar Coffee & flour than usual in order to enable you to sell some to your men the whole year round, by so doing you will save a great deal of money which otherwise would have to be paid our men in St Louis.

I want you to come up and see me as soon as you can do so without Injury to your trade, if you come before the Steam Boat arrives it is all the better, but by all means come up in her if you cant come sooner
You will receive a letter
Yours &c
Signed H Picotte

❖ ❖ ❖

Fort Pierre 10th March 1846.
Messrs P. Chouteau Jr & Co
St Louis Mo,
Gentlemen

As it is desirable that the supplies for next year's trade reach this country as early as practicable, I now dispatch you Devine Guion with the requisitions for the Different Posts, which you will please fill and forward as soon after the receipt of the present as possible. Mr Chouteau showed me a 3 pt wht Blanket last summer, which cost no more than the 2½ pt white, the sample was brought from a House in N. Orleans, they will answer very well for the trade, I ask for 300 pr for this post, which you will please forward, should it happen that you have more on hand send no other kind of 3 pt white as we have plenty, ask for those above only in case we should be opposed, one Hundred and fifty pairs of the same kind Blks, as also asked for Fort John, if they cannot be furnished please send up 2½ pt white in lieu thereof. The 1 pt French wht Blankets recd. last year are too [word?], please send us Lowell 1 ps white or a Blanket that will measure at least 1¼ by 1 yd, those recd. last year measured 11/8 by 1 yd. Forty Barrels of alcohol at least are required for the upper Posts, as you are aware of the importance of getting that article in the country I will say no more on the subject than this; if there had been some at Fort Union last year Mr Kipp would have traded 500 packs more than he will and I have no doubt the difference (from the small quantity which was at the Blackfeet) in Mr Culbertsons trade will be equally as great, the loss as you will observe will be very great this year, let us try therefore to make it up next year and the only way to do this is for you to send us up at least 40 barrels of that article by the Steam Boat or any other way which you may think expedient. We have had an extraordinary mild winter & the trade will suffer in Consequence, it is difficult to say what quantity of Robes will be traded in this district but I fear not more than 1000 packs at Fort John Mr Papin will I think trade from 800 to 1000 packs, no news from the upper posts since my last per Harvey. In case the water should be low and it is (as I said above) desirable that the supplies reach their destination as early as possible, I request you to make Choice of a small Boat to come up, by all means do not send up the [steamboat] Nimrod[14] as she is too large & therefore draws too much water.

You will receive a package for Messrs: Pratte & Cabanné, Mr Papin writes to you fully respecting the transfer of their goods at fort John. You will also receive Dr. Finches order on P & C favor Charles Carr. For 78.95 Dollars which you will please Collect. The order is not endorsed by Carr and the man is now at the Blackfeet in our employ, the amt is placed to his Cr. on our Books. I hope Mssrs P & C will not notice this informallity.

Please send up by the Steam Boat all the Lodges Tools, Kettles &c belonging to this Outfit.

You will receive inclusive the Balances due to men going down. Mr. Bouguin has made out his requisition which you will please fill and deliver at Vermillion, please Bale up the goods for fort John seperately as last year
Respfy Yours &c
Signed H Picotte
Agt U. M. O.

❖ ❖ ❖

Fort Pierre March 10 1846
Capt J. A. Sire
St Louis Mo
Dear Sir

I have on several occasions conversed with you on the subject of getting alcohol in the country and I request you particularly to manage some way or another to bring it up, our case is really a hard one, no alcohol no trade with the Assiniboins and Blackfeet. You will observe that I have asked for some provisions to be left at Bellevue, when you land them at that place, inquiry of Mr Sarpy if Mr Harding has delivd. him five Barrels of Potatoes which he promised me last fall on my way up, and if so, please bring them up, they are much wanted in addition to those asked for From St Louis.

Again I request you to bring up a few pieces of Hickory suitable ~~for~~ to make [word?] for waggons & Carts, no good wood for that purpose can be found in this country and we are put to great inconvenience & Labour on account of the bad wood we have to make use of.

You will find wood Chopped at the usual places.
Wishing you a speedy trip
Truly Yours &c
Signed H Picotte

❖ ❖ ❖

Fort Pierre 11th March 1846
Messrs. P Chouteau Jr & Co
St Louis
Gentlemen

A short time after closing our mail yesterday Deignian & Morin arrived with your letters which have been carefully read and duly noticed. I will endeavor to make our claims good against the different nations and bands of Indians for depredations, Maj Drips promises me all the aid in his power, it will be sometime before I can do this with the Blackfeet and Crows and some bands of Sioux, but no time will be lost, I will persevere and follow your instructions and I believe we will recover the greater part if not all of them. As it is necessary that we should have four or five Hundred Bushels of corn next winter at Fort John to oppose the Taos Pedlers[15] who are a great annoyance and ~~great~~ get [a] good many Robes with that article; I have agreed with Mr Papin that he should bring up next fall the Carts &c now at Kanzas with a light load of corn, for that reason if you have not disposed of them when you receive the present, do not do so unless you get near their original cost, should you see them you will please bring up the 200 Bus corn asked for in the requisition, if not, you can bring the corn only in case it can be done without any detention of the Boat. I have left instructions with Mr Papin not to advance any thing more to Bridger and Vasquez until we have had a final settlement with them & they have paid all [word?], which at Fort John I made particular inquiries about the navigation of the Platte and learn by persons well informed on the subject, that if there is not a full river in the north fork our boats will run some risk of not getting down although they may reach the south fork, for the reason it is agreed between Mr Papin & myself, that he will not leave with his boats unless there is a fair prospect of high water, if the contrary he is to put all his waggons and carts in good repair and keep his horses & oxen in good order. I am to do the same thing here we will cooperate and begin to haul the packs by the 1st May from Fort John to this place, when here I will have Boats and men ready to dispatch them as they arrive, and we have reason to believe that the last shipment will be no later than the 1st Septr. I hope however that we will not be to all this trouble and that Mr Papin will go down safely with his Boats.

It was agreed with Mr McKenzie & Capt Sire to both of whom I spoke on the subject last year that the expenses of keeping up Fort Clark was too great and it was expedient t[o] remove to *l'Ours que danse*, in conformity with my instructions in the subject, Mr Chardon effected the removal with little or no trouble leaving Mr Desautels at Fort Clark with such goods only as were necessary to trade Corn as the Rees at that time had no Robes. Since then Mr Chardon has sent a good equipment to the Rees and Desautel is trading with them Some of them grumble it is true but the corn is far from being as bad as Harvey represented it to you. The remarks you make concerning the amtt due to Harvey since 1840 is correct it is true that in our last settlement you did not see that amt to debit of outfit neither did you see to Cr. Outfit the amt due by Bridger & Vasquez which would more than Counterbalance it, in fact as we have no presadent to go by the thing was not done & every year thus far the difference pro & con was so trifling that it has never been taken into consideration, however when I was in St Louis, Mr Chouteau spoke to me on this subject, and as the estate of Mr Halsey was to be settled with, and Mr Papin is to Come in as a partner in this Outfit, it was understood that it should and it will be done according to your desire. I will start three Mackinaw Boats on or about the 1st April with all the Robes which will be here from the interior say 7 or 800 packs. The dressed deer Skins are a cash article here and at Fort John, they sell well ~~with~~ to our men and to the Oregan Emigrants. I have all along given plenty of salt with instructions to our traders not to spare it and make good Tongues. I am inclined to believe that the Tongues spoil in St Louis, I seen some last summer in a Brick Smoke House which admitted of but little air, and remarked at the time to Mr Whetten that they would spoil. Your instructions concerning wolf Skins come too late for this season, hereafter we will endeavour to have these skins cured as you desire, but think it very difficult to do so with large wolves. Major Drips writes to Maj Harvey requesting him by all means to send up the Yancton Goods, I would also request you to send them up if Maj Harvey desires it there are plenty of free people in the country Zephyr [?] in the number who will advise the Yanctons and make them believe if their goods does not come up the fault is ours they are getting troublesome on the subject and it would be a great disappointment [to] them if they do not receive them by the steam Boat. Even if I had proposed to sell them the goods here they would have objected for the reasons I state above, you are mistaken when you say they do not require woolen goods in [word?]. I could not make any arrangements with Kimcillir, try and hire him with Equipment, F. Robidoun and young Robidoun, and give them Komcellir for a month during trading season 400$. F Robidoux 400 a year J Robidax J. 300$ a year and Gurrimont 200$ a year, by so doing you will perhaps keep Old J. Robidoux from sending to oppose us.

Signed H Picotte
Agt U. M. O.

❖ ❖ ❖

Fort Pierre March 12th 1846.
Mr: Louis Freniere
Yanctons Post
dear Sir

I part to day Morrain & Degneau with dispatches for the Upper country, please hurry them up, and give them all necessary instructions, in order that they may pass the Ree camp, and arrive at Fort Clark in safety.

It is of importance that I should start three Mackinaw boats loaded with Robes for St. Louis, as early as possible for that reason you will so soon as there is any appearance of the ice breaking at your place please send me down a man with the news, I will then send up men sufficient to bring down 3 Mackinaw boats, which you will hurry to finish, and load with timber for the making of 4 more Boats. Yourself & men, now with you will remain until the arrival of Lanis with the Corn from the Mandanes.

Yours &c
For Honoré Picotte
A. R. Bouis

❖ ❖ ❖

Fort Pierre 12th March 1846
Francis A. Chardon Esqr
Fort Berthold
Dear Sir

Ten days ago I received your Letters from St: Louis by Deigneau, Morrin, the two men who are now going up to Fort Union with our dispatches. You will receive a Letter from Messrs. Chouteau Jr: & Co, who no doubt give you all the information Concerning the value of Robes &c. &c. I will however remark, that wolves skinned Cased are much more valuable than when cut under the belly, if practicable, please make your Indians raise the skin as above. As the Estate of Mr: Halsey is to be settled with, & Mr Papin is to come in the Outfit as a partner, it is necessary, and I request you to be very particular in making out your inventory it will also be necessary for you to make out an a/c of what money may be due to men at your post, who will remain in the Country, also an a/c of what may be due by individuals when you make out your inventory; the a/cts of each of your men, that are going down will not of course be included, please be very particular, I believe I am explicit enough to be well understood.

As it is ~~necessary~~ desirable that the supplies for next years trade reach their destination as early as possible, I yesterday started my Express for St: Louis, with the requisitions of the different posts, as yours has not been recd. I followed the Invoice of last year, only I asked for more Groceries than usual, when your requisition comes I will compare it with the one I sent to St: Louis, add such articles as I may not have asked for will be furnished from this place, packed up & kept in readiness for the Steamboat next spring, I thought it best to follow this course, rather than to detain the express longer. Please send me the Corn I asked by Jane's as soon as possible, we will I fear starve here before long.

I have determined according to the desire of Messrs. P. C. Jr. & Co to dispatch 3 Mackinaw boats in the beginning of April it appears that the earlyer the boats get to St: Louis the better market we find for them.

If you can provide some Aricara tobacco seed[16] send me some, I have promised a little to the Yanctons should the Rees being much dissatisfied at your removal I am willing to keep up Fort Clark with three men the year round, if you think there is the last danger that the Steamboat will have difficulty with them in passing, you will please send me down Garreau to meet the Boat here, if Garreau does not come, I will take it for granted that there is no risk.

If your Indians have made a good hunt and should want horses, I hope you have sent to Mr: Kipp for some, I am told he has many.

You will oblige me if you send me down a little sweet Corn & pumpkins.

Signed H. Picotte

❖ ❖ ❖

Fort Pierre 12 March 1846
James Kipp Esqr
Fort Union
Dr. Sir

The St Louis Express arrived two days ago & I hasten to start Seigneau & Morrin with your letters, Messrs, P. Chouteau Jr: & Co. write to you, and no doubt make you acquainted with the prices of Robes & Cloth. I will remark however that wolfs skins [word?] sell for much more in New York, than when cut under the belly, if practicable, please induce your Indians to skin them as above.

As the estate of Mr. Halsey is to be settled with, and Mr. Papin is to come in as a partner in the Outfit, it will be necessary, and I request you to be as particular in taking your Inventories this season, you will also make out a detailed a/c of the Balances due to carry individuals who will remain in the country, and visa verce those who are indebted to the Outfit, of course the a/cs of the men who will go down are not to be included, Messrs. P. C: Jr: & Co: request me particularly to have this done for the reasons mentioned above, you will please therefore not neglect it, and advise Messrs. Culbertson & Murry to do the same thing at their posts.

It appears that with a little pirsevearance we will be enabled to make the different Indian Nations pay us (that is the government will do so) for depredations, you will please therefore make out a/cts against the Crows for the horses they have stolen from us at different times, it will be necessary to have a few of those Indians at Fort Union by the time the Steam Boat got up, to acknowledge before Maj: Drips, who will go up with me, that the a/cts. are right, it also be necessary for you, to have the men from whom the horses were stolen at Fort Union, in order that Maj: Dr: may take their depositions, the number of Horses stolen by those people from us is considerable, and if we can substantiate our claims, the Government by a late law would be obliged to pay us. You will do the same with respect to the Assiniboins, if you have any claims against them, as for the Blackfeet it is too late to undertake it this season, but we would hereafter please also request Mr Denig to make out the a/cts against the Sioux who have for some years back stolen Horses from F. U. I will get those accounts acknowledged at this place and if necessary bring down the persons from whom stolen, but I believe Maj Drips will take their depositions at Fort Union you will receive herewith the account of merchandise stolen from Mr James Brieginn on White River it will be necessary for him to testify to it when Maj Drips goes up.

Please not neglect and send me per 1st opportunity Mr Chardons a/c at Blackfeet & Fort

Union Otft 1844. You will place to Cr. of Jacque Berger 259.83 Doll[ar]s collected by the House below from Union fur Co. & placed to Cr. of this outfit, when paid you will charge this post with the same. You will receive a/cs Morrin & Degneau, a/ct [word] them for [word] and sundry letters for the gentlemen above. You will as usual keep back your small furs & peltries & ship them down by the steam Boat.

Signed H Picotte

❖ ❖ ❖

Fort Pierre 12 March 1846.
Alexr Culbertson Esqr
Fort Lewis[17]
Dr. sir

Here is written the same as in Mr Kipp's letter from Page 1 to 17

I am flattered and thank you for your good opinion of me in giving my name to your Fort, but I request you to substitute *Lewis* in the place of Honoré which is much more suitable and appropriate by so doing you will oblige me.

The extraordinary mild weather we have had during the winter has caused the Buffaloe to move far in Land, we will not make as good a trade as I at first had reason to believe I hope that such is not the case with you. Buffaloe have been very plenty at the Platte & although Mr Papin trades much higher than we do here he will make I doubt not 12 or 13 packs very cheap

Signed H Picotte

❖ ❖ ❖

Fort Pierre 7th April 1846
P. D. Papin Esqr
Fort John
Dr. sir

Caryon & Morin arrived on the 29 ulto with all you sent in good order except the two Cats which were drowned in *Leue que Court* by the negligence of the men. I think they should be made to pay well for them & I request you to send me others pr 1st opportunity.[18] I have delayed until now expecting that Louison P. D. Picotte would arrive I would then have been able to send you the men you require, but as the weather Continues strong, no Calculations Can be made when they will be here therefore I think it best, to start your two men with the carts loaded with skins &c ahead, and so soon as I can scrape up 15 men, they will be dispatched with Instructions to make their way to Fort John with as little delay as possible & I have no doubt that they will reach that place as soon as the Carts. I am pleased to learn that the prospects of high water in the Platte this season are good, I have no doubt you will take advantage of the 1st rise & use every exertion to get your returns down by so doing it will be a great saving to the Outfit, when I had the pleasure of seeing you last, we came to a perfect understanding about the measures to be taken in case you Could not take down the returns by way of the Platte therefore I think it [un]necessary to say any thing more on this subject, except to request you, not to abandon the Idea of going down with Boats as long as there is a prospect of a risk in the River.

I see in a/c of sundries for'd Pratte & Cabanné a charge for 40$ for a horse furnished Raboin, from the date of the Charge (Mar 9th) I suppose the amt was not sent to St Louis as it was given after the departure of Mr Finch, you will therefore not neglect to send it down pr 1st opportunity, you should mention by whose order you paid Roboin the most.

As the estate of Mr Halsey is to be settled with and you are to come in as a partner in the Outfit, I request you to be very particular in taking the Inventory. The good articles Mr H purchased from Pratte & Cabanné are to be taken separately, it will also be necessary to make an a/c of what will be due to every man remaining in the Country & an a/c of what may be due by Individuals to the Outfit. I wish to be very particular in this. When you leave Fort John please give Instructions to the person remaining in charge of that post to trade during the summer every thing in the shape of a Robe [word] inferior or otherwise, provided they are paid for according to their value to be sent here by the 1st Sept next and as soon as they arrive I will take them down to St Louis. I mean by paying for them according to their value not to trade woolen goods & guns for them. The dressed deer Skins now sent you are very inferior & the price charged is large, but according to Contract we had to pay the same charge you to Bridger & Vasquez we sell them here No 1. 2$ No 2 1½ & No 3 1$. This however is no guide you say sell them to the Emigrants for cash, much

Cheaper. I wish you when you get in the settlements to report many fewer packs than you really have, it is Mr. Chouteaus wish that such should be the Case. In case you cannot go down the Platte, I wish you to Bear in mind that the men are not to be free until the returns reach St. Louis, therefore you will make them assist to bring the packs to this place

Truly Yours &c
Signed H Picotte

❖ ❖ ❖

Fort Pierre April 18. 1846
P. D. Papin Esqr
Fort John
Dear Sir

Mr Charles Primeau with 15 men will leave this morning for your place, I have not been able to send them down as J. Picotte[19] arrived from the Chayenne yesterday, I hope however they will be in time to answer all purposes. Seven men are to come back with Primeau as they are good as Drivers, the others you can send with the Boats if you think proper you will receive their a/cs herewith. I have every reason to believe that you will run down the Platte, but should it be otherwise, do not fail (after you have lost all hopes) to send me an express immediately thereafter as agreed upon when I saw you last. I wish you to have in mind to give orders to the person remaining in charge of Fort John not [to] neglect and trade all the Robes &c during the summer and send them to this place as I ordered you on my last. Tell Mr Hodgkiss if he is still desirous to have employment to come over with Mr P.

You will find provisions belonging to the outfit at Bellevue at the establishment of P. A. Sarpy.

Signed H Picotte

❖ ❖ ❖

Fort Pierre 2nd May 1846
Capt. J. A. Sire
Dr. Sir

Please let Mr. J Picotte have what provisions he may require to reach Bellevue. Please also leave at Mr Campbells Houses the following articles, viz.

3 Bbls Flour, 1 Bbl: Rice, 1 Bl Dried ap[p]les
3 Bbls Pork 1Bbl Navy bread 1 Bl Sugar, 1 sac coffee
3sacs [word] 1 Box soap

The letters from the upper posts were lost at upper Yanctonais Post by Mr Chardon Express, I am therefore unable to give you any news from that part of the country. By recent arrivals Mr. Papin informs me, that there is plenty of snow in the mountains, and from the rains we have lately had, I have every reason to believe he will get down the Platte with all his boats

Wishing you a speedy trip Yours T:
Signed H. Picotte

❖ ❖ ❖

Fort Pierre May 2 1846
Messrs. P. Chouteau Jr. & Co
St Louis
Gentlemen

After a delay of fifteen days, caused by stormy weather, I am at last enabled to startt Mr. J. Picotte with four Mackinaw boats loaded with robes &c a packing a/cts of which together with a/cts of men going down you will receive herewith.

I have already informed you that the mild winter we have had would effect the trade to our disadvantage, still I am in hopes to realize from one thousand to twelve hundred Packs in this district this season.

Mr. Chardon sent an express to Upper Yanctonais Post in April last, the river on his arrival oposite that place was full of drifting ice, and as he was unable to cross, he tied his letters to a tree and returned to Ft Clark, as soon as the weather permitted Freniere crossed the river and searched for the letters, but could not find them. I am therefore unable to give you a single word of news from the upper country. By recent arrivals Mr. Papin informs me that there is a great deal of snow in the mountains, and from the rains we have lately had I have every reason to believe he will get down the Platte with all his boats.

You will receive a small bundle of petrifactions [fossils] for Lieut. Carrolton, which Mr Clapp will please deliver, by Honoré Ayotte ~~with~~ of the men going down was formerly in the employ of Pratte & Cabanne at a salary of 20$ per month, should he wish to engage for this outfit you will please give him the same wages.

I draw on our favor of Honoré Ayotte for [blank] Doll[ar]s which you will please pay and charge to this outfit.

Signed H. Picotte

❖ ❖ ❖

Fort Pierre May 2. 1846
P. A. Sarpy Esqr
Bellevue
Dr. Sir

Please let Mr. J. Picotte have what provisions he may require from what you have belonging to this Outfit.

By so doing you will oblige Yours &c.

Signed H Picotte

❖ ❖ ❖

Fort Pierre 2 May 1846
Mr. Theophile Bruguire
Fort Vermillion
Dr Sir.

I received yours of the 17th April per Ayotte, and am sorry it is so bare of news, you do not even inform me what quantity of furs & robes you have on hand. Mr. J. Picotte leaves this morning for St Louis you will please ship all the robes on hand in his boats, including the 20 packs left by J Jewatt at your place last fall, and send down an account of the same to Messrs. P. Chouteau Jr. & Co. I send you Antoine Guion to take the place of Michelin, you will send the latter to St Louis with J Picotte and keep Guion until further orders. You will also keep a copy of what you ship to St Louis and send it up to this place pr: first opportunity as the twenty Packs of robes left at your place by Jewett have been charged to your post, you will therefore include them in your returns of this year. As it will be necessary for you to come up, to collect your credits from the Yanctons, and as I wish to see you on private business, I send Mr. Hamilton to take your place until your return with instructions to engage La Charite as interpreter for the time being, you will please therefore as soon as you can leave your post without injuring your trade come to this place, bring with you the list of Yanctons who are indebted to you.

You will receive 25 lb Powder.

Signed H Picotte

P.S. You will receive the a/cs Marcice Langlois & G Benoit

❖ ❖ ❖

Fort Pierre 2 May 1846
Mr. J. V. Hamilton
Dr. Sir

You will please come down with Mr. S. Picotte to Vermilion post; as I wish Mr. Bruguiere to come here, you will take charge of the post in his absence. You will hire La Cherité by the month until further orders, but enquire from him what he will take for a year, and let me know pr: 1st oportunity. Mr. Lewis Willcocks who goes down by the present conveyance it to take your place at Campbells, you will please give him all necessary instructions when you deliver your books to him.

Signed H Picotte

❖ ❖ ❖

Messrs. P. Chouteau Jr & Co
St Louis Mo
Gentlemen

I take the opportunity of Colin Lamont & Antoine Frenier who are going down in a skiff to write you a few words. Mr J. Picotte left here on the 2d. Inst, with four Mackinaw Boats loaded with Robes &c, by him I wrote to you fully respecting trade &c., nothing worthy of remark has occurred since that time, no news from Fort John, and any of the Upper Posts, however I expect Mr Kipp ~~daly~~ daily, the trade is not yet finished at this place, I hope we will make from 1000 to 1200 Packs. Lamont & Frenier promise me that they will come back, should they want any advces. Please let them have to the amount of 60$ each should they require that much. You will receive herewith the Blas [balance] due to each.

Signed H Picotte

❖ ❖ ❖

Fort Pierre June 6 1846
Mr James Bourdian
Fort John
Dear Sir,

An express arrived three days ago from Vermillion post with letters from St Louis informing me that the St Bt Genl. Brooke would not leave the latter place before the 20th May ~~next~~ last. Consequently I do not look for her arrival at this place before the 20th of the present; as this prove would be too long for Mr V. to stop her, he has determined upon going to Fort John immediately and take such goods from there as ~~sent~~ were sent him, having a memorandum for what he will require when he returns in Septr which memorandum you will please fill (sample the Groceries which will be sent from this place) & keep in readiness.

You will please furnish Mr Vasquez for a/c Bridger & Vasquez to the amt of (3000$). Three thousand Dollars at prices according to agreement a copy of which you will find herewith. He has made a small Bill with it, to which I refer you for the mode I follow to assertain the prices. You will observe that the freight is charged at the bottom without any advance the 50% is charged on the whole Bill [of] freight enclosed after you had ascertained the Cost price of the goods in the Country, on goods purchased from Pratte & Cabanne & Sybile & Co you will charge 25% advance & 5% Comn. on Cost price their 50% advance as per agreement & make no charge for freight. I have been this explicit to avoid any misunderstanding with Mr Vasquez when you make out his bills. If he should want one or more [word] waggons, you will let him have them at Inventory prices & no advances. As I have determined not to leave this place for St Louis before the 1st Octr next, you will wait for the return of Bridger & Vasquez which you will perceive per Copy of agreement he is to deliver at Fort John by the 25th [?] Septr next at latest, you will immediately after the recpt. of the above returns, send all the robes &c which you may have on hand to this place. Should Vasquez bring horses & mules you may keep all the mules and one half of the Running & Comn Horses if you want them. You will place Balance [in] the private a/c of James Bridger, 254.50 Dollars which amt has been Credited to Bridger & Vasquez on Fort Pierre Book.

Immediately upon the arrival of the StBoat I will dispatch 4 or 5 Carts lightly loaded with sugar Coffee flour & Bisquit, with orders to hurry on to Fort John as fast as possible therefore you may rely that you will receive these articles by the 5th July. Should any Beaver Hunters arrive at your place in the mountains try and detain them until the arrival of your groceries.

I wish you to be very particular in the recpt of Bridger & V's returns, go strictly according to Contract, the Buffaloe Running you will satisfy yourself are such by trying their speed & brand them with the Stamp inverted thus [inverted capital "A"] in order that I may know them, & these horses you should not sell for less than from 15 to 20 Robes

Signed H Picotte

❖ ❖ ❖

Fort Pierre 16th June 1846
Messrs P. Chouteau Jr & Co
St Louis Mo.
Gentlemen

Messrs. Primeau & Bouis will leave to morrow with two Mackinaw Boats loaded with Robes &c an a/c of which you will receive herewith also a/cs men going down. Victor Barager is going down "in Irons" for killing Napoléon McGuffin, he is to be well guarded until he can be deliver'd to the proper authorities, from what I can learn he is a great villain and committed murder in Cold Blood; the witnesses in the case are Charles Primeau, Mason Frake, Louis Vallé, Henry Collins, William Wilson & Joseph Turgeon. I refer you to Mr Primeau for further information on the subject. The account of Napoléon McGuffin and a Trunk containing his clothing are also sent you, he came some years ago apprentice to Mr Thornton Grimsley of your place who may perhaps give you some information where his relations are to be found. You will also secure a Box marked H. Hagdorn Care of Messrs. Anglisedt Egjen & Barth which you will please deliver. Your dispatches of the 4th May last were recd. on the 2d. Inst. and their contents certainly very much surprised me, for the present I refrain making any remarks thereon, but you will hear from me on the subject by return of Steam Boat, the letters destined for Messrs. Culbertson & Chardon I have not sent as I am daily expecting the arrival of both these gentlemen. Nothing from the upper Country since my last.

I learn that my nephew Mr Jos. Picotte is comming up [with] an outfit of merchandise to oppose us. I suppose others will join him, if this is the Case please try and make some arrangements with them and stop them from Comming up if possible. Charles Primeau has promised me to return (if he could) at the same salary he is now getting (say $800 a year) when he comes up please furnish him with 3 or 4 men and give him the means of purchasing 12 or 15 Amn. Horses in the upper part of the State. If Mr Papin can spare Frederick Laboue please ~~give him~~ hire him for this place at the same salary he is now getting, if Mr Papin should want him to steer down the Platte Boats next spring he can be sent there to perform that duty. Should my agent Mr Lebeau call on you for sixteen Hundred dollars, please let him have that amont & charge my account with the sum.

 Very resps. &c.
 Signed H Picotte

6

FORT PIERRE LETTER BOOK D

December 1, 1847–May 9, 1848

An eighteen-month gap in the letter books begins here. A change in transporting robes to Saint Louis began on the lower river in 1846. Mackinaw boats from the upper river now stopped at Fort Leavenworth, and the cargos were transferred to lower Missouri steam packets. This method provided a safer and more secure transportation into Saint Louis along the lower river. In July, the company acquired a new competitor when Harvey, Primeau and Company took out a license to trade on the upper Missouri. The partners of the new company were all experienced, former company employees: Alexander Harvey, Charles Primeau, Anthony R. Bouis, and Joseph Picotte. They had financial backing from Robert Campbell, and David D. Mitchell stood surety for their bond. Harvey, Primeau and Company would build a fort near Fort Pierre, reoccupy Fort Mortimer near Fort Union, and build a fort in Blackfeet country.

In the spring of 1846, the United States declared war on Mexico, a conflict that lasted through 1847. Iowa achieved statehood in December 1846 and became the twenty-ninth state in the Union. During the winter of 1846–1847, Captain Joseph LaBarge had the steamboat Martha *built in the boatyards in Cincinnati. Hauling company goods, the* Martha *made her maiden voyage on the Missouri in the spring of 1847. Competition with Harvey, Primeau and Company had been stiff, with both companies returning record robe harvests in the spring of 1847. The letter book narrative resumes in December 1847.*

❖ ❖ ❖

Fort Pierre Decr 1. 1847
Louison Frenier Esqr
Dear Sir

Your letter pr Indian was duly received, as also the one pr Tom Daurian In your last letter you mention a memorandum enclosed for what articles you wanted, but the mem. was not in the letter & consequently not received. Your equipment is put up, and I expect to start it on 2 Trains in 3 or 4 days; I am only waiting to get some kettles finished to send you, Mr McV will take charge of it to you & is to remain with you

Mr Picotte arrived a few days ago with 5 waggons, & has already started to White River, he brought some goods & a few horses which are very poor; so is of no use to send Indians here for horses unless they bring the Robes or pay beforehand.

The news from all quarters is good & Buf in great abundance everywhere, and I am much afraid we will be scarce of goods, therefore be hard with your good goods. I will write you fully by the trains

Yrs AD MCH [?]

❖ ❖ ❖

John C Picotte   Decr 9th 1847
D. Sir

I enclose you Invoice of all [word?] furnished pr Luzon [?] Defond on 4 pack animals, as these animals were heavily loaded it was impossible for me to send several Articles which you requested for Individuals, they shall be conveyed by a future opportunity.

Me Picotte will have arrived with you ere this reaches you, and from him you will receive all necessary information as to trade &c.

❖ ❖ ❖

Fort Pierre Decr 4 1847
P D Papin Esqr.

Your favor of 25th October pr Pulo [?] reached here in due time, and I have been compeled to detain him in consequence of the non arrival of the goods. Mr P only reached there on the 26, he writes pr this conveyance Mr Picotte have with him a Jennu, he is hard at work, I send you a few kettles & pans, in [word?] we can supply you with what you want of this article.

"Tashpa" arrived this morning he Met Mr Picotte on White River & deld. your letter to him, I send you all the Ammn. we can spare we are extremely short of Lead having the same quantity of it we have of Powder in fact I send you all that our present stock will admit of to fill the deficiency made you by B[word?].

Should Mr [Name?] make his [word?]—for horses [word?] will be of great advantage to us, as we shall not have near goods enough to meet the demands of the trade.

The horses lost by Manta have been found on White River, but it is extremely doubtful about our getting them, the Indian has traded two of them off I send you herewith Invoice of goods, also a/cs. of [Name?], and a/c of sundries ford. to Bissonette & Bordian which are chg. To your post.

Understanding [two words?] has left you I send you Joseph Boudein, said to be a good B[lack]Smith

We have neither Tar or Pitch for our Boats this spring, if you possibly can have some [word?] you will do us a great favor. Mr Picotte is under the impression that Castonje understands making it.

Your post is credited with 116.50 [word?] of R F Sleakton [word?] on [word?]

You have in your employ a Mulatto or Negro man named Charles Barton, this man is a slave, and belongs to some estate which Morton has control of, he has notified Mr Chouteau, that he holds us responsible for his return to St Louis, you could please keep an eye on him but not let him know it, and make as little advances as possible to him as I expect we shall have to pay Morton for his time.[1]

Respy.
D. D.

❖ ❖ ❖

Decr 2 1847
H Laboue Esqr
Dear Sir

Your Letters of 25th & 27th ulto pr Pouly was received yesterday and I dispatched him back to you without delay with all the goods as asked for in your Mem: that our present Stock will admit of sending. Mr Picotte arrived on 26th ulto. He brought but five Blankets [word?] [word?] & Beads were the principal articles he brought and had much difficulty in getting here. [word?] Blankets we are out of, all our traders are asking for them and should the present prospect of trade continue we shall not have near goods enough for the trade, however whenever you send for goods we shall send you as few as our stock will permit.

Mr Picotte has obtained a tin Smith who is now hard at work, and we shall very Shortly be able to supply you with Kettles Pans &c.

Mr Pouly remained 4 days in this Fort and has started to visit the posts he will visit you about the 15th I think, when he will arrange about the horses for the "Biens [name?]," the Smoke presented his [three words?] 20 Robes. I have given him a horse worth 3. The promise to pay you the 10 Robes as soon as he arrives with you. I wish you to tell your

Indians that we have [word?] American horses for 20 Robes, and it is useless to send them here, unless you receive 30 Robes. When they come with an order of only 20 Robes of the [word?] without one of the best horses they are dissatisfied, or else we must trust them for the balance, and run a risk in getting it. Mr P bought some five horses, but as they have been worked in the Waggons are tired & poor, and my wish is for them to improve [?] before I sell them, however he will explain all this to you when he visits you.

The only trader I have to send you is Hyatte, & B. Dischamp is the only spare man I have. I am hourly looking for the arrival of P[name?] from the states when I can possibly send you some more.

The only news I have of the Waggon & Cart you lent by Decatian, is that they have arrived at [two words?]

Enclosed you have Invoice & a/cts. men as for Groceries we are nearly out as the carts are very heavy loaded, when I send again I shall see what I can do for you. I also send two horses to aid the carts in the Snow.

A D [Andrew Dawson]
W D H [William D. Hodgkiss]

❖ ❖ ❖

Fort Pierre Decr 4 1847
Mr John Barradu
Dear Sir

I send you by Mr McElderry a new Pit Saw which Mr Picotte brot up. Mr Picotte wishes you to have the cross pieces for the Bottoms of the Boats at least 2 Inches thick and to get out all the [word?] for as many Boats as possible untill it is time to commence building.

The Nails Spikes Irons &c for the Boats will all be sent you in due time

[no signature]

❖ ❖ ❖

Fort Pierre Decr. 4. 1847
Louison Frenier Esqr
Dear Sir

Herewith you will receive Invoice of all the Merchandize [sent] to you on 3 Trains per Mr McElderry not having received your Mem. I do not know whether I have sent you every thing you require should there have been any omissions send me word by return of Moncrevie and they shall be sent you

I send you Mr McElderry to remain and clerk for you and assist in trading. Sibelle can be sent when you think he could be made useful. I also send you Mr. Meleau whom you can send out if you have a place for him with a small equipment, the rest of the men [word?] & [word?] are to assist you in building should you conclude to do so, or you can employ them should you not build in any way you think best.

Should you wish it you can retain two of the trains but the other I want you to send back, with Isadore & Moncravie, and send the Harness for all 3 back, for we have none left in the Fort, also send me all the meat by Moncrevie you can

Our goods are fast diminishing, what is the principal or leading articles, I must beg you to be as hard with them as possible, also of your Tobacco.

I have 3 Train Loads in readiness for the Mandans, & I am only waiting for Proveau to arrive, whom I expect hourly to send them, report says that the Tete Coupe will try and prevent me passing with them, should this be the case and you think there will be difficulty I shall have to pass you to go with the Trains untill they pass the upper Indians.

The man who came down from the Mandans and stopp'd at ~~your~~ [word struck out] visits you, you will send down with Moncrevie and should he meet the trains, why he can turn back and take the place of one of the men

Mr Picotte brot up but five Horses, they are poor as they have had to [word?] the Waggons, it will be of no use to send Indians here unless they pay you 30 Robes, beforehand. Indian horses we have none to sell.

[no signature]

❖ ❖ ❖

Fort Pierre Decr 1. 1847
Colin Campbell Esqr.
Dear Sir

I am now about starting to visit the different trading posts and expect to be absent from 40 days to 2 months, my object in starting so soon is to prevent the Traders from squandering the goods, being now convinced, that we shall not have near goods enough to meet the demand. We have now about 1000 packs traded at the different Posts; I have just received an Express from above, and the Oldest Indians say they never saw Buf so plenty. I must therefore beg of you to hold up your prices as well as you can, being well assured that in consequence of this Kind no one Knows better than you do how to mange things to the most advantage. Some of our traders in writing for goods say "if you cannot [send] such things as we ask for, send anything you have got every thing will bring Robes this winter."

I am told Alexis wants to get goods for dancing the Calumet.[2] I have no objection for him to get such things as he wants, he must get them at your post, but I want him to pay for them in horses as a change is to take place here next spring and I do not want him or any one else if I can help it to get in debt.

You can say to Rondelle I have read his letter & noticed the Contents, when he comes here I will do all in my power for him that is right or reasonable. I would send for him now but I am compelled to be absent for the time I have stated to you.

H[onoré] P[icotte]
W. D. H.

❖ ❖ ❖

Ft Pierre Decr 7 1847
C Campbell Esqr
Dear Sir

Annexed you have Mem. of Article sent you by Alexis.

I notice your remarks with respect to the Co if they say the Opposition gives five Robes, if they do so they act very foolishly in sacrificing goods in that way, for in my opinion there will not be near goods enough in the Country for the Robes.

The Horse you sent has been placed to Cr. of Yancton post.

Should you have no immediate use for Lafromboise please send him up, he will be of great service to me here.

Enclosed is a letter for you [word?] Mr P.
[no signature]

❖ ❖ ❖

Ft Pierre Decr 8 1847
Louison Frenier Esqr.
Dear Sir

I started Mr McElderry on the 5th with your equipment on 3 Trains, he only proceeded with them one day when he found it would be impossible to get along as the River is open in many places for a considerable distance, he did send his trains back and I now send a waggon with 3 Yoke of Oxen to proceed on with the goods. I also sent 2 mules & 1 Horse for your use. The waggon I would send back immediately, should you be encumbered with Robes or meat it would be well to send what you can in the Waggon, or it can bring a light send here [?].

[no signature]

❖ ❖ ❖

Fort Pierre Decr 8 / 47
Saml E McElderry:
Dear Sir

I received your note per the trains and regret that you were necessitated to send them back. I now send Larante with a waggon & 3 Yoke of Oxen, also 2 mules and 1 Horse, and trust that you will [word?] and without delay or accident.

I send Legris in the place of Welsh you have his A/c herewith

In the Waggon is the 2 Kegs [word?] and [two words?]

Respy.
[no signature]

❖ ❖ ❖

Ft Pierre Decr 9 1847
C Campbell Esqr
Dear Sir

Yours pr Laframboise is received, and I have in conformity thereto del[ivered]d. to the Indian ten [word?] Horses, the two best we have and Charged Sauce to your post.

I should keep Laframboise here for the present having immediate use for his services, he wishes you to send his things up here pr first oppy.

Mr Picotte left a men: to send you for of 1 ps White Berets and a Flannel shirt, the latter we have none of, let me know if the shirt is for yourself as I shall have to get one made, and I will send it with Blkts. pr next conveyance

[no signature]

❖ ❖ ❖

Ft Pierre Decr 11 1847
Jos Juett Esqr
Dear Sir
I annex you mem. of the Merchandize &c forwarded pr this conveyance, and regret that our present stock of Goods would not permit me to fill your requisition more fully.

The waggons brought in the meat in safety and the same has been passed to the order of your post.

This evening the "Fire Maker" arrived and deld. your letter of the 6th. I shall shew him the Horses tomorrow and try and satisfy him. As Mr Picotte will doubtless be with you when this reaches you, you will of course receive all instructions from him.

[no signature]

❖ ❖ ❖

Decr 12
J Jewett Esqr
The "Fire Maker" not finding any of our Horses to suit him took one [word?] Mr Laidlaw for the 30 Robes. I have also let him have a White Buf Robe for which he promises to pay you a horse coming on this arrival with you.

R[Name?]

❖ ❖ ❖

Decr 16. 1847
Honere Goulet Esqr
Dear Sir
I annex you mem. of articles which I forward you pr P[name?] & S[name?]. I send you all that you requested that is possible. Many of the articles, say 2 ½ pr White & Red Blankets, Chinese Yellow, Combs Flints, and Bridles [word?] &c, we have none in the Fort, in fact we have not 50 pr of Blankets here. Mr Picotte arrived here on the 27th of Novr & started again on the 2nd of December to visit the trading posts with a view to instruct his traders to hold firm to their prices, as it is most certainly ascertained that there is not one man good enough to trade all the Robes that will be made, he brought up no Blankets for the post. C[word?] Beads & Guns were the principal articles he brought, of the C[word?] I send you two pieces also 2 ps Calico & D[word?] &c. Dupes I send you all there is in the Fort, of Tobacco we have not as much as you ask for; that I now send you was brought back from the Yanctons.

We are hard run for horses, that is [word?] horses. I send you two horses for which you ought to get 20 Robes Ea[ch]. We have American Horses, and they were worked up in the waggons, and are so poor I feel certain they would never reach your post, however I would send you some.

[no signature]

❖ ❖ ❖

Ft Pierre Decr 15 1847
Louison Frenier Esqr
Dear Sir
John Parrada arrived here yesterday from the Shantee,[3] and states that there is between 30 & 40 Lodges of Indians encamped a few miles above here, they have between 30 & 40 packs of Robes and plenty of meat, they are very anxious to get a trader and have sent him here for that purpose. As these Indians are so close to you, I think it would be best for you to send to them and would propose (if you have no better use for him) your sending Maleau with goods for about 15 or 20 packs & some meat articles, when he has traded these, should he want more, there are men at the Shantee whom he can send here and I will supply him from this place, however I leave it entirely to you to arrange as you think best for the trade of these Indians.

There is no arrival from below yet; as soon as they do come I shall try the trains for the Mandans.

[no signature]

❖ ❖ ❖

Ft Pierre Decr 18. 1847
Francis A Chardon Esqr
Dear Sir
Your letter of 17th Novr. reached me the day after my arrival from St Louis and I assure you I am truly gratified at your fine prospects for trade, like [word?] you, nothing can prevent the opposition from trading their goods advantageously, the likes of Buffalo has not been

seen here for years and I am well opined, that there is not near goods enough in the country to trade all the Robes that will be made.

I have instructed Maj Drips in my absence to send you, what goods he possibly can, and only regret that it is will not be in my power to send you more. Mr Laidlaw arrived at this place only in the fall he brought several gentlemen with him among them is Mr Dawson[4] said to be a good accountant. I have told him as we have no employment for him here to go with the trains to you, if you have use for him why employ him (he appears willing himself useful) in [word?] why feed him & treat him well.

I would aid the Old woman with pleasure for you in going up, but the weather is so very cold that I fear both yours & her child would suffer, and I have therefore advised her not to attempt it.

Frederick Beeman[5] wishes to visit Germany it will require 400$ he has 100$ and [word?] lend him the Balance (say 300) will you go say halves in this affair. I feel a friend that if he lives and returns he will pay us.

I look for the Express up [word?] & Ant Morin will go through with it to fort Union

Truly Yours
H P
MDH

❖ ❖ ❖

Fort Pierre Decr 18 1847
James Kipp Esqr.
Dear Sir
I reached this place on the 27th Ulto, after a tedious trip with my engages I find that the prospects of trade could not be better. Buffalo have not been as abundant for years, and feel well assured that we have not goods enough to trade the Robes that will be made.

Chardon made a small requisition pr Steam Boat which was filled and brot up in my waggons I start them tomorrow on 2 Trains, he has written to me that he will not have near enough goods for the trade of his post, and I regret that our present stock will not admit of my sending him more.

I saw your family as I passd they were in good health; I have made arrangements with Cap [Joseph] Labarge of SB Marsha [Martha][6] to bring both yours and my wife up, I shall look for the Boat early, and shall send my Indian family off early in the spring. Would it not be well for you to do the same.

Antoine Morrin will bring up the Express I shall send him on with it to you, you will receive several letters herewith.
H P
MDH

❖ ❖ ❖

Fort Pierre Decr 18, 1847
Francis A Chardon Esqr
Dear Sir
I have the pleasure herewith to hand you Invoice & packing account of Merchandize which I start to your pack, hoping that all will safely reach you, the Indians told [Name?] on his way down that they would stop any goods we might send for you, or to the upper Country. Louison Frenier is trading with the Upper Yanctonais, the Trains have to pass his post. I have written to him if he should apprehend difficulty to go himself with the trains untill they pass upper Encampment of Indians, should however contrary to my expectations he [is] not be able to pass them, to send the Express with the letters and the Trains back.

I send you in the trains 4 [two words?] these I expect will find a ready market with you but I must request you to let Proveau have animals of some kind to bring the Trains back.

Michelle Lafferty goes up with Proveau he came up free and is now on his way to Ft Union, to hire for the Crow post, you will please send a man with him to take the letters &c for Fort Union, immediately on.
[no signature]

❖ ❖ ❖

Ft Pierre Decr 18 1847
Louison Frenier Esqr
Dear Sir
Proveau leaves me this morning in charge of two Trains loaded for Fort Berthold.[7] I wrote you pr Mr McElderry relative to passing these trains should you apprehend any difficulty. Since that time Bouis & Co. trains have passed up, and as they have not returned I am induced to believe they have passed without difficulty, and the Indians will certainly let ours pass also. However on their arrival with you, you will know what has *been* done, and what has

to be done. If you think you can pass them without risking the goods and animals too much Mr Picotte has instructed me to say to you, that he wishes you to leave your establishment in charge of Siebelle or McElderry a few days and proceed on with the Trains untill they pass the upper encampment of Indians, being convinced that if they can be passed at all you are the only one that can do it.

Should however you think that the Indians will not let them pass, and the risk too great, why [word?] Michelle Lafferty with the man, who came down from Chardon go on an take the letters, and send the Trains with the goods back to this place.

You will please give Proveau the File Shoes & Nails with the shoeing harness McElderry took from here. Proveau is furnished with Tobacco & Ammunition for making small presents to Indians.

It will be extremely mortifying to us if Bouis & Co. Trains pass on and ours do not, but I trust that with your exertion all will be well

[no signature]

❖ ❖ ❖

Fort Pierre Decr 27th 1847
Jno. C Rollette Esqr:
Dear Sir

Annexed you have Mem. of articles which I forward you pr Jervis Agend it comprises every thing that we have as asked for in the requisition made b Mr Picotte. I enclose your bill of Sundries which is forwarded herewith for Louis Peneau, which you will please collect. You mention sending 2 Robes for account of Peneau, these *have not been received.*

[no signature]

❖ ❖ ❖

Decr 29 1847
F. Laboue Esqr.
Dear Sir

Your favor of the 26th inst pr Pochet is received, and I delay no time in sending him back to you. I regret that it is not in my power to send you all you asked for, but the only reason for my not doing so, is because the articles are not in the Fort. You have herewith Invoices of what I send you.

I have sent you several articles not asked for in y[ou]r Mem: Such as [word?] Beads & Calico Domestic [word?] & spy Glasses, all of which in this plentiful time of Buffalo I hope you will be able to dispose of to great advantage. I assure you our stock of goods is very low, however we have plenty of Beads & cloth, if you should want more of these, send and I will supply you not only with these but anything else we have.

I send you a small supply of groceries, our present stock will not admit of sending more. Pochet has informed me you were scarce men I send you Bas Plante, he wintered last winter with Galpin and is a good man. Proveau brough a letter for you from St. Louis which will be handed you by Mr Picotte. Mr P. was detained a long while on White River otherwise he would have been with you ere this.

Buffalo, are all around us, and I have no doubt that we shall be able to trade all the goods we have got, at the Fort, there will not be near goods enough in the country to trade all the Robes that will be made.

Respy

MDH

❖ ❖ ❖

Fort Pierre Jany 4. 1848
Louison Freniere Esqr.
Dear Sir

I have your letter of the 19th Decr pr Moncrevie & Isidore, the waggon & oxen has reached me in safety. I am glad to notice the prospect for our Trains, and full satisfied that through your exertions they will safely reach their destination. I enclose you Invoice of Merchandize, which is now forwarded in charge of Moncrevie, he will leave some few articles with Malcon, an account of which I send you the whole is enclosed in your Bill.

Moncrevie tells me Malcon has but 14 lodges of Indians, I think myself it would be better for him to remove and trade at the Shantee. Sibelle will do well to send to the Tete Coupe, and Moncuvire you can send to the Mansse [?] Village to remain as long as our opponents keep a trader there. My own opinion is, from the Scarcity of Robes and the scarcity of goods the Indians will be obliged to come to us, and my advice is whatever the opposition may do, to remain firm in your prices, and incur as little expense in getting the Robes however you are on the spot, and leave it to your good judgment to pursue the most advantageous and profitable course.

As respects bringing your Robes down in the spring you can either trade skins and make Canoes, or your men with those of the Shantee can easily take a Boat up to you, should you adopt this latter plan send me word and I will sent a Cordell up to the Shantee for this purpose. I wish you to obtain from the Indians 20 or 30 lbs. of Buff Hair not that from the head but from the Sides & belly. I have a particular use for it.

There are several of your Indians who have Traps in their possession belonging to the Company, if you can possibly get the Indians to return them, without creating any difficulty with them, I wish you would do so. I enclose you a list of some of them.

I have given to Boyer an Am. horse with 30 robes and [word?] order to [word?] I [word?] for 10 Robes, both of which are charged to your post.

[no signature]

❖ ❖ ❖

Fort Pierre January 8. 1848
J V Hamilton Esqr
Dear Sir

Your favor of the 3rd ulto. Pr Proveau enclosing account of P. A. Sarpy is a hand. As for for LaCharité I think exactly as you do that he is an old Fool, and can harm us but little. My conscience does not reproach me any for the transaction of buying the Horses, for I can truly swear I took him at his own offer.

I send Lapelle & Lozier to you with 5 pack animals, on which I wish you to send me all the tradeable goods you can possible spare, we are out of every thing and can sell goods to better advantage here than at your post, you must try and make up the loss for me, even should you deprive yourself a little. I shall start the Express for St Louis early in Feby, at which time I wish you to have in readiness your requisition (which I wish to be as light as possible for 1848). Should you think in sending me goods it will deprive you of any trade for the present Of. [Outfit] you can make a separate requisition to be charged to Outfit 1847 [word?] which you can complete for trade for this season, and whatever should be left will of course be put in your Inventory of goods being on hand Of. '47 and will be transferred to Of. 1848.

I shall instruct the house with regard to your requisitions as above.

You are at liberty to draw on the Company for whatever amount may be due to Rubideau, provided he remains with you, untill he finishes his engagement, or untill such time as his services can be dispensed with.

Mrs Picotte and Mrs Kipp have intimated to me their intention of Coming up in the SteamBt, I have no doubt that your Lady when She hears it, will also wish to Come, and as there is every possibility of her doing so, would it not be well for you to dispose with the Society of at least [some] of your present Companions.[8] As you have lost old LaCharité I shall endeavor to find a substitute to take charge of the post.

[no signature]

❖ ❖ ❖

Ft Pierre Jany 8. 1848
Colin Campbell Esqr.
Dear Sir

Napelle & Losier leave me this day for the Vermillion to bring from that post all the goods that can be spared and I know that your Indians will neither stop or interfere in any way with them. Our Traders so far have all made good & profitable trades, and most of them are now very scarce of goods, and of many Articles the Fort is now destitute.

I have understood that your Indians are now in Buffalo; and there is my principal of them making a good trade, I must therefore beg of you to try hard and make the best you can of the goods you have now on hand and not to depend on the Fort for men, for there is none to give you. You can however tell your Indians to go ahead and have as many Robes in readiness as they please, and I will send for goods to be landed by the Boat at your place to finish the trade for Outfit 1847.

American Horses we are selling daily at 30 Robes each, no difference horses or mules, for that reason, I do not wish you to give any orders or send for any unless you get 30 Robes paid you in advance.

Should the weather continue fine and you can

spare a few days on receipt of this, I would like to see you here, I would willingly go and see you, but I am tired of travelling.

Your nephew is trading at the [word?] I think he will do well as a trader, he has sent us nearly 20 packs Robes

I send you herewith 1 Flanl Shirt 11 pr Sm White [word?] fr [two words?].

Since the foregoing the waggons has arrived from White River and I find that the Indians have mostly left that pass and gone towards the Platte, consequently I shall be in receipt of goods from that post, when I receive them I can supply you with a part of them.

Should you conclude to visit me, bring with you a man & a mule loaded with as much powder & Ball as you can spare, if you cannot do so immediately as soon as you can. We are very Scarce of men.

[no signature]

❖ ❖ ❖

Fort Pierre January 9 1848
Jos Jewett Esqr
Dear Sir

I enclose your Invoice of the Merchandize forwarded you per this conveyance, it comprises every thing that was mentioned in the requisition I brought from you as far as our present assortment of goods will admit of you sending.

You will notice that I have affixed prices to several articles, viz dressed Deer Skins 4 fine Robes [word?] 3 for a Robe, such as you cannot get this price for, have made into shirts and pantaloons, the "Mail shirt" I have sent not less than 8 Robes, some Fool Indian I have no doubt will give you much more for this, and of course, as it is for the interest of your post to get all you can, you will make the most of it. Medals 1 Robe Ea[ch] if no more can be got, small spy Glasses 2 Robes Ea, silver arm Bands less than 3 Robes pr pair will not pay us, Tin Cups 4 for a Robe, the War Bonnet 8 Robes. The copper kettles I have had made for such Indians as have "Medicine Ceremonies" to make and I would rather you would bring them back than to take less than 2 Robes.

I send you one of Nicelles horses which I have borrowed on account of those belonging to the Company being poor & tired, and I hope that the "Feather in the Ear" or whoever gets it will not get it for less than 35 Robes. I send you herewith the account of Barker, "Fire Maker" and "Pocamoggin Rouge" you will notice the "Fire Maker" got agreeable to [your] request in your letter, a White Buff skin for which he promised to pay you a horse, and I trust that you will be able to make him pay you, I do not want you to advance anything but what is actually necessary pr [word?].

The "Bad Lodge" brought two orders from Clement for 60 robes which are paid and charged to your post, it appears Mr. Bad Lodge was not altogether Satisfied with the Horses he got, and afterwards bragged he would be Smart enough for us, that 12 of [the] Robes for which he got an order were painted but have not yet del[ivere]d, find out if you can how many robes Clement *actually received* for which these orders were given.

After filling yours and the several requisitions for your people for groceries, I find that our stock will not admit of my sending more, independent of this the waggon is heavily loaded. When Schlegel comes in, let him bring 2 or 3 of your best mules and if any thing can be done in that line he will take it on. [word?] Pole Spikes, and a further Supply of Iron for Arrow Points[9] will be sent you. I want you to send me in the large [word?] Iron pan, I shall have use for it to make Sugar loaf &c.

I have detained your waggon because we were out of Boxes axes Tomahawks &c all of which we have had to get more.

I want you to send your waggon in as soon as you can, I want to haul Rollettes Baggage &c in before the River opens. The enclosed Letter for Mr Laboue you will please send immediately to him by LaPointe, who is to remain with him in place of one of his men whom I have immediate use for here. [Word?] recollect and not deceive me, but Send LaPointe immediately on. I send for Deschamp who is with Laboue to make me kegs, and shall be much displeased if I am disappointed

[no signature]

❖ ❖ ❖

Fort Pierre Jany 8, 1848
Jno. C. Rolette
Dear Sir

The waggon arrived from your post last Evening, and I learn from the men who came in with it, that the greater part of your Indians have left for the Sand Hills and Porcheans district. Now if this information is correct, there is no use for us to oppose our own people, and it is useless to follow them and I presume that you will call in your traders, and move every thing into your house, in which case you will inform me immediately and I shall be prepared to move you, Robes good[s] & all at one trip.

We have plenty of Indian & Buffalo all around us and we can dispose of all your goods to advantage here, and I can immediately place you at a post you will be satisfied with. At all events I want you to try and be at your houses by the 1st February so that Baptiste Picotte can come in to take the place of F. Behman who will start for St Louis.

[no signature]

❖ ❖ ❖

Fort Pierre Jany 21 1848
Louison Freniere
Dear Sir

Your letter per Turgeon was received this morning, and I dispatched F. Daurian without delay to you to contradict the report of our horses having been stolen, which report it seem will have an injurious effect upon your trade. *Our Horses have not been stolen*, we have plenty of Am & Indian Horses and mules, and at all our posts we have an advantage, many of which will be here shortly, independent of this I look for a supply from the Platte, and have sent below for Am Horses which will be here before the trade is finished. On the score of Horses therefore rest easy for it is as I have stated to you, and whenever an Indian gives you Robes, you can safely give an order, with a certainty that it will be paid. We have Indian horses for 10 and some for 15 Robes, mules for 20 Robes 2 Am for 30 Robes.

In two or 3 days I will send you the files and small articles which you ask for together with 6 prs scarlet & cloth. Meantime you would send me back as soon as possible by J[name?] a memo of such articles as you actually want or can trade, and I will send you as soon as we can such as we have.

Your letter is far from satisfactory in expressing your prospects or what you have done and I [word?] by that you will let me know by return of Daurian, what number of Robes you have traded and give me your opinion what will probably be the amt of your trade, and I whenever you do write I wish to be advised partic[ularl]y as to your prospects & &c.

Under the impression that your trade will be a good one, I am unwilling to risk it in Peroges or skin canoes. I have plenty of men, and in due time before the Ice Breaks I will send men to be in readiness to take a Boat from the Shantee to you, it will therefore be useless to incur the Expense of purchase of skins for canoes, should you however have Boat then they will answer to cover your boat.

We have been anxiously looking for Proveau to return from above but some Indians report that after you left the trains some 15 or 20 Indians pursued them, I am therefore a little uneasy, please let me know pr Tom what your opinion is about them.

We shall send the groceries you asked for in your letter pr Solomon with the C[name?].

You seem to think that a skin canoe or two and a pirouge will bring all your trade down, I think however, with what goods you have had, when I shall send you, and the orders you will give, I think I ought to calculate fully on 300 packs from you, and for that reason I shall certainly send you up a Boat, therefore be [two words?] the trouble and expense of making canoes or piroges.

[no signature]

❖ ❖ ❖

Jany 22 1848
Louison Freniere Esq
Dr Sir

As intimated in my letter to you yesterday pr Isadore, I herewith annex you Invoice of Post Groceries &c. which I for[war]d you on 1 pack animal pr Turgeon, which I trust will speedily & safely reach you, and that you will find a ready market for the Cloth the Flour which is still due to your post will be sent you by a future conveyance, our sugar & coffee is down, we have barely enough to last the Tables two weeks, and should you make sugar I assure you a cake or two of it would be very acceptable in the Spring.

I send you the [two words?], and hereafter [word?] you want any such articles sent you with to the person in charge of the Fort & not to Bayes. I do not charge you with these but shall expect payment for them in Sugar.

[no signature]

❖ ❖ ❖

Fort Pierre Feby 3. 1848
Colin Campbell Esqr
Dear Sir

I send Vapeur [word?] back to [you] with such articles as you asked for that we have, you have Bill herewith 2/2pr White Blankets we have none, and I send you the only pr Blue we have, I am hourly looking for Wasselle and perhaps on his return I shall be able to supply you with such Blankets as you want. Send when you want goods, and I will do my best for you.

I have Cr[edite]d you with the Mule & sent you a Horse in his place, the Horse cost 16 Robes, I got him at this price on acct of his having a Big foot if you can get the same for him sell him if you choose he catches Buff.

    Yours
[no signature]

❖ ❖ ❖

Fort Pierre Feby 5 1848
J V Hamilton
D Sir

Napelle arrived yesterday with yours of the 22d ulto. And the goods and animals all safe. Vermillion Post has received the proper credits.

I notice in your letter to Campbell the canoes purchased by LaCharite & Bircon, I cannot but commend your zeal in the Liquor affair, but I fear that your proceedings will only excite still greater animosity against us, and under this consideration must beg you to drop it, untill such time as the Agent may arrive, to whom you can make your representations of the case he can then act as he thinks proper.

Should Maj Drips on his arrival wish you require fresh animals or assistance in any way, you will aid him all in your power.

I want you to send up in April a cart with as many seed potatoes as you can spare if it is only 1 Bushel send them. I will return the cart to you with the Plough and as much meat and Tallow as they can take. Send me word should your [word?] meat & Tallow, Send word how much & I will send it pr Boats.

As for Plough Horses I have none to send you, you must do the best you can, and I think you are acting foolishly in trying to raise so much corn.

You will of course send your requisition per Maj for [word?] and as I before wrote you should you need goods to finish the trade of a/c '47 make a duplicate requisition or a/c present Oft [Outfit].

Provost who goes down with the Express returns [word?] on his way if you can send me by him a few more goods please do so, or animals if you have them to spare. You will forward to Messrs. P Chouteau Jr & Co. a copy of the contract with Bircon & L. C and represent the thing in the proper light. Do not forget when the Agent comes up if he has the Yancton. [word?] to try & have [word?] received for the 3 Horses which were stolen last fall.

[no signature]

❖ ❖ ❖

Colin Campbell Esqr
Dr Sir

[Word?] you have Invoice of Mdze which I send you per Maj. Drips.

Should Maj Drips leave with you a horse which I purchased from Galpin, I do not want you to dispose of him for less than 18 Robes, he can catch Buf

    Respy
[no signature]

❖ ❖ ❖

Fort Pierre Feby 8, 1848
Joseph Serritt [?]
Dear Sir

Your letter as well as all the things you sent pr Schlegel, were all safely received, I have detained him with his cart a few days to get the Bsmith work done, he now returns to you with the cart and what goods I can spare, and regret that it is not in my power to send you more. I could have sent you more but the news you send me that Villandré is coming with 40 pack animals loaded, makes it necessary for me to keep my goods at home so that I can compete with him when he does come, as I shall have all the Indians here. I am tired of receiving threats from my traders, I am surrounded with plenty of Indians who have Robes in Abundance, and I can sell all my goods here, without threats to opposition or trouble of any kind, and obtain my price for them. In the course of two or 3 weeks however, Mr Villandré, will have arrived and if you could send in then I will know whether it is in my power to send you a few more goods.

It is not in my power to send the waggon back, I have sent it with two others to Rollette, before Schlegel arrived I had promise to send all 3 of them to Laboue as soon as they came back from W River to lighten his canoes.

I expect Rollette and all his people in, in the course of 10 or 12 days, I will then send you 3 or 4 good men, should this not be enough for you, I wish when you are ready to start down, to do so with what you can and leave Schlegel, Mocravie or some trusty person in charge of what you leave, and I will get them here either by waggons or canoes as soon as I can. It would be well as soon as you can to send in all your carts loaded, I think your men will have time to bring them in and return to you in time for your canoes.

If you send I want you to send the Big kettle, I want it for Boats & making Sugar.

As long as you have goods, I wish you to supply your traders on the Moreau, those who are on the Chyenne when they get out of goods let their Indians come here.

I have told you above about bringing the returns, if you see proper to do so, why it is all right, however you are on the spot & I leave it all to your own good judgment to get the Returns here how as you think best, having every confidence that you will bring them safe.

I want the Packs to come down as soon as water will permit but I want you to recollect that I do not want the post broken up, as long as there is any trade to be made, therefore I think you had better come down yourself with a few canoes, and return and make the second trip.

I send you the Dauthers a/c for 3 Robes which please try and collect.

I regret having no sugar & coffee to send you, we have been drinking Corn Coffee for some time past.

Maj Drips has started down according to my promise to your Indians for horses, we shall have some 60 or 70 horses brought up this spring and should your Indians want let them give their Robes.

[no signature]

❖ ❖ ❖

Fort Pierre Feby 12. 1848
F Laboue Esqr
Dear Sir

Your 9th inst per Peche & Plante is before me, and I send them right back to you with all the Blankets I can spare. I regret it is not in my power to do more for you, it is time we have received goods back from Rollette & Vermillion but whether a few day's pass we have traded upward of 70 packs, most of which has been for blankets, we are crowded with Indians who are full of Robes, and the cry with them all is Blankets.

From some Indians who have just arrived from above I learn that Louison is less [word?] Indians and that he has plenty of goods left. I am certain you can get 15 or 20 prs of Blankets by sending to him, and I advise you to do so. I enclose your letter to him on the subject his Houses at the place called Wani tu, a few miles above the Old Ree Village.

I have sent three waggons to Rollette to move him in, they will be back in about 8 days, when I shall immediately send them to you, at the same time I will send you a few good men.

[no signature]

❖ ❖ ❖

Ft Pierre Feby 12 1848
Louison Freniere Esqr
Dear Sir

Understanding per Indians who have just arrived from your quarter, that your Indians have all left you, and that you have plenty of goods rem[ainin]g on hand, I have instructed Mr Laboue in case of need to send to you for a small supply of Blankets, should my information with regard to the Indians having left you be correct, you will oblige me by letting him have 15 or 20 prs if you can spare them.

I am now preparing a waggon to take Nails &

tools to the Shantee in all probability I shall send it as far as your place to bring the balance of your goods.

Before the breaking of the Ice I shall send 5 or 6 men to be in readiness to take a Boat up to you.

You can keep all your people Sebelle Moncreve &c untill you come down, they can all help you and I have no use for any of them here, as we have now here more than we want.

[no signature]

"Wrote pr Napels as above, to send goods pr waggons [he] can spare if no use for them why send all."

❖ ❖ ❖

Fort Pierre Feby 12 1848
Mr Jno Barratta
Dear Sir

From what Trugeon told me I expected to have seen you here, thinking that you do not intend coming, I now send the waggon with the things necessary for the Boats. As I have none to send you you will therefore have to rise Tallow & ashes should you not have Tallow enough, I expect you can get more from Louison if not why let me know and I will send it from here.

I want you to build me a good Skiff to carry the Men and a good quantity of luggage say 15 feet long and wide in proportion pr high.

I want you to send your waggon & skins with your driver and the waggon I now send to Louison bring down his goods. You can keep Malcon with you to help build your Boats.

It is my intention to send one of your Bts to Louison to bring him down as soon as the River opens. I will send men to you for that purpose in due time.

[no signature]

❖ ❖ ❖

Fort Pierre Feby 15 1848
Colin Campbell Esq
Dear Sir

Since receipt of yr letter pr Vapeur I am without any news from you, and am extremely anxious to hear from you as some Indians have arrived from Bouis and report the arrival of Villandre with 30 Am Horses and some goods. I wish you would send up one of your men as soon as you can and let me know particularly what Mr Villandre brot up and let me know if it is in your power how Bouis is off for goods, also your prospects &c &c

Should you be in want of pieces I send up and I will send you what I can, I can furnish you with animals from here.

The Following Indians are indebted to us & promise to pay you.

Mal de Cabrie [Bad Deer]
    3 ___ ___
    Bal on horse 5
Smutty Bear
    2 ½ prs Blks
The Flying Bird
    ___ & ___
    3 1/3 Yds Blue Cloth   1 pr 2 ½ pr W Blkts
    1 pr 2 ½ ___ Blks 4   1 pr 3 ___ 6 = 20
Blue Earth
    1 3 pr Wht Blks 1 shirt 4
Blue Cloth 1

You will please try & collect these a/cs some time ago we lost from the [word?] the following described animals, ye Indians may hear of or find them, in which case please try & recover them.

1 Bro Indian mare
1 " "   Horse   Spot Brand
1 White Am mare
1 Sorrel " "
1 Brown "   Horse
1 Sorrel " "   White Horse & sway Back

there was seven lost the others I cannot describe you will please let us know when any of the above Ind a/cts are paid to you.

[no signature]

❖ ❖ ❖

Fort Pierre Feby 16. 1848
Jos Jewett Esqr
Dear Sir

The continuation of the fine weather, induces me to believe that you would stand in need of your men to bring down your Boats. I therefore send you 5 men viz C. Chattellion, Louis Agard, Jos Brazeau, John Caufman, and Carlile Roberts to assist you, these are all I can spare, and it is my wish for you to bring every thing as far as where Moncrevie and Dupuis are, so that in case it is necessary to make the second trip it will be easier to make it from there. I however wish you before the pass is broken up to finish all the trade. I send you also Jno C Rollette who is willing to aid you in any way he can be [of] service & [word?]. Should you want more goods send, and I will send them to you.

[no signature]

❖ ❖ ❖

Feby 20th
Per Schlegel

Your favor per Schlegel of 17th inst is in hand and I am pleased to notice your good prospects of Trade.

I regret it is not in my power to send you a larger supply of Blankets, but I hope with what you will receive with Schlegel you will be able to realize your expectations of 600 packs. Should you want more Beads, kettles [word?] or Tobacco let me know and I will supply you with what we can spare.

There is plenty of Indians all around us, all of whom have more or less Robes.

Villandre has returned from St. Joseph, he brought 20 Am Horses besides the mules, he started with, he brought but few goods. Two days ago V passed here, on his way to the Moreau with 5 Am Horses and 7 animals lightly loaded principally your Calico Kettles and Tobacco these goods were a part of what Charles Primeau brought back from White River.

I must urge you not to break up your post untill the trade is completely finished, you recollect what happened last year, by your hurry to abandon your post, if you wish to visit Saint Louis there is ample time after the trade is finished.

I am told by the Indians, your traders will not receive their Robes [until you] give them orders; I want you and you to tell your traders to get all the Robes you can and give orders. I have plenty of Horses, and expect more from below next Month, the Horses that were too poor some time ago have all recruited [?] and are now in poor order, I also expect a large band up early with Maj Drips.

[no signature]

❖ ❖ ❖

Ft P Feby. 20. 1848
Colin Campbell Esqr
Dear Sir

I send Vapair back to you without delay with goods as pr Invoice. I send you all the capes Blankets we have, Colored Blankets we have none in the Fort. I am however daily in expectation of receiving some goods back from Louison, and among them I expect is some [word?] & Blkts, which I will put aside for you. The Scarlet Chiefs Coats will be made in the course of next week, you can send for them, I have kept Tison here, and send you Begrompe in his place. I want Tison to help down with the canoes, our returns last from F pr Cheyenne & Moreau Rivers will be very large, as soon as you can spare Begompe I wish you would send him back, I am aware that Tison is a good Ox Driver but I also know that in this S & P can take his place.

There is an encampment of Yanctonais on the Chappelle, as soon as you hear of a trader from the opposition being with them, if you are not able to send let me know

I had heard Primeaus to receipt of your letter that goods Bouis & Co received from below, and also what goods Chs Primeau are brought back from White River, be not alarmed, be firm in your prices, they cannot oppose you long as more of these have already passed on to Jo Picotte. I send you 3 Indian Horses @ 10 Robes Ea:

[no signature]

❖ ❖ ❖

Fort Pierre Feby 26 1848
Colin Campbell Esqr
Dear Sir

I send you per Napelle the 6 Chiefs Coats, you have bill annexed.

Naspelle is on his way to Saint Louis, as it is important that he should reach there without delay. I have to require that you will furnish him with a good animal that will answer his purpose. We are in want of some Red stone pipes, and I wish you to trade if possible for 50 provided you can get them without giving your woolen goods.

I have sent McElderry with a sm[all] equipment to trade with the Yanctonais on Snake River, he would like to have his squaw with him, if you can prevail on her to join him I wish you would do so.

Louison has returned, he brought only 3 pt White & Carped Blankets, should you want of these send for them.

[no signature]

❖ ❖ ❖

Fort Pierre Feby 26. 1848
Jas V Hamilton Esqr
Dear Sir

Circumstances render it necessary for me to send another Express to Saint Louis, and Napelle leaves me on his way there this day, on his arrival with you I wish you to aid him to get on as fast as possible by furnishing him with a fresh animal, should he require it, or rendering him any assistance he may want.

In due time I shall look for your Cart here with the articles I wrote you to send, Potatoes &c and hope you will be able to furnish me with a few animals when Proveau passes up.

I also wish you to send me 3 or 4 of your best Ot[t]er skins.

Our trade will be a large one, the accts we have received from all quarters are very flattering.

[no signature]

❖ ❖ ❖

Ft Pierre Feby 26/ 1848
P A Sarpy Esqr
Dear Sir

The bearer hereof H Nappelle is on his way to Saint Louis as Express from UM Outfit, it is important that he should reach his destination without delay, if on his arrival with you he should need a fresh animal you will please furnish him, or you will please render him such assistance as he may require to get on.

Respy S. C

❖ ❖ ❖

Fort Pierre Feby 27 1848
F Laboue Esqr
Dear Sir

I send you herewith the Three Waggons with the articles I mentioned to you in my last letter. I send you all the [word?] we have to spare, you will please cover the meat well, and let the men have Parfleches & sinews enough to make a canoe in case the Chayenne should be high on their return I send you La Lozier to assist you in your Boats. Benoist is able to help bring in the Carts.

I have now sent you as many men as you asked for, but should you bring down more canoes than you expected and require 3 or 4 men more let me know immediately and I will send them to you, at the same time should you require more goods send me word and such as we have are at your command

Tom Daurion guides the waggons to yr place he is on a trapping expedition, he is already sufficiently indebted to us therefore do not make him any advances.

[no signature]

❖ ❖ ❖

Ft Pierre Mar 2 1848
C Campbell Esqr
Dear Sir

I send St Pierre back to you, the weather will not admit of having the mast fixed, being in want of mules and a cart, I keep yours and have given your pair credit for the same. The ploughs will be fixed, and when it is time to use them, send St Pierre up and every thing will be in readiness, at the same time I will send you the Calf and Pigs, For [word?] who [word?] the Ree.

I have no Oxen here now except a few to haul my wood; the rest have all gone to the Moreau and will not be back under 3 weeks, at all events it is of no use to talk about Ploughing untill the winter is over and the Frost gets out of the ground, I have no idea that the ground will be fit for the Plough for at least 6 weeks.

I send you your molasses, also your Flour & Bread.

As for goods we have some of most every kind except Cold. Blkts, when you want send.

Your men have but little to do, let them as soon as you can put up your Robes & count them, you wrote me you had above 140 packs, from what I learn there appears to be some doubts about your having this many. I should like to receive an accurate account of what you have, as I shall in all probability want to ship your Robes by the first Boats, it would be well to have them [word?] and ready.

[no signature]

❖ ❖ ❖

Fort Pierre March 5 1848
Mr Honore Goulet
Dear Sir

I send Pacquitte back to you with 4 men, it is my wish that you will make Canoes as large as you can, and on your way down to put in Louison Frenieres returns, if possible and bring them as far as the Shantier. Loison has about 120 pks Robes & about 150 of meat & a few [word?], you will find Sebille with 3 more at Louisons houses, who will render you all the assistance they can. Should you however be too heavy loaded and afraid to risk taking these returns, I wish when you arrive at the Shantier for you to land your Robes and dry your canoes, and send with your men and the men I shall send from here to meet you one of the Boats to bring Louisons Robes. Sebille can bring the Boat back, while you and Pacquitte will remain to assist Parrada in building his Boats. I do not want you to come down untill you can bring every thing from the Shantier that is your returns, Louisons, send the Boats & timber &c, give yourself no uneasiness about your family, I will see that they are provided for.

I would have sent Louison to bring down his own returns, but we are surrounded with Indians and I cannot do it without him here.

[no signature]

❖ ❖ ❖

Ft Pierre Mar 10 1848
Sam E McElderry Esqr
Dear Sir

Maleau arrived here yesterday and bought me yours of 7th inst I bring him back to you with the carts, ~~I bring him back to~~ having every confidence in your judgment. I leave you to prosecute this trade in such manner as you shall think most likely to promote our interest.

You have Bill enclosed of the articles I send you. I have substituted stroud for S S Cloth not having the latter. I do not wish you to be in a hurry about sending in your carts only [if] you should want more goods in which case it would be best to send one or more of your [word?] Robes to put on them. I am at present scarce of men but hope when you send again to be able to spare you another.

Maleau says our opponents talk of receiving B[word?] Robes, I would much rather you would not do it, however there are sometimes cases when you are obliged to receive a part on his way, I am well assured that our opponents have had very few goods of any kind left, and you need not be apprehensive of their trouble you must so for. Horses those that I would take 10 Robes for are with unbroken Colts, and I have nobody at present to send with them, or old Horses that are too poor to travel. I shall receive plenty of Horses from below this month certainly and I would much rather if your Indians are able to pay for Horses of any kind they would deliver you their Robes and come with an order & get them here.

The two Horses Maleau brot I send back, you can sell these for 13 or even 12 if the Robes are prime. Maleau says he can get a good work horse & 3 Robes for one of them, it would be best to do so. I have been told the Indians intend collecting at the Oak Grove, should this be the case it would be well for you to get your Indians to move there [word?] with them, at that place you would then have them all convenient to you.

[no signature]

❖ ❖ ❖

Fort Pierre Mar 12 1848
J Jewett Esqr
Dear Sir

I have yours of 3d inst pr Dupuis. I have made every exertion to get from the Indians around us the number of Lodges you asked for, but without success, I send you the only two we have & 2 skins. I trust with these you will be able to make out, the other articles you asked for I send, you have mem. annexed.

Could not Mercia [?] trade you a Lodge or two if it is necessary. I think you will have plenty of time to send to him, however in this do as you think best

I send you two mules 21 Ind Horses, which I hope you will send back with your carts. I have sent S Saguire to Chayanne River near the Crossing to oppose Lamban who is trading there, if you have any goods left when you come down & he should be in want of them leave them with him, and bring me an account thereof.

I am pleased to notice your large returns & trust that in due time you will arrive here in Safely with them.

[no signature]

❖ ❖ ❖

Fort Pierre Mar 15 1848
F Laboue Esqr.
Dear Sir

Your favor of 10th inst pr Colin Lamont reached me yesterday, and he returns to you with 4 Men viz Jas Servais, Herbert Paude, James Adams & Bat Jacquemain to you in bringing your canoes. I send you also such of the Merchandize you requested that we have. Blankets we have none.

I have no doubt you will have plenty of water some time between this and May, should we however have to [word?] them, you see the situation of our Oxen, it will be late in May before we shall be able to do it.

I trust you will have your canoes in readiness and that you will keep your men by you to take advantage of starting whenever the water does come. The Express from Saint Louis has not yet arrived.

We are hourly looking for it, should it bring Letters for you they will be sent you pr first oppy.

Proveau will be back with some horses by the last of this month & Maj Drips will bring up a larger Band very early, therefore should your Indians have Robes to give for a good horse you can give them an order which will be paid in May at latest.

As soon as the river opens we shall receive a supply of Blankets fro. Ft Union

[no signature]

❖ ❖ ❖

Fort Pierre Mar 27. 1848
Colin Campbell Esq.
Dear Sir

Girard & Vapeur arrived this morning and brought me yours of 26th. I send them right back to you with all the goods we are able at this time to send you. I send you some Grey [word?] Cloth this we sell at the same price of scarlet, the Pastels, we sell at 3 Robes Ea, the silver arm Bands, [word?] at the price of 2 Robes pr pair and ought certainly to bring 3 Robes. Girard mentions your being in want of a [word?] I send you Moncrevie, he has been trading above with the Yanctonais and has done very well.

I wish you to send one of the mules with the Man, I send right back with all the White Bead you have, you can make the load up with sky Blue & any others you can spare. A for Indian or 10 Robe Horses we have none on hand, and they are much in demand here.

As regards Blankets we have none at all at present. I expect as soon as the river opens to receive a supply of blankets from Ft Union. Mr Kipp has promised to send them. I also expect from there some Tobacco & Coffee, therefore send up in 10 or 12 days and perhaps at the same time I shall be able to send you a few horses, as some may come in from the Outposts.

When Proveau comes I wish you if possible not to detain any of his horses. Here we have more & Indians who have given me 30 Robes [two words?] and I have to find them and their families untill they come you can say to your Indians Drips will be here soon, I have written to Drips, to bring 30 Hoses. I would much rather your Indians should wait untill he comes. You can also tell your Indians in 3 weeks I will be read[y] to send down the Ploughs & Oxen.

The corn I send you, I trust you will get paid for, we have but little, and are selling it hourly for 10 or 12 cups per Robe, your Indians have had plenty from us for nothing

We have plenty kettles Guns Axes Tomahawks & [word?], also Calico White Cotton if you can sell the Cotton at 4 Yds & the Calico at 5 1/3 for a Robe send for as much as you please.

In haste
Resp Yours
H P

❖ ❖ ❖

Fort Pierre April 3d 1848
Colin Campbell Esqr.
Dear Sir

I received yours of 31st ulto pr Girard yesterday. I now send him and Vizlot back to you with the articles you asked for, and in addition I have added 3 ps Cloth, and a little Tobacco. P[word?] we have no more, should however any come back from the posts they shall be sent you.

You can tell Messrs Rondelle & Alexis, our molasses is down and therefore unable to send them any.

I wish you to send one or both of these men back if you have no use for them with all the Iron wire you have, I have immediate use for it. Please let me know whether Bayeis Br in law Flying Bird has yet paid to you his credit.

I sent Pascal Cerre & Little Dog to the Yancton Camp to deliver our Horses which they found [if] they Refuse [word?] to give them up or pay for them. I think it would be well for you to consult the Chiefs about them, I am inclined to think that the agent will not hesitate to settle it for us, and now is the time for the Chiefs to act when they have plenty of Robes.

[no signature]

❖ ❖ ❖

Fort Pierre April 5th 1848
Saml Ellderry Esqr
Dear Sir
Yours of 27th Ulto only reached me yesterday Maleau having lost his way in coming in, I now annex Mem. of the articles forw[arde]d by him. I regret it is not in my power to send you the animals asked for but I have them not, and am compelled to an Ox wagon to you. I am however in of many some animals from the Platte and no doubt we shall have a number returned from the Outposts. I shall certainly have animals within a month and if your Indians have Robes to give you, you can give them orders which will certainly be paid in that time.

From what Maleau tells me I am inclined to believe that the Ox wagon will hardly be able to bring you and every thing in at one load, therefore if you have 12 or 15 packs on hand it would be well to send it in, and I think in that time I shall be able to send you some more goods should you require them, as I am in daily expectation of securing a supply of Blankets from Ft Union and should I have no doubt will bring considerable goods back, and perhaps at the same time I an send[ing] you a few horses.

I have sent you all the Blankets we have in the Ft., and you will notice I send you some Blanket Coats, these try and get 4 Robes each for, if they will not give that sell them for 2 Robes. An Indian called "One that Runs last or Again nen dou Ja" owes Balance on cloth to Monciere 1 Robe & Balance on Flying 6 Robes, for which he has promised to give his Lodge, please try and make him pay it

[no signature]

❖ ❖ ❖

Fort Pierre April 10 1848
Colin Campbell Esqr
Dear Sir
Your several favors per Proveau & Gerard are received. I now send you pr Laframboise some Cats & tin pans, you will also receive per him your Animals which McElderry sent in. McE had to pay $9 for his recovery which I have charged your account.

Mr "Handsome Bear" gave me a Horse for which I allowed him 20 Robes he then promised (but never gave) me 10 Robes with a [word?] to give an American horse. I let him draw a Drum for which he was to pay 5 Robes, you have his account herewith.

The Horses brought by Proveau did not last 5 minutes at 30 Robes each. I have no chance of sending Maj Drips word not to pass by your place. Your Indians can have what horse they want at *30 Robes* each *and* no less, if they take them by force I shall certainly get pay from the Government. I regret that I have no goods to send you, as I wrote you before we have plenty of Calico, cotton kettles, axes &c. Blankets we have none, but are hourly looking for the arrival of the Boat from Ft Union when I will send you a supply

I am now ready to send you down the Ploughs & Oxen if you wish them send up one of your men with Lassanoboise to help down with them and let me know how many men you want. The Coats we send you are small, but we have no other in case you cannot sell them send them back.

Hamilton sent the enclosed a/c against you which I have charged you with.

[no signature]

❖ ❖ ❖

April 17, 1848
Saml E McElderry:
Dear Sir

I enclose your Invoice of Merchandize which I forward you pr Maleau, I have sent you every thing you asked for as far as our present stock on hand will admit of, and have added several articles which I hope in the absence of other goods you will be able to dispose of for Robes.

I send you all the mules I have, I trust that will be enough to move you in, I do not wish you to dispose of any of these for they are all the work animals I have. I also send you two Indian horses as requested the one you can give to the Indian who gave Goulet the Robes, and the other to whoever pays for it.

As soon as you can consistently with our interests close your trade & come in.

H P
W D H

❖ ❖ ❖

Fort Pierre Apr 19. 1848
C Campbell Esqr
Dear Sir

Your letter per the "Boues Gache" & St Pierre are in hand, and in compliance with your request I forward you the Ploughs & Oxen, and such goods as we have to suit your trade, Invoice is annexed, You owe the Yanctons 23 days ploughing which I wish you to do for them, and on the 24th day after, [two words] I shall expect you to send me the Oxen back, as I have immediate use for them to go to the Platte.

I am looking every minute for the arrival of the Blankets from Ft Union, when they come I will send you all we can spare.

I thought ere this to have received the lost horses which your soldiers were to go & get if you can get them at a fair price, I have no objections should you do so, keep a description of them and what you get for each, as part of them are the property of Mr Laidlaw, who I suppose gave you his instructions on the subject.

St Pierre says you wanted to know from me if I intended abandoning the Yancton post, I do not altogether. I shall leave somebody there all summer if it is only one man, therefore I do not leave any thing sent up, but when you send the Oxen back I want you to send your waggon & all your carts & trains, which I shall have to send to the Platte

[no signature]

❖ ❖ ❖

Ft Pierre April 19. 1848
C E Galpin Esqr
Dear Sir

I send "Sionais" back to you with two men and such articles you sent for as we have.

The Boats have not yet come down from the Sta and it is my wish that you should send your Robes there provided you can do so without difficulty, if however there is a point on the Missouri where you can send them await the passing of the Boats, why do so and send them to the Shantier where they are and require them to stop for them. Should you not be able to get them to the River in time for the Boats you will haul them to L. River, trade skins make a canoe & come down with them

I am preparing to send very shortly 15 more Advances in.

I send you herewith [blank] Horses all we have, I have no objection to giving orders on receipt of Robes either for goods or Horses.

[no signature]

❖ ❖ ❖

Ft Pierre Apl 21. 1848
The person in charge of waggons
From Ft John

Mr. Jos Lamire who will hand you this is on his way to Ft John with instructions for Mr. Papin to bring all the Robes he can, to make a Baggage when at the "Bute Cach" or the last crossing of White River, and return and bring whatever is left to the Same place, there to await the arrival of my Trains, which I will start from here between the 15th & 20th of May as at which time you will be able to come on from there with all your returns

I do not suppose it will be necessary for you to send all your trains back you will know what you have left behind you will of course send back your best trains and enough so that they will not be too heavy loaded, what will enable them to come the faster

You will leave some good careful man in charge with all the spare men you have.

[no signature]

❖ ❖ ❖

Ft. Pierre April 23 1848
Colin Campbell Esqr
Dear Sir

I send Laframboise back to you with the Driver, & some Calico & Domestic. I have not had any [word?] & Blankets to send you another supply, however when I do I will send them.

I am told you have two Wild Horses, I wish you would have them caught and send them up, I can break them in the carts. I shall I think be ready to start my first Brigade of Boats by the first of May, by the first opportunity let me know how many packs you will have in readiness by that time, that I may make my calculations accordingly.

Tell "he who Strikes the Ree" I am sorry I cannot send him the calves he wanted, the Bull calf was altered by Maj Drips last summer, and the Heifer cannot be found. I must urge you to have your ploughing done without delay, as I do not want to be disappointed in the return of the trains to this place as it is of the utmost importance that all our Teams should start for the Platte by the 15th May.

[no signature]

❖ ❖ ❖

Fort Pierre Apl 30 1848
Mr Louis Lageire [?]
Dear Sir

I send you per Danville a few more goods Mem. of which you will find herewith. I wish that in case you find opposition for you to push the trade, and get all the Robes you possibly can. I will send to you again for the carts and some more goods which I expect from Goulet.

I want you to send me back Prairie as soon as you conveniently can, and let me know what you are likely to do, the two Indian Horses I send you, you can sell if you can get 10 or 12 Robes each for them.

[no signature]

❖ ❖ ❖

Fort Pierre May 1st 1848
Colin Campbell Esqr
Dear Sir

Moncrevir arrived here yesterday with the carts peltries Tongues &c which when examined shall appear as the credit of your post.

As you requested I send Morrin back with such goods as we have, I am hourly looking for the arrival of the Boat from Fort Union when I will send your the Blankets without delay for our trade is pretty much finished here.

Shall be glad to see you when Maj Drips arrives perhaps I will return with you on my way to meet the Steam Boat. I want you however to send me an Express (Lafromboise or Lamont) immediately and let me know how much meat you can furnish when the boat passes, I want you to have it tied up in readiness. I want to send a supply to the Vermillion and should like to get from you if possible 250 pieces.

You can tell Mr Rondelle that I shall be better able to make him an offer for the Robes when I see them, if he chooses he can deliver them to you and you can receipt to him for them if this does not suit him I will take them to St Louis for him per Steam Boat, charging only Freight and Ins[urance].

[no signature]

❖ ❖ ❖

Fort Pierre May 9. 1848
Mr Pierre Garreau[10]
Dear Sir

I send Constant Proveau with men to bring down the Returns from Ft Union, they have [word?] their 8 American horses which I send to be sold by you the price is 40 Robes each, these are all fine horses, and I have had particular care taken of them, that they might be sent to you in good order. Mr Culbertson informs me that the 4 Bears wishes to give one of these animals, you will please give him choice provided he has the wherewith to pay first, you will also please say to the 4 Bears that I have got the Otter skins he requested me to obtain for him which I will bring pr skin boat and I hope he will be able to pay me well for them, in case you cannot sell all these horses, you can furnish Proveau with one to take it to Ft Union, and you will please furnish Mr Proveau's party with a sufficient number of work animals to transport their Baggage Provisions &c. to Ft U, should you require to have these animals back from Ft Union Mr [Mc]E[lde]rry will send them to you. I have instructed them on the subject, you will please have all the riding saddles as 41 P[word?] that canter, I [word?] packed up and marked the Benton Oft 1828 and have [word?] made of the same in readiness for the Steam Boat.

I have instructed Mr. Desautel to furnish 1 man from his post to go up with Proveau to Fort Union, to come down with the Returns, you will also furnish each another from your post. Proveau and his party may not pass by the post of Mr Desautel, in which case it will be necessary for you to send two men with Mr. Proveau and you can send to Mr Desautel and get a man when you have need for him.

[no signature]

❖ ❖ ❖

Fort Pierre May 9 1848
Jos Desautele:

Your favor of 23rd of April was duly received pr Creely, I have to express my satisfaction therewith, and as you have now come I hope you will [word?] frequently.

Our opponents have notified me of Mr. Piere Vasquez, having taken your Boat, they are willing to pay us for it. I send Constant Proveau with men to Ft Union to bring down the Returns, and I am obliged to call upon your post to furnish him with 1 man in case Mr Proveau should not deem it prudent to visit your post I have instructed Mr Garrow to furnish 2 men from Ft Berthold and in case he requires it to call on you for 1 man.

Should you have more Riding Saddles at Ft Clark than are actually needed, I wish you to have them pack'd up and marked "Ft Berthold a/c 48" in readiness pr steam Boat

[no signature]

❖ ❖ ❖

Ft Pierre May 9. 1848
E T Denig Esqr
Dear Sir

Messrs Culbertson & Kipp arrived here yesterday in safety. Mr Kipps health has improved a little he proceded on to St. Louis this morning

I send Constant Proveau to you with 7 men from here and I have directed Messrs Desautell & Garrou each to furnish 1 man more, this number I trust will be enough to complete the crews of your Boats to bring down he Returns.

Should any thing have prevented you building the Boats which Mr Culbertson requested before the arrival of these men I must require that you will proceed and get them in readiness without delay.

Proveau is one of leaders & best steersman, Antoine Morrin is also a good steersman & Couvar can steer. It is my wish that Proveau should have the charge of the Boats, let Antoine Morrin take the lead Boat; and Mr. Lee can remain at Ft Union for the Steam Boat.

You will please observe Mr Culbertsons instructions with regard to the B[word?] Boats that is only to detain them untill the load can be properly reduced to 350 packs, and then come in without delay, in case the Boats should have started before Proveau arrives, you will please furnish him with a skiff to overtake them.

I trust you would have in readiness to ship to this place all the dress'd Elk & C[word?] you can spare.

Should Mr Garrau require to have the horses which he furnishes Proveau & party to carry his bedding &c send back your [word?] please do so.

[no signature]

7
FORT PIERRE LETTER BOOK E
February 12, 1849– December 4, 1850

The third and final gap in the letter books occurs from May 1848 through February 1849. In the spring of 1848, Pierre Chouteau, Jr., and Company reorganized once again. With a new stock redistribution, long-time company manager James Kipp was awarded a share of the enterprise. The company planned an expansion of forts and wintering posts along the Missouri River. Still locked in a competitive struggle along the river with Harvey, Primeau and Company, Pierre Chouteau, Jr., and Company decided it was time to buy out the competition. They made overtures in the late fall of 1848, but Robert Campbell and Alexander Harvey turned down the offer. In February of 1849, Pierre Chouteau, Jr., and Company renewed their trading license, which is where the letter book picks up again.

❖ ❖ ❖

Fort Pierre Feby 12 1849
Messrs P Chouteau Jr Co
Gent

The Express from Ft Union only reached here on the 7th inst, it left that place on the 14th Decr, the severe cold weather and the great depth of the snow, has caused this unusual delay in getting here, I have lost no time in having the papers put in order, and you will find herewith the requisitions for the different posts intended for the trade of 1849.

It has been the most severe winter that has been known at this place for years, the snow is laying in great depth throughout the Country, so as to cut off all communication with several of our posts, we have lost a number of our Cattle & Horses, and among the Indians the loss of Horses is very great.

As yet our trade has proceeded but slowly, in many places Buffalo are abundant, and the Indians have a large quantity of skins, but the weather is still too severe to dress them, from all I can learn we have but about 500 packs traded. We are powe[r]fully opposed by both Bouis & Co. & Benoise they are both pushing for the Robes, I still however feel confident we will have as many as both of them.

Maj Drips' Express left the Platte on the 1st Jany it was 30 days getting here, at the time he wrote he [had] 500 packs and Buffalo Plenty, he has oppositions to contend with.

Mr Culbertson thinks favorably as to our trade

above. Garreau & Desautel are both of the opinion they will make good traders, on the whole I feel certain we will make at least 5000 packs.

In the requisition for this post you will notice I have ordered only S S Cloth, Blue Stroud no longer sells with these Indians, we have now on hand upwards of 50 ps. I hope however to make the most of it off in the spring. Should you not be able to obtain the 6 ps White Blankets send in their place white English (not French) this preference I presume arises from being much larger.

Laboue & Campbell have both remarked to me of the superiority of our opponents goods. I am convinced however myself that in Cloth and Blankets we are at least equal to them, and in Guns & Beads really superior, in the articles of Tobacco we are far behind them, and cannot trade any in a camp when they have any [of] the Carrot Tobacco sent in of 48 is worthless the Indians will not give cords for it. I have ordered largely in the Grocery line, and would like even more of it as possible for the Boat to carry it. Since November last we have had none to sell, and had double the quantity been brought last year it would have been disposed of, it would make a difference of several thousand dollars on our payments as well as aid us in the trade.

The 1000 Bushel of corn I have ordered I hope will be brought, it is absolutely necessary that this place should have that quantity. Our traders have not been able to furnish the Fort with any meat this winter, and for near 2 months past we have subsisted on corn alone, our Traders are all calling for us, they say it is the only article [that] will get meat, and a quantity could be disposed of for Robes, on the Island last summer about 70 Bushels were raised, at the time our men were pulling it, a Band of Yanctons went there and carried all but about 30 Bushels, there is no calculation to be made on raising a crop on the Island and I conceive it only a useless expense to continue it

I also send you a requisition from Messrs Bridger & Vasquez, Maj Drips who sent it to me calls it an "additional requisition" this would imply that another had been sent. None has been received by me, they may however forward one to you direct, which I trust has been the case. I know they will stand in need of more than is called for in this "additional requisition" particularly Groceries, and should we have to equip them from what we receive it will make us extremely short, they have delivered about 200 Head of Horses at the Platte not one of which has been received at his post. My situation has been peculiarly embarrassing on acct of not having animals, the consequence is that some of my posts have been much neglected, and the trade of a large quantity of Robes lost to us. Maj Drips was aware of my situation, he had selected 40 Horses to send me by Maj [Joseph V.] Hamilton, but Mr Culbertson thought proper to countermand this. I have not received from Maj Drips the a/c of Messrs B & V, but I am certain we are now indebted to them rising $2000. Our opponents received 27 Am Horses on the 3rd inst from below, but they brought no news of Mr Laidlaw. I think he will stop at the Vermillion, until the snow diminishes, here is plenty of corn there to feed his animals.

Schlegel writes me he shall make a good trade at the Vermillion he has sent to me for goods but situated as I am without animals I cannot send them, he wishes if the post is abandoned to make some arrangement to retain it on his own account. I have written to him to forward his requisition and his proposals to you, you will therefore bring up another equipment on a/cc of 1849, arrange with him, or abandon the post as you may think proper, I send in Company with Decoteau, & w/ Bolduc this man is sent down by Mr Culbertson, he goes to St Louis, as evidence against Harvey for the burning of our Keel Boat. Langham started down for the same purpose but was unfortunately taken sick and went back to Ft Union he will however be down very early in the spring.

I send you Maj Matlocks[1] letter which he wrote to Mr Picotte for the Yancton Indians in Septr 1847. I understood he denied having written such a letter, and in his publication respecting the affair of the SB Martha he denied that the Government was indebted to those Indians.

I obtained it from the Indians through Mr Campbell, Wm H Cross who accompanies Decoteau, is our Tinner I have tried to rehire him, but he insists on going down it was his engagement with Maj Drips to go with the Express, he says he will return in the Steam Bt if you will arrange with him, I wish if possible for you to do so. A Tinner we must have, having large crews to fill for Bridger & Vasquez

& Ft John, Cross says some five tools more are required of which he will give you memo.

The a/c of Decoteau, Cross & Bolduc you will find herewith. I have drawn on you in favor of Mrs J Jackson, the wife of our Tailor (who was rehired for the hundred dollars) the whole is on a/c Oft 1848

[no signature]

❖ ❖ ❖

Ft Pierre March 9, 1849
Alexander Culbertson Esqr.
Dear Sir

Your several favors of 14th & 19th Decr last only reached here on the 7th ulto., I immediately put every thing in readiness and on the 12th dispatched Decoteau & Bolduc & Cross, they have had tolerable weather since they started and I have no doubt are by this time near St Louis.

I regret that as yet we have received no Express from below, and I am at a loss to account for the very unusual delay of Mr. Laboue. Mr Penison arrived from St Joseph in February he came up with Maj Mattock who has stop'd at the Vermillion, he states he saw Mr Laidlaw at the Bluffs, he had quarreled with his men who all left him but one, this was on his way down.

The winter has been an extraordinary one, that is for extreme cold and snow, the snow has fallen so deep that communications with our posts has been cut off for more than two months, the consequence has been the Indians have lost nearly all their horses, and altho Buffalo have been abundant they have not the means of killing them this want of Horses on our part will be a great loss to us, the fact is we have not been able to do any thing for the want of them, and the different posts have been neglected on this account. We have been starving all winter having to subsist on corn alone, which article is now exhausted and at present we have not 5 days provision in the Fort, and no prospect of relief.

Neither Laboue or Galpin has furnished the Fort with any meat this winter, and in fact about 300 ps received from Goulet & Sibelle is all we have received since you left

Laboue will make but a poor trade say 250 packs at most. Garpin & Goulet will each make about 300. Louison 100. Campbell has now 50 and may make 50 more. We received an Express from Maj Drips it left 1st Jany he had here 500 packs and he was contending with 4 oppositions, on the whole here and at the Platte our trade will not exceed 2000 packs. From the great depth of snow on White River it will be very late before Drips can get over, he intends to send here for Teams, but it will not be in my power to assist him any, we have lost about 40 head of Cattle and among them the most of our best work steers.

I must beg of you to have a Boat put in readiness to start at the earliest moment possible and send down to me all the meat & Tallow that can be spared from Ft Union, without some assistance of this kind I will be obliged to send my men on the Prairie to live.[2]

I trust you will use all exertion to get here as early as possible, there are some alterations & arrangements to make here, which will need your presence, and it is essentially necessary I should start as we concluded below as early as possible. Mr Grosclair &c came up with Mr Pearson he brought the melancholy news of the death of Mr Murray,[3] it appears he lingered untill some [time] in November

❖ ❖ ❖

Fort Pierre Mar 9 1849
P Garreau Esqr
Dear Sir

Your favor of Jany 1st after considerable delay reached here on the 7th Feby. I am glad to notice your good prospects of trade and trust they will be realized, the trade at this place will be but small, the winter has been unusually severe added to the great depth of the snow which has caused the Indians to lose more of their Horses, and altho' Buf have been abundant they have not had animals to kill them.

Mr Laidlaw started nearly 4 months to bring from the States a Band of 40 Horses, but as yet he has not returned. I am fearful some accident has happened that will prevent his coming back, we have no American Horses or Indian either on hand, but should Mr C return with the Horses [they] shall be sent as you desire. The spotted horse sent by Mr Sarpy, I sold, I knew he would not send you as he was extremely Old, the two Grey horses of Mr C are still here, which I will send with the rest if Mr L returns.

It is important that Dauphin, should get to

Ft Union without delay, please aid him all you can to get on.

Respy Yours
J K

❖ ❖ ❖

Fort Pierre Mar 9 1849
E. T. Denig Esqr
Dear Sir

In my letter to Mr Culbertson I have requested him to send me down a Boat as early as possible with all the Dried Meat & Tallow that can possibly be spared from your post, as Mr Culbertson might probably be detained above longer than he expected, I must request you to have every thing in readiness by the time of his arrival to send to me, if it is not in your power to do so before. This has been an extraordinary severe winter here and altho' Buf in many places have been and are still abundant, the loss of horses has been so great among the Indians, they have made but little more meat than enough for their own use. We have not therefore been able to trade the usual supply.

The want of Provisions and not having horses to prosecute the trade properly, added to mean Indians has rendered this post any thing but agreeable this winter.

❖ ❖ ❖

Fort Pierre Mar 30th 1849
Messrs P Chouteau Jr Co
Gentlemen

Since I wrote you on the 12th Ulto.; I am without advice from you, and am at a loss to account for the delay of Mr Laidlaw, the inconvenience has been very great in consequence of not receiving the horses, and will make a considerable difference in the amount of our trade.

Messrs Beauvais & Lutaman arrived yesterday from the Platte on their way to St Louis. Maj Drips trade there will be about 1000 packs in his letter pr Mr Beauvais I presume he has stated to you all the news.

Mr Langham started from Ft Union on 26th Decr and had proceeded as far as Ft Berthold when he was again taken sick and compelled to stop there, the letters were forwarded to Ft Clark & from thence to our post at the Upper Yanctonais, but from the great depth of snow above they only reached me last night, they contain additional instruction for Oft [Outfit] 49 which I forward herewith, also an additional one for Ft John which I trust will reach you in time to fill and forward pr [two words?] Our trade here will not exceed I think 1400 packs, but as the accounts from above are encouraging I am still in hopes that all our returns will make 5000 packs. Our opponents Messrs Penaire & Pearson are giving their goods to the Indians for the half Price and do, they must certainly have very considerable, and I have no idea they will ever return here, the Indians have still a great many good Robes and had we horses, we could command the most of them

The Trade of meat has been very small, and unless this post is relieved by Provisions from Ft Union early this spring, we shall have to send most of our people to the Prairie to live.

Maj Drips sends to me for Teams to assist him in bringing his return here for shipment but situated as I am at present I am totally unable to render him any.

I have not a horse or mule, and my Oxen are totally unable to perform a trip anywhere before the grass comes, and I have about 400 packs of my own to haul from Riviere Jacque & White River, however I shall use my exertion to have his Robes here in time for the S. Boat, at latest.

The prospect for high water is good, and I trust the Boat will reach us early.

I shall send you 4 Boats pr Mr Laboue by the 1st May if possible.

J P Cerre accompany Mess Beauvais & Harris, I send you his a/c there never has been an engagement with Mr C, he has been occupied a few weeks at the White River post last fall, since that time I have had nothing for him to do, you will please settle with him as your think proper. I have given Mr Beauvais a draft for $349 and Mr Harris for $368.60 both these are on account Oft 1848.

Respy Yours
J B

❖ ❖ ❖

Fort Pierre April 14 1849
Maj Drips
Dear Sir

Yours of 10th March per Beauvais reached me in due time, and [Name?] with Harris & P Cerre to their departure for St Louis in a canoe from Campbells on the 1st inst.

As you requested I gave them drafts for the amt due them and charged same to your post.

I am glad to notice your fine trade, and at the same time regret it is not in my power to send you the assistance you require to bring your returns from White River. I may be able in the course of 20 days to send from 13 to 18 carts which will be all I can do and for these I shall require 20 animals to bring them back as for Ox teams it is totally out of the question. I have not a yoke of Oxen that can perform a trip anywhere, and besides this I have 300 packs to haul from White river, and some 40 or 50 packs from the River Jacque.

Mr Laboue arrived 4 days ago from Chayenne with 300 packs, and I am so badly off for teams I have not been able to haul them in the Fort. Mr Laidlaw arrived from below on the 1st inst with 40 Horses & mules having been nearly 3 months on the road, fortunately he lost no animals, but they are generally in a miserable plight

As you requested I send Robinson over, his engagement and a/c LDH has enclosed to Mr Husband he is in debt $31.73. I presume he will reengage, he is very little acct as a trader

Our Steam Bt was building they wrote me, and they think she will be capacitated to carry our requisitions with ease. Mr Sarpy will come up as usual

[no signature]

❖ ❖ ❖

Fort Pierre May 9 1849
Jos Desautel Esqr.
Dear Sir

You will receive pr T[homas] Jeffries 12 Am Horses, these are all that can be spared from Ft Pierre, you will take from this for your Indians such of them that exceeding 5 as you will be able to dispose of to advantage, these Animals have just arrived from the states not in a very saleable condition, they are however all good Buffalo Horses, and I only regret that we have no more of them to send you.

The two Grays we talk'd of were purchased by the Sioux some time since therefore cannot be sent.

I send up a Jack belonging to myself which you will please send on to Ft Berthold, from which place I will take him up.

These Horses is as expected will be sold to the best advantage, say the usual price of Am. Horses, I have therefore stipulated no price, you will be guided by circumstances.

I expect that Maj Drips will bring from the Platte a large Band of Indians & California Horses, such as you can dispose of for from 10 to 20 Robes in it. I shall send you a band of them, and you may calculate on receiving the same by the 15th June, you can state this to your Indians.

The balance of the Horses after making your selection you will send on with the same men to [Name?] You will please forward to his post as soon as you can an a/c of the Horses you retain

[no signature]

❖ ❖ ❖

Ft Pierre May 9 1849
Messrs P Chouteau Jr Co
Gent.

Your esteemed favor of 30th of December only reached me on the 1st April at which time Mr Laidlaw arrived, the great depth of snow prevented his reaching here sooner. Mr L got here without losing any of his animals altho his long trip has made them cost us very high, they have all however been disposed of to a profit.

You will find enclosed Bills of Lading & packing account of Robes Furs & Peltries shipped you in 4 Mack Boats in charge of Mr Laboue you will find also the a/cs of men

Mr Culbertson has drawn on you in favor of C Campbell for $64 and I have drawn on you in favor of Francis Delaucourt for 283$ both on a/c of Oft 1848.

Mr McDonald accompanies M Laboue his a/c he will arrange with you

Mr Culbertson reached here a few days ago from above he goes with Mr Laboue to meet the Steam Boat.

The great depth of snow and the unusual

severity of the weather prevented the Indians above from making their usual quantity of Robes, but notwithstanding this our trade will be as I wrote you 5000 packs. Our opponents Messrs Bouis & Co will make on their *whole trade* about 1700 packs and Messrs Pearson & Benoit about 300 packs. I expect Maj Drips here with part of his returns about the 1st June at which time I shall start 4 Boats more.

I send you the accounts of Maj Matlack which I presume he will settle with you, the items of the ac at Vermillion I believe has been furnished the prices were annexed here at the same rate we always furnished him with goods. Mr Culbertson was charged here last fall with $130, and the same credited to Maj Matlach but since you have charged him with it I have taken it from his a/c here. Your instructions with regard to the shipment of Robes has been communicated to Mr Laboue and will be strictly addressed

[no signature]

❖ ❖ ❖

Fort Pierre June 15 1849
Messrs P Chouteau Jr Co
Gentn

You will receive herewith the Bills of Lading & packing accounts of Buf Robes shipped you in 4 more Boats in charge of Constant Provost. These Boats are fully manned and the present high stage of water inclines me to believe that they will reach you at an early day. The situation of the Fort is such, being completely destitute of provisions of all kinds has compelled me to send down every body that could be spared; Mr Culbertson started in May in expectation of meeting the Steamer, he proceeded as far as Vermillion, and as late as the 5th with no news had been received at that post he returned here on the 10th inst.

Boats #s 5 & 6 contain the returns from the Crow Post, which arrived here in charge of Maj Hamilton, we are daily looking for the Boats from Fort Union with the returns of that post & Fort Benton, a very fair trade will be made at Forts Berthold & Clark, and our trade at this post has rather exceeded our calculations, so that or whole trade will be rising 5000 packs.

The returns from Ft John have not yet reached here having been delayed by the constant rains. In addition to the accounts of the men which you have herewith I have drawn on you the following drafts

In favor
Servis Cartier   734.25
James Laird   25.25
Fr Laframboise   159.22
in favor
Sam McClintock   79.19
Toussaint Dagneau   40 "
Pierre Goulet   120 "

Should Francis Laframboise wish to rehire we do not wish you to make any arrangements or make him any advances; should we have use for his service in the fall we can rehire him here

[no signature]

❖ ❖ ❖

Fort Pierre June 24 1849
Messrs P Chouteau Jr Co
Gents

Since I wrote you on 11th inst pr Provost, the Boats from Ft Union bringing the returns of Ft Benton have arrived. Maj Drips has also reached here with his waggons with part of his returns, the whole is now shipped you in 6 Macaw Boats which I send in charge of Jon Sibelle.

You will find Bills of Lading, packing acct and a/cts of men herewith, all of which I trust you will find satisfactory and correct.

As yet we have no news of the Steamer, & this unusual delay causes no little inconvenience and expense.

The Teams of Maj Drips will leave here tomorrow for White River where the balance of Ft John returns are, and I hope to receive them in time to ship pr StemBt

There will be a draft presented to your deacon by Mr E. T. Denig on a/c 1848 Oft, in favor of Messrs [Name?] Primeau Co, we wish you to detain $100 of the amount to pay for 2 of our mules which Mr Harry has, these mules stray'd a short distance from Ft Benton, and was found by Mr H, who has thought proper to keep them.

❖ ❖ ❖

Fort Pierre July 25. 1849
Bruce Husband Esqr
Dr Sir

The waggons returned here from White River last evening, they will have to remain 2 or 3 days for some necessary repairs when they will start to you with the "Ft John Oft 1849," and the Outfit of Mr B[ridger] & Vasquez. I have let Ft Pierre have part of my Flour, Bread Sugar Coffee &c, a part of these articles will be returned to us in the fall after the return of the Steam Bt from the Bluffs, also some more corn will be sent to us. I must beg you however to use all care & economy with your Groceries, as we make them count in the ensuing trade. As soon as you possibly can after the arrival of Monta with you, you will move to the place where Bissonnette had the Baggage last winter and commence building. I am told there is plenty of good timber at that place, Monta knows the place well, and I have explained to him and to Rouelle the manner I want you to have the buildings constructed, you will of course build your store houses first.

You will receive herewith the Invoices and a/cts mens Equipment &c some of these men were intended for the Upper Post, and was exchanged at the moment of her departure, the Book stating the terms of their eng[agemen]t was sent above. I will obtain the price at the Office and bring them up with me.

I send Jo Jewitt he is hired as interpreter for the Fort, you know him, he will of course lend a hand at the building of the Fort.

Bayer is hired as Blacksmith & Trader Js B Moncrevir Clerk Trader &c, they will also assist you in any way you wish.

If Reynald is about and you can hire him on reasonable terms, do so, but if he asks more than you think he can earn, let him go.

I expect the SteBt down every hour, I shall go down on her, and without an accident will be with you by 1st Oct, should however any thing occur to delay me beyond the time, of sending out the equipment, send them out in charge of such traders as you shall deem less, in case of my not getting up in time you will have to arrange with McClasstey & Rule.

I wish you as soon as the meat gets good to trade above 100 ps. So as to load the waggon which will be sent from this place.

There is some [word?] Hicking Shirts in an Invoice you will have to get 10 yd Calico made by the women for the Indian Trade.

I send you Auguste back, do not let him [have] any thing but what is absolutely necessary, as I expect his master will send him up supplies by me.

It would be best for you not to open any of the goods untill you have a proper place to put them
[no signature]

❖ ❖ ❖

Fort Pierre Augt 2 1849
Messrs P Chouteau Jr Co.
Gents

The Steam Boat Amelia reach'd here this day from Ft Union, having performed the trip in the usual time. She has brought to this place all the returns of the Upper Country, and will take the most of them to the Bluffs. I shall detain the tongues for examination, as I fear they have been so long packed up some of them may have spoiled. Previous to the arrival of your Express bringing the unfortunate news of the loss of the Dahkota [word?] I had sent to Mr Denig and instructed him to prepare Boats for the transportation of the balance of our returns this was promptly done; I however met these Boats a short distance from the Little Mo and instructed them to continue on to Ft Berthold there to unload the Boats and remain untill our return, the water being still in a good stage I thought they would be more safe on board the steamer than in Mackinaws with inexperienced Patroons besides the men would be of good assistance in getting wood &c.

The Fort Benton & Crow Boats with the Outfits are now well on their way, these Boats notwithstanding the loss of our men, will be well manned, sufficiently so to ensure their safe & speedy arrival at their place of destination to guard against desertion I send 27 of the men from St Luis to the Blackfeet & 12 to the Crows, these with some free residenters from other posts made the crews double strong.

Fort Union is left pass as it should be with 5 or 6 men which is sufficient to do all the necessary work as you see altho' we have lost a great many men we have ample still to carry on our business.

Owing to the large amt of Mdze remaining on hand at Ft Benton I send up [our] best one Boat, which is ample to carry our Outfit for that post, on my way up I expected to see the articles which we would not want this season from the Outfit to remain at Ft Union where I hope they will remain safe for another Year.

Our Old Traders in the Upper districts are all reengaged at their former wages therefore I think our business will continue as usual, the Traders at fort Pierre are mostly reingaged, some I was compelled to discharge. Mr F Faujnein [?] was one of the latter his conduct during the past was such, I could not pass it over, it was clearly evident to me that he done all in his power to favor the opposition post in charge of his nephew Antoine, and I did not conceive it profitable business to pay him 800 to work for our opponents, there are a few more of his stripe whom I shall serve in he same way.

I cannot consistent with our interest be absent from Ft Pierre at present after accompanying Captain Finch as far as the Yancton, I will return and put in repair all my waggons so that should any thing happen to prevent our Boat from getting back we can transport the Outfit by land, this I hope however will not be the case, in fact I have every reason to think there will be sufficient water for her return.

We shall want at Fort Pierre some 80 head of cheap Horses, also at Ft Clark & Berthold about 20 Head, these I suppose you will send up by F Laboue, but I think [it] is doubtful whether he is a suitable Judge of horses to purchase them, as it requires some one who has experience in the business. I think it would be best for you to employ some man for this purpose, if you can get one you can rely upon, there is no necessity of buying high priced horses such ones as can catch Buffalo is all that is required

So soon as I can put my business in a proper train I will take a canoe and go down and meet the Amelia on the return, and so soon as the Outfits are all out, with proper traders instructions &c I will then proceed to St Louis, this will be about the 1st Decr. My present intention is to leave the post in charge of F Laboue and send Campbell to his Chayenne, Mr Laboue is no doubt a good trader but he must curtail his wants, as I am determined to carry in the business of this post with 50 men which will be about 40 less than usual, therefore you will only hire men more for the Upper Country which will be all sufficient unless something happens that I cannot foresee

Mr Denig & Mr Kipp have given me a power of authority to ask for them, the other Gentlemen will make their own arrangements.

Mr Provost who is now on board the Amelia will return with Cap Finch in charge of the men he is well known to you as an efficient man in that capacity, should the Old men wish to return and you feel disposed to employ him he might be useful at Ft Pierre.

Mr Kipp remains in charge of Fort Berthold, and from him no doubt a better state of things will appear at that post than under the management of Mr Garreau.

When Major Drips signed our articles of association he claimed his wages to the tune of [word?] it, this I promised him he should have, provided however it met with your approbation.

During my absence letters were received from Mr Husband who was left in charge of Fort John, stating that he had sold the same to the Government in compliance with instructions received from you for 4000, therefore enclose you the following drafts

P D Novaburgs check   4000.
H Stansburgs draft
on Rob Campbell   2000
E. A. Daicys   a/c   100   6100

there has been a immense emigration to California passing Ft John this season and Mr Husband has done a profitable business.

Mr Laboue drew on you at the Bluffs 3 d[ra]fts amt to 415 Dollars, the one in favor of C E Galpin for 160$ should be charged to Oft 49, the others to Gould for 150$ & Larpenteur for 115 to Oft 48.

I have this day drawn on you the following dfts
In favor H Pehonai $60 of 48
" " H Gould   100 " "
" "S E McElderry   125 " "
" "Brooks   45 " "
which you will please pay.

There are many things in regard to business which I would write but as they require much explanation, I think best to defer it untill I have the pleasure of seeing you

Yrs A C[ulbertson]

❖ ❖ ❖

Fort Pierre Juy 28 1849
Messrs Bridger Vasquez
Gent

We forward to the Platte this day in charge of Mr Monta your Outfit for the present season, as received here pr SB Amelia, the Invoice statements thereof & packing accounts are herewith, all of which we can hope will reach you in safety, and be found satisfactory & correct. We had hoped to have received a Band of Horses from you this spring, as this post is completely destitute of animals, but presume it has not been in your power to procure them in time, we hope however to be well supplied by you this summer & fall.

We have been advised by the house that Beaver has become almost worthless, bringing only 75¢ pr lb and the Wolf skins are only worth 50 c[ent]s, for the largest, while the smaller ones can hardly be sold at all

All are in want of a supply of dressed deer & Elk skins and hope to receive by the return waggons in the fall a supply from you

There is no news but what you will have heard pr the Emigrants, the last accounts the cholera was abating.

    Respy Yours
    A Culbertson
    Agt UMO

❖ ❖ ❖

Fort Pierre August 31st 1849
Joseph Desautel
Dear Sir

Your favor of 20th inst per Tom Jeffries is before me, and I have the files sent to Ann us you Invoice of Sundries as you requested the stats &c Bal of [word?] as [word?] belong to your Outfit, we left here by the steamer and I send them to you by this conveyance. Also your Invoice you will also receive a supply [of] his Pans which I send for your Corn & Pumpkin Trade, should there be a desirable article with you let me know & I will send you a further supply.

With regard to Horses for yourself no [two words?] I will supply you as I told you. When your Indians have Robes The two Horses for the Sans of Louis Defer would be sent now, but as we have them not they must wait until they come from below, they have been sent for and you may rest assured that they will be sent to fulfill my promise

Your Indians had better Keep quiet we have now the U.S. Dragoons[4] here and we have a perfect understanding with them, and any act of hostility on their part towards the whites will be justifiably chastened at my request.

You will please send Mr. Denig a copy of the Saint Louis a/c of men which was intended for your post per Steamer, you will find them in the same Book with your & [word?] a/c

I have now only to require you to Trade all the corn Pumpkins Beans &c you possibly can & be assured it is our determination to prosecute the Trade with all possible sign we have certainly been unfortunate this year in the [two words?] and rely on the economy, [word?] & perseverance of our Clerks with whatever opposition we may have

At the close of Oct. 49 we shall at least be able to Square a/c Your post has always shown a pr. Balance & I feel [text ends abruptly]

❖ ❖ ❖

Fort Pierre August 31st 1849
James Kipp Esqr
Dear Sir

Your esteemed favour of 20th instant per Thos. Jeffries came duly to hand I loose no time in starting mine back with the white Beads for Mr. Denig & you will receive every thing that you asked for as per Invoice enclosed

I send you as you will see a supply of Tin Pans, my impression is that they will readily comm and Corn and Pumpkins if they do so and you want a further supply let me know and they shall be forwarded to you

You will please send Mr. Denig a copy of the mens a/c. which came up from St Louis for your post. You will send them on the side of your Book which contains your packing a/c

The a/c which you sent against men ought to have come down when they came down stream. These men have all gone below, and no doubt but what the Co. have paid them, this with several other things that was reflected at Ft. Berthold is a loss of several hundred Dollars, for a small post this is too bad

I hope next year we will be able to receive a correct a/c of what F. Berthold makes & what it Shipped, together with a correct a/c with your men

You know our situation generally speaking with regard to provisions I must therefore request that you will have all the corn, Beans, Pumpkins &c that you possibly can with a view to supply this post.

The United States Dragoons under Capt. [Name?] are now here. We have sold out Fort John to Government on very advantageous terms, they have come here to look out a situation to establish a military Post, and any future depredations committed by Indians in this district will be promptly chastened at our request.

[no signature]

❖ ❖ ❖

Fort Pierre Sept 5 1849
Mr E M McKenzie
Dear Sir

You will proceed with the Equipment now under your charge to its place of destination Forks Chayenne you will occupy at once the same Houses which we had last winter, they doubtless will need some repairs which you will have done forthwith

You Know our situation as to animals and do not wish you to dispose of any at present You will Trade all the meat you possibly can and send it on without delay. The [word?] in your Outfit are sent for the purpose of Trading animals for the use of your post; and the sooner you trade them the better

The a/ct. of men you have in your Books it is our wish to pay our men in the Country but at the same time we do not wish them to go in debt

In proper time a Tariff will be sent you for the Trade of the present outfit. And as soon as soon as they came from the States, men and Traders to prosicute your Trade

Relying on your industry, economy & [word?] in the Indian trade I feel confident that you will do every thing to promote our interest & profit

Yours &c
A. Culbertson

❖ ❖ ❖

Fort Pierre Sept 31 1849
Messrs Chouteau Jr & Co
Gent

The steamer Amelia arrived here yesterday and has landed the Outfit for this post in safety.

I have this moment received an Express from Fort Union, by which it appears that the Beads shipped to that place as *White*, are all *Blue*. this is a serious mistake as to its effect on the trade. I have sent them back with what they asked for say 600 pounds to [word?] & 50 lbs to Ft Berthold this makes Ft Pierre extremely short and unless you can replace this 600 pounds to us our trade will suffer naturally. We also wish a fourth supply of Dark Blue Blankets, say 90 pair.

The US. Dragoons are now here, for information I refer you to Col Mackie [Lt. Col. Aeneas E. Mackay] who goes down in our Boat.

You will find herewith the packing a/c Bill of Lading a/cs of men and in fact all the papers appertaining to settlement of Outfit 1848, every thing is now shipped and I trust will reach you safely, and find a good market. In due time I shall look for the return of Mr Laboue, whom I trust will receive your particular instructions which it is to be hoped he will strictly follow.

In haste
Respy Yrs
A.C.

❖ ❖ ❖

Fort Pierre Augt 31 1949
V H Schlegel Esqr
Dr Sir

Your letter with the accompanying papers are all received per Amelia. In reply I have to state as to your desire of visiting this post that I think it more to the interest of the Concern for you to remain at home (the Vermillion), as for the purchase of to be made of Traversie, have nothing to do with him, neither with Messrs Brugiere & Ayotte. As you have received from St Louis a good Outfit, and I think all sufficient for your trade. I have hired Jos Brazeau you have his [word?] and a/c herewith, also the several a/cs you requested [be] sent you.

It is more than likely that I shall visit your post this winter.

Yrs Respy
A. C.

❖ ❖ ❖

Fort Pierre Novr 1849
E T Denig Esqr
Dr Sir

I avail myself of the present oppy offered by our friend Brugier who arrived here about the [word?], in company with Laboue Rouville and others from Saint Louis with a Band of poor horses for this trade a pair of which I now send to be disposed of at Ft Berthold where I think they will be disposed of to advantage when in order.

My letters from the House below is altogether void of news that might be called important particularly in regard to the termination of Oft "48" as only part of their returns had been received at the time of our last express the other as you are aware were left at the Bluffs untill the return of the Amelia from her second trip she arrived at St Louis about the 15th Septr as she passed [two words?] on the 10th. The Company has neglected sending us any a/c curt. whatever we are consequently completely unaware what losses we may sustain by first sinking the Dahkotan and then the burning of the Martha[5] in fact from present appearances I judge there will be no settlement untill the termination of the Agt. They however write in regard to Robes that there is no set price but that the opposition had offered at 275 for Robes & 200 for Calves. Intelligence has been received from Campbell who was in N York and trying to make sale that he was unable at that time to sell, upon the whole if we get $2.50 I think it is all, and even at that should the losses sustained by the Insurance company be not too heavy there will still be a Bal[ance] to be divided.

Mr Laidlaw has not yet arrived, and I think by my advice from the House it is doubtful whether he comes or not, he is talking of moving to Cal[ifornia] next spring,[6] this is most likely to be the final termination of the Old man as I perceived he was afflicted with the Gold fever which I am told is still raging thro'out the US, it has however not reached Fort Pierre, as for myself I saw its fatality when at Laramié last summer enough to keep clear of it. Hundreds of poor fellows are now stretched along the Route and many others will starve to death before they reach the Gold Region.

Buffalo is now plenty in this section, and should they continue every thing will be right in the spring. The Gentlemen of the House below have given me instructions to proceed to St Louis as soon as possible but circumstances will prevent my leaving before the 1st Decr. Mr Campbell will be left in charge with the asst. of Hodgkiss. I think every thing will go on well. Mr Laboue is in charge of Fks Chayenne, where I hope he will retrieve some of his lost character. I am unaware what stay I will be able to make below, but hope nothing will prevent my staying until spring, it is absolutely necessary that I should go down as they write from below they cannot send up a Boat on an uncertainty, and it is for me as the general Agent for advice in regard to what we intend doing, which we will continue or not as the expiration of the present Agt. The opposition here is going on as usual but I think this fall in Robes will stop their headway before a great while at least. I hope so. Your draft to them for Horses purchased by Hamilton was presented, but the Company according to instruction from me deducted $100 for Two mules taken by Harvey at Fort Benton which you know is altogether correct I would therefore advise that hereafter any thing they may want let their pay [be] in Robes, as their drafts will not be paid. Harvey took those mules knowing them to be our property. Consequently it is nothing more than right he should pay for them.

[no signature]

❖ ❖ ❖

Ft Pierre Nov 49
Mr Malcolm Clark
Dear Sir

The expedition from St Louis arrived here a few days since and among the number our friend Bruguire who leaves this for Ft Union, he has in charge some Am Horses for Ft Berthold. H. Morrin who accompanies him one of the party now leaving will no doubt continue as far as your post.

The steamer Amelia on her 2nd downward trip left here on the 1st Septr after delivering all her freight in good order, we had a visit from the Dragoon Col Macky [who] went down in our Boat.

With regard to Trade and the general management of Affairs of your fort we have already talked that over, and as I then said the result will depend a good deal on your judgment & management of the trade, during opposition we are obliged at times to deviate from several rules which we would not do under other circumstances, the "Motto" is now to get the Robes as cheap as possible and make your opponents pay as high as possible, as it is not likely you will hear from me shortly again I would recommend your starting as early as Water and circumstances will permit leaving in your judgment the most suitable clerk now at your post in charge during the summer or untill further orders.

[no signature]

❖ ❖ ❖

Fort Pierre Nov 1849
J V Hamilton Esqr
Dear Sir

The fall expedition from Saint Louis arrived here a few days since and camped there our friend Bruguire he leaves this day for the upper country and by him I avail myself of writing you.

I am now preparing to start for Saint Louis and Hence East, where I expect to spend the winter and now before I leave after giving you all the news, let me say a few words regarding the Trade &c &c you are as I told you last summer notwithstanding the efficient assistance of Meldrum & Hawthorn that a good deal depends on your perseverance and good management of the Trade &c in general, therefore I now enjoin upon you to let nothing escape your attention & vigilance, thus next spring when you will be able to say you come down with Flying Colors, with the whole of your returns safe at Ft Union, and that the opposition made nothing. Wake them up any hour and tell the Crows this is their last year which is likely to be the case.

[no signature]

❖ ❖ ❖

Ft Pierre Nov 15 /49
James Kipp Esqr
Dear Sir

Howard with the Macaw. Boat loaded with corn from Ft Clark arrived today. Your letter by that occasion was duly received and contents noticed, and at the same time was happy to hear of a fair prospect for a good trade this winter. The second expedition from St Louis with Horses arrived here abt the 1st inst, but I am sorry to say with a lot of the most miserably poor horses I ever seen come up, the 1st Band under charge of Mr Beauvais and the 2d under Rouville. Mr Brugiere one of the expedition has been waiting here by my instructions untill the arrival of Howard to start for the upper Country. I must forthwith hasten to start him with six of the best horses I have here which I hope will satisfy your Indians untill I can do better for them which will be in the spring when I intend sending for the other Mackinaw Boat which I hope you will endeavor to Save untill that time as you Know we will want it. And I wish you would let me Know by the Express the quantity of Corn you will be likely to trade, so that we will know what to order from below.

We are now well off at Ft Pierre for Provisions, we have traded a large quantity of meat, and I think from present appearances we are going to make a good trade.

I leave this on the 20th inst for St Louis and unless there is something to prevent I will return in Febuary.

Campbell remains in charge untill my return. Hoping to see you in the spring
I remain your friend
A. C. [Alexander Culbertson]

❖ ❖ ❖

Ft Pierre Novr 16. 1849
Jos Desautel Esqr
Ft Clark
Dear Sir

Your favor pr Jos Howard was duly received the mackinaw and contents arrived safely and in good order.

The expeditions from St Louis arrived here about the 1st inst, amongst the number was our friend Bruguire who leaves this morning with a few poor Horses for the Gros Ventres.

I have noticed your remarks and observations regarding the prospect of a good trade, the coming winter and hope your most sanguine wishes may be fully realized. The Expenses of that post this year you will see has now increased to some extent.

The equipment is also better selected in regard to quality and as well as in quantity being greater than former years, this however will be all for the better as it is the great desire of those concerned in this Country as well as those in St Louis that nothing should be lacking on our part to furnish every thing necessary to facilitate our Traders with the means of putting down the opposition, and obt[ainin]g the greater portion of the Robes if possible. And I now think you have the advantage altogether in your favor, and having every confidence in your well known character as an economical & [word?] Trader that nothing will be wanting on your part to obtain the principal part of the trade and send the Dobbys[7] back where they came from. The express from above will be down some time during the winter with the requisitions for the different posts and by it you will of course send yours, be particular in making it out so that there will be nothing lacking for the trade of 1850.

Our opponents here florish but poorly, and are now going down about as fast as they got up and there is hardly a doubt but this year will finish their [word?].

Be particular in letting me know by the Express the quantity of corn you will be able to let us have in the Spring. Sweet corn is in demand here.

Wishing you a good trade & pleasant winter
I remain Yrs Truly
[no signature]

❖ ❖ ❖

Fort Pierre Novr. 30. 1849
E T Denig Esqr
Dear Sir

Your Express pr Desnoyes & Brugiere reached here yesterday. Mr Culbertson departed as you will have been informed by Mr J Brugiere on the 19th and as he has started with a double set of fine animals it is useless to try and overtake him. I have received a letter from him "En Route" and from his progress he had then made on his journey, I think that he is now very near Council Bluffs, your letters will have consequently to remain for the next conveyance.

I am pleased to notice the flattering prospects of trade thro'out the Upper Country while I regard your misfortunes occasioned as it is, by the rascally Indians, this shall certainly be represented to the Troops. I think Mr Ree will receive a visit ere long.

L'Hereux is the only Boatbuilder we have at present, but I think Mr Kipp will upon reflection send his man to you. should however he not do so, let us know by the winter Express and as Mr Culbertson is to bring a Carpenter up with him, he will arrange it so that some person will be sent to build your Boats. I should advise you to have all your timber in readiness. I can only state that unless something unforseen occurs, Mr Culbertson will return here early in February, at which time I know it is his intention to start an Express above, and at which time he will fully reply to the different points of your letter.

Mr H writes you on business &c pr this conveyance
Respy Yours
[no signature]

❖ ❖ ❖

Ft P Novr 30 1849
James Kipp Esq
Dear Sir

Your favor of 9th inst pr Ft Union Express reached here yesterday

The prospect of Trade here so far is flattering but the weather is too fine for Buf to continue, we must however, if we have any winter at all, have it soon, in which case we shall do doubt make a good trade. Mr Denig has been very unfortunate in having one Trader wounded and Tom Jeffries killed, Mr J Brugiere and the man we sent with him will doubtless prove of great assistance, it is certainly hard that our best men are killed off this way by the rascally war parties, and we can get no redress, the fate of poor Jeffries shall be represented to the Troops, and I think Mr Ree will receive a visit.

Mr Denig will require somebody to build his Boats, we have nobody here except L'Hereux that can do it, and his services we cannot dispense with, you know it does not take long to build 9 Boats, let Mr Denig have every thing in readiness, your man could soon go & do it, if however you cannot spare him, let us know by the winter express & probably Mr Culbertson when he returns will be able to arrange in some way for him.

I am glad to notice your good trade of corn and hope that through you and Mr Desautels we shall get enough to prevent the necessity of ordering any pr steamer.

Respy &c
[no signature]

❖ ❖ ❖

Ft Pierre Novr 30 1849
Joseph Desautel Esqr
Dear Sir

I have yours of 11th pr Ft Union Express, and am glad to notice your continued good prospect of Trade.

The express arrived here afoot having left their animals somewhere on the road. I have directed them to look for them and try and get them as far as your place, where they can leave them to recruit.

The Fate of poor Tom Jeffries by the rascally Rees calls loudly for redress, and I assure you shall be properly represented to the Troops.

Mr Culbertson left as you were informed on the 19th he was well fitted out with animals &c and will doubtless make a quick trip. I look for his return 1st Feby at [word?]. We have nothing new here, the prospect so far of trade is flattering

Rspy Yours
[no signature]

❖ ❖ ❖

Fort Pierre February 1st /50
Messrs P. Chouteau Jr & Co
Gentlemen

Your esteemed favor of 29th of Decr. reached me last evening, the animals brought by the party, are in good order, and will meet with ready sale at 30 Robes Each, the Beads tho' rather late can be well disposed of profitably

The Express for Saint Louis could have started at a much earlier period, as the letters with requisitions &c were received here from Ft Union in Decr, but my instructions from Mr. Culbertson was to await the arrival of the express from Saint Louis.

For the prospects of Trade in the Upper Districts, I must refer you to the letters herewith from Messrs. Clark & Dennig, at Fort Berthold Mr. Kipp, calculated to make about the usual trade, at Ft Clark Mr. Desautelle will make most of the Robes, as our opponents are badly off both for Goods & Traders and Mr. D is of the opinion his trade will exceed that Outfit 48

From the Platte we have no news that can be relied upon. Major Drips not having sent any express, I am at a loss to account for this but think it probable he has addressed you direct per Government Mail. Indian Reports however state that there is no Buffalo on the Platte, and that both whites and Indians are starving there and but few Robes will be made.

In this district Buffalo have been and are still in great abundance, the Yanctonais & Yancktons will make a large number of Robes, and of these we shall get our full share

At Fork Chayenne Mr. LaBoue's Indians have left the district, in which the Buffalo were, and are now moving toward the Missouri, this is in consequence of a small War Party of Crows having made a descent upon them and took 125 of their best Horses, but a small trade can be calculated upon in this quarter. I regret to say that for the few Robes these Indians had, a useless and extravagant trade has been made the few Robes in this quarter would not justify it, they have given 2 1/3 yds. Blue Cloth together with other articles the full value of a robe as paid for a Robe. The very articles thus squandered Col[ored] d & wh[ite] Blankets & Cloth are the only articles which the Indians on the Mo. Trade, and of which I fear we shall be short, I have written Mr. Laboue fully on the subject, and as he has a great many more goods than he will want have requested him to send them in, particularly the above articles, as it is useless to sacrifice them there when we can get our price for them here. Altho' ample time has elapsed since I wrote him, he has not done so. At the Moreau Galpin is continuing with Jos. Picotte, I think an average trade will be made there. At White River a comparatively small trade will be made and Goulet writes me that our opponents have pushed him hard for what Robes he has traded.

At Present we have near 800 Packs traded, it is impossible to state with any accuracy, what will be the state of our trade, I can say to a certainty that it will exceed 1700 packs, so that if the Upper posts realise their expectations our returns will be about the same as last year.

I wrote to the different traders to let me know their prospects, and the probable quantity of goods they would have left, they write they cannot state with any certainty as it depends altogether on the Buffalo, should they Continue they will make good returns, and but few goods left, on the contrary small returns & plenty of goods. On the whole the prospects are fair, and a good average trade may be calculated upon.

In making the requisitions I have well considered upon the prospects, and think that all that is ordered will be required if the trade of 1850 should be good. Corn we shall not need any brot up as we have now about 800 Bushels in the Fort and Messrs. Kipp & Desautelle can furnish us to a Certainty with 700 Bushel more.

Major Hatton arrived here from W. Bouis a few days since, he has signed the liscence which is enclosed under Envelope to D. D. Mitchell Esqr.

[no signature]

❖ ❖ ❖

Fort Pierre April 11 /50
Messrs Chouteau Jr & Co
St Louis
Gent

I avail myself of the departure of Maj Hatton to write you, and as he goes down in a small Boat I am in hopes he will reach you previous to departure of Steamer.

Since I wrote you by the Express we have prosecuted the trade with all possible industry, and our calculation of exceeding 1700 packs will be realized, we have now traded 1600 packs, the Yanctons have yet 350 to trade and if our Boat gets up before our opponents we shall doubtless get the most of them. Our Blue Cloth is all traded and of Blkts we have only some 3 pr White Mac & Common, the latter are entirely too common, but as our opponents are completely out of goods we may get [word?] them off to a profit. Taking every thing into consideration I have thought proper to order some Cloth & Blankets to finish the Yancton trade, which together with some few articles omitted in the requisition you will find on Memo enclosed, Sugar & Coffee had become a considerable article of Trade, and should the Boat be able to carry it I should recommend an increase of this article. I have just received an Express from Maj Drips that Platte people have made but a small trade, the Maj writes that he shall only make 400 packs with which he says he should proceed to Westport[8] in waggons, unless otherwise instructed, I have sent the Express back to him, and as Mr Culbertson left no instructions on this subject he will of course adopt his own plan, he also states he shall send his requisition pr Government mail in time for Steamer.

About the middle of last month Jos Conesalie one of Mr Bouis traders was wantonly killed by an Indian while trading in the "Sans Arc" camp there was no provocation on the part of Conesalie mainly refusing to give 2 Yds Cloth for a Calf skin. Upward of 400 Lodges of Indians assembled here shortly after this event, Maj Hatten [William S. Hatton] held a council with them and demanded the murderer, they promised to either punish him themselves, or give him up, but my opinion is they will do nothing with the matter. The Indians are daily getting more hostile to the Whites, and that they assembled here with hostile intentions there is not a doubt, the chiefs themselves say they wish the Government to send Troops here, for they can no longer control their people, and that if this affair of Conesall is not noticed properly, they fear that Traders will meet with a like fate next winter. Old Swan, whom you know as one of our best friends, [says] that they came here with a view of killing somebody with [a] Horse and nothing but the head men taking our part prevented them doing it, it will be well for the Steam Boat to be cautious and to be prepared for any emergency, we shall however send some person to meet the Boat.

The Indians have killed a number of our cattle this was done while Maj Hatten was here, he requested us to keep an account of them which has been done.

I enclose you a statement of Maj Hattens a/c which will be settled with you

The River only Broke up yesterday as soon as our canoes get down and the Robes in order I shall dispatch 4 Boats in charge of Mr Beauvais.

[no signature]

❖ ❖ ❖

Fort Pierre May 10 1850
Maj A Drips
Scotts Bluff
Dear Sir

I received on my arrival here your several communications, the contents of which have been noticed, particularly the one requesting the transportation of your packs to lower post. It is however now too late to say any thing about the proprity or impropriety of the responsibility you have assumed in adopting a measure which has been and always will be censured in regard to the transportation of Fort John outfit.

The concern has been reorganised as yet no one has signed but Picotte and myself being the only two present. Picotte will be up in (for a few days) the Boat which I expect about the 10th June, he will take charge of Ft. Pierre and I of the upper Country.

Should Messr P Vasques, make their appearance endeavor to get as much [as] you can from [them] towards towards liquidating their a/cts as possible and we finsih arrangements for furnishing them with goods will be entered into.

A copy of my Instructions from the House is being sent.
Respy Yours &c
Alex Culbertson
For UMO

❖ ❖ ❖

Fort Pierre May 10 1850
Andrew Drips Esqr
Dear Sir

Your several favors of 23rd. 28. & 30th April per [Name?] was received here yesterday, I have duly noticed the contents, as your waggons have already started in with your returns & therefore, it is now too late to recall them. Messrs. P Chouteau Jr & Co. advised you on this subject under date of 19th March and it was my wish as well as my own that if your returns could not be made by water that they should be brought to this place for shipment, in their letter to me they say "we write this day to Maj Drips, in answer to several of his communications, in regard to the manner of bringing in his returns, we are positive that they should not come any other way than by Ft Pierre except there should be plenty of water to bring them down the Platte the expense always incurred at any other point than Ft Pierre are always enormous and have to be paid in Cash when we can do any thing necessary (being prepared) at Ft Pierre.

If you find an opportunity of writing to him on your way please do so and impress on the mind of Maj Drips of what he ought to do, and write him by mail."

It will not be in the power of Mr Hodgkiss to render you your a/c current from Ft Pierre by this conveyance, but as soon as he receives the necessary papers from St Louis it shall be done it is a matter of regret that M Husband did not forward the a/cs of all debts, due to and by the Outfit, you will please have his attention to per enclosed conveyance.

Messr P C Jr Co. wrote "we recommend every clerk in the employ of the Outfit since 1849 shall render correct accounts of the true situation of their respective offer as new arrangements are never entered into, & altogether a different interest. All debts (we mean good debts) must be transformed, for or against the Oft 1850. The Inventories also should be taken in the usual manner, the goods at their actual cost, [word?] & transportation & the horses mules & cattle of all kinds as well as Forts, establishments and articles in use at their actual value, and that value based upon the Inventories of '47 & 1849.

[no signature]

❖ ❖ ❖

Ft Pierre May 11 1850
Maj Andrew Drips
Dear Sir

Since closing the letters, I recollect that I have neglected stating to you what to pay in each for Robes, you can give as high as $1.75 (say one Dollar seventy five cents) perhaps you can get them at less, if so of course you will do it, but more than this from the present appearances, we would not be justified in paying unless it should be for a small one if very superior for which you would give as high as two Dollars, it would not be worth while to give more than the above for Robes, and the [word?] unless you see some particular object in doing so.
In haste, yrs
A C
For UMO

❖ ❖ ❖

Fort Pierre May 17. 1850
Messrs. P. Chouteau Jr Co.
St Louis
Gents

You have herewith the Bills of Lading, Packing a/c, and the a/cts of Men in two Mackinaw Boats, in charge of Mr. F. Laboue, all of which I hope will reach you safely and be found correct.

Since I wrote you pr Mr Beauvais I have drawn on you as follows

    In favor of Atn Morrin   for $85.00
    " " " Colin Campbell   "   100.00
    " " " Francis Laframboise " 241.61

The whole is on a/c of Upper Mo. Outfit 1849

as yet the River remains in a very low stage, and we are without any advices from the upper posts. The Boats from these posts will no doubt arrive here in due time, when they shall immediately proceed on, in charge of careful patroons

[no signature]

❖ ❖ ❖

Fort Pierre June 13th 1850
Messrs. Pierre Chouteau Jr. & Co.
Saint Louis
Gent.

You will please receive herewith the Bills Lading Packing a/c & accounts men pr six Mackinaws in charge of Major J Hamilton, these Boats contain the returns of Ft. Union and its dependants, the whole being an a/c of U. Mo. Outfit 1849

Major Hamilton has been instructed to turn the whole over to Messrs D. & J. D. McDonald on his arrival at Saint Joseph pr shipment to you as per orders of Mr. Alexander Culbertson

The Steamer El Passo arrived here safely on the 5th, she proceeded above the next day, we look for her return here by the 19th, when I shall write you fully with all the papers appertaining to the Outfit

    Respectfully Your Obt Servant
    Wm. D. Hodgkiss
    Clk U.Mo.Out.

❖ ❖ ❖

"El Passo"
Fort Pierre June 30. 1850
Messrs P Chouteau Jr Co.
St Louis
Gent

I have the pleasure to hand you herewith Bills Lading and packing a/cs of Robes Furs & Peltries & Tongues shipped to your address pr. El Passo all of which belongs to UMO. 1849. I have also shipped pr same conveyance all that has been traded per Oft. 1850 the same is charged to a/c current with oft '49 which is also herewith. Mr Larpenteur[9] will ship all his returns per "Ell Passo" and I have instructed him to forward you a specific account as to the Ofts they belong

You will find the whole of the Oft '49 papers herewith, and as we have given them particular attention I hope that nothing has been omitted, and that all will be satisfactory and correct.

It is my wish that you could write to Culbertson and Denig, and impress upon their mind the necessity of having good wood cut on the River for our next annual steamer, we lost this year at least 7 days by not having wood at readiness, the only and Cheapest way to do it is to give to each Brigade of Boats with return, 10 or 12 good axes, with instructions to cut good wood, wherever they are weather or land bound, they should know too what kind of wood is [word?], in all cases [word?] long, if ash Cedar or Dry Cotton wood is about, no [word?], if Green Cotton wood, it should be stripped of the Bark, split & put up in "echiquelle" [a checker pattern] let them also to know the value of Elk Horns, and be made to trade them, and not to give away to strangers all they collect, nor permit their men to pack them in on Company animals, and then sell or give them to whom they please, the men engaged as hunters should be made [to] collect them whenever they can, and they should also be made [to] save all the Deer & Elk skins and deliver them to the Company in place of trafficking the same on their own a/c, they are hired at high wages, and the Company furnishes them with ammunition & animals[10] I should like you to send back Paul Eutard with 6 stout work horses for our Saw Mill expressly, and as many more for our trade as you can, the Saw Mill is up and doing well, and is certainly a great acquisition to this Fort. I mention Eutard as he is the only man we have down who is a careful man with animals.

I wish you to buy and collect for me all the horses you possibly can those you can get at a price not exceeding $40. I will send down with Eutard, [word?] or Provisions for them.

On Board is a Bay of some Corn for Mr Sarpy & Captn Sire, also some dried meat for the Office.

Mr Desautel will give you a d[oub]le Bar[rel] Gun left to Champagne to be repaired and come up by next springs Steamer.

Captn Burly is a good man *but no Pilot*, and the

Boat "El Passo" suits the oft well, he is anxious for you to buy out his partners with whom it appears he is not on the best of terms, in order to get the 1st Pilot to go up the Milk River, I promised that the time we were proceeding from Ft Union there & back should not be considered in the trip to Fort Union, he is a pretty good Pilot, but lacks his ease as [John] Durack will inform you

Durack is a good Captain and I take pleasure in recommending him to you.

I trust that you will credit the present Oft with the Freight which the El Passo carries for Oft 1849 as well as the Cabin Passages of Messrs Clark F Culbertson Desautel Beheman Js P Lafevre. I notified Mr Culbertson that we should charge for all Cabin Passengers of Oft 49, and told him to arrange with them accordingly, which I understood from Mr Denig had been done. As for Mr Culbertsons [word?], I told him I would make no charge, but for him to write you in the subject. Captn Stillman who goes up and down in the Boat should be made [to] pay for his passage. Mr Culbertson writes me to say that should Messrs Clark Culbertson & Desautel come up in the Fall, it would be less for them to ride their own horses and eat their own provisions on the route, as we will know better when they get here what use we shall have for them, and the value of their services.

Sebille is not worth the powder that would below him up, therefore let him remain in St Louis, all we want is 2 or 3 good men to come with horses.

The Lodges which you charged, as so Skin Lodges pr "El Passo" $14 and to them was attributed the Cholera were thrown overboard, for they they were certainly, independant of the disease, worthless.

You will see by Ft Pierre Inventory that it is impossible to haul the Govt Stores &c. I shall wait Mr Papins arrival with Maj Drips Trains to take his up to its destination, and I am in hopes by the time his teams start (those sent down by Maj Drips) you will have received the Beads from Europe, and that we shall be in possession of them to start with our first Ofts. Mr Culbertson has arranged for the Crow Post in future, and I signed to say the Oft has no further use for the Services of Maj Hamilton.

I offered J Blafer $375 pr year he refused to take it, when he comes back he will be loaded with Mdze Horses &c to speculate upon, if he wants to hire from you do not give him more than $25 per.

Mr Behman goes down, he is behind his time to commence when he returns, I promised he should receive advances for $400 which you will please hand him on a/c of Oft '50, he of course returns at his own Expense.

I have drawn on you as follows a/c of 49
F Rondelle $446   F Deteulle   29.73
P Mire   125.20   V H Schlege   230.98
[no signature]

❖ ❖ ❖

Fort Pierre July 13 1850
Messrs P Chouteau Jr Co.
Saint Louis
Gentn.

Since the departure of the "El Passo" we have been busily engaged in reexamining our accounts &c and find that several things have been omitted that should have been noticed in the communication made you.

It appears that when Maj Drips sent here his Inventory of Stock and amount of returns he neglected to send a Bal[ance] Sheet of debts due at Ft John, or the amts due to the men who went down with his waggons, of course we have not been able to send you amts Transfers Comp, but I still hope that a correct account of every thing was hand[ed] you by Mr Husband, and thus you will be able to let me know what amt UMO 1850 is responsible for the unsettled transactions of Ft John oft. 49.

I forward you herewith a letter which I received from Maj Drips. I consider Ft John in good hands as long as he remains in charge, at present I have no confidential person to spare from this post, whom I could send to take his place. Another object in letting him remain there for the present, is in case of the arrival of Bridger, Vasquez, is for him to make a settlement with them, he is well acquainted with all our arrangements with them, and it is evident they wish if possible to avoid fulfilling their part of the Contract made with them which on our part has been Strictly Complied with. Maj Drips will [two words?] will prevent their [word?] any imposition. I shall however as soon as Jno Broulliard who is now out with a trading party returns, start him with a few men to assist the Major.

You will of course perceive the Bal due by B & V $266 is not in the a/c of transfers as well as the a/c of Colin Campbell for $400. Should these amts be collected they shall be placed to Cr[edit] of UMO 1847, there [are] also some a/cts due by Indians, should any of them be collected, agreeable to an old established procedure they of course belong to UMO 1850

Mr Campbell in spite of your letter, and his persuasion of Mr Culbertson & others, would go to St Louis to see after his claims, and I think it is questionable whether he will return.

I am daily in expectation of seeing Mr Papin and I am in hopes that when he does come he will have in charge the trains that carry all the returns of Ft John, should he not bring these trains, in the present scarcity of Oxen & Horses here, I do [not] see how the equipment to Ft John is to be transported.

In looking over the Inventory of Ft John, I should believe I have brought more goods, than that post will require. Should Maj Drips have sent you his requisition since my departure, please send it to me. I will fill it from here, and should there be any remaining out of what I brought up for the post I will keep them here, where I am in hopes we shall be able to dispose of them to advantage.

I learn from Mr Jas. Picotte who has just paid me a visit that they could only obtain of all colors of Beads about 800 lbs, but that they have the promise of a full supply to be sent during the summer to St Joseph, from thence they will bring them by land. It is to be hoped that we shall not wish no disappointment in our supply, for if our opponents get there it gives them a great advantage over us.

Mr Jas Picotte tells me that his Bouis & Primeau are heartily Sick of their connection with Harvey, he says that in 1848, they authorised Harvey when he went to St Louis to make a contract with R[obert] Campbell, for two years and under the impression that it was made for this term, they signed the article of association, they awaited the arrival of Harvey this season under the impression that the partnership was dissolved by liquidation and it was their intention to withdraw from him on some terms or other, when to their great surprise Mr H produced the "Article" and they found themselves bound for another Year, he tells me however that Mr H will find himself alone another year for they positively will not associate themselves with him again.

On examination of this Fort, I find all the Buildings more or less decayed and must be either rebuilt or repaired, for that reason I have most of the hands up the River procuring Timber and rafting it. I have now 400 saw logs and nothing will prevent us having the Fort completely renewed but the want of proper horses to work our Saw Mill as I have already written you.

If you send up Mr Laboue I do not know what use I shall make of him. I have seen Indians from all the Bands, he has usually traded with, and they say if I want them to trade to us their Robes we [are] to send him as the Trader, but still should you have him and send him up, start him late, say in December with some good Indian Ponies with orders to take his own time and bring his animals here in good order.

I have already stated to you about J. B. Lafeve, in my section pr "El Paso" on reflection I must request that he is not rehired on any terms

Mr Beauvais will no doubt wish to rehire, should you do so I must [word?] the price he got last year (it being principally cash) is enough for him, upon the whole we can do without him, being plenty of equally efficient Traders who remain in the Country & spend their wages.

We are much in want of the article of Blue Cotton Drilling, say Indigo Blue *fast color* 1 1/10 wide, but if you could obtain it or have it manufactured the same width as S S Blue Cloth it would be better, it should also have a white Border similar to S S Cloth, it will trade for very nearly the same as Cloth, we notify you this early, to give you time to arrange for this article, if you can obtain it, we shall require at least Ten thousand Yard.

I shall close this letter as Dr Evans will certainly take passage Lgr down with Las Page   I shall endeavor to ship by him 106 packs of Robes which I have now on the Bank of the River 1 mile from here, convenient for him to land and take if he will. If I do ship by him I shall forward in another envelope the packing a/c & Bill of Lading.

I have now two trading expeditions out, and have no doubt that should LaBarge refuse to take these I can start a Mackinaw by September with at least 200 packs

[no signature]

❖ ❖ ❖

July 10 [1850]

I have prevailed on Captn Labarge to take our packs, and you will find Packing a/c & Bill of Lading enclosed.

I have drawn on you in favor of Jos LaBarge for Fifty Dollars, on a/c of of. /50

There is a difference of 1 pack in the a/c of the Clerk of the Boat & ours of 1 pack. I believe our a/c is correct, if so as Capt LaBge will keep them separate you will receive the 106 packs.

H P
WDSo

❖ ❖ ❖

Fort Pierre July 20 1850.
Messrs P Chouteau Jr Co.
St Louis
Gentn.

Since writing you pr Steamer St Ange Maj Drips has arrived here from the Platte, and after a conversation with him with regard to our future movements in that quarter I find they will have to be entirely different from what we have calculated in past

With regard to the future location of the Post, I find it will never do to put it on White River as proposed by Mr C, the frequent visits of war parties there has entirely withdrawn the Indians, and no inducements could be made them even to Return the post must therefore remain where it is, or at some more suitable point in the Platte River which Maj Drips will point out to you.

Should Mr Papin arrive here having left before this reaches you, I shall send him to build houses low down on White R for the Brulles that usually frequent that place. I consider it all important that Maj Drips should return to the Platte, and I should like you to make arrangements with him for this Post. I can either employ Mr Papin as above or at the Yanctons. You will furnish Maj Drips with such Aricaris corn &c that he wants, the few goods that will be necessary to complete his equipment I will contrive to send him from here, I must beg of you to let me know what arrangements you make at the earliest moment possible. Mr Culbertson and myself have only disposed of our share as yet, to Mr Denig, and as I have no doubt Maj Drips can do well for us in the Platte should he not come in, interested [if] we can afford to give him a good salary.

It is much to be regretted that Ft John was ever disposed of, as we now say that by proper management money can be coin'd there.

I have now come to the conclusion that it is better hereafter that the Platte Equipment comes by way of Kanzas, for several reasons. 1st to bring men up as they ususually come by Steam Bt, they have generally several minor advances, goods of all kinds are now plenty on the Platte, and are disposed of at low rates, and wages to laboring men are high, now you must still advance these men, and sell at the prices there, or they will leave you and we of course lose our advances. 2d, there is no necessity for the equipment being there before the 1st November when if you hire men you get them at a low rate, with but Small advances, and the emigration having passed you can always be sure of them untill spring, when the the trade is finished, when if they do leave, you can always get your returns taken to Westport, or any other point you may select, at a reasonable price in the Contractors waggons, by making a handy arrangement with him in St Louis. 3rd. the constant rains and deep snows for the last two years have washed out the roads in such a manner between this and the Platte makes it killing to animals, therefore let it be understood that in future the business of such post be carried on by the way of Kanzas.

Upon enquiry and investigation I find that the Platte Post has been much neglected during the past Season and thus justice has not been done Maj Drips, his returns even left at this post, thus a promise was made him on the arrival of the "Amelia" with the Fort Pierre Oft they would be sent to him, this was not done, he also left a Memo. for corn and other articles to be sent, this was also neglected, he labored under every disadvantage not being there, every body knows that the principal profit made at that post is on [word?] corn &c and had these have been sent him [word?] to request, I feel satisfied that a much better return would have taken place, it is my wish therefore that Maj Drips return to that Post when interested or him [?]

In case the Platte Teams have started up to Ft Pierre when Maj Drips gets down, please furnish him with 3 or 4 waggons to take up Groceries, and when the teams get up I will send his Oft across and if his teams are still at Kanzas let him take them up the Platte, and from whence send me such of them as are abl[e] to come here, and I will make from my own enough to carry the Outfit.

Forts Clark & Berthold are well provided for, if Mr Desautel returns from Canada, I should prefer your letting him come to me to make his arrangements, if Mr Kipp insists on coming up, he can only take care of Fort Berthold, altho' it is as I have stated provided for, however I have no objections to his coming up to stay at that post, under such a salary as you think the trade of that post will justify.

As for Rouville I see no necessity of having him he is not wanted by anybody, and he is anything but a profitable trader.

Mr Culbertson proceeded to the Crow Post in the Boat, this post will be in charge of Mr Meldrum,[11] and from his well known capacity, and the arrangements we have made, I think it will be profitably conducted. I find for the last two years that some leading men of the Company when travelli[n]g instead of attending to their business, have sought only pleasure, this is the reason why some have been censured while if those most interested had attended to the interests of the Oft it would have been [word?].

I send with Maj Drips Provensal if Maj Drips meets any party at the Bluffs or St Joseph he will send him back, should he however go to St Louis, let him return pr first opportunity.

If you have not already bought the Horses for our Saw Mill, they need not be purchased, as I am well provided now, having got such animals from Maj Drips and his party as I wanted.

Maj Drips left James M McClaskey in charge of Ft John, he intends going to Detroit this fall, I shall start some one from here to relieve him on the 10th of August at the same time I shall send such Mdze as the post is in immediate want of.

I should like you to see Mr McClaskey on his return and make arrangements with him. Maj D can inform you particularly as to his qualifications. I have made a calculation of the Expense of bringing the Fort John Outfit to this place & starting it from Kanzas and find the difference in Freight men &c 1500$ in favor of the latter. Now put the waggons in complete repair at Ft John and sent down in careful hands, they can be started back at a very trifling expense.

I know we charter the Boat & the Oft could come here under the same expense but still if we send from Kanzas, with a smaller Boat will do as [well] or we can bring up that enough more to this or the upper post in such articles as we always need that will realize us a handsome Profit.

[no signature]

❖ ❖ ❖

Fort Pierre Augt 14 1850
Jas McClaskey Esqr
Dear Sir

Maj Drips reached this place in due time safely, he remained here only 3 days and then proceeded to Sant Louis, he informed me that he had left you in charge at Ft John, and as it was your intention to visit your friends this fall he as unable to secure your services for a longer period than the 1st Septr. I have delayed sending to relieve you untill the latest moment possible having been advised under date of 18th June that Mr Papin would leave in a few days for this place with the teams of Ft John by which it was my intention to have forwarded the Oft for that post for the ensuing trade, having however been disappointed in the arrival of those teams, I now forward to you 3 Carts, containing such articles as are deemed necessary for the immediate wants of the post. I think however on receipt of this you will [word?] and remain in charge of the post, for I feel very certain that we shall very shortly receive news from below, when I will immediately send to you again, and shall by that time be enabled to make suitable arrangements for filling your place, should you still be resolved on going, but I might assure you, if you remain, that you will lose nothing by so doing.

In the event however of your resigning the charge of the post, I see no other person with you, better adapted to take its charge than Mr J. B. Moncravie;

as is always usual with us in such cases of this kind you will of course take a correct Inventory of every thing you leave, and put his written acknowledgement of his having received the same, you will please duplicate, one of which you will please forward to here the other if you go down hand to Messrs P Chouteau Jr Co.

I send with the Carts Colin Lamont, Jno Broulliard, Nicholas Tenceau, David Butler, these men are to return with the waggons & whatever Oxen steers and horses you may send, also Charles Bernard, Arthur Augre, Alfred Henauld, to stay at Ft John, provided their services are not required, to bring back the wagons animals &c.

I want you to send me without fail two heavy horse waggons, with all the Oxen & steers that are likely to be fit to work this winter, which I will keep here to replace such of my own Oxen as I will have to send over with the Oft.

I send you back Ft John Ledgers which was brought here by Mr Drips, you have also the mens a/c, [word?] you will note, they have all raised considerable advances, and I request that you make only such [word?] advances to them as they actually need.

The requisition of Oxen for Ft John called for 100, but we find that it will be impossible (not having received the requisition in time to send this many at present) being short of the proper [word?] Iron, should you have the proper [word?] Bar Iron, or any old tire, that is Suitable for ____, please send enough for 100 [word?], let Boyer select it.

I am in hopes that Messrts Bridger & Vasques have in this made some returns to you and that you will communicate some favorable accounts from these gentlemen. Should they have delivered you any Deer Skins you will please forward us part of the same. I shall also expect you to write me by return of Mr Lamont fully in all things connected with our prospects for the coming trade &c &c.

Maj Drips requested me to say to you that he had hired Michelle Boyer July 4th @ $20 pr mo[nth]. Should any thing occur such as sickness or any thing else to prevent Mr Moncravie from taking charge of the post, you will retain Mr Broulland and place him in charge, of course pursuing the same courses with him in taking acknowledgements of what you have left in charge.

It is also my wish to have traded for this post all the Indian Horses & mules possible, say to give in value of 10 to 15 Robes for Horses according to their quality & 20 Robes for good mules, that is in Mdze about usual of trading of robes.

[no signature]

❖ ❖ ❖

Fort Pierre Augt 16. 1850
Messrs P Chouteau Jr Co.
Saint Louis
Gent

I have to acknowledge receipt of your esteemed favor of 24th June which I received yesterday pr hands of Mr Papin

Mr Papin arrived here safely with the Beads & Horses, altho I regret to state that the Horses are in any thing but a good plight, occasioned by the extreme heat and working them, the waggons hired by Mr Sarpy at the Bluffs was entirely too heavy and not at all calculated for Horses. Mr Papin was obliged to work his horses one after the other untill the whole of them have been completely used up. I assure you I am much astonished that you should send me up here 28 head of Horses to transport [word?] Beads, when I thought it was perfectly understood between us that you would either buy or lease a pasture for the purpose of putting in the Horses you would buy whenever they were offered you on fair and reasonable terms, and for them to remain there untill such time as I needed them & sent for them, and at the same time having 13 waggons 88 Oxen & 10 head of horses & mules (which it seems you were then at a loss to know what to do with) at your disposal, out of which I am convinced Mr P could have selected Teams to have brought up twice the weight, and performed the trip in much less time, as it is these Horses, cost us delivered here $60.50 cash we shall no doubt lose some of them, we can get but the established price of 30 Robes each for them, and we are therefore bound to lose money on them. The horses are here at a time the Indians have no Robes to pay for them, nor will they have for months to come, they see them daily want to buy them on credit, and frequently when refused they are tempted to steal them, now had this pasture as we contemplated been procured and the Horses remained in it, can surely I can easily at the proper time sent Proveau, Massele or Guitard to bring up what I want, the Indians will then have the means to pay for them, and we dispose of them to a profit, the fact is I came up here to make money and with your cooperation I intend to do it. Mr Papin was compelled to buy carts from Bruguire at River Sioux[12] where the waggons turned back, at an extravagant price, and to bring a cart from the Vermillion, which puts them to a great disadvantage and me to the trouble and expense of sending it back, however these things could not be foreseen and was done for the best.

I shall start the Beads for Ft Union without delay and have no doubt they will reach their destination in time for the trade. It is to be hoped that there will be no disappointment in the Beads for this post, you make no mention of the Pigeon Egg Beads (white) cannot they be obtained? we hope also that we shall get the silver Lace for our Chiefs Coats.

Since I wrote you respecting Blue Cotton to take the place of Cloth I have obtained a sample of the quality of the article we want together with another sample of Blue Mixed, also the sample of an article (Hodgkiss calls it Duggis) we forward you these samples herewith and remark thereon, please let us know from you this fall if possible about them whether they can be obtained at about our limits so that we can make our calculations with regard to them when we make our requisitions. You will also find memo for a few articles which we want this fall.

I have started 3 Carts with men and such articles of Mdze. As are needed at the Platte we have no news from our people there since Maj Drips left.

Mr Papin says he did not receive the Saddle Blkts & Bridles as charged in your Invoice, we presume they have been left, and will be sent by some other party, he [word?] on you for $226. Freight of Horses passage &c in this draft is included $19 for the passage of Rouelle & Lady we presume pt of this is chargeable to Mr R. The men who came up have been charged the difference of Cabin Passage. Durack of course reported to you the circumstance of Harvey having taken our wood which we bought up [word?] at Brugieres, he ought to have made [to] pay well for it Brugiere was to be paid $73 for his Carts & [word?] which he let Mr Papin have, Mrs P A Sarpy is to settled with him.

Mr P. made an a/c with Mrs P A Sarpy in which he paid $30, also one with McDonald for $79.08 on which he paid $20.

Since my last we have had a great deal of sickness, some decided cases of Cholera, we have lost two men and many of the Indians have also died, the heat has been intense, our cattle have all been more or less sick and a great many have died, and I find it will be impossible for me to send the Ft John Oft over unless trains from below come here, or go up the Platte with lighter loads so that they can come here after it, in which case I will render them all the assistance in my power. The Sickness evidently Cholera prevails throughout the whole Indian Country, and whenever it commences in a village they immediately scatter, and at this time it is impossible to find more than 3 or 4 Lodges together, it is therefore not in my power to state to you with regard to prospects of the coming trade.

Under existing circumstances I shall detain Mr Papin here either untill the waggons arrive, or I hear from you again, should the waggons arrive here he will go over with the Oft to Ft John when if Maj D arrives there he will of course take charge of the post and Mr P be instructed to go & build houses for the Platte at some elegeble point, on the other hand should I hear that Maj D has gone up the Platte with the Teams I will send Mr P to build at some suitable place on Cold River, and again should Maj D not come up, and Mr P take charge at the Platte I shall select some suitable person to send to the Brulles in his place

For the reasons which I gave you in my letter pr Maj D. I should prefer the returns of the Platte going into Kanzas, but if you insist on their coming this way let me know in time that I may give the necessary instructions to the person in charge there, so that they can provide themselves with Teams for the purpose, having already lost so many of our work Oxen here, I shall not be able I shall not be able to render them any assistance, having barely enough to answer the purposes of this post.

In conforming with your request I have examined the Tobacco, it is pretty much the same thing from both houses, admittedly a better article than we have had heretofore, but all we have opened as yet is more or less mouldy. I am of the opinion this can be remedied by care in putting it up, the quality is good enough and with the exception of the mould we have no complaint to make

The Powder in quality answers well, it is somewhat lumpy in some of the Kegs, this can be avoided by having the Kegs thoroughly dry when they are filled.

Your remarks with regard to the Tongues shall receive all the attention in our power, that is we shall write to all the posts on the Subject, and recommend to all persons at the Outposts to be particular, you are aware that but a small part of these are Cured at the Fort, however in future we shall examine them all here, and will ship only such as we think perfectly sound.

We have heard that S Martin has deserted from Ft Berthold, should there be any debts which was assumed to pay for him unpaid please stop them. Pascal Segmann did have a few days since there was $12 assumed to pay for him. Stop this.

Altho' we have suffered much from sickness warm weather, the business of the Fort has not suffered any, we have more Hay and Coal than was ever made here in any one season before, and Timber at our gates for all the repairs & improvements of the Fort besides for our Posts next Spring, therefore should there be any trade made this winter, there is nothing to prevent all hands from prosecuting it to advantage.

I hope I shall soon have the pleasure of hearing from you again, and think when I do I shall hear that you have been enabled to procure the contemplated pasture for the Horses; having horses here now is only risking them in fact tempting the Indians to Steal them, no Indian will have good Robes enough to pay for a horse for 4 mo[nth]s to come, in the meantime the cool weather will let in and the Indians get over their alarm of the sickness, when we shall be able to judge of our coming prospects, if favorable, I can easily send Hassler Proveau or Guitard to bring whatever animals I may require.

From the upper Posts I am without advices, from the Vermillion I learn that Mr Larpenter still continues busily and should he live will in all probability quit the Post,[13] I have only Schlegel to depend upon there, as long as Larpenter remains when he leaves I will send some one else, for altho' Schlegel has promised fair, there are so many temptations at that place, I cannot implicitly rely upon him.

Trly Yrs
H P

❖ ❖ ❖

Fort Pierre Augt 30 /50
Alexander Culbertson Esqr
Dear Sir

You will receive herewith per Evan [i.e., Owen] McKenzie[14] Invoice of White pound Beads, now having pack animals to spare I send a waggon and hope they will reach you safely and without delay. The Beads were [word?] agreeable to your requisition, but not one pound as yet has been sent for this district. I was in immediate want of a few, and have reserved out of your lot 450 pounds, knowing that in taking your Inventory you had more remaining on hand than you expected, and believing what I now send you will be amply sufficient for your trade. As yet our opponents have not received a pound of their Beads, and if they get them at all, it will be very late, Primeau leaves without any.

I have received from the Platte and Saint Louis about 40 head of good American horses, 28 of these were brought up by Mr Papin, the extreme heat, Flies, Mosquitoes & the transporting of the Beads have so used them up that they are not in order to do anything at present. I however am taking particular care of them and by the time Messrs Kipp or Clark arrives shall have them in fine order, so that I can exchange for their tired horses.

As work horses and mules are very high at this place, I should like you to send Guitard and a man or two back immediately with all the work Horses and mules you possibly can, we are extremely bad off for most animals for the post, and you cannot send me a good work horse but what will bring from $50 to 60. Mules are worth from 75 to 80$, I am actually selling at this price every day, and after our trade is finished, by sending them over to the Platte with spring we can get for mules from $100 to 120 in Gold or in Exchange for five Am Horses that are only a little fatigued or tender footed, and can be recruited in a short time.

The description and price of the animals I send with McKenzie is herewith, and I wish if you send me any horses to send a like document.

Should you when McKenzie arrives not have received any horses or have none that you can send me, please build a small Post and send Eutard immediately down, I want him to bring me what Corn they Can from Fts Berthold & Clark. You will of course advise me what could be the prospect of getting Horses from you this Fall and I hope by your exertions I shall receive a good band

Chateannd who goes up with McKenzie is a good carpenter he is hired as a voyageur, as we were not in need of another carpenter, if you should have any use for him at his trade, keep him and send some other man in his place with Paul. We have had a great deal of Sickness here (Cholera) this summer, several white and numbers of Indians have died, the weather is now getting cooler, and we are in hopes it will soon cease.

The papers for the settlement of Oft 1848 are forwarded you herewith by which you will perceive that Outfit lost rising $1000, our opponents sold their Robes of last year in New York at $2.80 which netted them $2.60 consequently they made a profit, while yours you will perceive that [have] been shipped only netted about $2.28 for the [word?], hence this loss. The house I know would have given the Oft $2.70, the price and the saving in Shipg. Expense Commissions &c would have made a difference to Oft '48 of $25000. This year the house has bought our opponents Robes at $2.70 all sound. I do not know what instructions you have given them with regard to prices, but if they give you the [word?], it will be to great advantage, but if they [word?] them Oft 49 must lose by the transaction.

I hope you and Mr Denig will bear this in mind, and if you do not go down empower me to make such arrangements as will be satisfactory & profitable.

Our summers trade here has been a favorable one, we have already shipped on a/c present Outfit as follows, mostly summer Robes, those from here and the Vermillion do not cost us more than 55 cent Packs.

From Ft Berthold	235	
Ft Clark	814	
Ft Pierre	2231	
Vermillion	1088	4368.

320 Packs of these we succeeded in Shpg pr Steamer St. Ange.

Maj Drips also done well for us on the Platte having made about 3500$ clear (after taking Inventory) in fine horses & Gold, the present Oft assumed above $4000 for Oft 49 in this district most of which we have already paid. Altho the sickness has considerably retarded our Ft work, still we have accomplished a great deal, we have put up a large and fine stable, the Frames for the new Row of buildings is finished and ready to put up. We have upwards of 2800 [word?] logs at our gate, Cedar timber for a new Ice house, more Coal and Hay than Ft Pierre ever had before, our waggon Carts [word?] Saddles all in the most Complete order. Our Iron, Tin and sheet Iron will all be worked up in two weeks more; so that when the trade commences all hands will be employed to make Bouis & Co sweat.

I send you a few of the latest papers we have received, Congress was still in Session, the slave question was not decided, in fact nothing has been done, a man arrived at Ft Lookout a few days ago who left below a long time after Mr Papin, reports the death of President Taylor on the 4th July. Campbell went to St Peters of course done nothing, his nephew Laframboise arrived here a few days ago, he left him with the Indians, intending to remain out untill the sickness subsides.

We have as yet of but few Buffalo, the sickness here has scattered the Indians so, we can make no calculation with regard to prospects of trade, it is however early yet, as soon as the cold weather sets in, they will no doubt come together again, when all will be right.

It is McKenzie's wish I believe to remain with you above for reasons which he will explain to you.

Sepr. 3. Mr McKenzie has just sent Paul Leutard back to me with a letter stating that he finds it impossible to proceed with the waggons, and requesting me to send him additional animals, and pack Saddles, as he is put to considerable inconvenience it being so bad off for animals, I have complied with his request, you will find memo. of the animals, Pack Saddles, &c herewith

Truly Yrs
[no signature]

1 Sorrel Ind Horse	15	R[word?]	
1 Brown "	15	"	"
2 Good mules	20	"	Ea.

❖ ❖ ❖

Fort Pierre Oct 5 1850
Andrew Drips Esqr
Dear Sir

Your favor pr Raboin of 25th ulto reached me on the 3d inst; I was then making preparations to start Mr Beauvais with all the Teams that I thought would reach you. Mr Beauvais has a long and tedious trip up, having only arrived here 7 days ago, he lost some Oxen on his route, many are in such a crippled state that they cannot perform the trip, and having lost since you left upwards of 20 head by sickness, of my own, and the balance being out with the equipments renders it impossible for me to send you more than the 7 waggons at this time, however when Mr McKenzie arrives I expect my teams will all be in, when I shall send you by him and Campbell 3 certainly and perhaps 4 more waggons loaded with corn & Provisions, and forward you also such things as Rouville brings with him for your post. I have thought it less for Rulo and all hands to remain with the waggons the whole of the Route for the safety of the Oft, as many of the Indians are inclined to be troublesome

I have no other traders but Beauvais & Provelliard to send you at present, I think that Rouville & Campbell will soon be here, these with the above two, and what you have I am in hopes you will be able to make out with, but if I can do any thing more for you in this line I certainly shall.

I should recommend your [word?] on Messrs Ward & P on debauching men, there is certainly some of them that you can bring back, that you can pay in the Country, and in this way, we can hold out liberal inducements.

The men I send you by Mr Beauvais are all my best men, and men that there is no danger of going to my opposition, and Morrin can trade well, and Charles Morin & the two Counars, can also trade if you should require it. Lafferté who goes is a great Carpenter and I think will answer your purpose well. I send Mr Goulet, he is a good faithful old man and is a good Blacksmith. I recommend this old man to your good care. I have other Blacksmiths here, but as they have nothing due them, I am certain they would desert as soon as they reach the Platte. I hope you will be able to send me back my steersman back on time in the Spring, Viz. and Morrin, Chas Morin two Connards. I should also like Mr Beauvais to take down a brigade of Boats, unless you can prevail on him to stay in charge during the summer, and come over here yourself and go down in the Boats, which I should prefer, unless you have made arrangements with the Company. The Brulles & Ogalallas have been dying in such number this summer that I have not dared as yet to establish a post on White River. I am however making preparations to build houses where you and I found Primeau 3 years ago. I will send Laboue to take charge as soon as he comes, he will be able to extend his trade as far up as Porcupine Cr. I think myself it will be well to our interest to keep the Indians as low down as possible, that is near *us* when we have but one reasonable opposition.

I do not think it will be in my power to visit the Platte, as from all appearances we shall be surrounded with Indians all winter, consequently I cannot leave. I must therefore beg that you will let me hear from you as soon as you can, and let me know what arrangements has been made for your returns, and also for your requisition. [Name?] is to return to Fort Pierre in time to go down with the Express if he wishes, and we ought to be in the receipt of your requisition early in January. Should Fisk not wish to come, keep him untill spring when he wishes to go to California. In order to secure him to you, I have made some sacrifice which Mr B will explain to you

Your woman has remained quietly with me all summer, her relations only among here a short time since, since which she has disposed of her animals & sundry Mdze to them.

I think it would be well to apply to the Officer in Command at Laramié and see if he cannot do something to stop the desertion of our men. I enclose you a letter which if you approve of it you will sign & direct to him. I am confident if he would take it in hand, it would have a good effect.

You will find enclosed your Invoice of every thing sent you pr Mr P, as well as mens a/cs, also a copy of the License your Inventory &c.

You will please send me pr earliest conveyance all the Gold & silver Lace &c that you have, we were unable to procure from below in sufficiency for our

Chiefs Coats, please also send me all the a/cs of your men &c that you brot from the states

[no signature]

❖ ❖ ❖

Fort Pierre October 23 1850
Alexr Culbertson Esqr
Dear Sir

Since my advices to you under dates of 31st Augt pr McKenzie, we are without any accounts from you, but of course take it for granted that "Alls well" or we would have been informed otherwise.

Our parties from below have all arrived Mr Clark leaves tomorrow with the intention of proceeding as fast as possible to Ft Benton, where I presume you will find his services acceptable.

Our old friend Kipp came in Co. with Mr Clark and would have proceeded to take charge at Ft Berthold but the severe and dangerous illness of his nephew Mr Jos Desautel will delay him for some time longer.[15]

It is with pleasure that I can state that the prospects in this district are very flattering and should they be *anything like realised* I think our trade will be large & profitable.

Maj Drips has returned to the Platte here we have already recd. an Express from him, he will be powerfully opposed, my impression is that if his district does not make a profit we shall make both ends meet, and from the arrangements we have made that a very profitable business will be done after the trade with the emigrants. The Vermillion Post I am convinced will make a profit this year, and I hope that Fts Clark and Berthold will do the same. In your district wherever you have remained in charge yourself the most favorable results have ensued and therefore look for similar results this season.

All the returns of Oft 49 got down safely without insurance, untill they then reshipp'd pr Steamer, this was a saving of several thousand dollars, I am in favor of adopting the same plan for our returns next summer therefore it is best for us to build good Boats, not too large, man them well, with good and careful men, and by timely arrangements we can always send down Five Thousand packs pr SteamBt, so that I conceive there is not much risk. My plan has always been to pack my Best Calves & [word?] Robes seperate, and make the lower tiers of the Boats of these, I wish you would attend to this, for the loss is generally the lower tiers, and if we do lose, we had much better lose these than our prime Robes.

Mr Clark it appears was much dissatisfied with being charged with the passage of himself and family. I told you & Mr Denig that this would be done, and certainly understood Mr D that he had communicated the same to Mr Clark. I of course have no objections to you refunding this to Mr C, provided it is done at expense of Oft 1849.

Messrs Choteau Jr Co have rendered us this a/c for the present Oft up to this time, the whole Inventories, Invoices advances to men &c amount to $162000. While we have a credit against this for debts assumed, returns made &c for $22000, they have posted our returns to our Credit at 2.70 for Robes [three words?] all [word?], this is a favorable state of things so far and from the manner we are paying off our men & Traders here we shall (comparatively with former years) have had very small cash payments to make.

I send pr Mr Clark some good Lace, Invoise of which & a/cs of men are forwarded to Mr Denig

We have no news of Importance from below, the death of Genl [Zachary] Taylor has greatly retarded the progress of things, nothing has been done, nor do I think will be, with Mitchells bill for the general Treaty with Indians.

[no signature]

❖ ❖ ❖

Fort Pierre Octr 23. 1850
E. T. Denig Esqr
Dear Sir

You have herewith Invoice of sundries forwarded by, and furnished Mr Clark, together with that Gentlemans a/c and also that of P Gellavin who goes up with him

I had hoped that by this time I should have received from you an acknowledgment of the receipt of the Beads pr McKenzie it would be a great satisfaction for me to have learnt that they reached you safely and in time for their destination. I am however in hopes that the return of my men is delayed by their bringing me a band of horses with [word?] Jaquais which I assume you will be [find] very acceptable.

The prospects in this quarter could not be better for a large and profitable trade, and I feel very confident that these prospects will be realised. Our opponents as yet have not received their Beads and their arrival here in time to send forward to their upper posts is extremely doubtful.

Mr Clark will give you all the news, and in the hopes of soon hearing from & of good prospects in your quarter

I remain Respy Yours
[no signature]

❖ ❖ ❖

Fort Pierre Octr 23. 50
Andrew Dawson Esqr
Dear Sir

I think it necessary to inform you that Mr Desautel arrived here a few days ago in a very low state of health and from all appearances at present there is but little chance of his recovering, his uncle Mr Kipp is here with [him], and intends to remain with him untill his fate is decided, the Beads and some Chiefs Coats for your post will be sent if possible pr Mr K. Your having been associated with Mr Desautel for some time in the trade of Ft Clark and your familiarity with the manner which the business of your post requires to be conducted, gives me every confidence that should your Indians make Robes, that you will make a good and profitable trade.

I must beg of you to Keep me constantly advised (when opportunity occurs) of your movements & prospects, as well as that of our opponents
[no signature]

❖ ❖ ❖

Fort Pierre Octr 23 1850
Andrew Drips Esqr
Dear Sir

I have this pleasure under date of 5th inst pr Mr Beauvais who no doubt will have been a long time with you when you receive this. Rouville only reached here on the 20th and it was necessary for him to delay a few days to rest his teams. I send you by him two waggons which contain the Mdze sent you from St Louis and as much Groceries & Corn from here as he could Carry

I regret it is not in my power to send you another waggon loaded with [word?], but I have not actually the team, however should you stand in need of more Corn or Groceries you can get them if you can send the conveyance for them.

You have Invoice and packing a/ct of the whole herewith.

I have drawn on you in favor of Pierre Dening for (24$) Twenty four dollars, which you will please pay and charge this post, this man with Louis J Fotue goes on with Rouville they are to assist him on the way, they came here from below with Mr Beauvais and it is their intention to proceed to California if they render Mr Rouville satisfactory service you will please settle with them, they will be satisfied with a pr Pantaloons each, should you require their services untill spring I am of opinion you can get them for a low price
[no signature]

❖ ❖ ❖

Fort Pierre Decr 4 1850
Messrs P Chouteau Jr Co.
Saint Louis
Gent.

I have to acknowledge the receipt of your several favors from 16th July to Sept 4th all of which have received an attentive perusal

On the last of October I started an Express to you, but it turned back from the River Jacque the men having encountered (as they say) a war party of Pawnees, it was too late in season when they set [out] and I thought it useless to start another. Mr Beauvais reached here in safety with his teams, altho' a long time on the road, he took the Ft Jno over. Mr Rouville was found at St Joseph by Mr Behman, and where he remained some time after Mr B's arrival there, running the Outfit to great expense for nothing his teams were all in good order, he met with no detention on the road and he ought to have arrived here long before he did. I started him immediately with waggons loaded with Groceries & Corn to the Platte, when to judge from his trifling conduct on his trip here, he will not arrive untill the latter part of the winter.

Maj Drips arrived at his post in 19 days from

Kanzas, he sent an Express which arrived and went back again before Mr Rouville got here, the Maj was engaged in moving his Post, and calculated to be in comfortable quarters before the Cold weather, he will be powerfully opposed, and I therefore do not calculate that any thing of consequence will be done in the Invoice, but I am glad that you arranged with him, for there is not the least doubt that he will do a profitable business with the emigration.

As matters stand I am glad that the Oft 1850 did not assume the debt of B & Vasquez. I received a letter from McCloskey in September he says "I have just seen Mr Bridger, I stated to him that I had all the a/cts and was authorized to settle with them, he replied that if Chouteau Jr Co had any settlement to make with them they must each come to their Fort on Blacks Fork or wait untill they have them in St Louis when the Law would settle it. Vasques I am told will be in late this fall to get an equipment from [Name?] the Sutler, if Maj D sees him he may come to some arrangement, there is no doubt of their ability to pay if they had the disposition. I kept the principal part of Ft Jno Oft here merely sending sufficient to complete the assortment, I think it will all be profitably disposed of here with the exception of the Ammunition & Tobacco.

Mr Campbell returned here in Sept from St Peters he is hired for the trade and is now located alongside of Bouis in charge of Yancton Oft. It is to be regretted that he ever went to St P, as he took a party of Yanctons along with him who saw how trade is carried on there, the consequence is they are much dissatisfied with our prices, and cause us no little trouble, he contemplates returning there in the spring. Campbell told me he had drawn on you for $100 on his own a/c.

With regard to my not advising you more fully as to hiring traders, having been absent from here two years when I just arrived I thought we had enough. I feel certain however that you wanted him F Laboue and that you would use your own discretion as to [the] person to take charge of [word?] expectations might come up. I am pleased however that you did not hire Goulet, as the advances you would have had to make him was more than he is worth, in writing that Clark & Desautel would have to come upon their own expense, I thought certainly from that, you would understand that no engagement had been made with them. I also thought I had fully explained myself as regards charging of passages, when at Ft Union I told both Culbertson & Denig, that the charge would be made, and if they did not want the individuals charged, I would charge Oft '49. Mr Denig gave me to understand that he had [word?] it to the individuals and that all was right. I therefore again say that if these amts are refunded it will be done at expense of Oft 1849.

As to [steamboat] Captn Stillman he was of no service with boat and all he done, any gentleman would have done, who was found as he was with [word?] & Cigars, I thought Mr Sarpy took Mr Denad as security for the [word?] he got as well for his expenses, this debt ought to be paid. I have myself urged the matter about cutting wood for the Steamer above, as also about the conduct of the hunters & men about skins &c and thought that your influence united with mine might effect our object, however Mr Denigs self sufficiency and independence are such that he will pursue his own course without standing instructions to the contrary. Jno B Lafene is trading for Mr P[eter] A Sarpy with the Poncas and I am truly glad he did not come here his conduct among the Indians last winter was of serious injury to us. Ronville is rehired and is of course good for the advances you made him.

Mr Wilcocks arrived here on the 22d ulto from St Peters having left this place on the 6th Oct. Mr M brought down a band of horses he was unfortunately robbed of 10 of them by a war party of Crows previous to his arrival at Ft Union. Mr Denig will in all probability be able to get them back as the village where the Indians belonged is encamped near Ft Union, he brought 20 head to this place which has been of great service to us. Mr Culbertson anticipated sending us another band in the spring which will supply on their way Fts Berthold & Clark, thereby saving the post the trouble and the Oft the expense and risk in taking them from here.

The prospects at Ft Benton when the Express left could not be stated, as the Indians were yet far off, but as they will all winter in the vicinity of the Fort is to be expected that an average trade will be made.

Denig writes that his prospects are favorable he has 50 pks seasonal Robes traded from the Crees.

But little has been done at Ft Berthold only 10 pks on hand. Mr Dawson has done well at the Rees, he has sent us down 300 Bushel of corn, and will be able to give us our principal supply for Oft 1851, to come down on Steamer, he has also on hand 105 packs Robes

For ourselves we have pretty good prospects, at most of our posts Buffalo are plenty, we have now traded rising 600 packs and from all appearances, altho our Oft is large, I think we shall need it all

In the requisitions which are forwarded herewith I have reduced the quantity of Clark and substituted *in value* the Blue D Drilling under the expectation that you have been able to procure the article agreeable to our instructions, we calculate that each peace will contain 40 yards should they not contain so many, you will please increase the number of pieces accordingly in addition to what is in the requisition herewith, about 40 pr will be required for ft Jno & Vermillion. We have ordered lightly of the Cornelian Pigeon Egg Beads, as [it] is a nice article we are of the opinion it will take, altho you say "if we order any we must be certain they will sell["], this we certainly cannot vouch for at present, of other kind of Beads we want only such as are asked for in the requisitions, part of the Blue Beads sent us this year as well as some of the Oft '49 are not the article wanted, they are not the right color or size, we therefore request you send us only such as we send you sample herewith.

You will notice that the greater part of of the Guns received are "Chase" NW Fusils, the Belgian Guns sent heretofore will [do] very well if it was not for the Lock, and we must beg of you, to try and have them with better Locks, or we do not want them at all, the fault lies in the Frisen, it will make fire for a day or two only when the Indian is sure to bring it back to us, when our Blacksmith must either line the Frisen with steel, or we must give them another Gun, which he will again return, we think you can have this altered by representing to the manufacture that if not done we shall not want any more Belgian Guns.[16] The Powder Horns we want of good shape and for the right side, there is only one horn on [an] animal, that is fit to make a powder horn, but we get horns made of both, consequently one half at least remains on hand, we want good shaped ones and for the right side only, or none at all.

You could please have "Caybee" to manufacture the Squaw axes as I think he is the only one that will make the right article.

We wrote you on examination of the Tobacco sent us this year that we had no complaint to make except that it was mouldy, at that time we had only examined 4 packages, since we have opened a number both of the Bales & Boxes and find that it primarily is of a quantity inferior to that we looked at at first, we know that you have been greatly imposed upon, as the most of it is of very inferior quality and not the article we first looked at.

Mr M will shew you upon it

You perhaps will be surprised that we should order stone Coal but on calulation we find that it will be cheaper to bring this on the Steamer, than to make charcoal here, would [i.e., wood] is very scarce and besides saving the wood for our fires the men could be more profitably occupied.[17]

The shingles we could have made here but was in time to secure Oft from the weather.

The Corn mules [mills] usually sent here do not last a season and have been told that a superior article is manufactured at "Vide Poche" [St. Louis] by Chouteau or [two words?] our information he could try and get what we have wanted from there.

I have written to Mr Larpenter and requested him to send his requisition by this Express and let you know his trade prospects [at the post on Vermillion River]. Maj Drips as he is now to operate from Kanzas, will no doubt send you in time he has been well supplied with Groceries & Corn from here and is instructed to send here for more if he wants it

Mr Wilcox goes down with the Express he will return pr Steamer and I think is a competent person to take charge of the men in the Boat, you will notice by his a/c that his time does not expire untill 4th May, you will please pay him the whole of his wages, he will make up the time he is absent on his own business in his next years engagement, arrangements will be made with him when he comes up by Mr C for the Bfoot Post

I wish on receipt of this you would hire two Old very good [men] and send them to me, with 4 or 5 Horses to cost from 40 to 35 Ea. I want to hear from [you] particularly with regard to the accounts from California, if still [a] good many of our men wish to go there, I would prefer paying them off in Old Horses Carts Saddles &c than to pay them cash in St Louis in case they go I shall need more men to take down the returns, and I will advise you thereof upon the spring of the river, at the same time I can advise you what number of horses I shall require to pay for the Robes I shall have accrued in advance from Inventory.

I am satisfied that I have plenty of capable men to take charge of the returns, I have therefore decided not to insure untill they are reship[p]ed pr Steamer, your instructions to be observed on their arrival near St J will inquire to the person in charge. In case Mr McDonald in consequence of his misfortune be unable to attend to the shipment, I think Mr Beauvais would be a competent person, he has his family living in St J, he is now with Maj Drips but I expect him here early in the spring and will send him in charge of the first Brigade of Boats. Should however contrary to my expectations he not come here in time we can easily fix upon some other competent person

Mr Kipp was detained here untill late in November in consequence of the illness of his nephew M Desautel who died on the 15th ulto. Mr Desautel made a will by which he bequeaths a part of his money to his aunt Mrs Kipp the balance is to be paid at certain periods to his children. With respect to engaging Mr Culbertson for my post I could never see why he was ever engaged, I have never heard that he rendered the least service to the Company, therefore if he comes up he ought to come as passenger. Mr Culbertson is the agent for the Upper Country, he may want him, for my post I have no use for him. In looking over the requisition from Ft Alexander, I think the order for "Hudson Bay" Blankets too heavy, I think that 50 yds of each kind will be enough, and in case you have no "Hudsons Bay" and send them in the place do not send more than 50 pcs of each. I think also that 100 short Fusils will be enough.

The mechanics asked for in Ft Union requisition are ordered because none has been ordered at Ft Benton & Ft Alexander

As regards the transportation of Oft 1851 I hope that you will charter a good fast Boat, and even buy one, and that you will have *one* Pilot on board that Knows the River [Text ends abruptly.]

NOTES

Introduction

1. The location is important even apart from the fur trade. In 1743, on a bluff above the river, explorers led by the Chevalier de la Vérendrye—while guests of a nearby Arikara village—buried a lead tablet bearing the arms and inscription of the king of France to mark a key point in their travels. Herbert S. Schell, *History of South Dakota*, 4th ed., rev. John E. Miller (Pierre: South Dakota Historical Society Press, 2004), pp. 26–30; Charles E. DeLand, "The Vérendrye Explorations and Discoveries Leading to the Planting of the Fort Pierre Tablet," *South Dakota Historical Collections* 7 (1914): 99–322.

2. The Bad River originally appeared on maps as the Little Missouri and was still labeled as such on a map drawn by Indian guide Michael DeSomet in 1855 for a survey expedition led by Lieutenant G. K. Warren. Lewis and Clark renamed the stream the Teton River for the western Sioux or Lakota people, also called Tetons, who frequented the area, and it went by that name during the time covered in these letter books. The present name, Bad River, is a translation of the Lakota name, *Wakpa Sica*, given as a consequence of a flood in which many Sioux were drowned in about 1728, as calculated from a winter count. Rex C. Myers, "Exploration and the Fur Trade," in *A New South Dakota History* (Sioux Falls, S.Dak.: Center for Western Studies, Augustana College, 2005), p. 65; Gary E. Moulton, ed., *The Journals of the Lewis and Clark Expedition*, 13 vols. (Lincoln: University of Nebraska Press, 1983–2001), 3:109; Virginia Driving Hawk Sneve, ed., *South Dakota Geographic Names* (Sioux Falls, S.Dak.: Brevet Press, 1973), p. 139.

3. William Clark described this council and its proceedings in Volume 3 of *Journals of Lewis and Clark*, pp. 107–14. James P. Ronda, *Lewis and Clark among the Indians* (Lincoln: University of Nebraska Press, 1984), pp. 28–41, offers an account of this meeting and its consequences. Black Buffalo is usually called Black Bull today.

4. R. Peter Winham and Edward J. Lueck, "Cultures of the Middle Missouri," in *Plains Indians, A.D. 500–1500: The Archaeological Past of Historic Groups*, ed. Karl H. Schlesier (Norman: University of Oklahoma Press, 1994), p. 169; W. Raymond Wood, "Plains Trade in Prehistoric and Protohistoric Intertribal Relations," in *Anthropology on the Great Plains*, ed. Wood and Margot Liberty (Lincoln: University of Nebraska Press, 1980), pp. 98–109; William R. Nester, *The Arikara War: The First Plains Indian War, 1823* (Missoula, Mont.: Mountain Press, 2001), pp. 6–7.

5. For more on the Missouri River trade before Lewis and Clark, *see* A. P. Nasatir, *Before Lewis and Clark: Documents Illustrating the History of the Missouri, 1785–1804*, 2 vols. (Saint Louis: Saint Louis Historical Documents Foundation, 1952), and W. Raymond Wood, *Prologue to Lewis and Clark: The Mackay and Evans Expedition* (Norman: University of Oklahoma Press, 2003).

6. The life and accomplishments of Manuel Lisa are chronicled in Richard Edward Oglesby, *Manual Lisa and the Opening of the Missouri Fur Trade* (Norman: University of Oklahoma Press, 1963). For an account of life at Fort Manuel, *see* John C. Luttig, *Journal of a Fur-Trading Expedition up the Missouri River* (New York: Argosy-Antiquarian, 1964). G. Hubert Smith excavated the post for the Smithsonian Institution in 1965 and 1966. *See* Smith and John Ludwickson, *Fort Manuel: The Archeology of an Upper Missouri Trading Post of 1812–1813*, South Dakota Archaeological Assoc., Special Publication, No. 7 (Vermillion, 1981).

7. Frederick T. Wilson, "Old Fort Pierre and its Neighbors," *South Dakota Historical Collections* 1 (1902): 257–311; Mallery, "Pictographs of the North American Indians: A Preliminary Paper," in U.S., Bureau of Ethnology, *Fourth Annual Report to the Secretary of the Smithsonian Institution, 1882–1883* (Washington, D.C.: Government Printing Office, 1886), p. 109.

8. Michael M. Casler and W. Raymond Wood are preparing a history of the Columbia Fur Company, "The Rise and Fall of the Columbia Fur Company: Rethinking the Fur Trade on the Northern Great Plains."

9. Hiram M. Chittenden, *The American Fur Trade of the Far West*, 2 vols. (Lincoln: University of Nebraska Press, 1986), 1:167, 1:325–29; John E. Sunder, *The Fur Trade on the Upper Missouri, 1840–1865* (Norman: University of Oklahoma Press, 1965), p. 5.

10. Maximilian, Prince of Wied, *The North American Journals of Prince Maximilian of Wied*, 3 vols., ed. Stephen S. Witte and Marsha V. Gallagher, (Norman: University of Oklahoma Press, 2010), 2:155–56, fig. 9.3; Audubon, *Audubon and His Journals*, 2 vols., ed. Maria R. Audubon (New York: Dover Publications, 1960), 1:525–28; Edward Harris, *Up the Missouri with Audubon: The Journal of Edward Harris* (Norman: University of Oklahoma Press, 1951), p. 83. The painter George Catlin also visited the new fort in 1832. He described six hundred Indian lodges pitched nearby, and he painted Fort Pierre and the prairie around it bristling with tipis. George Catlin, *Letters and Notes on the North American Indians*, 2 vols. in one. (North Dighton, Mass.: JG Press, 1995), 1:233–98.

11. Galpin, quoted in G. Hubert Smith, *Fort Pierre II (39ST217): A Historic Trading Post in the Oahe Dam Area, South Dakota*, Smithsonian Institution, Bureau of American Ethnology, Bulletin no. 176 (Washington: Government Printing Office, 1960), pp. 92–93. Smith, an archaeologist, excavated Fort Pierre II in June and July 1956.

12. Smith, *Fort Pierre II*, p. 87.

13. Ibid., p. 108.

14. DeLand, "Editorial Notes on 'Old Fort Pierre and its Neighbors,'" *South Dakota Historical Collections* 1 (1902): 365–66, map.

15. Ibid., p. 378, map opposite p. 281; Smith, *Fort Pierre II*, p. 96.

16. Harold H. Schuler, *A Bridge Apart: History of Early Pierre and Fort Pierre* (Pierre, S.Dak.: By the Author, 1987), pp. 72–75.

17. Smith, *Fort Pierre II*, p. 90.

Chapter 1. Fort Tecumseh Journal

1. The Cheyenne Indians were major clients of the Bad River posts at this time. Both the Sheyenne River in North Dakota and the Cheyenne River in South Dakota are named for them. They were noted as long-distance traders and middlemen between the Missouri River tribes and more remote peoples. David J. Wishart, *Great Plains Indians* (Lincoln: University of Nebraska Press, 2016), p. 52; Joseph Jablow, *The Cheyenne in Plains Indian Trade Relations 1795–1840* (Lincoln: University of Nebraska Press, 1994), pp. 58–60.

2. The writer does not identify himself, but it is Jacob Halsey, a clerk and trader of the Upper Missouri Outfit. Historian Hiram M. Chittenden labeled him "a valuable man but given to hard drink, which eventually ruined his constitution" (*The American Fur Trade of the Far West*, 2 vols. [Lincoln: University of Nebraska Press, 1986], 1:391).

3. Most large posts of the American Fur Company on the Missouri River had "Navy Yards," where mackinaws and *bateaux* were built for river transportation. The Fort Tecumseh Navy Yard was fifteen miles upstream at the mouth of Chantier Creek. Harold H. Schuler, *Fort Pierre Chouteau* (Vermillion: University of South Dakota Press, 1990), pp. 32–33; Doane Robinson, Notes to "Fort Tecumseh and Fort Pierre Journal and Letter Books," ed. Charles E. DeLand, *South Dakota Historical Collections* 9 (1918): 95n10.

4. "Papin's house" is P. D. Papin and Company's nearby Fort Teton. It was built in about 1828 immediately south of the mouth of the Bad River and some two miles south of Fort Tecumseh. Charles E. DeLand, "Editorial Notes on 'Old Fort Pierre and its Neighbors,'" *South Dakota Historical Collections* 1 (1902): 374.

5. The Yankton Indians, one of the major divisions of the Sioux Indians, were major clients of the Bad River posts at this time. Herbert S. Schell, *History of South Dakota*, 4th ed., rev. John E. Miller (Pierre: South Dakota Historical Society Press, 2004), pp. 19–22. The Yankton, along with the Yanktonai and Assiniboine, make up the middle Sioux tribes, according to Herbert T. Hoover, "Native Peoples," in *A New South Dakota History*, ed. Harry F. Thompson (Sioux Falls, S.Dak.: Center for Western Studies, Augustana College, 2005), p. 44.

6. The Little Cheyenne enters the Missouri River from the east a few miles above the mouth of the Cheyenne River, in what is now western Potter County, South Dakota. Schuler, *Fort Pierre Chouteau*, p. 44.

7. The location is near the junction of the Cheyenne and Belle Fourche rivers in today's Meade County, South Dakota. Ibid.

8. Council Bluffs is not the community in present-day Iowa but a locale on the opposite (west) bank of the Missouri River in what is now Nebraska, some twenty-nine air miles north of the mouth of the Platte River where many trading posts were built. It gained its name from the fact that Lewis and Clark counseled with the Otoe and Missouri Indians at this locality on August 2, 1804. Gary E. Moulton, ed., *The Journals of the Lewis and Clark Expedition*, 13 vols.

(Lincoln: University of Nebraska Press, 1983–2001), 2:435–38; Chittenden, *American Fur Trade*, 2:924.

9. Hollowwood may have been on the Bad River, fifty to sixty miles southwest of Fort Pierre, according to Schuler, *Fort Pierre Chouteau*, p. 44. Robinson in 1918 cites two informants, one of whom identified Hollowwood as being a camping place on Medicine Creek, almost directly south of Fort Pierre, and the other who said it was much farther away but could give no precise information. Robinson, Notes to "Fort Tecumseh," p. 97n22. Gail DeBuse Potter lists it in 2007 as an Oglala post on the Bad River, southwest of Fort Pierre near the vanished town of Van Metre, South Dakota. Potter, "Trading Posts of the Central Plains," *Museum of the Fur Trade Quarterly* 43 (Fall/Winter 2007): 81.

10. James Noble was a clerk. L. Cerre may have been Michael Sylvester Cerre, nicknamed "Lami," who was a cousin of the Saint Louis Chouteaus. Annie Heloise Abel, ed., *Chardon's Journal at Fort Clark, 1834–1839*, by F. A. Chardon (Pierre: South Dakota Department of History, 1932), p. 209n45; Robinson, Notes to "Fort Tecumseh," p. 97n23.

11. Apple River, today's Apple Creek in Bismarck, North Dakota, enters the Missouri from the east. There was a small post here for the upper Yanktonai trade. Robinson, Notes to "Fort Tecumseh," p. 96n18.

12. Duke Friedrich Paul Wilhelm von Württemberg (1797–1860) was on his second expedition to America, which took him as far as Fort Union in present-day North Dakota. After returning to Germany from his first trip, he was accompanied by Jean Baptiste ("Pomp") Charbonneau, who spent time with the prince at his castle until coming back to America with the second expedition. Hans von Sachsen Altenberg and Robert L. Dyer, *Duke Paul of Württemberg on the Missouri Frontier: 1823, 1830, and 1851* (Boonville, Mo.: Pekitanoui Publications, 1998), pp. 27, 32–33; Marion Tinling, *Sacagawea's Son: The Life of Jean Baptiste Charbonneau* (Missoula, Mont.: Mountain Press Publishing, 2001), pp. 31–37; Louis C. Butscher, "A Brief Biography of Prince Paul Wilhelm of Württemberg (1797–1860)," *New Mexico Historical Review* 17 (July 1942): 181–225; John Francis McDermott, "The Reconstruction of a 'Lost' Archive: The Diaries and Sketches of Prince Paul Wilhelm of Württemberg," *Manuscripts* 30 (1978): 167–78.

13. *Cabri* was French *patois* for the pronghorn, or antelope. Cabri Creek is today's Antelope Creek, entering the Missouri from the west a few miles downstream from the cities of Pierre and modern-day Fort Pierre.

14. This post was at the mouth of the James River, near the present-day city of Yankton in Yankton County, South Dakota. Potter, "Trading Posts of the Central Plains," p. 77.

15. The Mandan Indians were then living in two earth-lodge villages near the mouth of the Knife River, in what is now Mercer County, North Dakota.

16. The text refers to the Niobrara River in northeastern Nebraska, also known as the Running Water River to early French traders. "Niobrara" comes from its Omaha-Ponca name *Ni obthatha ke*, meaning "Spreading water river." J. T. Link, *The Origin of the Place Names of Nebraska*, Nebraska Geological Survey, Second Series, Bulletin no. 7 ([Lincoln], 1933), pp. 78–79.

17. Frederick Laboue was a clerk trader who spent most of his time trading with the Sioux. During the winter of 1831–1832, when he was at a post on the Cherry River, Laboue got into an argument with F. Quenel, who was subsequently killed in a fight. Laboue then put the corpse up against a tree and shot it several times. Colin Campbell placed him in irons and sent him to Saint Louis to stand trial for murder. He was acquitted and would return to the upper Missouri in April 1832. Charles E. Hanson, Jr., "Frederick Laboue and His River," *Museum of the Fur Trade Quarterly* 27 (Spring/Summer 1991): 1–7.

18. There were two Dr. Lanes in Saint Louis at this time, Dr. William Carr Lane and his cousin, Dr. Hardage Lane. William Lane was the first mayor of Saint Louis and was elected to that office nine times. Halsey is probably referring to Hardage Lane, who practiced medicine in Saint Louis for more than twenty-five years and was a successful physician. J. Thomas Scharf, *History of Saint Louis City and County: From the Earliest Periods to the Present Day*, 2 vols. (Philadelphia: Louis H. Everts, 1883), 2:1521–22.

19. The Columbia Fur Company built Fort Lookout in about 1822 on the west side of the Missouri, ten or twelve miles above present-day Chamberlain, South Dakota. DeLand, "Notes on 'Old Fort Pierre,'" p. 43; John E. Sunder, *The Fur Trade on the Upper Missouri, 1840–1865* (Norman: University of Oklahoma Press, 1965), p. 38; Chittenden, *American Fur Trade*, 2:928.

20. The Ponca Indians were then living near the mouth

20. ...of the Niobrara River. James H. Howard, *The Ponca Tribe* (Lincoln: University of Nebraska Press, 1995), p. 2.
21. The Heart River enters the Missouri near the city of Mandan in Morton County, North Dakota.
22. The journal's description of the Mandans as people of light complexion, some with blue eyes and light hair, adds historical context to what Bernard DeVoto calls "the Welsh Indian myth," or the idea that somewhere in North America was an Indian tribe descended from a lost Welsh colony. Bernard DeVoto, *The Course of Empire* (Boston: Houghton Mifflin Co., 1952), pp. 68–73, 77–79. For a thorough exploration of this myth, *see* James D. McLaird, "The Welsh, the Vikings, and the Lost Tribes of Israel on the Northern Plains: The Legend of the White Mandan," *South Dakota History* 18 (Winter 1988): 245–73.
23. Syphilis was a serious problem among fur traders and Indians alike on the upper Missouri.
24. Halsey is writing in 1830. Seven years later, another devastating smallpox epidemic would diminish the remaining Mandans from sixteen hundred people to one hundred sixty-one individuals. Waldman, *Atlas of the North American Indian*, pp. 206–7.
25. The Assiniboine Indians lived to the northwest of the Mandan villages at this time. David Miller et al., *The History of the Assiniboine and Sioux Tribes of the Fort Peck Indian Reservation, 1600–2012* (Poplar, Mont.: Fort Peck Community College, 2012), pp. 14–65.
26. Both names allude to the Hidatsa Indians, who lived above the Mandans in villages around the mouth of the Knife River. Stanley A. Ahler, Thomas D. Thiessen, Michael K. Trimble, *People of the Willows: The Prehistory and Early History of the Hidatsa Indians* (Grand Forks: University of North Dakota Press, 1991), pp. 12–13.
27. William Dickson was the Métis son of Robert Dickson and a Sioux mother. The elder Dickson had been a Hudson's Bay Company trader at Lake Traverse and a former partner in the Columbia Fur Company. The son's post at the Vermillion and James rivers was built for the Sioux trade. Robinson, Notes to "Fort Tecumseh," p. 100n32; Grace Lee Nute, "Hudson's Bay Company Posts in the Minnesota Country," *Minnesota History* 22 (Sept. 1941): 282; William R. Swagerty, "A View from the Bottom Up," *Montana, The Magazine of Western History* 43 (Winter 1993): 28; David Lavender, *The Fist in the Wilderness* (New York: Doubleday & Co., 1964), p. 389; Abel, *Chardon's Journal*, p. 228n83.
28. The Arikara (Sahnish) villages were just above the mouth of the Grand River, but they deserted them in 1823 after being attacked by Colonel Henry Leavenworth following their own attack on a fur-trading expedition. *See* William R. Nester, *The Arikara War: The First Plains Indian War, 1823* (Missoula, Mont.: Mountain Press, 2001), p. 23.
29. Doane Robinson suggested that "Sanchannas" is a corruption of "Yanktonnas," a variation of Yanktonai. He noted that the passage refers to trader Daniel Lamont's establishment on Apple River in recognized Yanktonai territory. This group's name for themselves has been variously interpreted to mean "little dwellers at the end" or "little Yanktons" or "end village." Robinson, Notes to "Fort Tecumseh," p. 108n42. Herbert T. Hoover, "Native Peoples," in *A New South Dakota History*, ed. Harry F. Thompson (Sioux Falls, S.Dak.: Center for Western Studies, Augustana College, 2005), p. 45.
30. Each post had large fur presses to press furs into bales for shipment down river; there were ten buffalo robes per pack; eighty to one hundred beaver furs; or sixty otter pelts. Swagerty, Introduction to *Chardon's Journal at Fort Clark, 1834–1839*, by F. A. Chardon (Lincoln: University of Nebraska Press, 1997), pp. xxiii–xxiv.
31. The traders used drift wood as fire wood.
32. This phrase is another way of rendering the French name for the Niobrara River.
33. The text probably refers to today's Medicine Knoll, a prominent glacial moraine near the town of Blunt, South Dakota. Cartographer Joseph Nicollet calculated its distance from the Missouri River crossing near Fort Pierre at eighteen miles and, during his 1839 journey, recorded both its Dakota name, *Paha Wakan*, and the French translation, *Butte de Medicine*. Joseph Nicollet, *Joseph Nicollet on the Plains and Prairies: The Expeditions of 1838–39 with Journals, Letters, and Notes on the Dakota Indians*, ed. Edmund C. Gray and Martha Coleman Bray (Saint Paul: Minnesota Historical Society, 1993), pp. 172–73, map.
34. Ree is another name for the Arikara Indians. The Arikaras spoke a dialect of Northern Caddoan that their relatives, the Pawnee of eastern Nebraska, could understand. *See* the journal entry for June 21, 1830, and a letter from Fort Tecumseh dated December 30, 1830, for more evidence of the close ties between the Pawnees and Arikaras. Douglas R. Parks, "Caddoan Languages," in *Handbook of North American*

Indians, Vol. 13, part 1: *Plains*, ed. Raymond J. DeMallie (Washington, D.C.: Smithsonian Institution, 2001), pp. 80-81.

35. Cordage, or oakum, was a fiber, loosely twisted into a rope-like material and impregnated with tar, used to caulk the planks in the hulls of mackinaws and keelboats.

36. Thomas L. Sarpy was a well-known trader on the upper Missouri River. Later, Halsey reports his death when a barrel of gunpowder exploded in January 1832 at the Oglala post at the confluence of Rapid Creek and the Cheyenne River. Archaeologists' efforts to locate the ruins of the Oglala Post have to date been fruitless.

37. Emillian Primeau, brother of Charles, would later be killed at the Apple River post in present North Dakota in 1836. Robinson, Notes to "Fort Tecumseh," p. 115n59.

38. In the early nineteenth century, the northern groups of the western Sioux, or Lakota, Indians were sometimes known as Saones (Sawons), but by the mid-nineteenth century, that group had broken into four separate groups, the Blackfeet, Hunkpapas, Sans Arcs, and Two Kettles. The Minneconjous were sometimes considered a Saone band, as well. Raymond J. DeMallie, "Sioux until 1850," in *Handbook of North American Indians*, Vol. 13, part 2: *Plains*, ed. DeMallie (Washington, D.C.: Smithsonian Institution, 2001), p. 757; Herbert T. Hoover, "Native Peoples," in *A New South Dakota History*, ed. Harry F. Thompson (Sioux Falls, S.Dak.: Center for Western Studies, Augustana College, 2005), p. 44.

39. Hugh Glass, one of the legendary mountain men, had been grievously wounded by a grizzly bear in 1823 and left for dead. He crawled across what is now South Dakota to the safety of Fort Kiowa on the Missouri River to recover from his wounds. Most of the facts of his life are unknown, and books written about him are mostly based on speculation and conjecture. This reference is one of only four made to him during his time on the upper Missouri, and it records the longest period of time he was in one place, four days. In 1823, Glass was at Tilton's Post at the Mandan villages in search of Jim Bridger and John S. Fitzgerald, the men who abandoned him in South Dakota. In a letter written by Kenneth McKenzie, Glass is mentioned at Fort Floyd at the mouth of the White Earth River in the fall of 1828, requesting supplies. He was employed as a hunter at Fort Union, and the entry here shows he was sent down for horses. Prince Maximilian states that James A. Hamilton (Palmer) wrote a biography of Hugh Glass based on interviews with him while he was a hunter at Fort Union, but the biography has never been located. Hugh Glass, Colin Rose, and Hilain Menard were killed by the Arikaras shortly after leaving Fort Cass in the winter of 1832-1833. Chittenden, *American Fur Trade*, 1:330; Aubrey L. Haines, "Hugh Glass," in *The Mountain Men and the Fur Trade of the Far West*, 10 vols., ed. LeRoy R. Hafen (Glendale, Calif.: Arthur H. Clark, 1965-1972), 6:161-71; Willis Blenkinsop, "Edward Rose," ibid., 9:344-45; Robinson, Notes to "Fort Tecumseh," p. 119n70; Maximilian, Prince of Wied, *The North American Journals of Maximilian, Prince of Wied*, 3 vols., ed. Stephen S. Witte and Marsha V. Gallagher (Norman: University of Oklahoma Press, 2008-2012), 2:115, 115nM55, 127-28, 235. The only surviving letter written by Hugh Glass is in the State Archives Collection of the South Dakota State Historical Society, Pierre. James D. McLaird, *Hugh Glass: Grizzly Survivor*, South Dakota Biography Series, no. 5 (Pierre: South Dakota Historical Society Press, 2016), addresses the Hugh Glass legend in its historical context.

40. Glass and the Fort Union men had been dispatched to Fort Tecumseh to secure horses and equipment for mountain expeditions that Kenneth McKenzie was planning. McKenzie to the Gentleman in Charge of Fort Tecumseh for the American Fur Company, May 5, 1830, Chouteau Family Papers, Saint Louis, Mo. For a history of Fort Union, built in 1828, see Barton H. Barbour, *Fort Union and the Upper Missouri Fur Trade* (Norman: University of Oklahoma Press, 2001), and Erwin N. Thompson, *Fort Union Trading Post: Fur Trade Empire on the Upper Missouri* (Medora, N. Dak.: Theodore Roosevelt Nature & History Assoc., 1986). Today, the National Park Service maintains a replica of the post, built on its original site, as Fort Union Trading Post National Historic Site.

41. Joseph Garreau adopted Pierre, whose mother was an Arikara woman, after her Arikara husband's death. All of Joseph's family was involved in the fur trade on the upper Missouri. W. Raymond Wood, "A Permanent Presence: The Family of Joseph Garreau and the Upper Missouri River Fur Trade," *South Dakota History* 43 (Summer 2013): 91-117.

42. There are two Medicine Rivers (or Creeks) in the vicinity of Forts Tecumseh and Pierre. "Little" Medicine Creek flows into the Missouri from the

north about fourteen miles east of the city of Pierre; the other enters the Missouri from the south, about thirty-eight air miles southeast of the city, just above the Grand Detour.

43. The Big Bend is an alternative term for the Grand Detour and is still used today to refer to that area of the Missouri River in central South Dakota, roughly halfway between Chamberlain and Pierre. One of the best-known landmarks on the Missouri, it is a meander of the Missouri River that makes a loop of about thirty miles, separated at its narrowest point by a neck of land only twenty-two hundred feet across. R. F. Diffendal, Jr., *Great Plains Geology* (Lincoln: University of Nebraska Press, 2017), pp. 87–88; William E. Lass, *Navigating the Missouri: Steamboating on Nature's Highway, 1819-1935* (Norman, Okla.: Arthur H. Clark Co., 2008), p. 21.

44. Colin Campbell was a clerk and interpreter at various posts around Fort Pierre. At one point, he had a small post on the Elm River, north of present-day Aberdeen, South Dakota. Abel, *Chardon's Journal*, p. 227n81; Donald Jackson, *Voyages of the Steamboat Yellow Stone* (New York: Ticknor & Fields, 1985), p. 168; Schuler, *Fort Pierre Chouteau*, p. 43.

45. Cabanné's establishment or trading post was on the Missouri River twenty-three air miles above the mouth of the Platte River. For its history, *see* Richard E. Jensen, *The Fontenelle and Cabanné Trading Posts: The History and Archeology of Two Missouri River Sites, 1822-1838* (Lincoln: Nebraska State Historical Society, 1998), pp. 10–16.

46. "Belview," more commonly Bellevue, was a trading post on the west bank of the Missouri River nine miles above the mouth of the Platte River. Joshua Pilcher began trading on the site in about 1822, and it remained an important post for many years. Ibid.

47. Long after the Lewis and Clark Expedition, William Clark served as superintendent of Indian Affairs in Saint Louis from 1822 until his death in 1838. Jay H. Buckley, *William Clark: Indian Diplomat* (Norman: University of Oklahoma Press, 2008), p. xiv.

48. Also referred to as the Mahaws, these are the Omaha Indians, then living in what is now northeastern Nebraska and adjacent lands in Iowa. Mark J. Awakuni-Swetland, "Omahas," in *Encyclopedia of the Great Plains*, ed. David J. Wishart (Lincoln: University of Nebraska Press, 2004), pp. 586–87.

49. Fur companies would hire Indian warriors to police the forts during trade to maintain order. They were also employed to try to recover stolen horses and prevent looting of the post gardens. *See*, for example, William Laidlaw's letter of February 15, 1832, to David D. Mitchell (Fort Tecumseh letter book), in which the traders are grateful that a soldier society of the Oglalas kept order after an explosion of gunpowder destroyed a trading post near the Black Hills.

50. The Blackfeet here are not the Blackfeet Indian tribe of Montana but the Sihasapa, or Blackfeet division of the Lakotas, of which the Brulés mentioned here are another division. There are seven subtribes or divisions of the Lakotas: Oglala, Brulé, Two Kettle, Sans Arc, Blackfeet, Hunkpapa, and Minneconjou. Sihasapa translates as "black moccasin people." Schell, *History of South Dakota*, p. 19; Hoover, "Native Peoples," p. 46.

51. 1st Lt. Jonathan L. Bean of the United States Army was the Indian agent; his honorific title was "Major." Robinson, Notes to "Fort Tecumseh," p. 135n103.

52. James Archdale Hamilton Palmer (?–1840) is one of the more mysterious figures of the upper Missouri fur trade. He was of English descent and left England under mysterious circumstances. This notation is the first reference to him in any of the upper Missouri letter books, coming three years before he is noticed working at Fort Union for Kenneth McKenzie. Thompson, *Fort Union*, pp. 20–21; Ray H. Mattison, "James A. Hamilton (Palmer)," in *Mountain Men and the Fur Trade*, 3:163–66.

53. Ponca Creek begins in what is now southern South Dakota and then flows through part of Nebraska to enter the Missouri River a few miles above the Niobrara River in Holt County.

54. The Hunkpapas (Honcpapas) are another division of the Lakotas, or western Sioux. Their name translates variously as "Campers at the horn," "those who camp at the horn entrance," "end of the camp circle," or "end village people" (Hoover, "Native Peoples," p. 46).

55. Fort Clark, built about halfway between Fort Pierre and Fort Union, was erected by James Kipp in 1831 below the mouth of the Knife River, adjoining the Mandan village of Mih-tutta-hang-kusch in what is today Mercer County, North Dakota, where its ruins are preserved in Fort Clark State Historic Site. W. Raymond Wood, William J. Hunt, and Randy H. Williams, *Fort Clark and its Indian Neighbors: A Trading Post on the Upper Missouri River* (Norman: University of Oklahoma Press, 2011), p. 76.

56. Loisel spoke of the James River as the river *Bois Blanc*, or White Wood, as early as 1804 in discussing the narrow portage that separates it from the Sheyenne in what is now North Dakota. *See*

A. P. Nasatir, *Before Lewis and Clark: Documents Illustrating the History of the Missouri, 1785–1804*, 2 vols. (Saint Louis: Saint Louis Historical Documents Foundation, 1952), 2:737; Annie Heloise Abel, "Trudeau's Description of the Upper Missouri," *Mississippi Valley Historical Review* 8 (June 1921): p. 161n46.

57. Animal fats were an item in the trade sent downriver to Saint Louis and used in making soap and candles.

58. Straw Cabin Creek is possibly the Little Blue River, a small stream entering the Missouri in Jackson County of western Missouri. William Clark's journal entry of June 24, 1804, mentions passing a stream named "Hay Cabbin Creek from the camps of Straw built on it" (quoted in Moulton, *Journals of Lewis and Clark*, p. 2:319). The expedition's Joseph Whitehouse calls the creek "Straw Hill River" (ibid., 11:29); John Ordway calls it "the Creek of the Hay Cabbins" (ibid., 9:16); and Patrick Gass calls it "Depie," perhaps from the French *de paille*, "of straw" (ibid, 10:16, 16n1). As late as 1839, cartographer Joseph Nicollet still records the name of the stream as Hay Cabin Creek, but he also uses the name by which it is known today, Little Blue River. Joseph N. Nicollet, "Joseph N. Nicollet's 1839 Manuscript Maps of the Missouri River and Upper Mississippi Basin," comp. W. Raymond Wood, Illinois State Museum Scientific Papers, Vol. 24 (Springfield, 1993), pl. 13.

59. Kenneth McKenzie sent William Henry Vanderburgh in the spring of 1829 to fulfill the promise to Hugh Glass to supply the trappers at the rendezvous in the mountains. In the summer of 1830, Vanderburgh and his party fought the battle with the Blackfeet, but there is little information about his movements or who accompanied him to the mountains. Chittenden, *American Fur Trade*, 1:330.

60. The Bijou Hills are a group of buttes lining the Missouri River in South Dakota, about thirty miles above the Fort Randall Dam near the Nebraska border. John Paul Gries, *Roadside Geology of South Dakota* (Missoula, Mont.: Mountain Press Publishing Co., 1996), p. 118.

61. Saint Louis families of French descent, such as the Chouteaus, remained keenly interested in the politics of France, as this passage suggests. The insurrection brought Louis-Philippe, the Duke of Orleans, to the throne of France. On July 26, Charles X published ordinances that many thought contrary to the spirit of the Charter of 1814, the constitution that King Louis XVIII had put in place. Demonstrations followed, and Charles abdicated. David Pinkney, *The French Revolution of 1830* (Princeton: Princeton University Press, 1972), pp. 73–108.

62. Given the short time it took to make a round trip from Fort Tecumseh, the island in question is most likely Cedar Island a few miles upstream from the Grand Detour, thirty-five river miles below the Teton River. Regis Loisel and Hugh Heney built a trading post on the island in 1801; it was abandoned in 1804. Manuel Lisa's Missouri Fur Company occupied the buildings in 1809, rebuilt after a fire the next year, and continued operating there until 1813. Trader Joseph Brazeau may have occupied the post from 1819 to 1821. Potter, "Trading Posts of the Central Plains," pp. 75–76.

63. In his journal entries of June 5 and June 7, 1833, Maximilian reports passing an island with an earthen village, "île au Village de terre," a short way north of Fort Pierre on the same day his party left the fort to journey on to Fort Union. This locality is not identifiable today. Maximilian, *Journals*, 2:164–66, 164nM20.

64. Alexis Thibeau is listed as a "Patron" (a steersman or master of a keelboat or mackinaw) in the 1832 roster of men employed by the American Fur Company on the upper Missouri. Jackson, *Voyages*, p. 168.

65. Etienne Provost had been in the West for many years by this time. Here, he is preparing to take supplies to William Henry Vanderburgh and his men wintering on the Powder River. Leroy R. Hafen, "Etienne Provost," *Mountain Men and the Fur Trade*, 6:371–85; Harvey L. Carter, "William H. Vanderburgh," ibid., 7:315–20.

66. Ash Wood Point may refer to Ash Point, a feature mentioned in steamboat captain Joseph A. Sire's journal for the 1843 trip of the *Omega*; it was a few miles up the Missouri from the Cheyenne River. Sire, *For Wood and Water: Steamboating on the Missouri River*, ed. Mark H. Bettis (Hermann, Mo.: Wein Press, 2000), p. 73.

67. Cimmerians Island is Simoneau's Island, penciled in on Maximilian's copy of William Clark's route maps. It was later named Fort George Island. Captain Sire refers to Simoneau's Island in his 1841 log for the steamer *Trapper* and in the 1843 log for the *Omega*. The island was approximately opposite the mouth of (little) Medicine Creek and Fort George, the fort opposing Fort Pierre. Sire, *Wood and Water*, pp. 18, 43, 72; Gary E. Moulton, ed., *The Journals of the Lewis and Clark Expedition*, Vol. 1: *Atlas of the Lewis and Clark Expedition* (Lincoln: University of Nebraska Press, 1983), map 23.

68. Cherry Creek joins the Cheyenne River north and west of Fort Pierre. Schuler, *Fort Pierre Chouteau*, p. 44; DeLand, "Notes on 'Old Fort Pierre,'" p. 376.
69. The location is uncertain, but the Otoe Indians were then living on the Platte River in eastern Nebraska. Wishart, *Great Plains Indians*, p. 31; Chittenden, *American Fur Trade*, 2:859–60.
70. The average steamboat consumed ten cords of wood in one day, so it was important to have a ready supply for the boats. These men were going to cut timber on three islands, Fort Vermillion, Farm Island, and at the Moreau River. Schuler, *Fort Pierre Chouteau*, p. 107.
71. "Roy's Isle" is penciled in on Prince Maximilian's copy of William Clark's maps at the location of what was called Farm Island by residents of Fort Pierre. Moulton, *Journals of the Lewis and Clark Expedition*, vol. 1, map 23.
72. For a history of Fort Clark, *see* Wood, Hunt, and Williams, *Fort Clark and its Indian Neighbors*.
73. Copies of men's accounts were sent along to other posts as men were transferred in order to track their purchases against wages.
74. Capt. Joseph Sire recorded that Crooks' Point was between Okobojo Creek and the Cheyenne River. Sire, *Wood and Water*, p. 123.
75. For more on interments, *see* Michael M. Casler, "Fur Traders as Undertakers on the Upper Missouri," *Museum of the Fur Trade Quarterly* 43 (Fall/Winter 2007): 107–14.
76. A surround, sometimes small, as described here, and sometimes much more elaborate, was an impoundment method of hunting buffalo. Cartographer Joseph Nicollet encountered three hundred lodges of Yankton, Sisseton, and Yanktonai hunters preparing for a surround near the Sheyenne River in present-day North Dakota during his 1839 travels across the region. Joseph Nicollet, "Report Intended to Illustrate a Map of the Hydrological Basin of the Upper Mississippi River," *United States Senate Report* 237, 26th Cong., 2nd sess., 16 Feb. 1841, p. 48.
77. This new structure would be Fort Pierre Chouteau.
78. James Bird was one of the Blackfeet interpreters. DeLand and Robinson, Notes to "Fort Tecumseh," p. 155n139.
79. The child was a boy who, along with his mother and infant sister, would perish of smallpox at Fort Union in 1837. Jacob Halsey never mentioned their names. Michael M. Casler, "'This Outrageous Desease'—Charles Larpenteur's Observations of the 1837 Smallpox Epidemic," *Rocky Mountain Fur Trade Journal* 10 (2016): 18–35.
80. This trip was the second one up the Missouri for the *Yellow Stone*; its first voyage was in 1831, when the steamboat went only as far as Fort Tecumseh, returning to Saint Louis with a cargo of robes, furs, and ten thousand pounds of buffalo tongues. In 1832, after departing new Fort Pierre on June 5, the steamer covered the six hundred river miles to Fort Union in twelve days. Lass, *Navigating*, pp. 81–83; Michael M. Casler, *Steamboats of the Fort Union Fur Trade: An Illustrated Listing of Steamboats on the Upper Missouri River, 1831–1867* (Williston, N.Dak.: Fort Union Assoc., 1999), pp. 8, 37; Jackson, *Voyages*, pp. 38–40.
81. Lake Traverse lies on the South Dakota-Minnesota border and drains to the north by the Bois de Sioux River, the headwaters of the Red River of the North. In 1822, the Columbia Fur Company built Fort Washington on the east shore of the lake. The American Fur Company took over the post in 1827 and abandoned and burned it in 1838. Grace Lee Nute, "Posts in the Minnesota Fur-Trading Area, 1660–1855," *Minnesota History* 11 (Dec. 1930): 379.
82. "Pork eater" is the English translation of the French *mangeur du lard*, alluding to "the staple diet of salt pork and fat, corn and pea soup" fed to unskilled laborers (Ben Innis, *How t' Talk Trapper* [Williston, N.Dak.: Sitting Bull Trading Post, 1983], p. 18). The term was often applied to newcomers to the fur trade. Gabriel Franchère was the Canadian recruiter of pork eaters for the American Fur Company in Montréal. Abel, *Chardon's Journal*, p. 216n62; Lavender, *Fist in the Wilderness*, p. 389.
83. Narcisse Le Clerc, ex-company employee, began operating in 1831 as an opposition trader. Chittenden, *American Fur Trade*, 1:348–50.
84. George Catlin and Abraham Bogard were on their way to Saint Louis after Catlin's ascent of the Missouri as far as Fort Union. Catlin discusses his arrival in a passage in which he also describes the fort and Laidlaw's hospitality. Catlin, *North American Indians*, 1:233–34.
85. "Bear river" could be the Bear Creek in Oglala territory that American Fur Company employee Basil Clement traveled along during a journey back to Fort Pierre from Fort Laramie in 1844. He encountered Bear Creek shortly after crossing the White River and its Badlands. Early archaeology reports list

Bear Creek as one of the fossil-rich areas of the Badlands, near modern-day Scenic and immediately north of the Pine Ridge Indian Reservation, which is still home to the Oglalas. The creek feeds into the Cheyenne River. Charles Edmund DeLand, "Basil Clement (Claymore): The Mountain Trappers," *South Dakota Historical Collections* 11 (1922): 346; Cleophas C. O'Harra, "The White River Badlands," South Dakota School of Mines, Department of Geology, Bulletin no. 13 (Rapid City, Nov. 1920), pp. 52, 54.

86. Meredith Martin, M.D., arrived in Saint Louis in 1828 and studied in the office of Dr. Bernard G. Farrar until entering the University of Pennsylvania, graduating in 1832. Secretary of War Lewis Cass then appointed him to vaccinate the Indians of Sioux country around Fort Pierre for smallpox, but he ran out of cow pox material before he could finish. He returned to Saint Louis in November 1832, joining the practice of Dr. Farrar until he retired. "Physicians of Early St. Louis," freepages.history.rootsweb.ancestry.com/~earlystlouis/physicians.html.

87. Hanging the gates suggests that the fort's construction was now essentially complete, although men had begun transferring goods to it from Fort Tecumseh seven months earlier. *See* the entry for March 26, 1832.

88. "Daubing" is a term for whitewashing the buildings.

89. Still known as Beaver Creek, this stream enters the Missouri River from the east in Emmons County, North Dakota.

90. "Serpent river" is probably a reference to the stream known today as Snake Creek, which flows into the James River near present-day Redfield, South Dakota. Cartographer Joseph Nicollet, on his 1839 journey from Fort Pierre toward the northeast, marked it on his map with both its Dakota name, *Wamdushka Wakpa*, and its French translation, "*Riv. au Serpent*" (Nicollet, *Plains and Prairies*, pp. 171–7.

91. There is a difference between a "dispatch" and an "express." Dispatches were generally between posts, or temporary trading locations near the tribes, and forts. Men on foot or horseback carried them for much of the year. In winter, the carriers used "dog trains" (dog sleds). Dispatches were mostly local in nature. The winter express mentioned in this passage was a different matter, consisting of bundles of letters, trade good orders, and other information critical for doing business. The express extended from the farthest forts upriver (Fort McKenzie and later Fort Benton) and ran along the frozen Missouri River from fort to fort. Men and dogs were exchanged at each post. The most reliable men were chosen for these missions and were not allowed to carry any messages except those relating to business. Innis, *How t' Talk Trapper*, p. 11.

92. Vanderburgh and Pillon (or Pilou) were killed about six miles from Alder Gulch in present day Montana. Leroy R. Hafen, ed., *Fur Traders, Trappers, and Mountain Men of the Upper Missouri* (Lincoln: University of Nebraska Press, 1995), pp. 103–4; Paul C. Phillips, "William Henry Vanderburgh: Fur Trader," *Mississippi Valley Historical Review* 30 (Dec. 1943): 392–93.

93. The Oglalas, whose name for themselves translates roughly, "They scatter their own," are one of the divisions of the western Sioux, or Lakotas. In some records, the term "Teton" was limited specifically to the Oglalas and Brulés, just as the five northern bands of Lakotas were often referred to as Saones. Hoover, "Native Peoples," pp. 45–46.

94. All forts on the upper Missouri had gardens to supplement the heavy meat diet of the traders. Bloomfield Farm was a much larger operation than most. Originally on an island called Roy's Island, the place became known as Farm Island. Robinson, Notes to "Fort Tecumseh," p. 157n144; Schuler, *Fort Pierre Chouteau*, p. 69; David Wishart, "Agriculture at the Trading Posts on the Upper Missouri Prior to 1843," *Agricultural History* 47 (Jan. 1973): 61–63.

95. "Tonala Caxal" might be a garbled reference to a point on the Missouri River that Joseph Sire mentioned repeatedly in his steamer logs as "Touchon Kaksa." If so, it was on the Missouri River between the Moreau and Little Cheyenne rivers, north of Fort Pierre. Sire, *Wood and Water*, pp. 46, 57, 94, 123.

96. David Adams was a beaver trapper and later a small trader. He first came west with Captain Benjamin Bonneville in 1832. Charles E. Hanson, Jr., ed., *The David Adams Journals* (Chadron, Nebr.: Museum of the Fur Trade, 1994), pp. 1–2.

97. Both the *Yellow Stone* and the new *Assiniboine* arrived at Fort Pierre in 1833. The *Yellow Stone* transferred its cargo to the *Assiniboine* and, after loading with furs, returned to Saint Louis. The *Assiniboine*, carrying Prince Maximilian and Karl Bodmer, continued on to Fort Union. Lass, *Navigating*, p. 83; Casler, *Steamboats*, pp. 12, 18, 37; Jackson, *Voyages*, pp. 79, 95.

Chapter 2. Fort Tecumseh Letter Book

1. Richard T. Holliday was the clerk/trader at the Arikara post; his brother James is listed as a clerk/trader at Fort Tecumseh at this time. The brothers had come over to the Upper Missouri Outfit from the Columbia Fur Company in 1827. Annie Heloise Abel, ed., *Chardon's Journal at Fort Clark, 1834-1839*, by F. A. Chardon (Pierre: South Dakota Department of History, 1932), pp. 227-228n81; Doane Robinson, Notes to "Fort Tecumseh and Fort Pierre Journal and Letter Books," ed. Charles E. DeLand, *South Dakota Historical Collections* 9 (1918): 96n15; Dale R. Morgan, *The West of William H. Ashley, 1822-1838* (Denver: Old West Publishing, 1964), pp. 72-73, 249n218.
2. Robert Dickson had been a North West Company trader at Lake Traverse. Robinson, Notes to "Fort Tecumseh," p. 100n32.
3. A pitsaw was a long, two-handled saw used to cut lumber over a pit. One man stood in the pit, and the other stood above the log being sawed, giving rise to the terms "top dog" and "under dog."
4. The forts on the upper Missouri all maintained small libraries; this passage suggests that the men had either read or loaned out most of their books.
5. Alexander Harvey would have a long and troubled career as a fur trader on the upper Missouri. Hiram M. Chittenden, *The American Fur Trade of the Far West*, 2 vols. (Lincoln: University of Nebraska Press, 1986), 2:683-88.
6. The Blackfeet interpreter was Jacques Berger (a.k.a. Jacob Berger), a former Hudson's Bay Company employee. Berger had by this time spent some twenty-five years in Indian country and spoke the Blackfeet language. The treaty McKenzie mentions was never a government-sponsored treaty but rather one between the Blackfeet and McKenzie as a representative of the American Fur Company's Upper Missouri Outfit. In the fall, McKenzie dispatched James Kipp to build Fort Piegan at the mouth of the Marias River. David Smyth, "Jacques Berger, Fur Trader," *The Beaver* 69 (June/July 1989): 44-46; Chittenden, *American Fur Trade*, 1:332-34.
7. "Eau-qui-Courre" is another reference to the Niobrara River. *See* the Fort Tecumseh journal entry of March 14, 1830, which speaks of trading with the Sioux and Poncas near the head of the Niobrara.
8. Bear Butte, northeast of the Black Hills in Meade County, South Dakota, is a sacred locality for the Lakota Sioux and Cheyenne Indians. It rises more than twelve hundred feet from the surrounding prairie. "Bear Hill" is an exact rendering of the Lakota name, Mato Paha (sometimes spelled Mahto Paha). The Cheyennes also call it Noavasse, "Medicine Lodge." Carl Waldman, *Atlas of the North American Indian*, 3d ed. (New York: Infobase Publishing, 2009), p. 274; John Paul Gries, *Roadside Geology of South Dakota* (Missoula, Mont.: Mountain Press Publishing Co., 1996), pp. 162-63.
9. This statement is the source of the idea that Chouteau ordered that a new fort be built.
10. Michel Gravelle had gone to Washington in 1831-1832 to serve as an interpreter for an Indian delegation from the upper Missouri. Charles Larpenteur, *The Original Journal of Charles Larpenteur*, ed. Michael M. Casler, transc. and ann. Erwin N. Thompson (Chadron, Nebr.: Museum Assoc. of the American Frontier, 2007), p. 50n23.
11. Isidoro Sandoval, a Spaniard, was one of many who quarreled with hot-tempered fur trader Alexander Harvey, who eventually killed him. *See* John E. Sunder, *The Fur Trade on the Upper Missouri, 1840-1865* (Norman: University of Oklahoma Press, 1965), pp. 87-88; Chittenden, *American Fur Trade*, 2:684-85.
12. *Compos mentis* is Latin for "of sound mind." *Maladroit* is French for "awkward" or "clumsy."
13. Alexis Balley worked for the Upper Mississippi Outfit, and as part of the merger of the Columbia Fur Company with the American Fur Company, he took over the forts along the Saint Peter's (Minnesota) River.
14. The idea to build and use a steamboat originated with Kenneth McKenzie, who was supported by Pierre Chouteau, Jr.; Jean P. Cabanné and Bernard Pratte were against the expense. Ironically, with the success of the *Yellow Stone*, Bernard Pratte is listed as the owner of the next steamboat, the *Assiniboine*. Donald Jackson, *Voyages of the Steamboat Yellow Stone* (New York: Ticknor & Fields, 1985), p. 3; Michael M. Casler, *Steamboats of the Fort Union Fur Trade: An Illustrated Listing of Steamboats on the Upper Missouri River, 1831-1867* (Williston, N.Dak.: Fort Union Assoc., 1999), p. 6; Records of the Bureau of Marine Inspection and Navigation, "Enrollment record of the Steamboat *Assiniboine*," vol. 7939-B, Record Group 41, National Archives.
15. The Blacksnake Hills are along the Missouri River in the vicinity of present-day Saint Joseph, Missouri, the locale of a trading post that Joseph Roubidoux established for the company in 1826. They are a distinct landmark on cartographer Joseph N.

Nicollet's map of 1839. Chittenden, *American Fur Trade*, 2:924; Joseph N. Nicollet, *Joseph N. Nicollet's 1839 Manuscript Maps of the Missouri River and Upper Mississippi Basin*, comp. W. Raymond Wood, Illinois State Museum Scientific Papers, vol. 24 (Springfield, 1993), pl. 21.

16. The Hudson's Bay Company had a number of posts along the Qu'Appelle River in Saskatchewan, so it is difficult to identify the post in question.
17. Joseph Rolette was the head of the Upper Mississippi Outfit headquartered at Prairie du Chien.
18. Competitors called the former Columbia Fur Company men "Englishmen" because they had nearly all learned the trade in the North West Company of Montreal. Abel, Introduction to *Chardon's Journal*, p. xvii.
19. James Kipp built Fort Piegan at the mouth of the Marias River in present Chouteau County, Montana, in the fall of 1831; it was abandoned the following spring. Here, he is reported as passing the Musselshell River, in central Montana, about halfway to his goal. W. Raymond Wood, "James Kipp: Upper Missouri River Fur Trader and Missouri Farmer," *North Dakota History* 77 (Nos. 1–2, 2011), pp. 7–8.
20. These statements support the fact that Fort Union was built in the fall of 1828 and not in 1829 as some historians believe.
21. Epechimons may be a corruption of "apishamore," possibly derived from an Ojibway term for something to lie on. It came to refer to a skin or cloth saddle blanket and was applied sometimes to raw buffalo hides as well. Ben A. Innis, *How T' Talk Trapper* (Williston, N.Dak.: Sitting Bull Trading Post, 1983), p. 3; *Webster's New International Dictionary*, 2d ed., unabridged (Cambridge, Mass.: G & C. Merriam Co., 1934), s.v. "apishamore."
22. Crooks, Laidlaw, and Lamont were all from the area around Greenock, Scotland, and apparently they subscribed to a hometown paper.
23. Andrew Drips, the United States Indian agent from 1842 to 1846, was an employee of the Upper Missouri Outfit at this time. Abel, *Chardon's Journal*, p. 260n247.
24. Alexander was Kenneth McKenzie's eldest son born by an unknown Indian woman and left behind in the Selkirk Colony when McKenzie migrated to Saint Louis in 1822. Abel, *Chardon's Journal*, p. 215n60.
25. Pierre Ortubise was listed as an interpreter at the White River post. Abel, *Chardon's Journal*, p. 228n81; William R. Swagerty, "A View from the Bottom Up," *Montana, the Magazine of Western History* 43 (Winter 1993): 20.

Chapter 3. Fort Pierre Letter Book A

1. The traders were headed to Fort Washington on Lake Traverse, the source of the Red River. Grace Lee Nute, "Posts in the Minnesota Fur-Trading Area, 1660–1855," *Minnesota History* 11 (Dec. 1930): 379.
2. These *engagés* may have been hired in Montréal, but Bernard Pratte appears to have made the articles of agreement at Prairie du Chien. Other employees, including Laidlaw and Honoré Picotte, would lead the *engagés* to Fort Pierre.
3. A long-time cook at Fort Clark, Leclaire was also known as "Old Baptiste." During Maximilian's stay there during the winter of 1833–1834, LeClair judged that the prince had come down with scurvy and began giving him a broth of wild onions (*Allium mutabile* Mich.) mixed with small white flowers (*Allium reticulatum*), and within four days, the prince began to recover. Annie Heloise Abel, ed., *Chardon's Journal at Fort Clark, 1834–1839*, by F. A. Chardon (Pierre: South Dakota Department of History, 1932), p. 312n443; Michael M. Casler, transc. and ann., "Letters from the Fur Trade: Kenneth McKenzie's Letters to Prince Maximilian at Fort Clark, 1833–1834," *Museum of the Fur Trade Quarterly* 41 (Spring 2005): 14n14.
4. Jedediah S. Smith, David Jackson, and William Sublette had bought a mountain trapping business from William H. Ashley in July 1826. Hiram M. Chittenden, *The American Fur Trade of the Far West*, 2 vols. (Lincoln: University of Nebraska Press, 1986), 1:253.
5. For further details on the trip upriver and the construction of Fort McKenzie, *see* Chittenden, *American Fur Trade*, 1:335–36.
6. The "Hill without design" refers to the Cote sans dessein, an erosional remnant, or "lost island," on the north bank of the Missouri River in Callaway County, Missouri.

Chapter 4. Fort Pierre Letter Book B

1. A *parfleche* was an animal skin, usually bison, folded in much the same manner as a mailing envelope, in which Indians kept various goods, including dried foods.
2. The portrait was of Kipp's wife from the Mandan country, who, after Catlin's departure downriver, commanded her husband to retrieve it, believing it had caused her to have a nosebleed. Kipp caught up with Catlin downriver and recovered the offending portrait. Maximilian, Prince of Wied, *The North American Journals of Prince Maximilian of Wied*,

Vol. 3: *September 1833–August 1834*, ed. Stephen S. Witte and Marsha V. Gallagher (Norman: University of Oklahoma Press, 2012), p. 182; W. Raymond Wood, "James Kipp: Upper Missouri River Fur Trader and Missouri Farmer," *North Dakota History* 77, nos. 1–2 (2011): 9.

3. Dog Island is not identifiable, but the context suggests it was a Missouri River island north of Fort Pierre near the mouth of the Grand River where the Arikara village was located.

4. M. P. Lafferrier was a storekeeper and trader at Fort Union. Charles Larpenteur, *The Original Journal of Charles Larpenteur*, ed. Michael M. Casler, transc. and ann. Erwin N. Thompson (Chadron, Nebr.: Museum Assoc. of the American Frontier, 2007), p. 49n14.

5. The *Assiniboine* was the second in a series of steamboats that the Western Department of the American Fur Company owned and operated on the upper Missouri River. Michael M. Casler, *Steamboats of the Fort Union Fur Trade: An Illustrated Listing of Steamboats on the Upper Missouri River, 1831–1867* (Williston, N.Dak.: Fort Union Assoc., 1999), pp. 12, 18–19.

6. At this point, traders from Sublette and Campbell arrived to oppose the Upper Missouri Outfit. Formed by fur-trade veterans William Sublette and Robert Campbell, the firm was the chief competitor of the American Fur Company on the upper Missouri River during the 1830s. John E. Sunder, *The Fur Trade on the Upper Missouri, 1840–1865* (Norman: University of Oklahoma Press, 1965), p. 54; Hiram M. Chittenden, *The American Fur Trade of the Far West*, 2 vols. (Lincoln: University of Nebraska Press, 1986), 2:928, 931.

7. The post, built near the mouth of the Teton River, would last one year before the company sold out to the American Fur Company. Charles E. DeLand, "Editorial Notes on 'Old Fort Pierre and its Neighbors,'" *South Dakota Historical Collections* 1 (1902): 375–76.

8. Lac qui Parle is a lake on the upper reaches of the Minnesota River, where former Columbia Fur Company trader Joseph Renville ran Fort Adams trading post. The French name, "the lake that talks," is a direct translation of the Dakota name, Mde Iyedan. Warren Upham, *Minnesota Geographic Names: Their Origin and Historic Significance* (Saint Paul: Minnesota Historical Society, 1969), p. 288.

9. Alexander Kennedy was a clerk at Fort Clark; in the fall of 1834, he would be sent to winter at Fort Assiniboine on the Poplar River. Annie Heloise Abel, ed., *Chardon's Journal at Fort Clark, 1834–1839*, by F. A. Chardon (Pierre: South Dakota Department of History, 1932), pp. 207n33, 323–30.

10. The letter books refer several times to the prices for such horses, and a letter of May 9, 1849, discusses American horses in the larger context of Indian ponies and California horses that are being brought up from the Platte River country.

11. Cordells were large ropes that were used to pull keelboats up the Missouri River. In most cases, they were several hundred feet long and required a crew of twenty to forty men to pull the boat. Leland D. Baldwin, *The Keelboat Age on Western Waters* (Pittsburgh: University of Pittsburgh Press, 1980), p. 64.

12. As occurs elsewhere, this letter appears to be out of chronological order, just as in the original letter book.

13. The letter refers to the June rise of the Missouri River, as snowmelt from the mountains arrived to boost the level of the river. Melting snow from the plains and spring rains also cause a rise earlier in the year. William E. Lass, *Navigating the Missouri: Steamboating on Nature's Highway, 1819–1935* (Norman, Okla.: Arthur H. Clark Co., 2008), p. 20.

14. Prairie du Chien was the headquarters of Joseph Rolette's Upper Mississippi Outfit near the Fox River in Wisconsin, the point where the traveling *engagés* would arrive on the Mississippi River.

15. This French phrase translates as "to stop by briefly" or "to breeze through."

16. The company built Fort Cass in the fall of 1832 on the south bank of the Yellowstone River, a few miles downstream from the mouth of the Bighorn River; it was abandoned in 1835. Chittenden, *American Fur Trade*, 2:938.

17. Bent's "Old" Fort was in present-day southeastern Colorado, on the north bank of the Arkansas River. Built in 1833, it was destroyed in 1849. Robert H. Roberts, *Encyclopedia of Historic Forts: The Military, Pioneer, and Trading Posts of the United States* (New York: Macmillan Publishing Co., 1988), pp. 101–03; Chittenden, *American Fur Trade*, 1:50–52.

18. This French phrase means "cost what it may."

19. Chardon built Fort Jackson in December 1833 on the Missouri River just above the mouth of the Poplar River in modern Roosevelt County, Montana. Chittenden, *American Fur Trade*, 2:935.

20. Mary was Laidlaw's Sioux wife. Ray H. Mattison, "William Laidlaw," in *The Mountain Men and the Fur Trade of the Far West*, 10 vols., ed. LeRoy R. Hafen (Glendale, Calif.: Arthur H. Clark Co., 1965–1972), 3:172. For a description, *see* George Catlin, *Letters and Notes on the North American Indians*, 2 vols. in one. (North Dighton, Mass.: JG Press, 1995), 1:233–34.

21. The Forest River, once called Big Salt River, enters the Red River of the North in Walsh County, North Dakota.

22. The reference is to buffalo ponies that were specially trained for hunting bison. For accounts of such training, *see* George Bird Grinnell, *When Buffalo Ran* (Norman: University of Oklahoma Press, 1966), pp. 41–51, and Frank B. Linderman, *Red Mother* (New York: John Day Co., 1932), pp. 93–95.

23. During the fur-trade era, Plains tribes would request traders at the forts to care for their dead, which the traders did. They would later be paid for their services. Michael M. Casler, "Fur Traders as Undertakers on the Upper Missouri," *Museum of the Fur Trade Quarterly* 43 (Fall/Winter 2007): 112–13.

24. The Sans Arc are a division of the western Sioux, or Lakotas. The French name is a translation of the Lakota name, Itazipco, meaning "those without bows" or "no bows" (Herbert T. Hoover, "Native Peoples," in *A New South Dakota History*, ed. Harry F. Thomson [Sioux Falls, S.Dak.: Center for Western Studies, Augustana College, 2005], p. 46).

25. A *pockamogan* was a war club, mainly for ceremonial use, made in the shape of a gunstock and often fitted with a dag blade.

26. *Mauvais terre*, French for "bad lands," was a term applied to highly eroded landscapes at various locales in the Northern Plains. The reference makes it clear that this location is in the White River Badlands, part of which now make up Badlands National Park.

27. Catlinite pipes came from the renowned quarry in present-day southwestern Minnesota. The widely traded pipestone was later named for painter George Catlin, who first made mineralogists aware of it in about 1839. Waldo R. Wedel and George C. Frison, "Environment and Subsistence," in *Handbook of North American Indians*, Vol. 13, part 1: *Plains*, ed. Raymond J. DeMallie (Washington, D.C.: Smithsonian Institution, 2001), pp. 49–50.

28. The steamboat *Assiniboine* caught fire and burned near the mouth of the Cannonball River on June 1, 1835. The fire destroyed the natural history specimens that Prince Maximilian had left at Fort Union to be shipped after his own departure downriver. Casler, *Steamboats*, pp. 18–19.

29. William N. Fulkerson was the United States Indian agent for the Mandans.

Chapter 5. Fort Pierre Letter Book C

1. William Sublette founded Fort William in 1834; after its purchase in 1841, the company renamed it Fort John for company partner John B. Sarpy. It became a major stop on the Oregon Trail and assumed the name Fort Laramie in 1849 when the United States Army purchased it. Built at the confluence of the Laramie and North Platte rivers, it is today the National Park Service's Fort Laramie National Historic Site. *See* David Lavender, *Fort Laramie and the Changing Frontier*, National Park Service, Handbook no. 118 (Washington, D.C., 1983); LeRoy R. Hafen and Francis Marion Young, *Fort Laramie and the Pageant of the West* (Glendale, Calif.: Arthur H. Clark Co., 1938), pp. 17–134.

2. This entry clearly reveals that both carts, which were mainly used to transport goods between posts on the Missouri River, and wagons were used to carry goods between Fort Pierre and Fort John.

3. For more about Major Joseph V. Hamilton, *see* Doane Robinson, Notes to "Fort Tecumseh and Fort Pierre Journal and Letter Books," ed. Charles E. DeLand, *South Dakota Historical Collections* 9 (1918): 177n189.

4. In 1841, Lancaster P. Lupton built Fort Platte on the south side of the North Platte River about a mile west of its confluence with the Laramie River, but it was abandoned in 1845 after the construction of Fort Bernard, some eight miles farther east. Charles E. Hanson, Jr., and Veronica Sue Walters, "The Early Fur Trade in Northwestern Nebraska," *Nebraska History* 57 (Fall 1976): 298.

5. The Minneconjou (also Miniconjou or Minikowaju) make up a division of the western Sioux, or Lakotas. Their name for themselves translates as "planters beside the water" or "they plant beside the stream" (Herbert T. Hoover, "Native Peoples," in *A New South Dakota History*, ed. Harry F. Thompson [Sioux Falls, S.Dak.: Center for Western Studies, Augustana College, 2005], p. 46).

6. Pierre Louis Vasquez (1798–1868), sometimes referred to as "Old Vaskiss," was in partnership with mountain man Jim Bridger, who operated Fort Bridger on Black's Fork of the Green River at this time. Charles Larpenteur, *The Original Journal of Charles Larpenteur*, ed. Michael M. Casler, transc. and ann. by Erwin N. Thompson (Chadron, Nebr.:

Museum Assoc. of the American Frontier, 2007), p. 11n16.
7. One of five brothers, all of whom were involved in the fur trade, Marcelin St. Vrain built a post on the Platte River. Robinson, Notes to "Fort Tecumseh," p. 206n243.
8. Fort George was on the west bank of the Missouri River seventeen river miles downstream from the mouth of the Bad River, a little below the mouth of (little) Medicine Creek. The Union Fur Company built it in 1842 to compete with the Upper Missouri Outfit; the company collapsed in 1845. W. Raymond Wood, "Fort George and the Union Fur Company on the Upper Missouri River," *South Dakota History* 45 (Winter 2015): 305–26.
9. The Wind River Mountains are in western Wyoming.
10. L'ours qui dance ("Dancing Bear Creek") entered the Missouri opposite Fort Berthold and the Hidatsa village of Like-a-Fishhook in what is now Mercer County, North Dakota.
11. Fort Bernard was on the Oregon Trail beside the North Platte River eight miles downstream from Fort Laramie, in present-day Goshen County, Wyoming. Hafen and Young, *Fort Laramie*, pp. 118–23.
12. The fur trade operated on a hierarchy that dictated where employees sat in the dining halls at the forts. The "first table" was for the *bourgeois* and head clerks; being seated at the second table reflected lower status.
13. Théophile Bruguière was an interpreter for United States Indian Agent Andrew Drips and a nephew of James Kipp. Constant R. Marks, "Theophile Brugiere," *South Dakota Historical Collections* 4 (1908): 262–70; W. Raymond Wood, "James Kipp: Upper Missouri River Fur Trader and Missouri Farmer," *North Dakota History* 77, nos. 1–2 (2011): 10–11.
14. Over time, steamboat tonnage capacity grew to handle the increasing amounts of trade goods and government supplies going upriver. The *Nimrod* drew 210 tons. Michael M. Casler, *Steamboats of the Fort Union Fur Trade: An Illustrated Listing of Steamboats on the Upper Missouri River, 1831–1867* (Williston, N.Dak.: Fort Union Assoc., 1999), p. 31.
15. The Taos Peddlers were traders from New Mexico who followed the Taos Trail to Colorado to trade whiskey for furs; here they were trading corn for robes. Just as this letter indicates, Lakota historian Josephine Waggoner speaks of Lakota people trading with "Mexicans" on the Platte for seed corn, giving two robes for one peck of corn in 1853. The Sioux also traded furs for Navajo blankets with these peddlers, and some Sioux believed it was these traders who introduced a devastating outbreak of cholera. Waggoner said that a Brule Sioux trader named Swift Bear also went to the Southwest to trade, suggesting the commerce may have been two ways. Josephine Waggoner, *Witness: A Húnkpapha Historian's Strong-Heart Song of the Lakotas*, ed. Emily Levine (Lincoln: University of Nebraska Press, 2013), pp. 468–70.
16. The reference is to a species of wild tobacco (*Nicotiana quadrivalvis* Pursh), also known as Indian tobacco. Melvin R. Gilmore, *Uses of Plants by the Indians of the Upper Missouri* (Lincoln: University of Nebraska Press, 1977), pp. 61–62.
17. Fort Lewis was built to replace Fort Chardon, which had been near the mouth of the Judith River. The location for Fort Lewis was found to be unfavorable, and it was torn down and moved to the site of Fort Benton, where it was renamed after Missouri senator Thomas Hart Benton. Hiram M. Chittenden, *History of the American Fur Trade of the Far West*, 2 vols. (Lincoln: University of Nebraska Press, 1986), 2:937.
18. Cats were invaluable for catching mice and rats in the fur-trade posts on the river; these rodents consumed much of the corn on which the men lived. W. Raymond Wood, "Cats! Their Lives and Lore on the Missouri River," *Museum of the Fur Trade Quarterly* 47 (Fall 2011): 6–10.
19. Joseph ("Henry") Picotte was Honoré Picotte's nephew. Both had the nickname "Henry," which leads to confusion in some fur-trade documents.

Chapter 6. Fort Pierre Letter Book D

1. Slaves occasionally show up in documents of the fur trade as economic commodities for their owners or as property of an estate.
2. The calumet was a long and complex ceremony that many Plains Indians performed to foster trade between tribes or different bands of the same tribe. It took place over four days and involved ritual feasting and gift giving. Mark A. Eifler, "Calumet," in *Encyclopedia of the Great Plains*, ed. David J. Wishart (Lincoln: University of Nebraska Press, 2004), p. 569.
3. The reference is slang for the navy yard on Chantier Creek.
4. Andrew Dawson was an important figure in the upper Missouri fur trade. *See* Leslie Wischmann and Andrew Erskine Dawson, *This Far-Off Wild*

Land: The Upper Missouri Letters of Andrew Dawson (Norman: Arthur H. Clark Co., 2013).

5. Frederick Behman was a clerk on the upper Missouri from 1843 to 1856, and two watercolors of Forts Pierre and Union from a bird's-eye view with remarkable detail are attributed to him. John C. Ewers, "Folk Art in the Fur Trade of the Upper Missouri," *Prologue: The Journal of the National Archives* 4 (Summer 1972): 108; Harold H. Schuler, *Fort Pierre Chouteau* (Vermillion: University of South Dakota Press, 1990), p. 40.

6. The *Martha* was newly constructed, and Captain Joseph LaBarge brought his wife, Pelagie, with him on this 1847 trip, making her the first white woman to arrive at the forts of the upper Missouri. Michael M. Casler, *Steamboats of the Fort Union Fur Trade: An Illustrated Listing of Steamboats on the Upper Missouri River, 1831–1867* (Williston, N.Dak.: Fort Union Assoc., 1999), p. 29.

7. James Kipp built Fort Berthold in 1845 on the north side of the Hidatsa earth-lodge village of Like-a-Fishhook, opposite Dancing Bear Creek in today's Mercer County, North Dakota. G. Hubert Smith, *Like-a-Fishhook Village and Fort Berthold, Garrison Reservoir, North Dakota*, National Park Service, Anthropological Papers, no. 2, (Washington, D.C.,1972), pp. 3–20.

8. For whatever reason, the women mentioned in this reference never made the trip upriver.

9. Iron was also used for barrel hoops.

10. It is curious that the letter is addressed to Garreau, who is not known to have been able to read or write. Rudolf Friedrich Kurz, *The Journal of Rudolf Friedrich Kurz*, Bureau of American Ethnology, Bulletin no.115 (Washington, D.C.: Government Printing Office, 1937), p. 79.

Chapter 7. Fort Pierre Letter Book E

1. Gideon C. Matlock was Indian agent for the upper Missouri. Annie Heloise Abel, ed., *Chardon's Journal at Fort Clark, 1834–1839*, by F. A. Chardon (Pierre: South Dakota Department of History, 1932), p. 265n250.

2. When food ran low in the depth of winter, forts on the upper Missouri would send out a number of men with the horses to fend for themselves on the prairies. Rudolf Friedrich Kurz, *The Journal of Rudolf Friedrich Kurz*, Bureau of American Ethnology, Bulletin no. 115 (Washington, D.C.: Government Printing Office, 1937), pp. 305–6.

3. James Murray was the Scottish-born *bourgeois* of the Upper Missouri Outfit's Fort Alexander. James Kipp became the guardian of his orphaned daughter, Margaret. W. Raymond Wood, "James Kipp: Upper Missouri River Fur Trader and Missouri Farmer," *North Dakota History* 77, nos. 1–2 (2011): 20.

4. When the United States Army purchased Fort John (Laramie), military planners considered various routes for resupplying the fort. An escort of mounted rifles along with wagons left Fort John on August 17, 1849, to develop a northern supply route from Fort Pierre, and while this route was shorter than the southern route, the long winters on the northern Plains made it impractical. Douglas C. McChristian, "Fort Laramie and the U. S. Army on the High Plains 1849–1890," National Park Service Historic Resources Study, Fort Laramie National Historic Site (Feb. 2003), pp. 18–19, 48n18.

5. The *Dacotah* was built in Saint Louis in 1849; there is no documentation to confirm that it sank. On the night of May 17, 1849, fire broke out among the steamboats moored at the Saint Louis levee, where the *Martha* had already been in preparation for its annual trip up the Missouri. A total of twenty-three steamboats and the business district burned in what became known as the "Great Fire." Hiram M. Chittenden, *History of Early Steamboat Navigation on the Missouri River* (Minneapolis: Ross & Haines, 1962), pp. 185–87; William M. Lytle and Forrest R. Holdcamper, *Merchant Steam Vessels of the United States, 1790–1868: "The Lytle-Holdcamper List,"* rev. & ed. C. Bradford Mitchell (Staten Island, N.Y.: Steamship Historical Society of America, 1975), p. 50.

6. After spending twenty-seven years in the fur trade, Laidlaw retired shortly after this, and he and his Sioux wife, Mary Ann, lived in Liberty, Missouri, never reaching California. He died in 1852 at the age of fifty-two. He is buried in Mount Zion Cemetery at Mosby, Missouri. Ray H. Mattison, "William Laidlaw," in *The Mountain Men and the Fur Trade of the Far West*, 10 vols., ed. LeRoy R. Hafen (Glendale, Calif.: Arthur H. Clark Co., 1965–1972), 3:167–72; Dale L. Morgan, ed., *The West of William H. Ashley, 1822–1838* (Denver: Old West Publishing, 1964), p. 59. *See also* Wood, "James Kipp," p. 4.

7. This name referred to traders of the short-lived Union Fur Company, who used adobe to erect Fort Mortimer, near Fort Union. W. Raymond Wood, "Fort George and the Union Fur Company on the Upper Missouri River," *South Dakota History* 45 (Winter 2015): 309–10.

8. Westport was an early landing and port that later became part of Kansas City, Missouri. C. P. Deatherage, *Early History of Greater Kansas City, Missouri and Kansas: The Prophetic City at the Mouth of the Kaw*, Diamond Jubilee ed. (Kansas City, Mo.: Interstate Publishing Co., 1927), pp. 247–70.
9. Charles Larpenteur had been a trader for the Upper Missouri Outfit since coming over from Sublette and Campbell when they sold out in 1833; Larpenteur began his career at Fort Union under Kenneth McKenzie.
10. By contract, hunters hired at the forts kept the "head, hide, and horns" for later sale. This practice provided them extra income.
11. Robert Meldrum was associated with the Crow tribe for many years and worked for the American Fur Company. Born in Scotland in 1804, he accompanied his parents to Canada in 1812, then to Kentucky in 1816. He joined Ashley's expedition to the Rocky Mountains in 1825, remaining there for the next five years. About 1830, he joined the Upper Missouri Outfit and was assigned to Fort Cass, the Crow post on the Yellowstone. Meldrum is buried in an unmarked grave at Fort Union. Lewis Henry Morgan, *The Indian Journals, 1859–62*, ed. Leslie A. White (New York: Dover Publications, 1993), pp. 167, 191; Mark H. Brown, *The Plainsmen of the Yellowstone: A History of the Yellowstone Basin* (Lincoln: University of Nebraska Press, 1961), p. 54.
12. "River Sioux" is the Big Sioux River, which enters the Missouri at modern-day Sioux City, Iowa. Théophile Bruguière was a trader in its vicinity for most of his career on the Missouri River. Constant R. Marks, "Theophile Brugiere," *South Dakota Historical Collections* 4 (1908): 263–70.
13. Charles Larpenteur had been in poor health since early 1847, when he had apparently suffered a heart attack. Charles Larpenteur, *The Original Journal of Charles Larpenteur*, ed. Michael M. Casler, transc. and ann. Erwin N. Thompson (Chadron, Nebr.: Museum Assoc. of the American Frontier, 2007), pp. 74–75.
14. Owen McKenzie was the third son of Kenneth McKenzie and was born at Fort Union of an unnamed Assiniboine woman. He was killed in 1861 by Malcolm Clark. Chittenden, *Early Steamboat Navigation*, pp. 233–34n; Abel, *Chardon's Journal*, p. 215n60.
15. Kipp's nephew died at Fort Pierre on November 15, and Kipp remained with him until his death. Wood, "James Kipp," p. 16.
16. A comprehensive list of firearms identified at Fort Union through documentary and archaeological sources shows guns of unknown Belgian manufacturers, as well as many of American make. The frizzen worked with the flint to make the spark that discharged the firearm. William Jefferson Hunt, Jr., "Firearms and the Upper Missouri Fur Trade Frontier: Weapons and Related Materials from Fort Union Trading Post National Historic Site (23WI17), North Dakota" (Ph.D. diss., University of Pennsylvania, 1989), pp. 133, 481–82; Carl P. Russell, *Guns on the Early Frontiers: A History of Firearms from Colonial Times through the Years of the Western Fur Trade* (Berkeley: University of California Press, 1957), pp. 288–89; Charles E. Hanson, Jr., *The Northwest Gun* (Lincoln: Nebraska State Historical Society, 1992), p. 25n61; James A. Hanson and Dick Harmon, *Firearms of the Fur Trade* (Chadron, Nebr.: Museum of the Fur Trade, 2011), pp. 321, 339–40, 358–59.
17. After thirty years of occupation, the area had been denuded of grass and timber. *See* Harold H. Schuler, *Fort Pierre Chouteau* (Vermillion: University of South Dakota Press, 1990), pp. 133–36.

BIBLIOGRAPHY

Abel, Annie Heloise, ed. *Chardon's Journal at Fort Clark, 1834–1839*, by F. A. Chardon. Pierre: South Dakota Department of History, 1932.

Ahler, Stanley A., Thomas D. Thiessen, and Michael K. Trimble. *People of the Willows: The Prehistory and Early History of the Hidatsa Indians*. Grand Forks: University of North Dakota Press, 1991.

Altenberg, Hans von Sachsen, and Robert L. Dyer. *Duke Paul of Württemberg on the Missouri Frontier: 1823, 1830, and 1851*. Boonville, Mo.: Pekitanoui Publications, 1998.

Audubon, John James. *Audubon and His Journals*. 2 vols. Ed. Maria R. Audubon. New York: Dover Publications, 1960.

Awakuni-Swetland, J. "Omahas." In *Encyclopedia of the Great Plains*. Ed. David J. Wishart. Lincoln: University of Nebraska Press, 2004, pp. 586–87.

Baldwin, Leland D. *The Keelboat Age on Western Waters*. Pittsburgh: University of Pittsburgh Press, 1980.

Barbour, Barton H. *Fort Union and the Upper Missouri Fur Trade*. Norman: University of Oklahoma Press, 2001.

Blenkinsop, Willis. "Edward Rose." In *The Mountain Men and the Fur Trade of the Far West*, ed. Leroy R. Hafen. Vol. 9, pp. 335–45. Glendale, Calif.: Arthur H. Clark Co., 1972.

Brown, Mark H. *The Plainsmen of the Yellowstone: A History of the Yellowstone Basin*. Lincoln: University of Nebraska Press, 1961.

Buckley, Jay H. *William Clark: Indian Diplomat*. Norman: University of Oklahoma Press, 2008.

Butscher, Louis C. "A Brief Biography of Prince Paul Wilhelm of Württemberg (1797–1860)." *New Mexico Historical Review* 17 (July 1942): 181–225.

Carter, Harvey L. "William H. Vanderburgh." In *The Mountain Men and the Fur Trade of the Far West*, ed. Leroy R. Hafen. Vol. 7, pp. 315–20. Glendale, Calif.: Arthur H. Clark Co., 1969.

Casler, Michael M. "Fur Traders as Undertakers on the Upper Missouri." *Museum of the Fur Trade Quarterly* 43 (Fall/Winter 2007): 107–114.

———, ed. "Letters from the Fur Trade: Kenneth McKenzie's Letters to Prince Maximilian at Fort Clark, 1833–1834." *Museum of the Fur Trade Quarterly* 41 (Spring 2005): 9–14.

———. *Steamboats of the Fort Union Fur Trade: An Illustrated Listing of Steamboats on the Upper Missouri River, 1831–1867*. Williston, N.Dak.: Fort Union Assoc., 1999.

———. "'This Outrageous Desease'—Charles Larpenteur's Observations of the 1837 Smallpox Epidemic." *Rocky Mountain Fur Trade Journal* 10 (2016): 18–35.

———, and W. Raymond Wood. "The Rise and Fall of the Columbia Fur Company: Rethinking the Fur Trade on the Northern Great Plains." Ms. in preparation, 2017.

Catlin, George. *Letters and Notes on the North American Indians*, 2 vols. in one. North Dighton, Mass.: JG Press, 1995.

Chardon, Francis A. *Chardon's Journal at Fort Clark, 1834–1839*, ed. Annie Heloise Abel. Pierre: South Dakota Department of History, 1932.

Chittenden, Hiram M. *The American Fur Trade of the Far West*. 2 vols. Lincoln: University of Nebraska Press, 1986.

———. *History of Early Steamboat Navigation on the Missouri River*. Minneapolis: Ross & Haines, 1962.

Deatherage, C. P. *Early History of Greater Kansas City, Missouri and Kansas: The Prophetic City at the Mouth of the Kaw*. Diamond Jubilee ed. Kansas City, Mo.: Interstate Publishing Co., 1927.

DeLand, Charles Edmund. "Basil Clement (Claymore): The Mountain Trappers." *South Dakota Historical Collections* 11 (1922): 245–389.

———. "Editorial Notes on 'Old Fort Pierre and its Neighbors.'" *South Dakota Historical Collections* 1 (1902): 317–79.

———. "The Verendrye Explorations and Discoveries Leading to the Planting of the Fort Pierre Tablet." *South Dakota Historical Collections* 7 (1914): 99–322.

———, ed. "Fort Tecumseh and Fort Pierre Journal and Letter Books." Notes by Doane Robinson. *South Dakota Historical Collection* 9 (1918): 69–239.

DeMallie, Raymond J. "Sioux until 1850." In *Handbook of North American Indians*. Vol. 13, pt 2: *Plains*. Ed. DeMallie. Washington, D.C.: Smithsonian Institution, 2001, pp. 718–60.

DeVoto, Bernard. *The Course of Empire*. Boston: Houghton Mifflin Co., 1952.

Diffendal, R. F., Jr. *Great Plains Geology*. Lincoln: University of Nebraska Press, 2017.

"Enrollment Record of the Steamboat *Assiniboine*." Records of the Bureau of Marine Inspection and Navigation, vol. 7939-B, Record Group 41, National Archives, Washington, D.C.

Eifler, Mark A. "Calumet." In *Encyclopedia of the Great Plains*. Ed. David J. Wishart. Lincoln: University of Nebraska Press, 2004, p. 569.

Ewers, John C. "Folk Art in the Fur Trade of the Upper Missouri." *Prologue, The Journal of the National Archives* 4 (Summer 1972): 99–108.

Fosha, Michael, and James K. Haug, *The 1997-2001 Excavations at Fort Pierre Chouteau*. 2 vols. South Dakota State Historical Society, Archaeological Research Center, Research Report no. 3 ([Rapid City], 2010).

Gilmore, Melvin R. *Uses of Plants by the Indians of the Upper Missouri*. Lincoln: University of Nebraska Press, 1977.

Gries, John Paul. *Roadside Geology of South Dakota*. Missoula, Mont.: Mountain Publishing Co., 1996.

Grinnell, George Bird. *When Buffalo Ran*. Norman: University of Oklahoma Press, 1966.

Hafen, LeRoy H., ed. *Fur Traders, Trappers, and Mountain Men of the Upper Missouri*. Lincoln: University of Nebraska Press, 1995.

———. *The Mountain Men and the Fur Trade of the Far West*. 10 vols. Glendale, Calif.: Arthur H. Clark Co., 1965–1972.

———. *Trappers of the Far West*. Lincoln: University of Nebraska Press, 1983.

Haines, Aubrey L. "Hugh Glass." In *The Mountain Men and the Fur Trade of the Far West*, ed. Leroy R. Hafen. Vol. 6, pp. 161–71. Glendale, Calif.: Arthur H. Clark Co., 1968.

Hanson, Charles E., Jr. "Frederick Laboue and His River." *Museum of the Fur Trade Quarterly* 27 (Spring/Summer 1991): 1–24.

———. *The Northwest Gun*. Lincoln: Nebraska State Historical Society, 1992.

———, ed. *The David Adams Journals*. Chadron, Neb.: Museum of the Fur Trade, 1994.

———, and Veronica Sue Walters. "The Early Fur Trade in Northwestern Nebraska." *Nebraska History* 57 (Fall 1976): 291–314.

Hanson, James A. *The Encyclopedia of Trade Goods*, Vol. 4: *Clothing & Textiles of the Fur Trade*. Chadron, Neb.: Museum of the Fur Trade, 2014.

Hanson, James A., and Dick Harmon. *The Encyclopedia of Trade Goods*, Vol. 1: *Firearms of the Fur Trade*. Chadron, Neb.: Museum of the Fur Trade, 2011.

Harris, Edward. *Up the Missouri with Audubon: The Journal of Edward Harris*. Norman: University of Oklahoma Press, 1951.

Hassrick, Royal B. *The Sioux: Life and Customs of a Warrior Society*. Norman: University of Oklahoma Press, 1964.

Howard, James H. *The Ponca Tribe*. Lincoln: University of Nebraska Press, 1995.

Hunt, William Jefferson, Jr. "Firearms and the Upper Missouri Fur Trade Frontier: Weapons and Related Materials from Fort Union Trading Post National Historic Site (23WI17), North Dakota." Ph.D. diss., University of Pennsylvania, 1989.

Innis, Ben A. *How T' Talk Trapper*. Williston, N.Dak.: Sitting Bull Trading Post, 1983.

Jablow, Joseph. *The Cheyenne in Plains Indian Trade Relations, 1795-1840*. Lincoln: University of Nebraska Press, 1994.

Jackson, Donald. *Voyages of the Steamboat Yellow Stone*. New York: Ticknor & Fields, 1985.

Jensen, Richard E. *The Fontenelle and Cabanné Trading Posts: The History and Archeology of Two Missouri River Sites, 1822-1838*. Lincoln: Nebraska State Historical Society, 1998.

Kennedy, Michael Stephen, ed. *The Assiniboines: From the Accounts of the Old Ones Told to First Boy (James Larpenteur Long)*. Norman: University of Oklahoma Press, 1961.

Kurz, Rudolf Friedrich. *The Journal of Rudolf Friedrich Kurz*. Bureau of American Ethnology, Bulletin no. 115. Washington, D.C.: Government Printing Office, 1937.

Landry, Clay J. "Hugh Glass: The Rest of the Story." *Rocky Mountain Fur Trade Journal* 10 (2016): 1–17.

Larpenteur, Charles. *The Original Journal of Charles Larpenteur*. Ed. Michael M. Casler. Transc. & ann. Erwin N. Thompson. Chadron, Nebr.: Museum Association of the American Frontier, 2007.

Lass, William E. *Navigating the Missouri: Steamboating on Natures Highway, 1819-1935*. Norman: Arthur H. Clark Co., 2008.

Lavender, David. *The Fist in the Wilderness*. New York: Doubleday & Co., 1964.

———. *Fort Laramie and the Changing Frontier*. United States National Park Service, Handbook no. 118. Washington, D.C., 1983.

Linderman, Frank B. *Red Mother*. New York: John Day Co., 1932.

Link, J. T. *The Origin of the Place Names of Nebraska*. Nebraska Geological Survey, Bulletin no. 7, Second Series. [Lincoln], 1933.

Luttig, John C. *Journal of a Fur-Trading Expedition up*

the Missouri River. New York: Argosy-Antiquarian, 1964.

Lytle, William M., and Forrest R. Holdcamper. *Merchant Steam Vessels of the United States, 1790–1868: "The Lytle-Holdcamper List."* Rev. & ed. C. Bradford Mitchell. Staten Island, N.Y.: Steamship Historical Society of America, 1975.

McChristian, Douglas C. "Fort Laramie and the U. S. Army on the High Plains, 1849–1890," U.S., National Park Service, Historic Resources Study, Fort Laramie National Historic Site, Feb. 2003.

McDermott, John Francis. "The Reconstruction of a 'Lost' Archive: The Diaries and Sketches of Prince Paul Wilhelm of Württemberg," *Manuscripts* 30, (Summer 1978): 167–78.

McKenzie, Kenneth, to the Gentleman in Charge of Fort Tecumseh for the American Fur Company, May 5, 1830. Chouteau Family Papers. Missouri History Museum, Saint Louis, Mo.

McLaird, James D. *Hugh Glass: Grizzly Survivor*. South Dakota Biography Series, no. 5. Pierre: South Dakota Historical Society Press, 2016.

———. "The Welsh, the Vikings, and the Lost Tribes of Israel on the Northern Plains: The Legend of the White Mandan." *South Dakota History* 18 (Winter 1988): 245–73.

Mallery, Garrick. *Pictographs of the North American Indians: A Preliminary Paper*. In U.S., Smithsonian Institution, Bureau of American Ethnology, Fourth Annual Report (Washington, D.C.: Government Printing Office, 1886): 13–256.

Marks, Constant R. "Theophile Brugiere." *South Dakota Historical Collections* 4 (1908): 263–70.

Mattison, Ray H. "James A. Hamilton (Palmer)." In *The Mountain Men and the Fur Trade of the Far West*. Ed. Leroy R. Hafen. Vol. 3, pp. 163–66. Glendale, Calif.: Arthur H. Clark Co., 1966.

———. "William Laidlaw." In *The Mountain Men and the Fur Trade of the Far West*. Ed. LeRoy R. Hafen. Vol. 3, pp. 167–72. Glendale, Calif.: Arthur H. Clark Co., 1966.

Maximilian, Prince of Wied. *The North American Journals of Prince Maximilian of Wied*. Vol. 2: *April–September 1833*. Ed. Stephen S. Witte and Marsha V. Gallagher. Norman: University of Oklahoma Press, 2010.

———. *The North American Journals of Prince Maximilian of Wied*. Vol. 3: *September 1833–August 1834*. Ed. Stephen S. Witte and Marsha V. Gallagher. Norman: University of Oklahoma Press, 2012.

Miller, David, Dennis Smith, Joseph McGeshick, James Shanley, and Caleb Shields. *The History of the Assiniboine and Sioux Tribes of the Fort Peck Indian Reservation: 1600–2012*. Poplar, Mont.: Fort Peck Community College, 2012.

Morgan, Dale L., ed. *The West of William H. Ashley, 1822–1838*. Denver: Old West Publishing, 1964.

Morgan, Lewis Henry. *The Indian Journals, 1859–62*. Ed. Leslie A. White. New York: Dover Publications, 1993.

Moulton, Gary E., ed. *The Journals of the Lewis and Clark Expedition*. Vol. 1: *Atlas of the Lewis and Clark Expedition*. Lincoln: University of Nebraska Press, 1983.

———. *The Journals of the Lewis and Clark Expedition*. Vol. 2: *August 30, 1803–August 24, 1804*. Lincoln: University of Nebraska Press, 1986.

———. *The Journals of Lewis and Clark*. Vol. 3: *August 25, 1804–April 6, 1805*. Lincoln: University of Nebraska Press, 1987.

———. *The Journals of Lewis and Clark*. Vol. 9: *The Journals of John Ordway, May 14, 1804–September 23, 1806, and Charles Floyd, May 14–August 18, 1804*. Lincoln: University of Nebraska Press, 1995.

———. *The Journals of Lewis and Clark*. Vol. 10: *The Journal of Patrick Gass, May 14, 1804–September 23, 1806*. Lincoln: University of Nebraska Press, 1996.

———. *The Journals of Lewis and Clark*. Vol. 11: *The Journals of John Whitehouse, May 14, 1804–April 2, 1806*. Lincoln: University of Nebraska Press, 1997.

Nasatir, A. P., ed. *Before Lewis and Clark: Documents Illustrating the History of the Missouri, 1785–1804*. 2 vols. Saint Louis: Saint Louis Historical Documents Foundation, 1952.

Nester, William R. *The Arikara War: The First Plains Indian War, 1823*. Missoula, Mont.: Mountain Press, 2001.

Nicollet, Joseph N. *Joseph Nicollet on the Plains and Prairies: The Expeditions of 1838–39 with Journals, Letters, and Notes on the Dakota Indians*. Ed. Edmund C. Bray and Martha Coleman Bray. Saint Paul: Minnesota Historical Society, 1993.

———. *Joseph N. Nicollet's 1839 Manuscript Maps of the Missouri River and Upper Mississippi Basin*. Comp. W. Raymond Wood. Illinois State Museum Scientific Papers, no. 24. Springfield, 1993.

———. *Report Intended to Illustrate a Map of the Hydrological Basin of the Upper Mississippi River*. U.S., Congress, Senate, Senate Report no. 237, 26th Cong., 2nd sess. (16 Feb. 1841): 48.

Nute, Grace Lee. "Hudson's Bay Company Posts in the Minnesota Country." *Minnesota History* 22 (Sept. 1941): 270–89.

———. "Posts in the Minnesota Fur-Trading Area, 1660–1855," *Minnesota History* 11 (Dec. 1930): 353–85.

Oglesby, Richard Edward. *Manual Lisa and the Opening of the Missouri Fur Trade*. Norman: University of Oklahoma Press, 1963.

O'Harra, Cleophas C. *The White River Badlands*. South Dakota School of Mines, Bulletin no. 13. Rapid City, 1920.

Patton, Margaret Maurine. "Geophysical Surveys and Archaeological Insights at Fort Pierre Chouteau: A Frontier Trading Post on the Middle Missouri." M.A. thesis, University of Arkansas, 2013.

Phillips, Paul C. "William Henry Vanderburgh: Fur Trader." *Mississippi Valley Historical Review* 30 (Dec. 1943): 377–94.

Pinkney, David. *The French Revolution of 1830*. Princeton: Princeton University Press, 1972.

Potter, Gail DeBuse. "Trading Posts of the Central Plains." *Museum of the Fur Trade Quarterly* 43 (Fall/Winter 2007): 75–81.

Roberts, Robert H. *Encyclopedia of Historic Forts: The Military, Pioneer, and Trading Posts of the United States*. New York: Macmillan Publishing Co., 1988.

Robinson, Doane. Notes to "Fort Tecumseh and Fort Pierre Journal and Letter Books," ed. Charles E. DeLand. *South Dakota Historical Collections* 9 (1918): 69–239.

Ronda, James P. *Lewis and Clark among the Indians*. Lincoln: University of Nebraska Press, 1984.

Russell, Carl P. *Guns on the Early Frontiers: A History of Firearms from Colonial Times through the Years of the Western Fur Trade*. Berkeley: University of California Press, 1957.

Scharf, J. Thomas. *History of Saint Louis City and County: From the Earliest Periods to the Present Day*. Vol. 2. Philadelphia: Louis H. Everts, 1883.

Schell, Herbert S. *History of South Dakota*. 4th ed., rev. John E. Miller. Pierre: South Dakota Historical Society Press, 2004.

Schlesier, Karl H., ed. *Plains Indians, A.D. 500–1500: The Archaeological Past of Historic Groups*. Norman: University of Oklahoma Press, 1994.

Schuler, Harold H. *A Bridge Apart: History of Early Pierre and Fort Pierre*. Pierre, S.Dak.: By the Author, 1987.

———. *Fort Pierre Chouteau*. Vermillion: University of South Dakota Press, 1990.

Sire, Joseph A. *For Wood and Water: Steamboating on the Missouri River*. Ed. Mark H. Bettis. Hermann, Mo.: The Wein Press, 2000.

Smith, G. Hubert. *Fort Pierre II (39ST217): A Historic Trading Post in the Oahe Dam Area, South Dakota*. Smithsonian Institution. Bureau of American Ethnology, Bulletin no. 176 (Washington, D.C.: Government Printing Office, 1960)

———. *Like-a-Fishhook Village and Fort Berthold, Garrison Reservoir, North Dakota*. U.S., National Park Service, Anthropological Papers, no. 2 (Washington, D.C., 1972).

———, and John Ludwickson. *Fort Manuel: The Archeology of an Upper Missouri Trading Post of 1812–1813*. South Dakota Archaeological Association, Special Publication, no. 7 (Vermillion, 1981).

Smyth, David, "Jacques Berger, Fur Trader." *The Beaver* 69 (June/July 1989): 39–50.

Sneve, Virginia Driving Hawk, ed. *South Dakota Geographic Names*. Sioux Falls, S.Dak.: Brevet Press, 1973.

Sunder, John E. *The Fur Trade on the Upper Missouri, 1840–1865*. Norman: University of Oklahoma Press, 1965.

Swagerty, William R. Introduction to *Chardon's Journal at Fort Clark, 1834–1839*. Ed. Annie Heloise Abel. Lincoln: University of Nebraska Press, 1997.

———. "A View From the Bottom Up: The Work Force of the American Fur Company on the Upper Missouri in the 1830s." *Montana, the Magazine of Western History* 43 (Winter 1993): 18–33.

Thompson, Erwin N. *Fort Union Trading Post, Fur Trade Empire on the Upper Missouri*. Medora, N.Dak.: Theodore Roosevelt Nature & History Assoc., 1986.

Thompson, Harry F., ed. *A New South Dakota History*. Sioux Falls, S.Dak.: Center for Western Studies, Augustana College, 2005.

Tinling, Marion. *Sacagawea's Son: The Life of Jean Baptiste Charbonneau*. Missoula, Mont.: Mountain Press Publishing, 2001.

Upham, Warren. *Minnesota Geographic Names: Their Origin and Historic Significance*. Saint Paul: Minnesota Historical Society, 1969.

Waldman, Carl. *Atlas of the North American Indian*. 3d ed. New York: Infobase Publishing, 2009.

Wilson, Frederick T. "Old Fort Pierre and its Neighbors." *South Dakota Historical Collections* 1 (1902): 258–311.

Wischmann, Leslie, and Andrew Erskine Dawson, *This Far-Off Wild Land: The Upper Missouri Letters of Andrew Dawson*. Norman, Okla.: Arthur H. Clark, 2013.

Wishart, David. "Agriculture at the Trading Posts on the Upper Missouri prior to 1843." *Agriculture History* 47 (Jan. 1973): 57–62.

———. *Great Plains Indians*. Lincoln: University of Nebraska Press, 2016.

———, ed. *Encyclopedia of the Great Plains*. Lincoln: University of Nebraska Press, 2004.

Wood, W. Raymond. "Cats! Their Lives and Lore on the Missouri River." *Museum of the Fur Trade Quarterly* 47 (Fall 2011): 6–10.

———."Fort George and the Union Fur Company on the Upper Missouri River." *South Dakota History* 45 (Winter 2015): 305–26.

———. "James Kipp: Upper Missouri River Fur Trader and Missouri Farmer." *North Dakota History* 77, nos. 1–2 (2011): 2–35.

———. "A Permanent Presence: The Family of Joseph Garreau and the Upper Missouri River Fur Trade." *South Dakota History* 43 (Summer 2013): 91–117.

———. "Plains Trade in Prehistoric and Protohistoric Intertribal Relations." In *Anthropology on the Great Plains*. Ed. W. Raymond Wood and Margot Liberty. Lincoln: University of Nebraska Press, 1980.

———. *Prologue to Lewis and Clark: The Mackay and Evans Expedition*. Norman: University of Oklahoma Press, 2003.

———, William J. Hunt, and Randy H. Williams. *Fort Clark and Its Indian Neighbors: A Trading Post on the Upper Missouri River*. Norman: University of Oklahoma Press, 2011.

INDEX

LB stands for letter books. Identifier (u/i) is used when no first name or other information was given. Spelling variations are shown in (parentheses). PS stands for photo section [with unnumbered page in brackets].

Abel, Annie H., xi
Adams, David (trapper), 53, 243n96
Adams, James, 197
African Americans (mulatto/Negro/slaves), ix, 12, 32, 76, 96, 182, 226, 248n1
Agard, Louis, 193
Alcohol (liquor). *See* Whiskey; Wine
American Declaration of Independence, 21
American Fur Company: acquisition of Ft. Lookout, 2; acquisition of Ft. Washington, 242n81; arrival of Pierre Chouteau, vii; construction of boats, 263n3; importance of Ft. Pierre to, ix, 3; letter books, xi–xii; letters to (in Ft. Pierre LB), 93; letters to (in Ft. Tecumseh LB), 68–69; mentions in Ft. Pierre LB, 99, 129, 133; mentions in Ft. Tecumseh LB, 70; merger with Columbia Fur Company, 3, 244n13; ownership of steamboats, vii, 246n5; recruitment of Canadian *engagés*, 242n82; reorganization, 155; treaty with the Blackfeet, 244n6
American Indians. *See* individual tribes
American Revolution, 63
Angé (Augé), Henry (Henri), 17–20, 48, 93, 123, 131, 140, 147
Animals. *See* Cats; Dog sleds/dog trains; Horses and mules; Oxen
Apple River (Apple Creek), 8, 30, 36, 77, 79, 86–87, 100, 237n11, 238n29, 239n37
Arapaho Indians, 1
Arikara (Arriccarra, Ree) Indians, 238n34; as hub of intertribal trade, 1–2; hostilities/attacks on traders, 23, 43, 60–61, 215–16, 238n28, 239n39; intertribal rivalry/warfare, 20, 73, 75–78, 89; stealing from traders, viii, 23, 29, 58, 87; trading post/traders living with, 26–27, 31–33, 56–57, 109–10, 114; trading robes/furs, 68, 72, 88–89, 164; trading with, 18–19, 24–25, 40, 47, 72, 81, 86, 99, 163, 173, 175, 231–32; villages (Ree Village), 11, 44, 60, 129, 235n1, 246n3
Arkansas (Arkanzes) River, 125, 155, 246n17
Ashley, William H., 245n4, 250n11
Ash Wood Point (Ash Point?), 241n66
Assiniboine (fort/post), 84, 85, 249n9
Assiniboine (steamboat), 53, 114, 115, 116, 121, 125, 129, 149, 150, 243n97, 244n14, 246n5, 247n28

Assiniboine Indians, 10, 11, 89, 236n5, 238n25, 250n14, 1674
Astor, John Jacob, 3, 4, 155
Avaripe (Alvaripe), Mr., 16,17
Ayotte, Honoré, 177–78, 212

Badlands National Park, 247n26
Bad River (Wakpa Sica, aka Teton River), ix, xii, 1–5, 235n2, 236n1, 236nn4–5, 237n9, 248n8
Bailey, Alexis, 78, 81, 244n13
Baird (u/i), 15
Barratta, John, 193
Barton, Charles (slave), ix, 182
Bary, Joseph, 8, 32–33, 94
Bastian, P., 132
Battle of Platte Bridge, viii
Bayeis (u/i), 198
Bean, Jonathan L., 23–24, 30, 45–46, 60, 66, 69, 70–71, 73, 78, 81–82, 87–91, 99, 103–04, 130, 240n51
Bear Butte (Bear Hill, Mahto Paha), 244n8
Bear Hill, 71, 244n8
Bear River (Bear Creek?), 242n85
Beaugard (u/i), 116
Beauvais, Mr., 206–7, 214, 217, 219, 221, 228, 230, 233
Beaver/beaver trade/trappers, viii, 9, 21, 27, 29, 31–32, 42, 52–53, 62–63, 64, 67, 108, 243n96. *See also* Fur trade
Beaver Creek, 48–49
Beckwith (Beckwourth), James, viii, xiii, 129
Beemer, Mr., 25
Begué (Bigué, Bigéu), J. D., 50, 52, 110, 119
Behman, Frederick, 4, 150, 220, 230, 249n5, PS [8]
Belcom, Cyprian, 36, 39
Bellair, Francois, 100, 117, 119, 123, 135, 139
Belle Fourche River, 236n7
Bellehumeur (u/i), 44
Bellevue (Belview) trading post, 22, 168, 171–73, 177–78, 240n46
Belloires (u/i), 114
Benton, Thomas Hart, 248n17
Berger, Jacques (aka Jacob Berger), 244n6
Bernard Pratte and Company, 3, 155, 164–65, 172, 176, 177. *See also* Pratte, Bernard
Berthiencu, Joseph, 94

257

Berthold, Chouteau and Pratte (aka French Company), 2, 3
Bertrand, Etienne, 86, 92
Bighorn River, 2, 246n16
Big Sioux River (River Sioux), 250n12
Big Soldier (Yankton), 30
Bijou Hills, 241n60
Bijoux (u/i), 45
Billon (u/i), 105
Bird, James, 39, 98, 242n78
Biyer, Jacques, 130
Blackfeet Indians (of Montana): battle with Vanderburgh party, 29, 241n59; journal entries, 48, 66; mentions in Ft. Pierre LB, 118, 124, 126, 131, 162–66, 172–73, 175, 209; trading at Ft. McKenzie, 156; treaty with McKenzie, 244n6
Blackfeet (Sihasapa) Sioux Indians, 239n38, 240n50; journal entries, 37, 39, 43, 46, mentions in Ft. Pierre LB, 160
Blackfeet Post/fort, 181
Black Hills, 4–5, 65, 109–10, 240n49, 244n8
Black Snake Hills, 81, 244n15
Bloomfield farm (aka Farm Island), 50–52, 136, 138, 243n94
Blunt, S.Dak., 235n33
Bodmer, Karl, 3, 243n97, PS [1, 4]
Boenbomt (Bourbont), Auguste, 51–52
Bogart, Mr., 43, 98
Boillot, A. F., 94
Bondieu, Prudent, 51
Bonnetiere, André, 94
Bouchet, Pierre, 18, 19, 23
Bouchi (u/i), 61
Bouck, Mr., 20
Bouis, Antoine R., xiv, 158–63, 166, 174, 179, 181, 186–87, 193–94, 203, 208, 217, 221, 227, 231
Boulé, Edward, 94
Bourdan, J., 158
Boyle, James, 47
Brasseau, I., 26
Brasseau, Mr., viii, 25, 106, 109, 119
Braunsberg, Baron, 135, 137
Brazeau, Joseph ("Kiowa"), viii–ix, 2, 118, 151–52, 193, 212, 241n62
Bridger, Jim: abandonment of Hugh Glass, 239n39; arrival at Ft. John, viii, 161–62, 220; letters to, 161, 211; mentions in Ft. Pierre LB, 159, 161–62, 173, 176, 179, 204–5, 220, 224, 231; partnership with Vasquez, 247n6
Broit, Francois M., 94
Broken Leg (Brulé), 24
Brown, Mr., 42–44, 47–48, 50, 108

Brown, Mrs., 50
Brown, William L., 51, 96
Bruguière, Théophile, 171–72, 178, 213–14, 225, 248n13, 250n12
Brulé Sioux Indians, 240n50, 243n93; council with Lewis and Clark, 1; journal entries about, 13, 21, 23–27, 30–37, 39, 43–44, 47–49, 51–52; mentions in Ft. Pierre LB, 107, 124, 138–40, 145, 160–61; mentions in Ft. Tecumseh LB, 55, 65, 71, 78–79
Buffalo: abundant supply of, ix, 14–15, 28, 30, 32–33, 36–37, 48, 52, 57, 66, 73, 130, 185–87, 190, 203, 213, 232; disappearance of herds, 1, 46, 47, 49, 58, 60–61, 76–77, 81–82, 84–85, 103, 105, 107, 113, 115–17, 124–25, 131, 136, 138–39, 146–47, 167, 176, 216, 227; harvesting the tongue, 30–31, 37, 145, 147, 166, 174, 209, 219, 226, 242n80; hunting of, viii, 14–15, 17, 19–20, 35, 39, 41, 42–50, 121, 135, 143, 150, 179, 205, 207, 210, 242n76, 247n22; Indian migration in search of, vii; trading and harvesting meat, 13, 14–15, 17–18, 21, 24, 26–27, 29, 30–35, 37, 41, 43, 45–50, 55–57, 64–65, 89–90, 101, 103, 105–10, 112–13, 118–21, 125, 136, 141, 147, 165, 206; use in Indian ritual, 10–11
Buffalo robes: creating pressed packs, 13–16, 38, 39–40; insuring quality, 76, 158; loading wagons and carts, 157, 184; loss from fire, 84–86, 88; market value, 164–65, 167–68, 175, 178, 218, 227; quantities gathered, 7, 34, 41, 51–52, 63–64, 88–89, 94, 112, 125, 141, 144, 152, 159, 166, 172, 232; shipment of, 9, 20, 35, 41–42, 93, 95, 99, 138–39, 149, 164, 174, 177–78, 179, 195, 199, 208, 219, 229; trading for, 17–19, 33–34, 37–39, 57, 61, 68, 75–77, 81, 119–21, 127, 135, 140–41, 163, 173, 179, 182–85, 191–200, 211, 216, 224, 226, 248n15. *See also* Fur trade
Burly, Captain, 219–20

Cabanné (Cabanies, Cabaneé), Jean P.: journal entries, 22, 45, 60; letters to (in Ft. Pierre LB), 105; letters to (in Ft. Tecumseh LB), 66, 68, 73, 81–82, 84–85; location of trading post, 240n45; mentions in Ft. Pierre LB, 94, 98, 118, 122, 138, 159, 164–65, 172, 176–77, 179; mentions in Ft. Tecumseh LB, 78, 84–86; partnership with P. Chouteau, 155
California Gold Rush, ix, 210, 213
Calumet (Indian ceremony), 248n2
Campbell, Colin: arrest of Laboue for murder, 237n17; interpreter and clerk, 240n44; journal entries, 21, 32–33, 39–40, 44–45, 51–52; letters to (in Ft. Pierre LB), 117–18, 119, 123, 131, 134, 140–43, 148, 183–85, 188–89, 191, 193–95, 197–200; letters to (in Ft. Tecumseh LB), 90–91; mentions in Ft. Pierre LB, 109, 112, 126, 128, 131, 133–35, 137–38, 140, 143, 145, 147, 153, 177–78,

204–05, 207, 210, 213–14, 219, 221, 227–28, 231; mentions in Ft. Tecumseh LB, 59, 79, 83, 88
Campbell, Robert, ix, 181, 203, 210, 246n6, 250n9
Cannonball River, 247n28
Carr, Denion, 94
Carrier (Cassier), Michel, 20, 29, 58–59, 78, 96, 108, 140
Cartier, Servis, 208
Carts (*charettes*), transporting goods, ix; instructions for loading, 157; journal entries, 8, 20, 25–27, 43, 52, 56; mentions in Ft. Pierre LB, 99, 127, 142, 159, 160–61, 163, 173, 176, 179, 183, 191–96, 199–200, 207, 223–25, 227, 233; mentions in Ft. Tecumseh LB, 55
Casper, Wyo., viii
Cass, Lewis, 243n86
Castongi (u/i), 41
Catlin, George, 43, 98, 111, 113, 236n10, 242n84, 245n2, 247n27
Catlinite pipestone, 247n27
Cats, 176, 198, 248n18
Caufman, John, 193
Cedar Island, vii, 2, 8, 36–38, 47, 50–51, 52, 241n62
Cerré (u/i), 13–15, 18–19, 39, 49, 72, 75, 79, 110
Cerré, C. V., 43, 97
Cerré, G. P., 9, 43, 44–45, 107, 109, 206
Cerré, L., 8, 16–17, 19, 20–21, 23, 24–26, 237n10
Cerre, Michael Sylvester ("Lami"), 237n10
Cerre, Pascal L., 8, 26, 47, 48–49, 76–77, 86–87, 90, 93, 101, 106, 109–10, 112–13, 198, 207
Chamberlain, S.Dak., ix, 2
Champeau (u/i), 50
Chantier (boat yard), ix, 165
Chantier Creek, ix, 4, 236n3, 248n3
Charbonneau (Charboneaux, Charboncais), Jean Baptiste, 44, 108, 128, 237n12
Chardon, Francis A. (trader): Abel's edition of journal, xi; building Ft. Francis Chardon, 156; building Ft. Jackson, 126, 246n19; flogging Leclair for drunkenness, viii; journal entries, 14–25, 35; letters to (in Ft. Pierre LB), 137, 144, 147, 150–51, 158–59, 165–67, 174–75, 185–87; mentions in Ft. Pierre LB, 93, 96, 112, 117, 126, 145, 162–63, 173, 175, 177, 179; mentions in Ft. Tecumseh LB, 56, 77, 90; troubles with the Indians, 156
Charles X (king of France), 30, 241n61
Chattellion (Chatillion, Chatalion), C., 80, 111, 193
Chenie (u/i), 15, 25, 29–30, 31, 147
Cherry Creek, 242n68
Cherry River (Cherry Creek), 35–36, 39–40, 45, 48, 88–89, 100, 104, 119, 125–26, 139–43, 145, 148–49, 237n17, 242n68
Chesnie, Antoine, 21

Chevaliers, Baptiste, 114, 132
Cheyenne (Chyenne) Indians, viii, 1, 7, 10, 24–25, 68, 71, 78–80, 88, 109, 125, 138, 145, 236n1, 244n8
Cheyenne (Chyenne) Outfit/Establishment, 25, 31, 32, 50
Cheyenne (Chyenne) River, ix, 8–9, 14–15, 24, 26–27, 32–35, 39, 46, 48–50, 53, 56–58, 61, 65, 71, 78, 83–84, 86–87, 89–91, 101, 119–120, 123, 128, 130–131, 147, 160, 192, 194, 236n1, 236n7, 239n36, 241n66, 242n68, 242n74, 242n85, 243n95
Chittenden, Hiram M., 236n2
Chouquette, Julien, 27–28, 30
Chouteau, Pierre, Jr., PS [5]; letters, from Halsey, 83–84, 93–95; letters, from Laidlaw, xii, 69, 70–71, 72–73, 75, 81, 98, 103–04, 114–16, 121–22, 124–26, 135; letters, from Lamont, 59–61, 66, 67; letters, from Rolette, 75; and naming of Fort Pierre, vii, 3. *See also* Berthold, Chouteau and Pratte (aka French Company); Pierre Chouteau, Jr., and Company; Pratte, Chouteau and Company
Cibelle (u/i), 109
Cimmerians (Simoneau) Island, 34, 241n67
Clark, M., 163, 166
Clark, Mr., 216, 220, 226, 229–30, 231
Clark, Malcolm, 213, 250n14
Clark, William, viii; death, 156; journal entries, 22; letters, mentions in, 73, 74; Superintendent of Indian Affairs, 240n47
Clement, Basil, 242n85
Columbia Fur Company (aka Tilton, Dudley and Co.): construction of Ft. Lookout, 237n19; construction of Ft. Washington, 2, 242n81; establishment of Ft. Tecumseh, xii, 2–3; at Ft. Adams, 246n8; merger with American Fur Company, 3, 244n1, 244n13, 245n18; partnership changes, 155, 238n27; writing the history, 235n8
Comanche Indians, 1
Conesalie, Joseph, 217
Cote sans dessein ("Hill without design"), 99, 245n6
Council Bluffs, 236n8; journal entries, 8, 13, 18, 22–23, 33–34, 36, 41, 46, 48, 51, 53; mentions in Ft. Pierre LB, 99, 115–16, 119, 124, 205, 209–10, 213, 215, 223–24; mentions in Ft. Tecumseh LB, 60, 64, 68, 72, 78, 83, 88–89
Coy, A. F., 91
Crawford, Lewis, viii; journal entries, 48; letters to (in Ft. Pierre LB), 126–27, 128; mentions in Ft. Pierre LB, 97, 98–99, 107, 108, 110–11, 113, 114–17, 119, 121, 124, 127, 128, 133, 134, 150
Cree Indians, 231
Crooks, Ramsey, 9, 155, 245n22
Crook's Point, 37, 88, 242n74

Crow Indians: establishment of trade with, 2; Fort Cass trading post/supply boats, 163, 186, 208–09, 220, 223, 239n39, 250n11; mentions in Ft. Pierre LB, 126, 131, 134, 152, 165–66, 173, 209, 216, 231; mentions in Ft. Tecumseh LB, 68

Culbertson, Alexander: as *bourgeois* at Ft. Pierre Chouteau, 4; building Ft. Lewis, 156; letters from (in Ft. Pierre LB), 157–58, 211–12, 214, 217–18; letters to (in Ft. Pierre LB), 166, 176, 205, 206, 207–08, 226–27, 229; letters undecipherable, xiii–xiv; mentions in Ft. Pierre LB, 151–52, 159–60, 163–65, 172, 175, 179, 200–201, 203–04, 215–17, 219–23, 231, 233; mentions in Ft. Tecumseh LB, 78

Dacotah (steamboat), 249n5
Dafond (u/i), 143
Dagneau, Toussaint, 208
Dauphin (Dauphine), Pierre and J., 13, 31, 77, 88, 118, 119, 149, 150, 205–06
Dawson, Andrew, 183, 186, 230, 231, 248n4
Dear Hill, 123
Debruille, Michel, 9
Dechamps (u/i), 74
Decotemes (u/i), 114
Defond (Dufond), Baptiste, 24
DeGray, Charles, viii
Deigneau (u/i), 174
Delpai, Samuel, 47
Delude, Antoine, 48
Demant, Francois, 94
Demant, John, 94
Demaray, Louis, 43, 45–47
Denig, E. T., 116–17, 122, 126–27, 139–44, 146–47, 162, 175, 201, 206, 208–11, 213, 215, 219–20, 222–27, 229–31
Denoyer, Cyprian, 29–30, 33, 59
Derain, J. B., 24
Derocher (u/i), 14
Desautele, Joseph, 201
Deshonnette, J., 37, 80, 90, 91, 101, 142, 148
DeSomet, Michael, 235n2
Detaillier (Detailler, Detaille), Pierre, 20, 27–28, 57
DeVoto, Bernard, 238n22
Dickson, Madam, 19
Dickson, Robert (old Col.?), 57, 238n27, 244n2
Dickson, Thomas, 23–24, 27
Dickson, William: establishment of trading post, 29, 238n27; journal entries, 9, 11, 16–20, 23, 27, 39–41, 45, 52; letters to (in Ft. Pierre LB), 99, 105, 118, 119–20, 130–31, 134–35, 144–45, 146; mentions in Ft. Pierre LB, 93, 95, 97, 104, 119, 120, 123, 134, 140, 143–44, 147–48, 149; mentions in Ft. Tecumseh LB, 70, 73, 75, 78, 82

Dicoteaux (Decoteau) (trader), xiii, 46
Disease and illness. *See* Health, disease, illness
Dispatch, communications, 243n91
Dithonette (u/i), 26
Dog Island, 112, 246n3
Dog sleds/dog trains, ix, 8, 30, 32–33, 127, 128, 144, 243n91
Dog's Shadow (Indian), viii, 110
Dougherty, Major, 115
Dourian (Dourion, Dorion, Daurion), Baptiste, 8, 17–20, 24, 31, 33, 43
Dourion, Paul, 20
Drips, Andrew (Maj.): letters to (in Ft. Pierre LB), 207, 228–29, 230; mentions in Ft. Pierre LB, 163, 173–75, 186, 191–92, 194, 197–98, 200, 203–06, 208, 210, 216–17, 220–25, 230–33; US Indian agent, 245n23, 248n13. *See also* Fontenelle and Drips & Co.
Dubrielles, Mr., 130
Duchaim, Francois, 51
Duchonquette, Brasseau, 35, 37
Dumond, Thomas, 17, 20–21, 26–27, 69, 95–97, 111, 113, 131
Dupuis (u/i), 194, 196
Durack, John (Capt.), 220, 225
Durand, Nicholas, 42, 44, 95, 97
Durant, James, 43–44, 51
Dusseau, Alexis, 108

Engagés (fur-company employees): blacksmiths, 19–21, 27, 89, 94, 168, 209, 228, 232; boat builders, 15, 21, 27, 215; Canadian "pork-eaters," xii, 101, 105–6, 118–19, 124–26, 128, 131, 242n82, 245n2, 246n14; carpenters, 27, 32, 42, 44, 81, 94, 168, 215, 227, 228; cooks, ix, 76, 78, 94, 148, 245n3; deserters, xii, 9, 22, 43–44, 51, 70, 72, 77, 81–82, 84, 99, 116, 136, 138, 159–60, 163, 209, 226, 228; employment/recruitment, xii, 41–43, 93–99, 122; hierarchy of, 248n12; names of, xiv; payment for supplies, 41, 137, 242n73; wages/salary, 56, 59, 79, 81, 96–97, 100, 104, 107, 112, 116–17, 129–30, 132, 134, 141, 145–46, 148, 150–53, 157, 164, 168, 177, 179–80, 210, 219, 221–23, 232

Express, communications: bearers/couriers, 48, 171–72; defined/described, 243n91; Ft. Benton, 231; Ft. Pierre, 101, 108, 110, 127, 131, 162, 186, 191, 200, 203–5, 209, 214–15, 217, 228–29, 230–32; Ft. Tecumseh, 83, 86–87; Ft. Union, 83, 203, 212, 215–16; St. Louis, 48, 105–7, 112, 167, 175, 188, 195, 197, 216; upper Missouri, 177, 184, 195

Fairwell, Mr., 159

Fallons (u/i), 74

Farm Island (aka Bloomfield farm, Roy's Island), ix, 4, 50–52, 136, 138, 242n70–71, 243n94

Farrar, Bernard G. (Dr.), 243n86

Faye, Francois, 9

Feather in the Ear (Indian), 189

Fefer, Gabriel, 36

Fifie, Gabriel V., 37

Finch, Capt., 164, 210

Finch, Dr., 172, 176

Flying Bird (Indian), 193, 198

Fontenelle (Fontanelle, Fountinelle, Fountinelle, Fountanelle), Lucien, 40, 45, 53, 61, 68, 114–16, 122, 125, 130, 144

Fontenelle and Drips & Co., 89, 132, 138, 245n4

Forest River (Big Salt River), 128, 247n21

Fort Adams, 246n8

Fort Alexander, 249n3

Fort Benton, 156, 201, 208, 213, 229, 231, 233, 243n91, 248n17

Fort Benton (steamboat), 209

Fort Bernard, 165, 247n4, 248n11

Fort Berthold (Fort James): construction, 249n7; letters to (in Ft. Pierre LB), 166–67, 174–75; mentions in Ft. Pierre LB, 186, 201, 206–13, 216, 223, 226–27, 229, 231

Fort Bridger, 247n6

Fort Cass, 124, 126, 131, 153, 239n39, 246n16, 250n11

Fort Clark: journal entries, 26, 36, 45, 47, 48, 51, 52; letters, mentions in, 68, 86, 93–94, 95, 97, 98, 100, 106, 108, 116–17, 122, 129, 133–34, 150–52, 174, 177, 201, 206, 208, 214, 216, 223, 227, 229–32; letters to, 62, 70, 74, 96, 97, 106, 108, 110–11, 113, 137, 150–51, 158–59, 165, 214; letters undecipherable, xiii; maintaining a presence at, 175; merchandise for trade, 170–71; Prince Maximillian visits, 245n3; removal to l'Ours que danse, 173; requisition for merchandise, 170–71

Fort Clark State Historic Site, 240n55

Fort Floyd, xiv, 239n39

Fort Francis Chardon, 156

Fort Galpin, x, 4

Fort George, 156, 160, 241n67, 248n8

Fort Jackson, 126, 246n19

Fort James (renamed Fort Berthold), 166

Fort John (renamed Fort Laramie), 215–16; about the name, viii, 247n1; acquisition by Chouteau & Co., 156; arrival of Jim Bridger, viii, 161; letters, undecipherable, xiii; letters to (in Ft. Pierre LB), 158–60, 162–63, 166, 176–77, 178–79; mentions in Ft. Pierre LB, 157, 161, 164, 172–74, 178, 210, 212, 218; requisition for merchandise, 168–69; sale to the U. S. Army, ix–x, 156, 210, 212, 249n4

Fort Kiowa (Ft. Lookout), ix, 2, 239n39

Fort LaFramboise I, xii, 1–2

Fort LaFramboise II, 4

Fort Laramie (Fort John), 213, 228, 242n85

Fort Laramie National Historic Site, 247n1

Fort Leavenworth, 181

Fort Lewis, 156, 176, 248n17

Fort Lookout (renamed Fort Kiowa): construction by Columbia Fur Company, 2, 237n19; journal entries, 9, 35, 42, 45–46, 322; letters to (in Ft. Tecumseh LB), 70; mentions in Ft. Pierre LB, 94, 96, 103–04, 111, 113, 143, 148, 227; mentions in Ft. Tecumseh LB, 70–71, 77, 84–85, 89, 91; smallpox vaccinations, viii

Fort McKenzie, 156, 243n91

Fort Manuel, 2

Fort Mortimer, 156, 181, 249n7

Fort Piegan (Fort Peagon), 81, 244n6, 245n19

Fort Pierre Chouteau: area map, xv; building and naming, vii, 3–4; cutting pickets for, 37, 41–42, 44; *engagés* (Canadian "pork-eaters") route to, xii, 245n2, 246n14; hauling timber for, 58; letter books of, xi–xiv, 4; moving goods to, 38; recruitment of Canadian *engagés*, 41; repairs and sale to army, ix–x, 4; requisition for merchandise, 167–68. *See also* PS [1, 3, 4, 8]

Fort Platte, 159, 247n4

Fort Primeau, 4

Fort Raymond, 2

Fort Snelling, xii, 2, 98

Fort Sully, x, 4

Fort Tecumseh: area map, xv; arrival of Hugh Glass, xii; arrival of Pierre Chouteau, vii; Columbia takeover, 2–3; flooding and removal of property, 39, 243; journals and letter books of, xi–xiv, 4; letters to, 55–92; mentions in Ft. Pierre LB, 97, 115; replacement by Ft. Pierre, vii; steamboat service, 242n80

Fort Teton, 2–3, 236n4

Fort Union: construction, 3, 245n20; journal entries, 17, 21–23, 27, 32, 36, 39–43, 45, 48–49, 52; letter books of, xi, xiii; letters to (in Ft. Pierre LB), 95–96, 100, 106–8, 112–14, 117–18, 128–30, 133, 137, 151–53, 162, 164, 175–76; letters to (in Ft. Tecumseh LB), 73–74, 85–86; McKenzie as *bourgeois*, viii, ix, 155; mentions in Ft. Pierre LB, 93–94, 97–98, 106, 111, 115–16, 120, 124–25, 131–32, 138, 147–51, 161–62, 165–66, 172, 174–76, 186, 197–201, 203–6, 208–10, 212–16, 219–20, 225, 231; mentions in Ft. Tecumseh LB, 56, 58, 68, 75–76, 83; presence of George Catlin, 242n84; presence of Hugh Glass, 239n39–40; presence of James Palmer, 240n52; Prince Maximillian visits, 241n63;

Prince of Wattenburgh visits, 237n12; requisition for merchandise, 169–70; smallpox epidemic, 242n79; steamboat service, 156, 242n80, 243n97
Fort Union Trading Post National Historic Site, 239n40
Fort Vermillion, 143–44, 171–72, 178, 191–92, 200, 204–5, 208, 212, 225–27, 229, 238n27, 242n70
Fort Washington, 2, 242n81, 245n1
Fouchette, Baptiste, viii, 151–52
Fox, Livingston and Company (aka Union Fur Company), 156, 176, 248n8, 249n7
Fox River, xii, 115, 246n14
Franchère, Gabriel, 242n82
Frederick (u/i), 56, 58, 64–65, 71, 91, 142
French Company (aka Berthold, Chouteau and Pratte), 2–3
French Revolution, 30, 63
Frenier, Antoine, 178
Frenier (Funier), Narcisse (Narcess), 78, 99, 110
Freniere, Louison, 166, 186–87
Fulkerson, William N., 150–51, 247n29
Fur trade: establishing the upper Missouri posts, 1–5; growing competition, 156–57, 203–4, 213–15, 246n6; hierarchy of employees, 248n12; letter books and, xi–xii; St. Louis and, 1, 181, 242n80. *See also* Beaver/beaver trade/trappers; Buffalo robes

Gagin, Louis, 72, 77, 82
Gagnier, Louis, 9, 11, 26–27, 31, 84
Gagnin, Pierre, 69, 81
Gagnin, Pineau, 69
Gaillaucy, Phillip, 108
Gallieau, Baptiste, 36
Galpin, Charles E.: establishment of trading post, x, 4; letters to (in Ft. Pierre LB), 199, 210; mentions in Ft. Pierre LB, 187, 191, 205, 216
Gamlin, John B., 12
Gardner (Gardieu), Johnson, viii, 129, 139, 147, PS [3]
Garreau, Joseph, 239n41
Garreau, Pierre, 175, 200–201, 204, 205, 210, 239n41, 249n10, PS [7]
Garrow, Pierre, 18–19, 26, 52, 58, 86–87, 201
Gauslin, Pierre, viii, 25, 26
Gendion (u/i), 62
Gendron (servant/slave?), 89–90
Gens de paches (puches, pain) Indians, 37–38, 75–76, 77–78, 89–90, 123, 145
Gillaury, Philip, 151
Girard (u/i), 110
Giroux (slave?), 28, 30–31, 56–57, 61–62, 65, 67, 70
Glass, Hugh, viii, xii; biography of/letter by, PS [3], 239n39; journal entries, 17, 105; McKenzie expedition, 239n40, 241n59.
Gold (monetary), 226–27
Gold Rush: California, ix, 210, 213
Gordon, W., 23–24, 30–32, 34–35, 61–62, 64
Goslin (Gauslin, Golsin), Pierre, 24–25, 26
GossClaude, Justin, 165–67
Goulet, Honoré, 185, 196, 199, 200, 205, 216, 226, 228
Goulet, Pierre, 208
Grand Detour, 21, 25, 239n42, 241n62
Grand River, 2, PS [3], 238n28, 246n3
Grant, Cardinal, 24, 43, 45
Gravelles, Michel, 74
Gray, George, 86
"Gray Head." *See* Clark, William
Greenwood, C., 91, 110
Grondieu, Ignace, 69
Grossclaude (GossClaude), Justin, 129, 165–67
Grosventres (Minniterees), 11–12, 114, 134, 135, 137, 163, 214
Guerin, Denius Angé, 117
Guion, Antoine, 178
Guion, Devinie (Vincent), 48, 100–101, 171–72
Guitard (express courier), 48, 225, 226

Halemont, J., 114
Halsey, Jacob: author of Ft. Tecumseh journal, xiv, 7–53; correspondence with P. Chouteau, ix; drinking problem, 236n2; letters from (in Ft. Pierre LB), 106, 110–11, 113–14, 136–39, 148–53; letters from (in Ft. Tecumseh LB), 59, 62–63, 67, 69–71, 73–74, 79–81, 82–86, 94–100; mentions in Ft. Pierre LB, 104, 108, 116, 120–21, 142, 147, 174–76; mentions in Ft. Tecumseh LB, 57, 69, 78, 88; partnership with P. Chouteau, 155
Hamilton, H., 86
Hamilton, James A., 86, 89–92, 96, 100, 103, 106–8, 112–18, 137–38, 150–53, 158, 239n39
Hamilton, Joseph V., 178, 188, 191, 195, 204, 208, 213–14, 219–20
Hamilton, Mr., 23, 28–30, 32, 58, 74
Handsome Feather (Indian), 18
Harding, Ely (Eli), 111, 116
Harney, William S., 4
Harper, Robert F., 159
Hart, Benjamin, 94
Hart, Henry, 42, 75–76, 78, 95–97, 104, 119, 123, 131, 133
Harvey, Alexander, 68, 113, 130
Harvey, Primeau and Company, 181, 203, 208, 221
Hatton (Hatten), William S., 217

Haury, Alexander, 49
Hay, Mr., 20, 28, 30, 31, 33-35, 55-57
Hay Cabbin Creek, 241n58
Health, disease, illness: Brown drowning death, 50-51; Castongi illness, 41; children, illness and death, 37, 126, 242n79; cholera epidemic, viii, 115, 248n15; Chouquette illness, 27-28, 30; cold weather injuries, 124-28, 131; Deshonnette illness, 101; doctors, vii, 129, 172, 237n18, 243n86; Gamlin illness, 12; Halsey illness, 9, 22; Laidlaw illness, 99; Larpenteur heart attack, 250n13; Madam Dickson illness, 19; medicine, 12, 57, 59, 126; opium as trade good, 123; rabies, 77; Sarpy burns and death, 87-88; scurvy remedy and treatment, 245n3; sickness among the Indians, 227-28; smallpox, viii, 72, 156, 238n24, 242n79, 243n86; starvation, 12-13, 29, 45-46, 49, 52, 66, 91, 100, 107, 109, 131, 135-36, 138, 175, 205, 213, 216; steamboats and the spread of, 156; Vasseur illness, 18, 37; venereal disease, 10, 43, 94, 95
Heart River, 238n21
Hebert (Hilbert), Michel, 30, 32, 47
Heney, Hugh, 241n62
He that speaks the truth (Indian chief), 17
He who strikes the Ree (Indian), 200
Hidatsa Indians, 238n26, 248n10, 249n7
High Backed Wolf (Cheyenne), viii
Hill, Peter, 51-52, 132
Hodgkiss, William D., 164, 177, 183, 213, 218-19, 225
Holliday (Holiday), James M., 7-9, 12, 14-15, 17, 23, 25, 29, 78, 244n1
Holliday (Hilleday), Richard T., 16, 25-26, 27-29, 31-33, 56-57, 58-59, 60, 63-65, 69, 77-78, 83, 244n1
Hollowwood, 7-8, 71, 237n9
Horses and mules: bringing in a supply, viii, 81-83, 117, 161, 192, 204, 205, 207; buffalo runners, 121, 135, 143, 150, 179; hunting trips, viii, 15, 96, 205, 207, 210; Indian ponies, 221, 247n22; as pack animals, 7-8, 13-14, 16-17, 35-37, 40, 47-49; purchasing/prices, 79, 80, 108, 119, 127, 179, 188, 198, 207, 210, 219-20, 224, 226, 246n10; shoeing/taking care of, 27, 55, 58, 63, 67, 79, 101, 118, 134, 146-47, 172, 194; stolen by Indians, 10, 17-20, 26, 39, 43-44, 66, 69-71, 76, 78, 87, 90, 103, 105, 126, 131, 175, 190, 203; in trade, 118, 122, 159, 182-85, 188, 196, 200, 211, 224; transport by boat, 21; worn out, 9, 24-25, 30, 56-57, 61, 90, 106, 112, 128, 183, 205-07, 214, 224, 226. *See also* Oxen
Hudson's Bay Company, 2, 163, 238n27, 244n6, 245n16
Hunkpapa (Huncpapa, Honcpapa) Indians, 46, 239n38, 240n50, 240n54
Husband, Bruce, 207, 209-10, 218, 220

Illness and disease. *See* Health, disease, illness
Iowa, statehood, 181

Jackman, Baptiste, 130
Jackson (u/i), 95, 96, 129
Jackson, David, 245n4
Jackson, J., Mrs., 205
Jackson County, Mo., 241n58
Jacquemain, Baptiste, 197
James River, 75, 237n14, 238n27, 243n90. *See also* Riviere Bois Blanc; la Riviere a (au, O, le) Jacque(s)
Jeffries, Tom, 207, 211, 215-16
Jouett (Jewett, Juett, Jutt), Joseph, 7, 17, 20, 31, 38, 41-42, 160, 162, 178, 185, 189, 193, 196
Judith River, 156, 248n17

Kansas City, Mo., 250n8
Keel boats: *Acyes*, 122; *Argo*, 45, 46, 51, 116, 117, 129; *Atlas*, 46-47, 51; *Beaver*, 25, 73; cordage (oakum, caulking), 15, 41, 106, 168, 169, 170, 239n35; cordells, 121, 170, 188, 246n11; *En Route*, 98; *Flora*, 41, 100; *Fox*, 26, 62, 74; journal entries, 8, 10, 16, 21-23, 25-27, 40-41, 44-47, 50-52; *Louis Valle*, 25, 27, 35, 52, 70, 73; mentions in Ft. Pierre LB, 93-94, 98-100, 116-17, 121-22, 129, 149, 151-52, 162, 204; mentions in Ft. Tecumseh LB, 62, 68-70, 72-74; as Missouri River transportation, ix, 2, 156; *Musk Rat*, 25; *Otter*, 22; steersman/master (patron), 241n64; *Twin Male* (*Male Twin*), 41, 75, 93; *Twin Mules*, 23. *See also* Mackinaws
Kennedy, Alexander, 118-19, 132, 135, 246n9
Kenning, Paul, viii, 151
Kenny, M. (Dr.), 115
Kiowa Indians, 1
Kipp, James, 244n6, 245n19
Kipp, Margaret, 249n3

LaBarge, Joseph, 181, 249n6
LaBarge, Pelagie, 249n6
La Bouchanne (Ponca chief), 21
Laboue, Frederick: journal entries, 9, 14-16, 23, 25, 27-29, 39-40; letters to (in Ft. Pierre LB), 158-59, 160-61, 187, 192, 195, 197; letters to (in Ft. Tecumseh LB), 56, 78, 83; mentions in Ft. Pierre LB, 138-39, 157, 160, 180, 189, 204-8, 210, 212-13, 216, 218, 221, 228, 231; mentions in Ft. Tecumseh LB, 71-73; murder of F. Quenel, 39, 237n17
Laboue, H., 182
Laccovere, Pierre, 94
Lachapelle (Lachapele), Dominique, 123, 129, 131, 133, 135-36, 138, 142, 145, 149

Lachapelle (Lachapele), L.: journal entries, 16–17, 21, 23–24, 29, 44, 47–49; mentions in Ft. Tecumseh LB, 56, 64, 76–77, 79, 86–87, 89–90, 96–97, 100, 106, 114

Lacharite [La Charite, La Cherité] (interpreter), 31, 65, 77, 178, 188, 191

Lachauitay (u/i), 119

Lacomb, Amable, viii, 18, 26, 86

Lacompt, Joseph, 21, 48, 50, 77, 111

Lac qui Parle (*Mde Iyedan*, "the lake that talks"), 246n8

Lafayette, Marquis de, 63

Lafeve, J. B., 221

Lafferrier, M. P., 246n4

Lafieneu, Mr., 72

Lafierre (u/i), 27

Lafontain, J. B., 129

LaFramboise (nephew of Campbell), 227

LaFramboise [Laframboise, Lafromboise] (u/i), 184–85, 198, 200

LaFramboise, Francois (Francis, "Frank"), 2, 208, 219

LaFramboise, Joseph, xii, 1–2

LaFramboise Island, xii, 2

Lafraniere (u/i), 112

Lagrave, Louis, 13, 18, 21, 48, 51, 91, 105

Laidlaw, Mary Ann (Sioux), 135, 247n20, 249n6

Laidlaw, Robert, 37

Laidlaw, William: as *bourgeois* at Ft. Pierre Chouteau, vii–ix, 4, 242n84; correspondence with Honoré Picotte, viii; correspondence with P. Chouteau, xii; formation of Columbia Fur Company, 2; journal entries, 7–8, 9–10, 12, 14–16, 23–26, 28, 30–39, 41–47, 49–51; leaving Columbia Fur Company, 155; letter, transcription/translation, xiii–xiv; letters from (in Ft. Pierre LB), 93, 98, 100–101, 103–37; letters from (in Ft. Tecumseh LB), 63, 69–71, 73–92; letters to (in Ft. Pierre LB), 114, 139–49; letters to (in Ft. Tecumseh LB), 57–58; mentions in Ft. Pierre LB, 93–97, 99, 138, 148–49, 160, 185–86, 190, 204–07, 213; mentions in Ft. Tecumseh LB, 55, 57, 64–65, 85; origins in Scotland, 245n22; retirement, death, burial, 249n6. *See also* PS [7]

Lainvian (u/i), 39

Laird, James, 208

Lajuniss (u/i), 67

Lake Frances, 126

Lake Traverse (Lac Traverse), xii, 2–3, 41, 78, 238n27, 242n81, 245n1

Lakota Sioux Indians: Lewis and Clark encounter, 235n2; sacred sites, 244n8; tribal divisions, 239n38, 240n50, 240n54, 243n93, 247n5, 247n24; westward migration, vii

Lamont, Colin, 178, 197, 200, 224

Lamont, Daniel: building Ft. Pierre Chouteau, vii; formation of Columbia Fur Company, 2; journal entries, 8, 12, 16, 25, 28, 30, 32, 45, 52, 53; leaving Columbia Fur Company, 155; letters from (in Ft. Tecumseh LB), 56–68; letters to (in Ft. Pierre LB), 106, 108, 110–11; mentions in Ft. Pierre LB, 99–100, 103, 106, 107, 110, 113–14, 117–21, 124, 126, 128, 129, 132–33, 135, 144, 147, 149, 150, 151, 153; mentions in Ft. Tecumseh LB, 68, 72; origins in Scotland, 245n22; Ponca wife, 88; trading post on Apple River, 238n29

Landry, Charles, 94

Lane, Hardage (Dr.), 9, 237n18

Lane, William Carr (Dr.), 237n18

Langham, Mr., 59, 204, 206

Laramie River, 247n1, 247n4

Larpenteur, Charles, 210, 219, 232, 250n9, 250n13

Lataille (u/i), 12–13, 56

Latusiere, C., 152

Leavenworth, Henry, 238n28

Leblane, Henry, 130

Lebrun (u/i), viii, 140–41

Lebrun, Baptiste, 100

Lebrun, Boneventure, 86, 117, 147

Lebrun, Pierre, 69

Leccette, Michel, 94

Leclair, Baptiste ("Soyo"), 70, 94, 96, 245n3

Leclair, "Big," 141–43

Leclair, Oliver, viii; journal entries, 17, 18, 21, 24–27, 42; mentions in Ft. Pierre LB, 99, 124, 133, 138–40; mentions in Ft. Tecumseh LB, 69, 74, 76–79, 80, 83, 85, 89

Leclerc (Le Clerc), P. (A.) N. (Narcisse), 242n83; journal entries, 26–27, 35–36, 42, 52; mentions in Ft. Pierre LB, 96, 131, 147; mentions in Ft. Tecumseh LB, 68–69, 72–73, 79–82, 84–85, 87–88, 90–91

Legé (u/i), 55, 57

Legris (fur trapper), viii, 144, 184

Lemay, Joseph, 29–30, 34

Lemoin, Joseph, 94, 96

Leoulli, Francois, 72

Leston (u/i), 70

Letand (Letaud), Jacque, 7–8, 12, 21, 29–30, 34, 76–77, 83

Letter books, viii, xi–xii

Lewis and Clark Expedition of 1804–1806, vii, 1, 235n2, 236n8, 241n58

Liquor. *See* Whiskey; Wine

Lisa, Manuel, vii, 2, 156, 241n62

Little Blue River (aka Straw Cabin Creek?), 190

Little Cheyenne (Little Chyenne) River, 7–9, 12–13, 15, 47–49, 101, 107, 109, 112, 236n6

Little Crow (Mandan chief), 76
Little Dog (Indian), 198
Little Soldier (Yankton), 30, 51, 135
Livestock. See Horses and mules; Oxen
Loisel, Regis, 241n62
Longeau, Joseph, 15
Louis XVIII (king of France), 241n61
Louisiana Purchase of 1803, vii
Louison (Brulé), 8, 24, 35, 118, 192–96, 205
L'ours qui dance ("Dancing Bear Creek"), 248n10
Lupton, Lancaster P., 247n4
Lurty, Mr., 159, 160

McClaskey (McClasstey), James, 223–24, 290
McClintock, Sam, 208
McElderry, Samuel E., 183–84, 186–87, 194, 196, 198–99, 201, 210
Mackay (Mackie), Aeneas E., 212
McKenney (M Kenny), G. W. (Dr.), 115, 129
McKenzie, Alexander, 245n24
McKenzie, E. M., 212
McKenzie, Kenneth: Blackfeet treaty, 244n6; as *bourgeois* at Ft. Union, 240n52, 250n9; as *bourgeois* of Upper Missouri Outfit, 3, 155; building a steamboat, 244n14; closure of Ft. Clark, 173; dealings with Hugh Glass, 239nn39–40, 241n59; departure for St. Louis, 245n24; formation of Columbia Fur Company, 2–3; formation of P. Chouteau & Company, 156; journal entries, 21, 25–27, 28–30, 32–33, 39–40, 45; letters from (in Ft. Pierre LB), xiii–xiv, 99, 114; letters from (in Ft. Tecumseh LB), 55, 68–69, 92; letters to (in Ft. Pierre LB), 95–96, 128–29, 133; letters to (in Ft. Tecumseh LB), 73–74, 85–86, 90; mentions in Ft. Pierre LB, 94, 96–99, 103–4, 105, 107–08, 114, 116–18, 119–22, 125–26, 131, 134–38, 144, 150–53, 165, 226–29; mentions in Ft. Tecumseh LB, 56, 58, 59–62, 64, 66, 70–72, 74–77, 81–82, 87–88, 91
McKenzie, Owen, 250n12, 250n14
Mackinaws: construction, 236n3; mentions in Ft. Pierre LB, 115–16, 148–49, 151–52, 159, 165–66, 174–75, 177–79, 209, 214, 218–19, 222; as river transportation, ix; transport to St. Louis, 156, 181. See also Keel boats
McKnight, John, 21, 33, 62, 69, 78, 97, 129
Mackquie, A., 73
Mahaw (Mahas, Omaha) Indians, 22, 34, 240n48
Maladraite (u/i), 77
Maleau (u/i), 185, 196, 198–99
Mallery, Garrick, 2
Mandan, N.Dak., 238n21
Mandan Indians: contact with white traders, 1; intermarriage with whites, 245n2; journal entries, 9–12, 17, 20–21, 23, 26, 29–30, 34, 44, 46–47, 51–52; lifestyle and traditions, 10–11; mentions in Ft. Pierre LB, 94, 98, 108, 110–15, 118–19, 125, 127, 134, 136, 145–47, 174, 183, 185; mentions in Ft. Tecumseh LB, 59, 62, 67–68, 73–77, 84–85, 89; physical description, 238n22; smallpox epidemic, viii, 238n24; trading posts, 239n39, 240n55; villages on the Knife River, 237n15
Map, upper Missouri place names, xv, PS [2]
Marchand, Jean, 108
Martha (steamboat), 186, 204, 213, PS [6], 249nn5–6
Martin, Meredith (Dr.), viii, 45, 243n86
Martin, S. (deserter), 226
Mashed Testicles (Indian), viii
Matlock (Matlack), Gideon C., 204, 208, 249n1
Matthews, Alexander, 21, 27, 32, 75, 77, 81, 82
Maurice, Henry, viii, 152
Mauvis (Mauvaise) Boeuf (Brulé chief), 13
Maximillian, Prince of Wied, 3, 135, 239n39, 242n71, 243n97, 247n28
May, W. P., 17–18, 25, 27, 52–53, 106, 136, 141, 144, 147, 148, 150–51
May, W. P., Mrs., 144
Mayaneu (u/i), 96
Mayotte, Jacques, 27–28, 31
Meade County, S.Dak., 236n7
Medicine Hill, 14–15, 48, 50
Medicine/medical care. See Health, disease, illness
Menard, Hilain, 239n39
Ménard, Louis, 78, 96, 104, 117–18, 139–40, 141–42
Merchandise requisitions. See requisitions
Mexican War of 1846, 181
Miller, Peter, 86
Miller, William, 17–18, 20–21
Minneconjou Sioux Indians, 240n50
Minnesota River. See Saint Peter's River
Minniterees. See Grosventres
Mischall, Henry, 151
Missouri Fur Company (aka Saint Louis Fur Company), vii, 2, 156, 241n62
Missouri History Museum, xi
Missouri Indians, 236n8
Mitchell (Mitchel), David D.: appointed superintendent of Indian Affairs, 156; financial interests, 155, 181; journal entries, 23, 25–26, 33, 52–53; letters to (in Ft. Tecumseh LB), 59, 62–63, 64–65, 74–76, 87; mentions in Ft. Pierre LB, 217, 229; mentions in Ft. Tecumseh LB, 58, 64, 74, 77–78, 86, 89, 98, 100, 129
Moncravie (Moncrevie, Moncreve), J. B., 52, 130, 162, 183, 187, 193–94, 197, 200, 209, 223–24

Monigen, Louis, 47
Montaigne, Francois, 7–8, 12, 14, 77, 81, 84
Moreau River, 242n70
Morrin, Antoine, 174, 201
Mulatto/Negro/slaves, ix, 12, 32, 76, 96, 156, 182, 226, 248n1
Murray, Alexander H., PS [4]
Murray, James, 205, 249n3
Musselshell River, 81–82, 245n19

Neissell, Hipolite, 43
New Mexico: Taos Peddlers, 248n15
Nicollet, Joseph, 242n76, 243n90, 244n15
Nimrod (steamboat), 172, 248n14
Niobrara (Running Water) River, 71, 139, 237n16, 244n7
Noble, James, 7–9, 13, 14–15, 237n10
Northern Department (American Fur Company), 155
North West Company, 2, 244n2, 245n18

Obachon, Louis, 27, 56
Oglala (Oggallalla, Oggalles, Ogallallahs) Sioux Indians: hired as fort police, 240n49; journal entries, 25, 32, 35, 41, 44; as Lakota tribal division, 240n50, 243n93; mentions in Ft. Pierre LB, 112, 115, 131, 138–39, 142, 228; mentions in Ft. Tecumseh LB, 78–80, 83–85, 88; Pine Ridge reservation, 242n85
Oglala Post, ix: journal entries, 35, 37–39, 45–47, 49, 51; letters to (in Ft. Tecumseh LB), 90–91; locations of various, 237n9, 239n36; mentions in Ft. Pierre LB, 133, 140; mentions in Ft. Tecumseh LB, 71, 80, 87
Okobojo Creek, 242n74
Omega (steamboat), 241n67
Oregon Trail, 156, 247n1, 248n11
Ortubise, H., 136
Ortubise (Octubise), Pierre (interpreter), 245n25; journal entries, 40–41, 43, 46–48; mentions in Ft. Pierre LB, 93, 109, 110, 113, 117, 138, 143, 147–48; mentions in Ft. Tecumseh LB, 55, 57, 92
Otoe (Otto) Indians, 99, 172, 236n8, 242n69
Otto Establishment, 68–69, 83, 84, 92, 105, 138, 144
Oxen, 157, 173, 184, 187, 195, 197–99, 206–7, 221, 224–25, 228. *See also* Horses and mules

Palmer, James Archdale Hamilton, 240n52
Papin, Etienne, 94
Papin, Pierre Didier: arrival at Ft. Tecumseh, 3; journal entries, 7–9, 12–18, 22, 25–26, 28, 31, 38–39, 45, 48, 51–52; letters from (in Ft. Pierre LB), 149; letters to (in Ft. Pierre LB), 100–101, 112, 120–21, 123–24, 126, 132–33, 145, 162–63, 164, 166, 176–77, 182; letters to (in Ft. Tecumseh LB), 56, 57, 61–62, 65, 67, 79–80, 82–83, 90–91; mentions in Ft. Pierre LB, 94, 96, 101, 104, 109, 115–18, 122, 130, 140, 142, 147, 150–52, 172–77, 180, 199, 220–27; mentions in Ft. Tecumseh LB, 59, 62, 69, 72, 76, 77, 81, 86
Papin's House (P. D. Papin & Co.), 7, 9, 26, 28, 31, 236n4
Paquette, Albert, 8, 28, 67
Parker, James, 20, 29, 35, 69, 96
Parker, Janus, 108
Parkins (Parker), James (mulatto), ix, 32, 96
Parrada, John, 185, 196
Passiche, Joseph, 23
Paunee (Pawnee) Indians, viii, 19–20, 60, 71, 77, 78
Paur, David, 94
Pencinneau, F., 66
Philbert (Phillibert) (u/i), 30, 35
Philip I (king of France), 30, 63, 241n61
Phillips, Frederick, 86
Picotte, Baptiste, 190
Picotte, Honoré ("Henry"), 248n19: as *bourgeois* at Ft. Tecumseh, xii, 4, 245n1; as *bourgeois* of Sioux Outfit, 155–56; correspondence from W. Laidlaw, viii; formation of Columbia Fur Company, 2; journal entries, 15–17, 22–23, 25–26, 36–38, 41, 47–48, 52; letters from (in Ft. Pierre LB), 93–94, 161, 163–67, 172–80, 185–87; letters from (in Ft. Tecumseh LB), 83, 84–85; letters to (in Ft. Pierre LB), 106, 109–10, 120–21, 122, 134, 140, 147, 159–60; letters to (in Ft. Tecumseh LB), 76; mentions in Ft. Pierre LB, 96–97, 99, 100, 103–5, 107, 108, 112, 115–18, 120, 122, 126–29, 133, 140–46, 148–49, 151–53, 157, 160–62, 182–85; mentions in Ft. Tecumseh LB, 68, 72, 74–77, 79, 88–89, 91; merchandise requisitions, 167–71
Picotte, Jas., 221
Picotte, John C., 182, 194
Picotte, Joseph ("Henry"), 157–62, 177, 178, 179, 181, 216, 248n19
Picotte, Mr., 218
Picotte, Mrs., 188
Pierre Chouteau, Jr., and Company: acquisition of Ft. John, 156; acquisition of upper Missouri trade, 4, 155; formation and letter books of, xi–xii; letters, 219–23; letters from Hodgkiss, 219; letters from Picotte, 225–26; reorganization, 155–56, 203. *See also* Chouteau, Pierre, Jr.
Pilcher, Joshua, 16, 22, 64, 122, 124, 136, 148
Pillon (Pilou), A., 38, 243n92
Pincinneau and Company, 86
Pineau le Yancton (Indian), 14, 16–17, 18, 20, 23, 24, 33, 35, 41, 47–49, 69–70, 80, 96, 142
Pine Ridge Reservation, 242n85
Pipe (Yankton), 111

Pipestone, 160, 247n27
Piton, Louis, 16
Platte River, 3
Poplar River, 246n19
Portolance & Co., 86
Prairie du Chien, xii, 96, 115, 122, 245n2, 245n17, 246n14
Pratte, Bernard, 3, 4, 78, 96, 155, 244n14, 245n2. *See also* Bernard Pratte and Company
Pratte, Chouteau and Company, 4, 136-39, 143, 149-50, 151-52
Presley, Modest, viii, 150, 151
Preville, Louis, 92
Primeau, Charles: building fort near Ft. Pierre, 4, 181; journal entries, 15-16, 23-24, 26, 47, 50, 52-53; mentions in Ft. Pierre LB, 126, 145-48, 160, 162, 177, 179, 194, 226, 228
Primeau, Emillien: journal entries, 25, 33, 43, 45, 46, 48-51; killed at Apple River, 239n37; letters to (in Ft. Pierre LB), 101, 104, 108-11, 113; letters to (in Ft. Tecumseh LB), 55-57, 63; mentions in Ft. Pierre LB, 116, 121, 123-24, 138-39, 143, 144, 146; mentions in Ft. Tecumseh LB, 57, 65, 67, 99-100
Prouvoucier, Louis, 122
Proveau, Constant, 116, 162, 183, 186-88, 190, 195, 197-98, 200-201, 225-26
Provost, Etienne, 32-33, 35, 45, 65, 85-86, 90, 114, 119, 162, 191, 208, 210, 241n65

Qu'Appelle River, 245n16
Quenel, Francois, 8, 36, 39-40, 99, 237n17

Raboin, Antoine, 48, 105, 126, 176, 228
Raboin (Robain), Louison, 28-29
Railroads, 5
Rapid Creek, 239n36
Ray, Bernard ("old Mayonce"), 144
Recontre, Madam, 35
Recontre, Zephine, 28-29, 33-34, 59, 61, 63-64, 66, 70, 75, 81-82, 85, 89, 91
"Red Headed Chief." *See* Clark, William
Red River of the North, 242n81, 245n1, 247n21
Red Stone quarry, 160, 247n27
Ree, Mr., 215
Ree Indians. *See* Arikara (Arriccarra, Ree) Indians
Renville, Joseph, 2, 78, 246n8
Renville, Louis, 36
Requisitions: goods/merchandise, xiii, 79, 93, 164, 166-72, 175, 185-89, 203-04, 215-17, 225-26, 228, 232-33; for men, 64, 125; for oxen, 224
Richard, Madame, 69
Richard, Noel (Nowl), 29-30, 32, 36, 41, 69, 77-78, 81

la Riviere a (au, O, le) Jacque(s), 9, 11, 39, 40, 45, 48, 73, 75, 76, 81, 99, 160, 163, 206. *See also* James River; Riviere Bois Blanc
Riviere Bois Blanc, 27, 29, 45, 240n56. *See also* James River; la Riviere a (au, O, le) Jacque(s)
Riviere broache, 78
la Riviere Leau que course, 13
Riviere Platte. *See* Platte River
Riviere que Appell (Qu'Appelle), 78, 245n16
Roberts, Carlile, 193
Rocky Mountain expeditions, 115, 250n11
Rocky Mountain Outfit, 32, 94, 125, 144
Roland (u/i), 51
Rolette, Joseph, 73, 75, 78, 81-82, 190, PS [5], 245n17, 246n14
Roque, Mr., 106
Rose, Colin, 239n39
Rosson, Mr., 115
Roy, Francis (Francois), 8, 13, 25, 94, 124
Roy, Louis, 13
Roy's Island, 39, 41-42, 44, 48. *See also* Farm Island

Sachanna Indians, 12, 238n29
Sachanté (u/i), 67
Saint Louis: as center of fur trade, 1; express communications, 48, 105-7, 112, 167, 175, 188, 195, 197, 216; Indian deputation visit, 30, 58-59; transporting furs to, 156, 181, 242n80;
Saint Louis Fur Company. *See* Missouri Fur Company
Saint Peter's River (aka Minnesota River), ix, xii, 2-3, 244n13, 246n8
St. Pierre (u/i), 195
St. Vrain, Marcelin, 160, 248n7
Sand Hills, 190
Sandoval, Isidore, 74, 244n11
Sanford (Sanfords, Sandford), John F. A., 16, 69, 72, 74, 77, 81, 88, 94, 97
Sans Arc Indians, 140, 211, 217, 239n38, 240n50, 247n24
Saon (Saone/Sawon) Indians, 17-18, 23-27, 31-32, 36-40, 44-46, 50-51, 53, 70-71, 78, 84, 126, 136, 138-39, 148, 160, 239n38
Sarpy, John B., ix, 155, 163, 247n1
Sarpy, Mr., 205, 207, 219
Sarpy, Peter A., ix, 177-78, 188, 195, 224-25, 231
Sarpy, S. A., 171, 173
Sarpy, Thomas L., ix, 15-17, 20-21, 35, 70, 80, 83-88, 90, 104, 151-52, 239n36
Schlegel, V. H., 189, 191-92, 194, 204, 212, 226
Sebelle (Sebille), G., 33, 193, 196, 220
Seblond (u/i), 67
Segmann, Pascal, 226

Selkirk Colony, 245n24
Serpent river (Snake Creek?), 243n90
Serritt, Joseph, 191
Seviellé (Seveille), Louis, 77, 82
Shanks, C., 96
Sheppelands (u/i), 74
Sheyenne River, 236n1, 242n76
Sibelle, John, 59, 66, 103, 104, 187, 205
Sihasapa Sioux Indians, 240n50. *See also* Blackfeet (Sihasapa) Sioux Indians
Simonds, George, 100
Sioux City, Iowa, 250n12
Sioux Outfit, ix, 155–56
Sire, Joseph A., 155, 173, 177, 219, 241nn66–67, 243n95
Slaves/slavery. *See* Mulatto/Negro/slaves
Smith, Jackson & Sublette, 129, 245n4
Smith, Jedediah S., 245n4
Smith, Sublette & Co., 95–96
South Dakota State Historical Society, xii
Steamboats: adaptation to shallow water, 156, 172; *Assiniboine*, 53, 114–16, 121, 125, 129, 149–50, 243n97, 244n14, 246n5, 247n28; capacity, 248n14; *Dacotah*, 249n5; *Diana*, 148–49, 151–53; disease and, 148, 156; *El Passo*, 219–20; *General Brooke*, 165; goods moved on, ix, 2–5, 156, 181, 242n80; *Martha*, 204, 213, PS [6], 249nn5–6; *Nimrod*, 172, 248n14; *Omega*, 156, 241nn66–67; *St. Ange*, 222, 227; *St. Peter's*, 156; *Trapper*, 241n67; wood supply required, 242n70; *Yellow Stone* (American Fur Co.), vii, 38, 69, 121, 242n80, 243n97, 244n14.
Steboiné (u/i), 111
Stillman (steamboat captain), 220, 231
Straw Cabin Creek (Straw Hill River), 190
Sublette (Sublett), William, 52, 66, 95–96, 114–15, 118, 123–24, 129, 133, 245n4, 247n1, 250n9
Sublette & Campbell, ix, 137, 246n6, 250n9
Sublette & Co., 95–96, 114–15, 118, 123–24
Sully, Alfred, PS [8]

Taos Peddlers/Taos Trail, 173, 248n15
Taudière (fur trapper), 144
Teton Sioux Indians, 1. *See also* Lakota Sioux Indians
Thibeau, Alexis, 241n64
Thompson, William, 96
Tibaut, Alexis, 7, 13
Tilton, Dudley and Co. *See* Columbia Fur Company
Tilton, William P., 2
Tisdale, Amable, 94
Tobacco, 23, 175, 248n16
Tonala Caxal, 51, 243n95
Trapper (steamboat), 241n67

Trappers. *See* Beaver/beaver trade/trappers
Traverse, Alfred, 101, 116, 117
Trotten, Baptiste, 86
Turcot, Louis, 43–44, 51
Two Kettles Indians, 239n38, 240n50

Union Fur Company (aka Fox, Livingston and Company), 156, 176, 248n8, 249n7
United States Army: establishment of Ft. Sully, 4; purchase of Ft. John, 156, 247n1, 249n4; purchase of Ft. Pierre, ix–x, 4
Upper Mississippi Outfit, 244n13, 245n17, 246n14
Upper Missouri Outfit: Carpenter as trader, 250n9; Drips employed at, 245n23; formation and operation of, 3–4; Ft. Pierre becomes headquarters, ix, 156; growing competition, 246n6, 248n8; Halsey as clerk, 236n2; Holliday brothers as clerks, 244n1; McKenzie as head, 132, 155; Meldrum as employee, 250n11; mentions in Ft. Pierre LB, 93, 100, 106, 159, 166; mentions in Ft. Tecumseh LB, 86, 89; Murray as *bourgeois*, 249n3; treaty with the Blackfeet, 244n6

Vachard, Charles, 104, 122–23, 130, 133–34, 149
Vachard, Louis, 27, 30, 32, 34, 63
Vallin, A., 46, 148
Vanderburgh (Vanderburg), William Henry, 29, 32–33, 48, 60–61, 71, 112, 241n55, 241n59, 241n65, 243n92
Van Metre, S.Dak., 237n9
Vasquez, Pierre Louis ("Old Vaskiss"): letters to (in Ft. Pierre LB), 161, 211; mentions in Ft. Pierre LB, 159, 161–62, 173, 176, 179, 201; partnership with Bridger, 204, 209, 220, 231, 247n6
Vasseur, Joseph, 18, 21, 37, 42, 79, 96, 140, 146
Vérendrye, Louis-Joseph Gaultier de la, 235n1
Vermillion (pigment), 99, 159, 168, 169, 171
Vermillion farm, 138
Vermillion River, 9–10, 13, 21, 82, 188, 232
Villande, Joseph, 17
Vinette (u/i), 110
Vinitte, S. Delpant, 132
Vione, Francois, 17
Vissina, Joseph, 132

Waggoner, Josephine, 248n15
Warren, G. K., 235n2
Welch, Pierre, 75
Western Department (American Fur Company), xi, 3–4, 68–70, 98, 155, 246n5
Westport (port/landing), 222, 250n8
Whiskey: banned in Indian country, 155; drunkenness, 18, 78–79, 92, 93–94, 162; trade goods, 62, 81, 83, 120, 121,

125, 140, 163; trading with Indians, ix, 122, 123, 134, 143, 172–73

White River/White River post: establishment of opposition posts, ix; journal entries, 7–9, 13, 20, 25–29, 31, 33, 35, 37–41, 49, 52; letters to (in Ft. Tecumseh LB), 55–57, 61, 63, 67, 79–80, 82–83, 90–91; mentions in Ft. Pierre LB, 109, 112, 119, 124, 133, 142, 157–60, 162, 166, 175, 181–82, 187, 189, 194, 199, 205–09, 216, 222, 228; mentions in Ft. Tecumseh LB, 71, 87–89

White River Badlands (*Mauvais terre*), 247n26

Whitten, Mr., 138, 144

Wind River Mountains, 161–62, 248n9

Wine, 118–19, 123, 125, 128, 131, 134–35, 148

Winter, J. P., 15–17, 139

Württemberg (Wattenburgh), Friedrich Paul Wihelm von (Prince), 8–9, 237n12

Yankton, S.Dak., 237n14

Yankton (Yancton, Yanctonna, Yanktonnai, Sanchanna) Sioux Indians, viii, 3, 8, 13, 24, 32, 34, 36–37, 43–44, 48–50, 198, 204, 217, PS [4], 236n5, 238n29, 242n76

Yankton (Yancton) trading post, 28, 30–31, 35–36, 42, 43, 53, 95, 163, 174, 199, 237n11

Yellow Stone (steamboat), vii, 38, 69, 72, 121, 242n80, 243n97, 244n14

Yellowstone (Yellow Stone) River, 2, 64, 66, 68, 115, 119, 120–21